PHILIP'S NAVIGATOR

Camping and Caravanning

Atlas of Britain

www.philips-maps.co.uk

First published in 2014 by Philip's,
a division of Octopus Publishing Group Ltd
www.octopusbooks.co.uk
Carmelite House
50 Victoria Embankment
London EC4Y 0DZ
An Hachette UK Company
www.hachette.co.uk

Second edition 2016
First impression 2016

ISBN 978-1-84907-405-6

Cartography by Philip's
Copyright © 2016 Philip's

This product includes mapping data licensed from Ordnance Survey®, with the permission of the Controller of Her Majesty's Stationery Office. © Crown copyright 2016. All rights reserved. Licence number 100011710

Data for the speed cameras provided by PocketGPSWorld.com Ltd.

Data for the caravan sites provided by The Camping and Caravanning Club.

Information for the selection of Wildlife Trust nature reserves provided by The Wildlife Trusts.

Information for National Parks, Areas of Outstanding Natural Beauty, National Trails and Country Parks in Wales supplied by the Countryside Council for Wales.

Information for National Parks, Areas of Outstanding Natural Beauty, National Trails and Country Parks in England supplied by Natural England. Data for Regional Parks, Long Distance Footpaths and Country Parks in Scotland provided by Scottish Natural Heritage.

Information for Forest Parks supplied by the Forestry Commission.

Information for the RSPB reserves provided by the RSPB

Gaelic name forms used in the Western Isles provided by Comhairle nan Eilean.

Data for the National Nature Reserves in England provided by Natural England. Data for the National Nature Reserves in Wales provided by Countryside Council for Wales. Darparwyd data'n ymwneud â Gwarchodfeydd Natur Cenedlaethol Cymru gan Gyngor Cefn Gwlad Cymru.

Information on the location of National Nature Reserves in Scotland was provided by Scottish Natural Heritage.

Data for National Scenic Areas in Scotland provided by the Scottish Executive Office. Crown copyright material is reproduced with the permission of the Controller of HMSO and the Queen's Printer for Scotland. Licence number C02W0003960.

Photographic acknowledgements
Front cover and title page: Camping and Caravanning Club
Back cover top: Jim Holden / Alamy
Back cover bottom: Camping and Caravanning Club

Printed in China

Contents

Road map symbols

M25	Motorway
16 17	Motorway junctions – full access, restricted access
	Toll motorway
Pease Pottage Services	Motorway service area
	Motorway under construction
S	Primary route – dual, single carriageway, services – under construction, narrow
Cardiff	Primary destination
25 26	Numbered junctions – full, restricted access
	A road – dual, single carriageway – under construction, narrow
	B road – dual, single carriageway – under construction, narrow
	Minor road – dual, single carriageway
	Drive or track
	Urban side roads (height, weight and width restrictions not shown)
12'9 13'0 12'5	Height restriction, width restriction – feet and inches
2	Tunnel, weight restriction – tonnes
	Distance in miles
Toll	Roundabout, multi-level junction,
	Toll, steep gradient – points downhill
40 40	Speed camera – single, multiple
CLEVELAND WAY	National trail – England and Wales
GREAT GLEN WAY	Long distance footpath – Scotland
YATTON ROPLEY	Railway with station, level crossing, tunnel
	Preserved railway with level crossing, station, tunnel
	Tramway
	National boundary
	County or unitary authority boundary
	Car ferry, catamaran
	Passenger ferry, catamaran
	Hovercraft
V P	Internal ferry – car, passenger
✈ ✈	Principal airport, other airport or airfield
MENDIP HILLS	Area of outstanding natural beauty, National Forest – England and Wales, Forest park, National park, National scenic area – Scotland, Regional park
	Woodland
	Beach – sand, shingle
KENNET AND AVON CANAL	Navigable river or canal
6	Lock, flight of locks, canal bridge number
Ꞓ ℞ Ꞓ ℀ ℁	Caravan or camping sites – CCC* Club Site, Ready Camp Site, Camping in the Forest Site – CCC Certificated Site, Listed Site *Categories defined by The Camping and Caravanning Club of Great Britain
☼ P&R ▲965	Viewpoint, park and ride, spot height – in metres
	Linear antiquity
29 SY 80/70	Adjoining page number, OS National Grid reference – see page 402

Road map scale 1: 100 000 or 1.58 miles to 1 inch

```
0        1        2        3 miles
0    1    2    3    4    5 km
```

Road map scale (Isle of Man and parts of Scotland)
1: 200 000 or 3.15 miles to 1 inch

```
0      1      2      3      4      5      6 miles
0  1  2  3  4  5  6  7  8  9  10 km
```

Tourist information

BYLAND ABBEY ✠	Abbey or priory
WOODHENGE	Ancient monument
SEALIFE CENTRE	Aquarium or dolphinarium
CITY MUSEUM AND ART GALLERY	Art collection or museum
TATE ST IVES	Art gallery
1644 ⚔	Battle site and date
ABBOTSBURY SWANNERY	Bird sanctuary or aviary
BAMBURGH CASTLE	Castle
YORK MINSTER ✝	Cathedral
SANDHAM MEMORIAL CHAPEL	Church of interest
SEVEN SISTERS	Country park – England and Wales
LOCHORE MEADOWS	– Scotland
ROYAL BATH & WEST SHOWGROUND	County show ground
MONK PARK FARM	Farm park
HILLIER GARDENS AND ARBORETUM	Garden, arboretum
ST ANDREWS	Golf course – 18-hole
TYNTESFIELD	Historic house
SS GREAT BRITAIN	Historic ship
HATFIELD HOUSE	House and garden
CUMBERLAND PENCIL MUSEUM	Museum
MUSEUM OF DARTMOOR LIFE	– Local
NAT MARITIME MUSEUM	– Maritime or military

	⚓ Marina
SILVERSTONE	🏁 Motor racing circuit
	Nature reserves
HOLTON HEATH	– National nature reserve
BOYTON MARSHES	– RSPB reserve
DRAYCOTT SLEIGHTS	– Wildlife Trust reserve
	Ⓟ Picnic area
WEST SOMERSET RAILWAY	Preserved railway
THIRSK	🏇 Racecourse
LEAHILL TURRET	Roman antiquity
THRIGBY HALL	Safari park
FREEPORT BRAINTREE	🛒 Shopping village
MILLENNIUM STADIUM	Sports venue
ALTON TOWERS	Theme park
	Tourist information centres
	i – open all year
	i – open seasonally
NATIONAL RAILWAY MUSEUM	Transport collection
LEVANT MINE	World heritage site
HELMSLEY	△ Youth hostel
MARWELL	Zoo
SUTTON BANK VISITOR CENTRE	•:• Other place
GLENFIDDICH DISTILLERY	✦ of interest

Approach map symbols

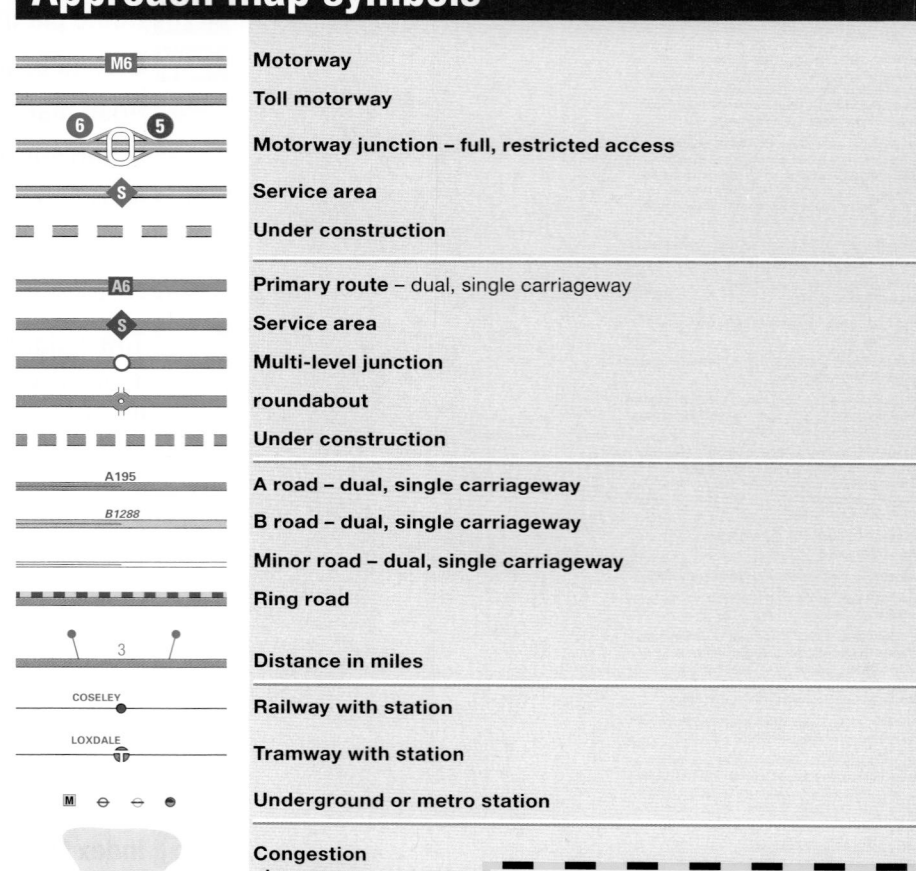

M6	Motorway
	Toll motorway
6 5	Motorway junction – full, restricted access
S	Service area
	Under construction
A6	Primary route – dual, single carriageway
S	Service area
	Multi-level junction
	roundabout
	Under construction
A195	A road – dual, single carriageway
B1288	B road – dual, single carriageway
	Minor road – dual, single carriageway
	Ring road
3	Distance in miles
COSELEY	Railway with station
LOXDALE	Tramway with station
M	Underground or metro station
	Congestion charge area

Speed Cameras

Fixed camera locations are shown using the 40 symbol. In congested areas the 40 symbol is used to show that there are two or more cameras on the road indicated.

Due to the restrictions of scale the camera locations are only approximate and cannot indicate the operating direction of the camera. Mobile camera sites, and cameras located on roads not included on the mapping are not shown. Where two or more cameras are shown on the same road, drivers are warned that this may indicate that a SPEC system is in operation. These cameras use the time taken to drive between the two camera positions to calculate the speed of the vehicle. At the time of going to press, some local authorities were considering decommissioning their speed cameras.

Load and vehicle restrictions – please read

Any information on height, width and weight restrictions in the UK as noted on pages 1–314 of this atlas has been derived from the relevant OS material used to compile this atlas. Any information on height, width and weight restrictions on the Isle of Man has been derived from the relevant information as supplied by the Isle of Man Highways Department. Where a warning sign is displayed, any height obstructions, including but not limited to low bridges and overhead cables, are shown in the atlas where such obstructions cross navigable roads selected for inclusion. Height restrictions lower than 16'6" and width restrictions narrower than 13 feet, are all shown in 3 inch multiples and have been rounded down where necessary. Weight restrictions indicate weak bridges and the maximum gross weight which could be supported is shown in tonnes. While every effort has been made to include all relevant and accurate information, due to limitations of scale a single symbol may be used to indicate more than one feature and it is not possible to show restrictions on urban side roads.

Our campsites, your great experiences

The Camping and Caravanning Club
The Friendly Club

campingandcaravanningclub.co.uk

READY Camp
FROM THE CAMPING AND CARAVANNING CLUB
www.readycamp.co.uk

CAMPING IN THE FOREST
www.campingintheforest.co.uk

Symbols explained

Understanding Club pitches

- **G** A grass-only pitch with no electric hook-up or other services.
- **A** A large grass-only pitch with no electric hook-up, where the unit measures more than 5m x 9m.
- **GWE** A grass pitch with electric hook-up.
- **HWE** A hardstanding pitch with electric hook-up.
- **A** A large pitch with electric hook-up for units that measure more than 5m x 9m.
- **HWE** A hardstanding pitch with electric hook-up plus fresh water and waste drainage. Some pitches may also have TV hook-up points.

Other symbols

- Touring caravans
- Motorhomes
- Trailer tents and folding campers
- Tents
- Camping Pods or Dens
- Camping Barn
- **HH** Holiday Homes and Exclusive Lodges
- **ACC** Alternative Accommodation/Self-catering
- **SP** Seasonal Pitches
- **SF** Storage facilities
- Difficult access or a difficult approach
- Open site
- Well-sheltered site
- Coastal
- Sea/loch view
- Dedicated accessible facilities
- Some accessible facilities
- No dedicated accessible facilities
- Parent and baby room
- Mother and baby room
- Family shower room
- Backpacker facilities
- **WC** Toilet
- Showers
- Washbasins
- Electric shaver sockets
- Drinking water taps
- Dishwashing facilities
- Washing machines
- Drying room
- **CDP** Chemical toilet disposal point
- **MHS** Motorhome Stop-off
- Shop
- **FF** Ice pack freezing
- Gas cylinders
- Battery charging
- Recreation hall
- **TV** Television room (not for hire)
- Wireless internet provider is Infinium
- Wireless internet
- Payphone
- Children's play area
- Ball games
- Swimming pool
- Boating
- Fishing facilities
- Tennis
- Takeaway
- Restaurant
- Bar
- Pets welcome
- Designated dog walk
- Pub within one mile
- **RC** Ready Camp

Camping in the Forest site specific symbols

- Select pitch - a larger pitch with electric hook-up and hardstanding
- Rally field
- Public transport
- Pets not permitted

Club Site Map Key

- ● Club Site
- ● Camping in the Forest Site

Club Site Philip's Map Key

 Club Site – we have over a 100 camp sites across the UK that you will find in the next 4 pages and within the maps.

 Ready Camp – pre-erected glamping tents on over 17 locations across the UK.

 Camping in the Forest Site – the Club works with the Forestry Commission to run these 16 sites in Britain's forest woodlands.

 Certificated Site – over 1600 smaller sites, accepting up to 5 caravans or motorhomes, plus tents – space permitting – they are exclusive to Club members only.

 Listed Site – these can range from huge holiday parks with entertainment to quiet commercial sites. The Club does not approve or recommend any of these sites.

Map locations

INVEREWE, DINGWALL, NAIRN, ROSEMARKIE, SPEYSIDE, SKYE, LOCH NESS SHORES, GLENMORE, TARLAND, ABERDEEN, GLENCOE, OBAN, DUNDEE, COBLELAND, SCONE, MILARROCHY BAY, LUSS, CASHEL, EDINBURGH, DUNBAR, GLASGOW, LAUDER, KILMARNOCK, JEDBURGH, BEADNELL BAY, DUNSTAN HILL, AYR, CULZEAN CASTLE, MOFFAT, BELLINGHAM, DUMFRIES, NEWCASTLE, LARNE, STRANRAER, CARLISLE, HALTWHISTLE, BELFAST, DERWENTWATER, KESWICK, TROUTBECK, BARNARD CASTLE, DELAMONT COUNTRY PARK, ESKDALE, KENDAL, RAVENGLASS, WINDERMERE, SCARBOROUGH, DOUGLAS, BRAITHWAITE FOLD, SLINGSBY, BOROUGHBRIDGE, SHERIFF HUTTON, CLITHEROE, YORK, BLACKPOOL, LEEDS, HULL, SOUTHPORT, CHORLEY, HUDDERSFIELD, SCUNTHORPE, DUBLIN, MANCHESTER, CROWDEN, SHEFFIELD, LIVERPOOL, DELAMERE FOREST, HAYFIELD, LINCOLN, MABLETHORPE, HOLYHEAD, CHESTER, LEEK, BAKEWELL, TEVERSAL, WOODHALL SPA, BEDDGELERT, WREXHAM, STOKE, ASHBOURNE, DERBY, NOTTINGHAM, BOSTON, LLANYSTUMDWY, BALA, OSWESTRY, ALTON, THE STAR, SANDRINGHAM, WEST RUNTON, CANNOCK CHASE, CONKERS, EBURY HILL, PETERBOROUGH, NORWICH, ABERYSTWYTH, DRAYTON MANOR, KINGSBURY WATER PARK, WOLVERHAMPTON, BIRMINGHAM, THETFORD FOREST, KESSINGLAND, WOLVERLEY, CLENT HILLS, HUNTINGDON, CARDIGAN BAY, St NEOTS, CAMBRIDGE, IPSWICH, St DAVIDS, RHANDIRMWYN, HEREFORD, BLACKMORE, GULLIVER'S MILTON KEYNES, POLSTEAD, BRACELANDS, WINCHCOMBE, CHIPPING NORTON, COLCHESTER, SWANSEA, OXFORD, THEOBALDS PARK, HERTFORD, KELVEDON HATCH, CARDIFF, POSTERN HILL, LONDON, BRISTOL, WALTON-ON-THAMES, DEVIZES, CHERTSEY, CHEDDAR, BASINGSTOKE, HORSLEY, OLDBURY HILL, CANTERBURY, LYNTON, MINEHEAD, SALISBURY, CROWBOROUGH, FOLKESTONE, UMBERLEIGH, TAUNTON, CHICHESTER, GRAFFHAM, SLINDON, TEIGN VALLEY BARLEY MEADOW, CHARMOUTH, VERWOOD, NORMAN'S BAY, BUDE, EXETER, MORETON, ADGESTONE, TREGURRIAN, TAVISTOCK, TORQUAY, CORFE CASTLE, DARTMOUTH, CALIFORNIA CROSS, SLAPTON SANDS, SENNEN COVE, ST IVES, VERYAN

NEW FOREST SITES
Aldridge Hill; Ashurst
Denny Wood & Matley Wood; Hollands Wood
Holmsley; Ocknell & Longbeech
Roundhill; Setthorns

The Camping and Caravanning Club
The Friendly Club

Scotland

Culzean Castle Club Site
Culzean, Maybole,
Ayrshire KA19 8JX
Tel: 01655 760627
Map reference:
Pg: 256 Grid Ref: G6
Open: 24 Mar – 24 Oct 2016
Pitches: 90

Dingwall Club Site
Jubilee Park Road, Dingwall,
Highlands IV15 9QZ
Tel: 01349 862236
Map reference:
Pg: 300 Grid Ref: D5
Open: 24 Mar – 24 Oct 2016
Pitches: 83

Dunbar Club Site
Oxwellmains, Dunbar,
East Lothian EH42 1WG
Tel: 01368 866881
Map reference:
Pg: 282 Grid Ref: F4
Open: 24 Mar – 24 Oct 2016
Pitches: 90

Glencoe Club Site
Glencoe, Ballachulish,
Argyll PH49 4LA
Tel: 01855 811397
Map reference:
Pg: 284 Grid Ref: B5
Open: 24 Mar – 24 Oct 2016
Pitches: 102

Inverewe Gardens Club Site
Poolewe, Achnasheen,
Highlands IV22 2LF
Tel: 01445 781249
Map reference:
Pg: 307 Grid Ref: L3
Open: 24 Mar – 24 Oct 2016
Pitches: 55

Jedburgh Club Site
Elliot Park, Jedburgh,
Borders TD8 6EF
Tel: 01835 863393
Map reference:
Pg: 262 Grid Ref: E5
Open: 24 Mar – 24 Oct 2016
Pitches: 50

Lauder Club Site
Carfraemill, Oxton, Lauder,
Borders TD2 6RA
Tel: 01578 750697
Map reference:
Pg: 271 Grid Ref: E10
Open: 24 Mar – 24 Oct 2016
Pitches: 60

Loch Ness Shores Club Site
Lower Foyers, Highland
IV2 6YH
Tel: 01456 486333
Map reference:
Pg: 300 Grid Ref: G4
Open: All year
Pitches: 99

Luss Club Site
Luss, Loch Lomond,
Alexandria, Nr Glasgow,
Scotland G83 8NT
Tel: 01436 860658
Map reference:
Pg: 277 Grid Ref: C7
Open: 24 Mar – 24 Oct 2016
Pitches: 90
Note: Member only Caravans
and Motorhomes

Milarrochy Bay Club Site
Milarrochy Bay, Balmaha,
Nr Drymen, Glasgow
G63 OAL
Tel: 01360 870236
Map reference:
Pg: 277 Grid Ref: C8
Open: 24 Mar – 24 Oct 2016
Pitches: 150

Moffat Club Site
Hammerlands,
Moffat DG10 9QL
Tel: 01683 220436
Map reference:
Pg: 248 Grid Ref: C3
Open: All year
Pitches: 180

Nairn Club Site
Delnies Wood, Nairn,
Inverness, Morayshire
IV12 5NX
Tel: 01667 455281
Map reference:
Pg: 301 Grid Ref: D8
Open: 1 Mar – 29 Oct 2016
Pitches: 75

Oban Club Site
Barcaldine by Connel, Argyll
PA37 1SG
Tel: 01631 720348
Map reference:
Pg: 284 Grid Ref: C3
Open: 24 Mar – 24 Oct 2016
Pitches: 75

Rosemarkie Club Site
Ness Road East, Rosemarkie,
Fortrose, Highlands IV10 8SE
Tel: 01381 621117
Map reference:
Pg: 301 Grid Ref: D7
Open: 24 Mar – 24 Oct 2016
Pitches: 60

Scone Club Site
Scone Palace Caravan Park,
Scone, Tayside PH2 6BB
Tel: 01738 552323
Map reference:
Pg: 286 Grid Ref: E5
Open: 1 Mar – 2 Jan 2017
Pitches: 120

Skye Club Site
Loch Greshornish, Bovre,
Arnisort, Edinbane, Portree,
Isle of Skye IV51 9PS
Tel: 01470 582230
Map reference:
Pg: 298 Grid Ref: D3
Open: 1 Apr – 9 Oct 2016
Pitches: 105

Speyside Club Site
Archiestown, Aberlour, Moray
AB38 9SL
Tel: 01340 810414
Map reference:
Pg: 302 Grid Ref: E2
Open: 24 Mar – 24 Oct 2016
Pitches: 75

Tarland by Deeside Club Site
Tarland by Aboyne,
Aberdeenshire AB34 4UP
Tel: 01339 881388
Map reference:
Pg: 292 Grid Ref: C6
Open: 1 Mar – 2 Jan 2017
Pitches: 52

Northern Ireland

Delamont Country Park Club Site
Downpatrick Road, Killyleagh,
Northern Ireland BT30 9TZ
Tel: 028 4482 1833
Map reference:
Pg: N/A Grid Ref: N/A
Open: 10 Mar – 31 Oct 2016
Pitches: 63

Northern England

Barnard Castle Club Site
Dockenflatts Lane, Lartington,
Barnard Castle, Cty Durham
DL12 9DG
Tel: 01833 630228
Map reference:
Pg: 223 Grid Ref: B10
Open: 3 Mar – 31 Oct 2016
Pitches: 90

Beadnell Bay Club Site
Beadnell, Chathill,
Northumberland NE67 5BX
Tel: 01665 720586
Map reference:
Pg: 264 Grid Ref: D6
Open: 17 Mar – 31 Oct 2016
Pitches: 150

Bellingham Club Site
Brown Rigg, Bellingham,
Hexham, Northumberland
NE48 2JY
Tel: 01434 220175
Map reference:
Pg: 251 Grid Ref: G8
Open: 1 Mar – 3 Jan 2017
Pitches: 70

Boroughbridge Club Site
Bar Lane, Roecliffe,
Boroughbridge, North
Yorkshire YO51 9LS
Tel: 01423 322683
Map reference:
Pg: 215 Grid Ref: F7
Open: All year
Pitches: 85

Braithwaite Fold Club Site
Glebe Rd, Bowness-On-
Windermere, Cumbria
LA23 3HB
Tel: 01539 442177
Map reference:
Pg: 221 Grid Ref: F7
Open: 4 Feb – 2 Jan 2017
Pitches: 65

Clitheroe Club Site
Edisford Road, Clitheroe,
Lancashire BB7 3LA
Tel: 01200 425294
Map reference:
Pg: 203 Grid Ref: E10
Open: 26 Feb – 31 Oct 2016
Pitches: 80

Crowden Club Site
Woodhead Road, Crowden,
Glossop SK13 1HZ
Tel: 01457 866057
Map reference:
Pg: 185 Grid Ref: B9
Open: 17 Mar – 31 Oct 2016
Pitches: 45

Derwentwater Club Site
Crow Park Road, Keswick,
Cumbria CA12 5EN
Tel: 01768 772579
Map reference:
Pg: 229 Grid Ref: G11
Open: 25 Feb – 2 Jan 2017
Pitches: 50

Dunstan Hill Club Site
Alnwick, Northumberland,
NE66 3TQ
Tel: 01665 576310
Map reference:
Pg: 264 Grid Ref: E6
Open: 17 Mar – 31 Oct 2016
Pitches: 150

Eskdale Club Site
Boot, Holmrook, Cumbria
CA19 1TH
Tel: 01946 723253
Map reference:
Pg: 220 Grid Ref: E3
Open: 1 Mar – 13 Jan 2017
Pitches: 80

Haltwhistle Club Site
Burnfoot Park Village,
Haltwhistle, Northumberland
NE49 OJP
Tel: 01434 320106
Map reference:
Pg: 240 Grid Ref: E5
Open: 24 Mar – 31 Oct 2016
Pitches: 50

Hayfield Club Site
Kinder Road, Hayfield,
High Peak, Derbyshire
SK22 2LE
Tel: 01663 745394
Map reference:
Pg: 185 Grid Ref: D8
Open: 17 Mar – 31 Oct 2016
Pitches: 90

Kendal Club Site
Millcrest, Shap Road, Kendal,
Cumbria LA9 6NY
Tel: 01539 741363
Map reference:
Pg: 221 Grid Ref: G10
Open: 24 Mar – 31 Oct 2016
Pitches: 50

Keswick Club Site
Crow Park Road, Keswick,
Cumbria CA12 5EP
Tel: 01768 772392
Map reference:
Pg: 229 Grid Ref: G11
Open: 18 Feb – 2 Jan 2017
Pitches: 250

Ravenglass Club Site
Ravenglass, Cumbria
CA18 1SR
Tel: 01229 717250
Map reference:
Pg: 219 Grid Ref: F11
Open: 1 Feb – 30 Nov
20 Dec – 2 Jan 2017
Pitches: 75

Scarborough Club Site
Field Lane, Burniston Road,
Scarborough, North Yorkshire
YO13 0DA
Tel: 01723 366212
Map reference:
Pg: 227 Grid Ref: G10
Open: 10 Mar – 31 Oct 2016
Pitches: 300

Sheriff Hutton Club Site
Bracken Hill, Sheriff Hutton,
North Yorkshire YO60 6QG
Tel: 01347 878660
Map reference:
Pg: 216 Grid Ref: F2
Open: 17 Mar – 31 Oct 2016
Pitches: 90

Slingsby Club Site
Railway Street, Slingsby,
North Yorkshire YO62 4AN
Tel: 01653 628335
Map reference:
Pg: 216 Grid Ref: D4
Open: 24 Mar – 31 Oct 2016
Pitches: 60

Troutbeck Club Site
Hutton Moor End, Troutbeck,
Penrith, Cumbria CA11 0SX
Tel: 01768 779149
Map reference:
Pg: 230 Grid Ref: F3
Open: 11 Mar – 6 Nov 2016
Pitches: 54

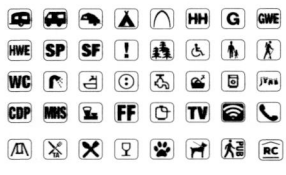

Windermere Club Site
Ashes Lane, Staveley, Kendal,
Cumbria LA8 9JS
Tel: 01539 821119
Map reference:
Pg: 221 Grid Ref: F9
Open: 11 Mar – 9 Jan 2017
Pitches: 250

Wales

Bala Club Site
Crynierth Caravan Park,
Cefn-Ddwysar, Bala,
Gwyned LL23 7LN
Tel: 01678 530324
Map reference:
Pg: 147 Grid Ref: B9
Open: 24 Mar – 31 Oct 2016
Pitches: 50

Cardigan Bay Club Site
Llwynhelyg, Cross Inn,
Llandysul, Ceredigion
SA44 6LW
Tel: 01545 560029
Map reference:
Pg: 111 Grid Ref: F7
Open: 24 Mar – 31 Oct 2016
Pitches: 90

Llanystumdwy Club Site
Tyddyn Sianel, Llanystumdwy,
Criccieth, Gwynedd LL52 0LS
Tel: 01766 522855
Map reference:
Pg: 145 Grid Ref: B9
Open: 24 Mar – 3 Oct 2016
Pitches: 70

Rhandirmwyn Club Site
Llandovery, Carmarthenshire
SA20 0NT
Tel: 01550 760257
Map reference:
Pg: 94 Grid Ref: C5
Open: 24 Mar – 31 Oct 2016
Pitches: 90

St David's Club Site
Dwr Cwmwdig, Berea,
St David's, Haverfordwest,
Pembrokeshire SA62 6DW
Tel: 01348 831376
Map reference:
Pg: 90 Grid Ref: E6
Open: 28 Apr – 3 Oct 2016
Pitches: 40

Central England

Alton, The Star Club Site
Cotton, Stoke-on-Trent,
Staffordshire ST10 3DW
Tel: 01538 702219
Map reference:
Pg: 169 Grid Ref: F9
Open: 1 Mar – 7 Nov 2016
Pitches: 195

Ashbourne Club Site
Belper Road (A517),
Hulland Ward, Bradley
Nr Ashbourne, Derbyshire
DE6 3EN
Tel: 01335 370855
Map reference:
Pg: 170 Grid Ref: F2
Open: 23 Mar – 31 Oct 2016
Pitches: 70

Bakewell Club Site
Hopping Lane, Youlgreave,
Bakewell, Derbyshire
DE45 1NA
Tel: 01629 636555
Map reference:
Pg: 170 Grid Ref: C2
Open: 17 Mar – 31 Oct 2016
Pitches: 100

Blackmore Club Site
No.2, Hanley Swan,
Worcestershire WR8 0EE
Tel: 01684 310280
Map reference:
Pg: 98 Grid Ref: C6
Open: All year
Pitches: 180

Cannock Chase Club Site
Old Youth Hostel, Wandon,
Rugeley, Staffordshire
WS15 1QW
Tel: 01889 582166
Map reference:
Pg: 151 Grid Ref: G10
Open: 17 Mar – 31 Oct 2016
Pitches: 60

Chipping Norton Club Site
Chipping Norton Road,
Chadlington, Chipping Norton,
Oxfordshire OX7 3PE
Tel: 01608 641993
Map reference:
Pg: 100 Grid Ref: G6
Open: 24 Mar – 31 Oct 2016
Pitches: 105

Clent Hills Club Site
Fieldhouse Lane, Romsley,
Halesowen, West Midlands
B62 0NH
Tel: 01562 710015
Map reference:
Pg: 117 Grid Ref: B9
Open: 24 Mar – 31 Oct 2016
Pitches: 95

Conkers, National Forest Club Site
50 Bath Lane, Moira,
Swadlincote, Derbyshire
DE12 6BD
Tel: 01283 224925
Map reference:
Pg: 152 Grid Ref: F6
Open: All year
Pitches: 90

Delamere Forest Club Site
Station Road, Delamere,
Northwich, Cheshire
CW8 2HZ
Tel: 01606 889231
Map reference:
Pg: 183 Grid Ref: G9
Open: All year
Pitches: 80

Drayton Manor Club Site
Drayton Manor, Nr Tamworth,
Staffordshire B78 3TW
Tel: 01827 260617
Map reference:
Pg: 134 Grid Ref: C3
Open: 11 Feb – 7 Nov 2016
Pitches: 90

Ebury Hill Club Site
Ring Bank, Haughton,
Shrewsbury SY4 4GB
Tel: 01743 709334
Map reference:
Pg: 149 Grid Ref: F10
Open: 24 Mar – 31 Oct 2016
Pitches: 100

Hereford Club Site
The Millpond, Little Tarrington,
Hereford HR1 4JA
Tel: 01432 890243
Map reference:
Pg: 98 Grid Ref: C2
Open: 4 Mar – 6 Nov 2016
Pitches: 102

Kingsbury Water Park Club Site
Bodymoor Heath Lane,
Sutton Coldfield,
West Midlands B76 0DY
Tel: 01827 874101
Map reference:
Pg: 134 Grid Ref: D4
Open: All year
Pitches: 150

Leek Club Site
Blackshaw Grange, Blackshaw
Moor, Leek, Staffordshire
ST13 8TL
Tel: 01538 300285
Map reference:
Pg: 169 Grid Ref: D8
Open: 17 Mar – 31 Oct 2016
Pitches: 70

Mablethorpe Club Site
Highfield, 120 Church Lane,
Mablethorpe, Lincolnshire
LN12 2NU
Tel: 01507 472374
Map reference:
Pg: 191 Grid Ref: E7
Open: 17 Mar – 31 Oct 2016
Pitches: 105

Oswestry Club Site
Cranberry Moss
Kinnerley, Oswestry,
Shropshire SY10 8DY
Tel: 01743 741118
Map reference:
Pg: 149 Grid Ref: E7
Open: All year
Pitches: 65

Teversal Club Site
Silverhill Lane, Teversal,
Notts NG17 3JJ
Tel: 01623 551838
Map reference:
Pg: 171 Grid Ref: C7
Open: All year
Pitches: 126

Winchcombe Club Site
Brooklands Farm, Alderton,
Nr Tewkesbury,
Gloucestershire
GL20 8NX
Tel: 01242 620259
Map reference:
Pg: 99 Grid Ref: E10
Open: 4 Mar – 9 Jan 2017
Pitches: 84

Wolverley Club Site
Brown Westhead Park,
Wolverley, Nr Kidderminster,
Worcestershire DY10 3PX
Tel: 01562 850909
Map reference:
Pg: 116 Grid Ref: B6
Open: 10 Mar – 31 Oct 2016
Pitches: 105

Woodhall Spa Club Site
Wellsyke Lane,
Kirkby-on-Bain, Woodhall Spa,
Lincolnshire
LN10 6YU
Tel: 01526 352911
Map reference:
Pg: 174 Grid Ref: C2
Open: 17 Mar – 31 Oct 2016
Pitches: 90

East Anglia

Cambridge Club Site
19 Cabbage Moor, Great
Shelford, Cambridgeshire
CB22 5NB
Tel: 01223 841185
Map reference:
Pg: 123 Grid Ref: G9
Open: 17 Mar – 31 Oct 2016
Pitches: 120

Kessingland Club Site
Whites Lane, Kessingland, Nr
Lowestoft, Suffolk NR33 7TF
Tel: 01502 742040
Map reference:
Pg: 143 Grid Ref: F10
Open: 17 Mar – 31 Oct 2016
Pitches: 90

Norwich Club Site
Martineau Lane, Norwich,
Norfolk NR1 2HX
Tel: 01603 620060
Map reference:
Pg: 142 Grid Ref: B4
Open: 17 Mar – 31 Oct 2016
Pitches: 50

Polstead Club Site
Holt Road, Bower House Tye,
Polstead, Suffolk CO6 5BZ
Tel: 01787 211969
Map reference:
Pg: 107 Grid Ref: C9
Open: 12 Feb – 12 Jan 2017
Pitches: 60

St Neots Club Site
Hardwick Road, Eynesbury,
St Neots, Cambridgeshire
PE19 2PR
Tel: 01480 474404
Map reference:
Pg: 122 Grid Ref: F3
Open: 17 Mar – 31 Oct 2016
Pitches: 180

Sandringham Club Site
The Sandringham Estate,
Double Lodges, Sandringham,
Norfolk PE35 6EA
Tel: 01485 542555
Map reference:
Pg: 158 Grid Ref: D3
Open: 15 Feb – 9 Jan 2017
Pitches: 275

Thetford Forest Club Site
Puddledock Farm, Great Hockham, Thetford, Norfolk IP24 1PA
Tel: 01953 498455
Map reference:
Pg: 141 Grid Ref: E8
Open: All year
Pitches: 150

West Runton Club Site
Holgate Lane, West Runton, Cromer, Norfolk NR27 9NW
Tel: 01263 837544
Map reference:
Pg: 177 Grid Ref: E11
Open: 17 Mar – 31 Oct 2016
Pitches: 200

South East England

Adgestone Club Site
Lower Road, Adgestone, Isle of Wight PO36 0HL
Tel: 01983 403432
Map reference:
Pg: 21 Grid Ref: D7
Open: 28 Apr – 3 Oct 2016
Pitches: 270

Canterbury Club Site
Bekesbourne Lane, Canterbury, Kent CT3 4AB
Tel: 01227 463216
Map reference:
Pg: 55 Grid Ref: B7
Open: All year
Pitches: 150

Chertsey Club Site
Bridge Road, Chertsey, Surrey KT16 8JX
Tel: 01932 562405
Map reference:
Pg: 66 Grid Ref: F5
Open: All year
Pitches: 150

Chichester Club Site
345 Main Road, Southbourne, Hampshire PO10 8JH
Tel: 01243 373202
Map reference:
Pg: 34 Grid Ref: F3
Open: 4 Feb – 14 Nov 2016
Pitches: 58

Crowborough Club Site
Goldsmith Recreation Ground, Bridge Road, Crowborough, Sussex TN6 2TN
Tel: 01892 664827
Map reference:
Pg: 52 Grid Ref: G4
Open: 17 Mar – 31 Oct 2016
Pitches: 90

Folkestone Club Site
The Warren, Folkestone, Kent CT19 6NQ
Tel: 01303 255093
Map reference:
Pg: 55 Grid Ref: F8
Open: 17 Mar – 31 Oct 2016
Pitches: 60

Graffham Club Site
Great Bury, Graffham, Petworth, West Sussex GU28 0QF
Tel: 01798 867476
Map reference:
Pg: 34 Grid Ref: D6
Open: 24 Mar – 31 Oct 2016
Pitches: 90

Gulliver's Milton Keynes Club Site
Frobisher Gate, Livingstone Drive, Milton Keynes MK15 0DT
Tel: 01908 679343
Map reference:
Pg: 103 Grid Ref: D7
Open: 24 Mar – 7 Nov 2016
Pitches: 90

Hertford Club Site
Mangrove Road (Not Ball Park), Hertford, Hertfordshire SG13 8AJ
Tel: 01992 586696
Map reference:
Pg: 86 Grid Ref: C4
Open: All year
Pitches: 250

Horsley Club Site
Ockham Road North, West Horsley, Surrey KT24 6PE
Tel: 01483 283273
Map reference:
Pg: 50 Grid Ref: B5
Open: 24 Mar – 31 Oct 2016
Pitches: 130

Kelvedon Hatch Club Site
Warren Lane, Doddinghurst, Brentwood, Essex CM15 0JG
Tel: 01277 372773
Map reference:
Pg: 87 Grid Ref: F9
Open: 17 Mar – 31 Oct 2016
Pitches: 90

Normans Bay Club Site
Normans Bay, Pevensey, East Sussex BN24 6PR
Tel: 01323 761190
Map reference:
Pg: 37 Grid Ref: F11
Open: 17 Mar – 31 Oct 2016
Pitches: 200

Oldbury Hill Club Site
Styants Bottom, Seal, Sevenoaks, Kent TN15 0ET
Tel: 01732 762728
Map reference:
Pg: 52 Grid Ref: B5
Open: 17 Mar – 31 Oct 2016
Pitches: 60

Oxford Club Site
426 Abingdon Road, Oxford OX1 4XG
Tel: 01865 244088
Map reference:
Pg: 83 Grid Ref: E8
Open: All year
Pitches: 85

Slindon Club Site
Slindon Park, Nr Arundel, Sussex BN18 0RG
Tel: 01243 814387
Map reference:
Pg: 35 Grid Ref: F7
Open: 24 Mar – 3 Oct 2016
Pitches: 40

Theobalds Park Club Site
Bulls Cross Ride, Waltham Cross, Hertfordshire EN7 5HS
Tel: 01992 620604
Map reference:
Pg: 86 Grid Ref: E4
Open: All year
Pitches: 90

Walton on Thames Club Site
Fieldcommon Lane, Walton on Thames, Surrey KT12 3QG
Tel: 01932 220392
Map reference:
Pg: 66 Grid Ref: F6
Open: 24 Mar – 31 Oct 2016
Pitches: 115
Note: Members Only Site

South West England

Bude Club Site
Gillards Moor, St Gennys, Bude, Cornwall EX23 0BG
Tel: 01840 230650
Map reference:
Pg: 11 Grid Ref: C9
Open: 28 Apr – 3 Oct 2016
Pitches: 100

California Cross Club Site
Modbury, Ivybridge, Devon PL21 0SG
Tel: 01548 821297
Map reference:
Pg: 8 Grid Ref: E4
Open: 28 Apr – 3 Oct 2016
Pitches: 80

Charmouth Club Site
Monkton Wyld Farm, Scotts Lane, Nr Charmouth, Dorset DT6 6DB
Tel: 01297 32965
Map reference:
Pg: 16 Grid Ref: B2
Open: 11 Mar – 31 Oct 2016
Pitches: 150

Cheddar, Mendip Heights Club Site
Mendip Heights, Townsend, Priddy Wells, Somerset BA5 3BP
Tel: 01749 870241
Map reference:
Pg: 44 Grid Ref: C4
Open: 11 Mar – 7 Nov 2016
Pitches: 90

Corfe Castle Club Site
Bucknowle, Wareham, Dorset BH20 5PQ
Tel: 01929 480280
Map reference:
Pg: 18 Grid Ref: E4
Open: 1 Mar – 31 Oct 2016
Pitches: 80

Dartmouth Club Site
Stoke Fleming, Dartmouth, Devon TQ6 0RF
Tel: 01803 770253
Map reference:
Pg: 9 Grid Ref: F7
Open: 24 Mar – 31 Oct 2016
Pitches: 90

Devizes Club Site
Spout Lane, Nr Seend, Melksham, Wiltshire SN12 6RN
Tel: 01380 828839
Map reference:
Pg: 62 Grid Ref: G2
Open: All year
Pitches: 90

Lynton Club Site
Lydiate Lane, Caffyn's Cross, Lynton, Devon EX35 6JS
Tel: 01598 752379
Map reference:
Pg: 41 Grid Ref: D8
Open: 24 Mar – 3 Oct 2016
Pitches: 105

Minehead Club Site
Hill Road, North Hill, Minehead, Somerset TA24 5LB
Tel: 01643 704138
Map reference:
Pg: 42 Grid Ref: D3
Open: 28 Apr – 3 Oct 2016
Pitches: 60

Moreton Club Site
Station Road, Moreton, Dorchester, Dorset DT2 8BB
Tel: 01305 853801
Map reference:
Pg: 17 Grid Ref: D11
Open: 24 Mar – 31 Oct 2016
Pitches: 120

Salisbury Club Site
Hudson's Field, Castle Road, Salisbury, Wiltshire SP1 3SA
Tel: 01722 320713
Map reference:
Pg: 46 Grid Ref: G6
Open: 24 Mar – 6 Jan 2017
Pitches: 150

Sennen Cove Club Site
Higher Tregiffian Farm, St Buryan, Penzance, Cornwall TR19 6JB
Tel: 01736 871588
Map reference:
Pg: 1 Grid Ref: D3
Open: 24 Mar – 31 Oct 2016
Pitches: 72

Slapton Sands Club Site
Middle Grounds, Slapton, Kingsbridge, Devon TQ7 2QW
Tel: 01548 580538
Map reference:
Pg: 8 Grid Ref: G6
Open: 24 Mar – 31 Oct 2016
Pitches: 115
Note: Member-only caravans

Tavistock Club Site
Higher Longford, Moorshop, Devon PL19 9LQ
Tel: 01822 618672
Map reference:
Pg: 12 Grid Ref: G6
Open: All year
Pitches: 80

Teign Valley, Barley Meadow Club Site
Crockernwell, Exeter, Devon EX6 6NR
Tel: 01647 281629
Map reference:
Pg: 13 Grid Ref: C10
Open: 10 Mar – 7 Nov 2016
Pitches: 63

Tregurrian Club Site
Nr Newquay, Cornwall TR8 4AE
Tel: 01637 860448
Map reference:
Pg: 4 Grid Ref: B6
Open: 10 Mar – 31 Oct 2016
Pitches: 90

Umberleigh Club Site
Over Weir, Umberleigh,
Devon EX37 9DU
Tel: 01769 560009
Map reference:
Pg: 25 Grid Ref: C10
Open: 24 Mar – 31 Oct 2016
Pitches: 60

Verwood Club Site
Sutton Hill, Woodlands,
Wimborne, Dorset
BH21 8NQ
Tel: 01202 822763
Map reference:
Pg: 31 Grid Ref: F9
Open: 24 Mar – 31 Oct 2016
Pitches: 150

Veryan Club Site
Tretheake, Veryan, Truro,
Cornwall TR2 5PP
Tel: 01872 501658
Map reference:
Pg: 5 Grid Ref: G8
Open: 24 Mar – 31 Oct 2016
Pitches: 150

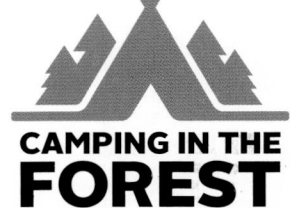

CAMPING IN THE FOREST

New Forest

Aldridge Hill CITF Site
Brockenhurst, Hampshire
SO42 7QD
Tel: 01590 623152
Map reference:
Pg: 32 Grid Ref: G3
Open: 26 May – 6 Jun 2016
23 Jun – 5 Sep
Pitches: 170

Ashurst CITF Site
Lyndhurst Road, Ashurst,
Hampshire SO40 7AR
Tel: 02380 292097
Map reference:
Pg: 32 Grid Ref: F4
Open: 17 Mar – 26 Sep 2016
Pitches: 280

Denny and Matley Wood CITF Sites
Beaulieu Road, Lyndhurst,
Hampshire SO43 7FZ
Tel: 02380 293144
Map reference:
Pg: 32 Grid Ref: F4
Open: 17 Mar – 26 Sep 2016
Pitches: 240

Denny Wood

Matley Wood

Hollands Wood CITF Site
Lyndhurst Road, Brockenhurst,
Hampshire SO42 7QH
Tel: 01590 622967
Map reference:
Pg: 32 Grid Ref: G4
Open: 17 Mar – 26 Sep 2016
Pitches: 600

Holmsley CITF Site
Forest Road, Thorney Hill,
Bransgore, Christchurch,
Dorset BH23 7EQ
Tel: 01425 674502
Map reference:
Pg: 19 Grid Ref: B10
Open: 17 Mar – 31 Oct 2016
Pitches: 600

Ocknell and Longbeech CITF Sites
Fritham, Hampshire SO43 7HH
Tel: 02380 812740
Map reference:
Pg: 32 Grid Ref: E2
Open: 17 Mar – 26 Sep 2016
Pitches: 480

Ocknell

Longbeech

Roundhill CITF Site
Beaulieu Road, Brockenhurst,
Hampshire SO42 7QL
Tel: 01590 624344
Map reference:
Pg: 32 Grid Ref: G4
Open: 17 Mar – 26 Sep 2016
Pitches: 500

Setthorns CITF Site
Wooton, New Milton,
Hampshire BH25 5WA
Tel: 01590 681020
Map reference:
Pg: 32 Grid Ref: G3
Open: All year
Pitches: 235

Forest of Dean

Bracelands CITF Site
Bracelands Drive, Christchurch,
Coleford, Gloucester GL16 7NP
Tel: 01594 837258
Map reference:
Pg: 79 Grid Ref: C9
Open: All year
Pitches: 520

Savernake Forest

Postern Hill CITF Site
Postern Hill, Marlborough,
Wiltshire SN8 4ND
Tel: 01672 515195
Map reference:
Pg: 63 Grid Ref: F7
Open: All Year
Pitches: 170

Snowdonia National Park

Beddgelert CITF Site
Beddgelert, Gwynedd LL55 4UU
Tel: 01766 890288
Map reference:
Pg: 163 Grid Ref: F9
Open: All Year
Pitches: 195

Loch Lomond and Trossachs National Park

Cashel CITF Site
Rowardennan G63 0AW
Tel: 01360 870234
Map reference:
Pg: 277 Grid Ref: C7
Open: 1 Mar – 24 Oct 2016
Pitches: 168

Cobleland CITF Site
Station Road, Gartmore,
Stirlingshire FK8 3RR
Tel: 01877 382392
Map reference:
Pg: 277 Grid Ref: B10
Open: 17 Mar – 24 Oct 2016
Pitches: 126

Cairngorms National Park

Glenmore CITF Site
Aviemore
Inverness-shire
PH22 1QU
01479 861271
Map reference:
Pg: 291 Grid Ref: C11
Open: All Year
Pitches: 206

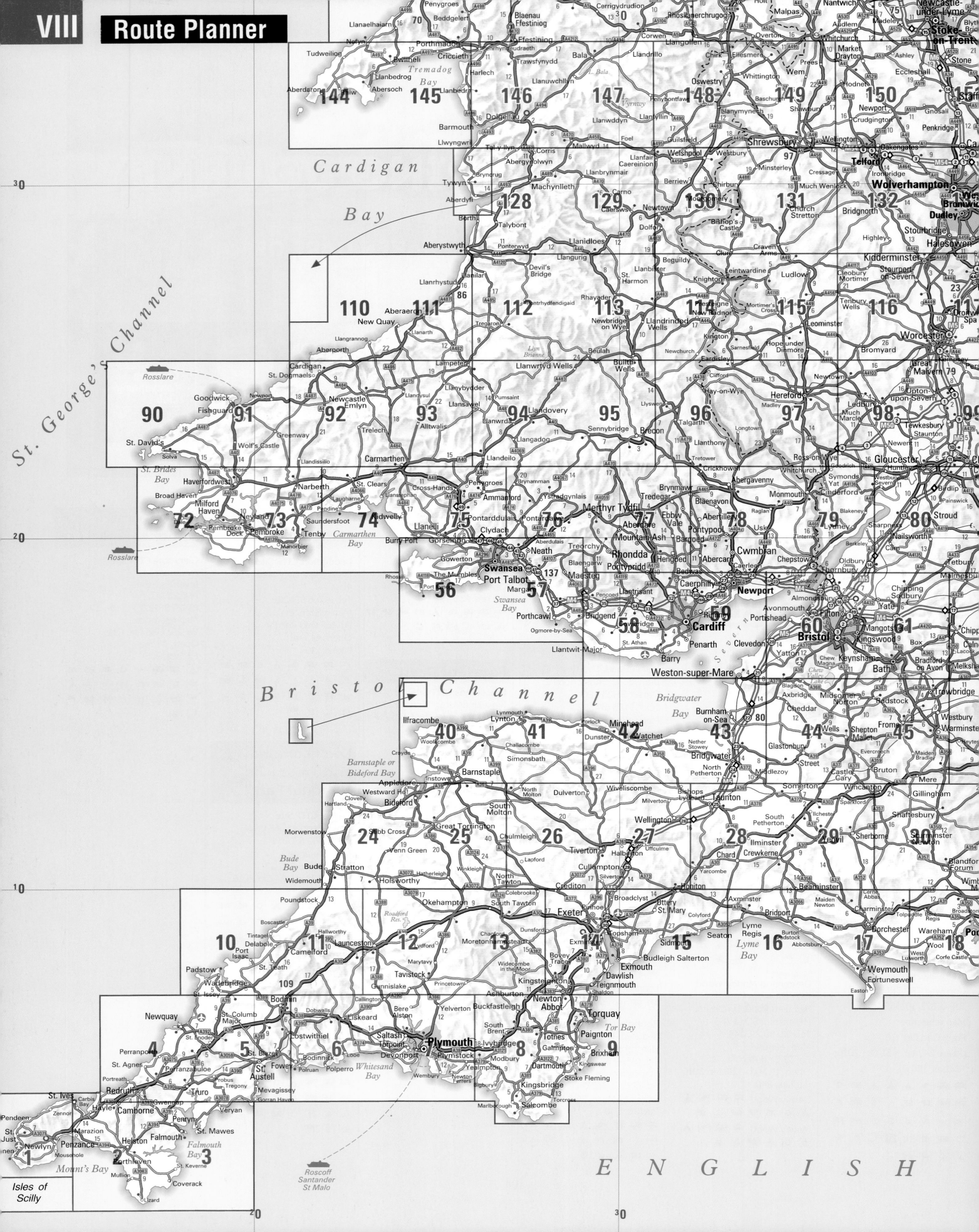

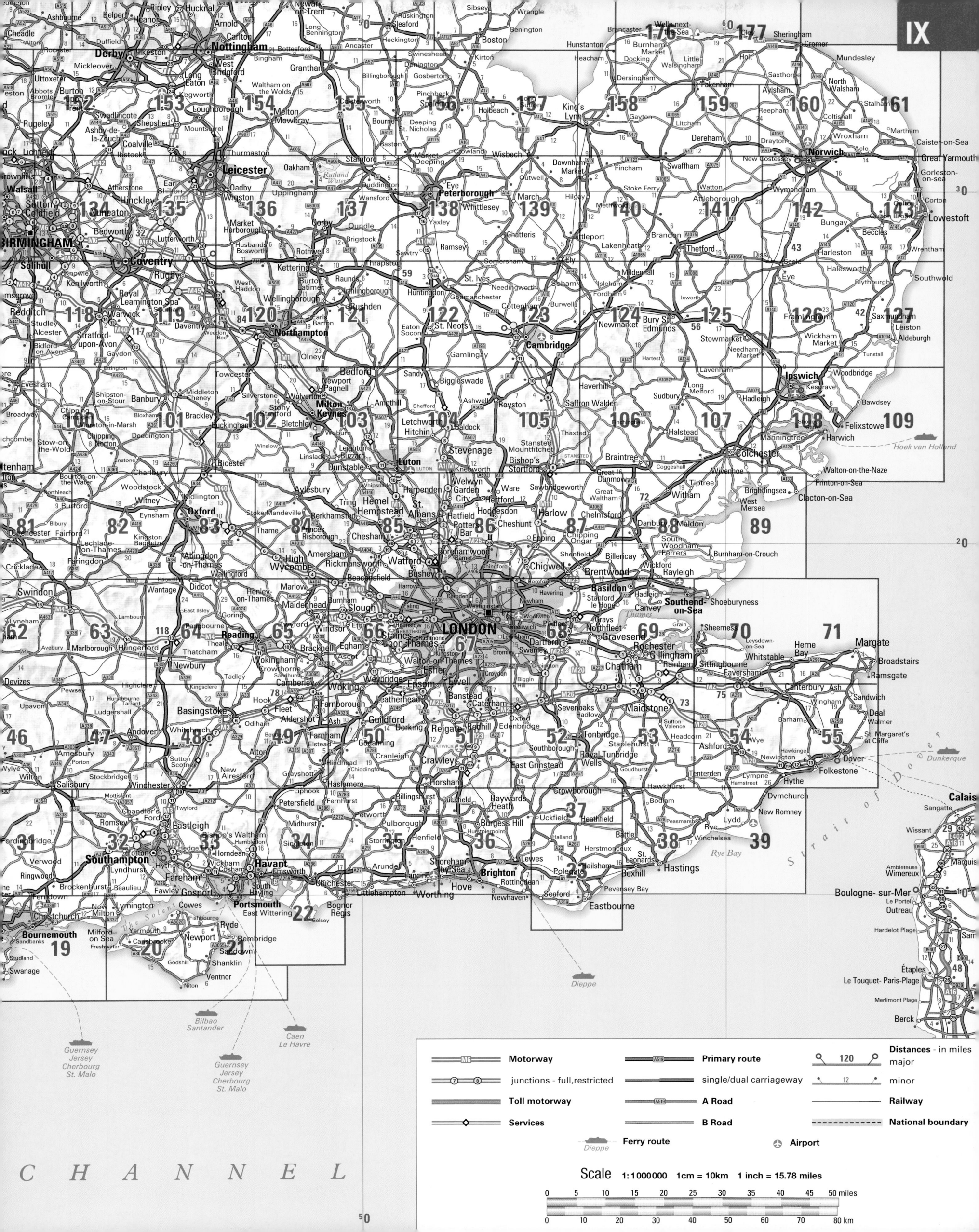

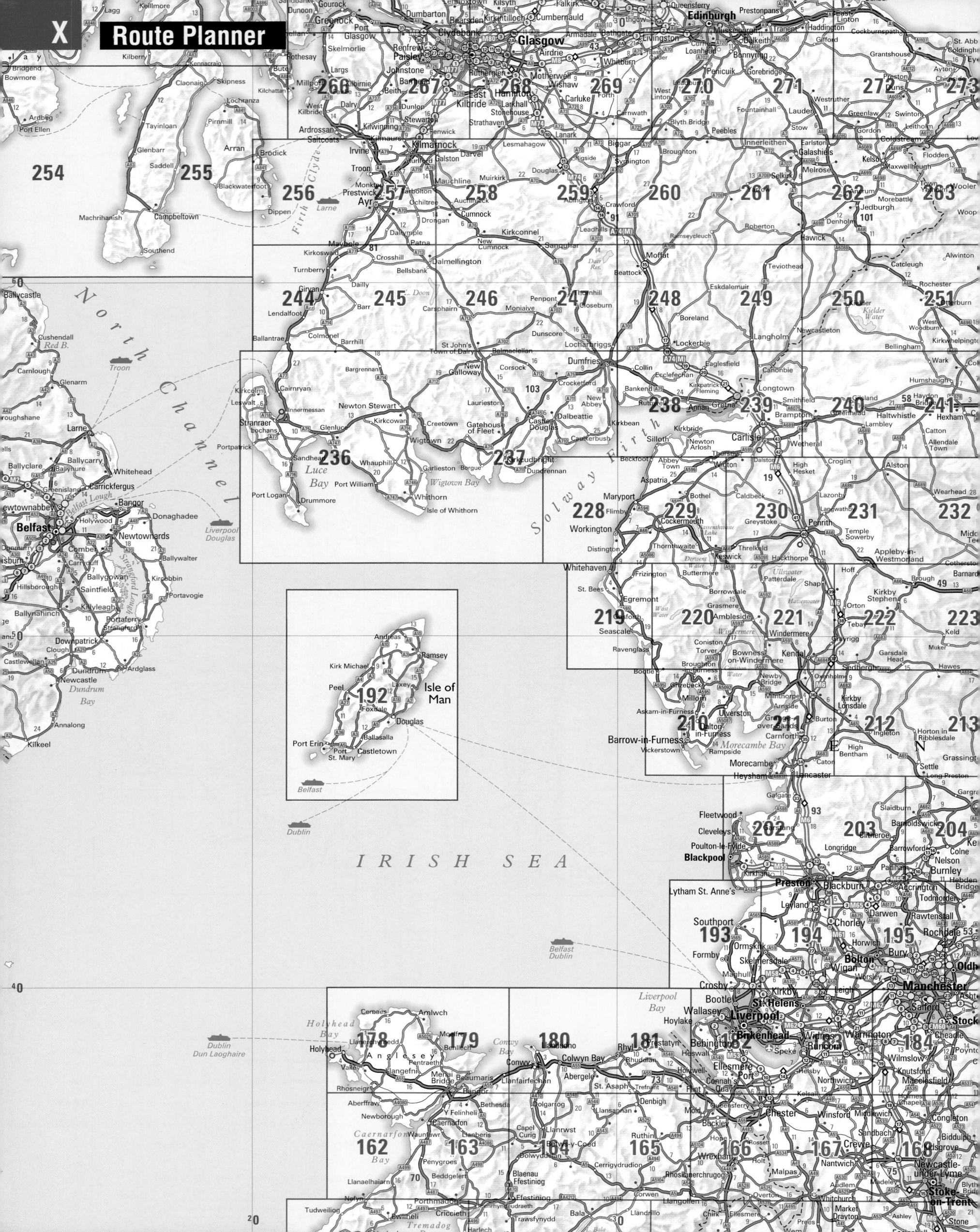

50

60

**NORTH
SEA**

Amsterdam

Berwick-upon-Tweed
Scremerston

Belford
Bamburgh
Seahouses
Beadnell
Charlton
264 **265**
Alnwick
Embleton
Longhoughton
Lesbury
Alnmouth
Warkworth
Amble

252 **253**
Longframlington
Widdrington
Longhorsley
Ashington
Pegswood
Newbiggin-by-the-Sea
Hartburn
Morpeth
Belsay
Bedlington
Whalton
Blyth
Ponteland
Cramlington
Whitley Bay
242 Longbenton Tynemouth
Newcastle-Upon-Tyne **243**
Jarrow South Shields
Whickham Gateshead
Sunderland
Washington
Consett Chester-le-Street
Lanchester Houghton-le-Spring
Durham Seaham
Hetton-le-Hole Peterlee
Willington **233** **234** Hartlepool **235**
Spennymoor Ferryhill Sedgefield
Bishop Auckland Trimdon
Newton Redcar
Aycliffe Billingham Marske-by-the-Sea
Stockton-on-Tees Saltburn-by-the-Sea
Darlington **Middlesbrough** Staithes
Bowes Thornaby-on-Tees Loftus
Yarm Guisborough
224 **225** Stokesley **226** Sleights **227** Robin Hood's Bay
Richmond Scotch Corner Whitby
Catterick
Reeth Northallerton
Leyburn Burniston
Bedale Scalby Scarborough
Masham Thirsk Kirkbymoorside
Sowerby Helmsley Thornton-le-Dale
Kirkby Malzeard Pickering Filey
214 **215** Hovingham **216** **217** **218**
Ripon Malton Snainton Flamborough
Pateley Bridge Boroughbridge Stillington Norton-on-Derwent
G L A N D Sledmere Bridlington
Knaresborough Fridaythorpe Rudston Burton Agnes
Harrogate Stamford Bridge Driffield Bridlington Bay
Ilkley Otley Wetherby York Pocklington
205 **206** **207** Bainton **208** **209**
Baildon Collingham Escrick Hutton Cranswick Skipsea
Bingley Saltaire Tadcaster Holme-on-Spalding-Moor North Frodingham Hornsea
Leeds Selby South Market Weighton Leven
Bradford Garforth Cave Beverley Aldbrough
Halifax Castleford Howden Cottingham Sproatley
Brighouse Pontefract Snaith Goole **Kingston upon Hull** Hedon
Dewsbury Wakefield Thorne Burton upon Stather Barrow upon Humber Keyingham Withernsea
19 **Huddersfield** **197** **198** **199** Barton-upon-Humber **200** **201** Patrington
Meltham Darton Adwick le Street Scunthorpe Ulceby Immingham Easington
Barnsley Hatfield Barnetby le Wold **Grimsby**
Holmfirth Wombwell Epworth Brigg Cleethorpes
Penistone Mexborough **Doncaster** Scotter Humberston
Stocksbridge Rotherham Bawtry Kirton in Lindsey Caistor North
Glossop **185** **186** **187** Maltby **188** Gainsborough **189** Market **190** North Somercotes Saltfleet
Sheffield Blyth Beckingham Rasen Binbrook Thoresby
Chesterfield Eckington Worksop Retford Walkeringham Faldingworth Louth Withern **191** Mablethorpe
Dronfield Sturton Wragby Scamblesby Sutton-on-Sea
Buxton Baslow Staveley Saxilby Horncastle Huttoft
Chesterfield Clowne Bolsover East Markham Alford
Bakewell Clay Cross Ollerton Sutton-on-Trent Bardney Partney Burgh le Marsh
Matlock Market Lincoln Woodhall Spa Spilsby Skegness
169 **170** Warsop **171** **172** **173** **174** Wrangle **175**
Wirksworth Alfreton Mansfield Collingham Coningsby Wainfleet All Saints
Ashbourne Belper Sutton in Ashfield Southwell Newark-on-Trent Sibsey
Ilkeston Hucknall Long Bennington Ruskington The Wash
Derby Arnold Sleaford Heckington Boston Hunstanton
Mickleover Carlton **Nottingham** Ancaster Benington **176** **177**
West Bridgford Bottesford Bingham Grantham Brancaster Wells-next-the-Sea Sheringham
Kirton Burnham Market Holt Cromer
Long Heacham Docking Walsingham Little
Bridgford Gosberton Hunstanton Mundesley
Dersingham Saxthorpe
North

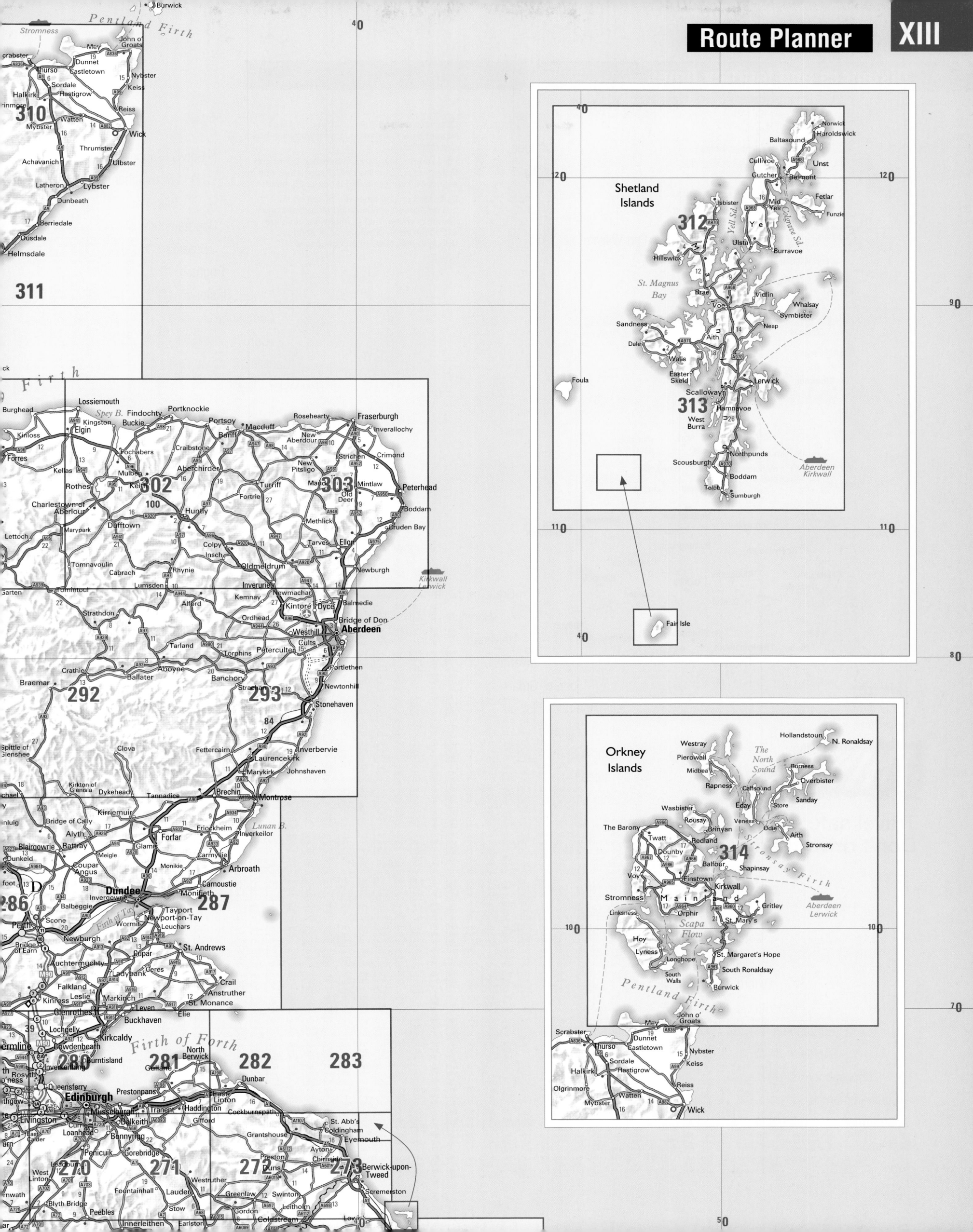

Distances and journey times

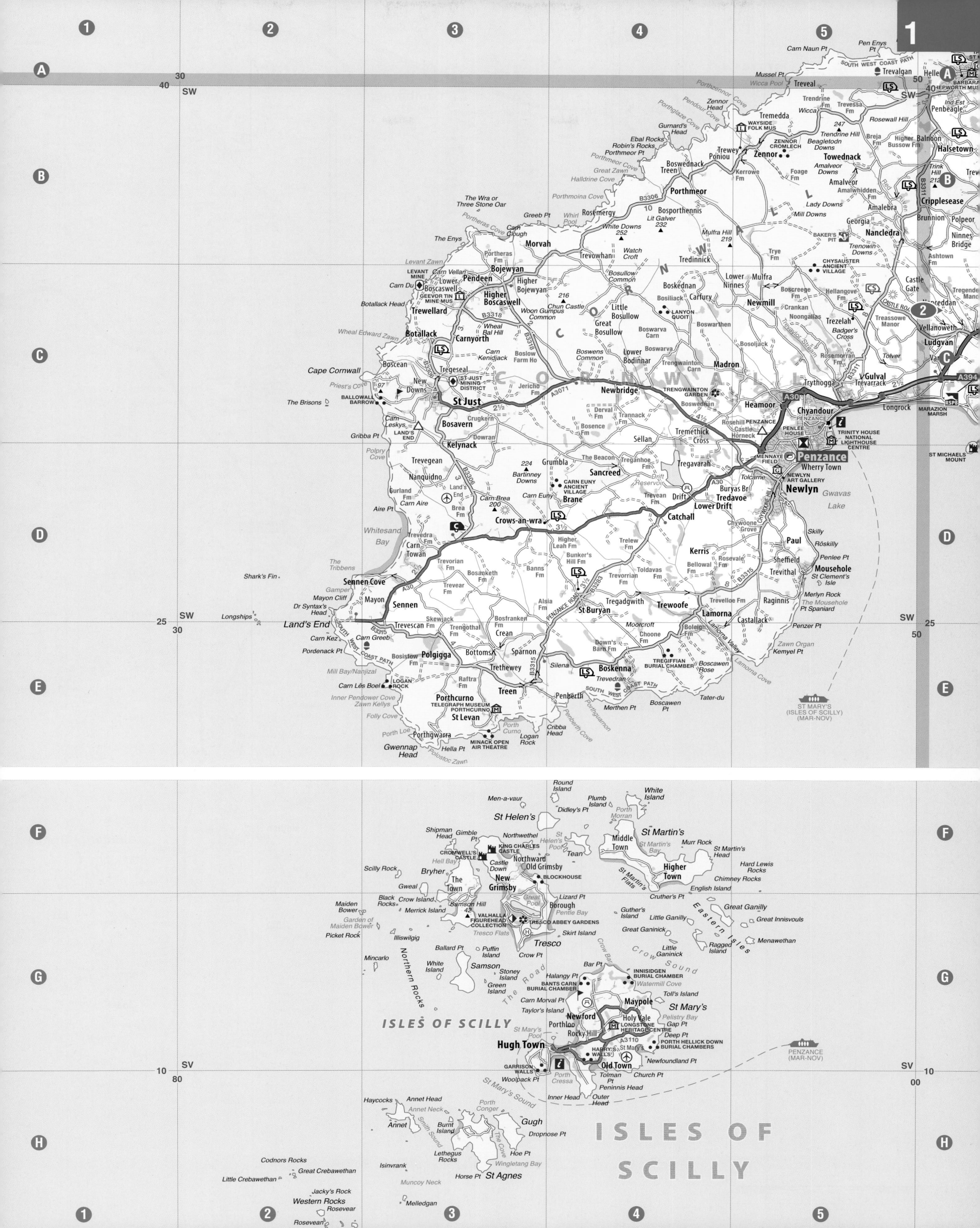

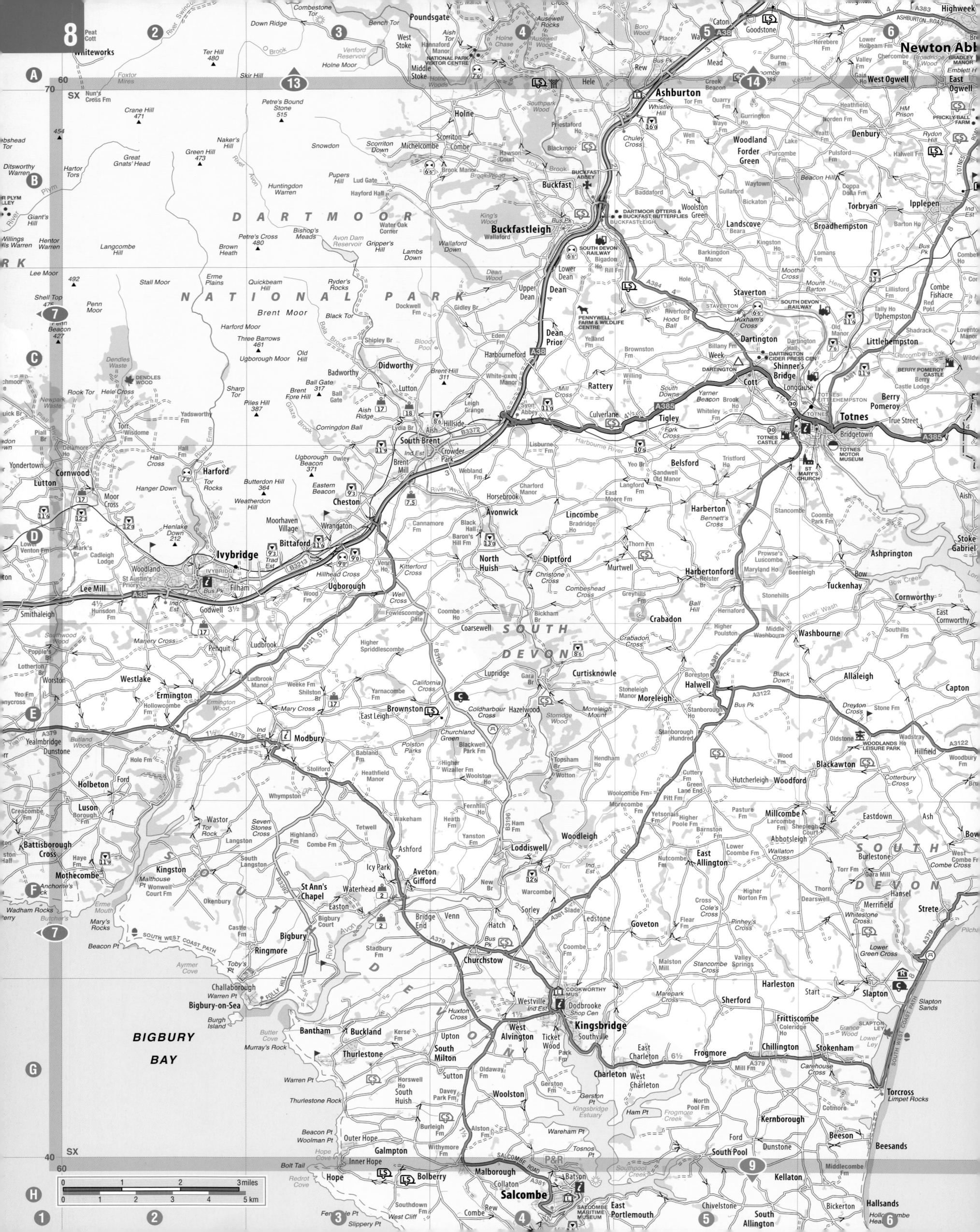

ABBOT
Knowles Hill
Lower Netherton
Combeinteignhead
Sheldon
SHALDON WILDLIFE TRUST
The Ness Ho
Newton Abbot
Buckland
Netherton
Higher Netherton
Combeinteignhead
The Beacon 169
Labrador Bay
Wolborough
Milber
Newtake
Haccombe
Trad Est
Teinginhead
14
Lower Gabwell
Higher Gabwell
15
10
70
SY
A
Aller Park
Langford Br
PLANT WORLD
Middle Rocombe
Blackaller's Cove
Abbotskerswell
Aller
Mile Cross
Stoneycombe
Coffinswell
Daccombe
Maidencombe
Rock Ho
Bell Rock
B
Dainton
Blair Hill
North Whilborough
Kingskerswell
Higher Rocombe Barton
Barton
Watcombe
Watcombe Head
Moles Cross
Edginswell
Kerswell Gardens
Combe Pafford
St Marychurch
BABBACOMBE
COMPTON CASTLE
Compton
Shiphay
Hele
Retail Pk
MODEL VILLAGE
BYGONES
BAY
Marldon
Widdicombe Fm
Chelston
Torre
Plainmoor
Babbacombe
Bus Pk
Torquay
Ellacombe
KENT'S CAVERN
Black Head
C
Cockington
Stantor Barton
TORQUAY
TORRE ABBEY
Wellswood
Anstey's Cove
Churscombe
Shorton
Preston
Livermead
LIVING COASTS
Lead Stone or Flat Rock
Daddyhole Cove
Thatcher Rock
Blagdon
Hollicombe
Peaked Tor Cove
ORBAY
Collaton St Mary
Primley
Paignton
TOR BAY
Windmill Hill
KIRKHAM HOUSE
St Michael's
Roundham Head
166
PAIGNTON ZOO
GOODRINGTON SANDS
P (APR - OCT)
Yalberton
Bus Pk
Goodrington
QUAYWEST
Saltern Cove
D
Port Bridge
Broadsands
Elberry Cove
Fishcombe Pt
BERRY HEAD
Waddeton
Galmpton
CHURSTON
BRIXHAM HERITAGE MUSEUM
THE GOLDEN HIND
BERRY HEAD
GREENWAY HALT
Churston Ferrers
Brixham
Cod Rock
Durl Head
Dittisham
Maypool
GREENWAY
Alston Fm
Higher Brixham
St Mary's Bay
Cott Fm
RIVER DART
DARTMOUTH STEAM RAILWAY
Sharkham Pt
SOUTH
Hillhead
Southdown Cliff
Old Mill Creek
BRIDGE
ROAD
Hillhead Fm
Man Sands
Crabrock Pt
DEVON
Woodown Fm
Woodhuish Fm
Cod Rocks
Long Sands
E
Dartmouth
NEWCOMEN ENGINE HO
Kingston
Scabbacombe Sands
Scabbacombe Head
Norton
STSAVIOUR'S CHURCH
Kingswear
COLETON FISHACRE GDN
Ivy Cove
BAYARD'S COVE FORT
Warfleet
KINGSWEAR
Pudcombe Cove
Cotton
P&R
Wheatland
DARTMOUTH CASTLE
Kelly's Cove
Newfoundland Cove
SY
50
Venn
Blackstone Pt
Compass Cove
Outer Froward Pt
Eastern Black Rock
10
F
Stoke Fleming
Combe Pt
Meg Rocks
Blackpool
Redlap Cove
Matthew's Pt
Leonard's Cove
Cove

F
Ho
South Huish
Davey Park Fm
Woolston
Gerston Fm
Gerston Fm
Charleton
North Pool Fm
Frogmore Creek
Torcross
Limpet Rocks
Burleigh Fm
Alston Fm
Kingsbridge Estuary
Ham Pt
Kernborough
Beeson
Galmpton
Withymore Fm
Wareham Pt
Ford
Dunstone
Beesands
er Hope
SALCOMBE ROAD
Tosnos
P&R
Southpool Creek
South Pc
8
Kellaton
Middlecombe
Malborough
Batson
Bolberry
Collaton
A381
Chivelstone
South Allington
Bickerton
Hallsands
Salcombe
SALCOMBE MARITIME MUSEUM
East Portlemouth
Hollowcombe Head
Soar
Rew
Combe
SALCOMBE
Mill Bay
South Sands
Nestley Pt
G
Cathole Cliff
OVERBECKS MUSEUM & GARDEN
Shag Rock
East Prawle
Gorah Rocks
Sleadon Rocks
Start Pt
Lantern Rock
Deckler's Cliff
Black Stone
Little Mew Stone
Ball Rock
Ballsaddle Rock
Bolt Head
Gammon Head
Langerstone Pt
START BAY
Prawle Pt
Sharpers Head
SX
35
SX
40
85
90
H

Hill Head

Blackfield

Calshot

Setley

Perrywood
Brockenhurst
Park

Hatchet
Gate

Otterwood

Swinesleys

Badminston
Common

Sprat's Down

Langley

Whitefield

Round
Hill

East
Boldre

Beutre

Keeping
Copse

Gatewood
Hill

West
Common

Stanswood

Battramsley

Sandy
Down

Dilton
Gardens

Hatchet
Moor

Newhouse
Copse

Ashen
Wood

Steam
Railway

Exbury
Gardens

Stanswood
Bay

Birchy
Hill

Boldre

Pilley
Bailey

Crockford
Bridge

Buckers
Hard

Maritime
Museum

Exbury

Stone

Shirley
holms

Battramsley
Cross

Bull
Hill

Norley
Inclosure

Newlands
Plantn

Horsemoor
Copse

Salternshill
Copse

Lepe

LEPE

Stansore Pt

Mount
Pleasant

St Austins

Portmore

Norleywood

South
Baddesley

East
End

Beck
Fm

Thorns
Fm

Lower
Exbury

Gins

Inchmery Ho

Stone Pt

Bowling
Green

Buckland

Walhampton

Pitts
Deep

Pylewell
Lake

Colgrims

North
Solent

Needs Ore Pt

Little
Marsh

Park
Shore

THE

Cowes Roads

Lymington

Pennington

Waterford

Pylewell Pt

Old Castle Pt

Cowes

East
Cowes

Springhill

Everton

Woodside

Lymington
Spit

Maritime
Museum

Gurnard

Osborne
Bay

Milford
on Sea

Lower
Pennington

Pennington
Marshes

Keyhaven

KEYHAVEN & PENNINGTON
MARSHES NATURE RESERVE

Newtown
River

Thorness Bay

Gurnard Ledge

Rew
Street

Northwood

Whippance
Fm

Hillis Corner

Somerton
Fm

Whippingham

Ludham
Cottage

King's Quay

Woodside

Hurst Beach

Sconce Pt

Yarmouth
Castle

Hamstead
Lower Hamstead

Newtown
Harbour

Old Town
Hall

Porchfield

Clamerkin
Lake

Little
Whitehouse

Mark's
Corner

Noke
Fm

Parkhurst

Parkhurst
Forest

Signal
Ho

Fairlee

Wootton
Common

BUTTERFLY
WORLD

The
Grange

Littletown

Wootton
Bridge

WOOTTON

Hurst Castle

FORT VICTORIA &
MARINE AQUARIUM

Cliff End

Bouldnor

Lee
Copse

Ningwood
Common

Shalfleet

Vittlefields
Fm

Forest
Side

Park
Green Fm

Gunville

Retail Pk

CLASSIC
BOAT MUS

Staplers

Blacklands

Brambles Chine

Colwell Bay

Norton

Yarmouth

Thorley
Brook

Ningwood

Ningwood
Manor Fm

Elm
Fm

Newpark
Fm

Hunny
Hill

Barton

Warden Point

Norton
Green

Thorley
Street

Thorley

Wellow

East Gate
Barn

Five Houses

Bulls
Wood

Fulholding
Fm

Great
Park

Carisbrooke

Newport

Doreshill
Lodge

RAVENS

Lynn
Fm

Combley
Great
Wood

Totland

Freshwater

Newbridge

Calbourne
Water Mill

Calbourne

Mudless
Fm

Newbarn
Fm

Apes
Down

Clatterford

CARISBROOKE
CASTLE & MUSEUM

Shide

Pan

New Close
Ho

ROBIN HILL
ADVENTURE PARK

Downend

Weston
Manor

Pound
Green

Easton

DIMBOLA
LODGE

Freshwater
Bay

Afton

Newport Road

Churchills
Fm

Westover
Fm

Tapnell
Fm

High
Wood

Bowcombe

Great Whitcombe
Manor

Standen
Ho

Arreton

Hatherwood Pt

Alum Bay

CHAIR
LIFT

THE NEEDLES
PARK

Warren
Fm

Totland Bay

TOTLAND
BAY

Weston

Shalcombe

CHESSELL
POTTERY BARNS

Westover
Plantn

Blackwater

St George's
Down

Merston
Manor

ARRETON
MANOR

ISLE OF WIGHT
MARITIME MUSEUM

The Needles

THE NEEDLES OLD
BATTERY

Main Bench

Compton Bay

Compton
Fm

Westover
Down

Brighstone
Forest

Gatcombe

Gatcombe

Long
Copse

Sheat
Manor

Chillerton

Rookley

ROOKLEY

Stickworth
Hall

Horringford

Scratchell's Bay

Shippards Chine

Hanover Pt

Brook

Long
Stone

Hulverstone

MOTTISTONE
MANOR GARDEN

Rock

Cheverton
Down

Cheverton
Fm

Rowborough
Fm

Lorden
Copse

Loverstone
Fm

Chillerton
Down

Ramsdown
Fm

Rookley
Green

Harts
Green

Bohemia
Corner

Little
Budbridge
Fm

Great
Budbridge Manor

Brook
Bay

Mottistone

Moortown

Brighstone

The Undercliff

Limerstone

Shorwell

Sandy Way

Wolverton
Manor

New
Barn Fm

Prestord

Cridmore

Lessiland
Moor Fm

Leechmore
Fm

French
Mill

Bedhill
Fm

Chilton Chine

Chilton
Fm 11

Yafford

Yafford
Ho

Bucks

Kingston

Dungewood
Fm

Corve
Fm

Godshill

NATURAL
HISTORY
CENTRE

MODEL
VILLAGE

Shanklin

NOSTALGIA
TOY MUSEUM

DONKEY
SANCTUARY

Sandfo

ISLE OF
WIGHT PEARL

Hardman Rock

Thorncross

Grange Chine

Sutton
Fm

Marsh
Green Fm

Samber
Hill

Little
Atherfield

Beckfield
Cross

Billingham
Manor

Bridge
Fm

Roud

OWL & FALCONRY
CENTRE

APPULDERCOMBE
HOUSE

Sheepwash
Fm

Span

Rew

Wroxall

Shepherd's Chine

Atherfield
Green

Atherfield Pt

Pyle

Chale
Green

Upper
Appleford Fm

Gotten
Manor

Ford
Fm

Bierley

Stenbury
Manor

Stenbury
Down

Southford

Nettlecombe

Week
Fm

Whale
Chine

St Catherine's
Down

Downcourt
Fm

Kingates

Jobsons
Fm

Whitwell

Dean
Fm

Chale Bay

Chale

St Catherine's
Hill 236

ST CATHERINE'S
ORATORY

Blackgang

BLACKGANG
CHINE

Niton

St Catherine's Pt

Waatershoot Bay

Knoles
Fm

Puckaster
Cove

Binnel Pt

St Lawrence

Binnel
Bay

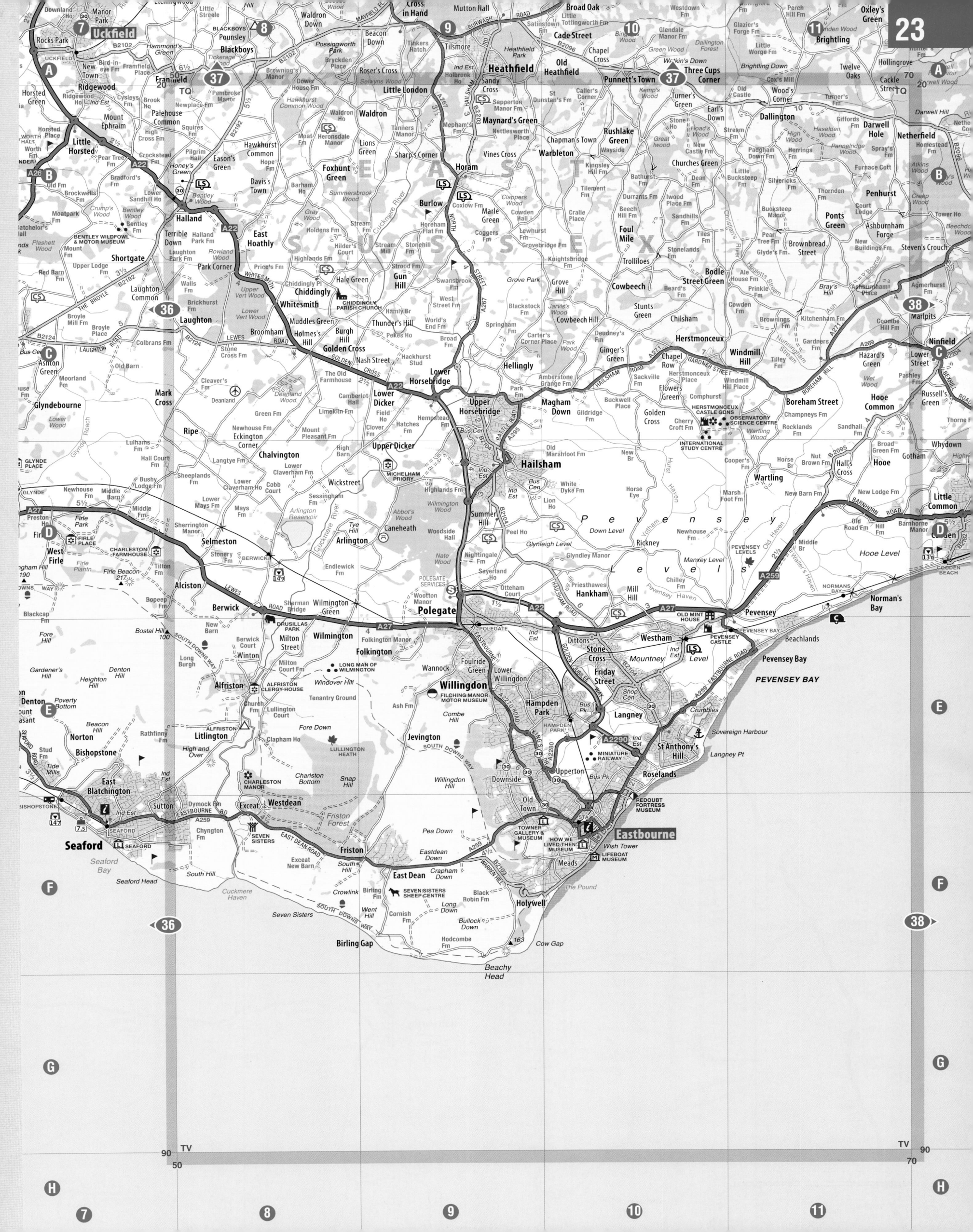

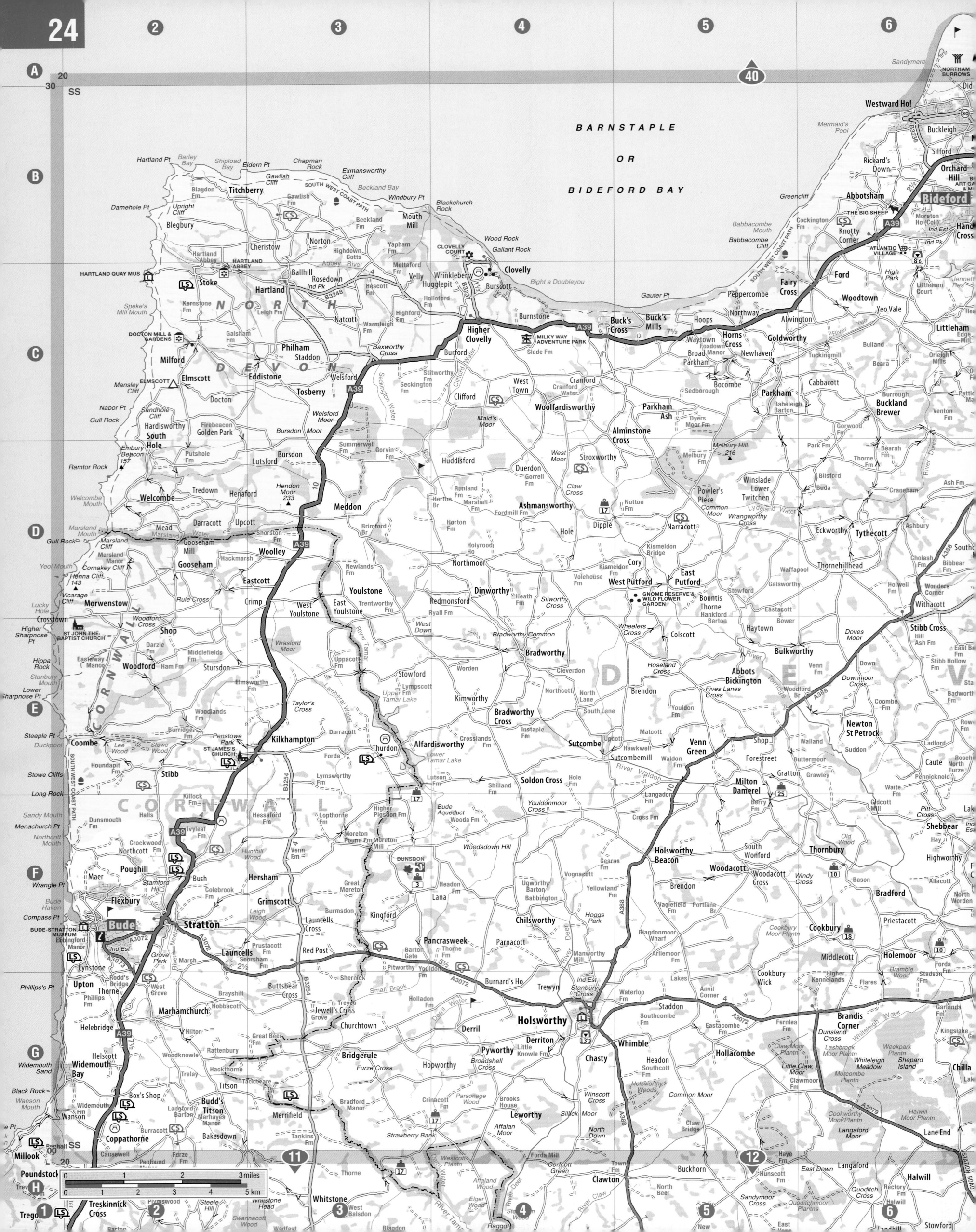

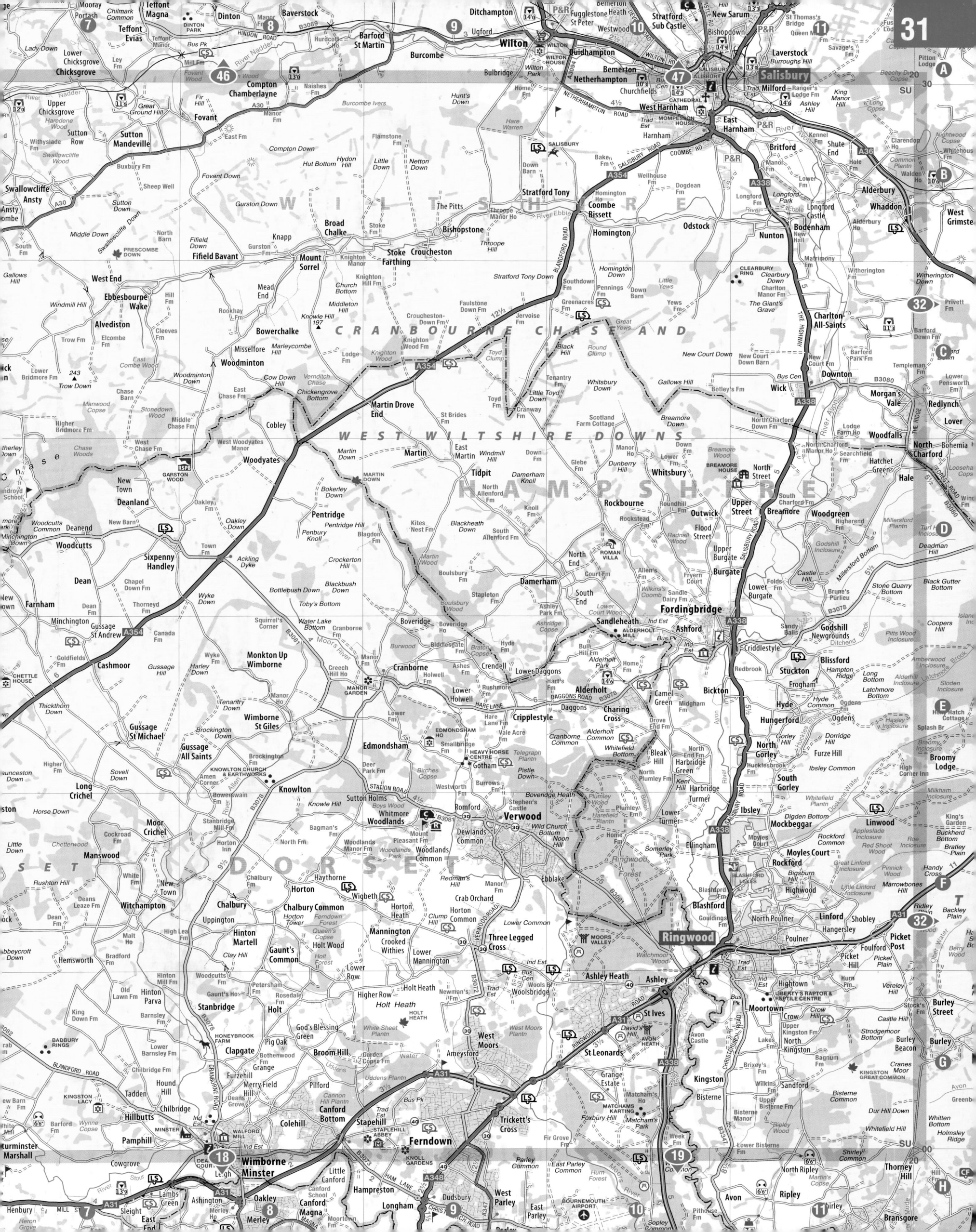

Lundy

Hen & Chickens
North West Pt
Seals' Rock
North East Pt
Gannets' Rock
Gannets' Bay
St James's Stone
Tibbetts Hill 138
Tibbett's Pt
LUNDY MARINE NATURE RESERVE
Jenny's Cove
Lundy Roads
Dead Cow Pt
Ackland's Moor 142
BIDEFORD (MAR-OCT)
ILFRACOMBE (MAR-OCT)
Halftide Rock
Beacon Hill
Castle Hill
Rat Island
South West Pt
Surf Pt

LUNDY (MAR-OCT)
Capstone Pt
Samson's Bay
Water Mouth
WATERMOUTH CASTLE
Rawn's Rocks
Blackstone Pt
Elwill Bay
Trentisho
SOUTH WEST COAST PATH
Hele Bay
Little Hangman 218
Gt Hangman 318
Holdstone Down 349
South Dean Fm
Trentishoe Down

Ilfracombe
Hele
OLD CORN MILL
Hole Fm
Goosewell
Hangman Pt
Lester Cliff
Girt Fm
Girl Down
Holdstone Fm
MUSEUM
Chambercombe
CHAMBERCOMBE MANOR
Kitstone Hill
10.9
Berrynarbor
Lee
Combe Martin
Knap Down
Verwill Fm
Stony Corner
Trentishoe Manor
Walner Fm
High

Bull Pt
Pensport Rock
Lee Bay
Shag Pt
Flat Pt
Lincombe
Higher Slade
NORTH DEVON
Sterridge
Warmscombe Fm
Ruggaton Fm
Bowden Fm
Smythen
Stoneditch Hill
Nutcombe
LONG
Westleigh
Truckwell
Dean
Cowley Wood
Rockham Bay
North Morte Fm
Higher Warcombe
Whitestone
Shaftsboro
Campscott Fm
Slade Resvr
Lower Slade
Oakridge Fm
Henstridge
Hempster Fm
WILDLIFE & DINOSAUR PARK
South Ley
A3123
Kentisbury
Higher Week Fm
Kentisbury Down

Morte Pt
North Morte Fm
Mortehoe
Borough Cross
Little Shelfin Fm
Two Pots
2 A3123
Ettiford Fm
Stapleton Fm
Berry Down
Berry Down Cross
Cleave Fm
Bugford
Stonecombe
Preston Ho
A39
Bridwick

Grunta Pool
Woolacombe
Mill Rock
Manor Fm
Trimstone
Willingcott
Cheglinch
Hore Down Fm
Outer Narracott Fm
Hillcrest Fm
Highlands Fm
Ford Fm
Northcote Fm
Patchole
Higher Week Fm
A39

Morte Bay
Ossaborough
Ivycott
Roadway
Bradwell
Dean Cross
Dean
Higher Aylescott
Fullabrook
Centery Fm
Little Silver
Collacott Fm
Dingles Fm
Wigmore Fm
Clifton Fm
East Down
Kentisbury Ford
Halls Cross
Hallsdown Fm
EXM

Black Rock
Putsborough Sand
Pickwell Down
Spreacombe Manor
North Downs
West Down
Burland Fm
Bowden Corner
Hewish Down
Churchill Cross
Churchill
Churchill Down
Arlington Beccott
Arlington
Huckham Fm
Besshill
White Cawsey

Baggy Pt
SOUTH WEST COAST PATH
Pickwell
Castle Street Fm
Buckland Down
Stoneyard Wood
Fullabrook Down
Metcombe Down
Garman's Down
ARLINGTON COURT
Arlington Court
Tidicombe
Rye Park

Vention
Putsborough
Buckland Down
Halsinger Down Ho
Beara Down
Patsford
Swindon Down
Okewill Cross
Deerpark Wood
Woolley Wood

Croyde Bay
Ora Hill
Forda
Darracott
Upcott
Incledon Fm
Georgeham
North Buckland
Nethercott
Halsinger
Winsham
Beara
Middle Marwood
Gipsy Corner
Plaistow Corner
Whiddon
Crockers Fm
Higher Muddiford
Muddiford
The Warren
Chilbridge Fm
Loxhore
Loxhore Cott

Croyde
Cross
South Hole Fm
Buckland Manor
Knowle
Boode
Marwood
MARWOOD HILL
Plaistow Mill
Guineaford
South Hill
Shirwell Cross
South Woolley Fm
Lower Loxhore

CROYDE ROAD
SAUNTON ROAD 4½
B3231
Lobb
Saunton
Sandy Lane Fm
SHOP CENT
Braunton
Pippacott
Luscott Barton
Whitehall
Prixford
Kingsheanton
BROOMHILL SCULPTURE GARDENS
Varley Fm
Shirwell
B3230
Waytown Fm
Youlston Wood
Bratt Flem
Town Fm
Birch

Saunton Sands
SOUTH WEST COAST PATH
Braunton
Braunton Down
Mainstone
Springfield Cross
Heanton Punchardon
West Ashford
Ashford
Upcott Ho
Burridge
Brightlycott Fm
Kingdon's Gardens
Sepscott Fm
Chelfham
Horridge
Hakeford
12'9
Bratton Cross
Birch
Stoke Rivers

Velator
Wrafton
Braunton Marsh
Knowl Water
A361 5
Bradiford
Raleigh
Pitt
Snapper
Northleigh
Middle Dean Fm
Dean Head
Gunn
Stone Cross

Braunton Burrows
SOUTH WEST COAST PATH
Chivenor
Penhill Pt
Chivenor
Allen's Rock
A40
Pilton
Pottington Ind Est
Derby
Waytown
Youlden Fm
Coombe Willesleigh
Goodleigh
Hutcherton Down

Horsey Island
Saltpill Duck Pond
Penhill
ST ANNE'S CHAPEL & MUSEUM
Barnstaple
MUSEUM OF BARNSTAPLE & NORTH DEVON
Westacott
East Acland
Birch
Accott

Airy Pt
LUNDY (MAR-OCT)
River Taw
Sticklepath
A3125
Bus Stn
P&R
Newport
Portmor
A60
Birch
Sandick
Sandick Cross

Sandymere
Crow Rock
Instow Sands
Yelland
Lower Yelland
B3233
WESTLEIGH
Fremington
Combrew
Bickington
Ind Est
Lake
Landkey
Harford
Hurscott

NORTHAM BURROWS
Crow Pt
Broad Sands
SOUTH WEST COAST PATH
Brake Plants
Brynsworthy
Roundswell
A361
Rumsam
Landkey Newland
Swimbridge Newland
Yeoland Ho
Riverton

Appledore
N DEVON MARITIME MUSEUM
7.5
THE QUAY
Worlington
Instow
INSTOW
Collacott Fm
Upcott Fm
Hollamoor Clump
Tawstock
A377
Bishops Tawton
17
Swimbridge
Yarnscott
Hannaford
Kerscott
High

Diddywell
Westleigh
River Torridge
TAPELEY PARK GARDENS
Coombe Fm
Trayhill
The Quay
Combe
St John's Chapel
Stonyland
Eastacombe
Prospect Corner
Downrew Ho
Horsewell
Hangman's Hill
Bydown Ho
Lane End Fm

Silford
Northam
Holmacott
Huish
Huish Moor
Rushcott Fm
Uppacott
Holmstone Manor
Lower

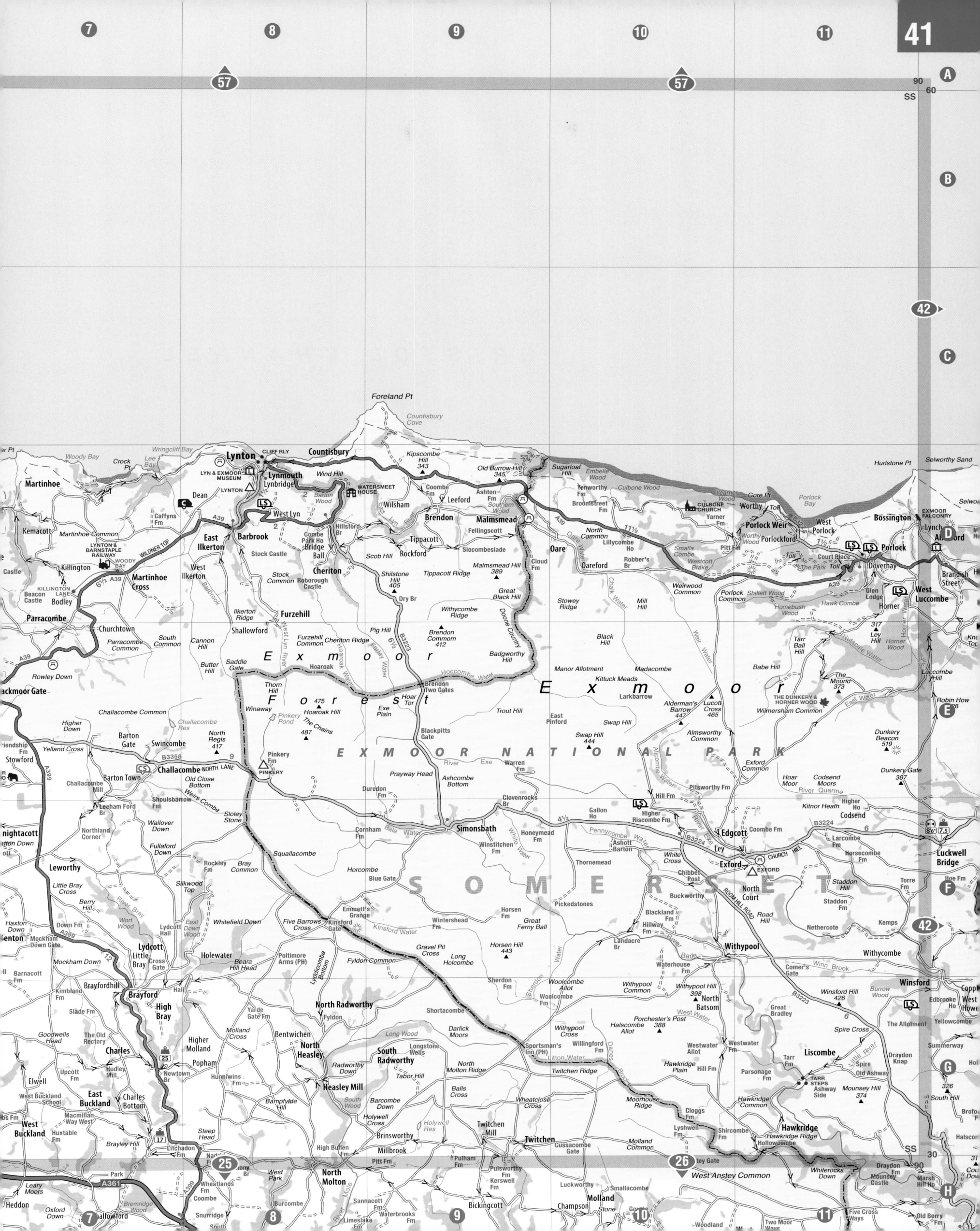

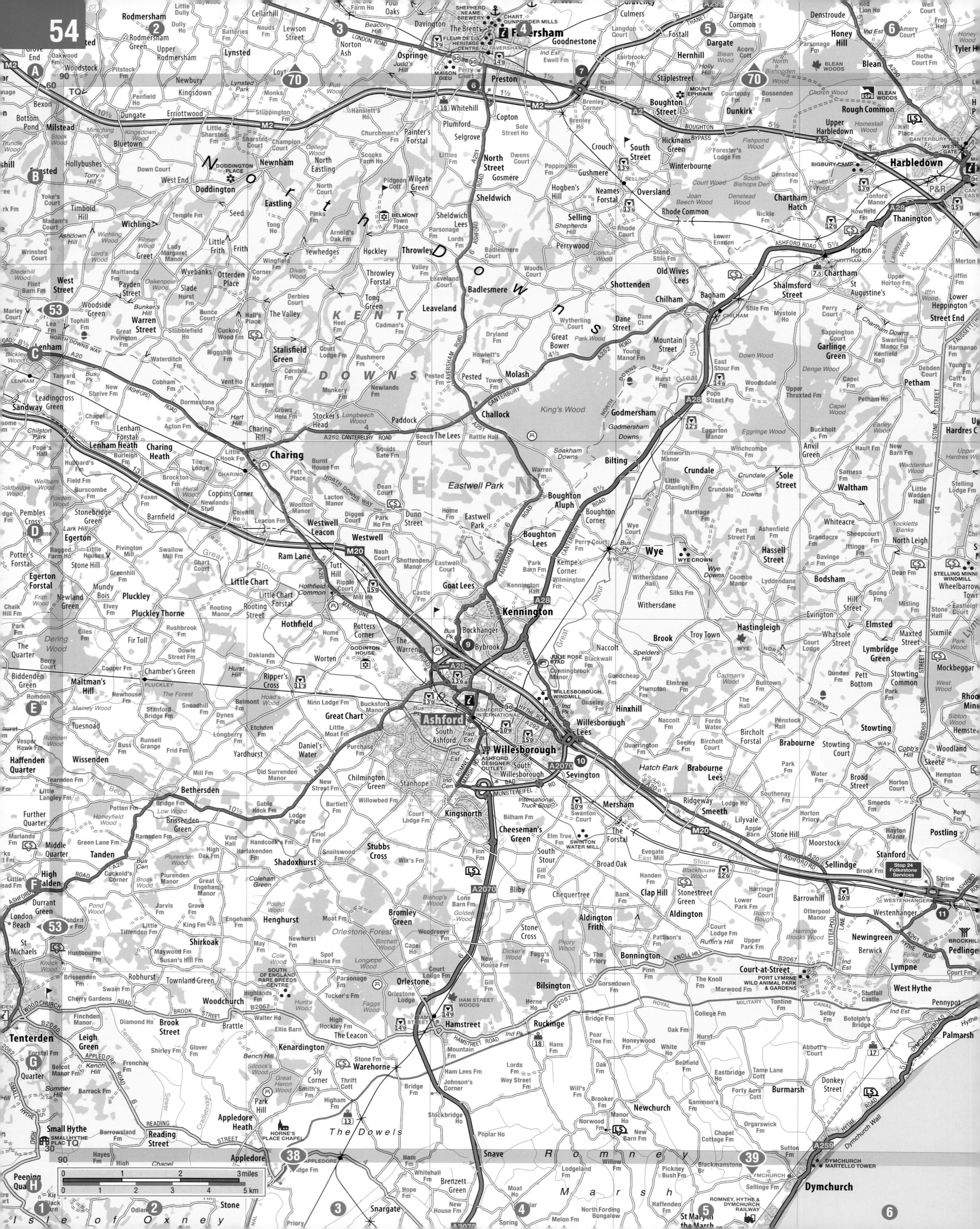

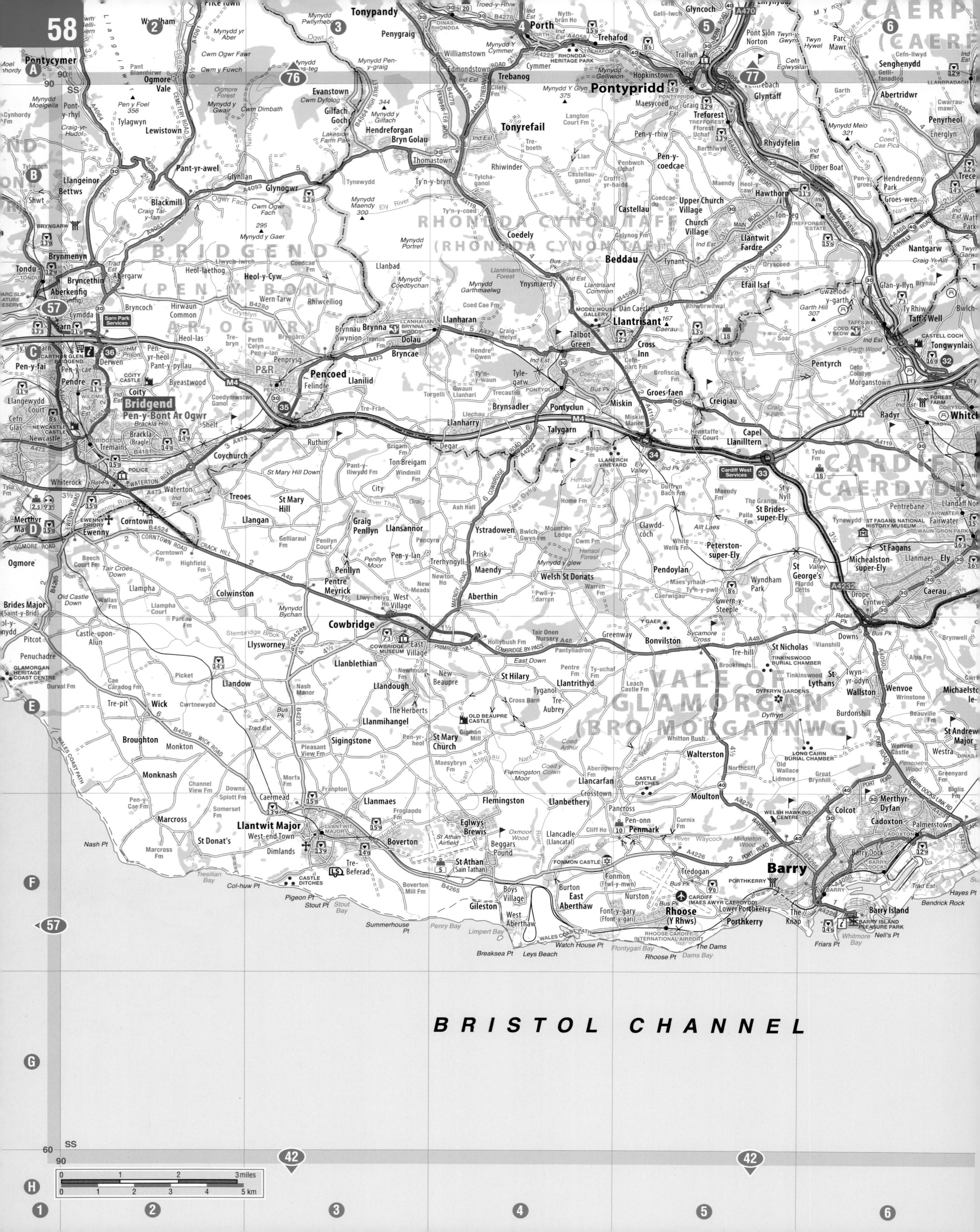

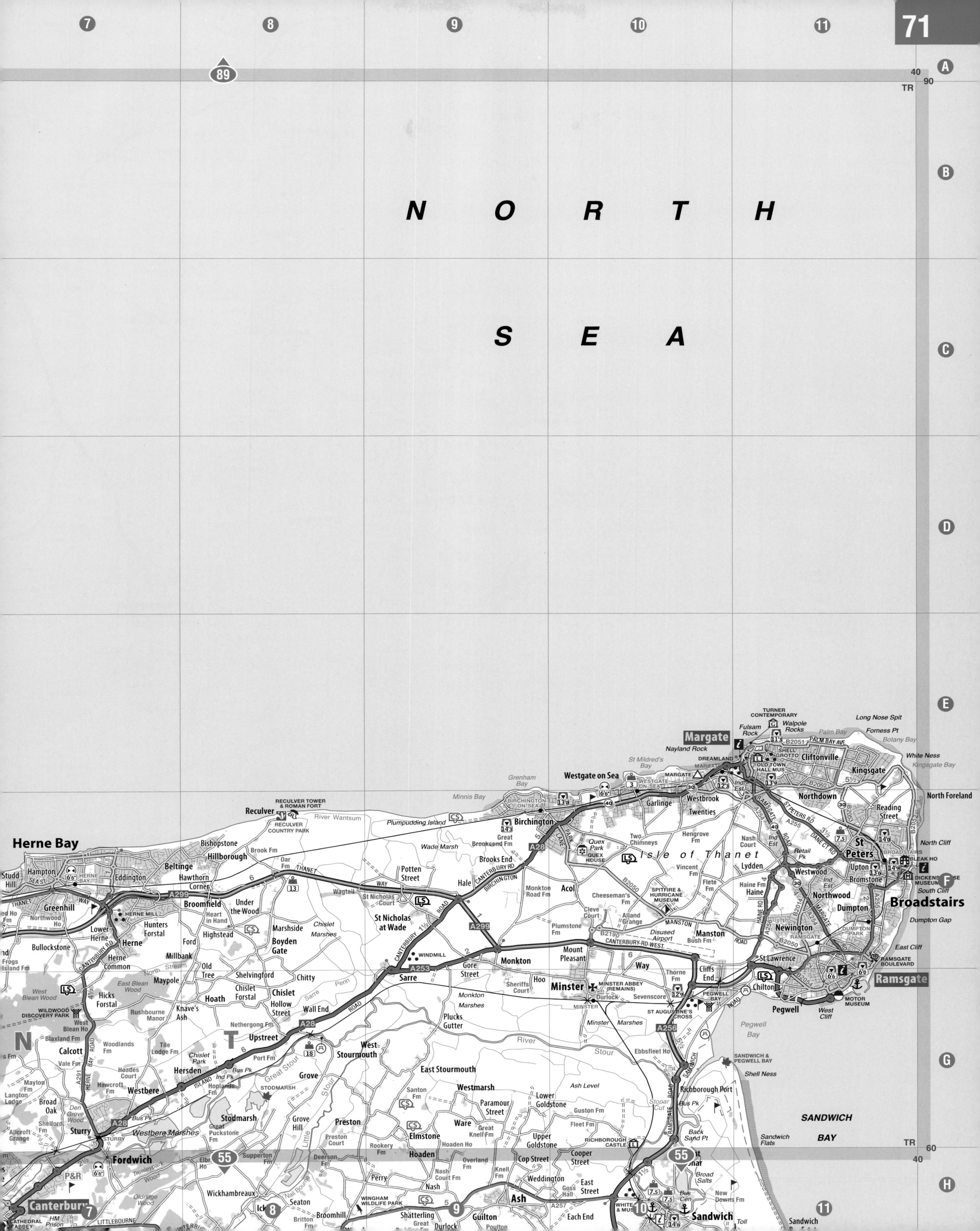

NORTH

SEA

Herne Bay

RECULVER TOWER
& ROMAN FORT
Reculver
RECULVER
COUNTRY PARK
River Wantsum
Plumpudding Island

Bishopstone
Hillborough
Brook Fm
Oar
Fm
Wade Marsh
Great
Brooksend Fm
Brooks End
Birchington

Margate
TURNER
CONTEMPORARY
Fulsam
Rock
Walpole
Rocks
Long Nose Spit
Forness Pt
Botany Bay
Palm Bay
White Ness
Kingsgate Bay
Nayland Rock
St Mildred's
Bay
DREAMLAND
SHELL
GROTTO
OLD TOWN
HALL MUS
Cliftonville
Kingsgate
Westgate on Sea
WESTGATE
ON SEA
Grenham
Bay
Minnis Bay
BIRCHINGTON
ON SEA
Garlinge
Westbrook
Twenties
MARGATE
Northdown
North Foreland
Reading
Street
North Cliff

Studd
Hill
Hampton
HERNE
BAY
Eddington
Beltinge
Hawthorn
Corner
THANET
Potten
Street
Hale
CANTERBURY RD
BIRCHINGTON
Monkton
Road Fm
Acol
Quex
Park
QUEX
HOUSE
Isle of Thanet
Two
Chimneys
Hengrove
Fm
Vincent
Fm
Nash
Court
Flete
Fm
ST PETERS RD
Ind
Est
Retail
Pk
St
Peters
BLEAK HO
DICKENS HOUSE
MUSEUM
South Cliff

Greenhill
WAY
HERNE MILL
Broomfield
Under the Wood
Heart in Hand
St Nicholas
Court
Wagtail
SPITFIRE & HURRICANE
MUSEUM
Lydden
Westwood
Ind
Est
Upton
Bromstone
Broadstairs

Lower
Herne
Hunters
Forstal
Highstead
Marshside
Boyden
Gate
Chislet
Marshes
St Nicholas
at Wade
A299
Cleve
Court
Alland
Grange
Cheeseman's
Fm
Haine Fm
Haine
Northwood
Dumpton
Dumpton Gap

Bullockstone
Herne
Ford
Old
Tree
WINDMILL
MANSTON
Plumstone
Fm
Disused
Airport
CANTERBURY RD WEST
Manston
Bush Fm
Newington
Ramsgate
East Cliff

West
Blean
Wood
Herne
Common
Millbank
Shelvingford
Chitty
A253
Gore
Street
Monkton
Mount
Pleasant
Way
Thorne
Fm
Cliffs
End
St Lawrence
RAMSGATE
BOULEVARD

WILDWOOD
DISCOVERY PARK
West
Blean Ho
Maypole
Hoath
Knave's
Ash
Chislet
Forstal
Chislet
Hollow
Street
Wall End
Sarre
Sheriffs
Court
Hoo
Minster
MINSTER ABBEY
(REMAINS)
Durlock
Sevenscore
St AUGUSTINE'S
CROSS
PEGWELL
BAY
Chilton
Pegwell
West
Cliff
MOTOR
MUSEUM

Blaxland Fm
Calcott
Vale Fm
Rushbourne
Manor
Nethergong
Pln
Upstreet
Port Fm
West
Stourmouth
Plucks
Gutter
Minster
Marshes
River
Stour
Ebbsfleet Ho
Stonar
Cut
Pegwell
Bay
SANDWICH &
PEGWELL BAY
Shell Ness

Mayton
Fm
Langton
Lodge
Broad
Oak
Shelford
Hawcroft
Fm
Sturry
Westbere Marshes
Hersden
Island
Pk
Hoplands
Fm
Grove
Stodmarsh
East Stourmouth
Westmarsh
Santon
Paramour
Street
Lower
Goldstone
Guston Fm
Ash Level
Back
Sand Pt
RICHBOROUGH
CASTLE
SANDWICH
BAY

Allcroft
Grange
Frogs
Island Fm
Stodmarsh
Great
Puckstone
Fm
Grove
Hill
Preston
Elmstone
Ware
Great
Knell Fm
Upper
Goldstone
RICHBOROUGH
CASTLE
Richborough Port

Fordwich
Supperton
Fm
Deerson
Fm
Hoaden Ho
Hoaden
Rookery
Fm
Nash
Court Fm
Cop Street
Cooper
Street
Sand
Sand Pt

Canterbury
HM
Prison
Wickhambreaux
Seaton
Broomhill
Shatterling
Durlock
Ash
Guilton
Poulton
A257
Each End
Weddington
East
Street
Goss
Hall
New
Downs Fm
WHITE
& MUS
Sandwich
Sandwich
Toll

ST BRIDES BAY

BAIE SAIN FFRAID

PEMBROKESHIRE COAST

NATIONAL PARK

PEMBROKESHIRE

COAST NATIONAL PARK

Milford Haven
Aberdaugleddyf

Milford Haven
Aberdaugleddau

CARMARTHEN BAY

BAE CAERFYRDDIN

IRISH SEA

MÔR IWERDDON

PEMBROKESHIRE COAST

NATIONAL PARK

ST BRIDES BAY

BAIE SAIN FFRAID

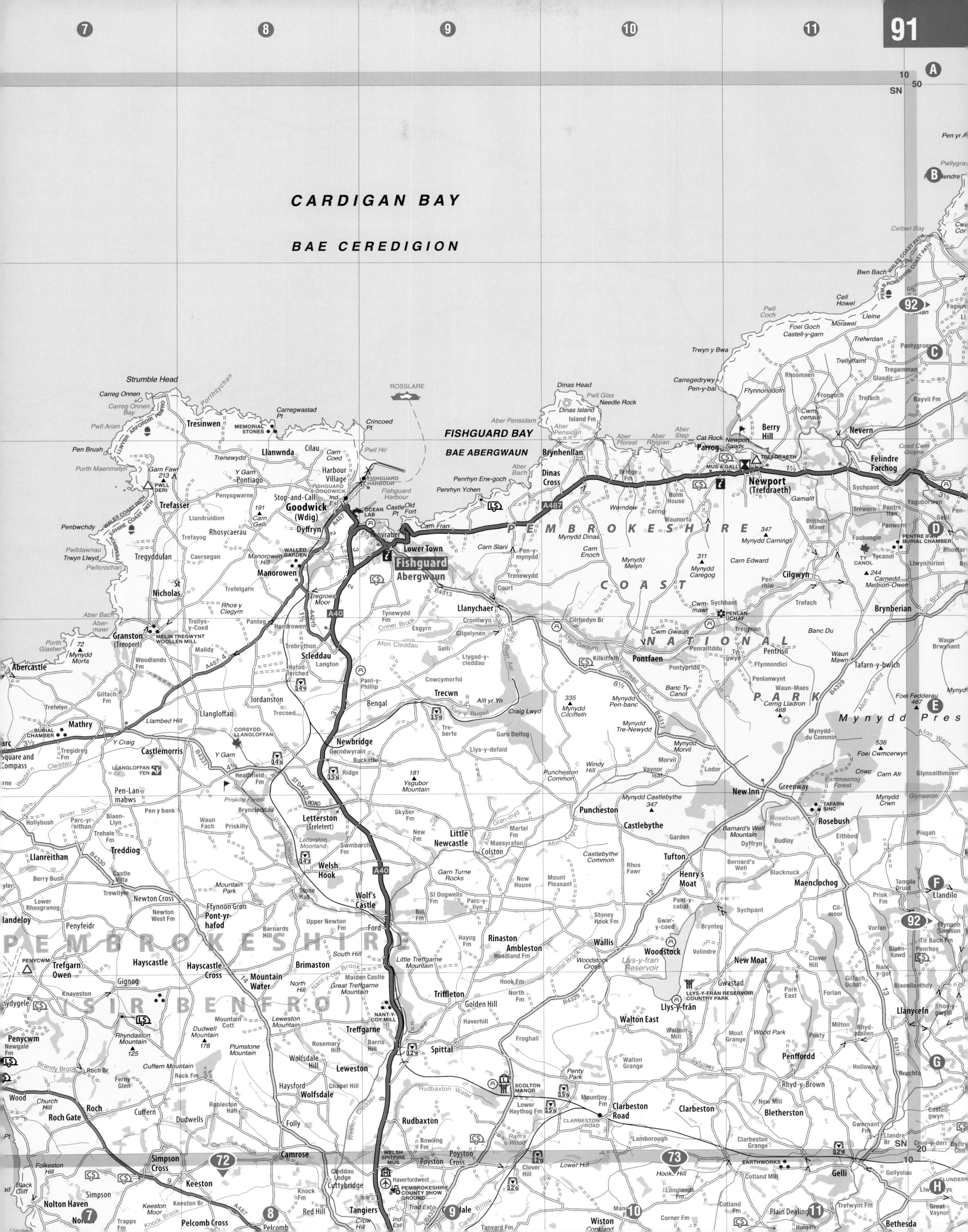

CARDIGAN BAY

BAE CEREDIGION

FISHGUARD BAY

BAE ABERGWAUN

PEMBROKESHIRE COAST

NATIONAL PARK

Mynydd Pres

PEMBROKESHIRE

(SIR BENFRO)

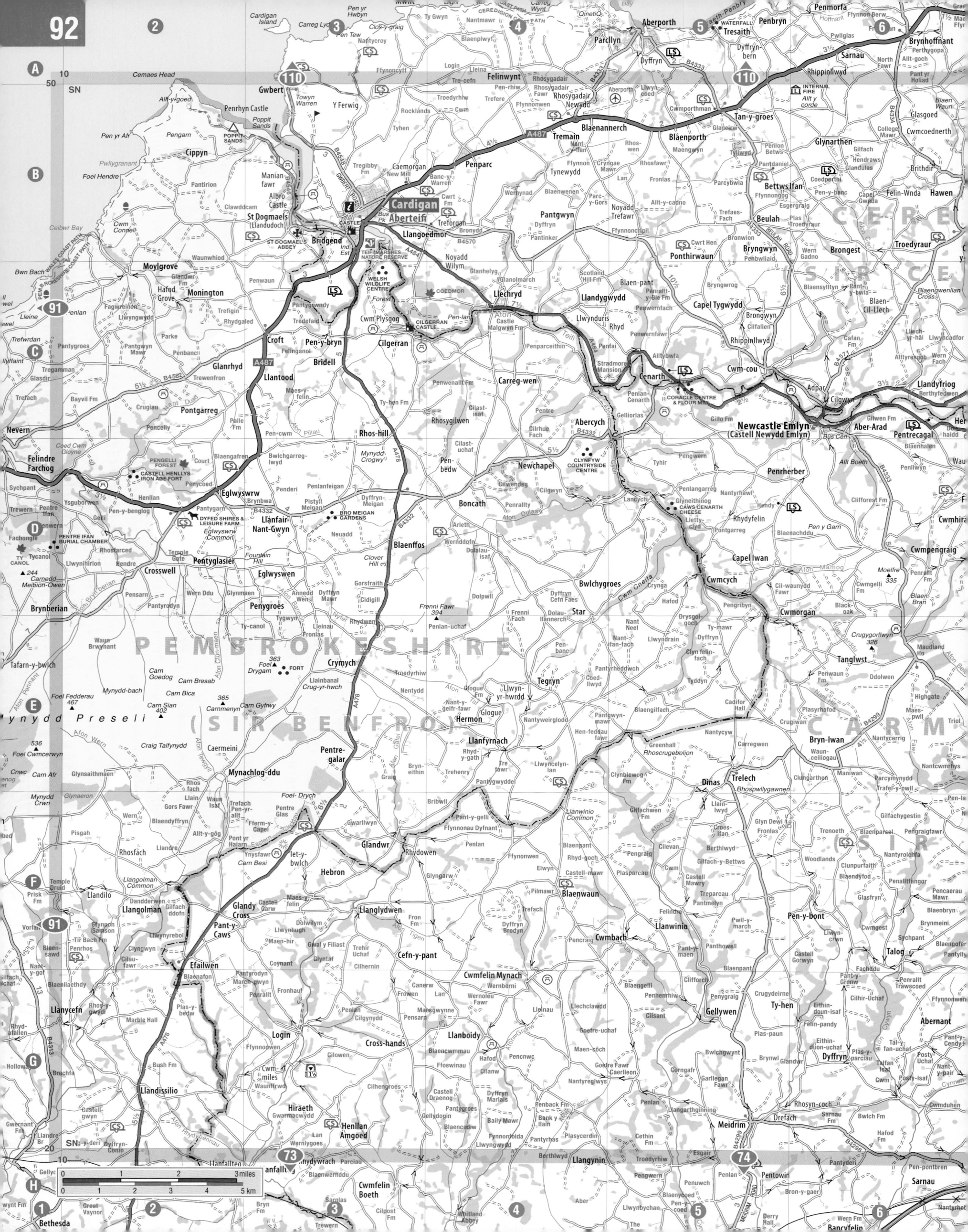

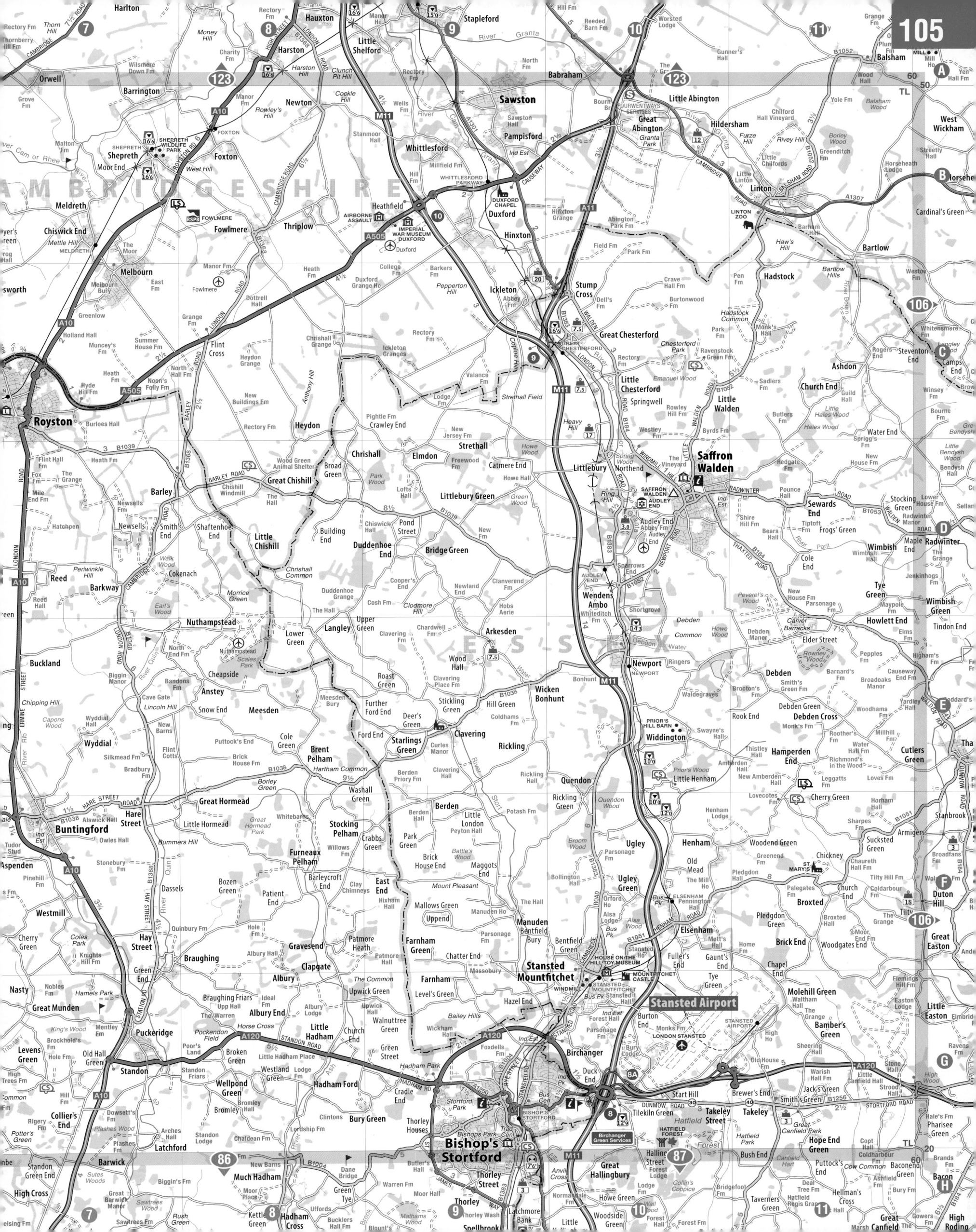

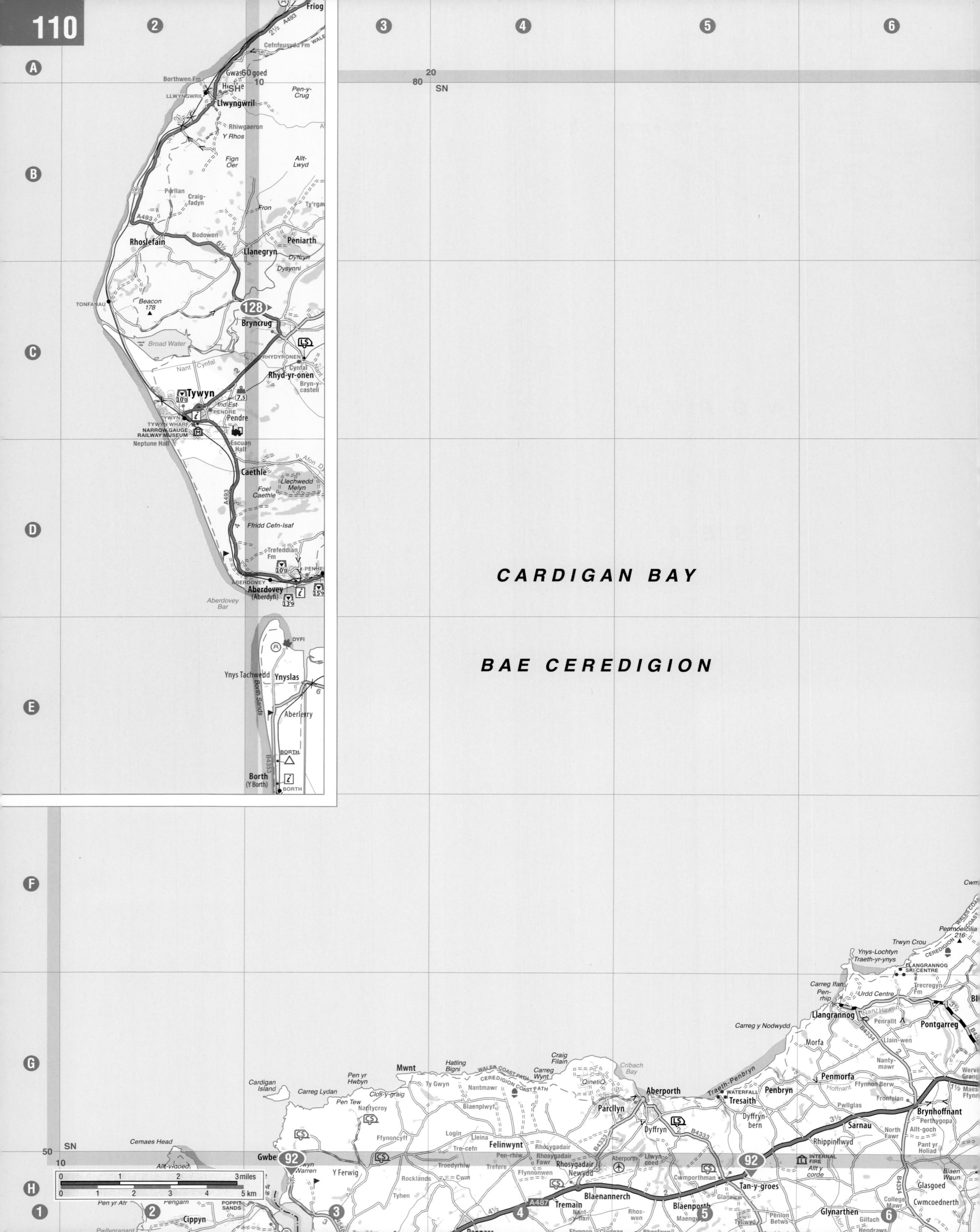

CARDIGAN BAY

BAE CEREDIGION

Friog
A493
Cefnfeusydd Fm
Gwas goed
60
10
Borthwen Fm
SH
LLWYNGWRIL
Llwyngwril
Pen-y-Crug
Allt-Lwyd
Rhiwgaeran
Y Rhos
Fign Oer
Craig-fadyn
Portlan
Bodowen
Peniarth
Rhoslefain
Llanegryn
Dyffryn
Dysynni
Fron
Ty'rgau
TONFANAU
Beacon 178
128
Bryncrug
Broad Water
Nant Cynfal
RHYDYRONEN
LS
Cynfal
Rhyd-yr-onen
Bryn-y-castell
Tywyn
7.5
Ind Est
PENDRE
Pendre
TYWYN WHARF
NARROW GAUGE
RAILWAY MUSEUM
Neptune Hall
Escuan Hall
Afon D
Caethle
Llechwedd Melyn
Foel Caethle
A493
Ffridd Cefn-Isaf
Trefeddian Fm
10.0
PENHE
ABERDOVEY
Aberdovey (Aberdyfi)
13.9
Aberdovey Bar
DYFI
Ynys Tachwedd
Ynyslas
Borth Sands
Aberleri
BORTH
Borth (Y Borth)
BORTH
B4353

20
80
SN

50
SN
10

Cemaes Head
Allt-y-goed
Pen yr Afr
Pengarn
Cippyn
POPPIT SANDS
Pwllynranant
Cardigan Island
Carreg Lydan
Pen Tew
Nantycroy
CS
Ffynoncyft
Login
Lleina
Tre-cefn
Gwbe
92
Y Ferwig
Y Warren
Troedyrhiw
Trefere
Rocklands
Cwm
Tyhen
Mwnt
Pen yr Hwbyn
Clos-y-graig
Nantmawr
Blaenplwyf
Ffynnonwen
Rhosygadair
Rhosygadair Fawr
Rhosgadair
Newydd
Tremain
Nant-y-ffin
Rhoswen
Blaenannerch
Hatling Bigni
Ty Gwyn
WALES COAST PATH
CEREDIGION COAST PATH
Craig Filain
Carreg Wynt
QinetiQ
Cribach Bay
Parcllyn
Dyffryn
LS
Aberporth
B4333
Llwyn-coed
Blaenporth
Maengwyn
Penlon Betws
A487
Glaneirw
Blaen Waun
Cwmporthman
Allt y corde
INTERNAL FIRE
Tan-y-groes
92
Aberporth
Tresaith
Penbryn
WATERFALL
Hoffnant
Ffynnon Berw
Pwllglas
Dyffryn-bern
Fronfelen
Sarnau
North Fawr
Rhippinllwyd
Perthygopa
Brynhoffnant
Allt-goch
Pant yr Holiad
Glynarthen
Gilfach
Hendraws
Glasgoed
Cwmcoednerth
College Mawr
B4334
Ynys-Lochtyn
Traeth-yr-ynys
Penmoelciliau
Trwyn Crou
216
LLANGRANNOG
SKI CENTRE
Carreg Ifan
Pen-rhip
Urdd Centre
Trecregyn Fm
CEREDIGION COAST PATH
Llangrannog
Peniallt
Llain-wen
Pontgarreg
B4334
Carreg y Nodwydd
Morfa
Penmorfa
Nanty-mawr
Wervil Grang
Maes
Ffynnon
Bl

Carreg Ifan
Penrhip

Traeth-Penbryn

0   1   2   3 miles
0   1   2   3   4   5 km

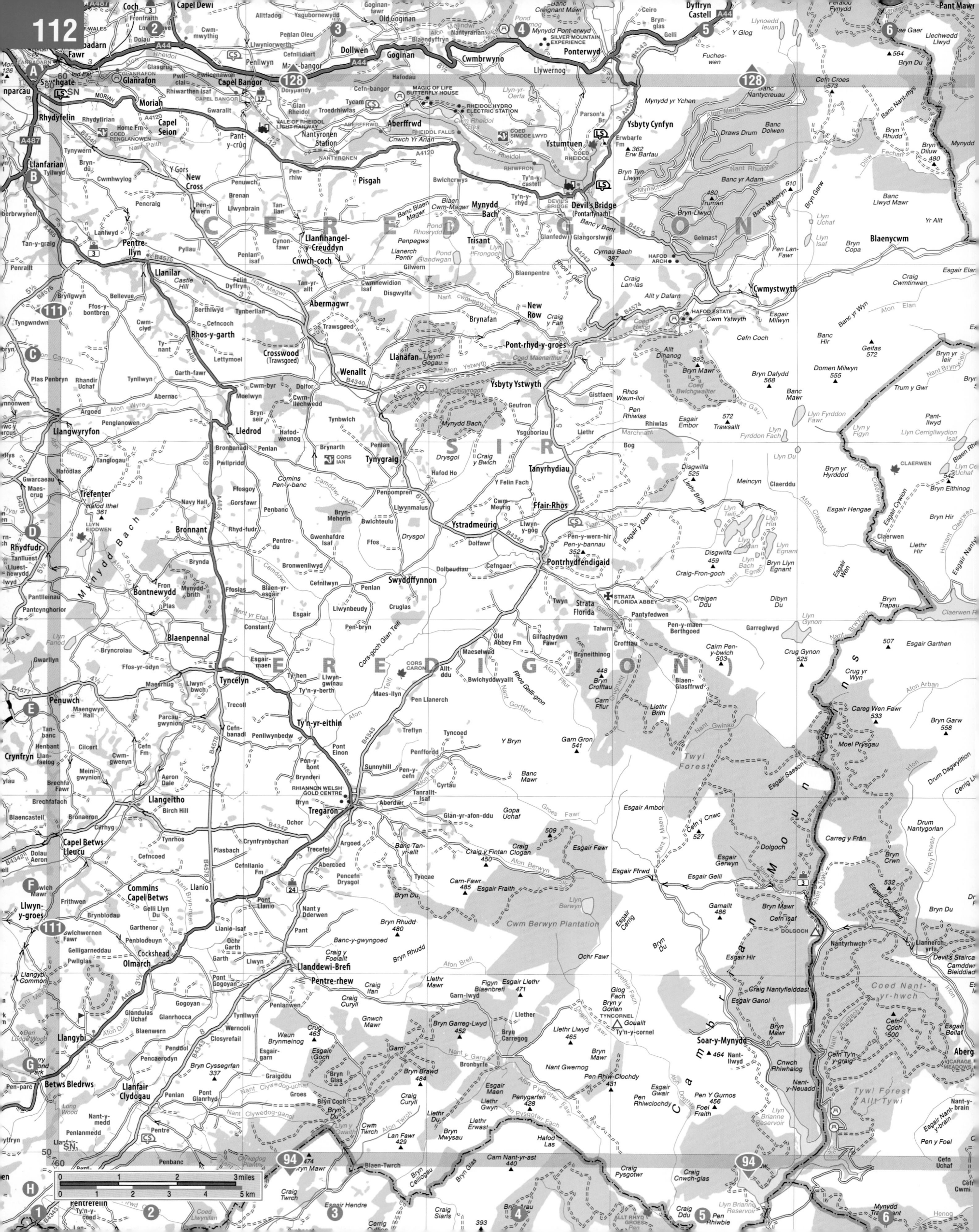

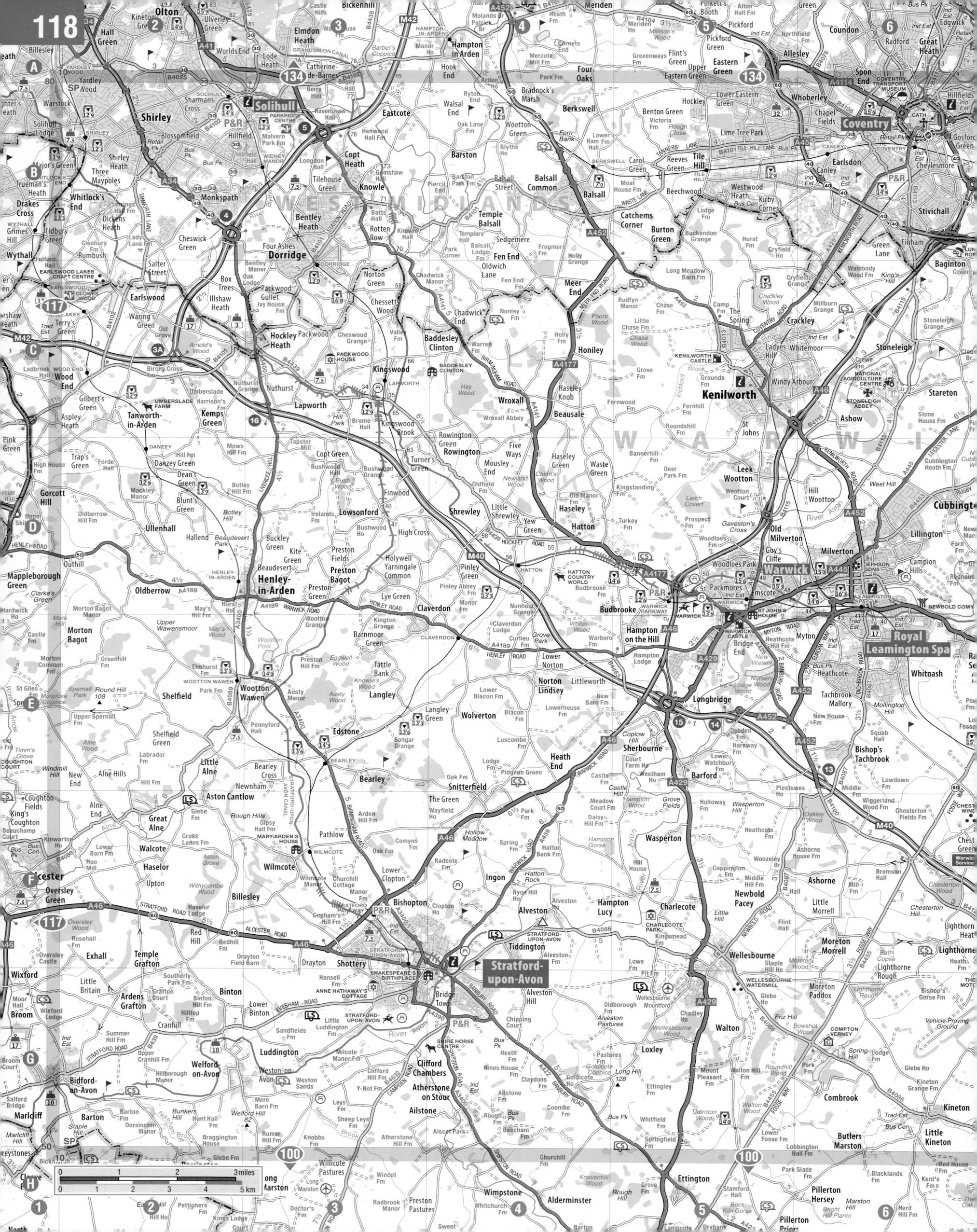

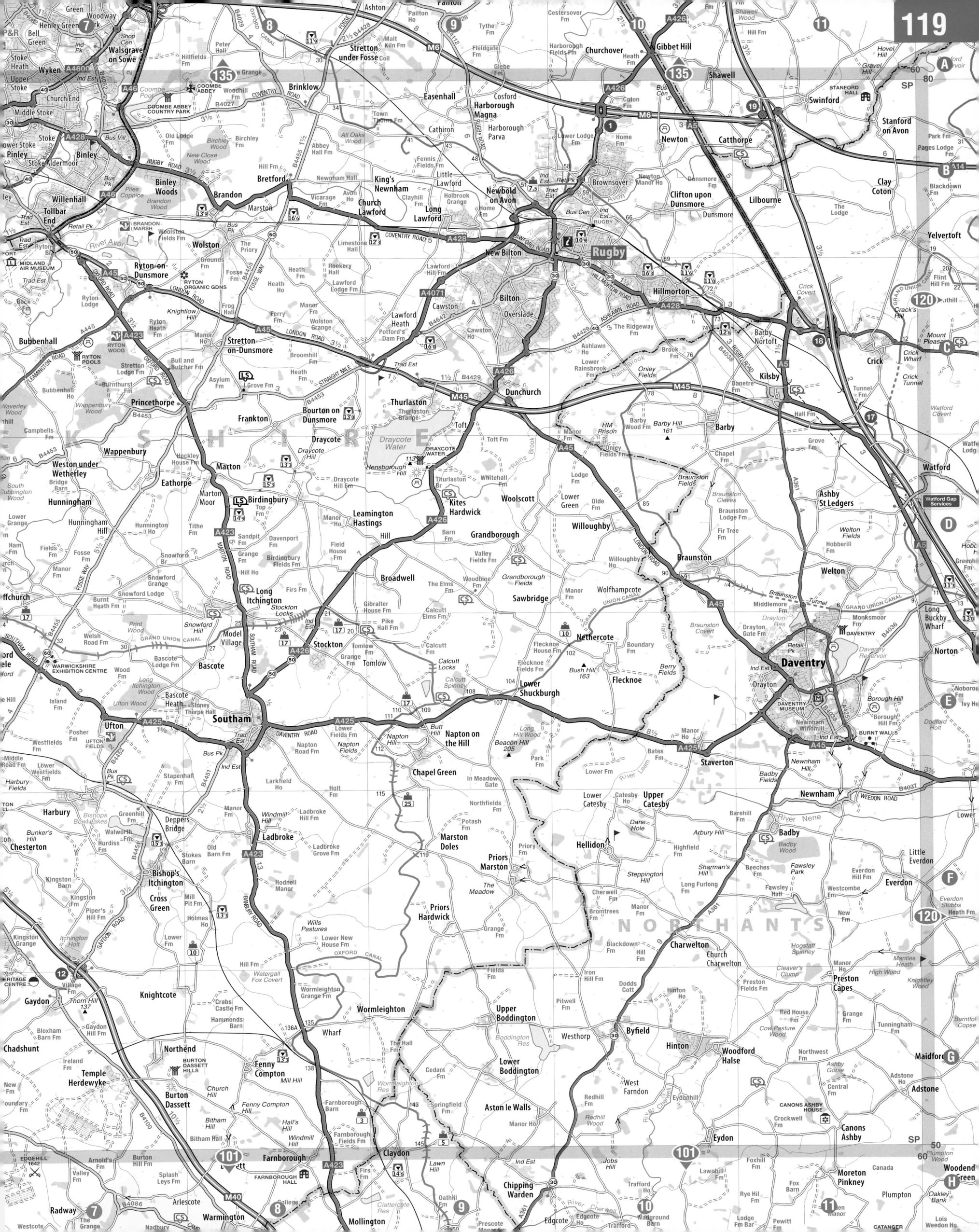

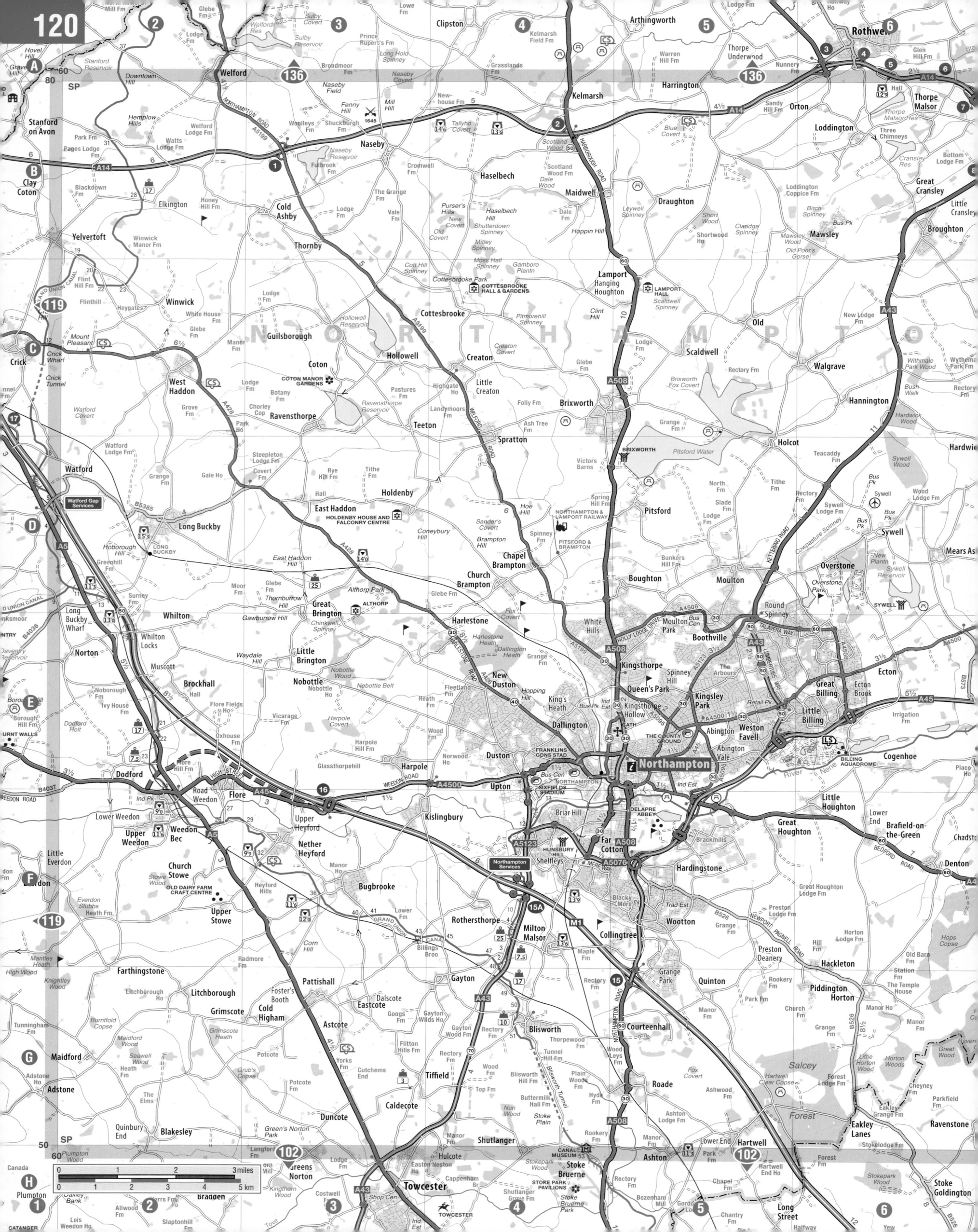

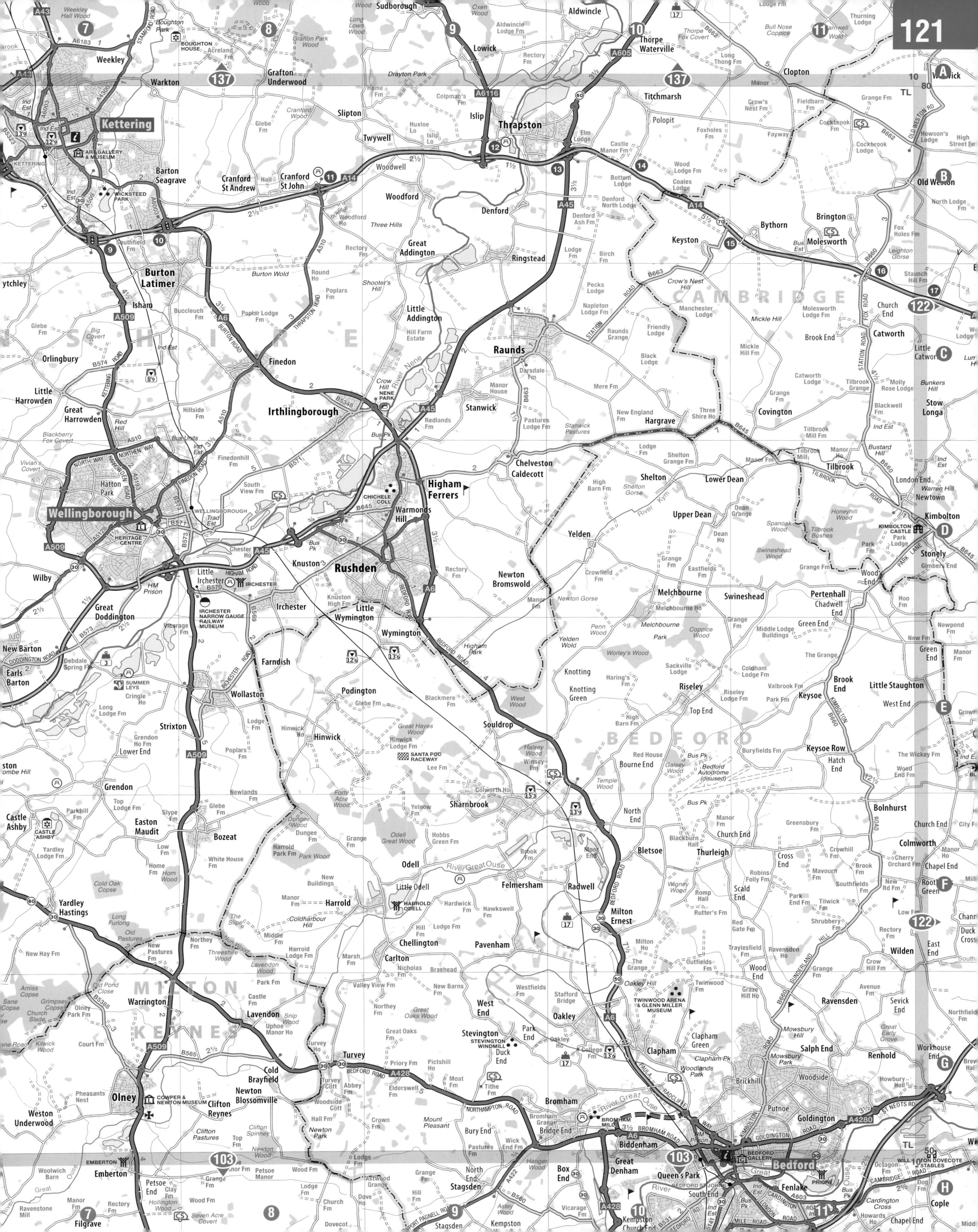

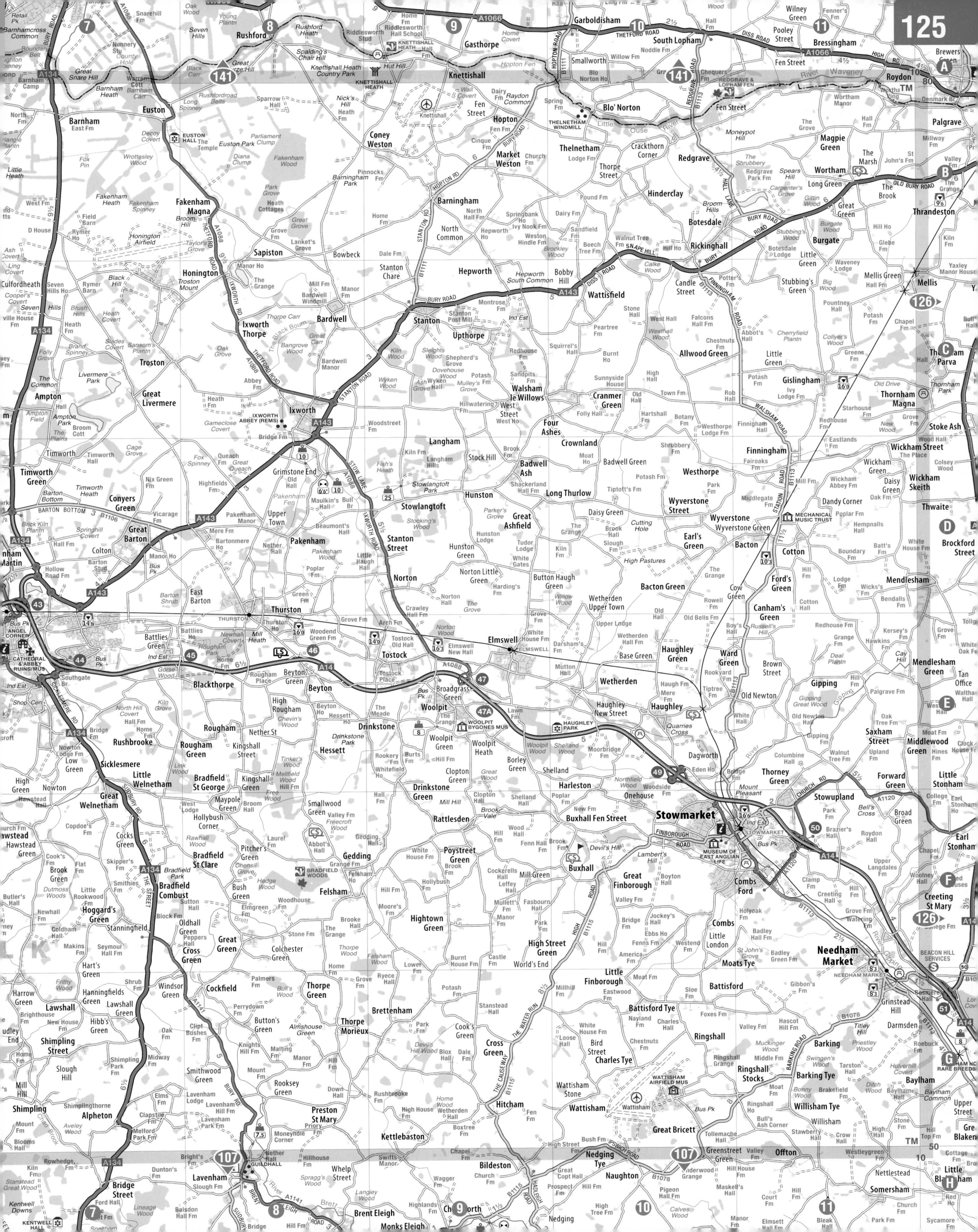

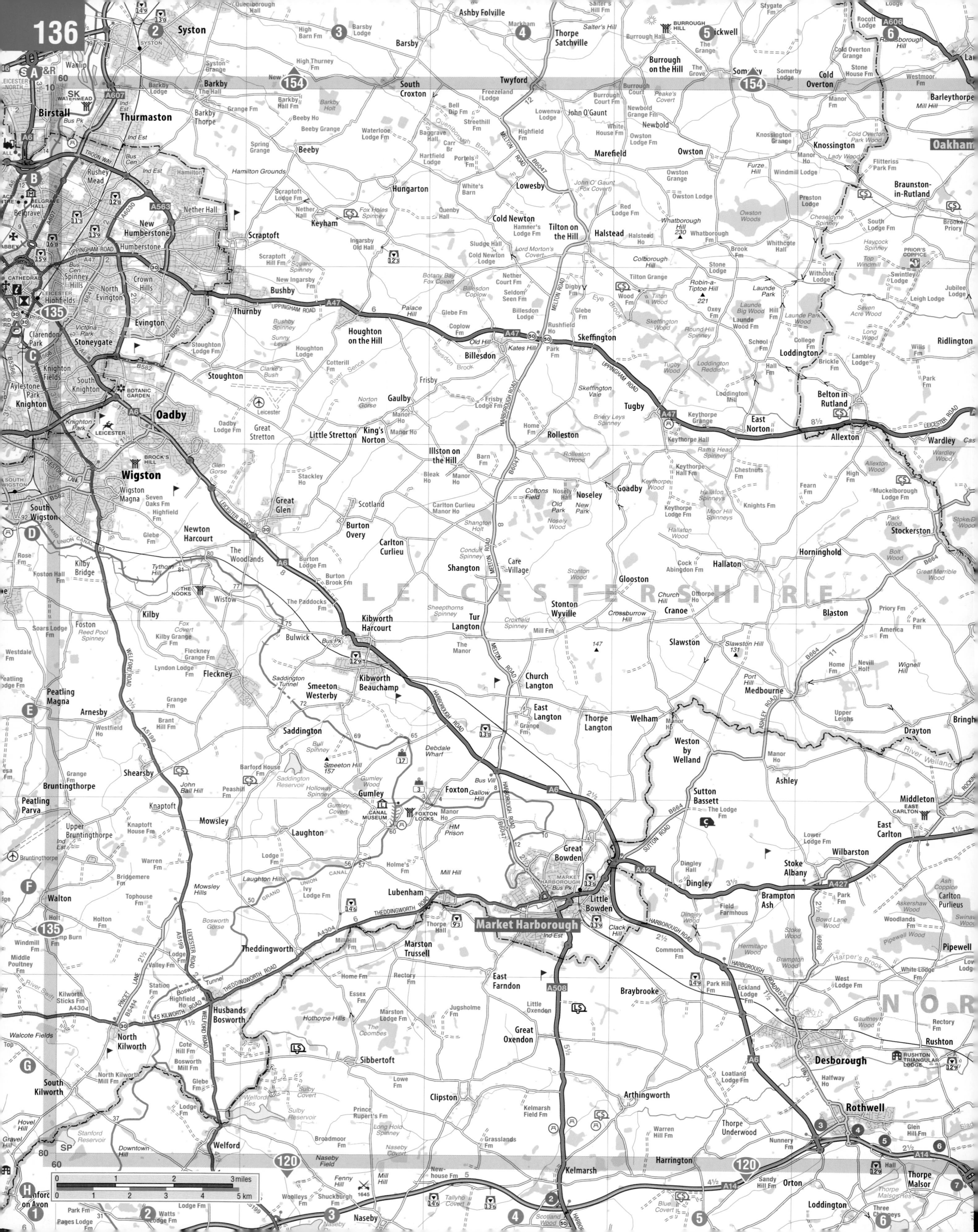

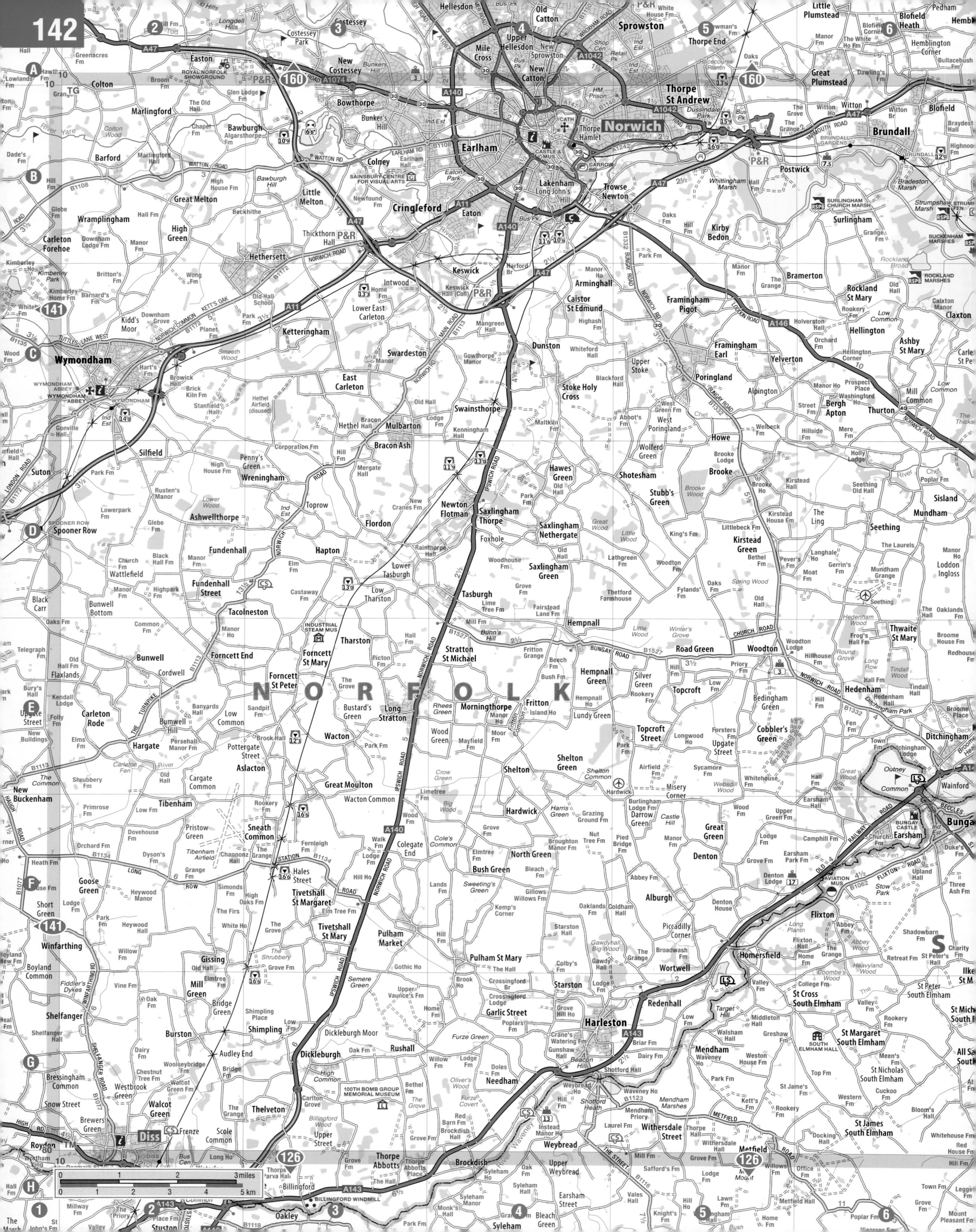

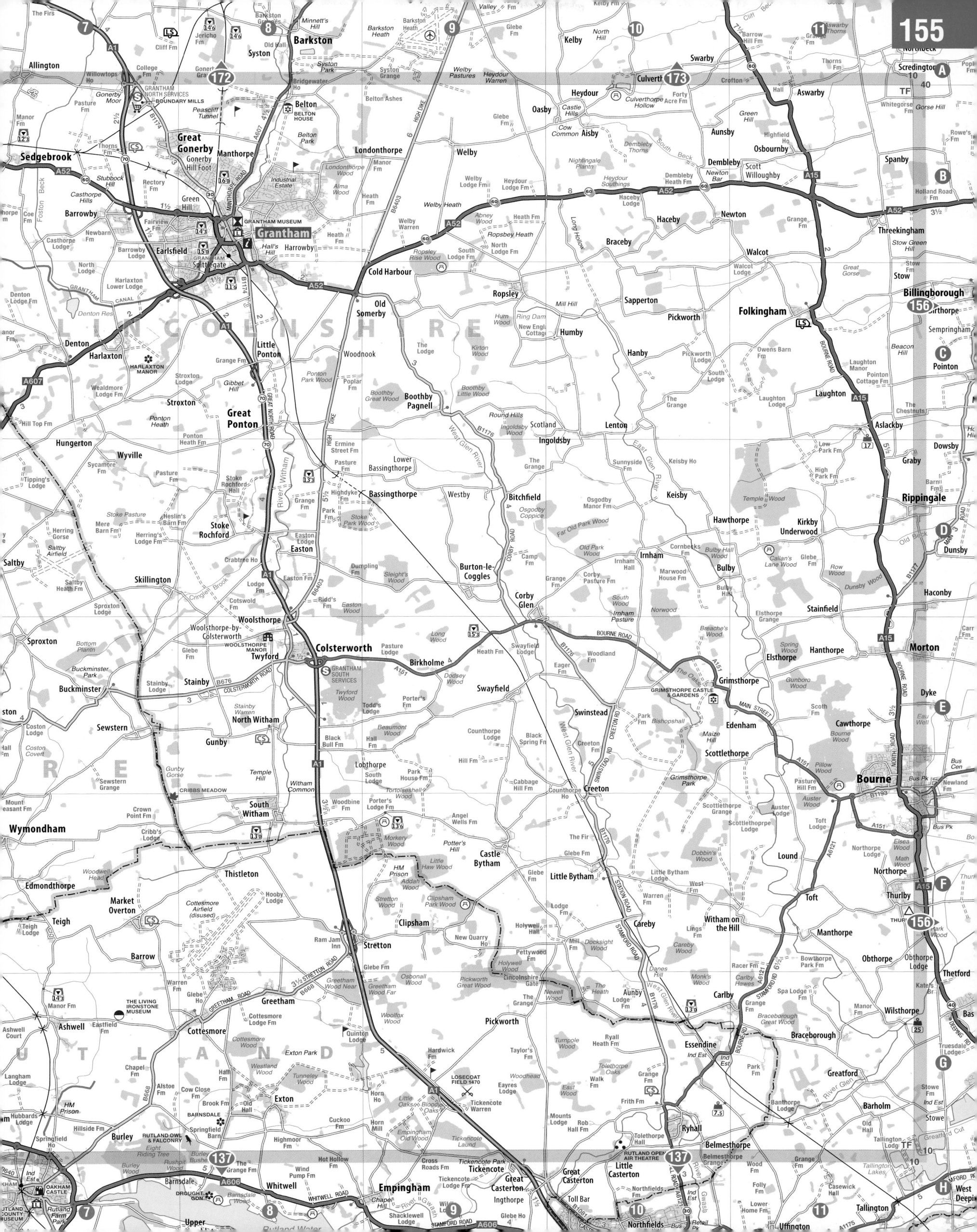

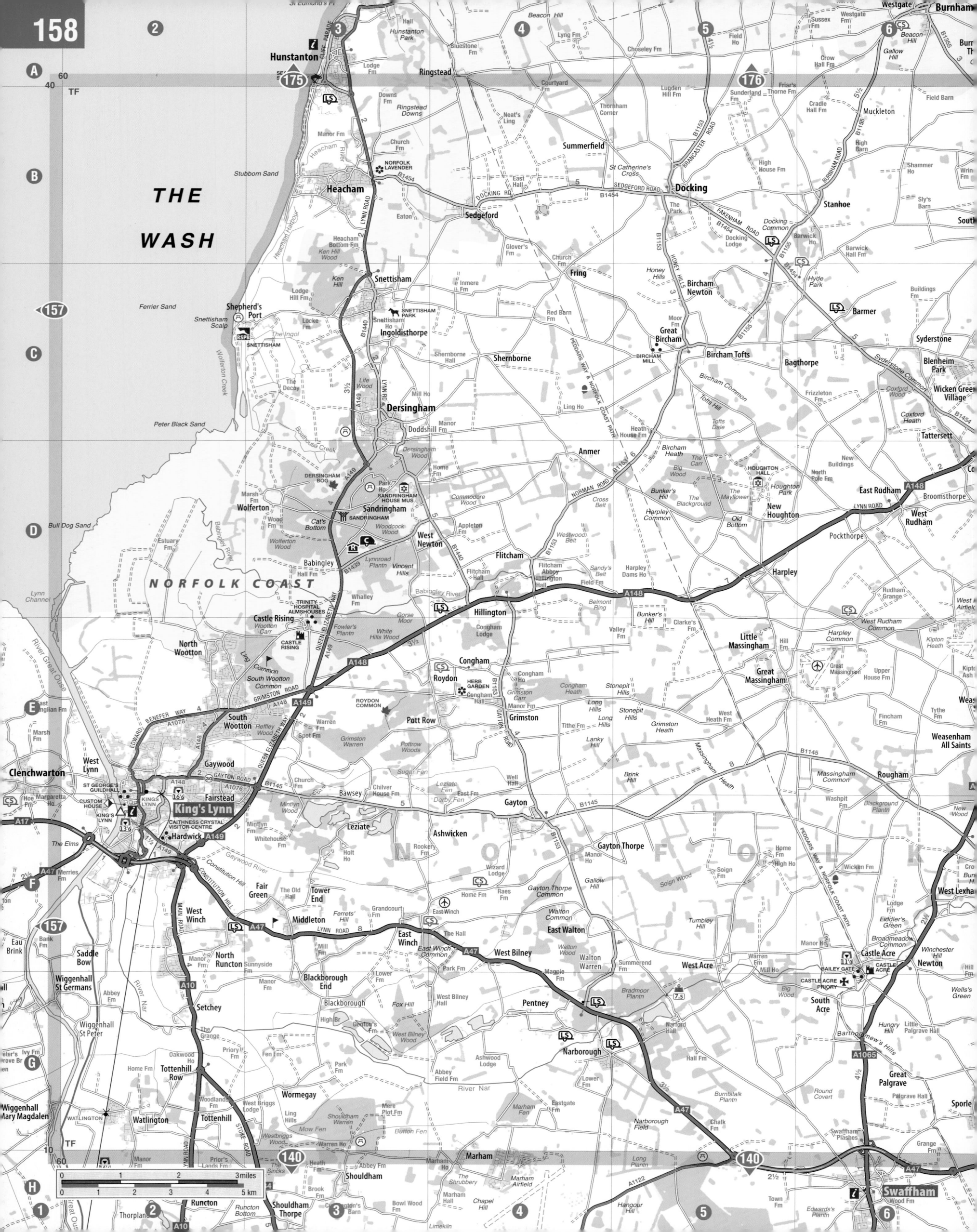

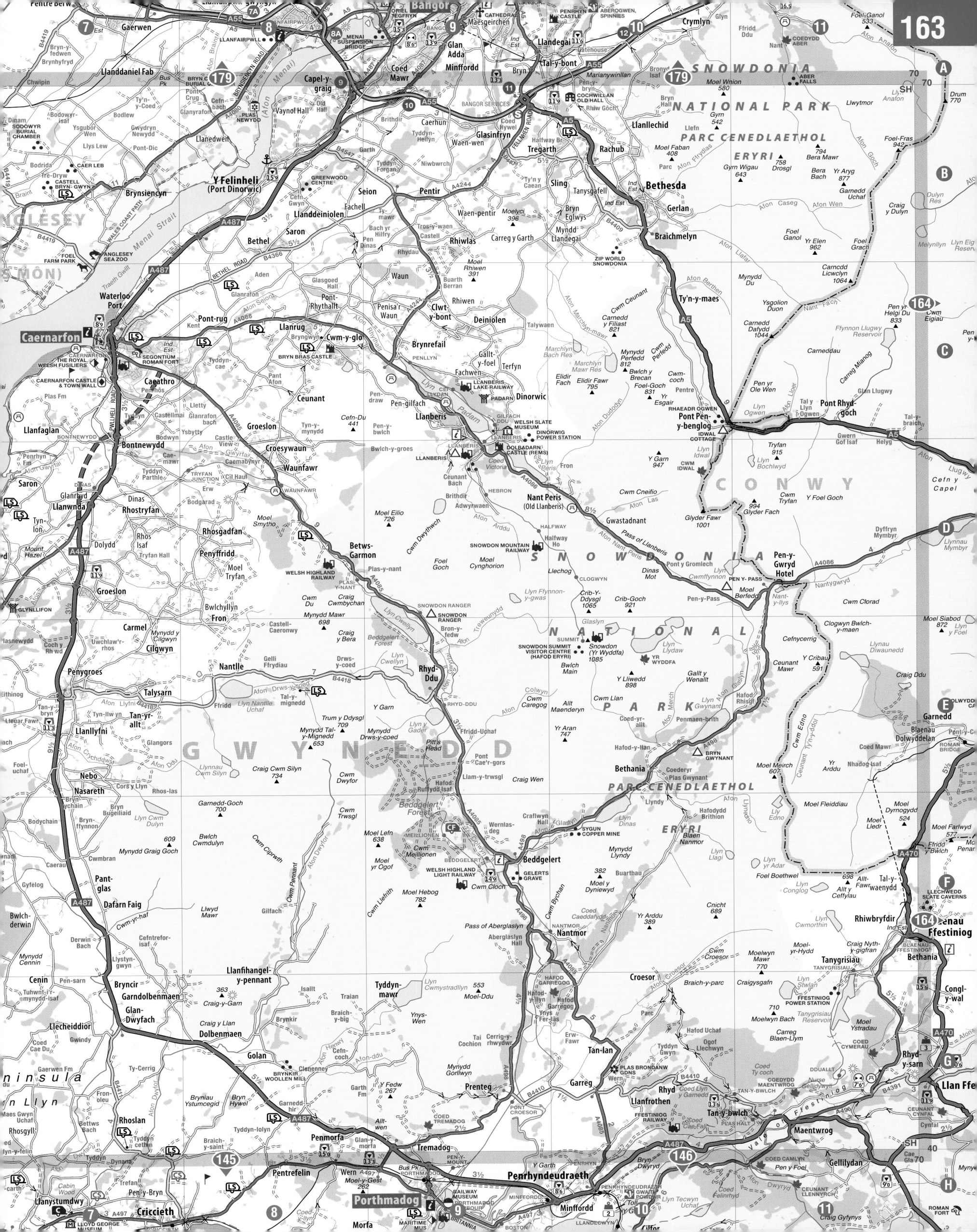

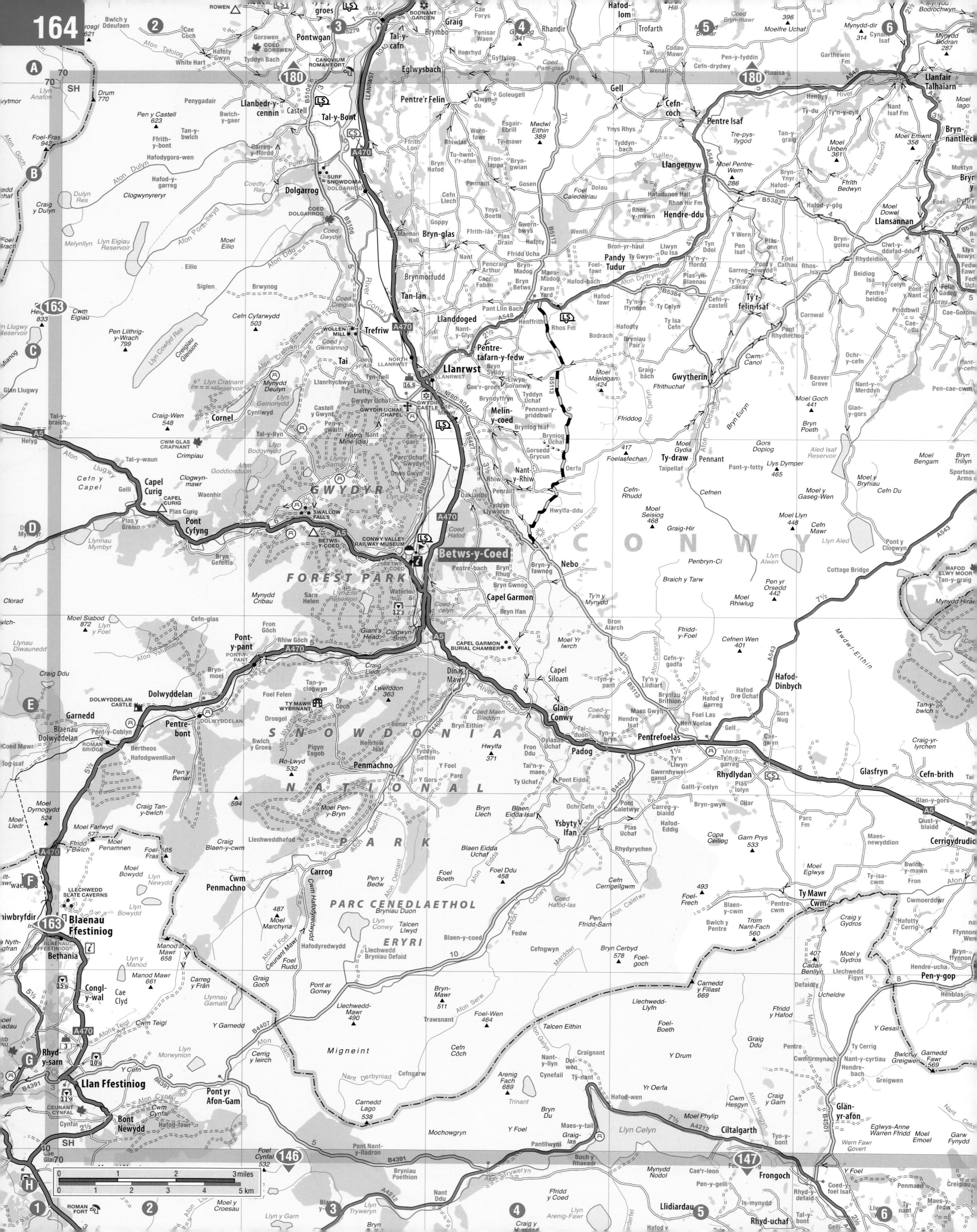

182

HOYLAKE
LIFEBOAT MUS

Hilbre
Island

Little
Hilbre
Island

RED ROCKS
MARSH

West
Kirby

Marine
Lake

Point of Ayr
(Yr Parlwr Du)

POINT OF AYR
DEE ESTUARY

Wild Road

Salisbury Middle

Talacre
Bus Pk

RSPB

Tanlan
Banks

Tanlan

Gronant

Gwespyr

Ffynnongroyw

WALES COAST PATH

Y-Ffrith

PRESTATYN ROAD

A548

VICTORIA ROAD

Rhyl
(Y Rhyl)

Prestatyn

Glasdir

Picton

Kelston
Fm

Mostyn
Quay

Mostyn Quay

SEAQUARIUM

Meliden
(Gallt Melyd)

Gwaenysgor

Llanasa

Glan-
yr-afon

Rhewl-
fawr

Pen-y-
ffordd

Garth

Afon y Garth

Kinmel Bay
(Bae Cinmel)

Pydew

Four
Winds Fm

Tan-yr-allt

Gop Hill
251

Axton

Mostyn

Trelogan

Wern
Fm

Rhewl-Mostyn

Glan-y-don

Towyn

Bryn
Cwnin Fm

Mia
Hall

153
Graig
Fawr

Bryniau

DYSERTH
WATERFALL

Trelawnyd

Marian

Walwen

Berthengam

Tre-Mostyn

Mynydd
Mostyn

Maes Pennant

Llannerch-y-môr

Ty-mawr

Llewerllyd

Bryn
Cwnin Fm

Dyserth

Henllan Hall

Sarn

Pentre-
ffynnon Hall

Belgrano

Retail
Pk

Pen-y-
ffordd

BODRHYDDAN
HALL

Rhuddlan

Long
Acre

Ochr-
y-foel

Moel
Hiraddug

Pen-y-
Cefn-isaf

Graig-
Arthur

MAEN
ACHWYFAN

Bryn-
coch

Whitford
(Chwitffordd)

The Marsh

Stokyn
Hall

Greenfield
(Maes-Glas)

River Gele

Hendre-
bach

Gofer

Cwm

Marian Cwm

Plas-
mawr

Plas
Captain

Llyn
Helyg

Glol

Garreg

Saith ffynnon

Golch

Mertyn
Hall

Greenfield Valley
Heritage Park

BASINGWERK
ABBEY

Walwen

Whels

Pen-y-
ffordd

Pengwern

Rhyfyddauddwr
Fm

Coed
Cwm

Pant-y-
dulath

Per-ffordd-llan

Lloc

Carmel

Per-y-
maes

Bryn Celyn

Bodryfn
Fawr

Ty'n-
y-llyn

Ty
Isa Fm

Ffyddion
Fm

Gorsedd

Pantasaph

Mwdwl-
eithin

Pen-y-
Ball Top

182

St
George

Bodelwyddan

Gwernigron
Fm

Plas
Coch Fm

Brynllithrig
Hall

Rhuallt

Pant-y-
Wacco

Elwybr-h ir

Pen-y-cefn

Naid-y-march

Smithy
Gate

Holywell
(Treffynnon)

Milwr

Dinorben

BODELWYDDAN
CASTLE

Bodelwyddan
Park

The Roe

Cae Rhys-h

Hartley
Fm

Calcoed

Pant

Brynford

Cefn
Fm

Bryn Madyn

Moelfre

Kinmel
Hall

Bus
Pk

CATHEDRAL

St Asaph
(Llanelwy)

Rhewl
Fm

Moel Maenefa
390

Bryngwyn
Hall

Caerwys
Hall

Croes-
wian

Babell

Calcot
Fm

Dolphin

Llongley

Glascoed

Groesffordd
Marli

Hendy
Fm

Eryl
Hall

Waen
Goleugoed

Plas
Coch

Tremeirchion

Bryntirion
Fm

Ty-
mawr

Caerwys

Ivy
House

Waen

Truly

Pwll-
clai

Pwll-
melyn

Bryn-y-pin

Bodysgaw
Fm

Ty'n-y-
ffordd

Glascoed
Fawr

Bryn
Asaph

Llannerch
Hall

Hafod-y-
coed

Cefn
Du

Lodge
Fm

Graig

Henblas

Maes-mynan Hall

Prysau

Mynydd-
llan

Pen-Uchar
Plwyf

Pentre
Halkyn

Windmill

Bron-
haul

Fron-
Fawr
230

Tan-
llan

Wigfair

Perthewig

Penuchagreen

Nantlys

Sodom

Nantgwilym

Wheeler

Afonwen

Ddol

Ysceifiog

Lixwm

Bwlch

Halkyn
Mountain

Rhes-y-
cae

Talgrwn

Tal-y-bryn

Hafod-
Green

Trefnant

AFONWEN CRAFT
ANTIQUE CENTRE

Bryn yr
Eithin

Fron-
haul

Walwen

Garneddwen

Halkyn
Mountain

Catch

Halkyn

Llannefydd

Graig

Plas
yn-Cefn

Bont-
newydd

Moel y Parc
398

Bodfari

AFONWEN
CRAFT
MILL

Moel-
y-crio

Berth-
ddu

Wern-
gaer

Mynydd
y Gyrt

Cefn Berain

Galltfaenan
Hall

Pen-cae-du

Pontruffydd
Fm

Pontruffydd
Hall

Geinas

The Grove
Hall

Bryn Golau

Coed-y-
mynydd Ucha

Pen-y-
felin

Nannerch

Pant-
ffuon

Beniar

Moel
Fodiar
390

Plas
Heaton
Hall

Plas
Heaton
Fm

Green

Penpalmant

Aifft

Waen

Nant Coed-
y-mynydd

Hafod-
y-maes

Penbedw

Hendre

Dyffryn
Aled

Cae'r
groes

Tenllan

Cae-
Drain

Plas
Brwyn

Meus
Drain

Dre-gôch

Pen-ucha'r
cwm

Firwood

Hendre
Uchaf

Nant-
isgillt Issaf

165

165

7

8

9

10

11

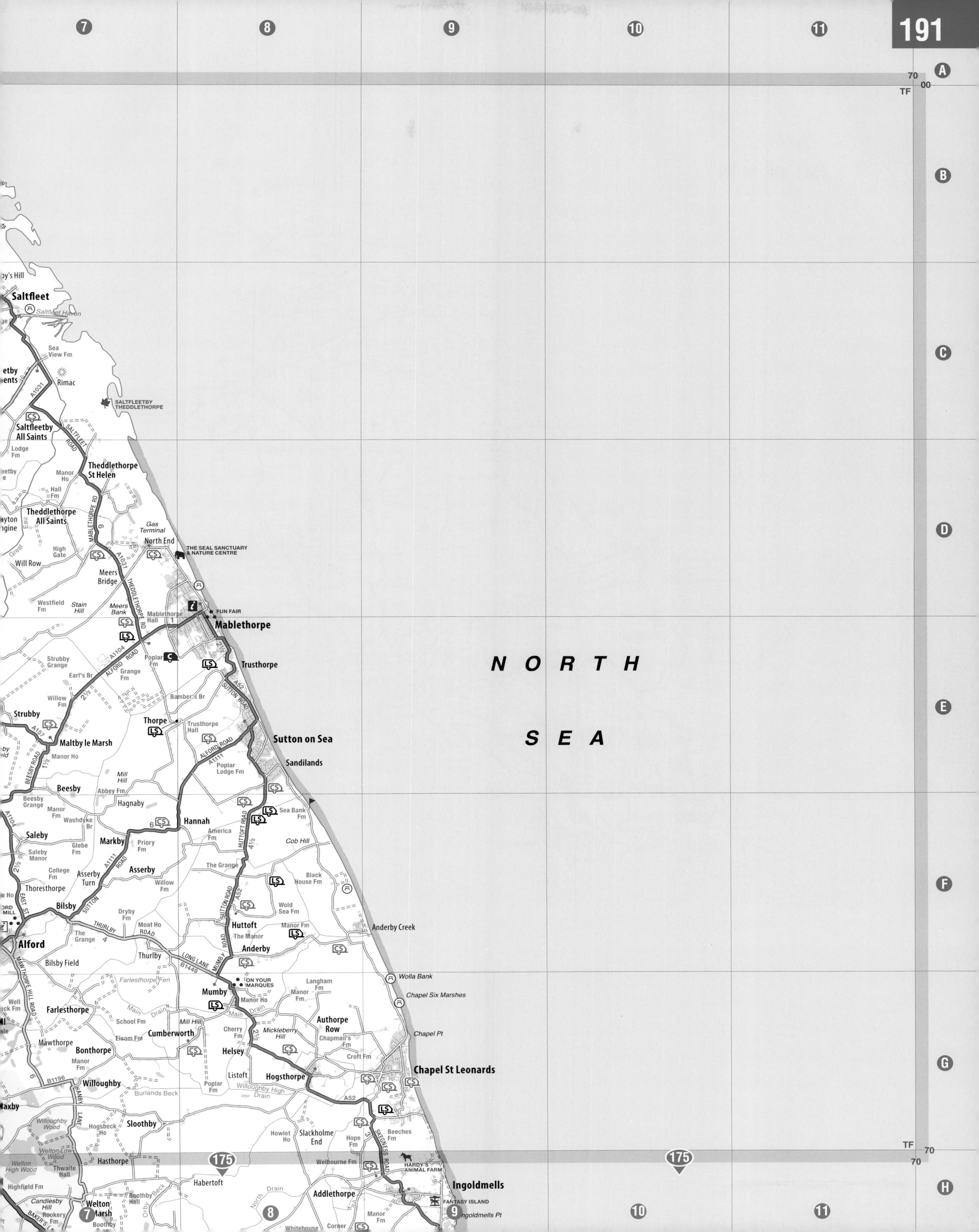

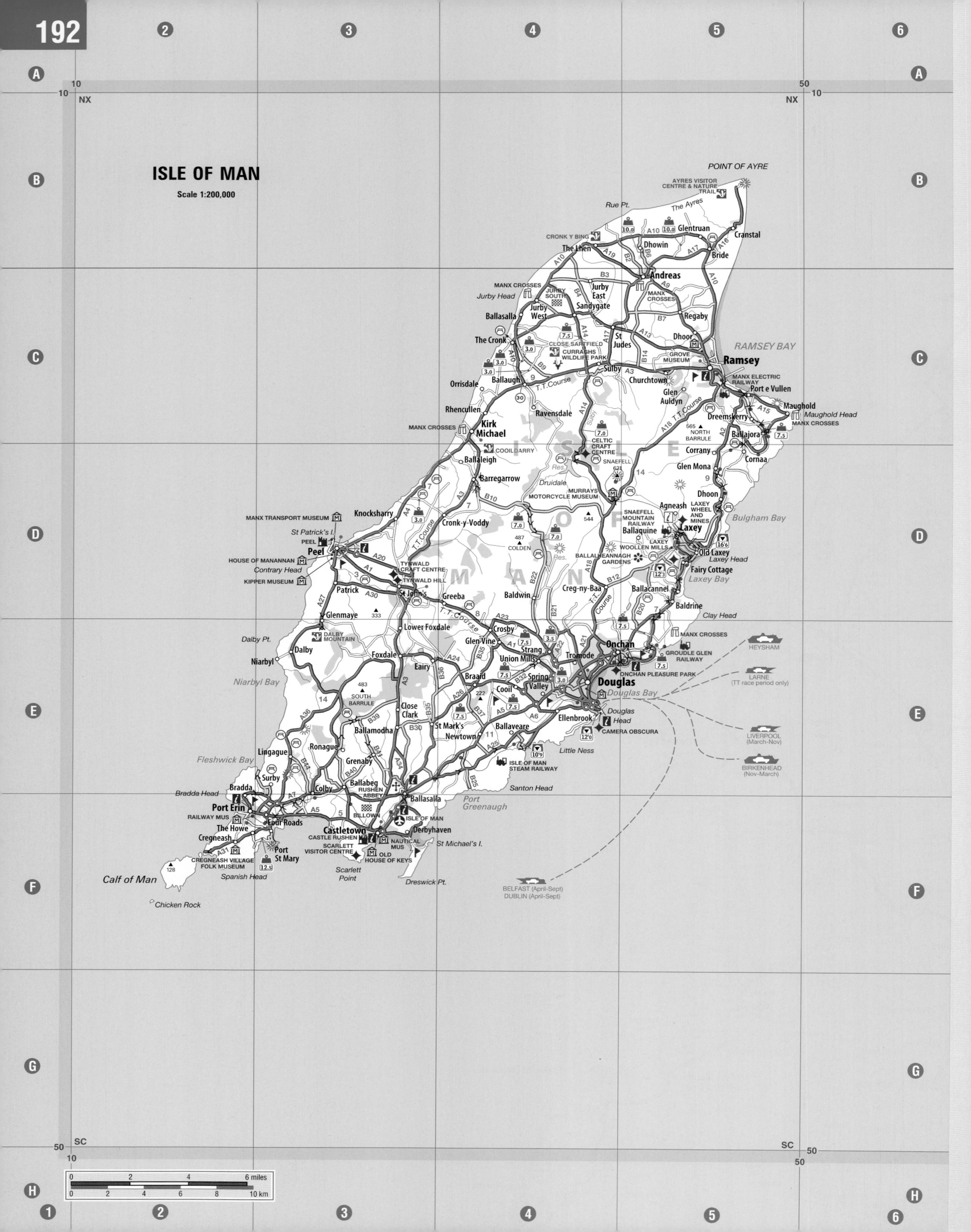

ISLE OF MAN

Scale 1:200,000

POINT OF AYRE

AYRES VISITOR
CENTRE & NATURE
TRAIL

Rue Pt.   The Ayres

CRONK Y BING   A10 10.0 Glentruan   Cranstal
                10.0   Bride
The Lhen   B22   Dhowin   A16
         A19 B22   A17
              B3   Andreas   A9
MANX CROSSES   Jurby Jurby   A10
Jurby Head   JURBY   South East   A10
              Ballasalla Jurby Sandygate MANX Regaby
              West   CROSSES
The Cronk   CLOSE SARTFIELD St A13 Dhoor
         7.5   CURRAGHS Judes   B14   GROVE
         3.0   WILDLIFE PARK   B14   MUSEUM RAMSEY BAY
Orrisdale   3.0   Sulby A3 Churchtown   Ramsey
         Ballaugh   9   MANX ELECTRIC
              T.T.Course Glen   Port e Vullen RAILWAY
Rhencullen 30   Auldyn
                   Ravensdale   A14   Dreemskerry Maughold
              Kirk   Sulby   A15 Maughold Head
MANX CROSSES Michael   565 NORTH MANX CROSSES
              7.0   CELTIC   BARRULE Ballajora 7.5
         Cooildarry   CRAFT 14   Cornaa
         Ballaleigh   CENTRE SNAEFELL Corrany
                        621   Glen Mona
         Barregarrow Druidale Res.   9
              B10   MURRAYS   Dhoon
              7   MOTORCYCLE MUSEUM   Agneash LAXEY WHEEL
MANX TRANSPORT MUSEUM 7   Cronk-y-Voddy 7.0 544 SNAEFELL AND MINES Bulgham Bay
              3.0   7.0 MOUNTAIN
St Patrick's I.   487   RAILWAY Ballaquine Laxey
PEEL   Knocksharry   A3 COLDEN Res. LAXEY 16.6
HOUSE OF MANANNAN Peel   B22 BALLALHEANNAGH WOOLLEN MILLS
Contrary Head TYNWALD A1   GARDENS Old Laxey
KIPPER MUSEUM CRAFT CENTRE A20   Baldwin 12.5 Laxey Head
         Patrick TYNWALD HILL Greeba B21   Fairy Cottage
         A30 St John's   Creg-ny-Baa B12 Laxey Bay
    Glenmaye 3   333   Ballacannel
Dalby Pt.   DALBY Lower Foxdale Crosby   B20 Baldrine
         MOUNTAIN   Glen Vine 7.5   7.5 Clay Head
    Dalby   3.5   Tromode MANX CROSSES
Niarbyl Foxdale A24 Strang Onchan
Niarbyl Bay Eairy   Union Mills GROUDLE GLEN HEYSHAM
         483   Spring 7.5 RAILWAY
         SOUTH   Braaid Valley 3.0 Douglas LARNE
         BARRULE A26 Cooil 222 A5 Douglas Bay (TT race period only)
    Lingague 14   Close B37 A6 Ellenbrook
    Ronague Clark 7.5 7.5 Douglas Head LIVERPOOL
    Surby   St Mark's Ballaveare CAMERA OBSCURA (March-Nov)
Fleshwick Bay Ballamodha B30 Newtown 11 Little Ness
    Colby   Grenaby   A25 BIRKENHEAD
Bradda Ballabeg 10.9 ISLE OF MAN (Nov-March)
Bradda Head RUSHEN STEAM RAILWAY
         ABBEY Ballasalla Port
Port Erin Four Roads Colby Greenaugh Santon Head
RAILWAY MUS A5 BILLOWN ISLE OF MAN
The Howe 5 Castletown Derbyhaven
Cregneash CASTLE RUSHEN NAUTICAL MUS
    Port SCARLETT OLD St Michael's I.
    St Mary VISITOR CENTRE HOUSE OF KEYS
CREGNEASH VILLAGE 12.5 Scarlett Dreswick Pt.
FOLK MUSEUM   Point
128   Spanish Head
Calf of Man

Chicken Rock

BELFAST (April-Sept)
DUBLIN (April-Sept)

0   2   4   6 miles
0 2 4 6 8 10 km

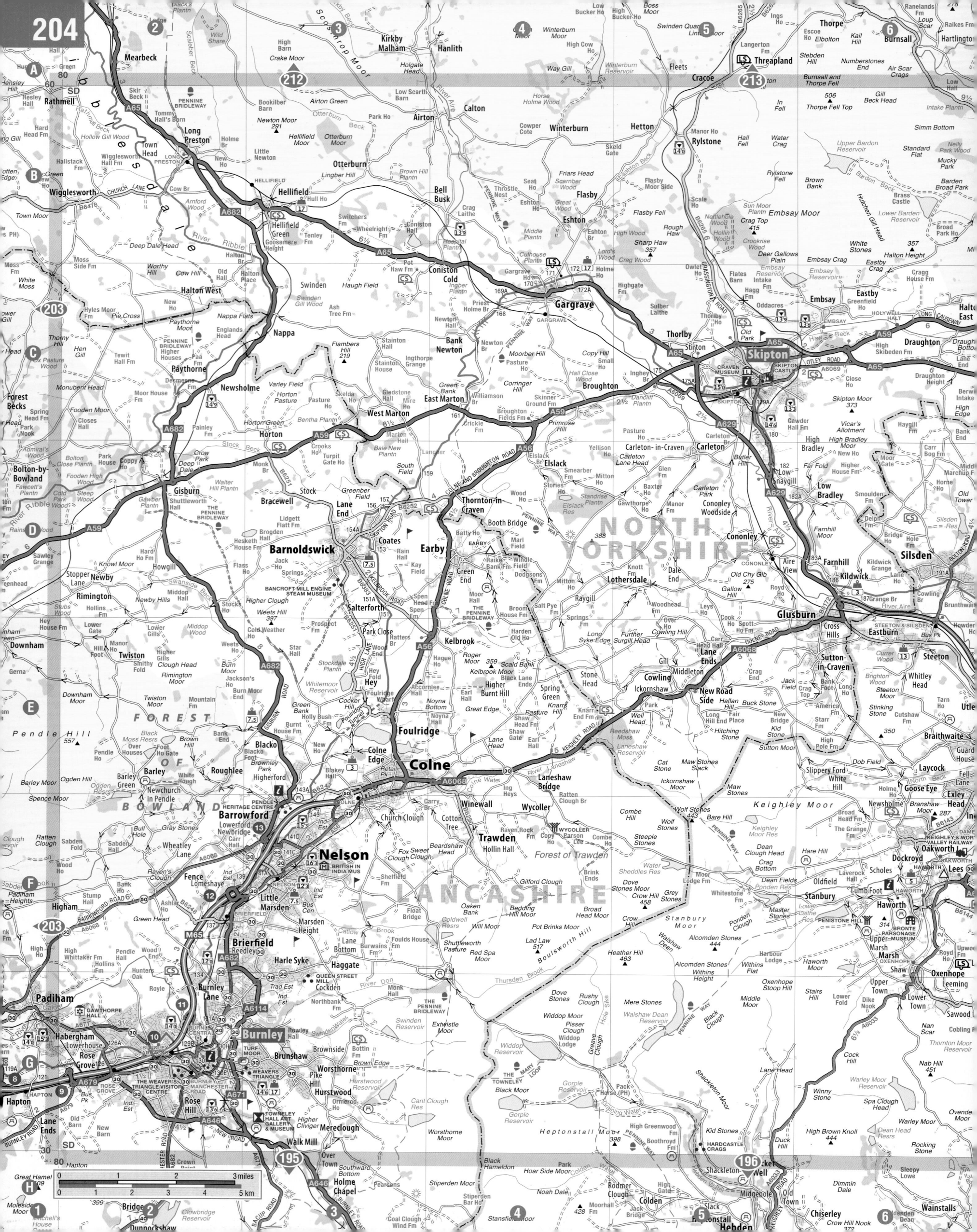

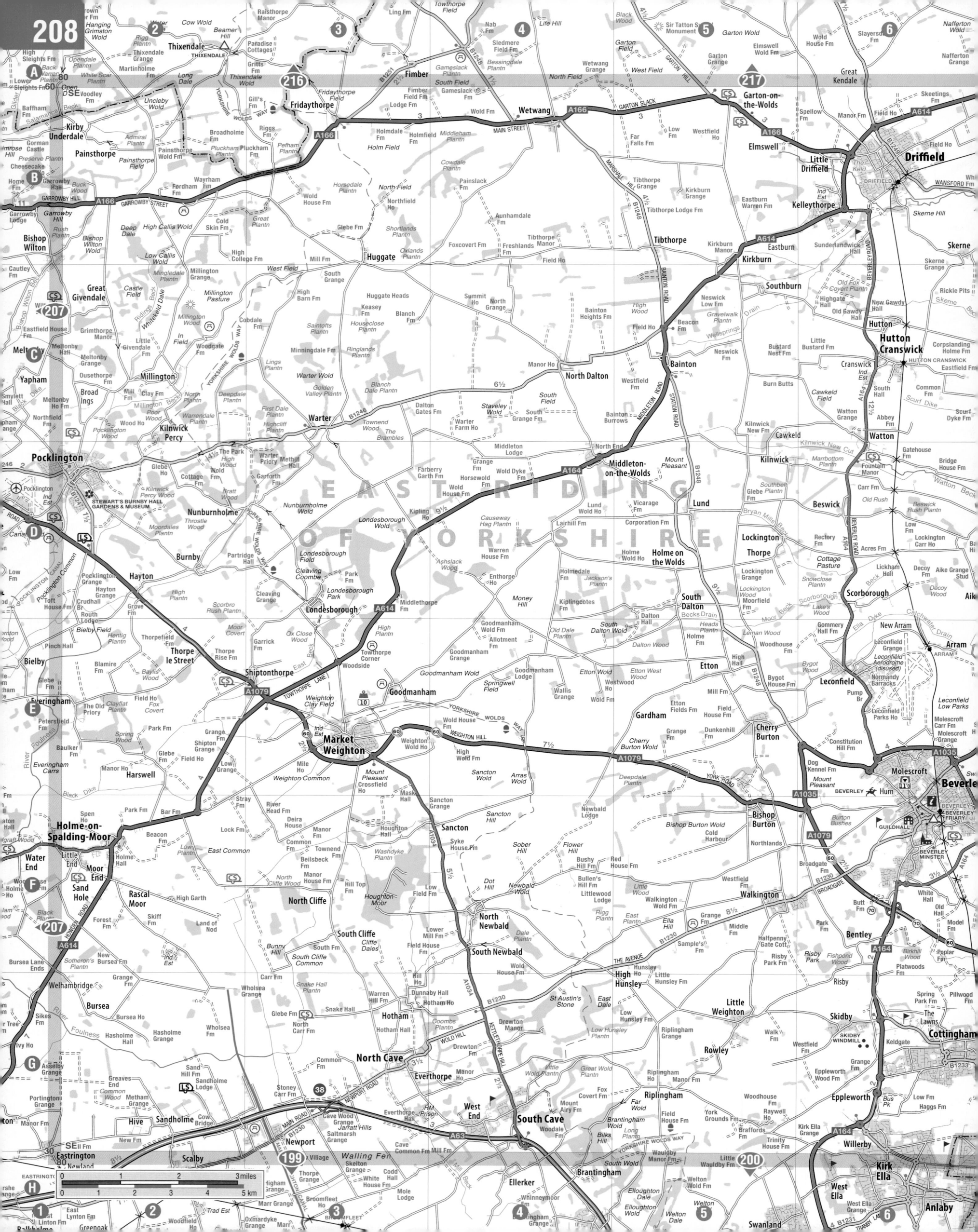

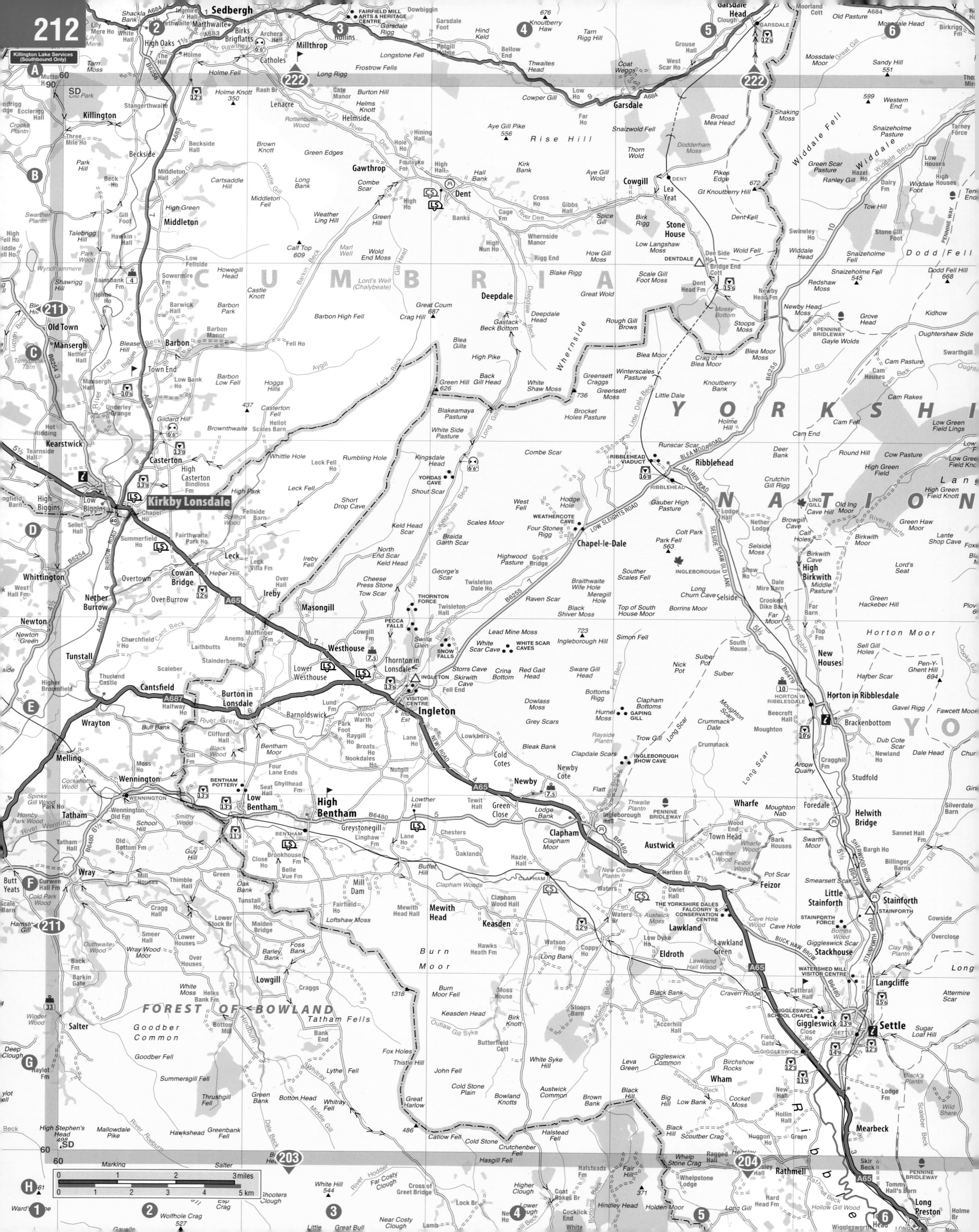

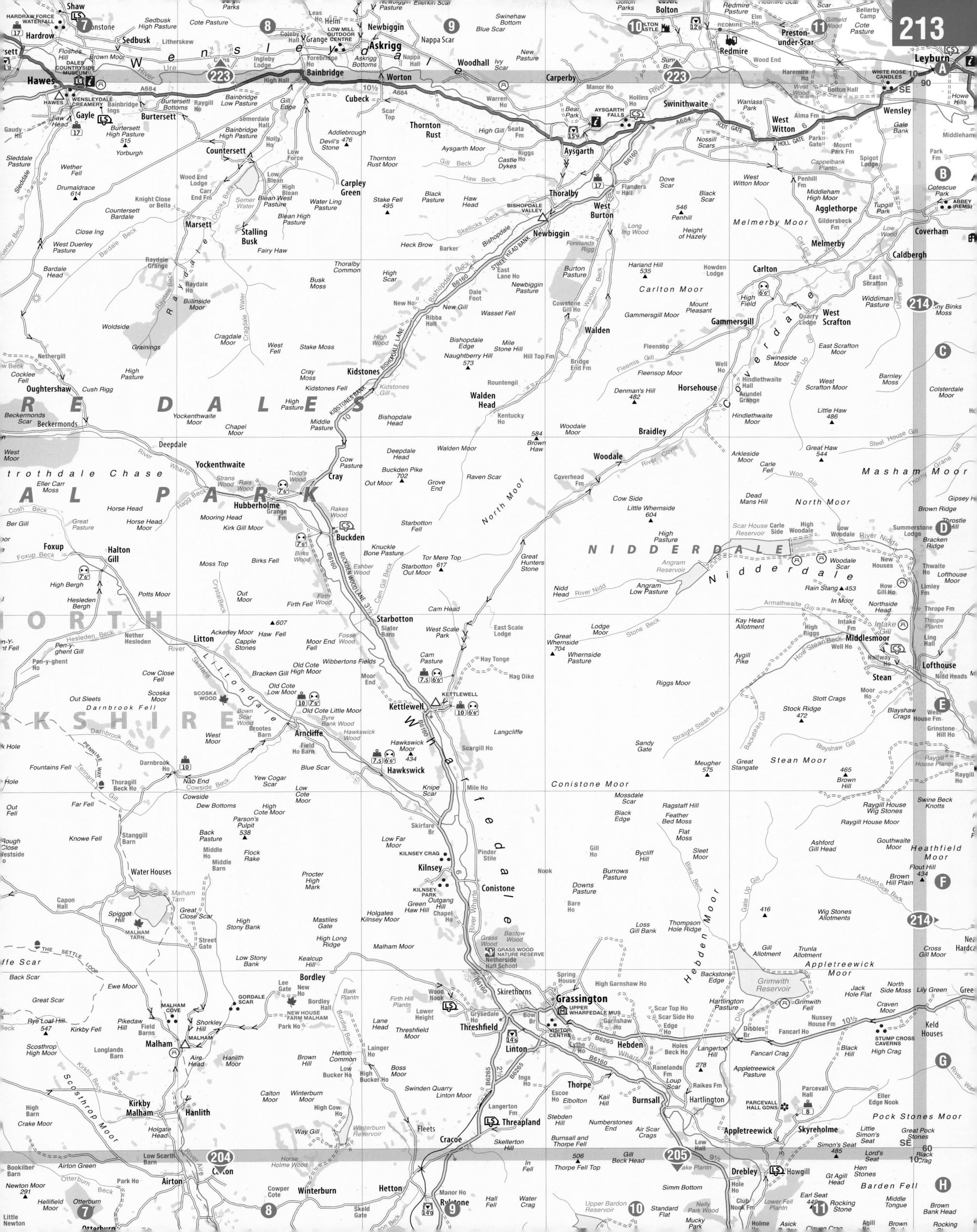

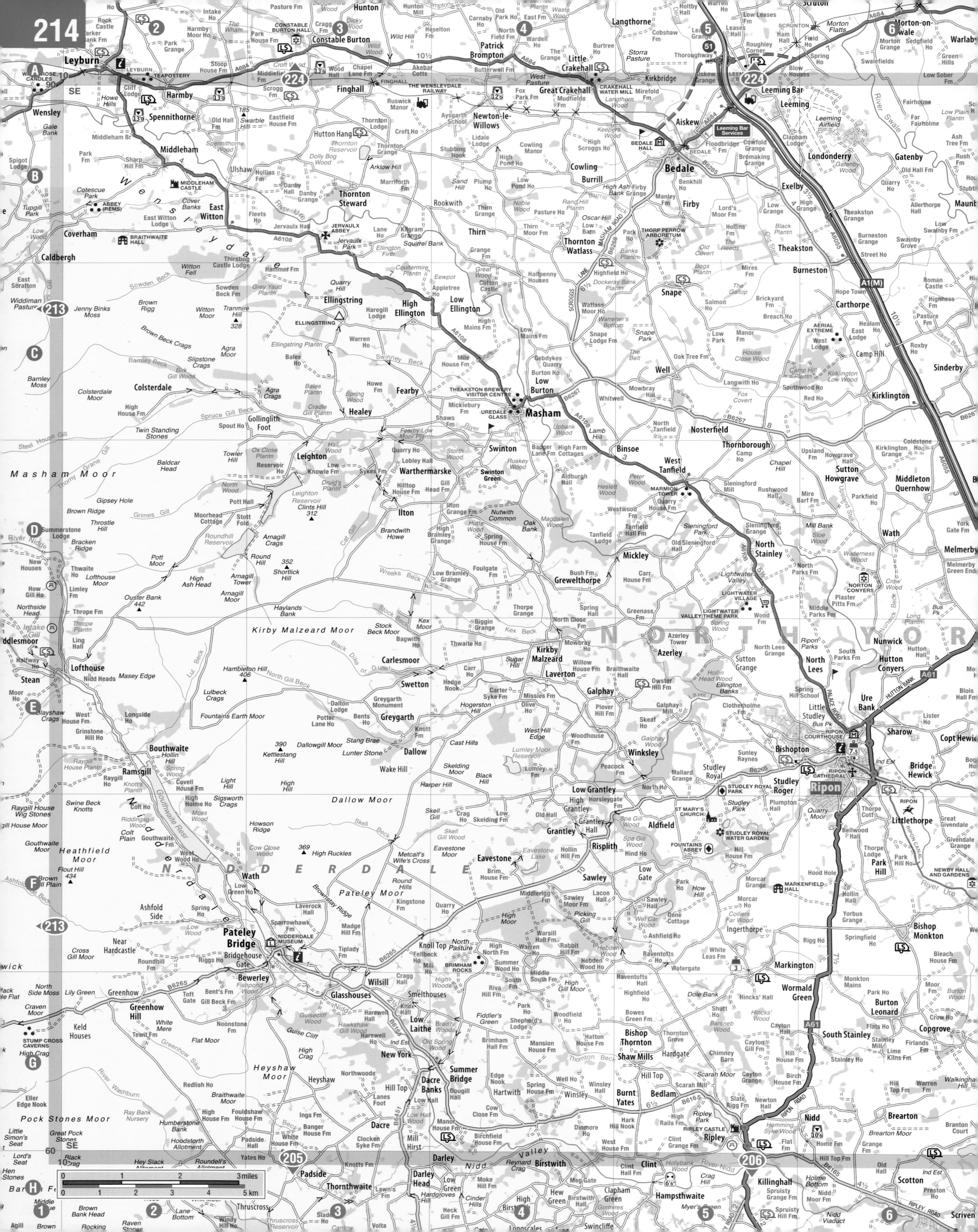

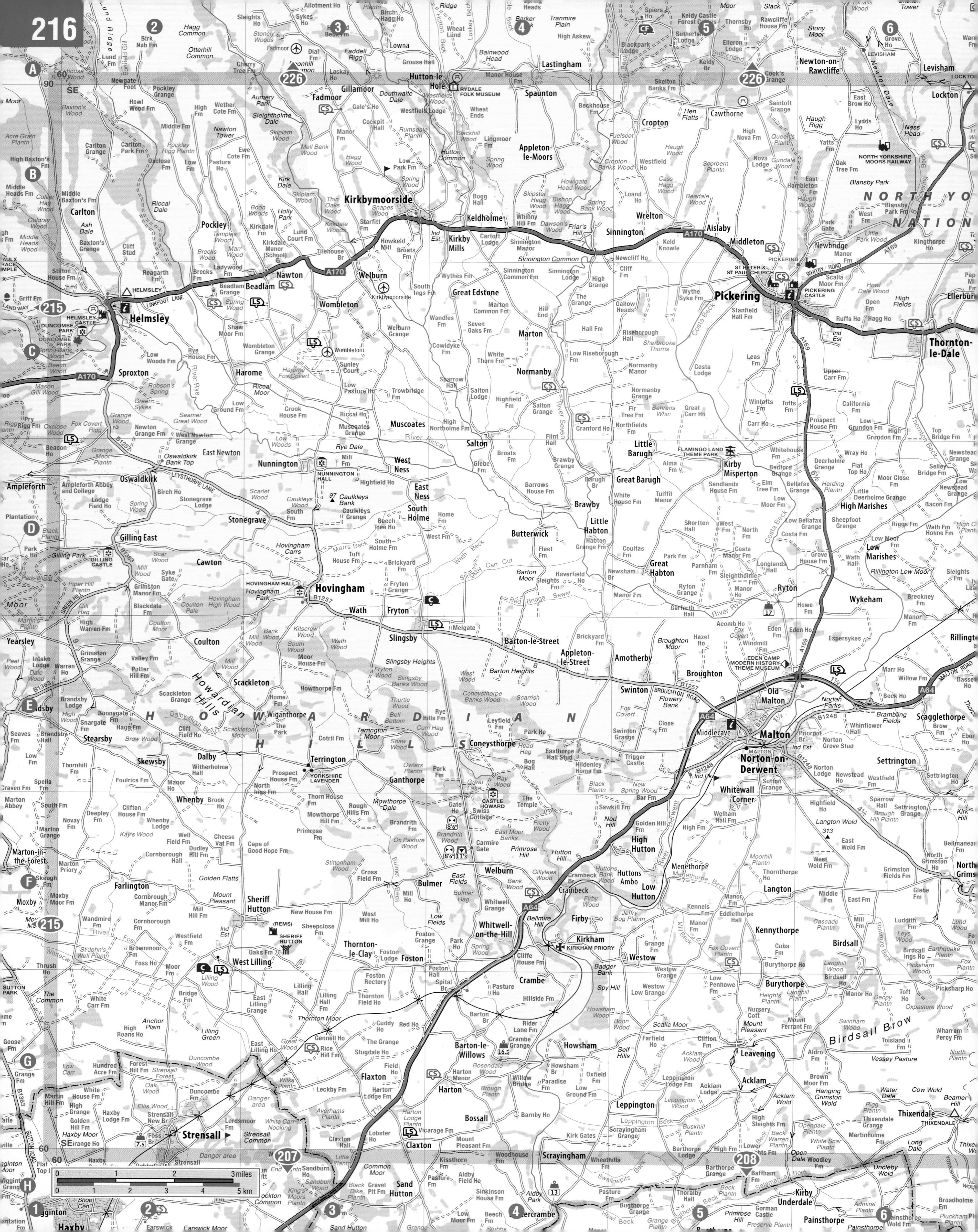

Helmsley · Kirkbymoorside · Pickering · Thornton-le-Dale · Hutton-le-Hole · Lastingham · Cropton · Appleton-le-Moors · Sinnington · Aislaby · Middleton · Newbridge · Newton-on-Rawcliffe · Levisham · Lockton

Beadlam · Nawton · Welburn · Great Edstone · Marton · Normanby · Kirby Misperton · Great Barugh · Little Barugh · Brawby · Salton · Muscoates · Nunnington · West Ness · East Ness · South Holme · Butterwick · Great Habton · Little Habton · Ryton · Wykeham · High Marishes · Low Marishes

Sproxton · Harome · Oswaldkirk · Gilling East · Cawton · Stonegrave · Hovingham · Wath · Fryton · Slingsby · Barton-le-Street · Appleton-le-Street · Amotherby · Swinton · Broughton · Old Malton · Malton · Norton-on-Derwent · Settrington

Ampleforth · Yearsley · Coulton · Scackleton · Terrington · Ganthorpe · Coneysthorpe · Castle Howard · Scagglethorpe

HOWARDIAN HILLS

Brandsby · Dalby · Skewsby · Whenby · Sheriff Hutton · Bulmer · Welburn · High Hutton · Low Hutton · Crambeck · Whitwell Corner · Langton · Birdsall

Marton-in-the-Forest · Farlington · West Lilling · Thornton-le-Clay · Foston · Crambe · Whitwell-on-the-Hill · Kirkham · Westow · Howsham · Leavening · Acklam · Burythorpe

Strensall · Flaxton · Harton · Bossall · Barton-le-Willows · Leppington · Thixendale · Kirby Underdale · Painsthorpe

NORTH YORKSHIRE MOORS RAILWAY · NORTH YORK[SHIRE] NATIONAL [PARK]

A170 · A169 · A64

NORTH

SEA

EAST RIDING

OF YORKSHIRE

FILEY

BAY

BRIDLINGTON

BAY

Yons Nab
Lebberston Cliff
Gristhorpe Cliff
Cunstone Nab
The Wyke
Cliff Fm
Newbiggin
Club Pt
Gristhorpe
Filey Field
Filey Brigg
Brigg End
Filey
Filey Sands
Carr Ho
Beacon Hill
Muston
Muston Grange
Muston Sands
Lowfield Fm
Hunmanby Sands
Royal Oak
Primrose Valley
Pilmoor Fm
Foxhill Fm
Airy Hill
Hunmanby Moor
Hunmanby Gap
Moor Fm
Hill Fm
Ind Est
Rosedale Fm
Moor Ho
Reighton Sands
Howe Fm
Barf Fm
Graffitoe Fm
Moor Fm
Reighton Gap
Vicarage Fm
Reighton
Speeton Sands
Dale Fm
Reighton Field
Speeton Hills
Speeton Cliffs
Buckton Cliffs
Hill Fm
Speeton Grange
Speeton
Speeton Moor
Speeton Gate
Bempton Cliffs
Scale Nab
Bartindale Fm
Speeton
Field Greenlands
Buckton Hall
Standard Hill
Cat Nab
Wandale Fm
Gull Nook
High Huntow Fm
Bempton Grange
Buckton
Wasters Plantn
Burton Fleming
Grindale Field
North Dale
Bempton
Dykes Plantn
Dane's Dyke
North Cliff
Thornwick Bay
FLAMBOROUGH CLIFFS NATURE RESERVE
Maidensgrave Fm
Grindale
Newsham Field
Butterwicks Fm
North Landing
North Moor
Cradle Head
Stottle Bank Nook
Finley Hill
Fox Covert Plantn
East Leys Fm
High Barn
Lynhams
The Crofts
Flatmere Plantn
Selwicks Bay
Flamborough Head
North Wood
Charlestone Fm
North Mount
Field Ho
LIGHTHOUSE ROAD
Flamborough Head
FLAMBOROUGH HEAD LIGHTHOUSE
Springdale Fm
East Crags Wood
High Easton Fm
Beacon Fm
Highcliffe Manor
High Stacks
Binsdale Fm
Eastfield Fm
Ind Est
Dane Dyke Fm
Beacon Hill
Boynton
Priory
SEWERBY HALL & GARDEN
Old Fall Plantn
Ruds
Thorpe Hall
Carr Plantn
West Lawn Wood
Fish Ponds Wood
Wandale Fm
BAYLE MUS
Old Town
Sewerby
BONDSVILLE MODEL VILLAGE
Sewerby Rocks
South Landing
Sands Wood
Temple Fm
High Wood
Bridlington
Bridlington
South Side Mount
Carnaby Temple
Hallowkiln Wood
West Hill
Ind Est
The Spa
OLD PENNY MEMORIES
Tufthill Fm
Wold Gate
Carnaby
Bessingby
Hilderthorpe
P&R
Haisthorpe Field
KINGSGATE
Haisthorpe
Thornholme Field
Wilsthorpe
South Sands
Burton Agnes Field
BRIDLINGTON BIRDS OF PREY Est & ANIMAL PARK
Carnaby Moor
Thornholme
Brackendale Fm
Auburn Fm
BURTON AGNES HALL
BURTON AGNES MANOR HOUSE
Oak Wood Fm
Harpham Grange
Burton Agnes
Burton Agnes Stud Fm
Demming Fm
Fraisthorpe
Harpham
Hords Covert
Burtoncarr Fm
Fraisthorpe Sands
Little Kelk Fm
Thornholme Field
Low Stonehills
Gransmoor Wood
Woodside Fm
Hamiltonhill Fm
Turtle Hill Fm
High Stonehills
Gransmoor Low Ho
Gransmoor
Barmston Sands
Great Kelk
Park Ho
Barmston
Lissett
Barmston Main Drain
Allison Lane End
Ulcome

0 1 2 3 miles
0 1 2 3 4 5 km

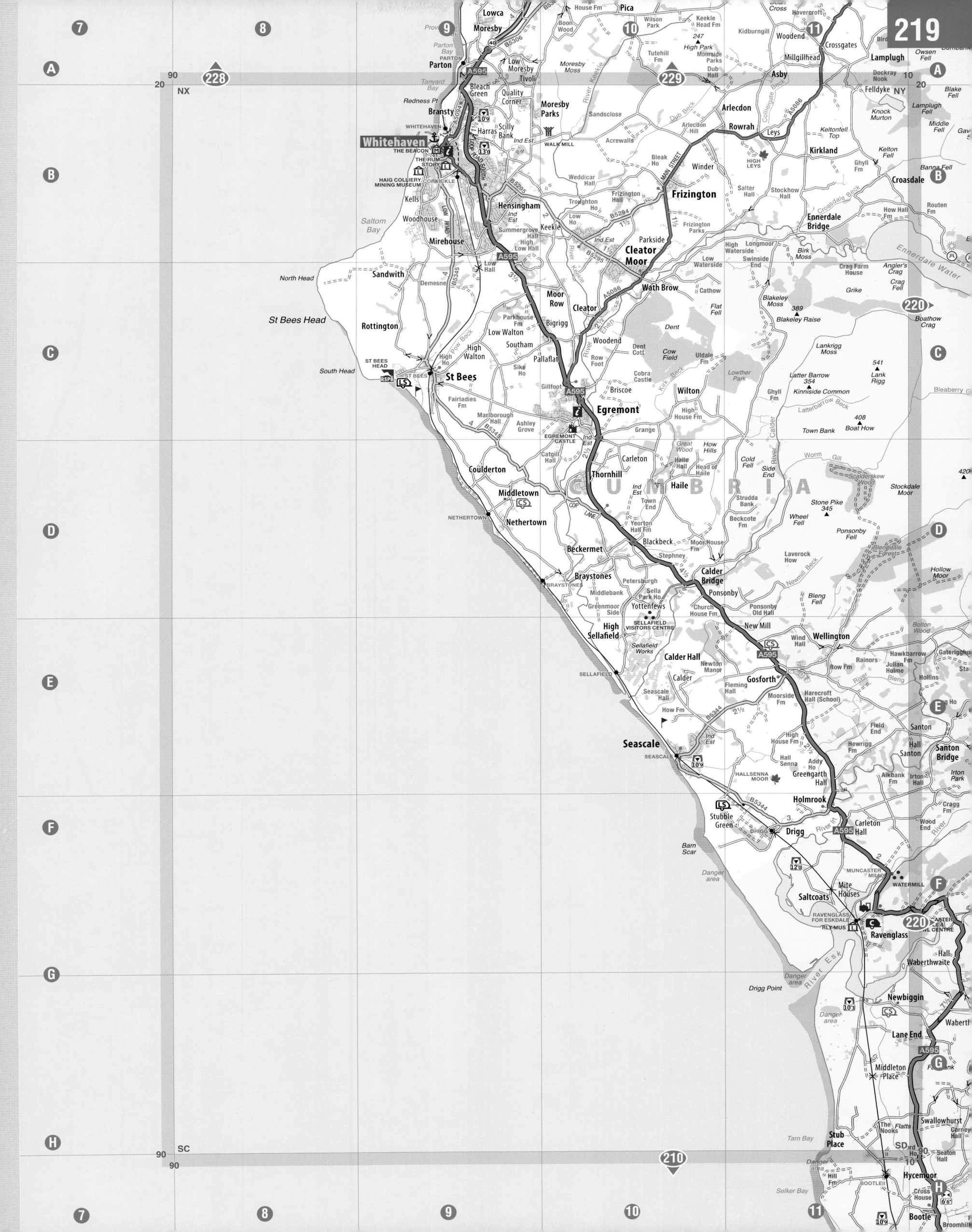

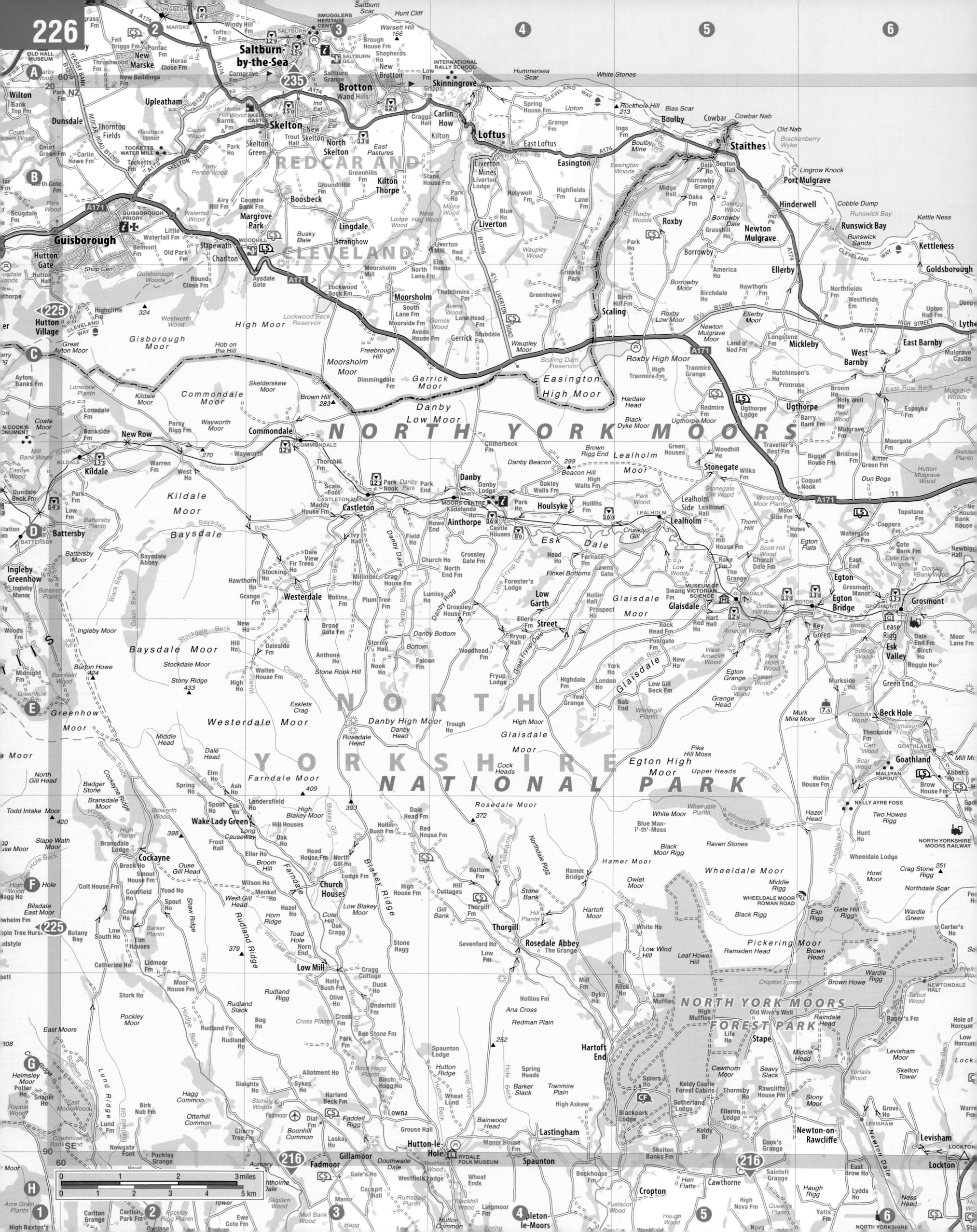

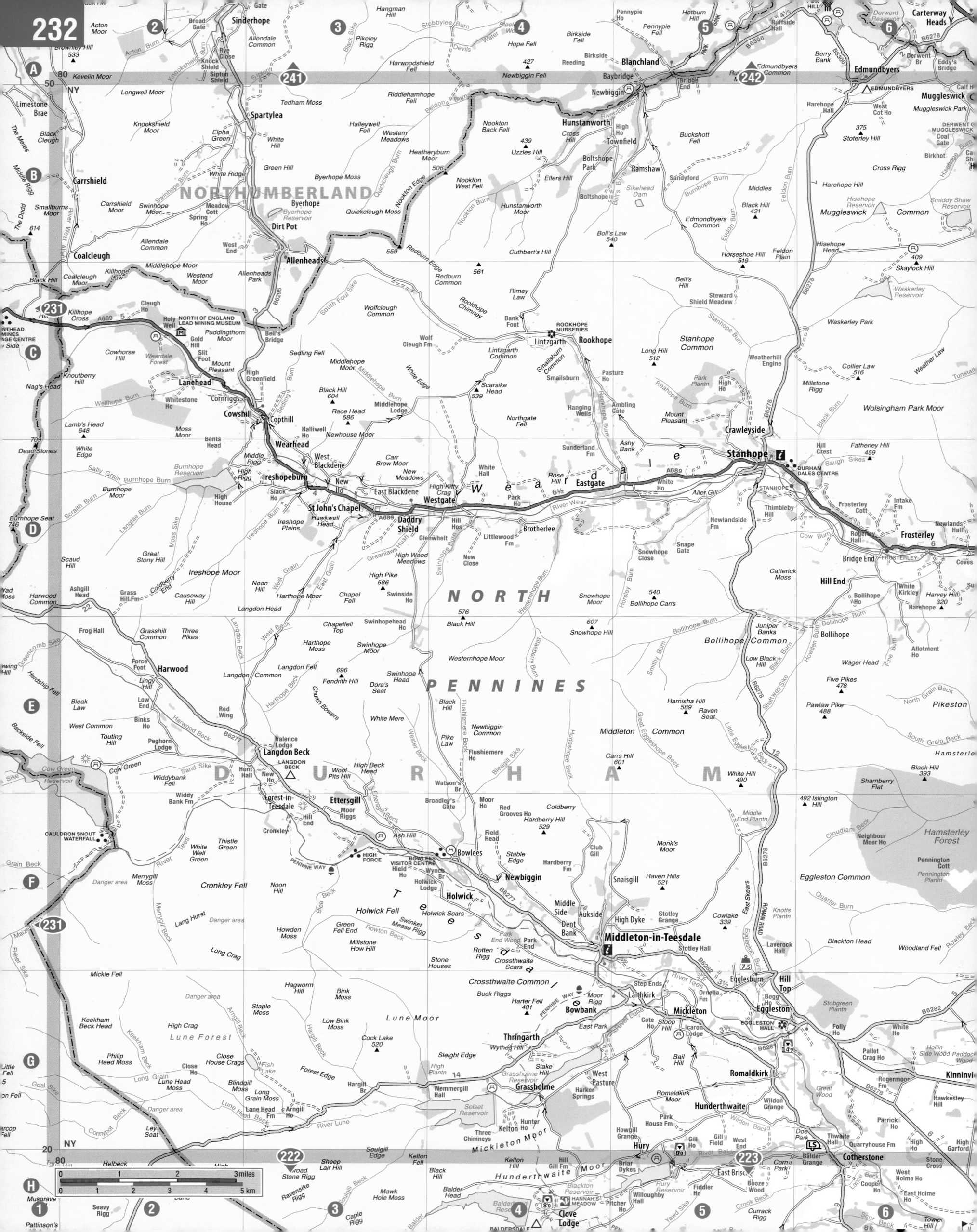

NORTH SEA

TEES BAY

Bran Sands
Grangetown Works
Coatham Marsh
Coatham
Warrenby
BRITISH STEEL REDCAR
Westfield
Redcar Racecourse
Dormanstown
Kirkleatham
Wilton Chemical Works
Lazenby
getown
Lackenby
Wilton
Wilton Castle
Lazenby Bank
Wilton Moor Plantn
242
Greystone Road
Court Green Wood
Dunsdale
Thornton Fields
Raisbeck Wood
Cargo Wood
Court Ho
Ho Fm

West Scar
Salt Scar
Redcar Rocks
The Flashes
REDCAR CENTRAL
Redcar
Mill Howle
REDCAR EAST
COAST ROAD
Scanbeck Howle
Marske-by-the-Sea
Stone Gap
Longbeck
Grewgrass Fm
Windy Hill Fm
Tofts Fm
MARSKE
Fell Briggs Fm
Pontac
Horse Close Fm
New Marske
Thrushwood
Yearby Wood
New Buildings Fm
Yearby
OLD HALL MUSEUM
Corngrave Fm
Saltburn-by-the-Sea
SMUGGLERS HERITAGE CENTRE
Saltburn Scar
Hunt Cliff
Warsett Hill 166
Brough House Fm
Shepherds Ho
Saltburn Grange
SALTBURN GILL
New Brotton
Brotton
Wand Hills
Low Farm
Skinningrove
INTERNATIONAL RALLY SCHOOL
Gripps
Hummersea Scar
White Stones
Craggs Hall
Kilton
Grange Fm
Spring House Fm
Upton
Rockhole Hill 213
Bias Scar
Boulby
Boulby Mine
Cowbar
Cowbar Nab
Old Nab
Brackenberry Wyke
Loftus
East Loftus
Staithes
Ings Fm
Upleatham
Skelton
SKELTON CASTLE
New Skelton
Skelton Green
Park Ho
East Pastures
Carlin How
A174
225
226
NZ 50
80
NZ 20
80

FIRTH

OF

CLYDE

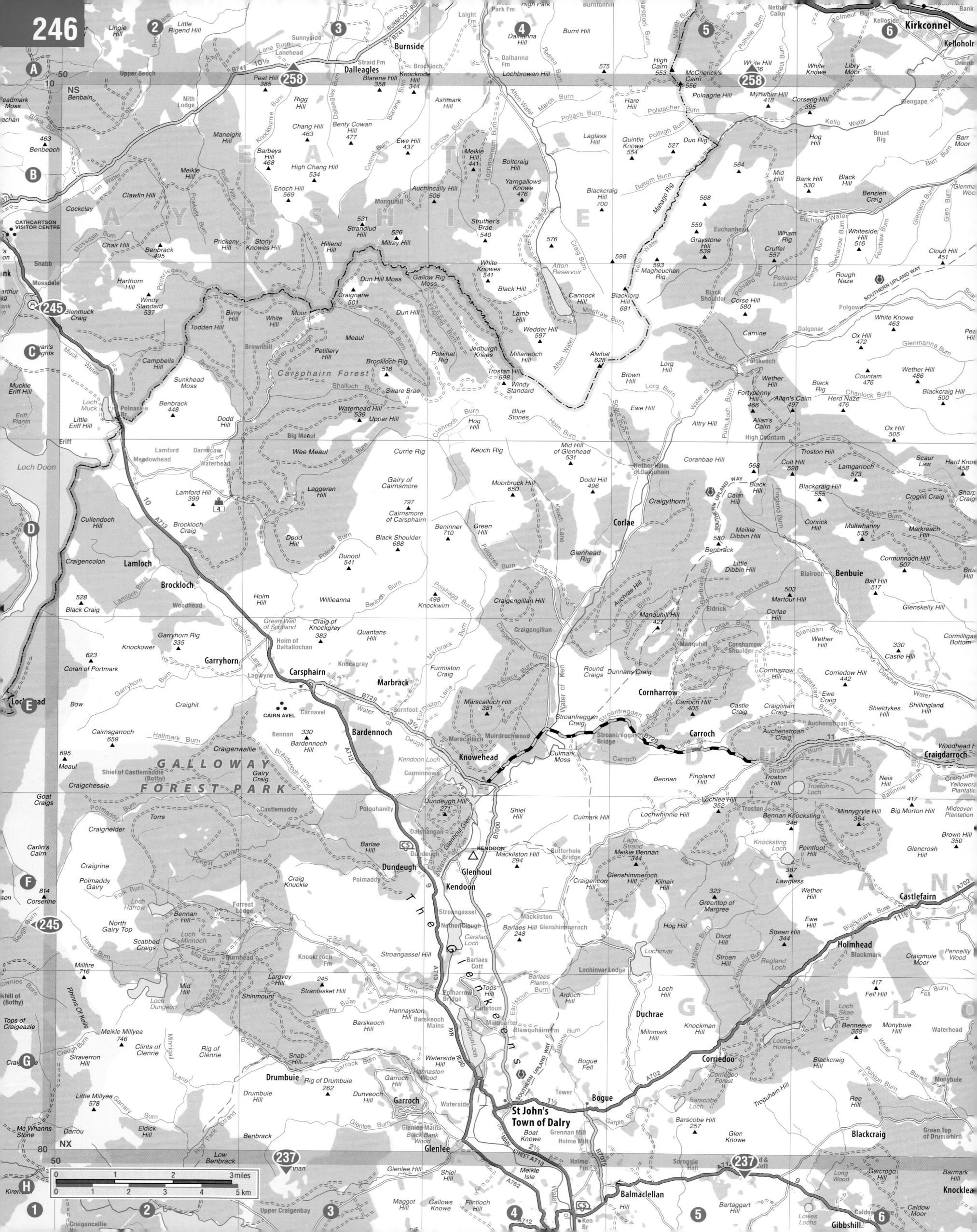

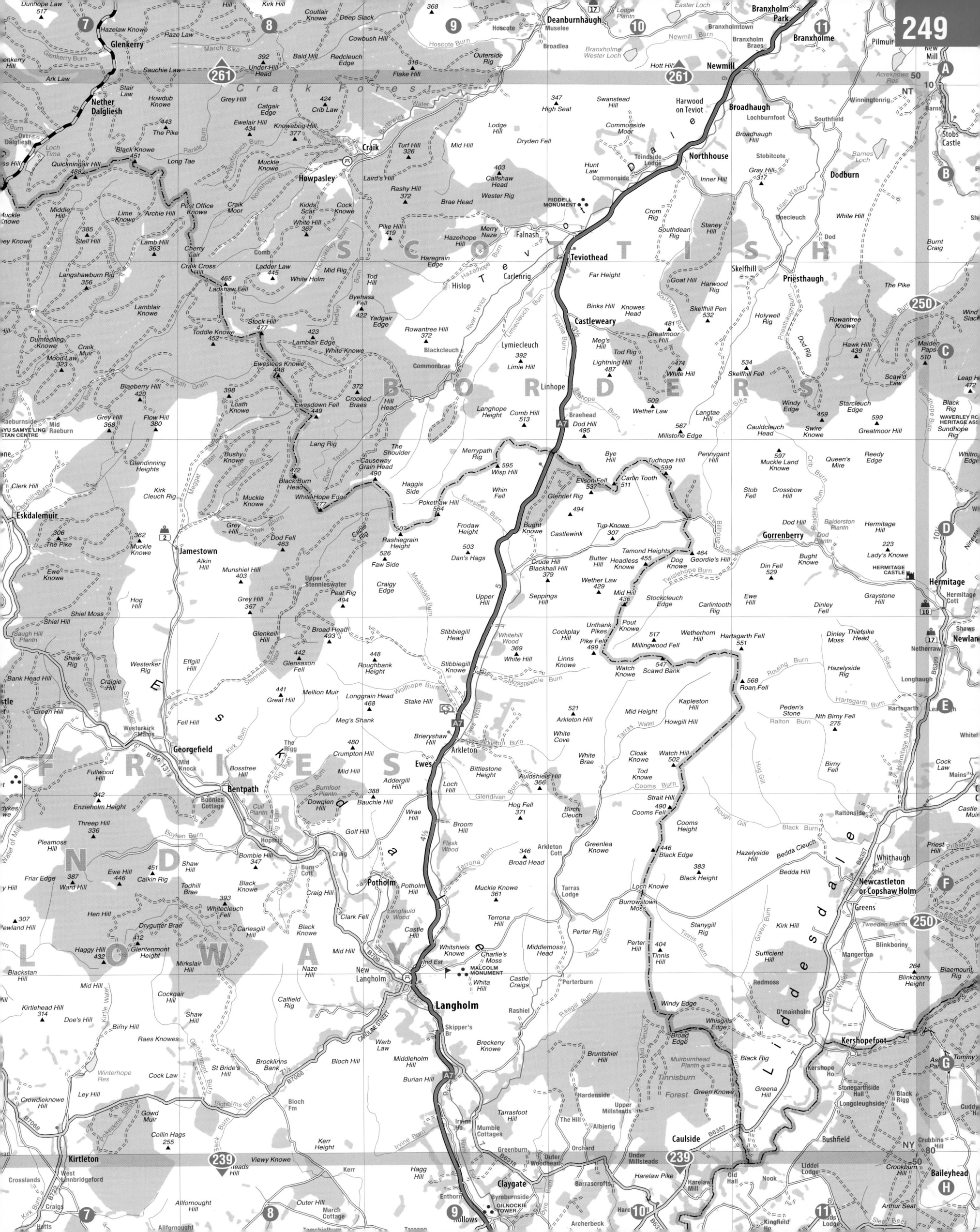

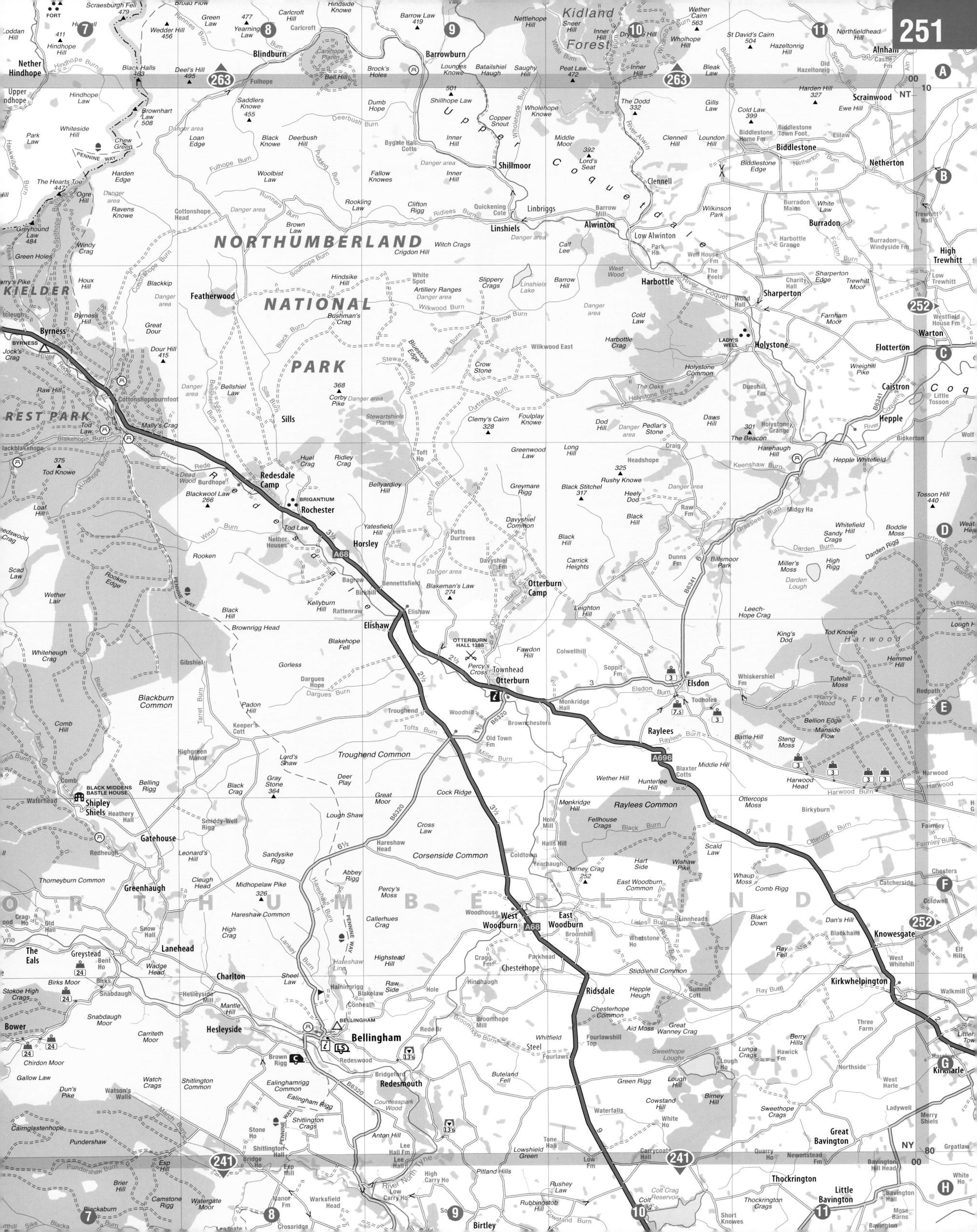

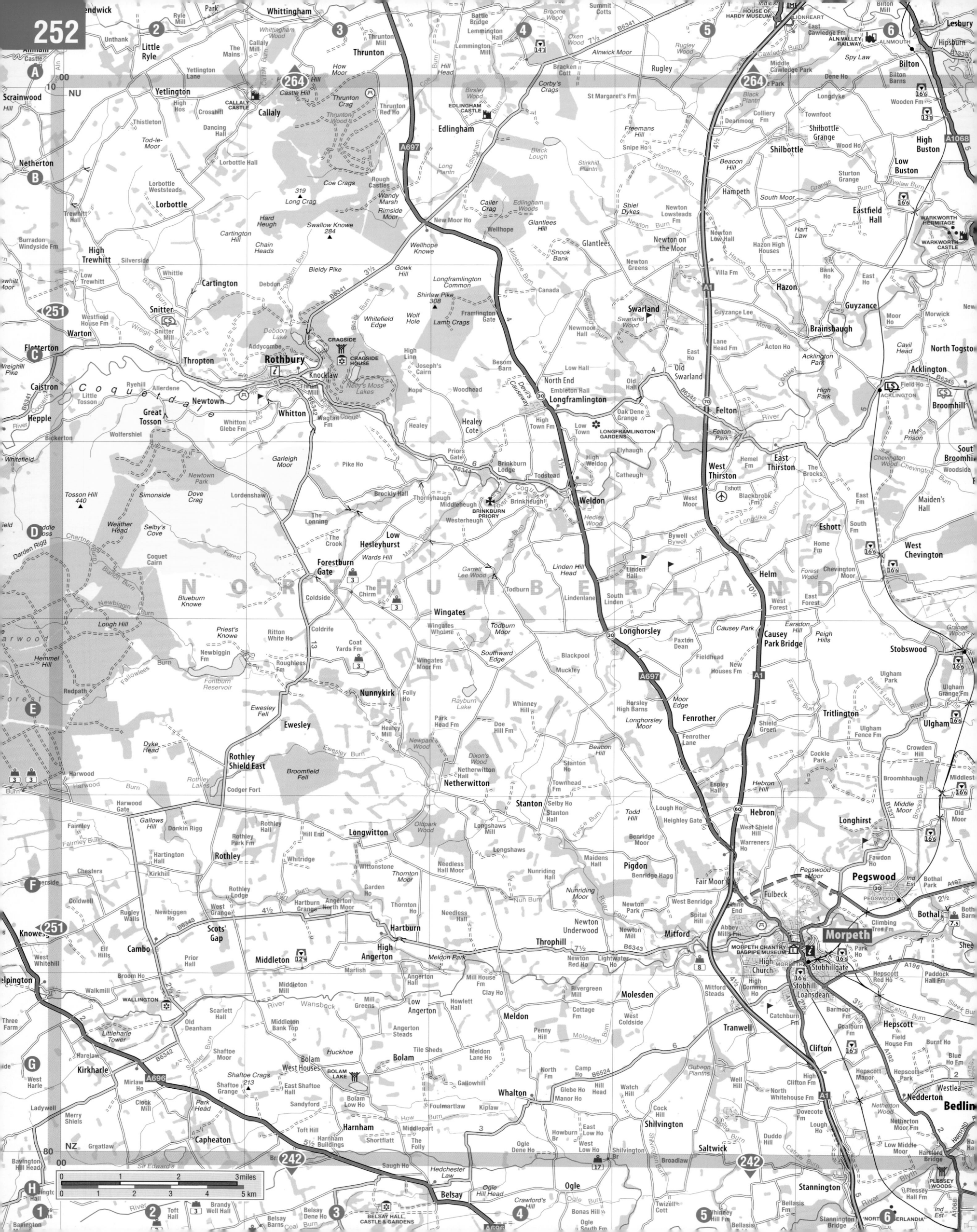

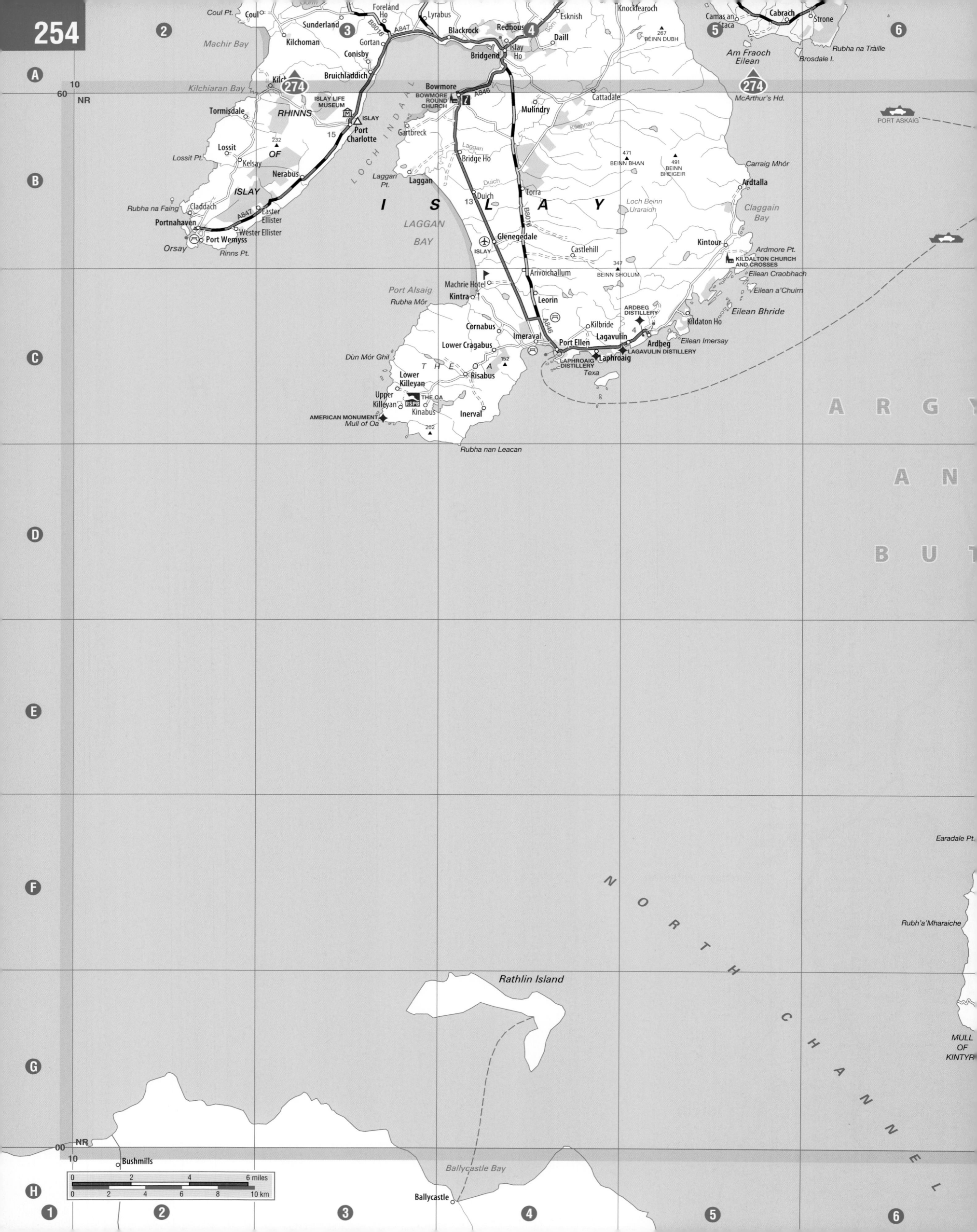

Coul Pt.
Coul
Foreland
Ho
Lyrabus
Esknish
Knockfearoch
267
BEINN DUBH
Camas an
Staca
Cabrach
Strone
Sunderland
Kilchoman
Gortan
B8018
A847
Blackrock
Redhouse
Daill
Conisby
Bridgend
Islay
Ho
Rubha na Tràille
Brosdale I.
Am Fraoch
Eilean
Bruichladdich
Bowmore
McArthur's Hd.
274
PORT ASKAIG
Kilchiaran Bay
274
BOWMORE
ROUND
CHURCH
A846
Tormisdale
ISLAY LIFE
MUSEUM
RHINNS
Mulindry
Cattadale
Port
Charlotte
ISLAY
15
Gartbreck
471
BEINN BHAN
491
BEINN
BHEIGEIR
Carraig Mhór
Lossit
232
Laggan
Bridge Ho
Laggan
Pt.
Laggan
Duich
Ardtalla
Lossit Pt.
Kelsay
Nerabus
Laggan
Duich
Torra
Loch Beinn
Uraraidh
Claggain
Bay
ISLAY
13
I S L A Y
B8016
Rubha na Faing
Claddach
Easter
Ellister
A847
LAGGAN
BAY
Kintour
Portnahaven
Wester Ellister
Glenegedale
Castlehill
347
Ardmore Pt.
Port Wemyss
ISLAY
BEINN SHOLUM
KILDALTON CHURCH
AND CROSSES
Orsay
Rinns Pt.
Arivoichallum
Eilean Craobhach
Eilean a'Chuirn
Port Alsaig
Machrie Hotel
Leorin
Eilean Bhride
Rubha Mór
Kintra
ARDBEG
DISTILLERY
Kilbride
Cornabus
Imeraval
Kilbride
Lagavulin
Kildaton Ho
Eilean Imersay
Lower Cragabus
Port Ellen
4
Ardbeg
Dùn Mór Ghil
152
LAPHROAIG
DISTILLERY
Laphroaig
LAGAVULIN DISTILLERY
THE OA
Risabus
Texa
Lower
Killeyan
Upper
Killeyan
RSPB
THE OA
Kinabus
Inerval
AMERICAN MONUMENT
Mull of Oa
202
A R G Y
Rubha nan Leacan
A N
B U T
Earadale Pt.
Rubh'a'Mharaiche
N
O
R
T
H
Rathlin Island
C
H
A
MULL
OF
KINTYRE
N
N
E
L
Bushmills
Ballycastle Bay

0   2   4   6 miles
0 2 4 6 8 10 km
Ballycastle

255
266
Ardrossan
ARDROSSAN TOWN
ARDROSSAN SOUTH BEACH
ARDROSSAN HARBOUR
BRODICK CAMPBELTOWN (May-Sept)
South Bay
NORTH AYRSHIRE MUSEUM
Saltcoats
Outer Nebbock

NS
00
40

Maol Donn
368

Glenshant Hill
Merkland
Creag Rosa
Torr Breac

Glen Rosa
Glenrosa
Merkland Wood
Merkland Pt
Wine Port

Cnocan Burn
A841

Glen Shurig
BRODICK CASTLE
Cladach
Old Quay
ARDROSSAN

THE STRING
BRODICK Burn
ISLE OF ARRAN HERITAGE MUSEUM
Brodick

Gaolthe
Glen Cloy
1½ A841

Glen Ormidale
Sgiath Bhán
255
Strathwhillan
Fairy Glen
Corriegills Pt
North Corriegills
South Corriegills
Dun Dubh

Cnoc Breac
Cnoc Dubh
Meall Buidhe
Clauchland Hills
Margnaheglish
Clauchlands Fm
Clauchlands
Clauchlands Pt
Kerr's Port
Hamilton Isle

Isle
Blairbeg
Clauchlands

Benlister Glen
Benlister Burn
Lamlash

of
The Ross
311
Monamore Br
Mullach Beag
Holy Island

Monamore Glen
Cordon
White Pt
314
Mullach Mór
Gortonallister
Pillar Rock Pt

Arran
A841
The Knowe Fm

Cnoc Dubh
Urie Loch
Auchencairn
Kingscross Pt
Kingscross

Dunvein
Knockenkelly
Sandbraes

NORTH
Glas Choirein
Allt Garbh
Borrach
North Kiscadale

Cnoc Donn
Cnoc an Fheidh
Cnoc Mór
South Kiscadale
Whiting Bay

Auchareoch
GLENASHDALE FALLS
Glenashdale Burn
Largymore

AYRSHIRE
Kilmory Water
Largymeanoch

Torr oh Mór
Cnoc Craobhach
Cnoc na Garbad
Cnoc na Comhairle
Largybeg
Largybeg Pt
Port na Gaillin

Torr a' Bannain
Margenaish Fm
Levencorroch Hill
Dippin Head

Southbank
East Bennan
West Bennan
Levencorroch
Auchenhew
Drumla
Dippin
Porta Leacach

STRUEY ROCKS
Port a'Ghillie Ghlais
Porta Buidhe
Kildonan
Port Dearg

Bennan Head
Sound of Pladda
Pladda

FIRTH
OF
CLYDE

NS
10
00

255
244
244

0   1   2   3 miles
0 1 2 3 4 5 km

Culzean Castle
Glasson Rock
Barwhin Pt
Maidenhead Bay
Morriston
Swan Pond
Culzean
Culzean Bay
Broad Craig

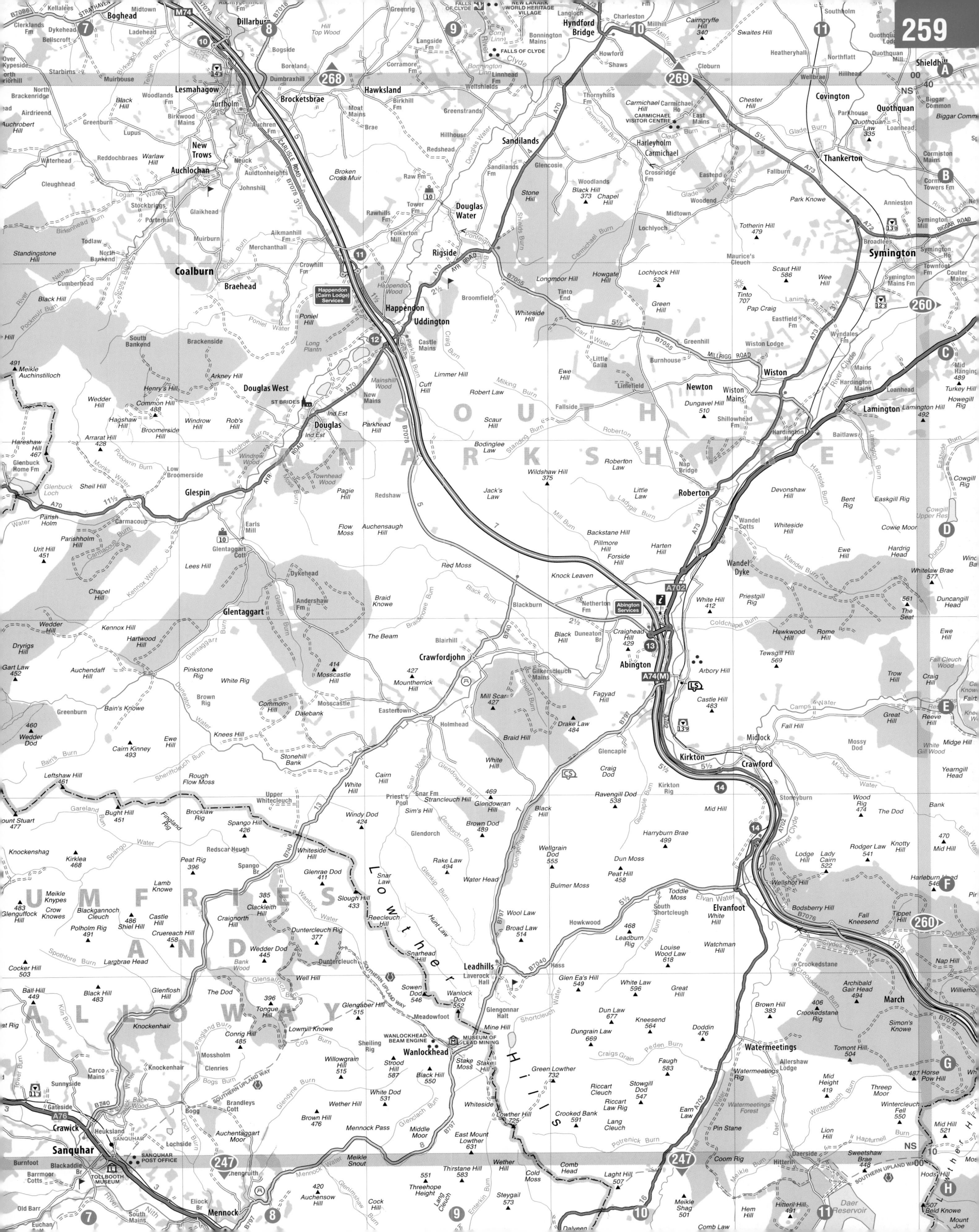

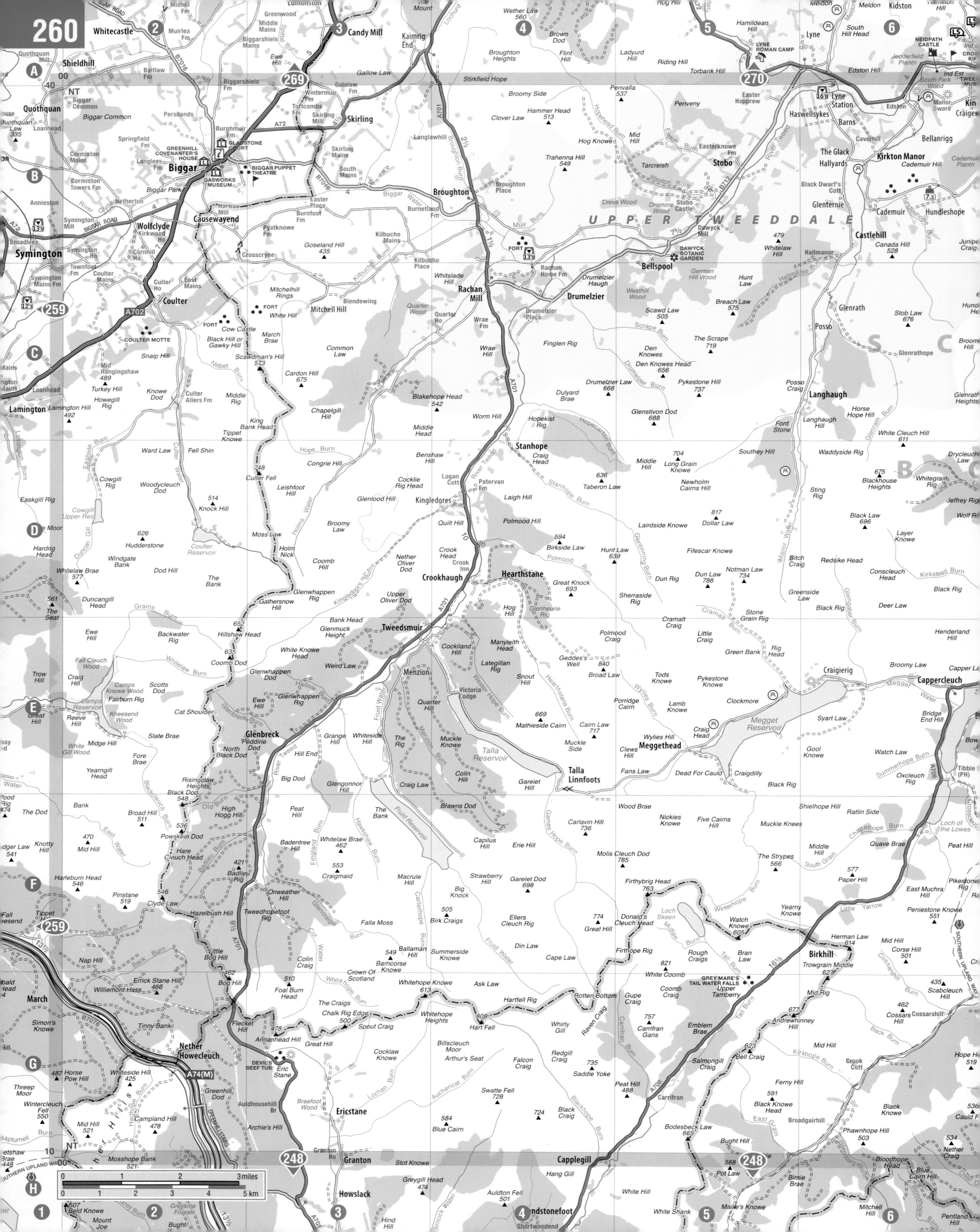

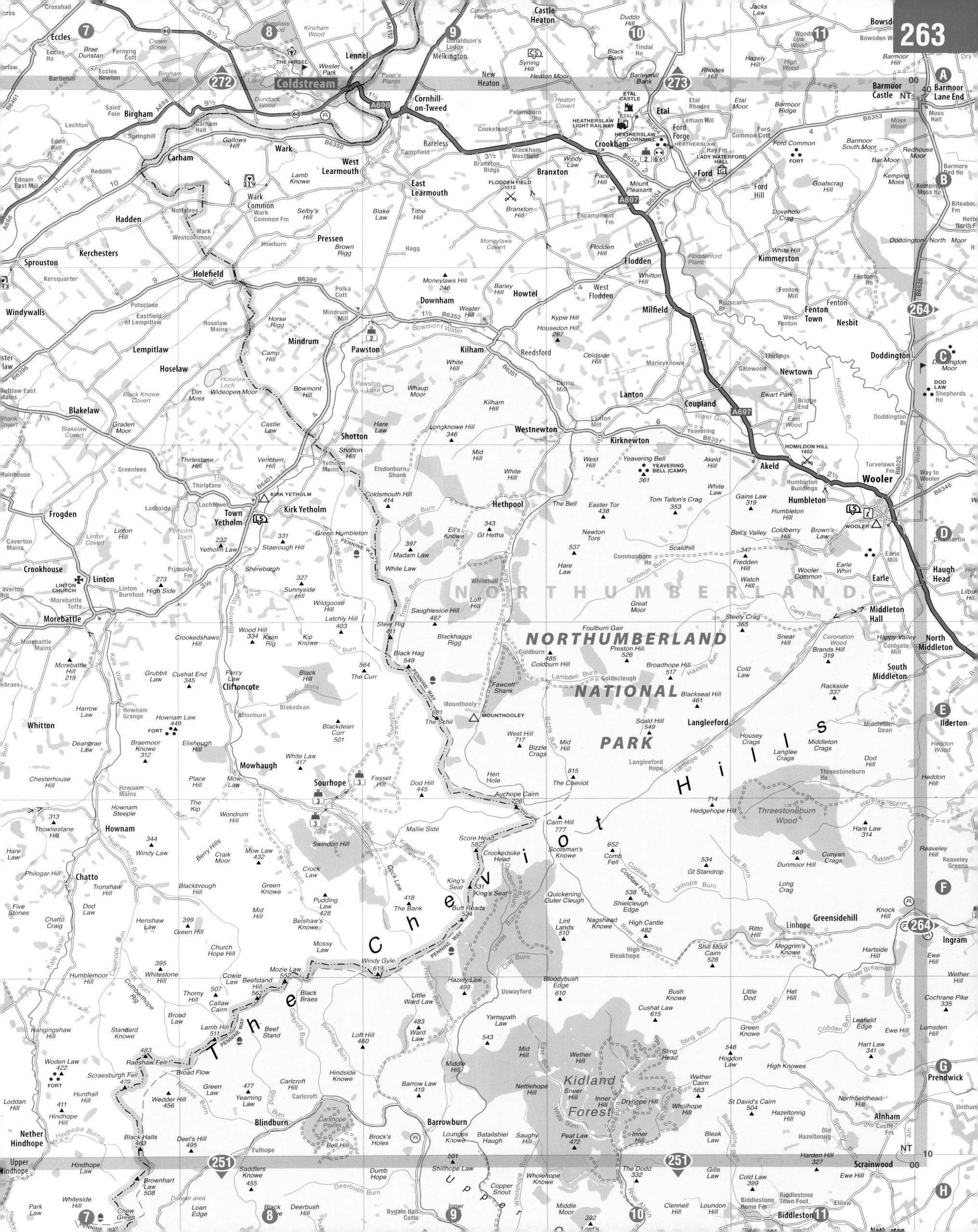

N O R T H

S E A

Castle Pt
BUNSTANBURGH
CASTLE
Queen
Margaret's Cove

Craster

Cullernose Pt

owick

Rumbling Kern

Howick
Haven

Sugar Sands

Low
Stead
Howdiemont Sands

houghton

Red Ends

Boulmer

Boulmer
Haven

Seaton Pt

Marden Rocks

mouth

Alnmouth
Bay

gstone

mbleton
Bay

n Pt

IONA ABBEY AND CATHEDRAL
IONA HERITAGE CENTRE
ST COLUMBA EXHIBITION
& WELCOME CENTRE

BEINN NA CROISE

Torrans

Leidle

Achnahard
Knokan
Eorabus
Lower
Ardtun
Lee

Kintra
Baile Mor
Aridhglas
BROLASS
Carsaig

Stac an
Aoineidh
ona
Slackneach
Fionnphort
Bunessan
Carsaig
Bay
Rubha
Dubh

Fidden
Tiraghoil
Loch
Assapol
CRUACHAN MIN
376
376

288
289

Erraid
Knockvologan
ROSS OF MULL
Uisken
Scoor

Soa I.
Ardalanish
Ardchiavaig
Malcolm's Pt.
CARSAIG ARCHES

125
Rubha nam
Braithrean

Eilean a'Chalmain

Rubh Ardalanish

OBAN

Torran Rocks

Dubh Artach

Rubh'a'Geadha

Kiloran Bay
Balnahard

Uragaig

KILORAN GARDENS
Kiloran

Kilchattan
Scalasaig

COLONSAY

Loch Staosnaig

Ardskenish
Garvard
Rubha Dubh

Balerominor

Corpach Bay

PRIORY

Dubh Eilean
Oronsay

Shian Bay
453
RAINBERG
MOR

Eilean nan Ron
Shian

318
R

Loch Righ
Mòr

Rubh'an t-Sàilein

(Summer Only)

Loch Tarbert

Rubha Lang-aoinidh

Rubha a'Mhail

U

Rubha Bholsa

Loch an Aircill

439

Lagg

Loch Lesgamail

J

Nave Island
Ardnave Pt.

364
SGARBH
BREAC

J U R A

785
755
J

Ardmenish

PAPS OF JURA

An Dùna

Gortantaoid
316
Bunnahabhain
BUNNAHABHAIN
DISTILLERY

Cnocbreac

JURA FOREST
Corran

Carraig Bhan
Ardnave
Kilnave

Killinallan

Gleann Astaile

Leargybreck
Knockrome
Ardfernal
Lowlandman
Bay

An Clachan
Sanaigmore
Garra
Eallabus

Caol Ila
561
Loch na Mile

Braigo
Leckgruinart
CAOL ILA DISTILLERY
Port Askaig
Feolin Ferry

Smaull
LOCH
GRUINART
FINLAGGAN
CENTRE
Keills
Keils
Craighouse

Ballinaby
Carnduncan
LOCH GRUINART NATURE
RESERVE VISITORS CENTRE
Craigens
Ballygrant
Camas an
Staca
ISLE OF JURA
DISTILLERY
Small Isles

Saligo Bay
Aoradh
Tighnacachla
Balole
Loch
Ballygrant
Lossit Lodge
Kilmeny
Gleann Ullibh
BRAT BHEINN
342
Crackaig

Saligo
Loch
Gorm
Foreland
Ho
Lyrabus
ISLAY
Knockfearoch
267
BEINN DUBH
Cabrach
Strone

Coul Pt.
Coull
Esknish
Daill
Rubha na Tràille

Machir Bay
Sunderland
Blackrock
Redhouses

Kilchoman
Gortan
Conisby
Bridgend
Islay
Ho
Am Fraoch
Eilean
Brosdale I.

Bruichladdich
Cattadale

Kilchiaran
Bowmore
Mulindry
's Hd.

Kilchiaran Bay
254
BOWMORE
ROUND
CHURCH
254

Tormisdale
ISLAY LIFE
MUSEUM

RHINS
OF
ISLAY
Port Charlotte
Gartbreck

471
BEINN BHAN
Carraig Mhór

Lossit Pt.
Laggan
Bridge Ho
491
BEINN

Nerabus
Kelsay

7   8   9   10   11

A
10
00
NT

B

C

D

E

F

G

NT
70
10

H

Lumsdaine

Fast Castle Head
Wheat Stack
Telegraph Hill
FAST CASTLE

Dowlaw Burn
Oatlee Hill

273

St Abb's Head
ST ABB'S HEAD
Horsecastle Bay

Coldingham Loch
Mire Loch

Bell Hill

Lumsdaine Moor
Cross

273

7   8   9   10   11

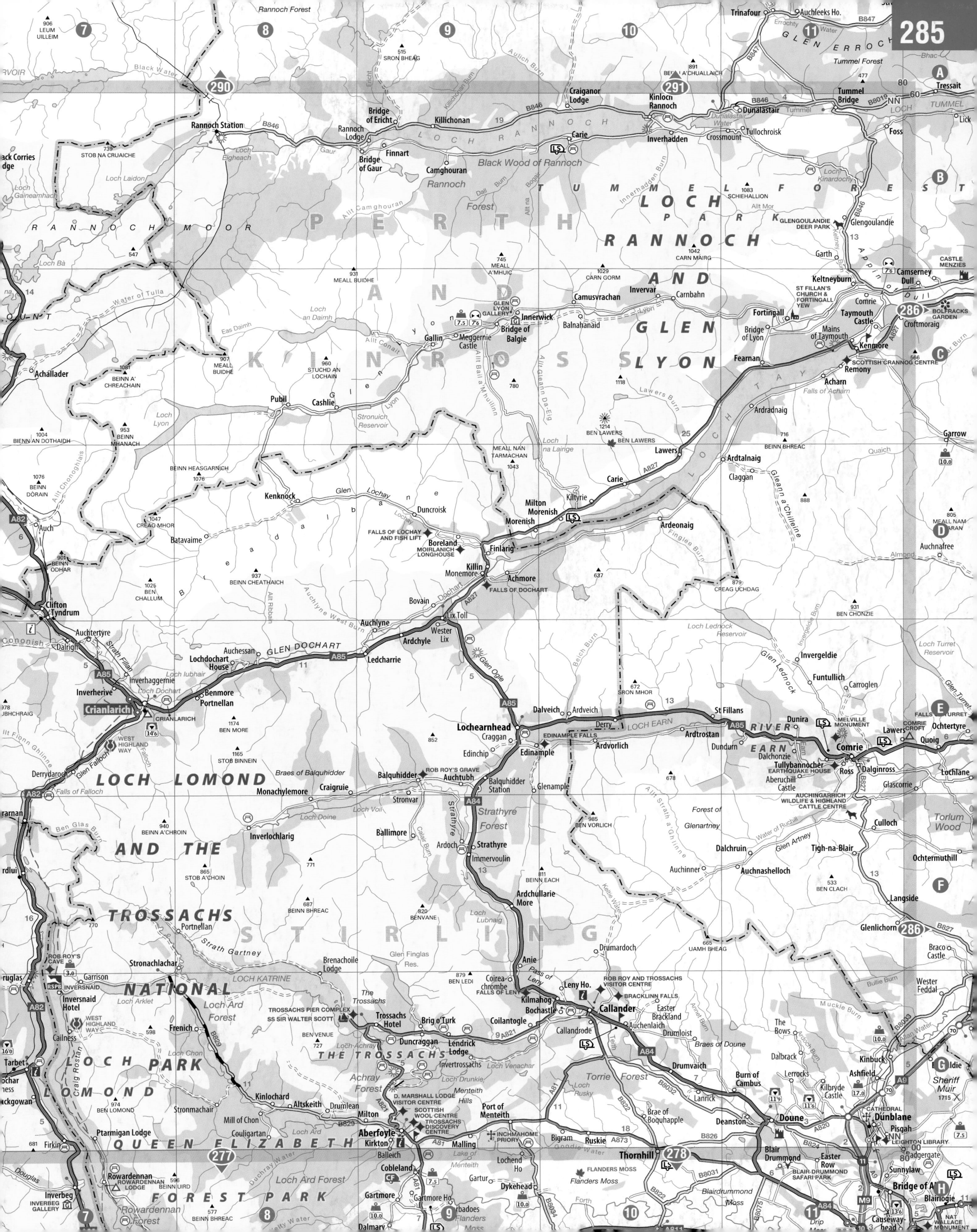

SANDAVORE
AN SGURR
Galmis

RUM

SOUND OF EIGG

294

Eilean nan Each

Gallanach
137 Port Mor

Muck

Sanna Point

Sanna Bay Sanna
Portuairk Achnaha
Point of Achosnich
Ardnamurchan
ARDNAMURCHAN LIGHTHOUSE

Cairns of Coll

Eilean Mor

Rubha Mor
Bousd
Sorisdale
Cornaigmore

An Acairseid

Ormsaigmore
Ormsaigbeg Kilchoan Bay

Cliad Bay

Arnabost Gallanach
Grishipoll
Clabhach B8071 **COLL**
Ballyhaugh Loch 73
104 Cliad

OBAN

Ardmore Bay Ardmore Pt.

Bloody

Hogh Bay
B8070
COLL Loch Eatharna
RSPB Arinagour
Totronald
Feall Acha
Bay Arileod Uig
Eilean
Ornsay

Glengorm
Castle
MULL MUSEUM

Calgary Pt.
Breachacha Friesland
Castle

Quinish Pt.
Rubha
an Aird
Croig **Tobermory**
Caliach Pt. Sunipol Cuin S AIRDE-BEINN
Caliach Penmore 292
Mill Dervaig
West Achnadrish
Ardhu THE OLD BYRE
Calgary HERITAGE CENTRE

CASTLEBAY
(Summer only)

Gunna
Calgary Bay

Crossapol Soa
Bay

Loch Breachacha

TIREE
Vaul Bay Salum Caolas
Cornaigmore Vaul Rubha Dubh
Kirkapol B8069
Cornaigbeg Ruaig
Kenovay Gott Bay
Imoluaig Gott Soa
Moss Scarinish
Heylipol TIREE
Crossapol Baugh B8065
Balinoe Heanish
Balemartine Rubha Traigh
West Mannal an Duin
Hynish Hynish Bay
141
Hynish

Treshnish Pt.
342
CARN MOR
Ensay
Rubh a'Chaoil
Haunn
Burg Kilninian
Achleck
23 Fanmore
390
Ballygown
EAS FORS
WATERFALL
424
Laggan BEINN NA DRISE
Lagganulva
Oskamull
ULVA
Ulva House Killi

LOCH TUATH

LOCH NA KEAL

Treshnish Isles
Fladda

Lunga

Eilean Dioghlum Baligortan
Gometra Bearnus 313 Ardalum
Gometra Ho.
Ho.

Bac Mor

INCH KENNETH
CHAPEL
Inch
Kenneth

ISLE OF
17 De
Eorsa

Little
Colonsay

Balnahard

Staffa **STAFFA**
FINGAL'S CAVE

MACKINNON'S CAVE Balmeanach
561

Erisgeir

Glen Seilisdeir
519
BEINN NA SREINE

ARDMEANACH
Tiroran
THE BURG Burg Kilfin
Bay

MACLEAN'S CROSS
Eilean
Annraidh
IONA ABBEY AND Rubha nan Cearc
CATHEDRAL
100
IONA HERITAGE CENTRE
ST COLUMBA EXHIBITION
& WELCOME CENTRE
Iona Kintra
Baile Mor Achnahard Knokan
Stac an
Aoineidh Aridhglas Eorabus 18
Sligneach Lower
Fionnphort A849 Ardtun
Fidden Tiraghoil Bunessan Lee
Knockvologan 376
CRUACHAN MIN

LOCH SCRIDAIN
Torrans

Loch na Lathaich

20 NM
20 Erraid **ROSS OF MULL** 274
Soa I. Uisken
Ardalanish Scoor
Ardchiavaig 125 Malcolm's Pt.
Eilean a'Chalmain Rubha nam
Braithean

Inset map (lower left):

Gunna

TIREE
Vaul Bay Salum Caolas
Sraid Cornaigmore Vaul Rubha
Ruadh Kirkapol Dubh
Balevullin Cornaigbeg B8069
Hough Kenovay Ruaig
Kilmoluaig Gott Soa
Moss Gott Bay
Kilkenneth Heylipol TIREE
Middleton Baugh B8065
Port Mor Barrapol Balinoe Crossapol Heanish
Loch Balephuil a'Phuill Balemartine Rubha Traigh
Balephuil B8067 Mannal an Duin
141 Hynish Bay
Balephuil West
Bay Port Snoig Hynish Hynish

CASTLEBAY
(Summer only) COLL

Scale:
0 2 4 6 miles
0 2 4 6 8 10 km

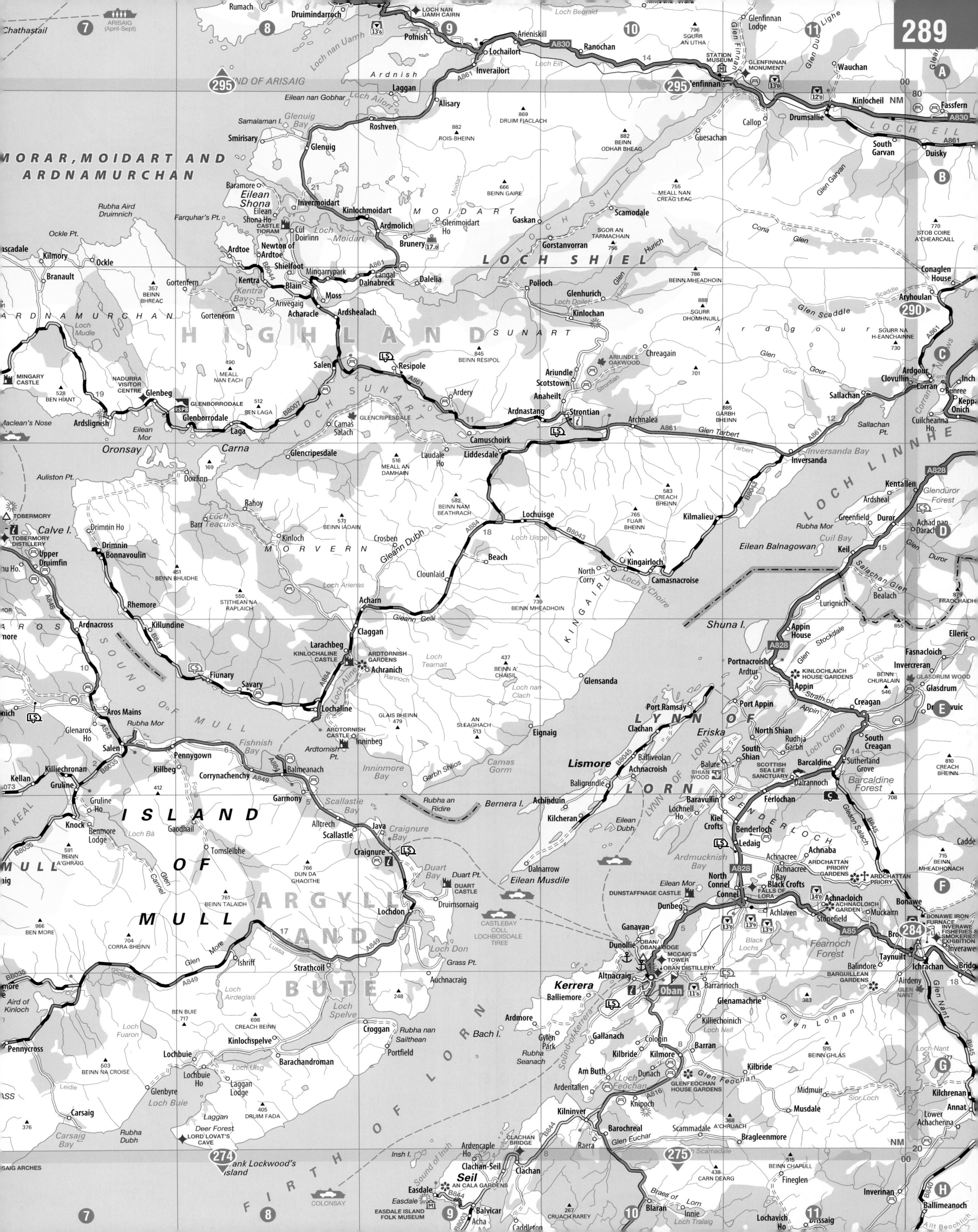

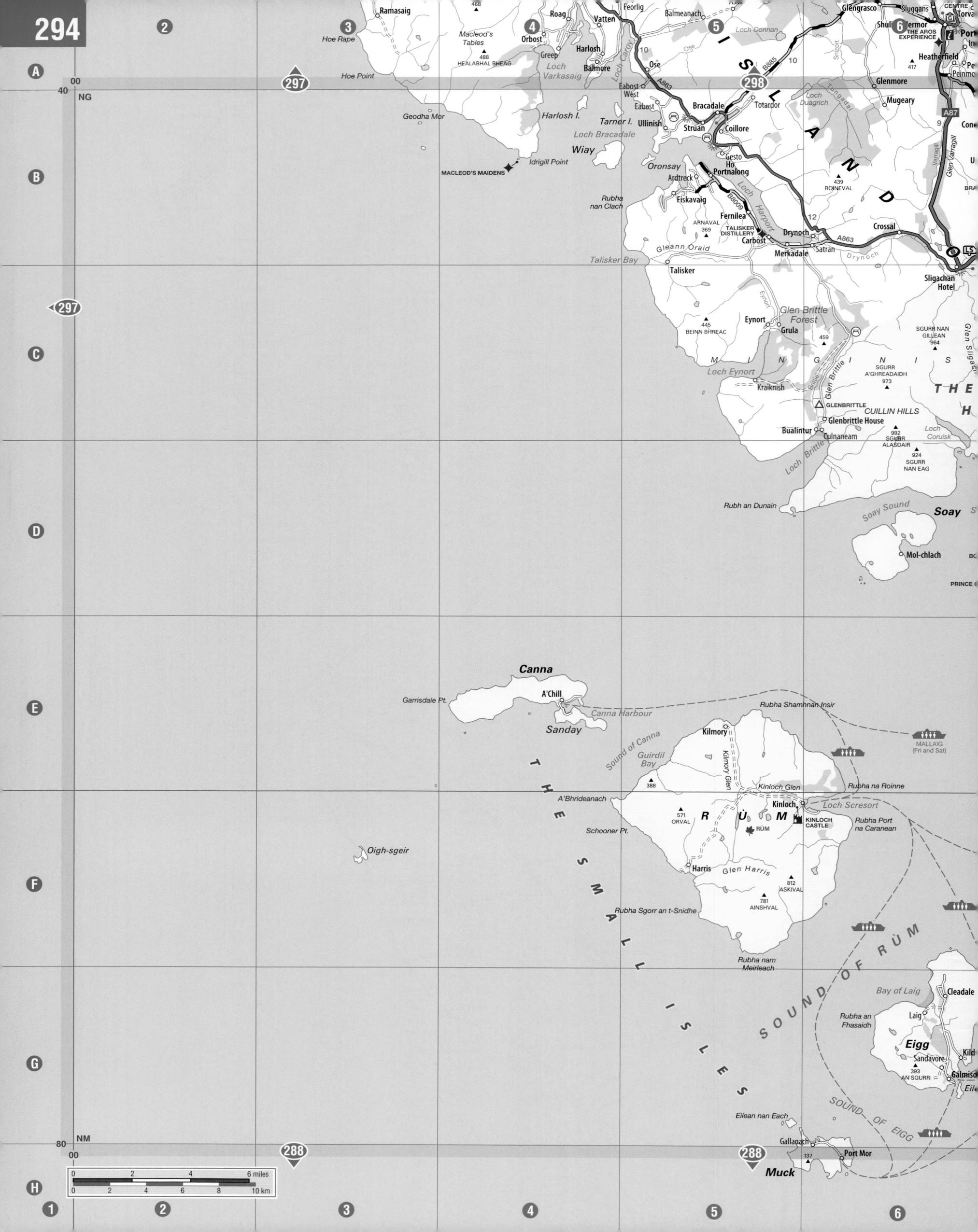

A

B

C

D

E

F

G

H

00
40
NG

297

Ramasaig
Roag
Feorlig
Balmeanach
Glengrasco
Sluggans
CENTRE
Torva
Shul
ermor
Port
THE AROS
EXPERIENCE
Vatten
Loch Connan
B885
Hoe Rape
Orbost
Harlosh
Loch Caroy
10
Heatherfield
417
Peinmo
Macleod's
Tables
Greep
Ose
Glenmore
Balmore
HEALABHAL BHEAG
Loch
Varkasaig
Eabost
West
Loch
Tungadal
Mugeary
A87
Hoe Point
Eabost
Bracadale
Totardor
Loch
Duagrich
9
Cone
Geodha Mor
Harlosh I.
Ullinish
Struan
Coillore
ISLAND
Tarner I.
Loch Bracadale
Gesto
Ho
439
ROINEVAL
BRA
Wiay
Oronsay
Ardtreck
Portnalong
Idrigill Point
Rubha
nan Clach
Fiskavaig
Fernilea
Loch Harport
B8009
12
Crossal
MACLEOD'S MAIDENS
ARNAVAL
369
TALISKER
DISTILLERY
Drynoch
A863
445
BEINN BHREAC
Carbost
Merkadale
Satran
Drynoch
Gleann Oraid
Talisker Bay
Sligachan
Hotel
LS
Talisker
Eynort
Glen Brittle
Forest
SGURR NAN
GILLEAN
964
Glen Sligach
459
SGURR
A'GHREADAIDH
973
THE
Grula
M I N G I N I S
H
Loch Eynort
Kraiknish
GLENBRITTLE
CUILLIN HILLS
Bualintur
Glenbrittle House
992
SGURR
ALASDAIR
Loch
Coruisk
Culnaneam
924
SGURR
NAN EAG
Rubh an Dunain
Soay Sound
Soay
S
Mol-chlach
BC
PRINCE C

Canna
A'Chill
Garrisdale Pt.
Rubha Shamhnan Insir
Canna Harbour
Kilmory
MALLAIG
(Fri and Sat)
Sanday
Sound of Canna
Guirdil
Bay
Kilmory Glen
Kinloch Glen
Rubha na Roinne
T
H
E
388
A'Bhrideanach
Kinloch
Loch Scresort
571
ORVAL
R Ü M
KINLOCH
CASTLE
Rubha Port
na Caranean
Oigh-sgeir
S
RÙM
Schooner Pt.
M
Harris
Glen Harris
812
ASKIVAL
A
781
AINSHVAL
Rubha Sgorr an t-Snidhe
L
L
Bay of Laig
Cleadale
Rubha an
Fhasaidh
Laig
Rubha nam
Meirleach
I
S
SOUND OF RÜM
Eigg
Sandavore
393
AN SGURR
Galmisd
Eil
L
E
S
SOUND OF EIGG
Eilean nan Each
Gallanach
288
288
NM
80

Port Mor
137
Muck

0   2   4   6 miles
0   2   4   6   8   10 km

1   2   3   4   5   6

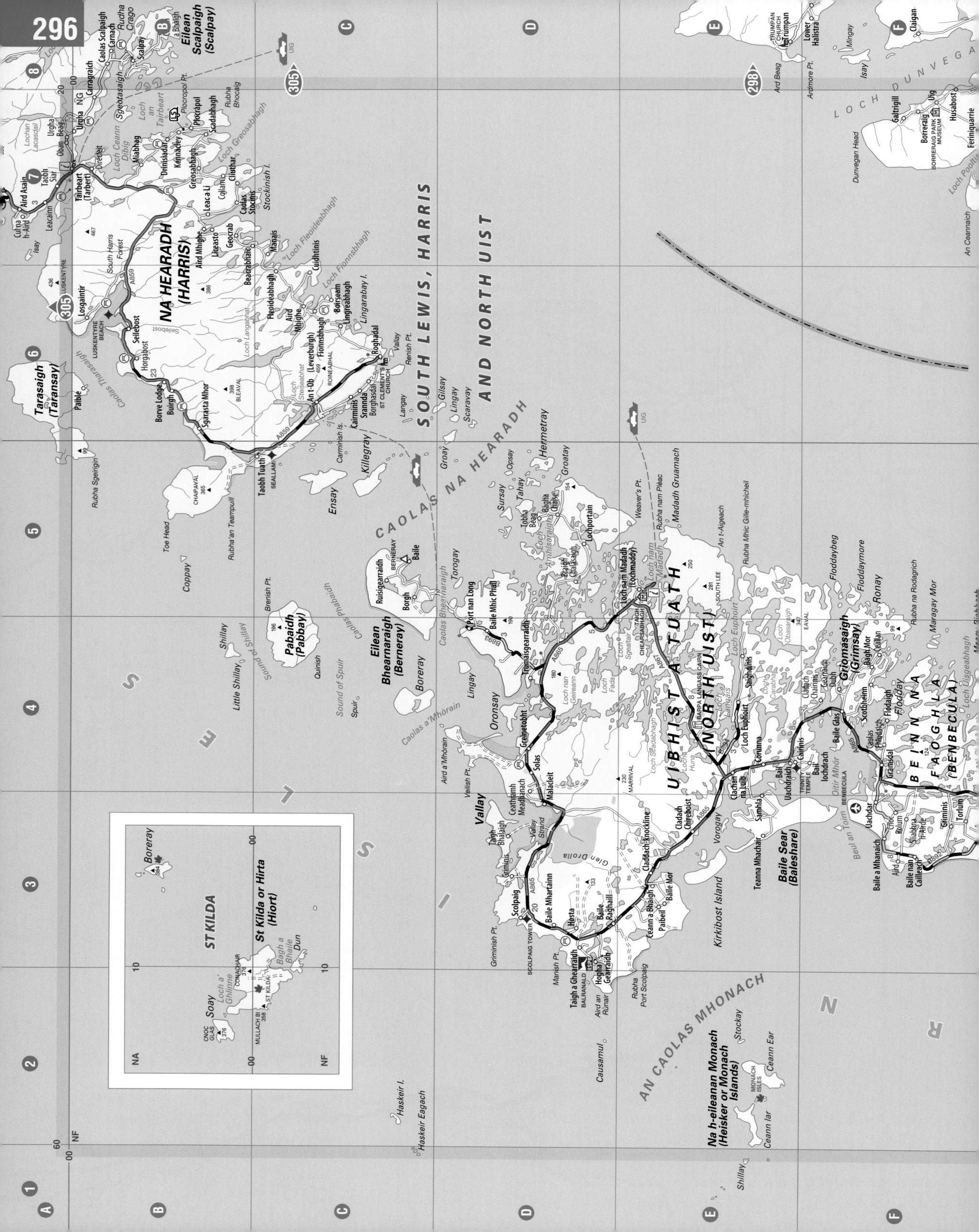

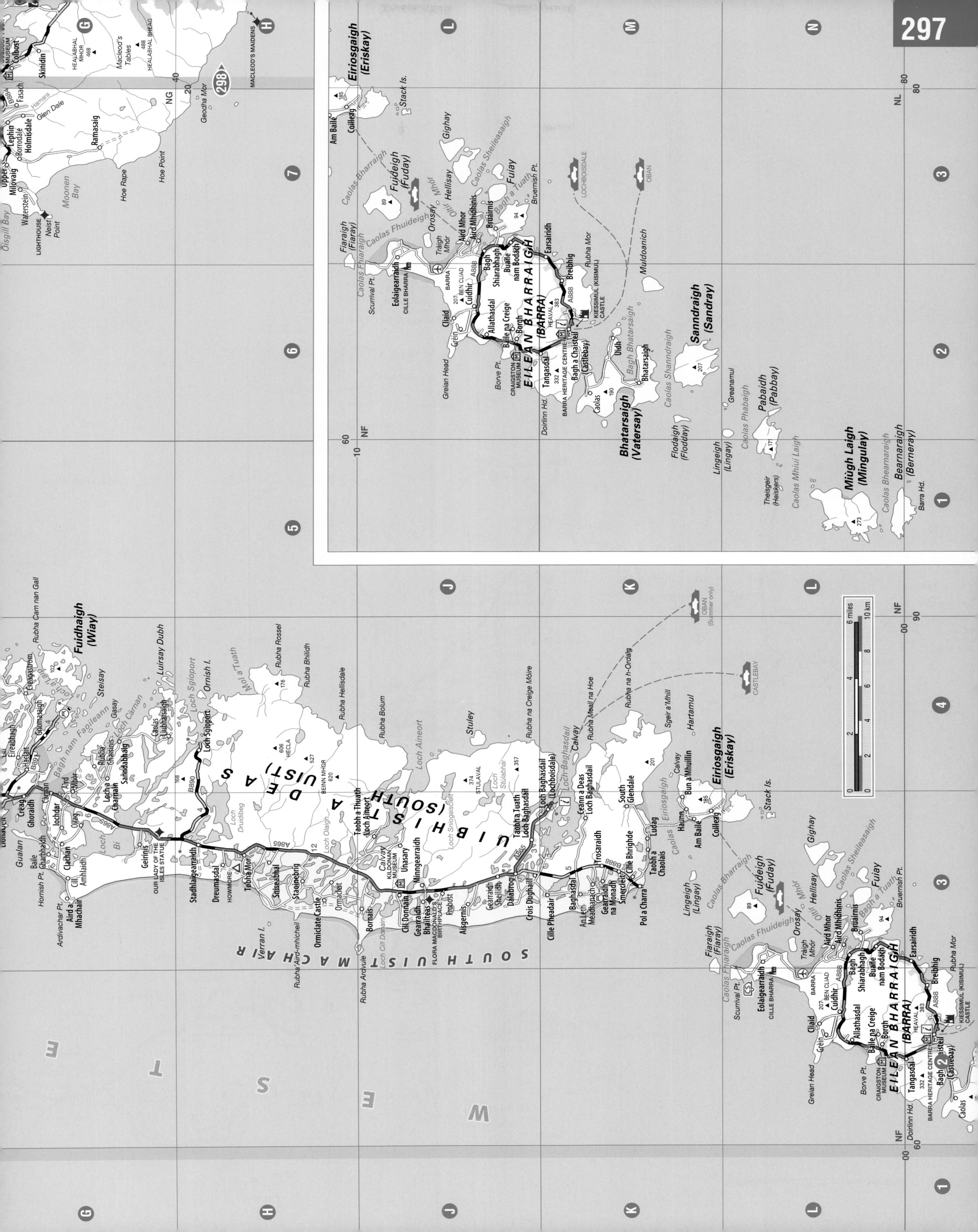

Top-right inset map (Barra and southern isles):

Eiriosgaigh (Eriskay)

Am Baile
Coilleag
Stack Is.

Caolas Bharraigh

Fiaraigh (Fiaray)
Fuideigh (Fuday)
Gighay

Caolas Fhuideigh
Orosay
Uidh Hellisay
Caolas Shelleasaigh
Fuiay

Traigh Mhòr
Àird Mhòr
Àird Mhidhinis
Bruaineis
Bàgh a Tuath
Bruernish Pt.

LOCHBOISDALE
OBAN

Fiaraigh (Fiaray)

Caolas Fhiaraigh

Scurrival Pt.

Eolaigearraidh
CILLE BHARRA

BARRA
BEN CLIAD
207
A888
Cuidhir

Grèin

Bàgh
Sharabhagh
Buaile
nam Bodach
Earsairidh

Cliaid

EILEAN BHARRAIGH (BARRA)

Breibhig
Rubha Mòr

Allathasdal
Baile na Creige
Borgh
HEAVAL
383
A888

KIESSIMUL (KISIMUL) CASTLE

Muldoanich

Bàgh Bhatarsaigh

Doirlinn Hd.
CRAIGSTON MUSEUM
Tangasdal
332

BARRA HERITAGE CENTRE
Bàgh a' Chaisteil (Castlebay)

Grean Head
Borve Pt.

Uidh
Caolas
Uidh
190

Caolas Shanndraigh

Sanndraigh (Sandray)

Bhatarsaigh (Vatersay)
Bhatarsaigh

207

Flodaigh (Flodday)

Caolas Phabaigh

Greanamul

Pabaidh (Pabbay)
177

Lingeigh (Lingay)

Caolas Mhiui Laigh

Theisgeir (Heisgers)

Miùgh Laigh (Mingulay)
273

Bearnaraigh (Berneray)

Caolas Bhearnaraigh
Barra Hd.

NL 80

NF 60

10

Left/main map — Skye area (top-left):

MUSEUM
Colbost
Skinidin
Healabhal Mhòr
488
Healabhal Bheag
Macleod's Tables

Upper
Milovaig
Lephin
Borrodale
Fasach
Hamara
Glen Dale
Ramasaig

MACLEOD'S MAIDENS

298

Waternish
Geodha Mòr

Holmisdale
Ordale
LIGHTHOUSE
Neist Point

Moonen Bay
Hoe Rape
Hoe Point

Oisgill Bay

NG 20

40

G
H
L
M
N

7

Main lower map — Uist / Barra:

Fuidhaigh (Wiay)

Rubha Càm nan Gall

Feagastrom
Stelsay
Luirsay Dubh

Orinsh I.
Mol a Tuath

Loch Sgioport

Loch Fagileann

Ornish I.

Rubha Rossel

Rubha Bhilidh

Rubha Hellisdale

176

Gormasaigh
Eireabhagh
Hàstat
Bàgh nam Faoileann

Stadhlaigearraidh
Howbeg

Ardivachar Pt.
Àird a Mhachair
Rubha Àird-mhichell
Verran I.

Geirinis
OUR LADY OF THE ISLES STATUE

HOWMORE

Ormiclate Castle

A865

Cladh
Loch Bì

Staoinebrig
Snaoisebrig

BEINN MHÒR
620

HECLA
606
527

Loch Druidibeg

Loch Sgioport

168

B890

Loch Carnan

Ormiclate

Loch Olaigh

UIBHIST A DEAS (SOUTH UIST)

Taobh a Tuath (Loch Aineort)
Minngearraidh
Uisgeabhagh

STULAVAL
374

Loch Stùlabhail

Loch Aineort

Stuley

Rubha Bolum

Rubha na Creige Mòire

OBAN (Summer only)

CASTLEBAY

SOUTH UIST MACHAIR

A865
12

Loch Cìll Donnáin

Bornais
Alasgernis

Cìll Donnain
Bhalltos
FLORA MACDONALD'S BIRTHPLACE
KILDONAN MUSEUM
Dalabrog

Gearraidh Sheilidh

Frobost

Geàrraidh na Monadh

Smeircleit

Crois Dùghaill

Baghasdail

Taobh a Chaolais

Cìle Bhrìghde

Pol a Charra

Cille Pheadair

An Leth Meadhanach

Taobh a Tuath Loch Baghasdail

Loch Baghasdail (Lochboisdale)

Ceann a Deas Loch Baghasdail

Calvay

Rubha Meall na Hoe
Rubha na h-Ordaig

Sgeir a' Mhill

Hartamul

201

Calvay
Bun a' Mhuillin
South Glendale

Eiriosgaigh (Eriskay)

Am Baile
Haunn
Coilleag
Stack Is.

Lùdag
Ludag

Caolas Eiriosgaigh

Caolas Bharraigh

Lingeigh (Lingay)

Fuideigh (Fuday)
Gighay

Caolas Fhuideigh
Orosay
Uidh Hellisay
Caolas Shelleasaigh
Fuiay

Traigh Mhòr
Àird Mhòr
Àird Mhidhinis
Bruaineis
Bàgh a Tuath
Bruernish Pt.

Fiaraigh (Fiaray)

Caolas Fhiaraigh

Scurrival Pt.

Eolaigearraidh
CILLE BHARRA

BARRA
BEN CLIAD
207
A888
Cuidhir

Grèin

Bàgh
Sharabhagh
Buaile
nam Bodach
Earsairidh

Cliaid

EILEAN BHARRAIGH (BARRA)

Breibhig
Rubha Mòr

Allathasdal
Baile na Creige
Borgh
HEAVAL
383
A888

KIESSIMUL (KISIMUL) CASTLE

Doirlinn Hd.
CRAIGSTON MUSEUM
Tangasdal
332
BARRA HERITAGE CENTRE
Bàgh a' Chaisteil (Castlebay)

Grean Head
Borve Pt.
Caolas

89

6 miles
4
2
0

10 km
8
6
4
2
0

J
K
L

4

3

H
J
K
L

1

2

3

M

S

E
F
S

W

M

NF 90

NF 00

NF 60

NF 00

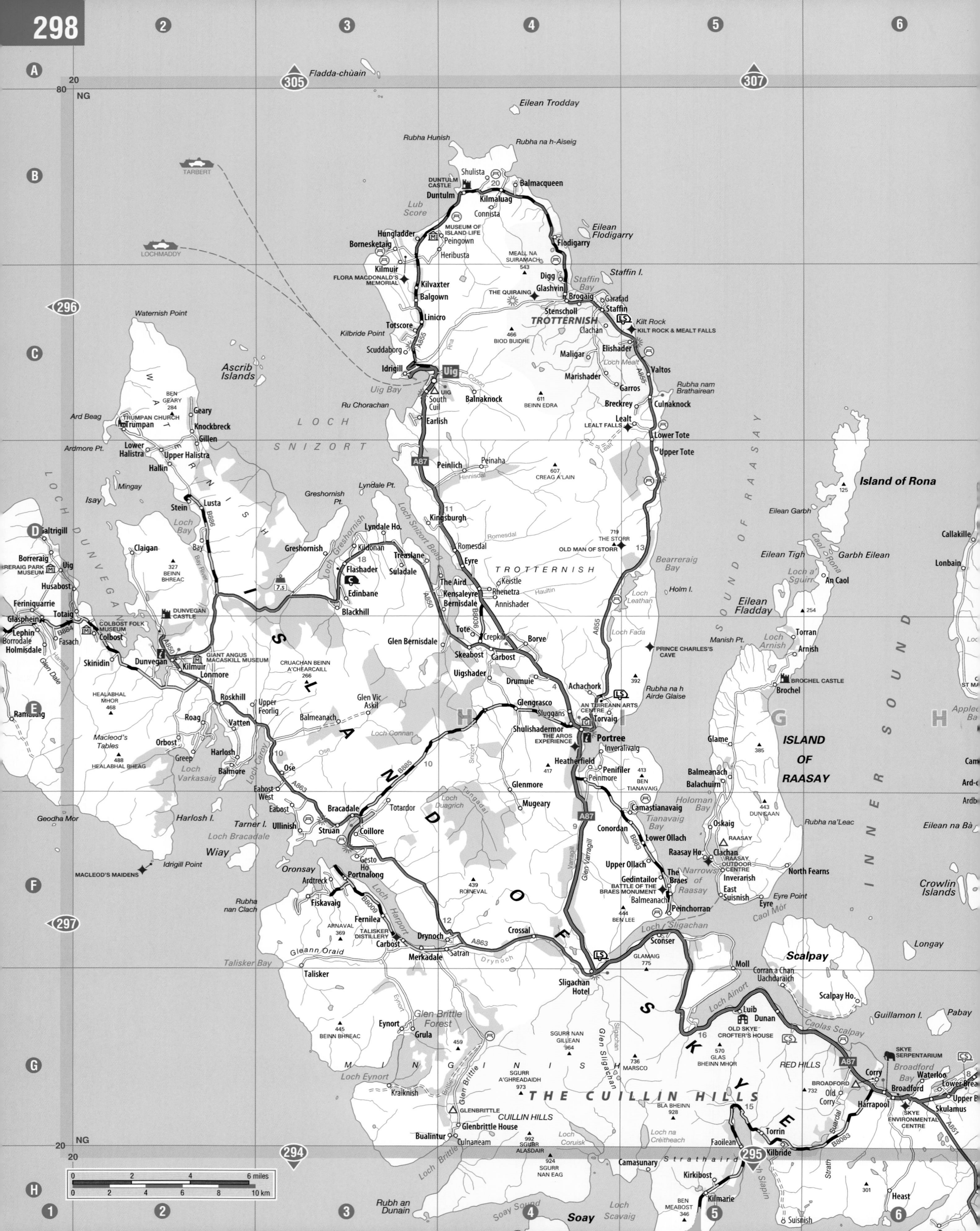

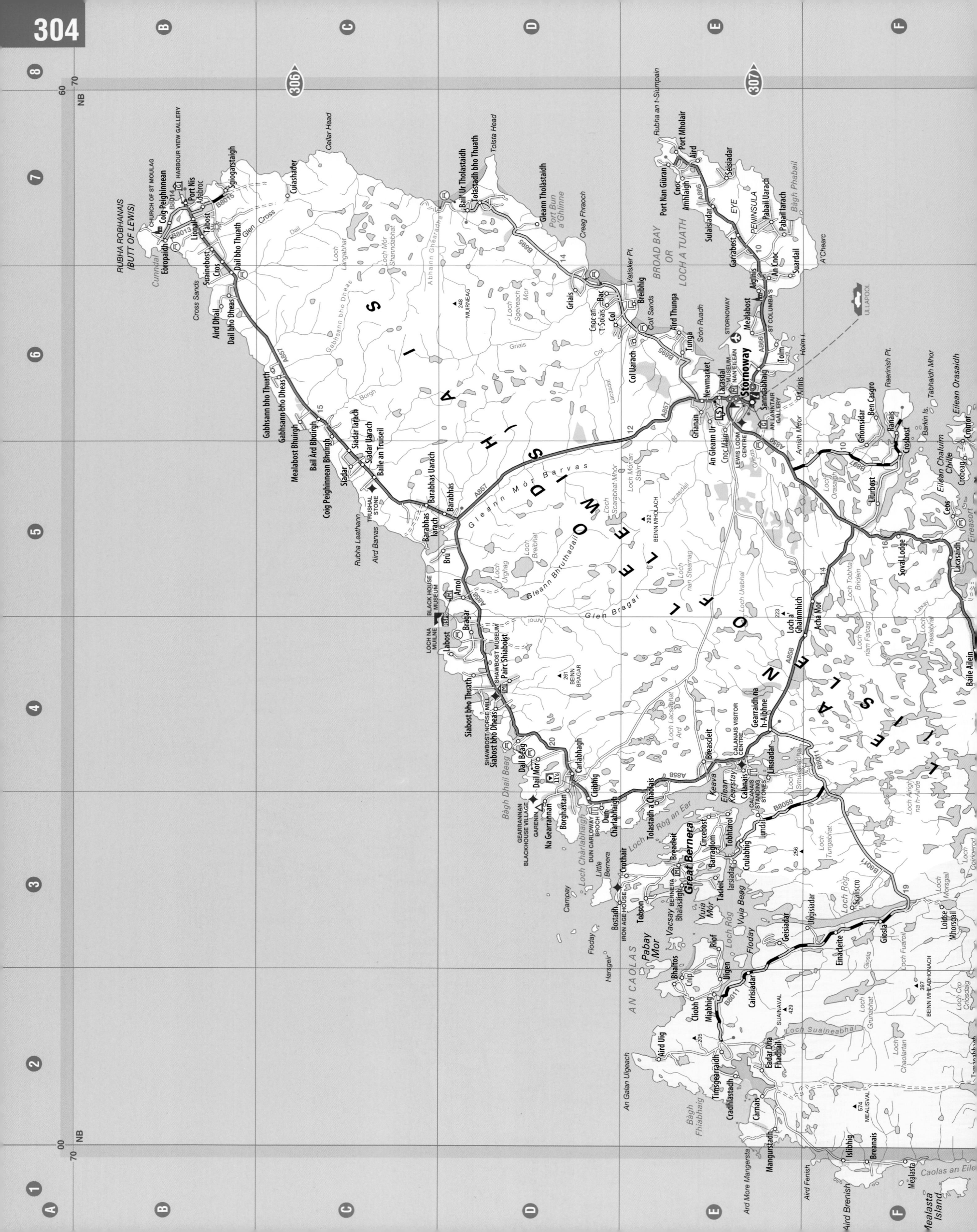

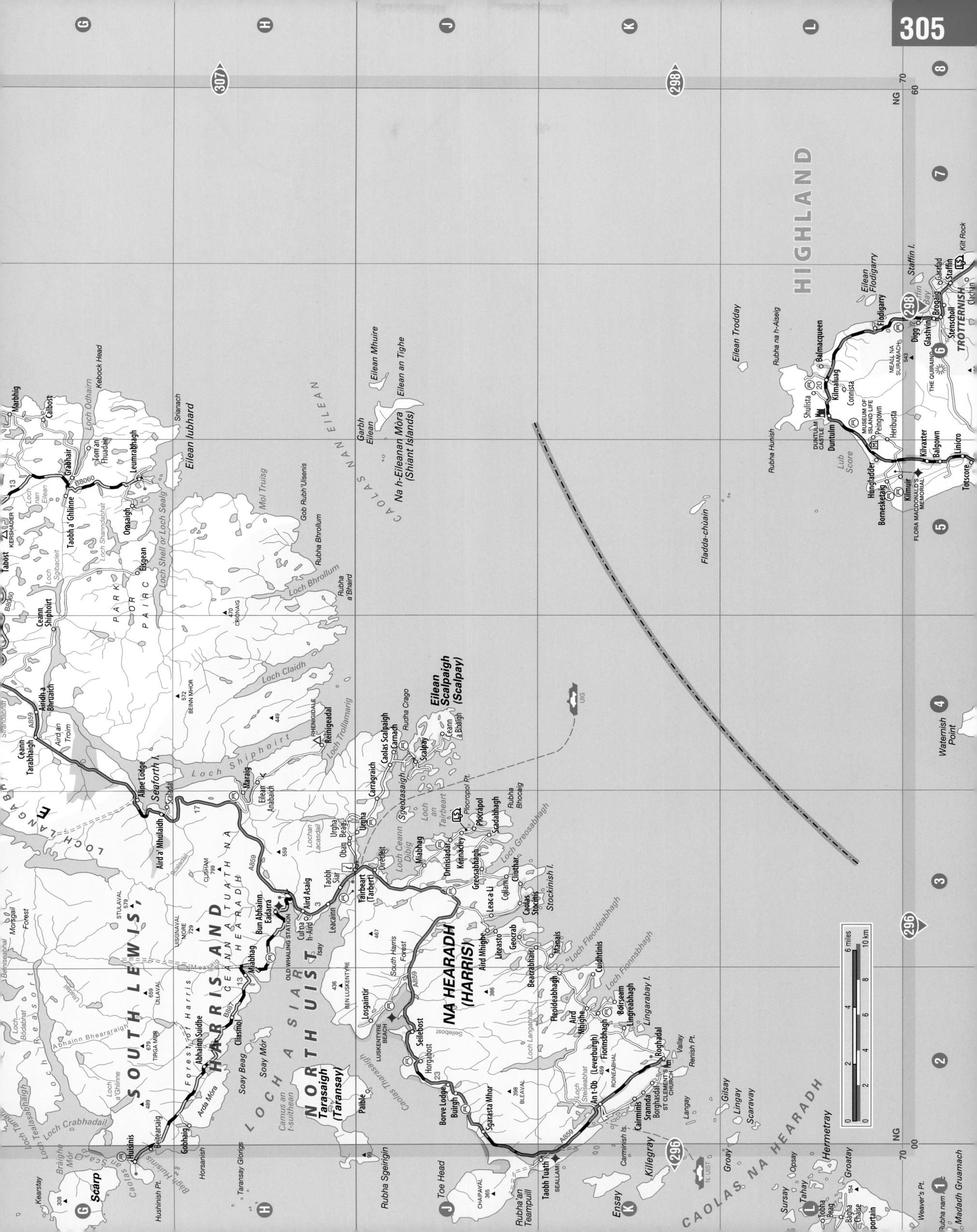

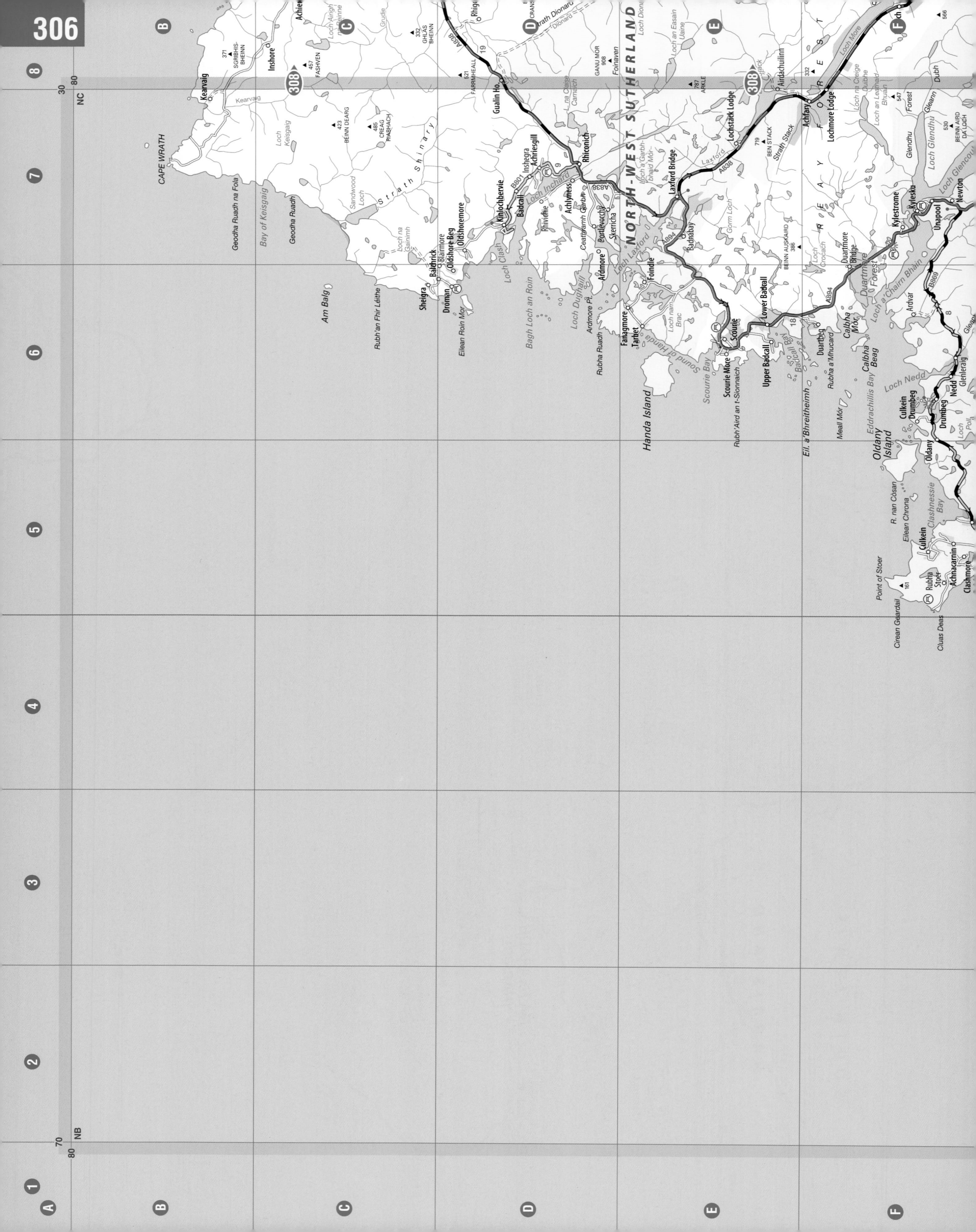

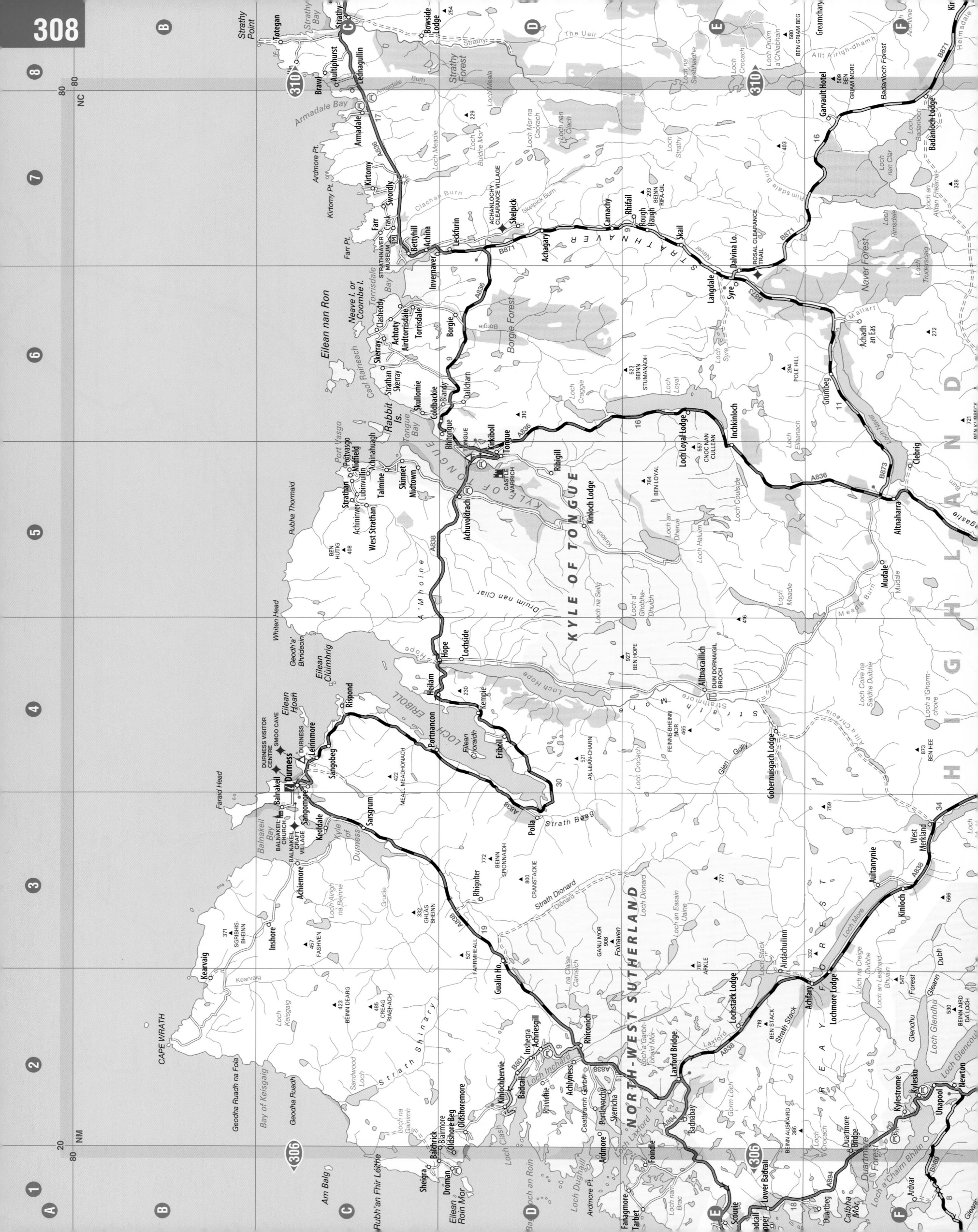

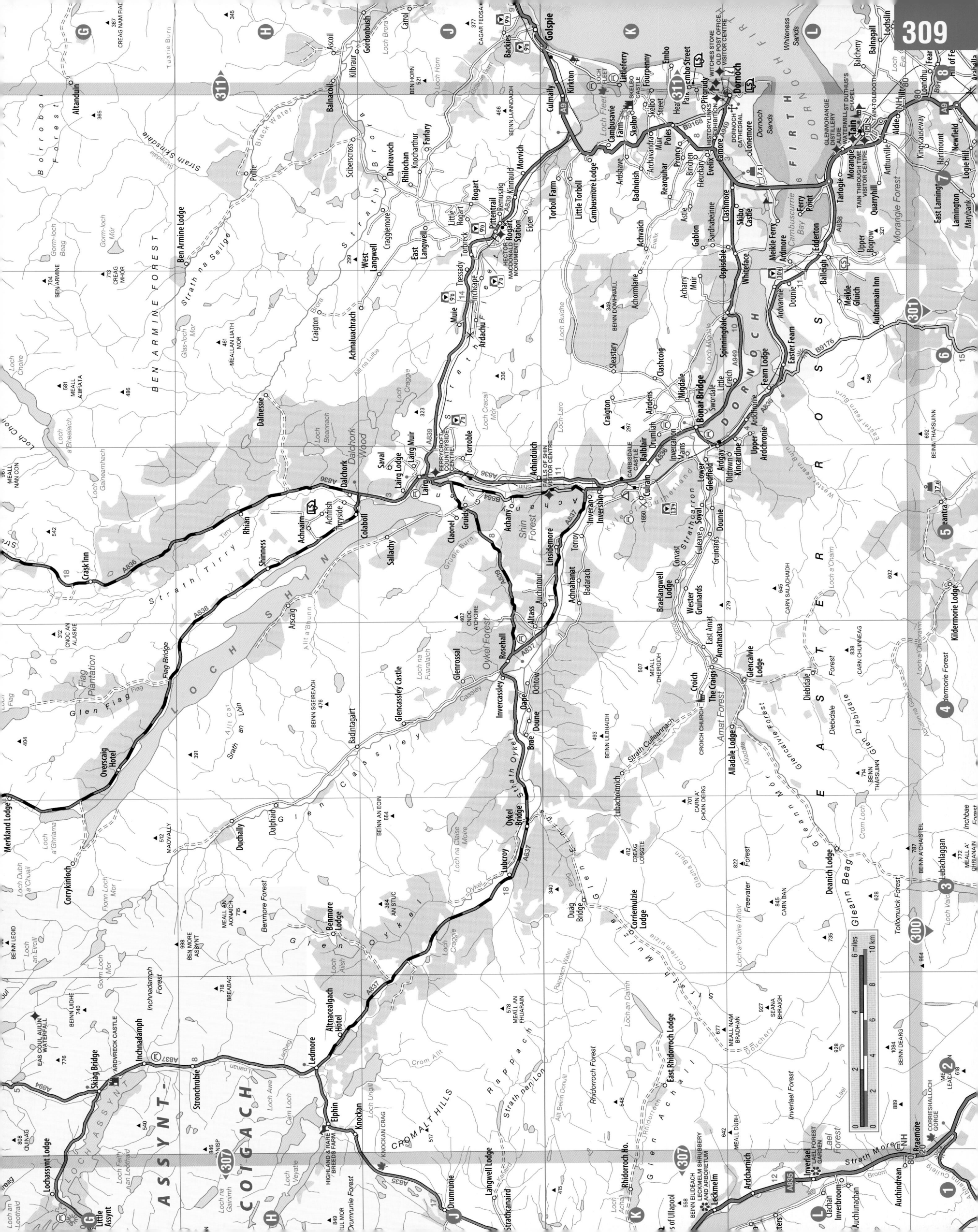

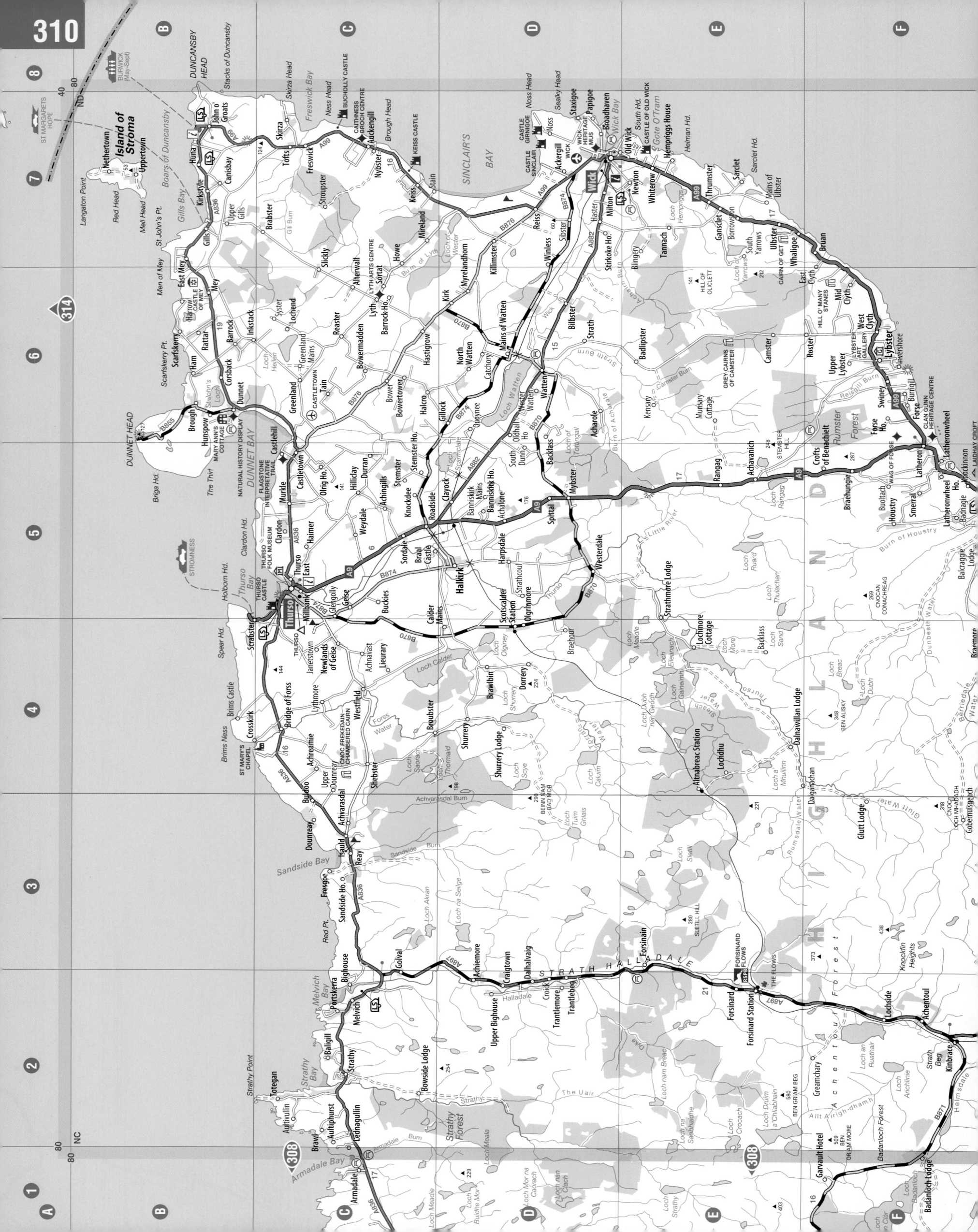

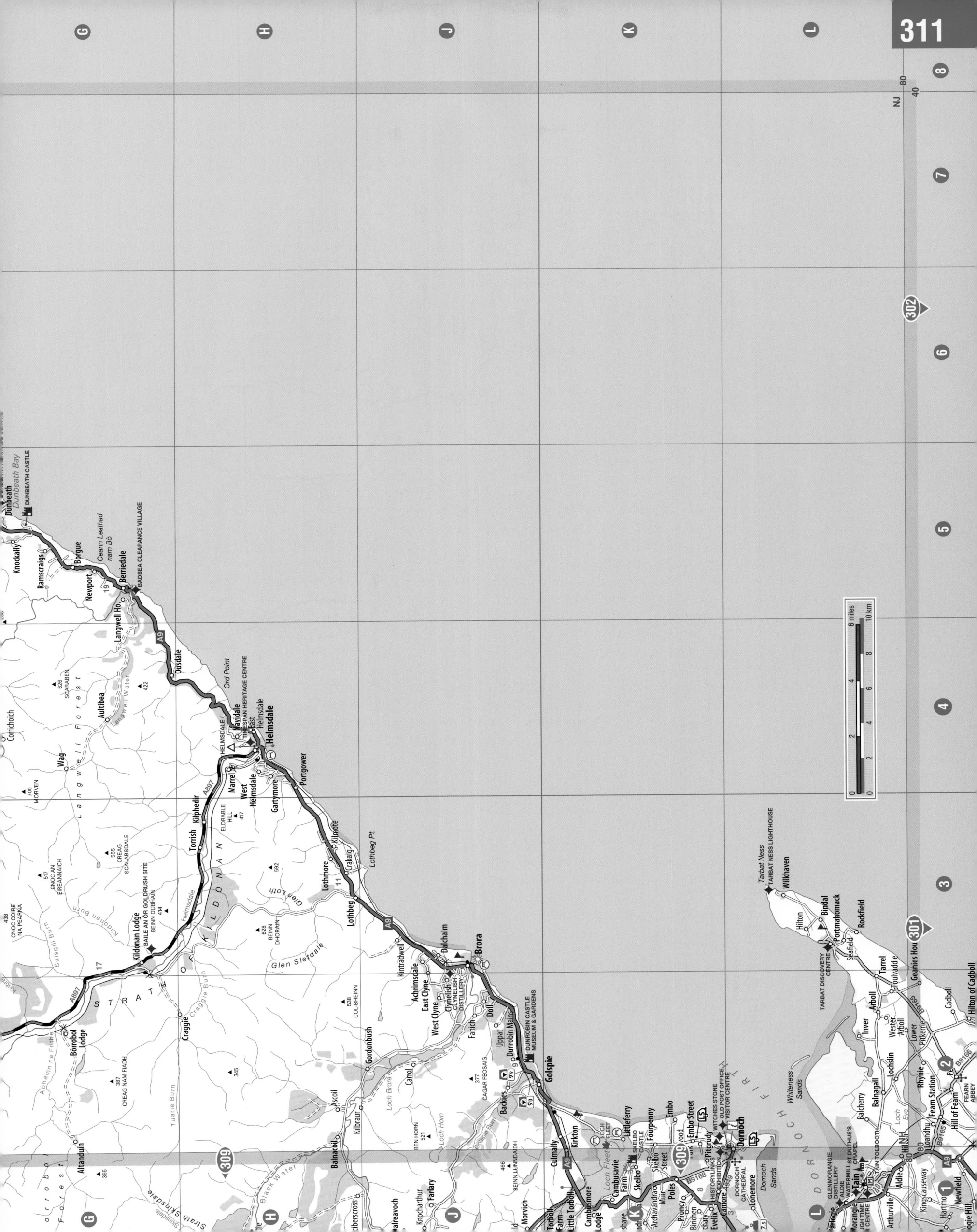

G   H   J   K   L

8
7
6
5
4
3
2
1

NJ 80 40

302

301

Dunbeath Bay
Dunbeath
DUNBEATH CASTLE
Knockally
Ramscraigs
Newport
Borgue
Ceann Leathad nam Bò
Berriedale
19
BADBEA CLEARANCE VILLAGE
Corrichoich
Langwell Ho.
A9
SCARABEN 626
Wag
Aultibea
Langwell Forest
Langwell Water
422
Ousdale
Ord Point
MORVEN 705
CREAG SCALABSDALE 595
CNOC AN ÉIREANNAICH 517
Navidale
THE SPAN HERITAGE CENTRE
Helmsdale
HELMSDALE
Helmsdale East
Marrel
West Helmsdale
Portgower
Torrish
Kilphedir
ELDRABLE HILL 417
Gartymore
A897
CNOC COIRE NA PEARNA 438
BAILE AN OR GOLDRUSH SITE
BENN DUBHAIN 414
Kildonan Lodge
17
STRATH OF KILDONAN
Kildonan Burn
Suisgill Burn
Kilmote
Lothmore
11
Crakaig
Lothbeg Pt.
Lothbeg
BENIN DHORAIN 628
592
Glen Loth
Glen Sletdale
Kintradwell
Dalchalm
A9
Brora
Borrobol Lodge
A897
Abhainn na Frithe
Black Water
STRATH
Achrimsdale
East Clyne
CLYNELISH DISTILLERY
Clynelish
West Clyne
Gordonbush
COL-BHEINN 538
Craggie
Craggie Burn
Carrol
Fanith
Doll
Uppat
DUNROBIN CASTLE MUSEUM & GARDENS
Altanduin
365
387
CREAG NAM FIADH
Ascoil
Loch Brora
377
Balnacoil
Kilbraur
BEN HORN 521
Loch Horn
CAGAR FEOSAIG
Backies
990
Golspie
99
Tuaile Burn
Knocharthur
Farlary
BENN LUNNDAIDH 466
Strath Shrisdale
345
Balnagall
Hilton
Portmahomack
Bindal
Rockfield
TARBAT DISCOVERY CENTRE
Seafield
Tarbat Ness
TARBAT NESS LIGHTHOUSE
Wilkhaven
Geanies Ho
Inver
Wester Arboll
Lower Pitkerrie
Arboll
Tarrel
Loans of Tullich
Cadboll
Hilton of Cadboll
Lochslin
Rhynie
Fearn Station
FEARN ABBEY
Hill of Fearn
Balchery
Loch Eye
Whiteness Sands
DORNOCH FIRTH
Dornoch Sands
Embo
Embo Street
Fourpenny
Littleferry
WITCHES STONE
OLD POST OFFICE
VISITOR CENTRE
Dornoch
DORNOCH CATHEDRAL
Embo Wood
Pitgrudy
Poles
SKELBO CASTLE
Skelbo Street
Skelbo
Cambusavie
Loch Fleet
Loch Fleet
Kirkton
Culmailly
Proncy
Clashmore
Cuthill
Morvich
Torboll
Little Torboll
Camblsmore
Birichen
Archvandra
Muir Street
Balnaluig
GLENMORANGIE DISTILLERY
Aldie
ST DUTHUS'S CHAPEL
DORNOCH
Tain
Newfield
Kingscauseway
Arthurville
A9
Harmo
Eagle Hill
NH
A836

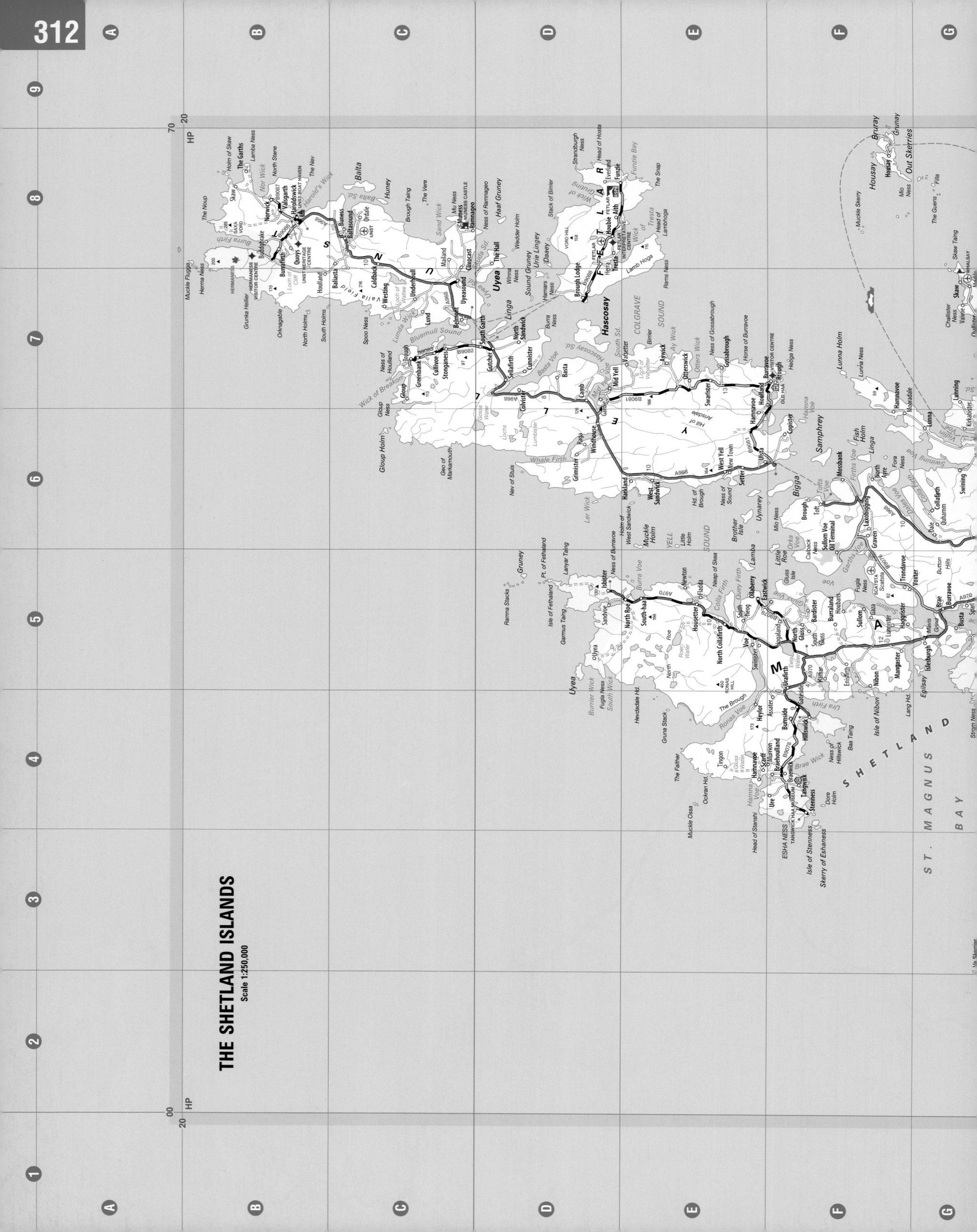

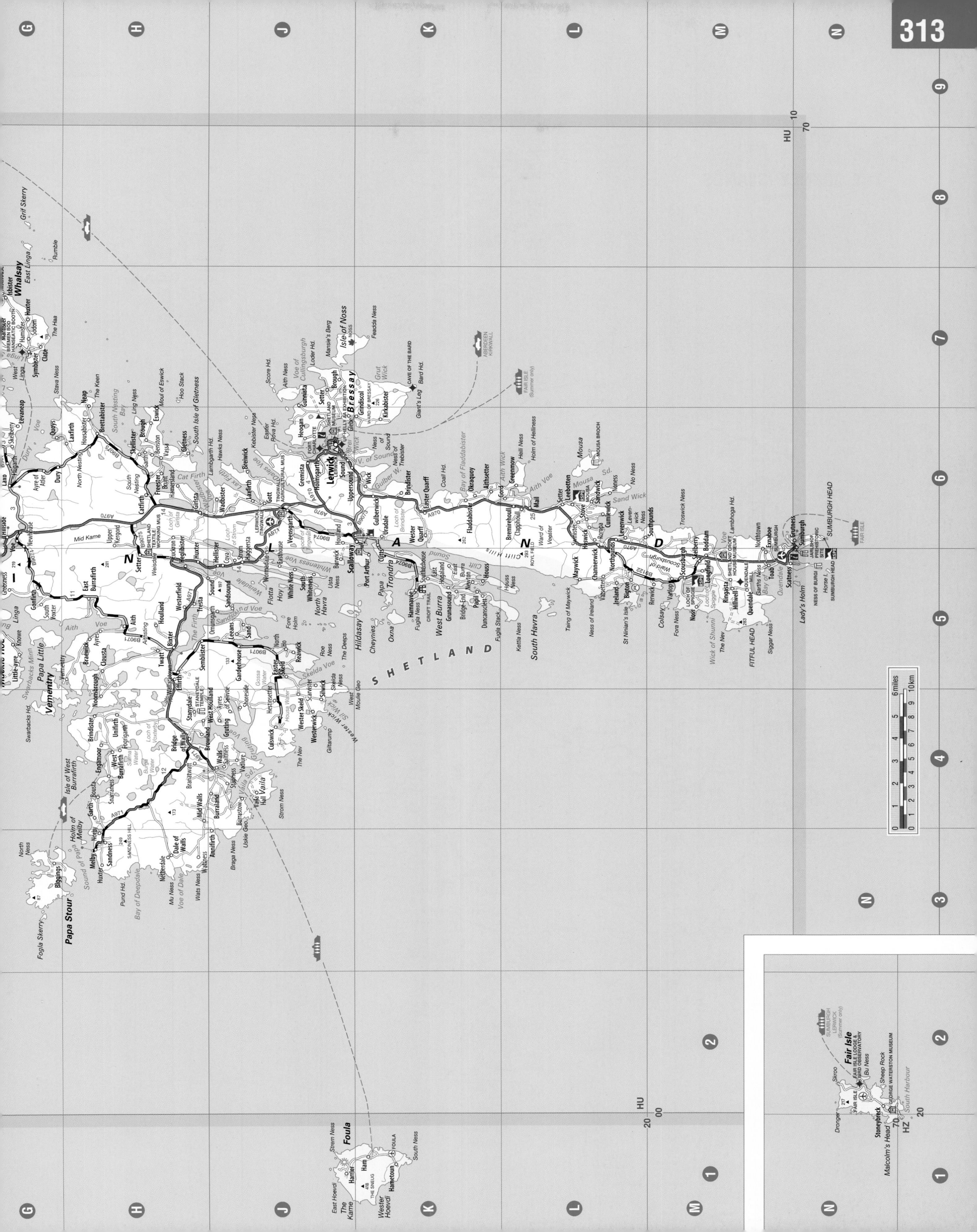

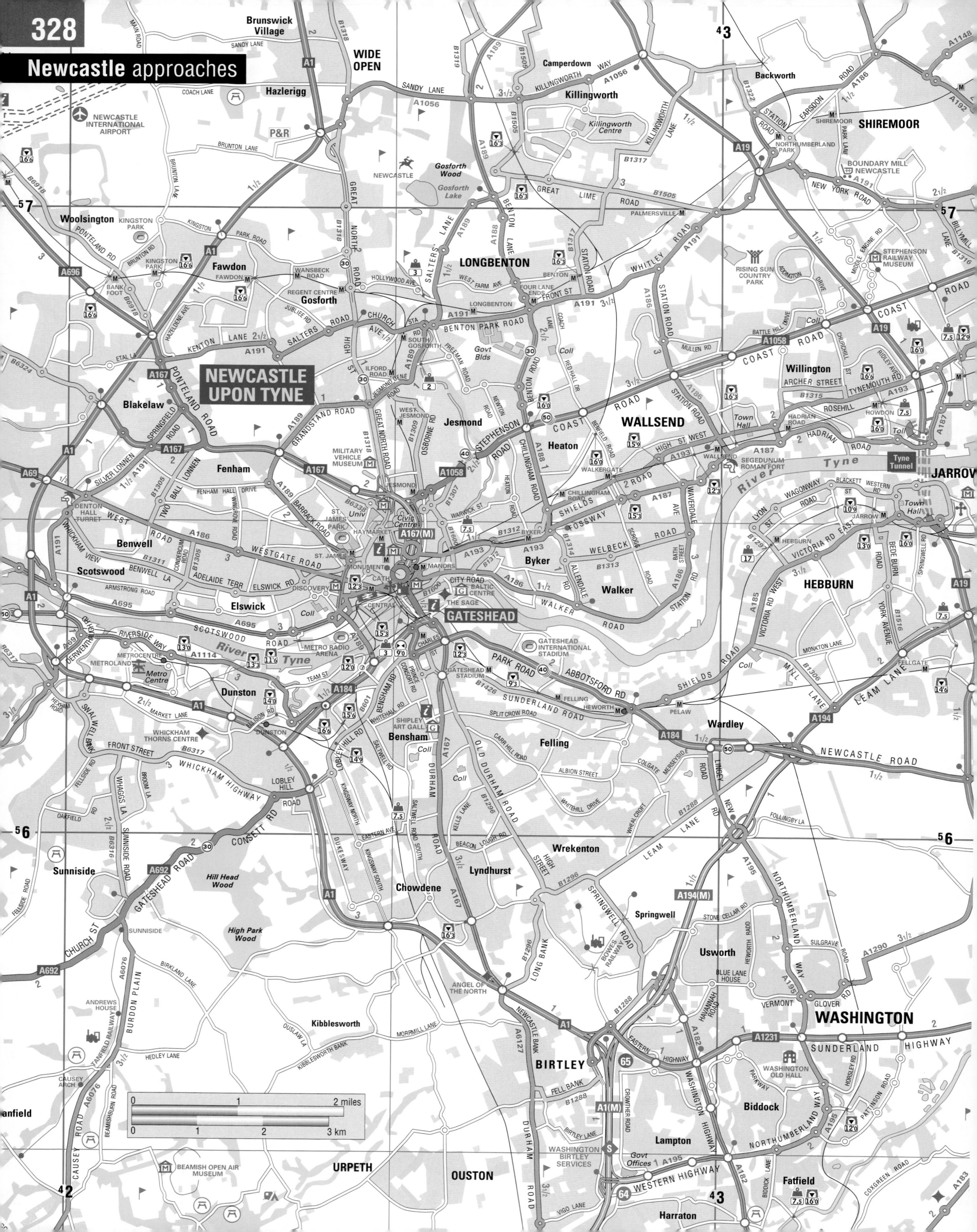

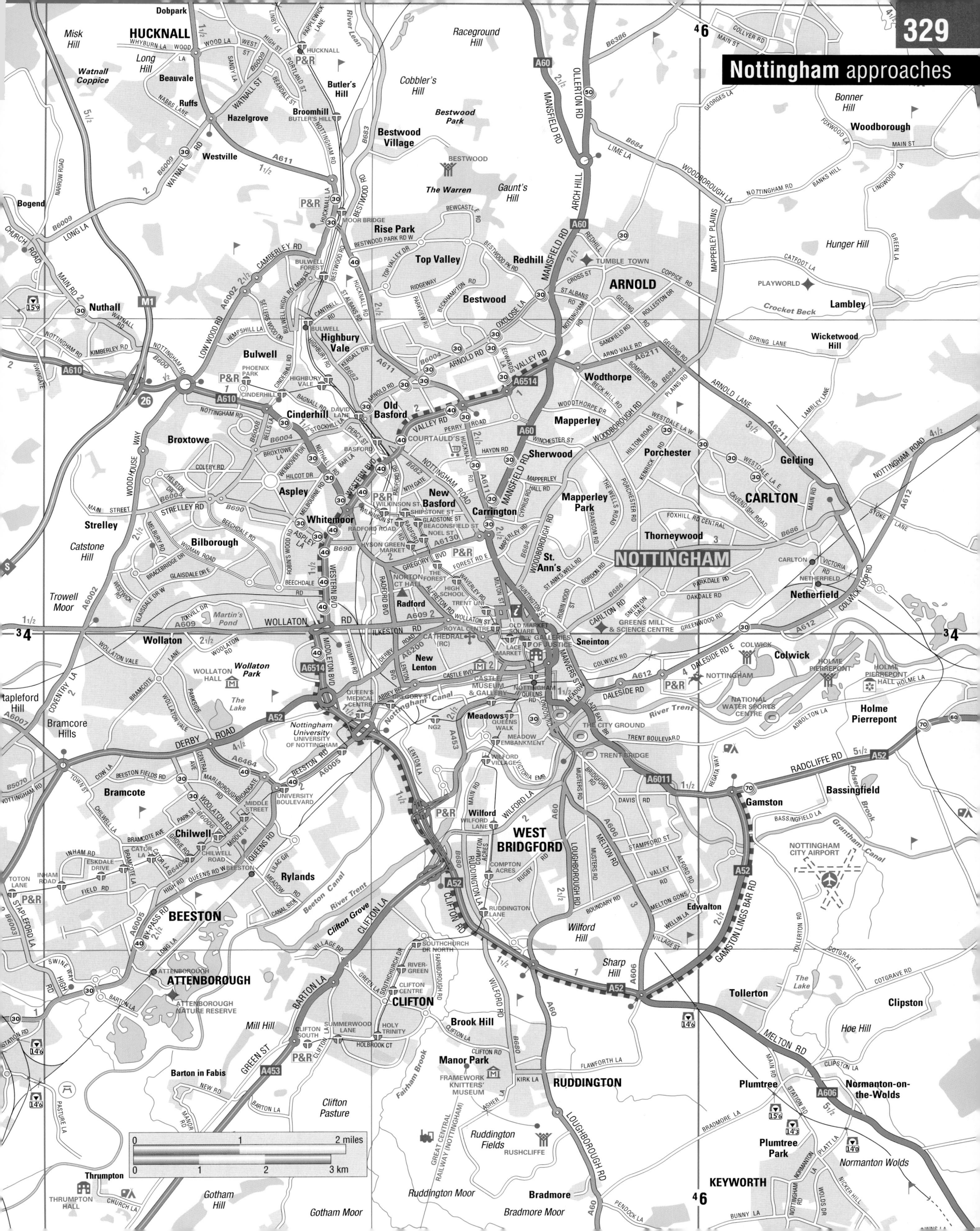

Aberdeen page 293 ● Aberystwyth page 128 ● Ashford page 54 ● Ayr page 257 ● Bangor page 179 ● Barrow-in-Furness page 210 ● Bath page 61 ● Berwick-upon-Tweed page 273

331

Town plan symbols

	Motorway
	Primary route – dual, single carriageway
	A road – dual, single carriageway
	B road – dual, single carriageway
	Minor through road
	One-way street
	Pedestrian roads
	Shopping streets
	Railway with station
	Tramway with station
	Underground or Metro station
H	Hospital
P	Parking
PO	Police, Post Office
	Shopmobility
▲	Youth hostel
	Bus or railway station building
	Shopping precinct or retail park
	Park
	Congestion charge zone

✝	Abbey or cathedral
	Ancient monument
	Aquarium
	Art gallery
	Bird collection or aviary
	Building of interest
	Castle
	Church of interest
	Cinema
	Garden
	Historic ship
	House
	House and garden
	Museum
	Preserved railway
	Roman antiquity
	Safari park
	Theatre
	Tourist information centre
	Zoo
✦	Other place of interest

Aberdeen
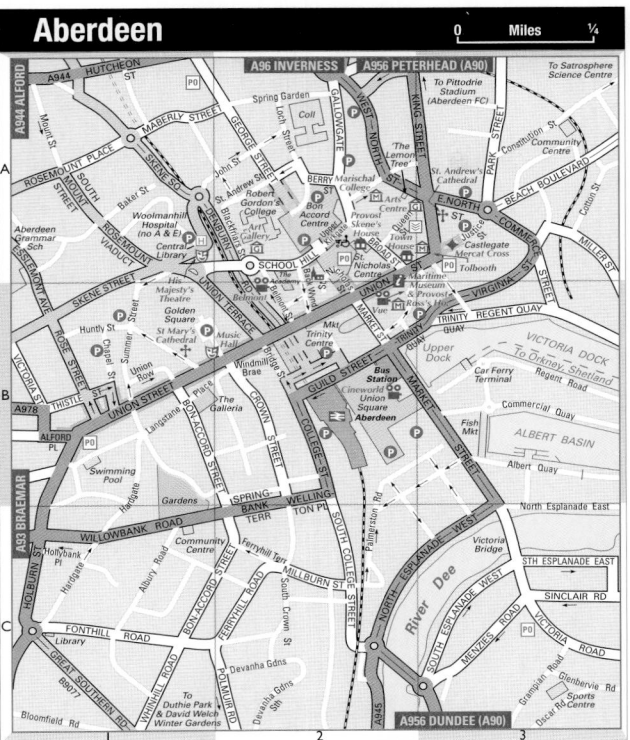

Aberystwyth
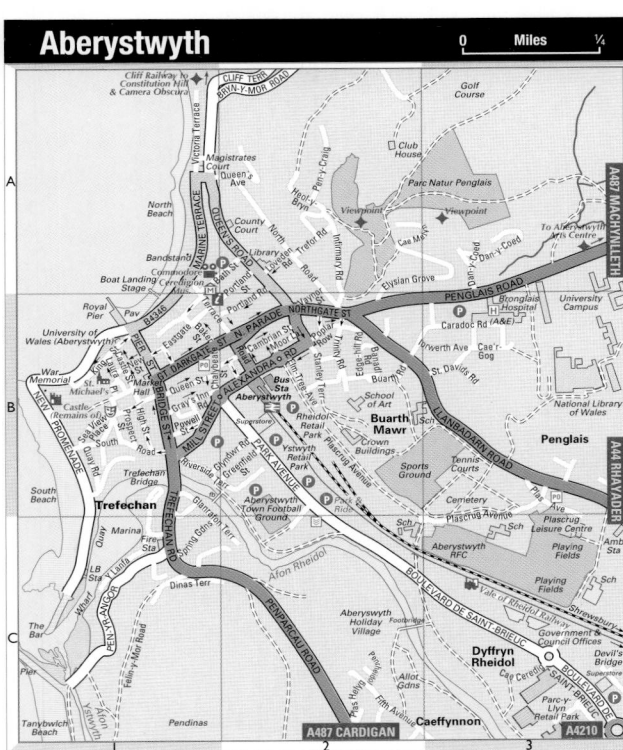

Ashford
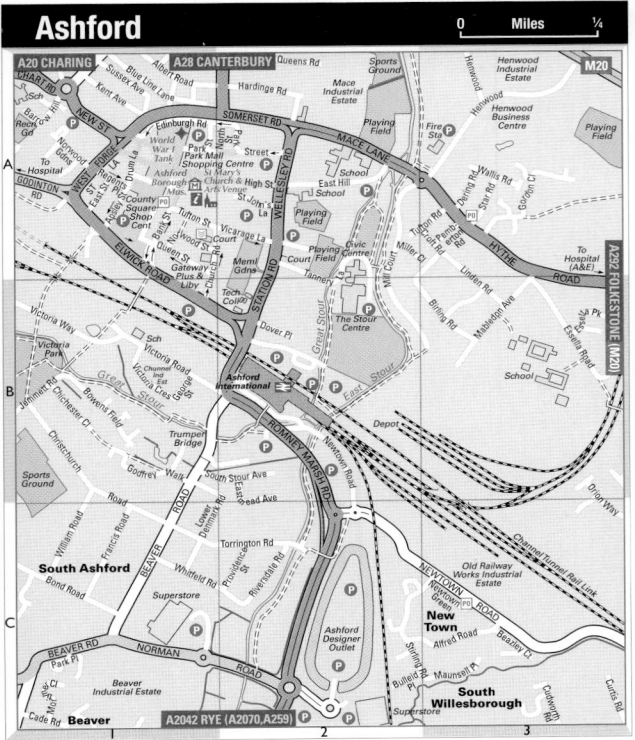

Ayr
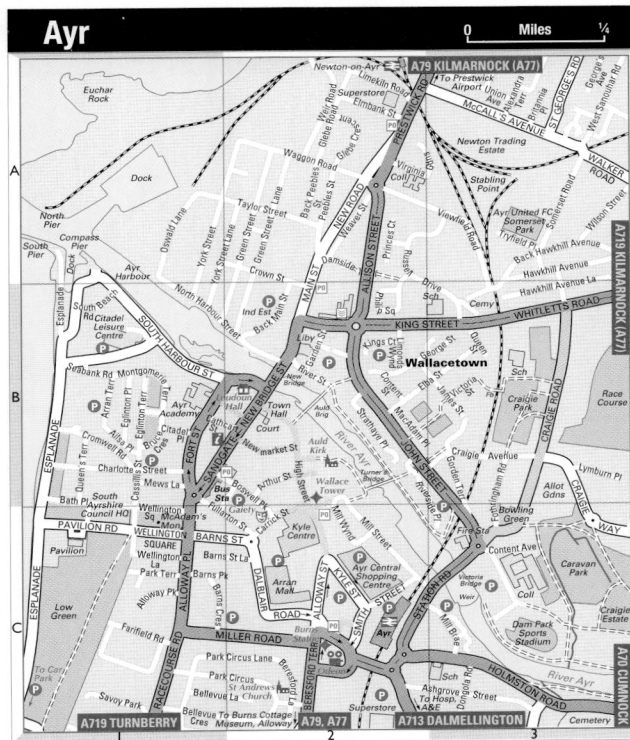

Bangor
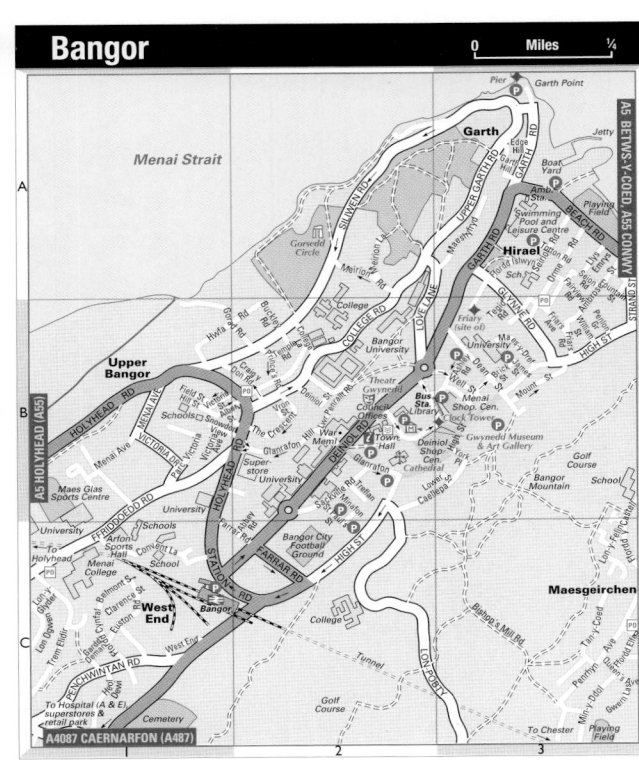

Barrow-in-Furness
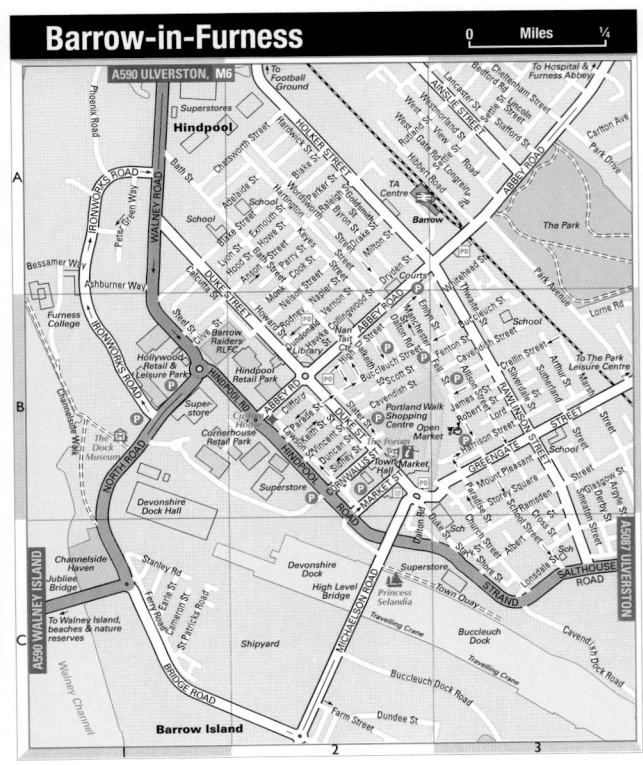

Bath
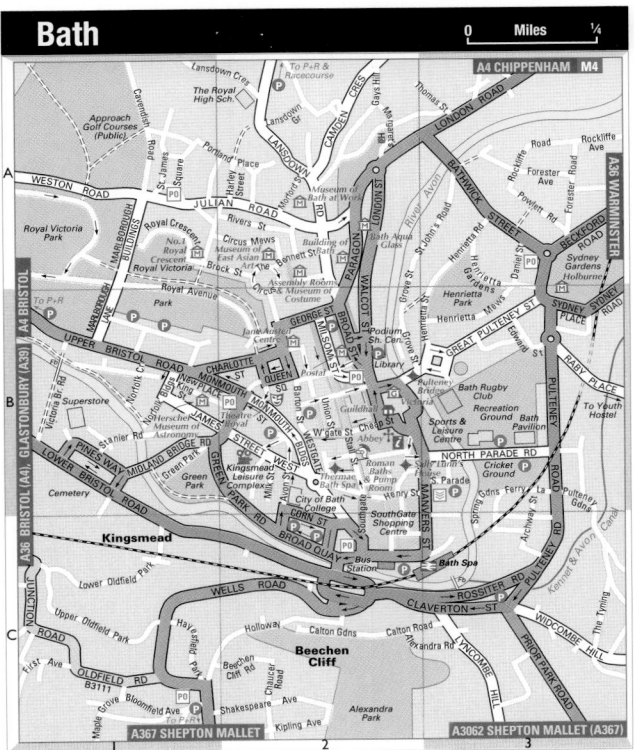

Berwick-upon-Tweed
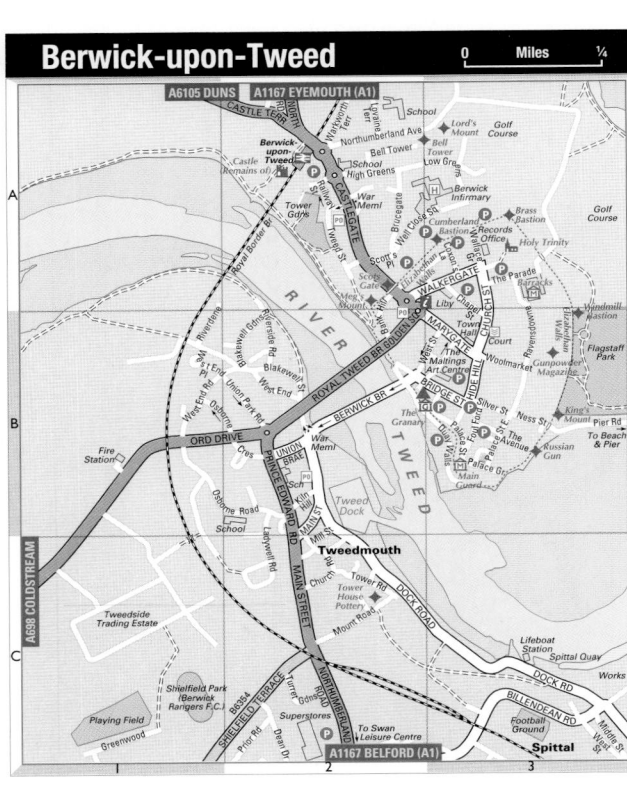

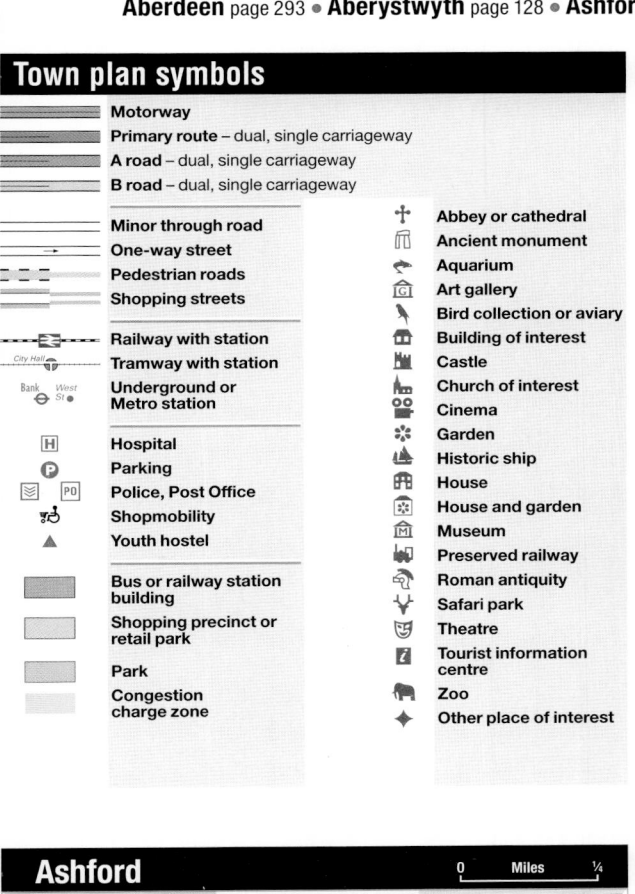

Birmingham

Blackpool

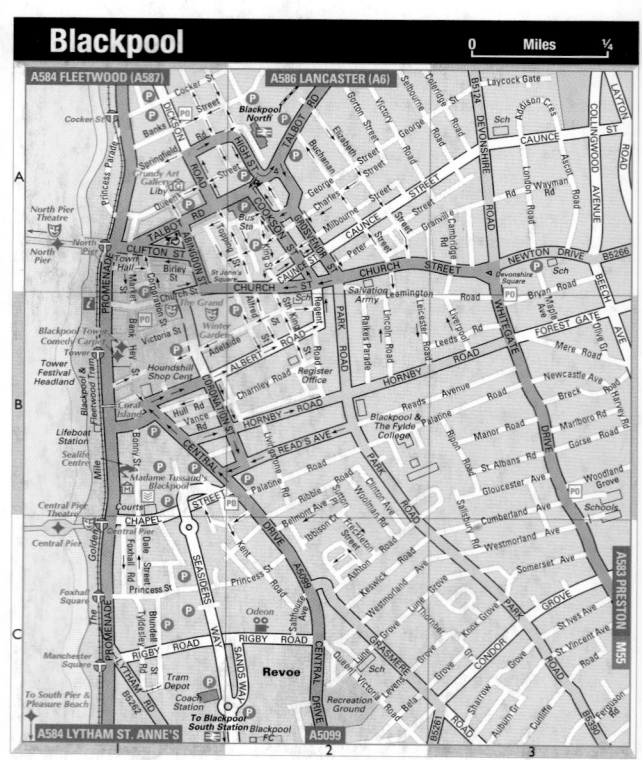

Bournemouth

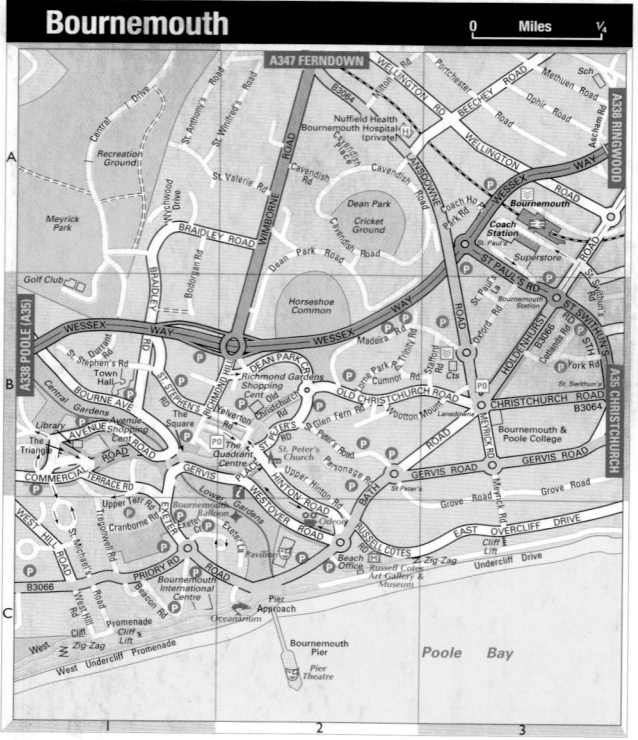

Bradford

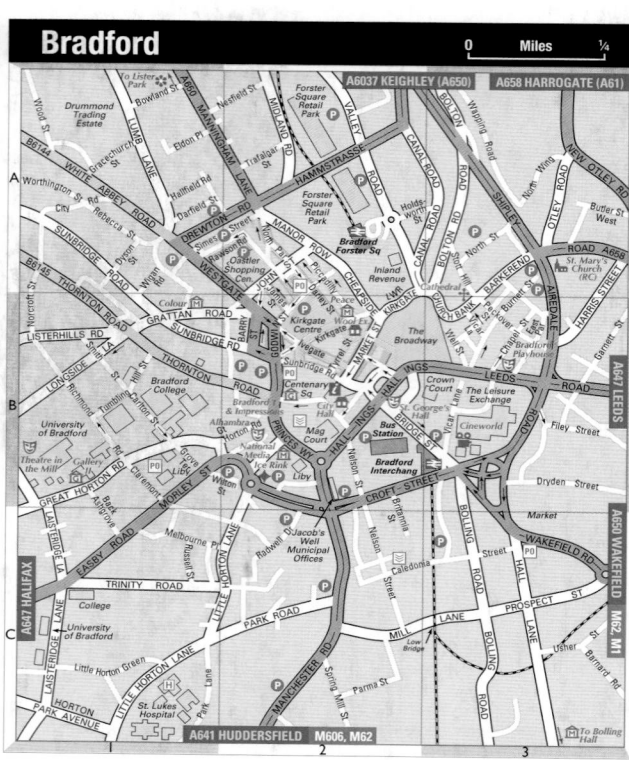

Brighton

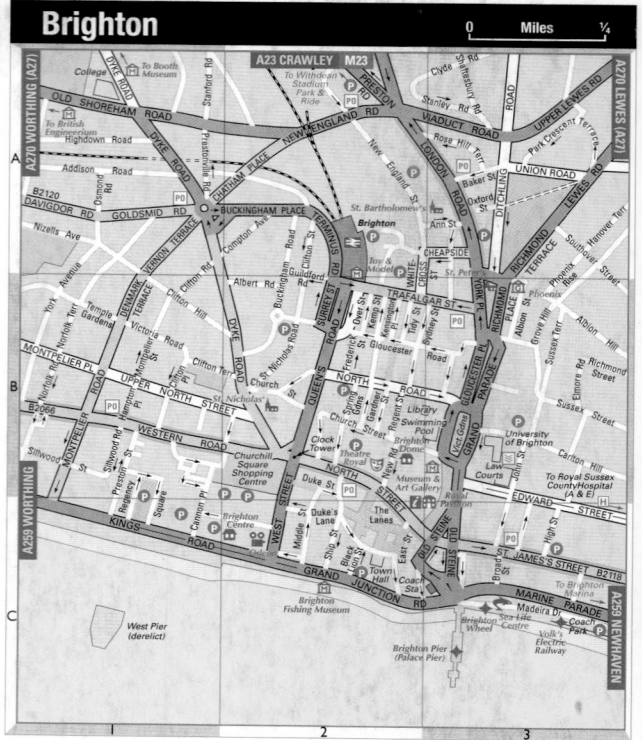

Bristol

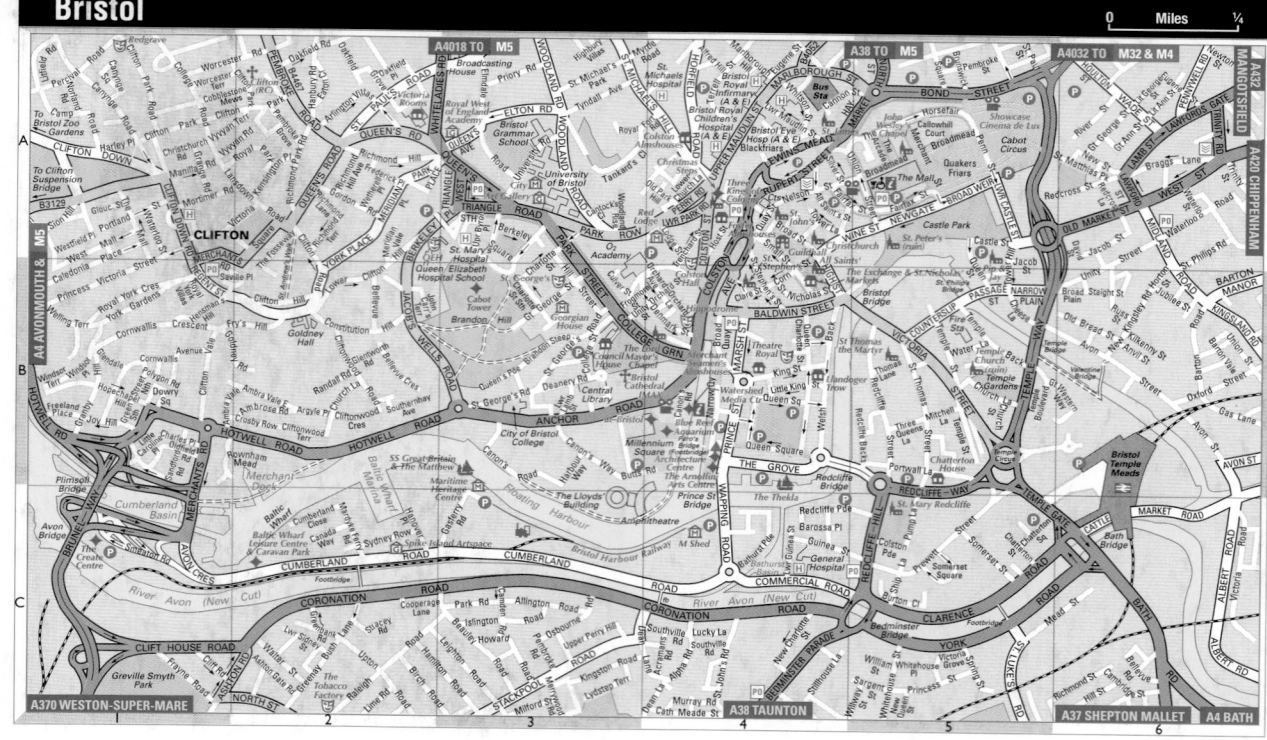

Bury St Edmunds

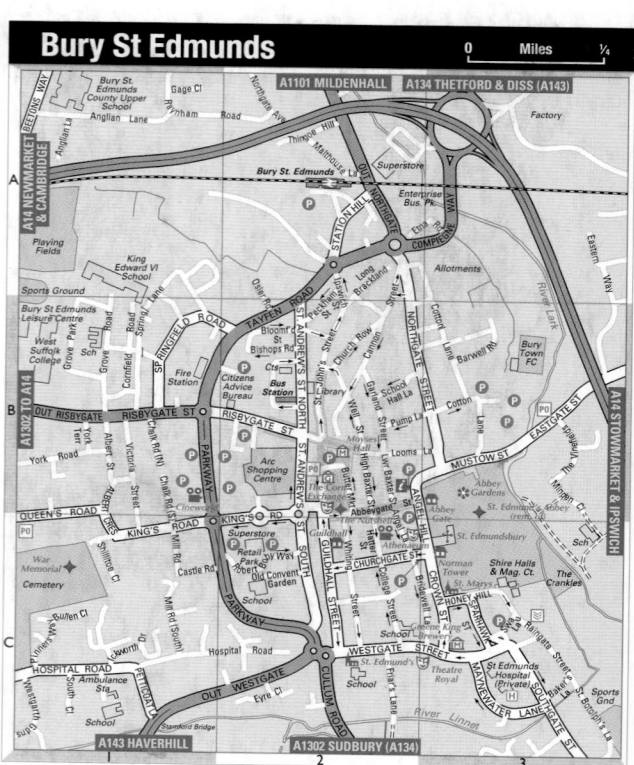

Cambridge page 123 • **Canterbury** page 54 • **Cardiff** page 59 • **Carlisle** page 239 • **Chelmsford** page 88 • **Cheltenham** page 99 • **Chester** page 166 • **Chichester** page 22 • **Colchester** page 107

333

Cambridge

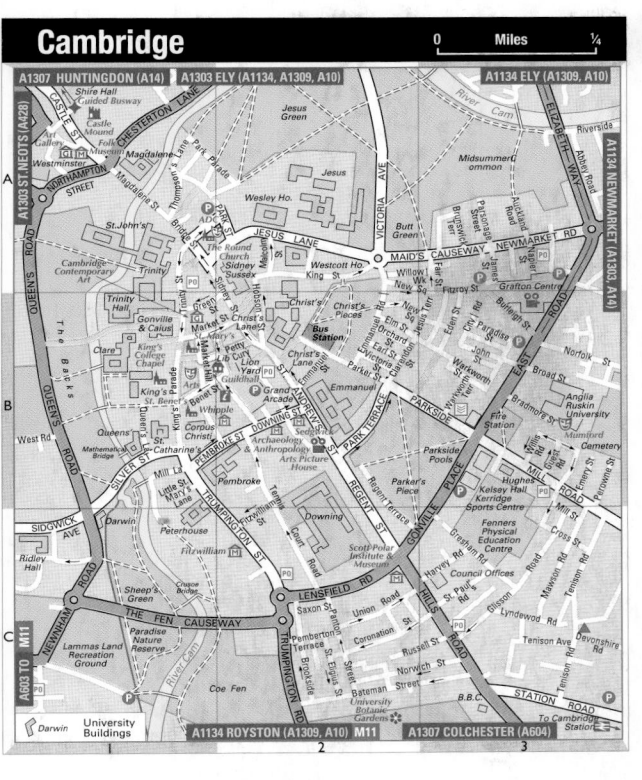

Canterbury

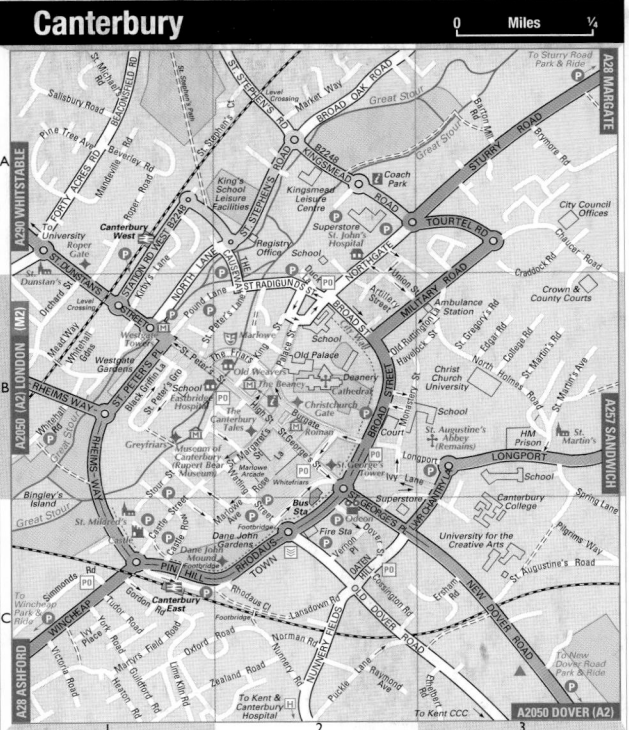

Cardiff / Caerdydd

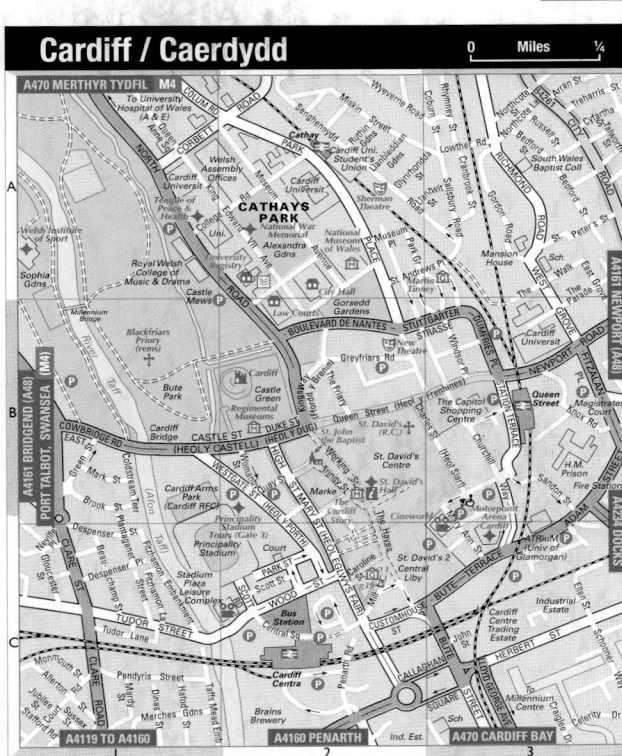

Carlisle

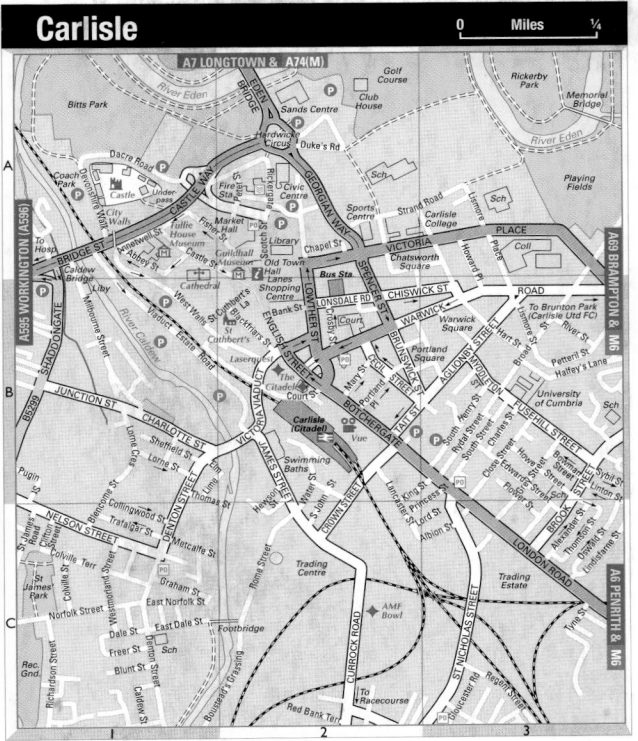

Chelmsford

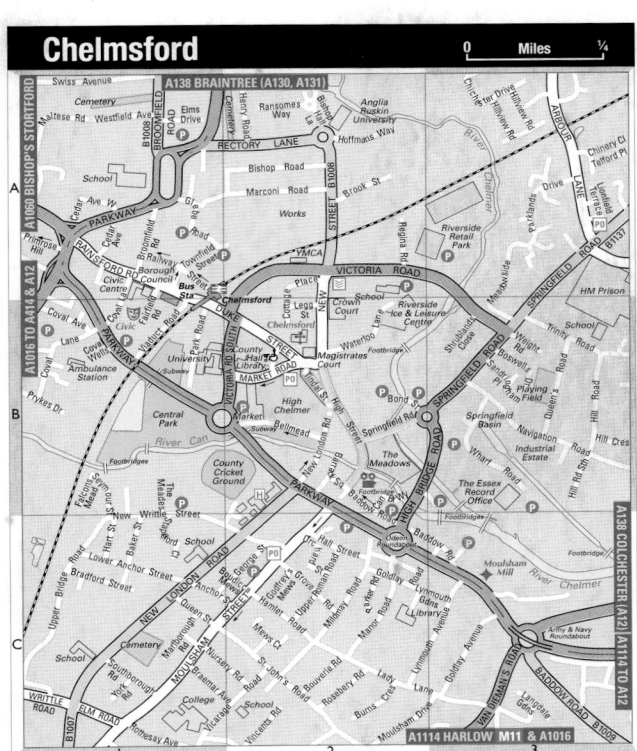

Cheltenham

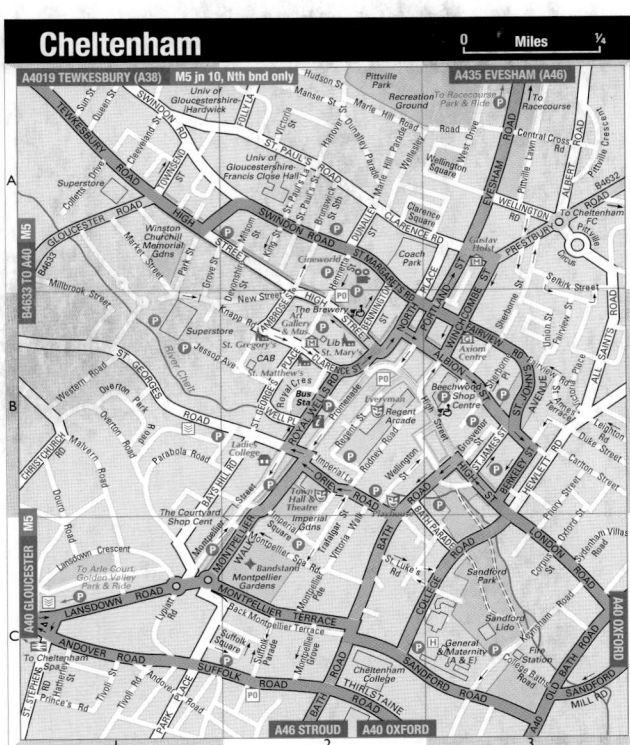

Chester

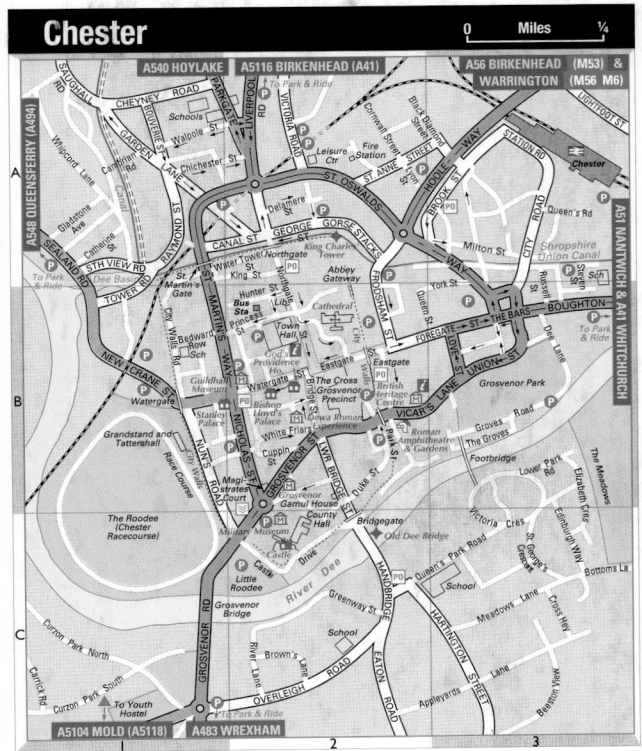

Chichester

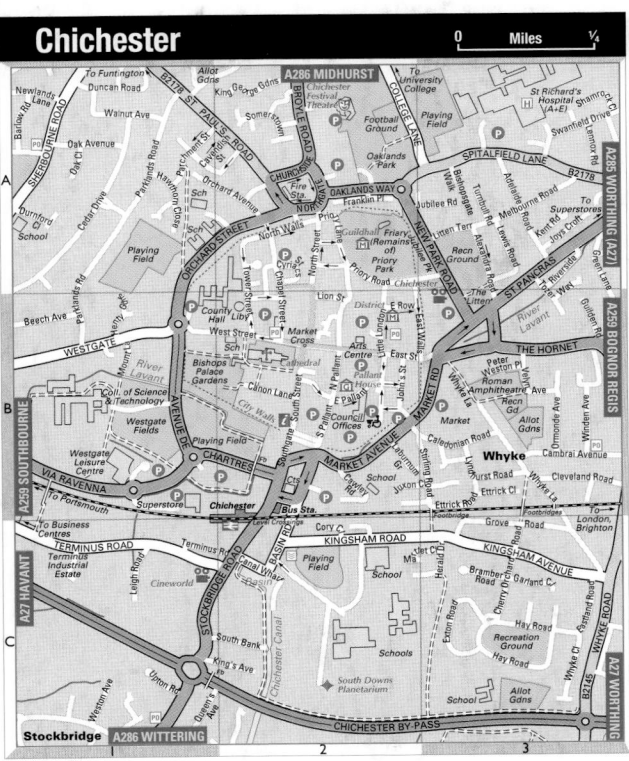

Colchester

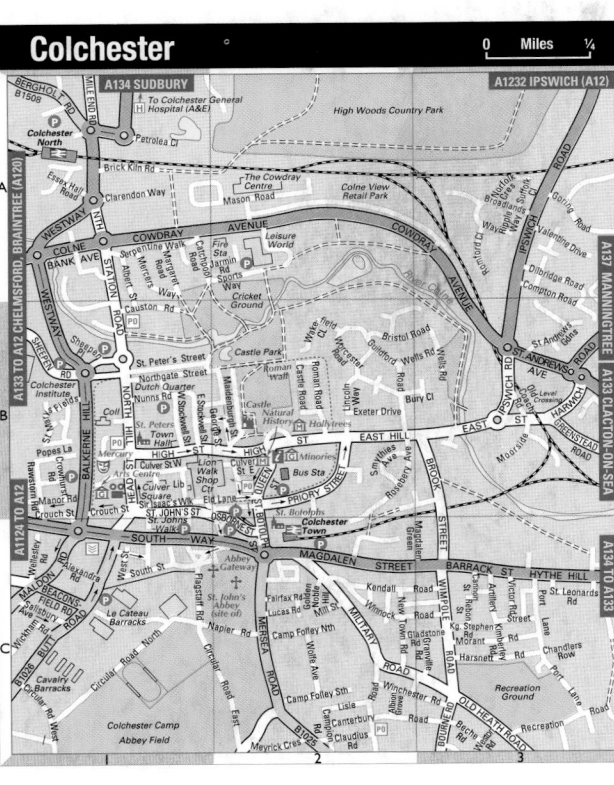

Fort William page 290 ● **Glasgow** page 267 ● **Gloucester** page 80 ● **Grimsby** page 201 ● **Hanley (Stoke-on-Tent)** page 168 ● **Harrogate** page 206 ● **Holyhead** page 178 ● **Hull** page 200

335

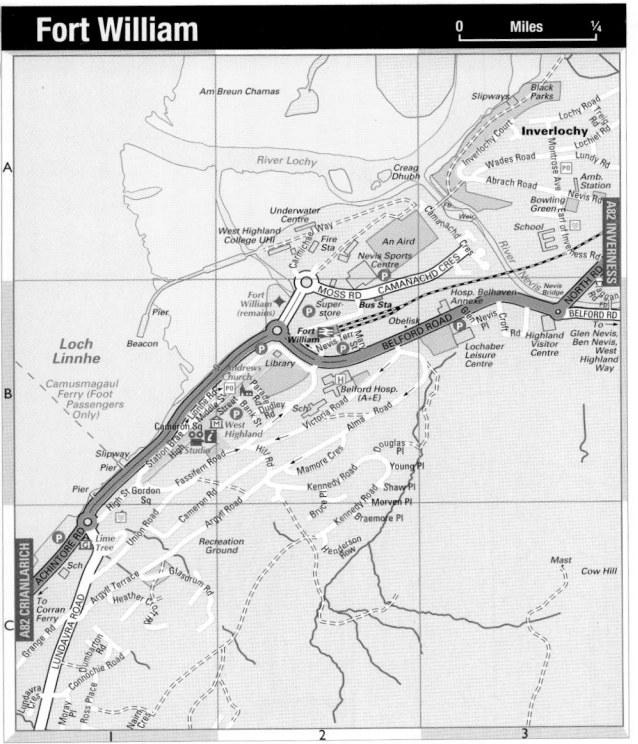

Fort William

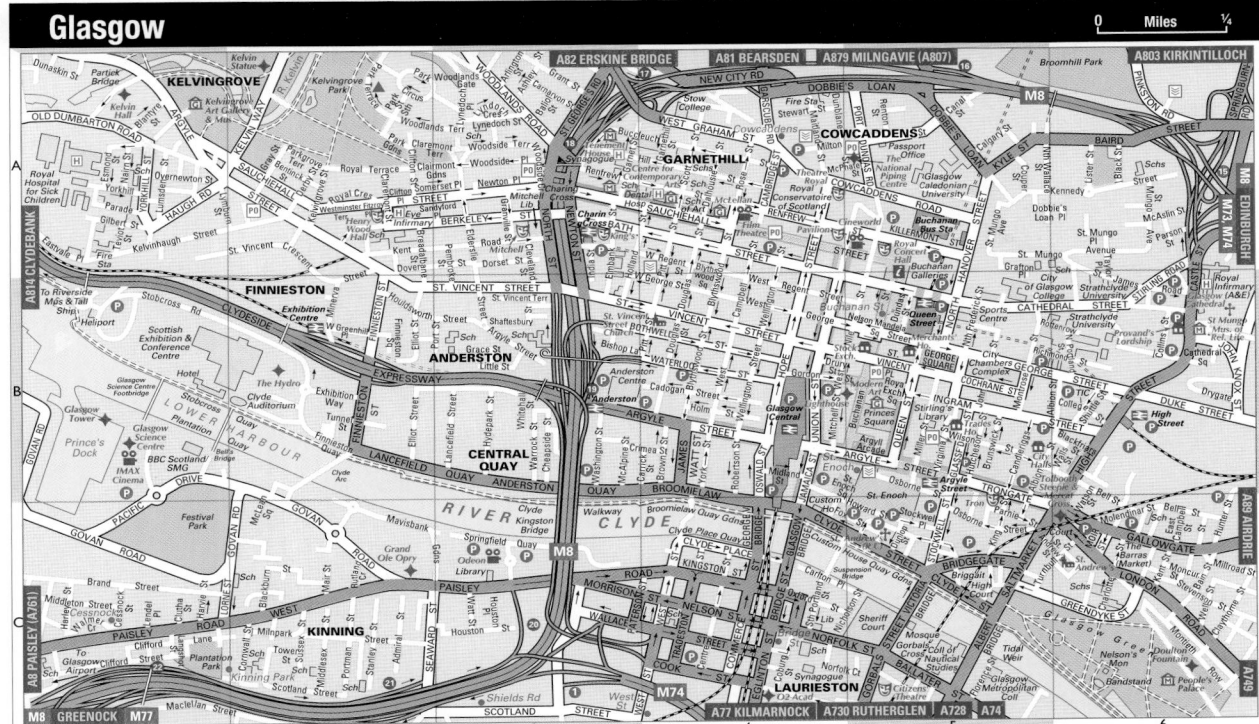

Glasgow

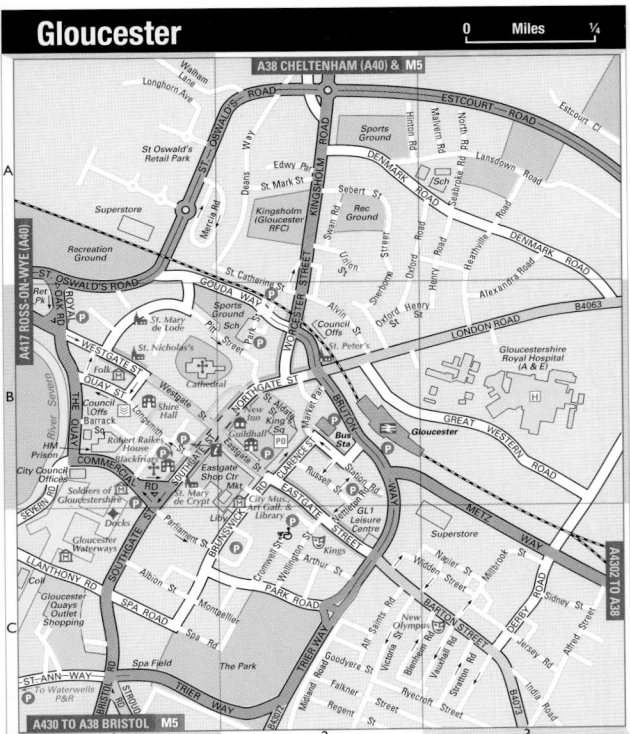

Gloucester

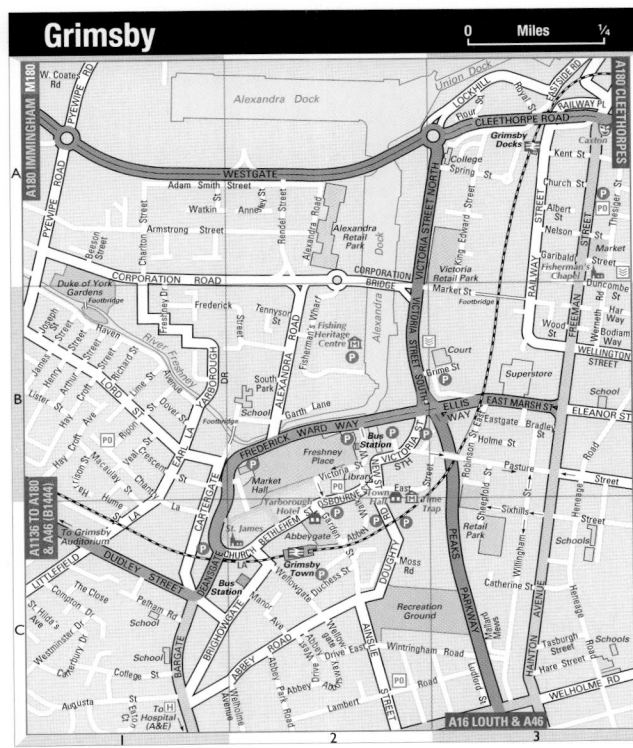

Grimsby

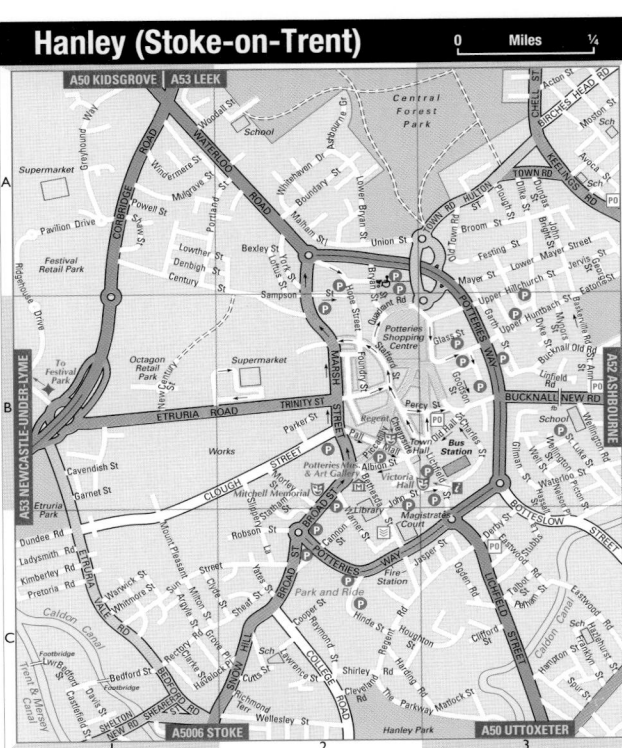

Hanley (Stoke-on-Trent)

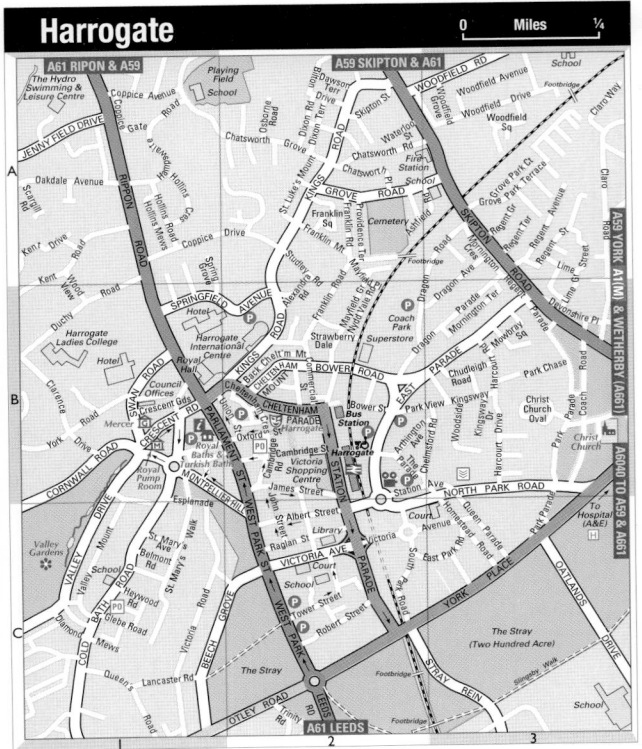

Harrogate

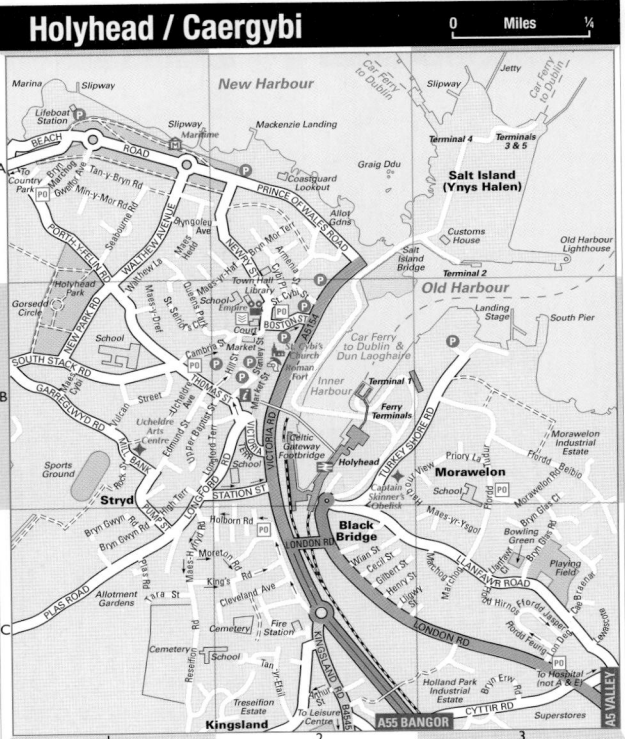

Holyhead / Caergybi

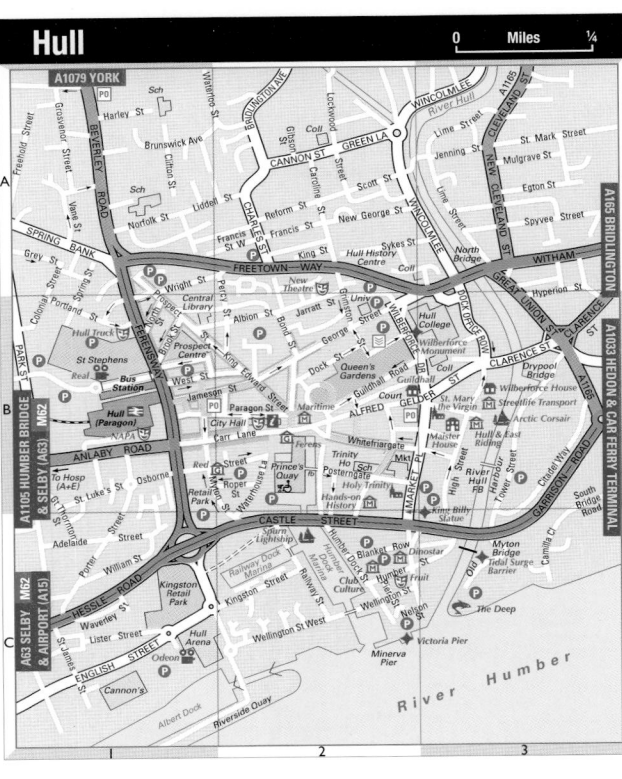

Hull

Inverness

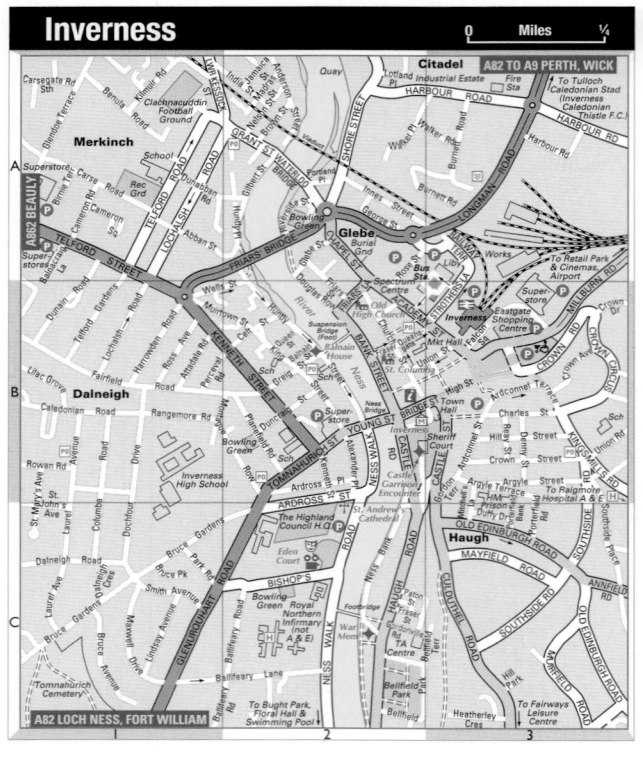

Ipswich

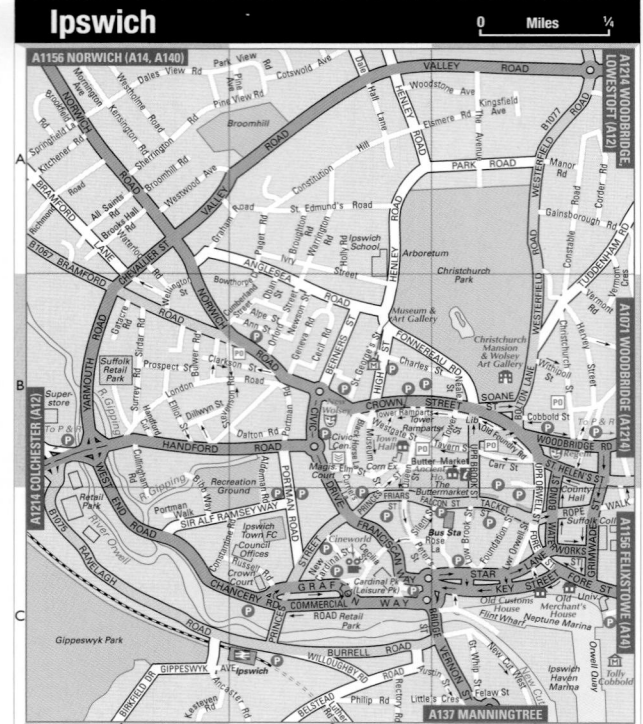

Kendal

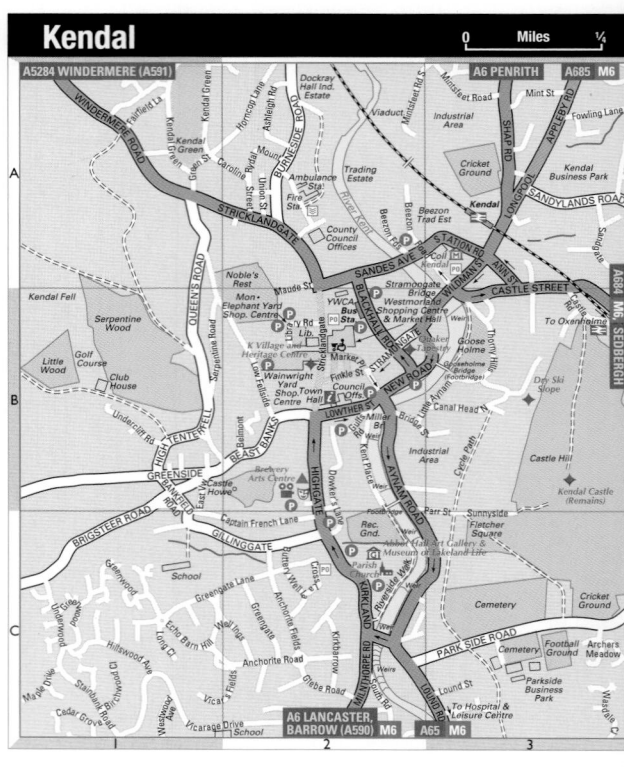

King's Lynn

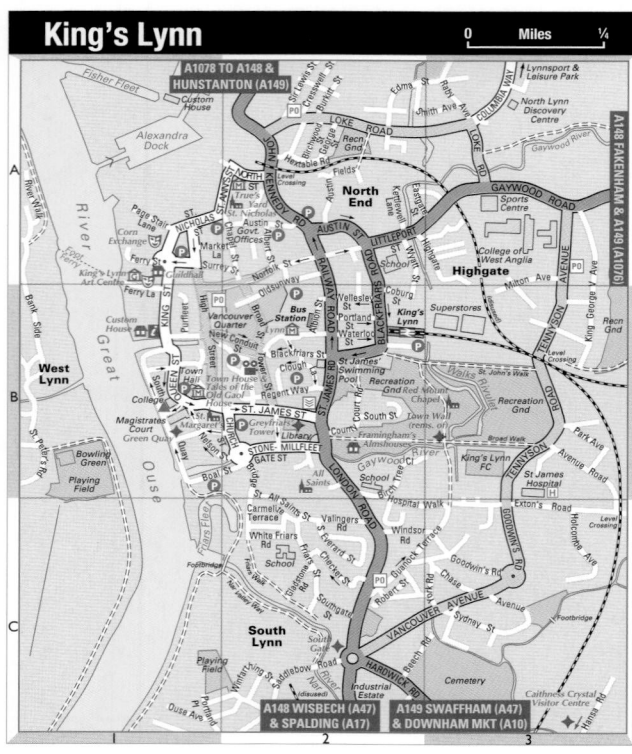

Leeds

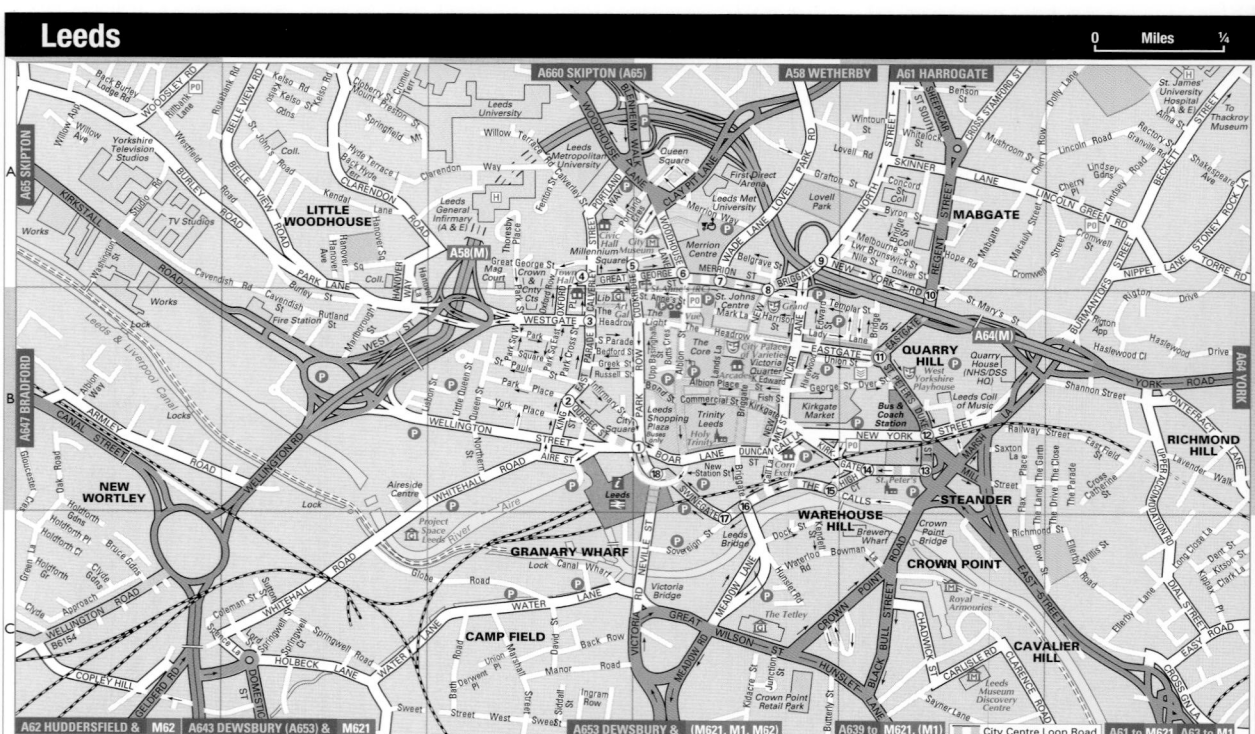

Lancaster

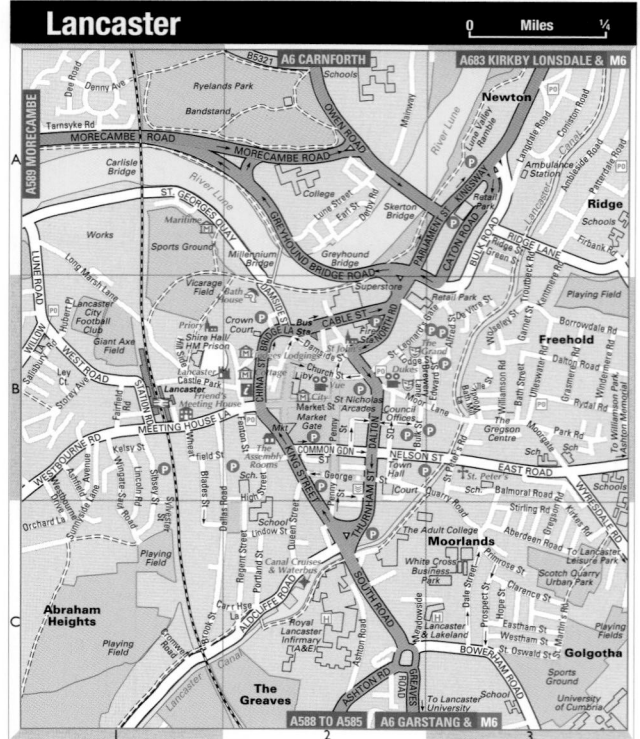

Leicester

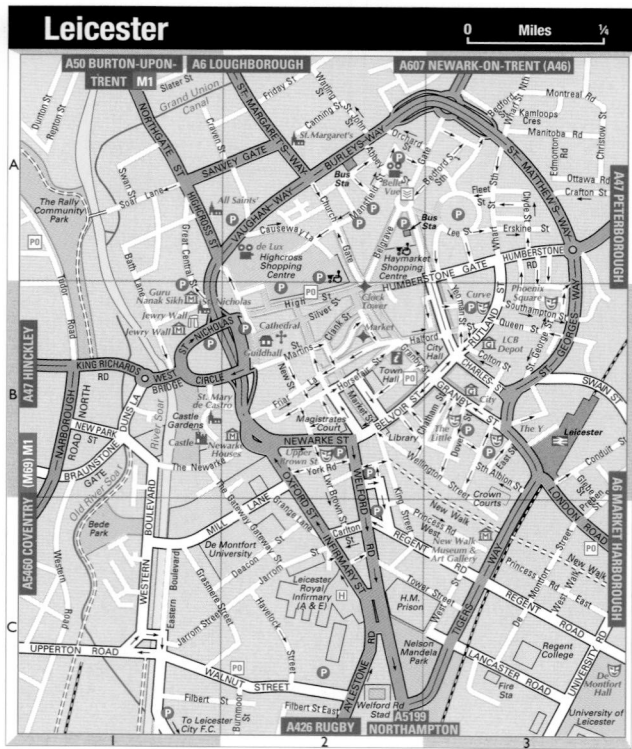

Lewes

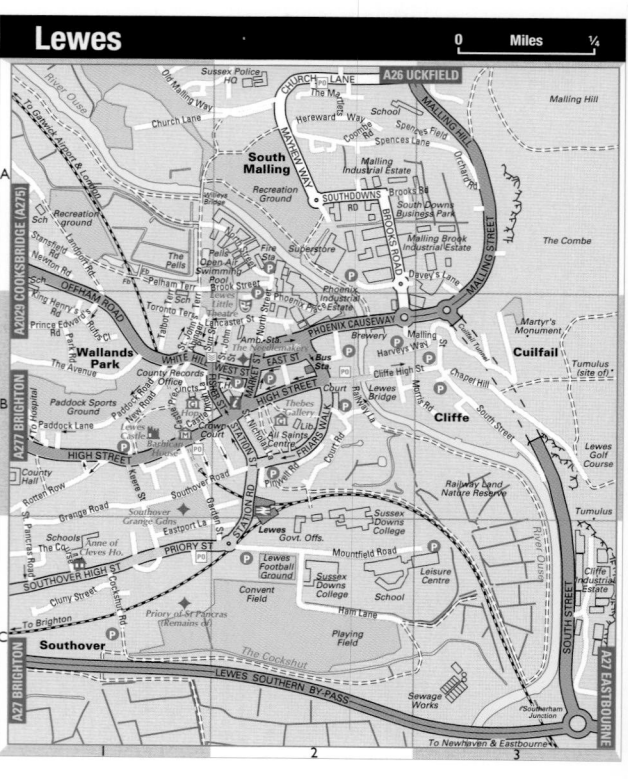

Lincoln page 189 ● **Liverpool** page 182 ● **Llandudno** page 180 ● **Llanelli** page 56 ● **Luton** page 103 ● **Macclesfield** page 184 ● **Manchester** page 184

337

Lincoln
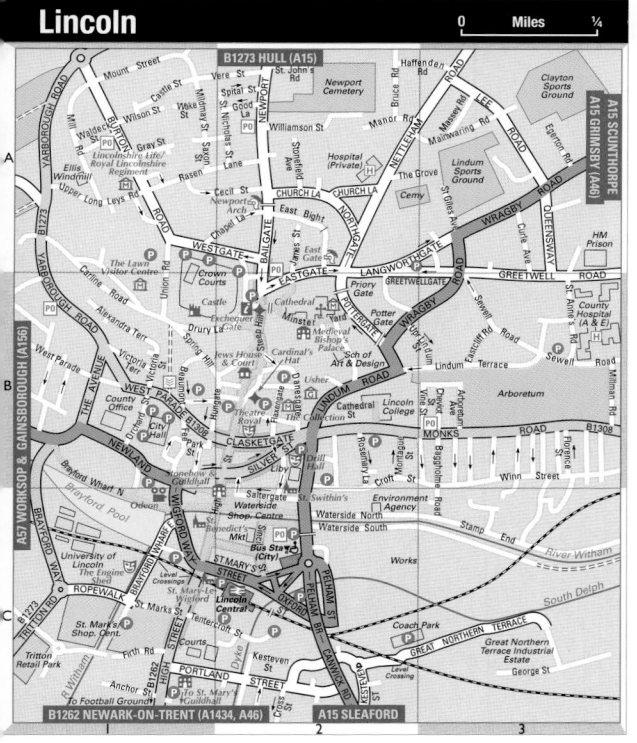

Liverpool

Llandudno
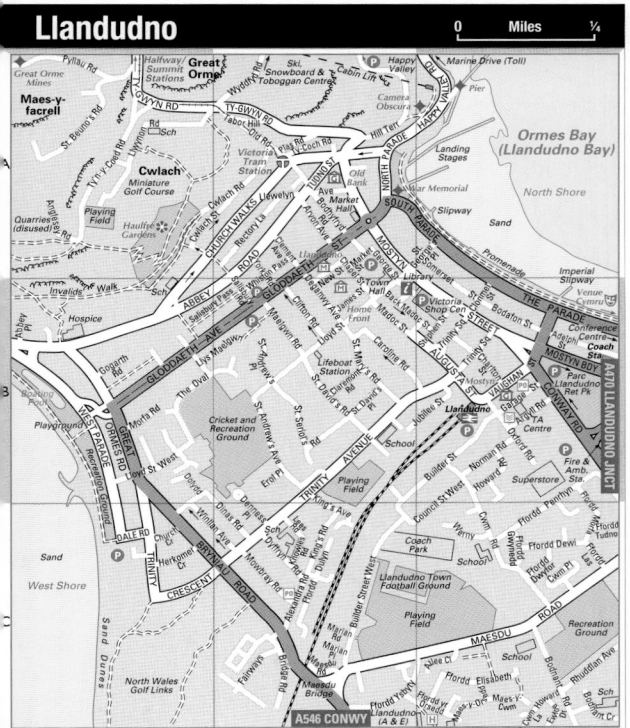

Llanelli
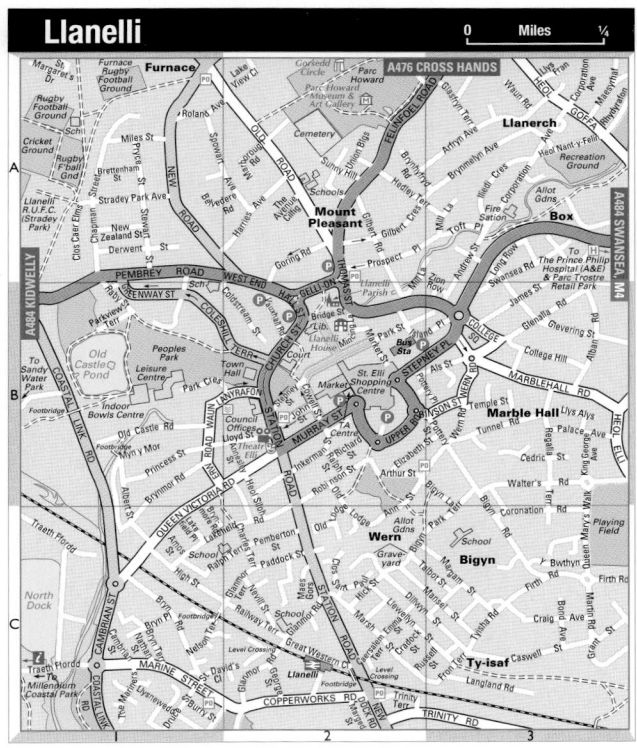

Luton
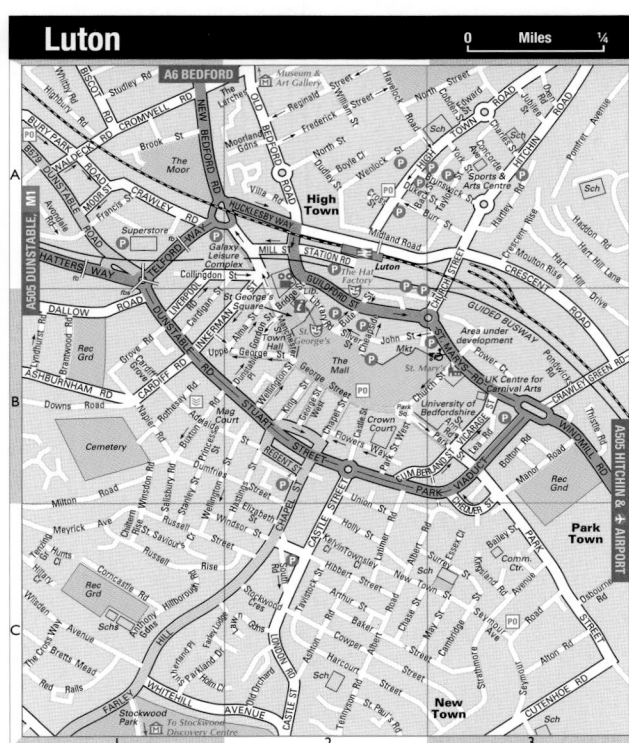

Macclesfield
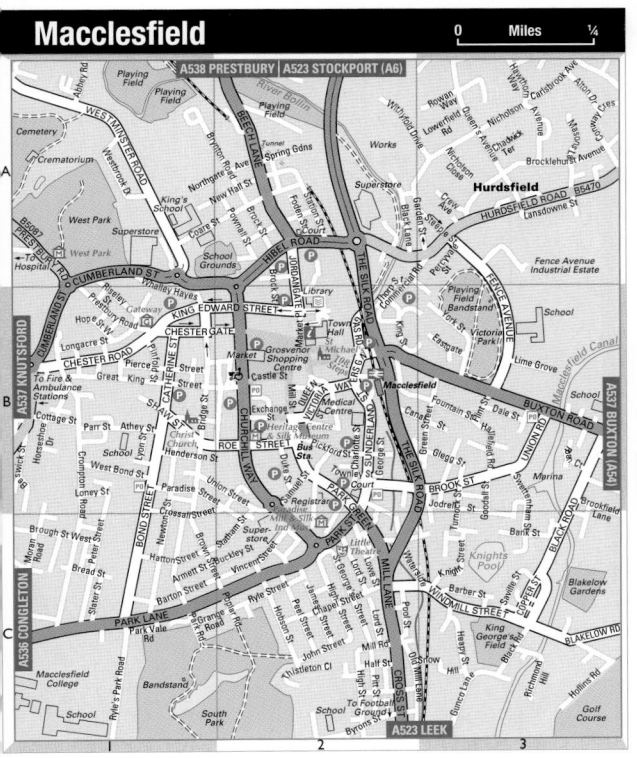

Manchester

Maidstone

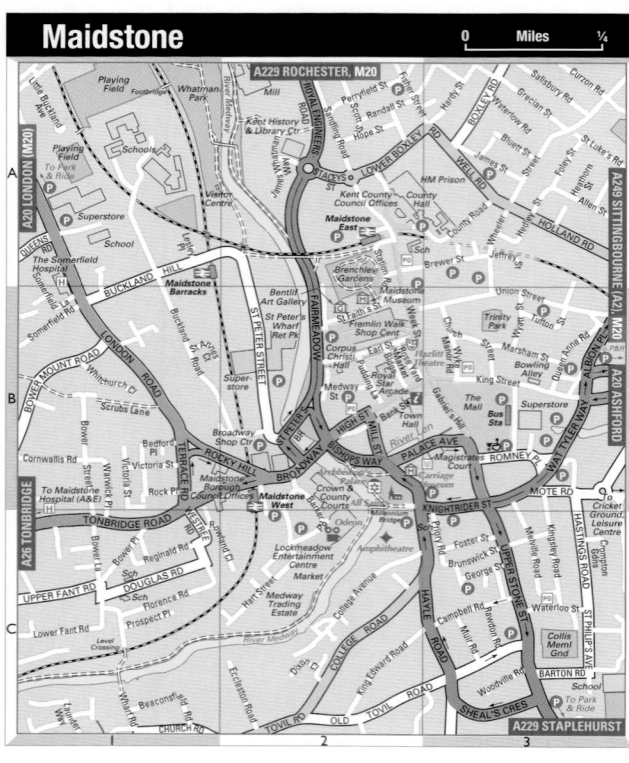

Merthyr Tydfil / Merthyr Tudful

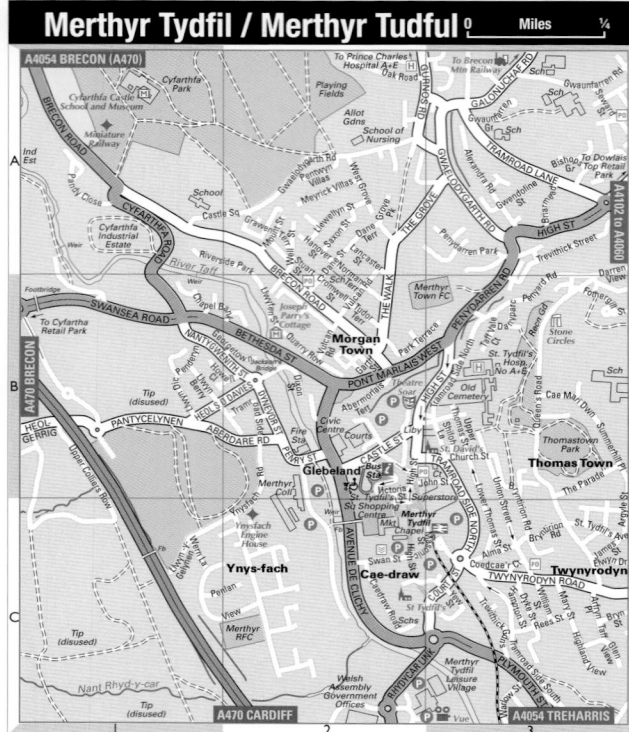

Middlesbrough

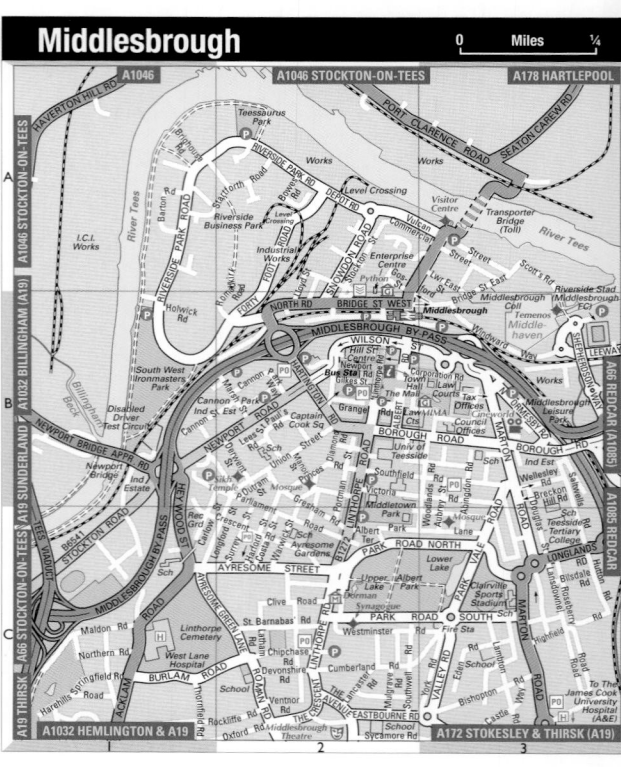

Milton Keynes

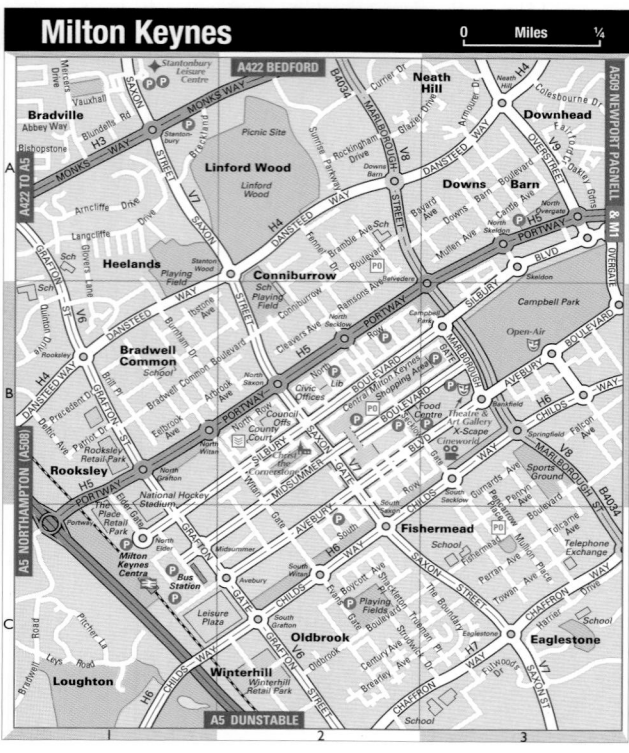

Newcastle upon Tyne

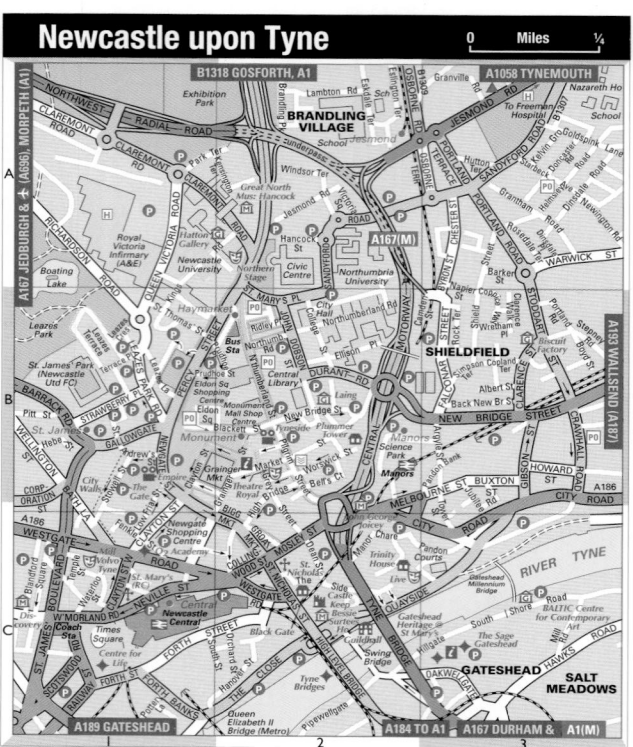

Newport / Casnewydd

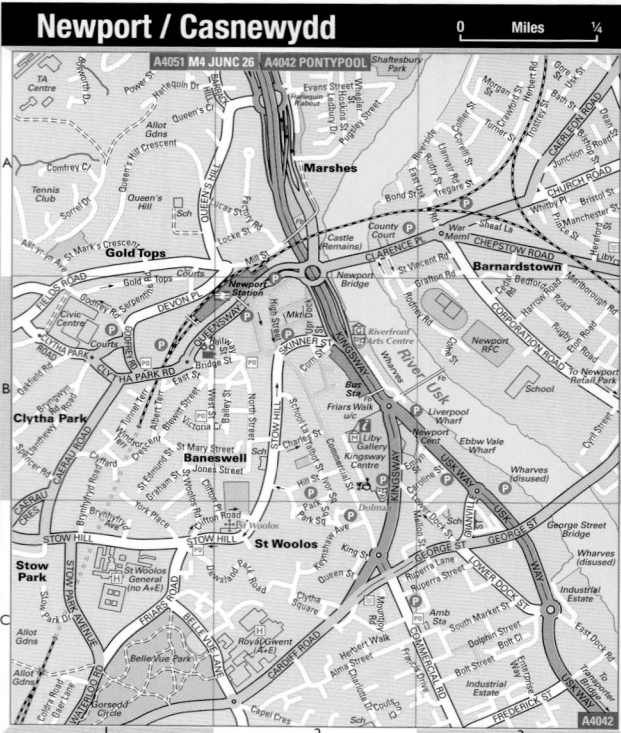

Newquay

Newtown / Y Drenewydd

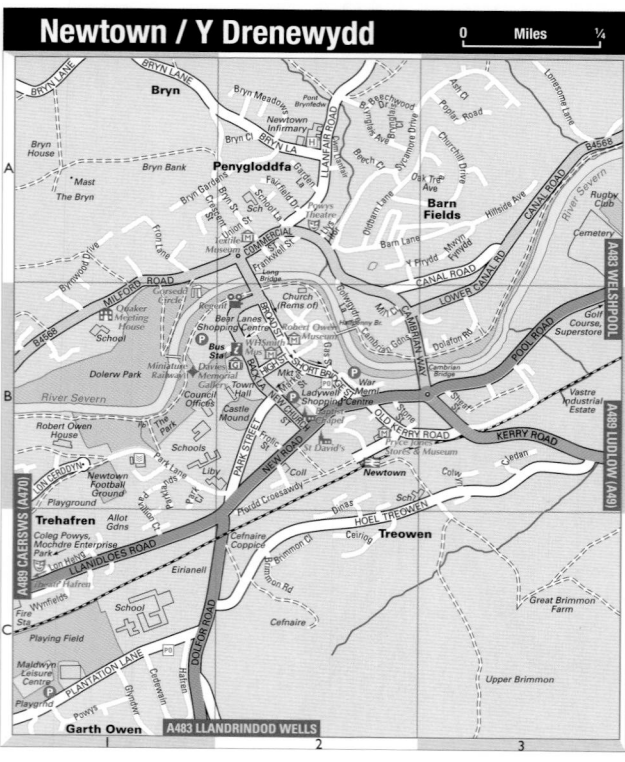

Northampton

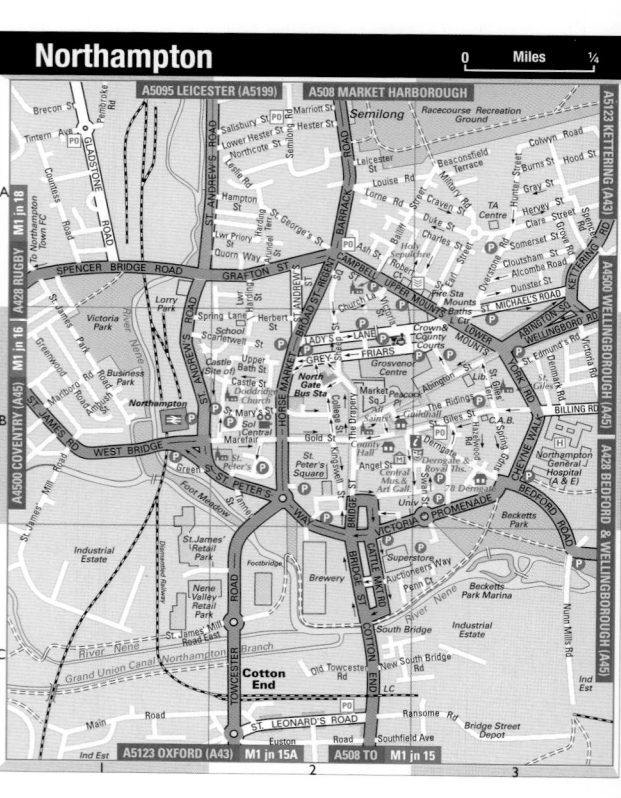

Norwich page 142 ● Nottingham page 153 ● Oban page 289 ● Oxford page 83 ● Perth page 286 ● Peterborough page 138 ● Plymouth page 7 ● Poole page 18 ● Portsmouth page 21

341

Norwich

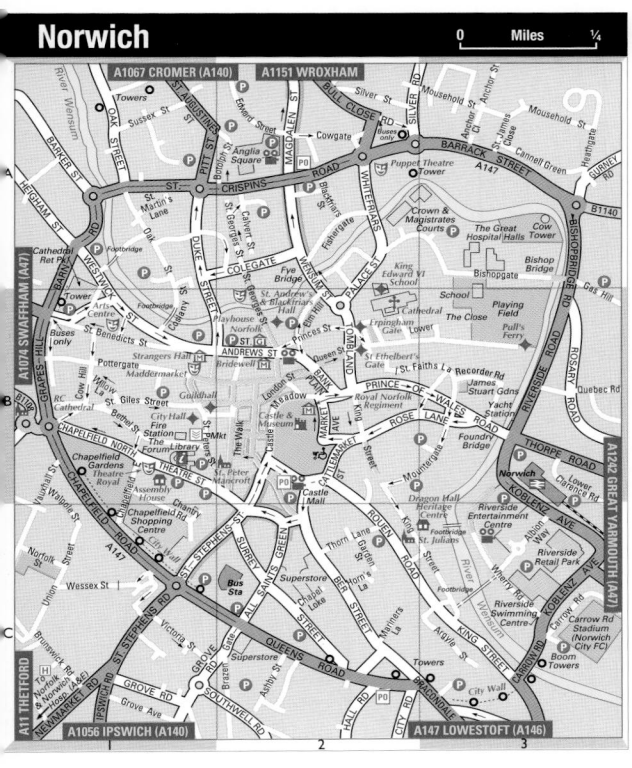

Nottingham

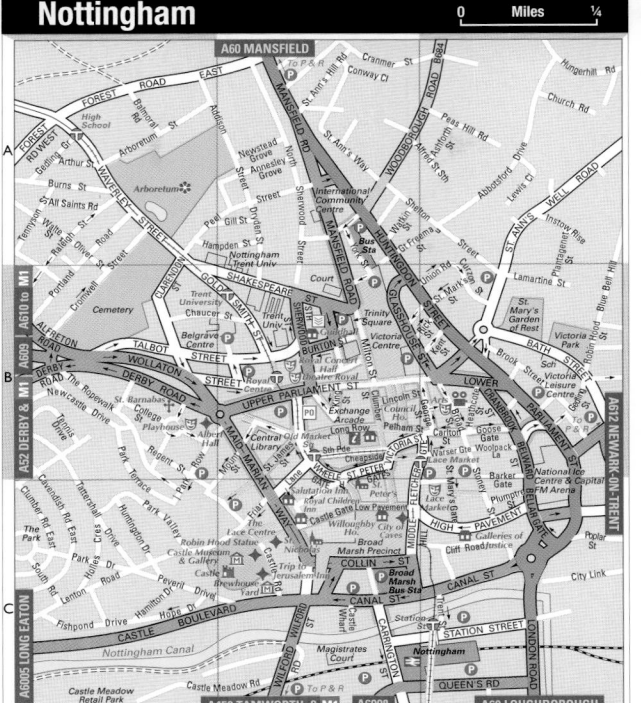

Oban

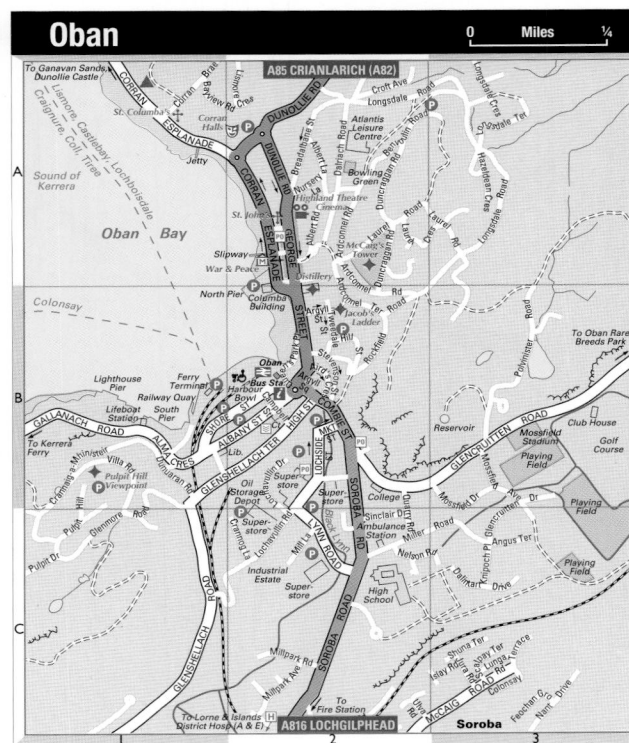

Oxford

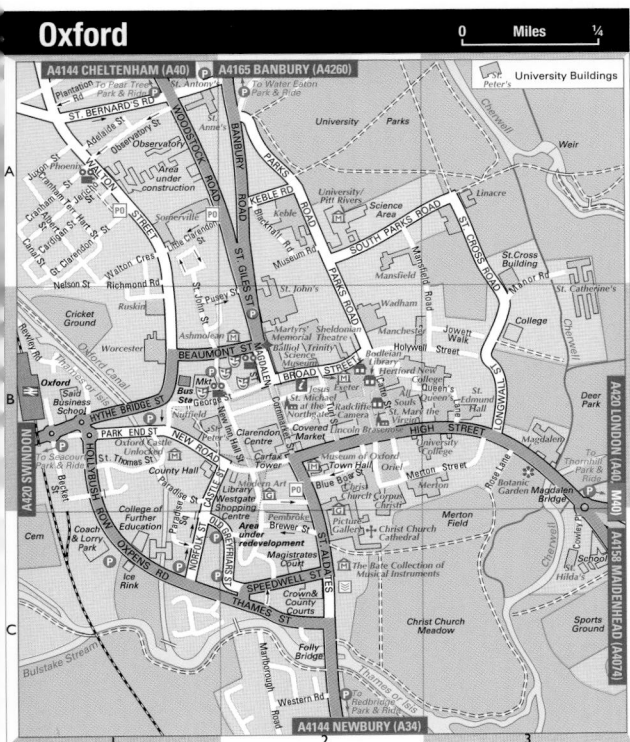

Perth

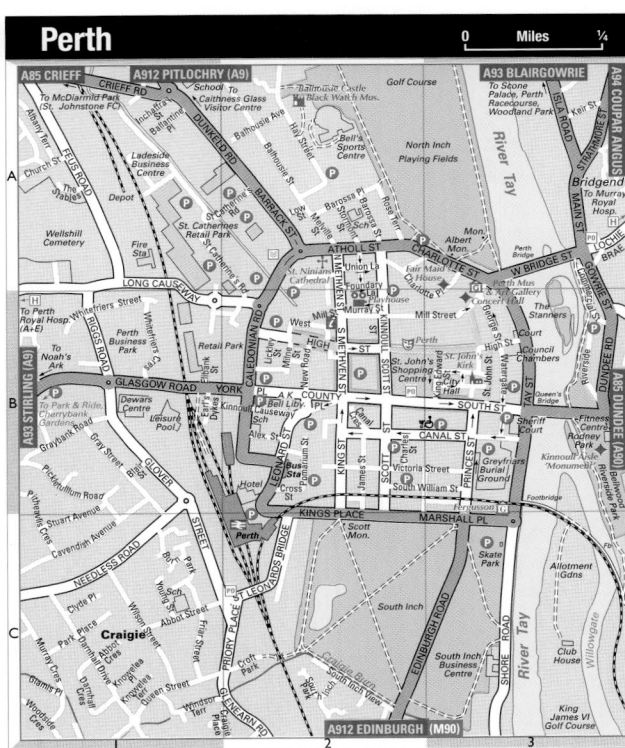

Peterborough

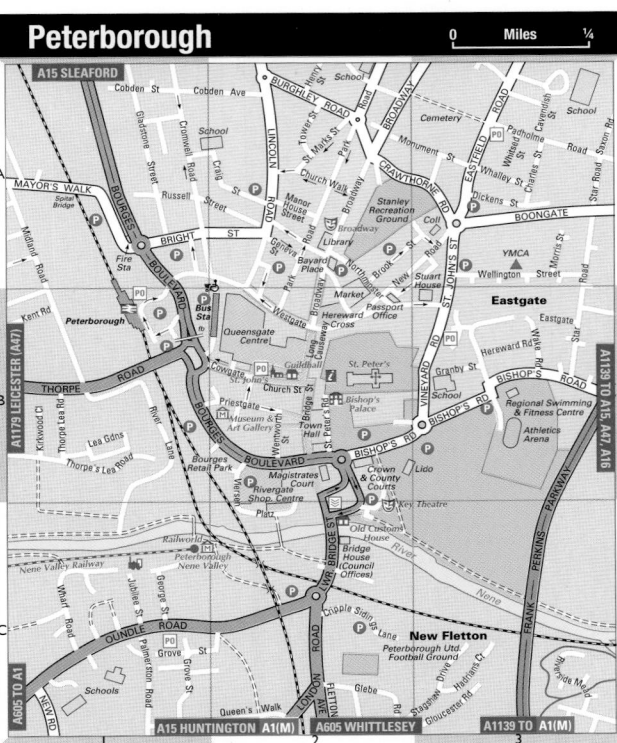

Plymouth

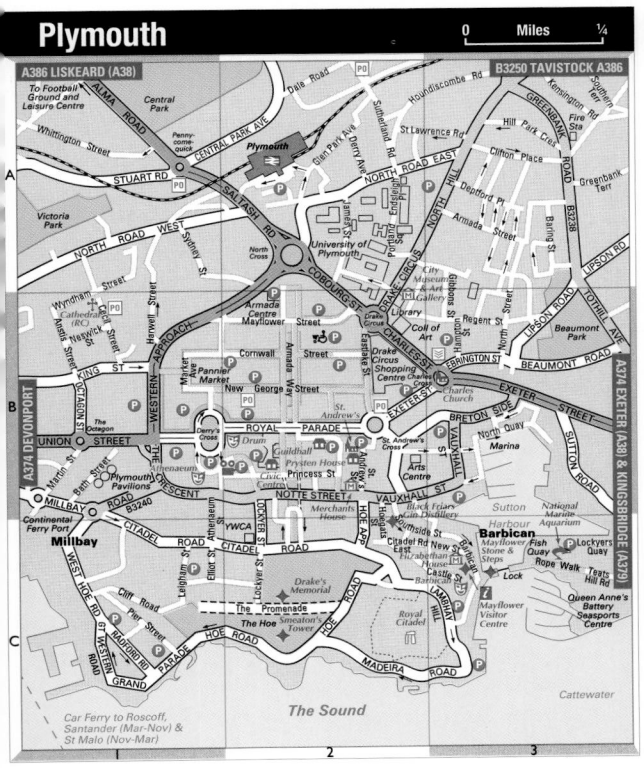

Poole

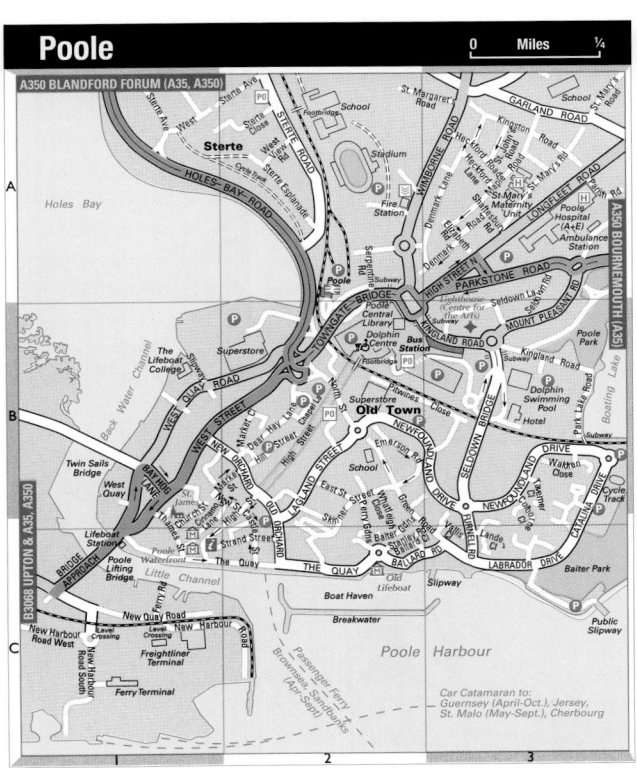

Portsmouth

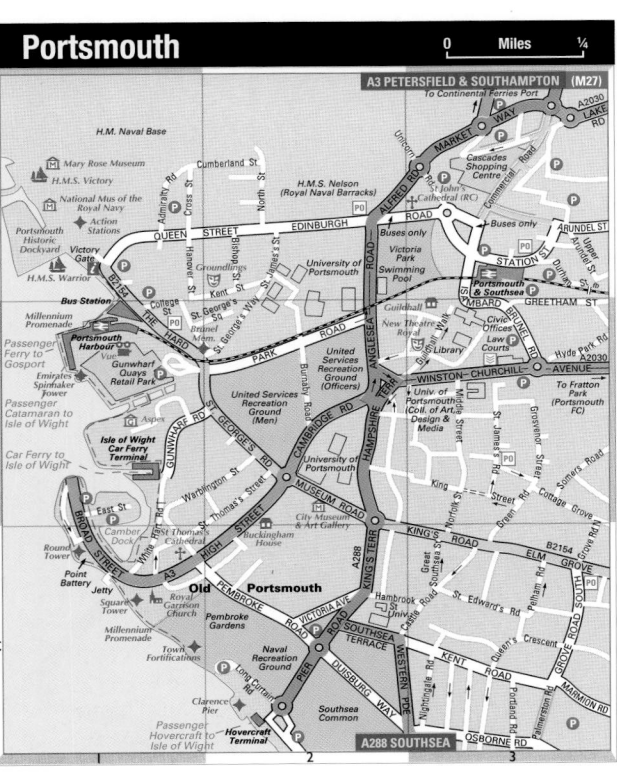

Preston

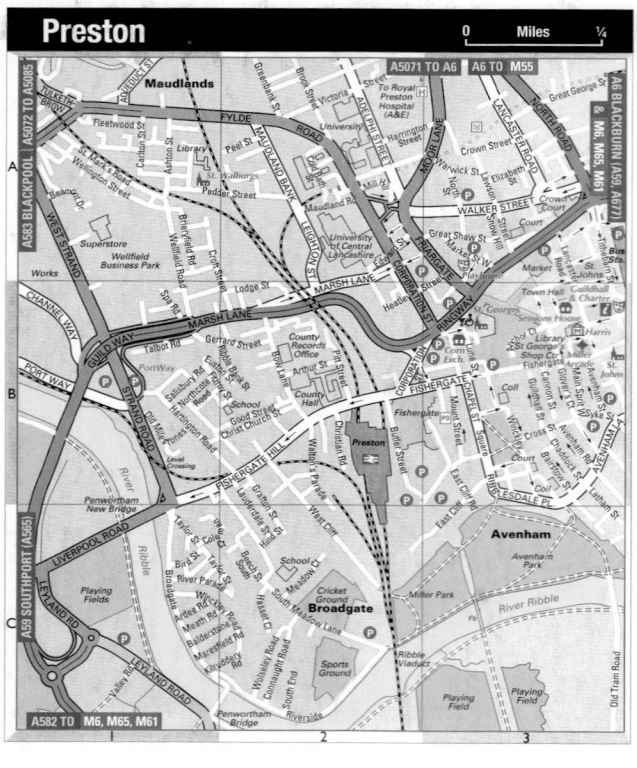

Reading

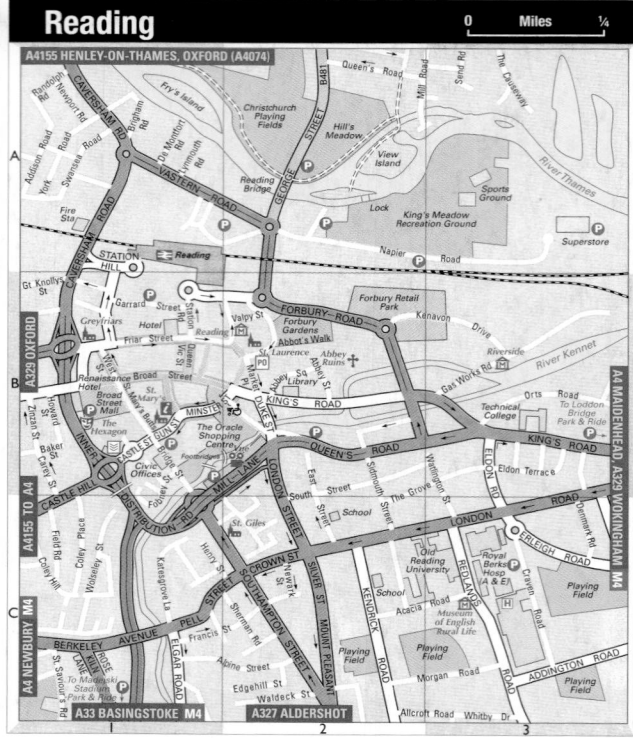

St Andrews

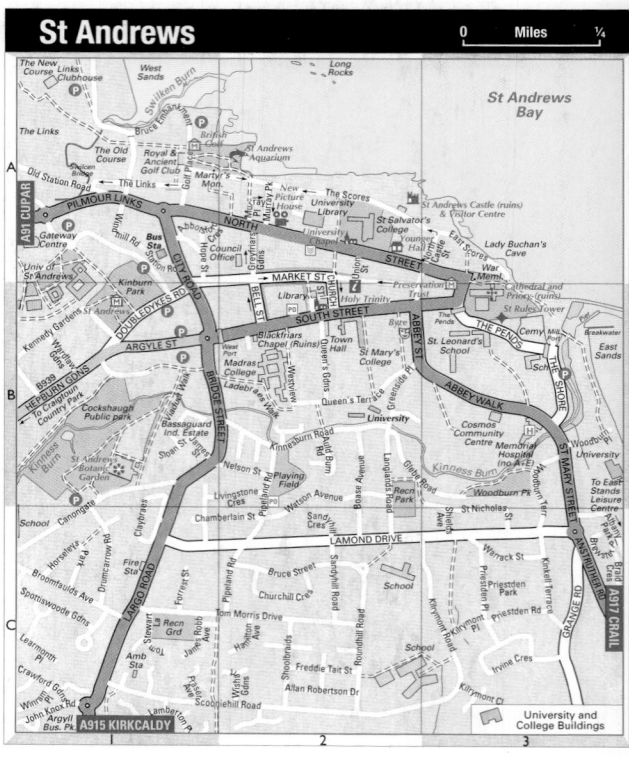

Salisbury

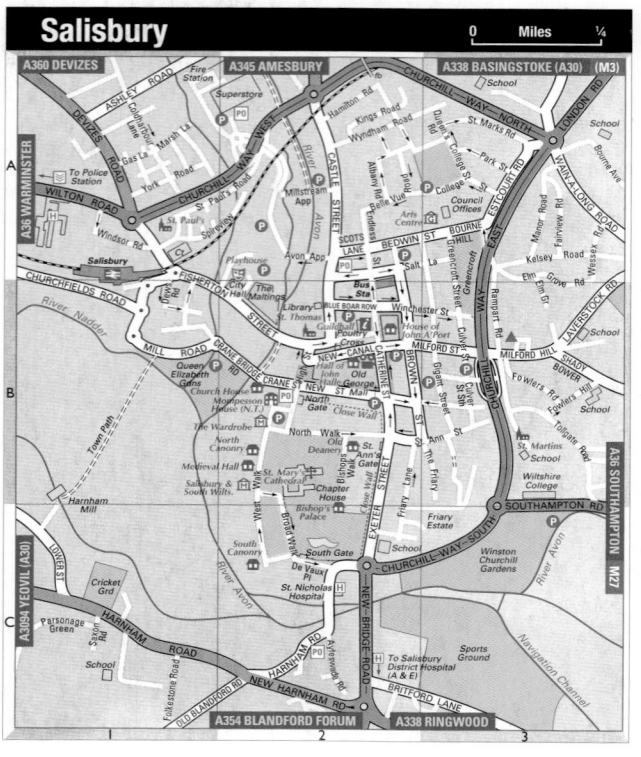

Scarborough

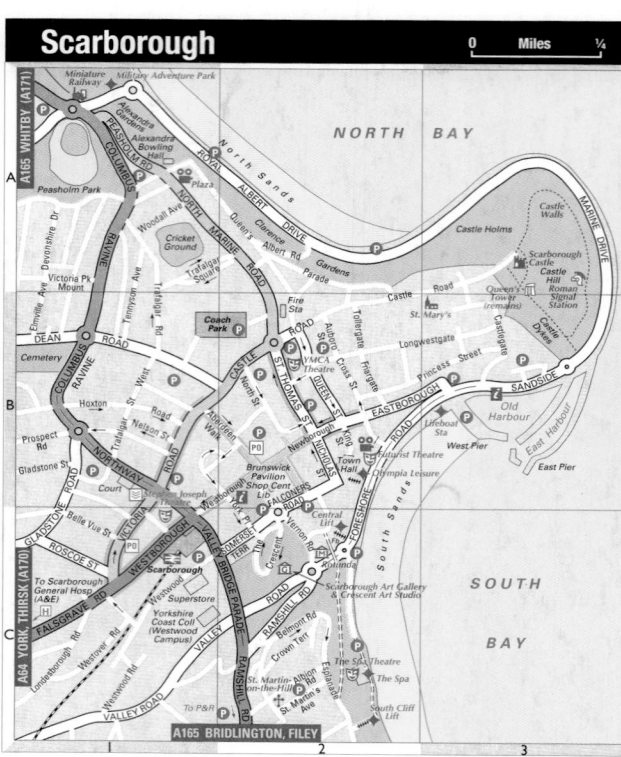

Shrewsbury

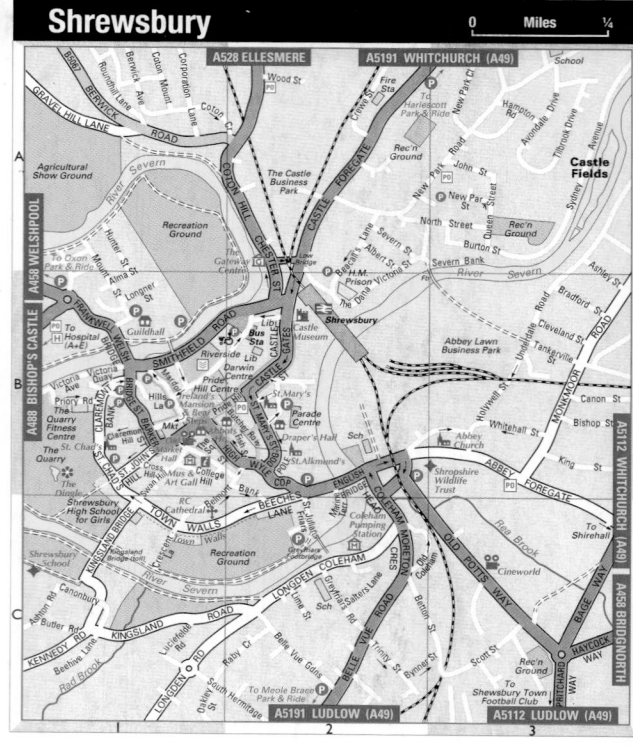

Sheffield

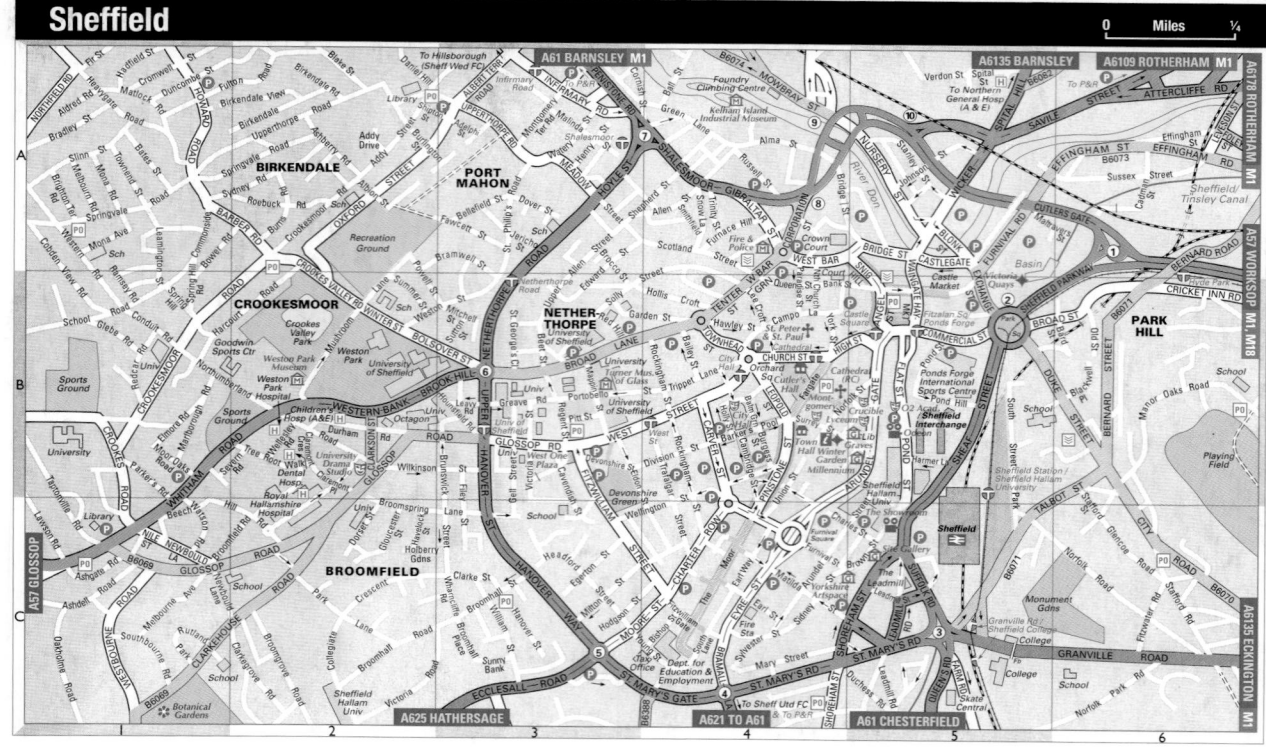

Southampton

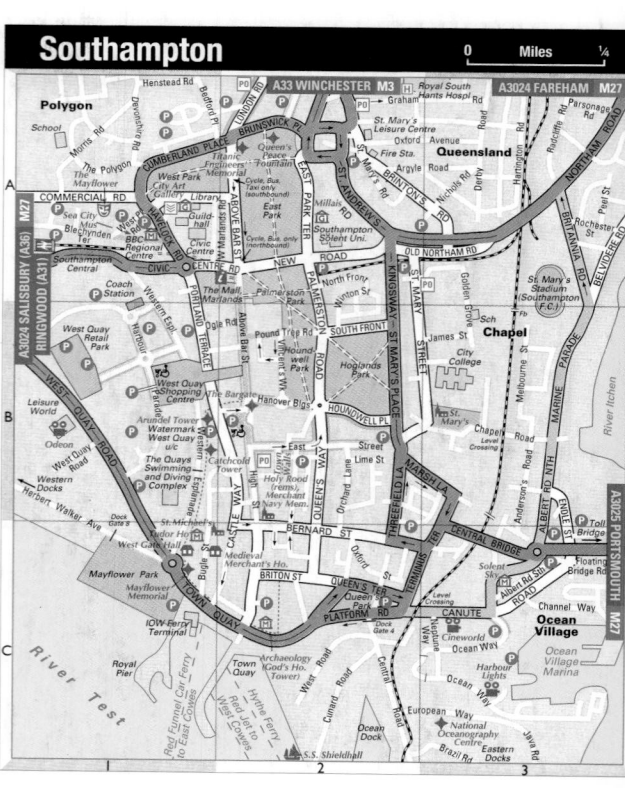

Southend page 69 ● Stirling page 278 ● Stoke page 168 ● Stratford-upon-Avon page 118 ● Sunderland page 243 ● Swansea page 56 ● Swindon page 63 ● Taunton page 28 ● Telford page 132

343

Southend-on-Sea
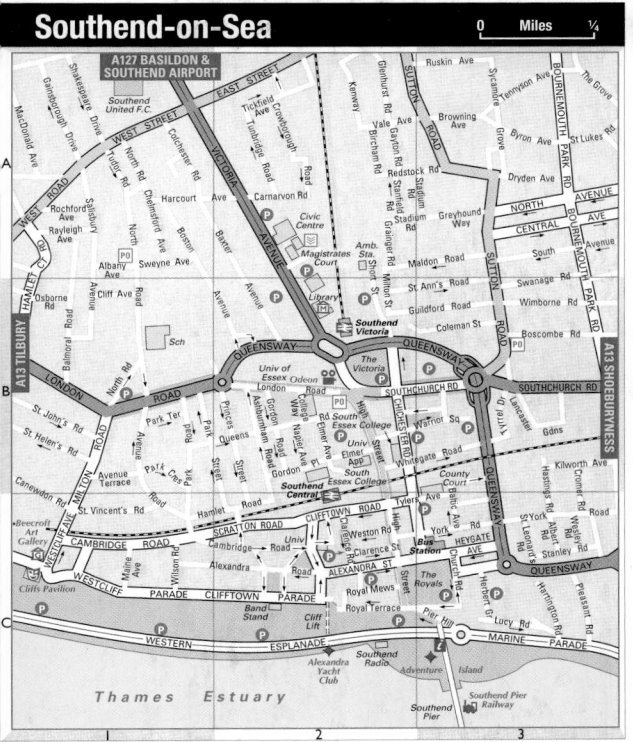

Stirling
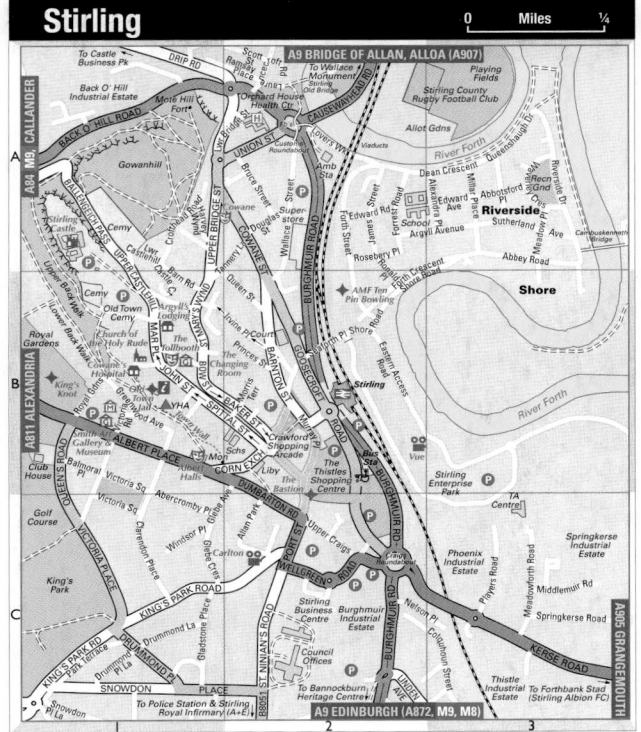

Stoke
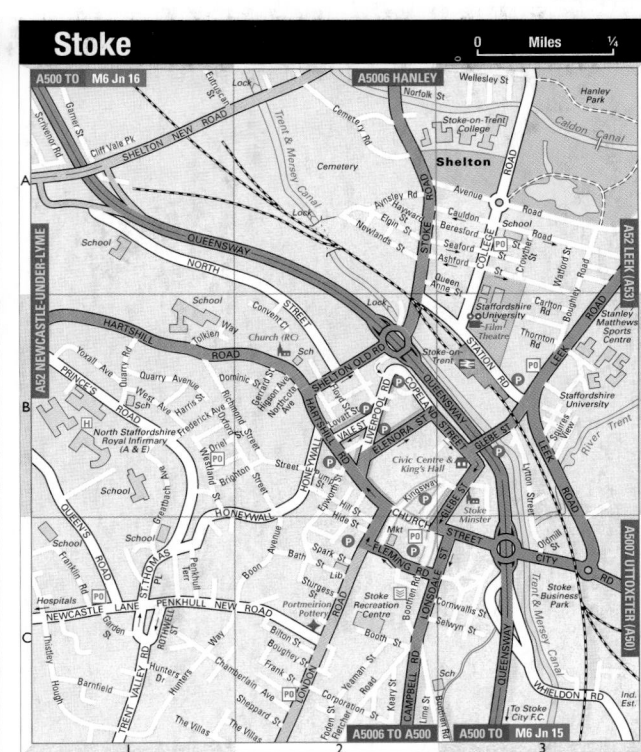

Stratford-upon-Avon
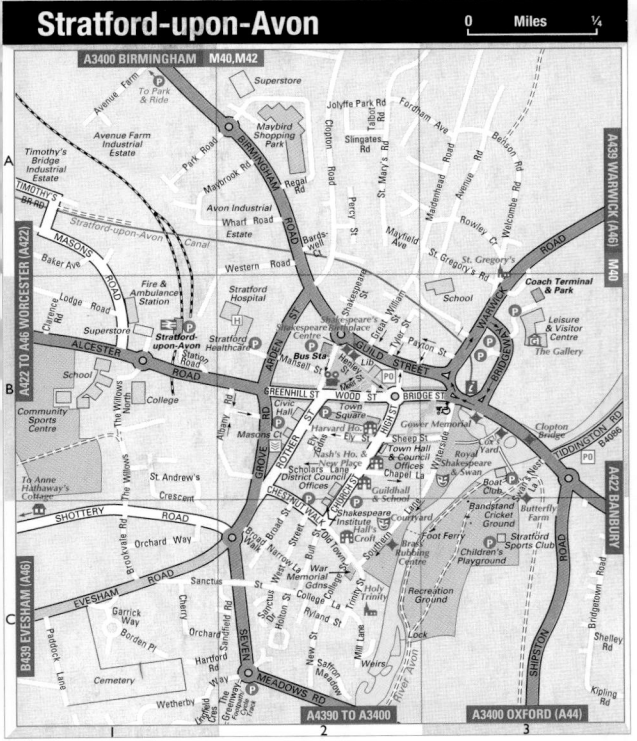

Sunderland
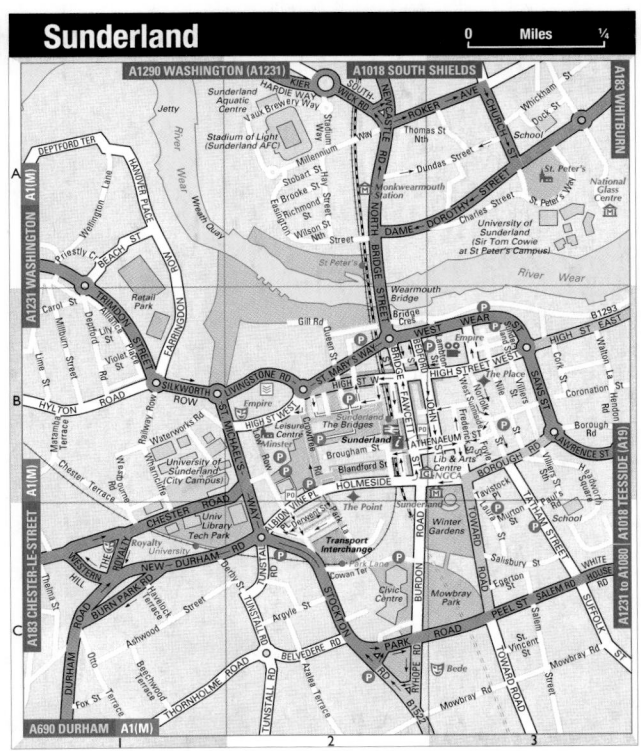

Swansea / Abertawe
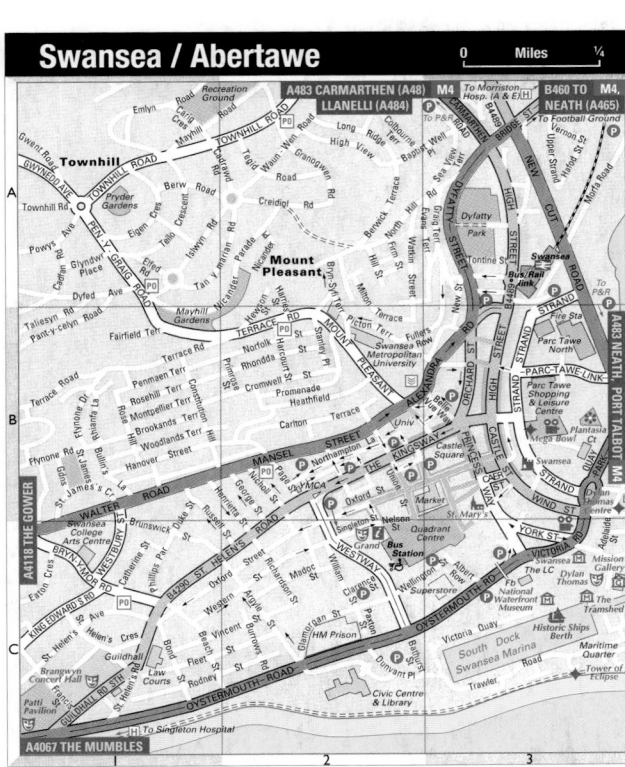

Swindon
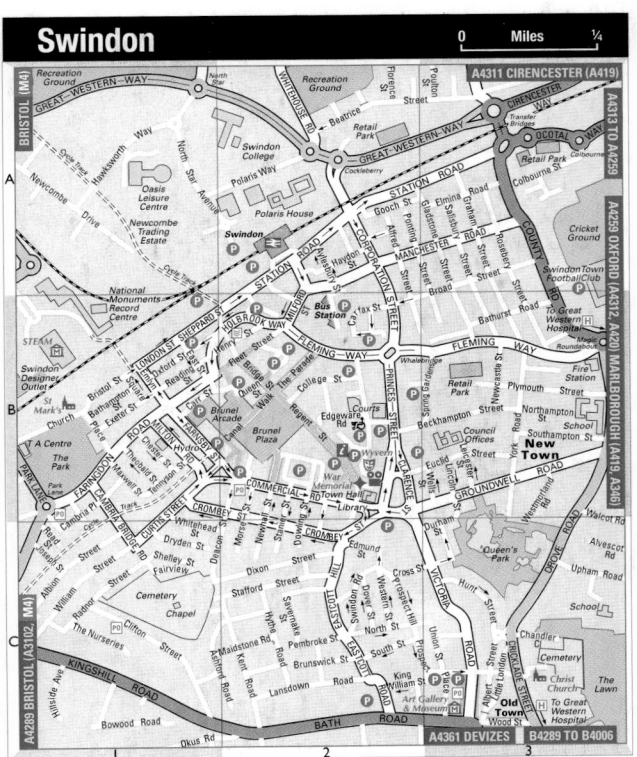

Taunton
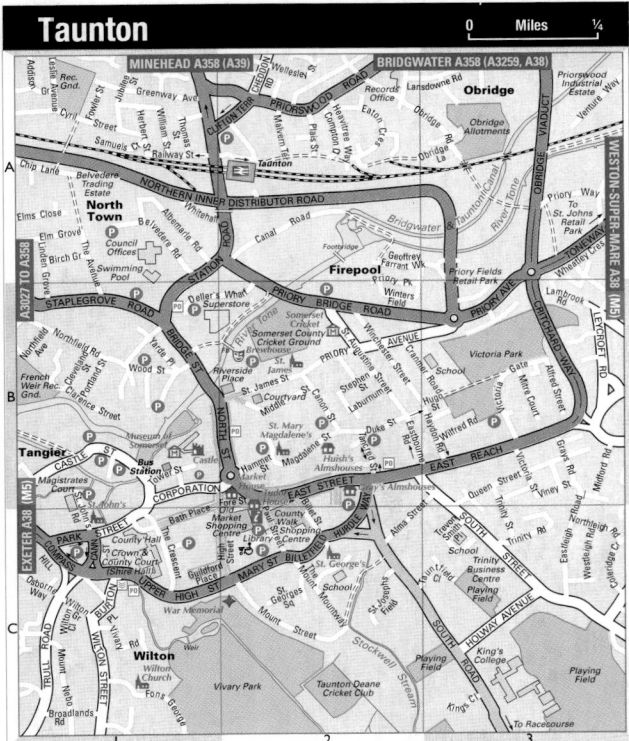

Telford
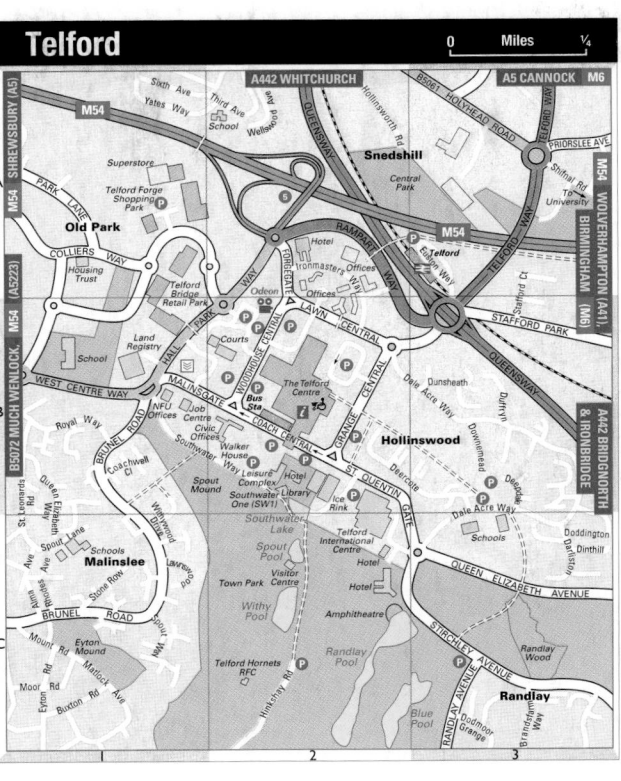

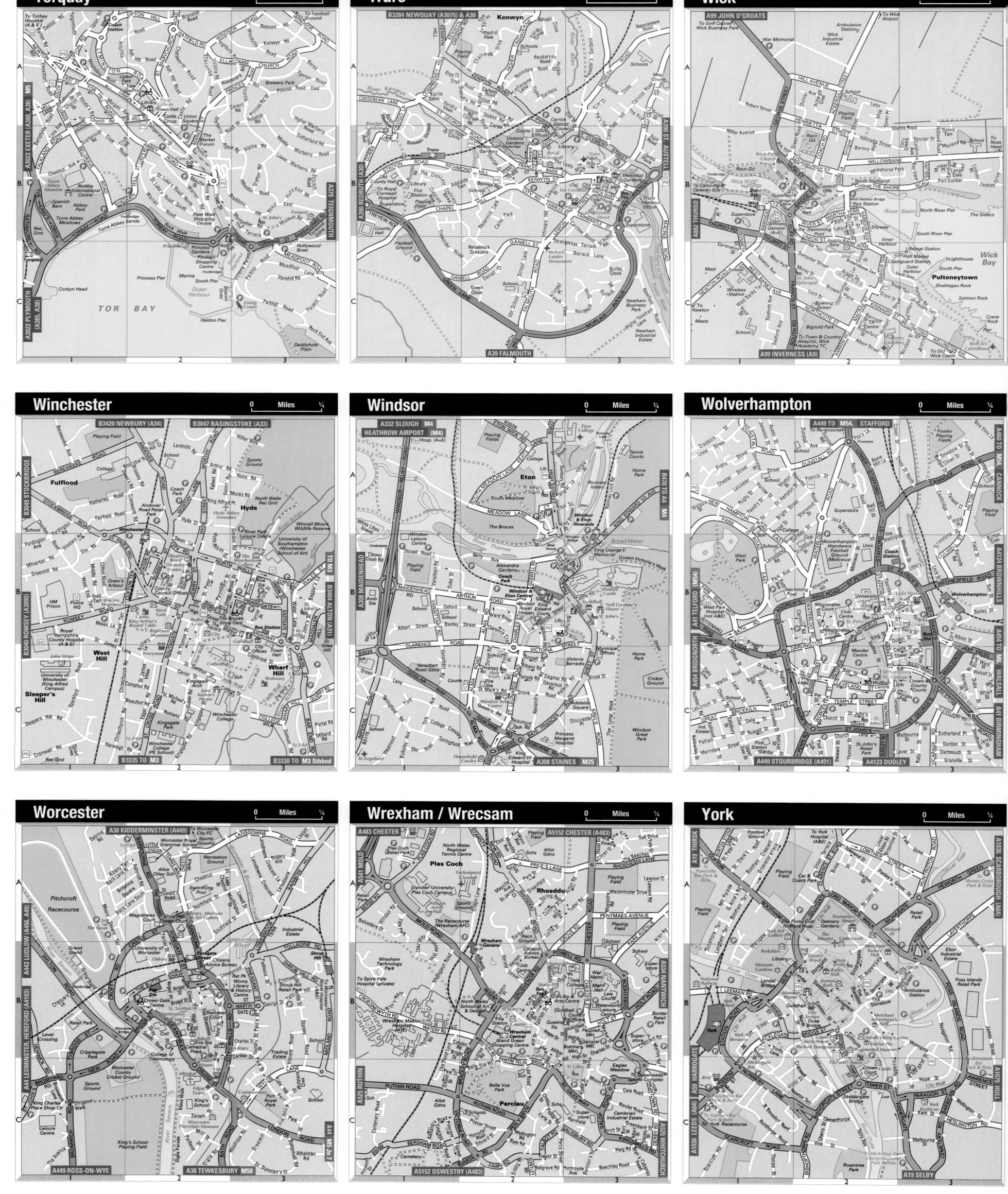

Aberdeen • Aberystwyth • Ashford • Ayr • Bangor • Barrow-in-Furness • Bath • Berwick-upon-Tweed • Birmingham 345

Town plan indexes

Aberdeen 331

Aberdeen ≷ B2
Aberdeen Grammar School A1
Academy, The B2
Albert Basin B3
Albert Quay B3
Albury Rd C1
Alford Pl B1
Art Gallery 🏛 A2
Arts Centre 🏛 A2
Back Wynd A2
Baker St A1
Beach Blvd A3
Belmont 🎦 B2
Belmont St B2
Berry St A2
Blackfriars St A2
Bloomfield Rd C1
Bon Accord Centre A2
Bon-Accord St B1/C1
Bridge St B2
Broad St A2
Bus Station B2
Car Ferry Terminal B3
Castlegate A3
Central Library A1
Chapel St B1
Cineworld 🎦 B2
College A2
College St B2
Commerce St A3
Commercial Quay B3
Community Centre A3/C1
Constitution St A3
Cotton St A3
Crown St B2
Denburn Rd A2
Devanha Gdns C2
Devanha Gdns South C2
East North St A3
Esslemont Ave A1
Ferryhill Rd C2
Ferryhill Terr C2
Fish Market B3
Fonthill Rd C1
Galleria, The B1
Gallowgate A2
George St A2
Glenbervie Rd C3
Golden Sq B1
Grampian Rd C3
Great Southern Rd C1
Guild St B2
Hardgate B1/C1
His Majesty's Theatre 🎭 A1
Holburn St C1
Hollybank Pl C1
Huntly St B1
Hutcheon St A1
Information Ctr ℹ B2
John St A2
Justice St A3
King St A2
Langstane Pl B1
Lemon Tree, The A2
Library C1
Loch St A2
Maberly St A1
Marischal College 🏛 A2
Maritime Mus & Provost Ross's Ho 🏛 B2
Market St B2/B3
Menzies Rd C3
Mercat Cross ✦ A3
Millburn St C2
Miller St A3
Market B2
Mount St A1
Music Hall 🎭 B1
North Esp East C3
North Esp West C2
Oscar Rd C3
Palmerston Rd C2
Park St A3
Police Station ▤ A2
Polmuir Rd C2
Post Office 📮 A1/A2/A3/B1/C3
Provost Skene's Ho 🏛 A2
Queen St A2
Regent Quay B3
Regent Road B3
Robert Gordon's Coll. A2
Rose St B1
Rosemount Pl A1
Rosemount Viaduct A1
St Andrew St A2
St Andrew's Cath ✝ A3
St Mary's Cathedral ✝ B1
St Nicholas Centre A2
St Nicholas St A2
School Hill A2
Sinclair Rd C3
Skene Sq A1
Skene St B1
South College St C2
South Crown St C2
South Esp East C3
South Esp West C3
South Mount St A1
Sports Centre C3
Spring Garden A2
Springbank Terr C2
Summer St B1
Swimming Pool B1
Thistle St B1
Tolbooth 🏛 A3
Town House 🏛 A2
Trinity Centre B2
Trinity Quay B3
Union Row B1
Union Square B2
Union St B1/B2
Upper Dock B3
Upper Kirkgate A2
Victoria Bridge C3
Victoria Dock B3
Victoria Rd C3
Victoria St B2
Virginia St A3
Vue 🎦 B2
Wellington Pl B2
West North St A2
Whinhill Rd C1
Willowbank Rd C1
Windmill Brae B2
Woolmanhill Hospl H A1

Aberystwyth 331

Aberystwyth Holiday Village C2
Aberystwyth RFC C3
Aberystwyth Sta ≷ B2
Aberystwyth Town Football Ground B2
Alexandra Rd B2
Ambulance Station C3
Baker St B1
Banadl Rd B2
Bandstand A1
Bath St A2
Boat Landing Stage A1
Bvd de Saint-Brieuc C3
Bridge St B1
Bronglais Hospital H B3
Bryn-y-Mor Rd A2
Buarth Rd B2
Bus Station B2
Cae Ceredig C3
Cae Melyn A2
Cae'r-Gog B3
Cambrian St B2
Caradoc Rd B3
Caravan Site C2
Castle (Remains of) 🏰 B1
Castle St B1
Cemetery B3
Ceredigion Mus 🏛 A1
Chalybeate St B1
Cliff Terr A2
Club House A1
Commodore 🎦 A1
County Court A2
Crown Buildings B2
Dan-y-Coed A3
Dinas Terr C1
Eastgate B1
Edge-hill Rd B2
Elm Tree Ave B2
Elysian Gr A2
Felin-y-Mor Rd C1
Fifth Ave C2
Fire Station C1
Glanrafon Terr B1
Glyndŵr Rd B2
Golf Course A3
Government & Council Offices C3
Gray's Inn Rd B1
Great Darkgate St B1
Greenfield St B2
Heol-y-Bryn A2
High St B1
Infirmary Rd A2
Information Ctr ℹ B1
Iorwerth Ave B3
King St B1
Lauraplace B1
Library B1
Lifeboat Station C1
Llanbadarn Rd B3
Loveden Rd A2
Magistrates Court A1
Marina C1
Marine Terr A1
Market Hall B1
Mill St B1
Moor La B2
National Liby of Wales B3
New Promenade B1
New St B1
North Beach A1
North Parade B2
North Rd A2
Northgate St B2
Parc Natur Penglais A3
Parc-y-Llyn Retail Pk C3
Park & Ride B2
Park Ave B2
Pavillion B1
Pendinas C1
Penglais Rd B3
Penrheidol C2
Pen-y-Craig A2
Pen-yr-angor C1
Pier St B1
Plas Ave B3
Plas Helyg C2
Plascrug Ave B2/C3
Plascrug Leisure Ctr C3
Police Station ▤ C2
Poplar Row B2
Portland Rd B2
Portland St A2
Post Office 📮 B1/B3
Powell St B1
Prospect St B1
Quay Rd B1
Queen St B1
Queen's Ave A2
Queen's Rd A2
Rheidol Retail Park B2
Riverside Terr B1
St Davids Rd B3
St Michael's ⛪ B1
School of Art B2
Seaview Pl B1
South Beach B1
South Rd B1
Sports Ground B2
Spring Gdns C1
Stanley Terr B2
Swimming Pool & L Ctr C3
Superstore B2/C3
Tanybwlch Beach C1
Tennis Courts B3
Terrace Rd B1
The Bar C1
Library A2
Trefechan Bridge B1
Trefechan Rd C2
Trefor Rd A2
Trinity Rd B2
University Campus B3
University of Wales (Aberystwyth) B1
Vale of Rheidol Railway 🚂 C3
Vaynor St B2
Victoria Terr A1
Viewpoint ✦ A2
Viewpoint ✦ A3
War Memorial B1
Wharf Quay C1
Y Lanfa C1
Ystwyth Retail Park B2

Ashford 331

Albert Rd A1
Alfred Rd C3
Apsley St A1
Ashford Borough Museum 🏛 A1
Ashford Int Sta ≷ B2
Bank St A1
Barrowhill Gdns A1
Beaver Industrial Est C1
Beaver Rd C1
Beazley Ct C3
Birling Rd B3
Blue Line La A1
Bond Rd C1
Bowens Field B1
Bulleid Pl C2
Cade Rd C1
Chart Rd A1
Chichester Cl B1
Christchurch Rd B1
Chunnel Industrial Est B1
Church Rd A1
Civic Centre A2
County Square Sh Ctr A1
Court A1
Court A2
Croft Rd A3
Cudworth Rd C3
Curtis Rd C3
Dering Rd A3
Dover Pl B2
Drum La A1
East Hill A2
East St A1
Eastmead Ave B2
Edinburgh Rd A1
Elwick Rd A1
Essella Pk B3
Essella Rd B3
Fire Sta A3
Forge La A1
Francis Rd C1
George St B1
Godfrey Walk B1
Gordon Cl A3
Hardinge Rd A2
Henwood A3
Henwood Bsns Ctr A3
Henwood Ind Est A3
High St A2
Hythe Rd A3
Information Ctr ℹ A1
Jemmett Rd B1
Kent Ave A1
Library A1
Linden Rd B3
Lower Denmark Rd C1
Mabledon Ave B3
Mace Industrial Est A2
Mace La A2
Maunsell Pl C3
McArthur Glen Designer Outlet C2
Memorial Gdns A2
Mill Ct A2
Miller Cl A2
Mortimer Cl C1
New St A1
Newtown Green C3
Newtown Rd B2/C3
Norman Rd C1
North St A2
Norwood Gdns A1
Norwood St A1
Old Railway Works Industrial Estate C3
Orion Way C3
Pk Mall Shopping Ctr A1
Park Pl A1
Park St A1/A2
Pemberton Rd A3
Police Station ▤ A1
Post Office 📮 A1/A3
Providence St C2
Queen St A1
Queens Rd A2
Regents Pl A1
Riversdale Rd C1
Romney Marsh Rd B2
St John's La A2
St Mary's Church & Arts Venue ⛪ A1
Somerset Rd A2
South Stour Ave B2
Star Rd A3
Station Rd B2
Stirling Rd C2
Stour Centre, The B2
Sussex Ave A1
Tannery La A2
Technical College B2
Torrington Rd C2
Trumper Bridge B1
Tufton Rd A3
Tufton St A1
Vicarage La A2
Victoria Cres B1
Victoria Park B1
Victoria Rd B1
Victoria Way B1
Wallis Rd A3
Wellesley Rd A2
West St A1
Whitfeld Rd C1
William Rd C1
World War I Tank ✦ A1

Ayr 331

Ailsa Pl B1
Alexandra Terr A3
Allison St B2
Alloway Pk C1
Alloway Pl C1
Alloway St C2
Arran Mall C2
Arran Terr B1
Arthur St B2
Ashgrove St C2
Auld Brig B2
Auld Kirk ⛪ B2
Ayr ≷ C2
Ayr Academy B1
Ayr Central Sh Ctr C2
Ayr Harbour A1
Ayr United FC A3
Back Hawkhill Ave A3
Back Main St B2
Back Peebles St A2
Barns Cres C1
Barns Pk C1
Barns St C1
Barns Street La C1
Bath Pl B1
Bellevue Cres C1
Bellevue La C1
Beresford La C2
Beresford Terr C2
Boswell Pk B2
Britannia Pl A3
Bruce Cres B1
Burns Statue ✦ C2
Bus Sta B1
Carrick St C2
Cassillis St B1
Cathcart St B1
Charlotte St B1
Citadel Leisure Ctr B1
Citadel Pl B1
Compass Pier A1
Content Ave C3
Content St B2
Craigie Ave B3
Craigie Rd B3
Craigie Way B3
Cromwell Rd B1
Crown St A2
Dalblair Rd C2
Dam Park Sports Stadium C3
Damside A2
Dongola Rd C3
Eglinton Pl B1
Eglinton Terr B1
Elba St B2
Elmbank St A2
Esplanade B1
Euchar Rock A1
Farifield Rd C1
Fort St B1
Fothringham Rd C3
Fullarton St C1
Gaiety 🎭 C2
Garden St B2
George St B2
George's Ave A3
Glebe Cres A2
Glebe Rd A2
Gorden Terr B3
Green St A2
Green Street La A2
Hawkhill Ave A3
Hawkhill Avenue La B3
High St B2
Holmston Rd C3
Information Ctr ℹ B1
James St B3
John St B2
King St B2
Kings Ct B2
Kyle Centre C2
Kyle St C2
Library B2
Limekiln Rd A2
Limonds Wynd B2
Loudoun Hall 🏛 B2
Lymburn Pl B3
Macadam Pl B2
Main St B2
Mcadam's Monument C1
Mccall's Ave A3
Mews La B1
Mill Brae C3
Mill St C2
Mill Wynd C2
Miller Rd C1
Montgomerie Terr B1
New Bridge B2
New Bridge St B2
New Rd A2
Newmarket St B2
Newton-on-Ayr Sta ≷ A2
North Harbour St B1
North Pier A1
Odeon 🎦 C2
Oswald La A1
Park Circus C1
Park Circus La C1
Park Terr C1
Pavilion Rd C1
Peebles St A2
Philip Sq B2
Police Station ▤ B2
Post Office 📮 A2/B2
Prestwick Rd B1
Princes Ct A2
Queen St B3
Queen's Terr B1
Racecourse Rd C1
River St B2
Riverside Pl B2
Russell Dr A2
St Andrews Church ⛪ C2
St George's Rd A3
Sandgate B1
Savoy Park C1
Seabank Rd B2
Smith St C2
Somerset Rd A3
South Beach Rd B1
South Harbour St B1
South Pier A1
Station Rd C2
Strathaye Pl B2
Taylor St A2
Town Hall B2
Tryfield Pl A3
Turner's Bridge B2
Union Ave A3
Victoria Bridge C3
Victoria St B3
Viewfield Rd A3
Virginia Gdns A2
Waggon Rd A2
Walker Rd A3
Wallace Tower ✦ B2
Weaver St A2
Weir Rd A2
Wellington La C1
Wellington Sq C1
West Sanouhar Rd A3
Whitletts Rd B3
Wilson St A3
York St A1
York Street La B1

Bangor 331

Abbey Rd C2
Albert St B1
Ambrose St A3
Ambulance Station A3
Arfon Sports Hall C1
Ashley Rd B3
Bangor City Football Ground C2
Bangor Mountain B3
Bangor Station ≷ C1
Bangor University B2
Beach Rd A3
Belmont St C1
Bishop's Mill Rd C3
Boat Yard A3
Brick St B3
Buckley Rd B2
Bus Station B3
Caellepa B2
Caernarfon Rd C1
Cathedral ✝ B2
Cemetery C1
Clarence St C1
Clock Tower ✦ B3
College B2/C2
College La B2
College Rd B2
Convent La C1
Council Offices B2
Craig y Don Rd B2
Dean St B3
Deiniol Rd B2
Deiniol Shopping Ctr B2
Deiniol St B2
Edge Hill A3
Euston Rd C1
Fairview Rd A3
Farrar Rd C2
Ffordd Cynfal C1
Ffordd Elfed C3
Ffordd Islwyn A3
Ffordd y Castell C3
Ffriddoedd Rd B1
Field St B1
Fountain St A3
Friars Ave B3
Friars Rd B3
Friary (Site of) ✦ B3
Gardd Deman C1
Garth Hill A3
Garth Point A3
Garth Rd A3
Glanrafon B2
Glanrafon Hill B2
Glynne Rd B3
Golf Course B3
Golf Course C2
Gorad Rd B1
Gorsedd Circle 🏛 A2
Gwern Las C3
Gwynedd Museum & Art Gallery 🏛 B2
Heol Dewi C1
High St B3/C2
Hill St B1
Holyhead Rd B1
Hwfa Rd B1
Information Ctr ℹ B2
James St B3
Library B2
Llys Emrys A3
Lon Ogwen C1
Lon-Pobty C2
Lon-y-Felin C3
Lon-y-Glyder C1
Love La B2
Lower Penrallt Rd B2
Lower St B2
Maes Glas Sports Ctr B1
Maes-y-Dref B3
Maeshyfryd A3
Meirion La A2
Meirion Rd A2
Menai Ave B1
Menai College C1
Menai Shopping Ctr B3
Min-y-Ddol C3
Minafon B2
Mount St B3
Orme Rd A3
Parc Victoria B1
Penchwintan Rd C1
Penlon Gr B3
Penrhyn Ave A3
Pier ✦ A3
Police Station ▤ B2
Post Office 📮 B2/B3/C1/C3
Prince's Rd B2
Queen's Ave C3
Sackville Rd B2
St Paul's St B2
Seion Rd A3
Seiriol Rd A3
Siliwen Rd A2
Snowdon View B1
Station Rd C1
Strand St B3
Swimming Pool and Leisure Centre A3
Tan-y-Coed C3
Tegid Rd B3
Temple Rd B2
The Crescent B2
Theatr Gwynedd 🎭 B2
Totton Rd A3
Town Hall B2
Treflan B2
Trem Elidir C1
Upper Garth Rd A3
Victoria Ave B1
Victoria Dr B1
Victoria St B1
Vron St B2
Well St B3
West End C1
William St B3
York Pl B3

Barrow-in-Furness 331

Abbey Rd A3/B2
Adelaide St A2
Ainslie St A3
Albert St C3
Allison St B3
Anson St A2
Argyle St B3
Arthur St B3
Ashburner Way A1
Barrow Raiders RLFC B1
Barrow Station ≷ A2
Bath St A1/B2
Bedford Rd A3
Bessamer Way A1
Blake St A1/A2
Bridge Rd C1
Buccleuch Dock C3
Buccleuch Dock Rd C2/C3
Buccleuch St B2/B3
Byron St A2
Calcutta St A1
Cameron St C1
Carlton Ave A3
Cavendish Dock Rd C3
Cavendish St B2/B3
Channelside Walk B1
Channelside Haven C1
Chatsworth St A2
Cheltenham St A3
Church St C3
Clifford St B2
Clive St B1
Collingwood St B2
Cook St A2
Cornerhouse Retail Pk B2
Cornwallis St B2
Courts A2
Crellin St B3
Cross St C3
Custom House ✦ B2
Dalkeith St B2
Dalton Rd B2/C2
Derby St B3
Devonshire Dock C2
Devonshire Dock Hall B1
Dock Museum, The 🏛 B1
Drake St A2
Dryden St A2
Duke St A1/B2/C3
Duncan St B2
Dundee St C2
Dundonald St B2
Earle St C1
Emlyn St B2
Exmouth St A2
Farm St C2
Fell St B3
Fenton St B3
Ferry Rd C1
Forum, The 🎭 B2
Furness College B1
Glasgow St B3
Goldsmith St A2
Greengate St B3
Hardwick St A2
Harrison St B2
Hartington St A2
Hawke St B2
Hibbert Rd A2
High Level Bridge C2
High St B2
Hindpool Retail Park B2
Hindpool Rd B2
Holker St A2
Hollywood Ret & L Pk B1
Hood St A2
Howard St B2
Howe St B2
Information Ctr ℹ B2
Ironworks Rd A1/B1
James St B3
Jubliee Bridge C1
Keith St B2
Keyes St A2
Lancaster St A3
Lawson St B2
Library B2
Lincoln St A3
Longreins Rd A3
Lonsdale St C3
Lord St B3
Lorne Rd B3
Lyon St A2
Manchester St B2
Market B2
Market St B2
Marsh St B3
Michaelson Rd C2
Milton St A2
Monk St B2
Mount Pleasant B3
Nan Tait Centre B2
Napier St B2
Nelson St B2
North Rd B1
Open Market B2
Parade St A2
Paradise St B3
Park Ave A3
Park Dr A3
Parker St A2
Parry St A2
Peter Green Way A1
Phoenix Rd A1
Police Station ▤ B2
Portland Walk Sh Ctr B2
Post Office 📮 A3/B2
Princess Selandia ⛵ C2
Raleigh St A2
Ramsden St B3
Rawlinson St B2
Robert St B3
Rodney St B2
Rutland St A2
St Patricks Rd C1
Salthouse Rd C3
School St B2
Scott St B2
Settle St A3
Shore St C3
Sidney St B2
Silverdale St B3
Slater St B2
Smeaton St B3
Stafford St A3
Stanley Rd C1
Stark St C3
Steel St B1
Storey Sq B3
Strand C3
Superstore A1/B1/C3
Sutherland St B3
TA Centre A2
The Park A3
Thwaite St B3
Town Hall B2
Town Quay C3
Vernon St B2
Vincent St B2
Walney Rd A1
West Gate Rd A2
West View Rd A3
Westmorland St A3
Whitehead St A3
Wordsworth St A2

Bath 331

Alexandra Park C2
Alexandra Rd C2
Approach Golf Courses (Public) A1
Bath Aqua Glass 🏛 A2
Archway St C3
Assembly Rooms & Mus of Costume 🏛 A2
Avon St B2
Barton St B2
Bath Abbey ✝ B2
Bath City College B2
Bath Pavilion B3
Bath Rugby Club B3
Bath Spa Station ≷ C3
Bathwick St A3
Beckford Road A3
Beechen Cliff Rd C2
Bennett St A2
Bloomfield Ave C1
Broad Quay C2
Broad St B2
Brock St A1
Building of Bath Museum 🏛 A2
Bus Station C2
Calton Gdns C2
Calton Rd C2
Camden Cr A2
Cavendish Rd A1
Cemetery B1
Charlotte St B2
Chaucer Rd C2
Cheap St B2
Circus Mews A2
Claverton St C2
Corn St C2
Cricket Ground B3
Daniel St A3
Edward St B3
Ferry La B3
First Ave C1
Forester Ave A3
Forester Rd A3
Gays Hill A2
George St B2
Great Pulteney St B3
Green Park B1
Green Park Rd B2
Grove St B2
Guildhall 🏛 B2
Harley St A2
Hayesfield Park C1
Henrietta Gdns A3
Henrietta Mews B3
Henrietta Park B3
Henrietta Rd A3
Henrietta St B3
Henry St B2
Herschel Museum of Astronomy 🏛 B1
Holburne Museum 🏛 B3
Holloway C2
Information Ctr ℹ B2
James St West B1/B2
Jane Austen Centre 🏛 B2
Julian Rd A1
Junction Rd C1
Kingsmead L Complex B2
Kipling Ave C2
Lansdown Cr A1
Lansdown Gr A2
Lansdown Rd A2
Library B2
London Rd A3
London St A2
Lower Bristol Rd B1
Lower Oldfield Park C1
Lyncombe Hill C3
Manvers St B3
Maple Gr C1
Margaret's Hill A2
Marlborough Bldgs A1
Marlborough La B1
Midland Bridge Rd B1
Milk St B2
Milsom St B2
Monmouth St B2
Morford St A2
Museum of Bath at Work 🏛 A2
Museum of East Asian Art 🏛 A2
New King St B1
No 1 Royal Cres 🏛 A1
Norfolk Bldgs B1
Norfolk Cr B1
North Parade Rd B3
Oldfield Rd C1
Paragon A2
Pines Way B1
Podium Shopping Ctr B2
Police Station ▤ B3
Portland Pl A2
Post Office 📮 A1/A3/B2/C1/C2
Postal Museum 🏛 B2
Powlett Rd A3
Prior Park Rd C3
Pulteney Bridge ✦ B2
Pulteney Gdns B3
Pulteney Rd B3/C3
Queen Sq B2
Raby Pl B3
Recreation Ground B3
Rivers St A2
Rockliffe Ave A3
Rockliffe Rd A3
Roman Baths & Pump Room 🏛 B2
Rossiter Rd C3
Royal Ave A1
Royal Cr A1
Royal High School, The A2
Royal Victoria Park A1
Sally Lunn's House ✦ B2
St James Sq A1
St John's Rd A3
Shakespeare Ave C2
Southgate C2
South Pde B3
Sports & Leisure Ctr B3
Spring Gdns C3
Stall St B2
Stanier Rd B1
Superstore B1
Sydney Gdns A3
Sydney Pl B3
Sydney Rd B3
Theatre Royal 🎭 B2
Thermae Bath Spa ✦ B2
The Tyning C3
Thomas St A3
Union St B2
Upper Bristol Rd B1
Upper Oldfield Park C1
Victoria Art Gallery 🏛 B2
Victoria Bridge Rd B1
Walcot St B2
Wells Rd C1
Westgate Buildings B2
Westgate St B2
Weston Rd A1
Widcombe Hill C3

Berwick-upon-Tweed 331

Bank Hill B2
Barracks 🏛 A3
Bell Tower ✦ A3
Bell Tower Pl A2
Berwick Br B2
Berwick Infirmary H A3
Berwick-upon-Tweed ≷ A2
Billendean Rd C3
Blakewell Gdns B2
Blakewell St B2
Brass Bastion ✦ A3
Bridge St B3
Brucegate St A2
Castle (Remains of) 🏰 A2
Castle Terr A2
Castlegate A2
Chapel St A3
Church Rd C2
Church St B3
Court B3
Coxon's La A3
Cumberland Bastion ✦ A3
Dean Dr C2
Dock Rd C2/C3
Elizabethan Walls A2/B3
Fire Station B1
Flagstaff Park B3
Football Ground C3
Foul Ford B3
Golden Sq B2
Golf Course A3
Greenwood C1
Gunpowder Magazine ✦ B3
Hide Hill B3
High Greens A2
Holy Trinity ⛪ A3
Information Ctr ℹ A2
Kiln Hill B2
King's Mount ✦ B3
Ladywell Rd C2
Library A3
Lifeboat Station C3
Lord's Mount ✦ A3
Lovaine Terr A2
Low Greens A3
Main Guard 🏛 B3
Main St B2/C2
Maltings Art Ctr, The B3
Marygate B3
Meg's Mount ✦ A2
Middle St C3
Mill St C2
Mount Rd C2
Museum B3
Ness St B3
North Rd A2
Northumberland Ave A2
Northumberland Rd C2
Ord Dr B1
Osborne Cr C2
Osborne Rd B1
Palace Gr B3
Palace St B3
Palace St East B3
Pier Rd B3
Playing Field C1
Police Station ▤ B3
Post Office 📮 A2/B2/B2
Prince Edward Rd B2
Prior Rd C2
Quay Walls B3
Railway St A2
Ravensdowne B3
Records Office A3
Riverdene B1
Riverside Rd B2
Royal Border Br A2
Royal Tweed Br B2
Russian Gun ✦ B3
Scots Gate ✦ A2
Scott's Pl A2
Shielfield Park (Berwick Rangers FC) C1
Shielfield Terr C2
Silver St B3
Spittal Quay C3
Superstores C2
The Avenue B3
The Granary ✦ B3
The Parade A3
Tower Gdns A2
Tower Ho Pottery ✦ C2
Tower Rd C2
Town Hall B3
Turret Gdns C2
Tweed Dock B2
Tweed St A2
Tweedside Trading Est C1
Union Brae B2
Union Park Rd B2
Walkergate A3
Wallace Gr A3
War Memorial A2
War Memorial B2
Warkworth Terr A2
Well Close Sq A2
West End B2
West End Pl B1
West End Rd B1
West St B3
West St C3
Windmill Bastion ✦ B3
Woolmarket B3
Works C3

Birmingham 332

Abbey St A2
Aberdeen St A1
Acorn Gr B2
Adams St A5
Adderley St C5
Albert St B4/B5
Albion St B2
Alcester St C5
Aldgate Gr A3
Alexandra Theatre 🎭 C3
All Saint's St A2
All Saints Rd A2
Allcock St C5
Allesley St A4
Allison St C4
Alma Cr B6
Alston Rd C1
Arcadian Centre C4
Arthur St C6
Assay Office 🏛 B3
Aston Expressway A5
Aston Science Park B5
Aston St B4
Aston University B4/B5
Avenue Rd A5
BT Tower ✦ B3
Bacchus Rd A1
Bagot St B4
Banbury St B5

Barford Rd. B1
Barford St. C4
Barn St. C5
Barnwell Rd. C6
Barr St. A3
Barrack St. B5
Barwick St. B4
Bath Row. C3
Beaufort Rd. C1
Belmont Row. B5
Benson Rd. A1
Berkley St. C3
Bexhill Gr. C3
Birchall St. C5
Birmingham City FC. . .C6
Birmingham City
  Hospital (A&E) H. . . .A1
Bishopsgate St. C3
Blews St. A4
Bloomsbury St. B5
Blucher St. C3
Bordesley St. C4
Bowyer St. C5
Bradburne Way. A4
Bradford St. C5
Branston St. A3
Brearley St. A4
Brewery St. A4
Bridge St. A3
Bridge St. C3
Bridge St West. A4
Brindley Dr. B3
Broad St. C2
Broad St UGC ⛶. C2
Broadway Plaza ✦. . . .C2
Bromley St. C5
Bromsgrove St. C4
Brookfield Rd. A2
Browning St. C2
Bryant St. A1
Buckingham St. A3
Bullring. C4
Bull St. B4
Cambridge St. C3
Camden Dr. B3
Camden St. B2
Cannon St. C4
Cardigan St. B5
Carlisle St. A1
Carlyle Rd. C1
Caroline St. B3
Carver St. B2
Cato St. A6
Cattell Rd. C6
Cattells Gr. A6
Cawdor Cr. C1
Cecil St. B4
Cemetery. A2/B2
Cemetery La. A2
Ctr Link Industrial Est. .B3
Charlotte St. B3
Cheapside. C4
Chester St. A5
Children's Hospital
  (A&E) H. B4
Church St. B4
Claremont Rd. A2
Clarendon Rd. C1
Clark St. C1
Clement St. B3
Clissold St. B2
Cleveland St. C4
Coach Station. C5
College St. B2
Colmore Circus. B4
Colmore Row. B4
Commercial St. C3
Constitution Hill. B3
Convention Ctr, The. . .C3
Cope St. B2
Coplow St. B1
Corporation St. B4
Council House 🏛. B3
County Court. B4
Coveley Gr. A2
Coventry Rd. C6
Coventry St. C5
Cox St. B3
Crabtree Rd. A2
Cregoe St. C3
Crescent Ave. A2
Crescent Theatre 🎭. . .B2
Cromwell St. A6
Cromwell St. B3
Curzon St. B5
Cuthbert Rd. B1
Dale End. B4
Dart St. C6
Dartmouth Circus. . . .A4
Dartmouth Middleway A5
Dental Hospital H. . . .B4
Deritend. A6
Devon St. A6
Devonshire St. A1
Digbeth Civic Hall. . . .C4
Digbeth High St. C4
Dolman St. B6
Dover St. A1
Duchess Rd. C2
Duddeston ≥. B6
Duddeston Manor Rd. .B5
Duddeston Mill Rd. . . .B6
Duddeston Mill
  Trading Estate. B6
Dudley Rd. B1
Edgbaston Sh Ctr. C2
Edmund St. B3
Edward St. B2
Elkington St. A4
Ellen St. A3
Ellis St. C3
Erskine St. B6
Essex St. C4
Eyre St. B1
Farm Croft. A3
Farm St. A3
Fazeley St. B4/C4/C5
Felstead Way. B5
Finstall Cl. B5

Five Ways. C2
Fleet St. B3
Floodgate St. C5
Ford St. A2
Fore St. C4
Forster St. B5
Francis Rd. C2
Francis St. A4
Frankfort St. A4
Frederick St. B3
Freeth St. C1
Freightliner Terminal. .B6
Garrison La. C6
Garrison St. B6
Gas St. C3
Geach St. A4
George St. B3
George St West. B2
Gibb St. C5
Gillott Rd. B1
Gilby Rd. C1
Glover St. C5
Goode Ave. A1
Goodrick Way. A6
Gordon St. B6
Graham St. B3
Granville St. C3
Gray St. C5
Great Barr St. C5
Great Charles St. B3
Great Francis St. B6
Great Hampton Row. .A3
Great Hampton St. . . .A3
Great King St. A3
Great Lister St. A5
Great Tindal St. C2
Green La. C6
Green St. C5
Greenway St. C6
Grosvenor St West. . .A3
Guest Gr. A3
Guild Cl. C2
Guildford Dr. A4
Guthrie Cl. A3
Hagley Rd. C1
Hall St. B3
Hampton St. A3
Handsworth New Rd. .A1
Hanley St. A4
Harford St. A3
Harmer Rd. A1
Harold Rd. C1
Hatchett St. A4
Heath Mill La. C5
Heath St. A1
Heath St. B1
Heath St South. B1
Heaton St. A2
Heneage St. B5
Henrietta St. B4
Herbert Rd. C6
High St. C4
High St. B5
Hilden Rd. B5
Hill St. C3/C4
Hindlow Cl. B6
Hingeston St. B2
Hippodrome
  Theatre 🎭. C4
HM Prison. A1
Hockley Circus. A2
Hockley Hill. A3
Hockley St. A3
Holliday St. C3
Holloway Circus. C4
Holloway Head. C3
Holt St. A5
Hooper St. B1
Horse Fair. C4
Hospital St. A4
Howard St. A4
Howe St. B5
Hubert St. A5
Hunters Rd. A2
Hunters Vale. A3
Huntly Rd. C1
Hurst St. C4
Icknield Port Rd. B1
Icknield Sq. B2
Icknield St. A2/B2
Ikon Gallery 🏛. C3
Information Ctr 🅸. . . .C4
Inge St. C4
Irving St. C3
Ivy La. C5
James Watt
  Queensway. B4
Jennens Rd. B5
Jewellery Quarter ≥. .A3
Jewellery Quarter
  Museum 🏛. A3
John Bright St. C4
Keeley St. C6
Kellett Rd. B5
Kent St. C4
Kenyon St. B3
Key Hill. A2
Kilby Ave. C2
King Edwards Rd. B2
King Edwards Rd. C3
Kingston Rd. C6
Kirby Rd. A1
Ladywood Arts & L Ctr.B1
Ladywood
  Middleway. C2/C3
Ladywood Rd. C1
Lancaster St. B4
Landor St. B6
Law Courts. B3
Lawford Cl. B5
Lawley Middleway. . . .B5
Ledbury Cl. C2
Ledsam St. C2
Lees St. A1
Legge La. B3
Lennox St. A3
Library. A6/B2
Library Walk. B2
Lighthorne Ave. B2
Link St. B1
Lionel St. B3

Lister St. B5
Little Ann St. C5
Little Hall Rd. C6
Liverpool St. C5
Livery St. B3/B4
Lodge Rd. A1
Lord St. A5
Love La. A5
Loveday St. B4
Lower Dartmouth St. .C1
Lower Loveday St. . . .B4
Lower Tower St. A4
Lower Trinty St. C5
Ludgate Hill. B3
Mailbox Centre & BBC.C3
Margaret St. B3
Markby Rd. A1
Marroway St. C1
Maxstoke St. C6
Melvina Rd. B6
Meriden St. C4
Metropolitan (RC) ✝. .B4
Midland St. B6
Milk St. C5
Mill St. A5
Millennium Point. B5
Miller St. A4
Milton St. A4
Moat La. C4
Montague Rd. C1
Montague St. C5
Monument Rd. C1
Moor Street ≥. C4
Moor St Queensway. .C4
Moorsom St. A4
Morville St. C2
Mosborough Cr. A3
Moseley St. C5
Mott St. A3
Mus & Art Gallery 🏛. .B3
Musgrave Rd. A1
National Indoor
  Arena ✦. C2
National Sea Life
  Centre ✦. C2
Navigation St. C3
Nechell's Park Rd. . . .A6
Nechells Parkway. . . .B5
Nechells Pl. A6
New Bartholomew St. .C4
New Canal St. C5
New John St West. . . .A3
New Spring St. B2
New St. C4
New Street ≥. C4
New Summer St. A4
New Town Row. A4
Newhall Hill. B3
Newhall St. B3
Newton St. B4
Newtown. A4
Noel Rd. C1
Norman St. A1
Northbrook St. B1
Northwood St. B3
Norton St. A2
Old Crown House 🏛. .C5
Old Rep Theatre,
  The 🎭. C4
Old Snow Hill. B4
Oliver Rd. C1
Oliver St. A5
Osler St. C1
Oxford St. C5
Pallasades Centre. . . .C4
Palmer St. C5
Paradise Circus. C3
Paradise St. C3
Park Rd. A2
Park St. C4
Pavilions Centre. C4
Paxton Rd. A2
Peel St. A1
Penn St. B5
Pershore St. C4
Phillips St. A4
Pickford St. C5
Pinfold St. C3
Pitsford St. A2
Plough & Harrow Rd. .C1
Police Station
  🏢. A4/B1/B4/C2/C4
Pope St. B2
Portland Rd. C1
Post Office 🏤. .A3/A5/B1/
  . . . .B3/B4/B5/C2/C3/C5
Preston Rd. A1
Price St. B4
Princip St. B4
Printing House St. B4
Priory Queensway. . . .B4
Pritchett St. A4
Proctor St. A5
Queensway. B3
Radnor St. A2
Rea St. C4
Regent Pl. B3
Register Office. C1
Repertory Theatre 🎭. .C3
Reservoir Rd. A1
Richard St. A5
River St. C5
Rocky La. A5/A6
Rodney Cl. C1
Roseberry St. B2
Rotton Park St. B1
Rupert St. A5
Ruston St. C2
Ryland St. C2
St Andrew's Ind Est. . .C6
St Andrew's St. C5
St Bolton St. C5
St Chads Queensway. .B4
St Clements Rd. A6
St George's St. A3
St James Pl. B5
St Marks Cr. B2
St Martin's ♥. C4
St Paul's ♥. B3

St Paul's ♥. B3
St Paul's Sq. B3
St Philip's ✝. B4
St Stephen's St. A4
St Thomas' Peace
  Garden ❀. C3
St Vincent St. C2
Saltley Rd. A6
Sand Pits Pde. B3
Severn St. C3
Shadwell St. B4
Sheepcote St. C2
Shefford St. A4
Sherborne St. C2
Shylton's Croft. C2
Skipton Rd. C2
Smallbrook
  Queensway. C4
Smith St. A3
Snow Hill ≥. B4
Snow Hill Queensway. .B4
Soho, Benson Rd ≥. .A1
South Rd. A2
Spencer St. B3
Spring Hill. B2
Staniforth St. B4
Station St. C4
Steelhouse La. B4
Stephenson St. C4
Steward St. B2
Stirling Rd. C1
Stour St. B1
Suffolk St. C3
Summer Hill Rd. B2
Summer Hill St. B2
Summer Hill Terr. B2
Summer La. A4
Summer Row. B3
Summerfield Cr. B1
Summerfield Park. . . .B1
Sutton St. C3
Swallow St. C3
Sydney Rd. C6
Symphony Hall 🎭. . . .C3
Talbot St. A1
Temple Row. C4
Temple St. C4
Templefield St. C6
Tenby St. B3
Tenby St North. B2
Tennant St. C2/C3
The Crescent. A2
Thimble Mill La. A6
Thinktank (Science &
  Discovery) 🏛. B5
Thomas St. A4
Thorpe St. C4
Tilton Rd. C6
Tower St. A4
Town Hall 🏛. C3
Trent St. C5
Turner's Buildings. . . .A1
Unett St. A3
Union Terr. B5
Upper Trinity St. C5
Uxbridge St. A3
Vauxhall Gr. A5
Vauxhall Rd. B5
Vernon Rd. C1
Vesey St. B4
Viaduct St. B5
Victoria Sq. C3
Villa St. A3
Vittoria St. B3
Vyse St. B3
Walter St. A6
Wardlow Rd. A5
Warstone La. B2
Washington St. C3
Water St. B3
Waterworks Rd. C1
Watery La. C5
Well St. A3
Western Rd. B1
Wharf St. A3
Wheeler St. A3
Whitehouse St. A5
Whitmore St. A2
Whittall St. B4
Wholesale Market. . . .C4
Wiggin St. B1
Willes Rd. A1
Windsor Industrial Est A5
Windsor St. A5
Windsor St. B5
Winson Green Rd. . . .A1
Witton St. C6
Wolseley St. C6
Woodcock St. B5

Blackpool 332

Abingdon St. A1
Addison Cr. A3
Adelaide St. B1
Albert Rd. B2
Alfred St. B2
Ascot Rd. A3
Ashton Rd. C2
Auburn Gr. C2
Bank Hey St. B1
Banks St. A1
Beech Ave. A3
Bela Gr. C2
Belmont Ave. C2
Birley St. B1
Blackpool &
  Fleetwood Tram. . . .B1
Blackpool & The Fylde
  College. A1
Blackpool FC. C2
Blackpool North ≥. . .A2
Blackpool Tower ✦. . .B1
Blundell St. B1
Bonny St. B1
Breck Rd. C2
Bryan Rd. C2
Buchanan St. B2
Bus Station. B2
Cambridge Rd. A3

Caunce St. A2/A3
Central Dr. B1/C2
Central Pier ✦. C1
Central Pier ⛴. C1
Central Pier
  Theatre 🎭. C1
Chapel St. C1
Charles St. A2
Charnley Rd. B2
Church St. A1/A2
Clinton Ave. B2
Coach Station. . . .A2/C1
Cocker St. A1
Cocker St ⛴. A1
Coleridge Rd. A3
Collingwood Ave. A3
Comedy Carpet ✦. . . .B1
Condor Gr. C3
Cookson St. A2
Coronation St. B1
Corporation St. B1
Courts. B1
Cumberland Ave. A3
Cunliffe Rd. A3
Dale St. C1
Devonshire Rd. A3
Devonshire Sq. A3
Dickson Rd. A1
Elizabeth St. A2
Ferguson Rd. C2
Forest Gate. B3
Foxhall Rd. C1
Foxhall Sq ⛴. C1
Freckleton St. B3
George St. A2
Gloucester Ave. C3
Golden Mile, The. C1
Gorse Rd. C3
Gorton St. A2
Grand Theatre, The 🎭.B1
Granville Rd. A3
Grasmere Rd. C3
Grosvenor St. A2
Grundy Art Gallery 🏛.A1
Harvey Rd. C3
Hornby Rd. B2
Houndshill Sh Ctr. B1
Hull Rd. B1
Ibbison Ct. C1
Information Ctr 🅸. . . .A1
Kent Rd. C2
Keswick Rd. C2
King St. A2
Knox Gr. C3
Laycock Gate. A3
Layton Rd. A3
Leamington Rd. B2
Leeds Rd. B2
Leicester Rd. B2
Levens Gr. C2
Library. A1
Lifeboat Station. A1
Lincoln Rd. B2
Liverpool Rd. B2
Livingstone Rd. B2
London Rd. A3
Lune Gr. C2
Lytham Rd. C1
Madame Tussaud's
  Blackpool ✦. C1
Manchester Sq ⛴. . . .C1
Manor Rd. B3
Maple Ave. A3
Market St. B1
Marlboro Rd. C3
Mere Rd. A3
Milbourne St. A2
Newcastle Ave. B3
Newton Dr. A3
North Pier ✦. A1
North Pier ⛴. A1
North Pier Theatre 🎭.A1
Odeon 🎦. B2
Olive Gr. B3
Palatine Rd. B2
Park Rd. B2/C3
Peter St. A2
Police Station 🏢. B1
Post Office 🏤
  . . . .A1/A3/B1/B2/B3
Princess Pde. A1
Princess St. C1/C2
Promenade. A1/C1
Queen St. A1
Queen Victoria Rd. . . .C2
Raikes Pde. B2
Reads Ave. B2
Regent Rd. B2
Register Office. B2
Ribble Rd. B2
Rigby Rd. C1/C2
Ripon Rd. B3
St Albans Rd. B3
St John's Square. B1
St Ives Ave. C3
St Vincent Ave. C3
Salisbury Rd. B3
Salthouse Ave. C2
Salvation Army Ctr. . . .B2
Sands Way. C1
Sealife Centre ✦. B1
Seasiders Way. C1
Selbourne Rd. A2
Sharrow Gr. C3
Somerset Ave. C3
Springfield Rd. A1
South King St. B2
Sutton Pl. B2
Talbot Rd. A1/A2
Thornber Gr. C2
Topping St. B1
Tower ⛴. B1
Town Hall. A1
Tram Depot. C1
Tyldesley Rd. C1
Vance Rd. B1
Victoria St. B1
Victory Rd. A2
Wayman Rd. A3
Westmorland Ave. . .C2/C3

Whitegate Dr. B3
Winter Gardens
  Theatre 🎭. B1
Woodland St. B3
Woolman Rd. B2

Bournemouth 332

Ascham Rd. A3
Avenue Rd. B1
Ave Shopping Centre. .B1
Bath Rd. C2
Beacon Rd. C1
Beach Office. C1
Beechey Rd. A3
Bodorgan Rd. B2
Bourne Ave. B2
Bournemouth. A3
Bournemouth &
  Poole College. B3
Bournemouth
  Balloon ✦. C2
Bournemouth Int Ctr. .C1
Bournemouth Pier. . . .C1
Bournemouth Sta ≥. .B3
Braidley Rd. A2
Cavendish Place. A2
Cavendish Rd. A2
Central Drive. A2
Central Gdns. B2
Christchurch Rd. B3
Cliff Lift. C1/C3
Coach House Pl. A3
Coach Station. A3
Commercial Rd. B1
Cotlands Rd. B3
Courts. B2
Cranborne Rd. C1
Cricket Ground. A1
Cumnor Rd. B2
Dean Park. B2
Dean Park Cr. B2
Dean Park Rd. B2
Durrant Rd. A1
East Overcliff Dr. C3
Exeter Cr. C1
Exeter La. C1
Exeter Rd. C1
Gervis Place. B1
Gervis Rd. C3
Glen Fern Rd. B2
Golf Club. A3
Grove Rd. B3
Hinton Rd. C2
Holdenhurst Rd. B3
Horseshoe Common . .B2
Nuffield Health
  Bournemouth Hospital
  (private) H. A2
Information Ctr 🅸. . . .C2
Lansdowne ♥. B3
Lansdowne Rd. B3
Lorne Park Rd. B2
Lower Gdns. B1/C2
Madeira Rd. B2
Methuen Rd. A3
Meyrick Park. A1
Meyrick Rd. B3
Milton Rd. A2
Oceanarium ✦. C2
Odeon Cinema 🎦. . . .B2
Old Christchurch Rd. .B2
Ophir Rd. A3
Oxford Rd. B3
Park Rd. A3
Parsonage Rd. B2
Pavilion 🎭. C2
Pier Approach. C2
Pier Theatre 🎭. C2
Police Station 🏢. . .A3/B3
Portchester Rd. A3
Post Office 🏤. . . .B1/B3
Priory Rd. C1
Quadrant, The. C1
Recreation Ground . . .A1
Richmond Gardens
  Shopping Centre. . . .B2
Richmond Hill Rd. B2
Russell-Cotes Art Gallery
  & Museum 🏛. C2
Russell-Cotes Rd. C2
St Anthony's Rd. A2
St Michael's Rd. C1
St Paul's ♥. A3
St Paul's La. A3
St Paul's Rd. B3
St Peter's ✝. B2
St Peter's Rd. B2
St Stephen's Rd. . . .B1/B2
St Swithun's ♥. B3
St Swithun's Rd. B3
St Swithun's Rd South. .B3
St Valerie Rd. A2
St Winifred's Rd. A2
Stafford Rd. B3
Terrace Rd. B1
The Square. B1
The Triangle. B1
Town Hall. B1
Tregonwell Rd. B1
Trinity Rd. B2
Undercliff Drive. C3
Upper Hinton Rd. B2
Upper Terr Rd. C1
Wellington Rd. A2/A3
Wessex Way. . . .A3/B1/B2
West Cliff Promenade. .C1
West Hill Rd. C1
West Undercliff Prom. .C1
Westover Rd. B2
Wimborne Rd. A2
Wootton Mount. B2
Wychwood Dr. A1
Yelverton Rd. B2
York Rd. B3
Zig-Zag Walks. C1/C3

Bradford 332

Alhambra 🎭. B1
Back Ashgrove. B1
Barkerend Rd. B1
Barnard St. C3
Barry St. C1
Bolling Rd. C3
Bolton Rd. B1
Bowland St. A1
Bradford 1 🎦. B2
Bradford College. C1
Bradford Forster
  Sq ≥. A2
Bradford
  Interchange ≥. B2
Bradford Playhouse 🎭.C3
Bridge St. B2
Britannia St. B2
Burnett St. B2
Bus Station. B2
Butler St West. B1
Caledonia St. C2
Canal Rd. A2
Carlton St. B1
Cathedral ✝. B2
Centenary Sq. B2
Chapel St. B2
Cheapside. B2
Church Bank. B2
Cineworld 🎦. A2
City Hall 🏛. B2
City Rd. A1
Claremont. C1
Colour Museum 🏛. . . .C1
Croft St. B2
Crown Court. B2
Darfield St. A1
Darley St. B2
Drewton Rd. A1
Drummond Trading
  Estate. C1
Dryden St. B3
Dyson St. A1
Easby Rd. C1
East Parade. B2
Eldon Pl. A1
Filey St. B3
Forster Square Ret Pk.A2
Gallery II 🏛. A2
Garnett St. B3
Godwin St. B2
Gracechurch St. A1
Grattan Rd. B1
Great Horton Rd. . .B1/B2
Grove Terr. B1
Hall Ings. B2
Hall La. C3
Hallfield Rd. A1
Hammstrasse. A2
Harris St. B3
Holdsworth St. A2
Ice Rink ✦. B2
Impressions 🏛. B2
Information Ctr 🅸. . . .B2
Ivegate. B2
Inland Revenue. A2
Jacob's Well. C2
James St. B2
John St. A2
Kirkgate. B2
Kirkgate Centre. B2
Laisteridge La. C1
Leeds Rd. B3
Library. B1/B2
Listerhills Rd. B1
Little Horton La. C1
Little Horton Gn. C1
Longside La. B1
Lower Kirkgate. B2
Lumb La. A1
Magistrates Court. . . .B2
Manchester Rd. C2
Manningham La. A1
Manor Row. B2
Market. B2
Market St. B2
Melbourne Place. C1
Midland Rd. A1
Mill La. C2
Morley St. C1
Mus & Art Gallery 🏛. .B3
Nelson St. B2/C2
Nesfield St. A1
New Otley Rd. B3
Norcroft St. B1
North Parade. B2
North St. A2
North Wing. A2
Oastler Shopping Ctr. .A2
Otley Rd. B3
Park Ave. C1
Park La. C1
Park Rd. C2
Parma St. C2
Peace Museum 🏛. . . .B2
Peckover St. B2
Piccadilly. B2
Police Station 🏢. . .B2/C2
Post Office 🏤
  . . . .A2/B1/B2/C3
Princes Way. B2
Prospect St. C1
Radwell Drive. C1
Rawson Rd. A1
Rebecca St. A1
Richmond Rd. C1
Russell St. C1
St George's Hall 🎭. . . .B2
St Lukes Hospital H. . .C1
St Mary's. A1
Shipley Airedale
  Rd. A3/B3
Simes St. A1
Smith St. B1
Spring Mill St. C1
Stott Hill. B2
Sunbridge Rd. . .A1/B1/B2
The Leisure Exchange.B3

Theatre in the Mill 🎭. .B1
Thornton Rd. A1/B1
Trafalgar St. A2
Trinity Rd. C1
Tumbling Hill St. B1
Tyrrel St. B2
Univ of Bradford. .B1/C1
Usher St. C3
Valley Rd. A2
Vicar La. B2
Wakefield Rd. C3
Wapping Rd. B3
Westgate. A1
White Abbey Rd. A1
Wigan St. A1
Wilton St. B1
Wood St. A1
Wool Exchange 🏛. . . .B2
Worthington St. A1

Brighton 332

Addison Rd. A1
Albert Rd. B2
Albion Hill. B3
Albion St. B3
Ann St. A3
Baker St. A3
Black Lion St. C2
Brighton 🎦. B2
Brighton Centre 🏛. . . .C2
Brighton Fishing
  Museum 🏛. C2
Brighton Pier
  (Palace Pier) ✦. C3
Brighton Wheel ✦. . . .C3
Broad St. C3
Buckingham Pl. A1
Buckingham Rd. B2
Cannon Pl. C1
Carlton Hill. B3
Chatham Pl. A1
Cheapside. A3
Church St. B2
Churchill Sq Sh Ctr. . .B2
Clifton Hill. B1
Clifton Pl. B1
Clifton Rd. B1
Clifton St. B1
Clifton Terr. B1
Clock Tower. B2
Coach Station. C3
Clyde Rd. A3
Coach Park. C3
Compton Ave. A2
Davigdor Rd. A1
Denmark Terr. B1
Ditchling Rd. A3
Dome 🎭. B2
Duke St. B2
Duke's La. C2
Dyke Rd. A1/B2
East St. C2
Edward St. B3
Elmore Rd. B3
Frederick St. B2
Gardner St. B2
Gloucester Pl. B3
Gloucester Rd. B2
Goldsmid Rd. A1
Grand Junction Rd. . . .C2
Grand Pde. B3
Grove Hill. B3
Guildford St. B2
Hampton Pl. B1
Hanover Terr. A3
High St. C3
Highdown Rd. A1
Information Ctr 🅸. . . .C2
John St. B3
Kemp St. B2
Kensington Pl. B2
Kings Rd. C1
Law Courts. B3
Lewes Rd. A3
Library. B2
London Rd. A3
Madeira Dr. C3
Marine Pde. C3
Middle St. C2
Montpelier Pl. B1
Montpelier Rd. B1
Montpelier St. B1
Mus & Art Gallery 🏛. .B3
New England Rd. A2
New England St. A2
New Rd. B2
Nizells Ave. A1
Norfolk Rd. B1
Norfolk Terr. B1
North Rd. B2
North St. C2
Odeon 🎦. C2
Old Shoreham Rd. . . .A1
Old Steine. C3
Osmond Rd. A1
Over St. B2
Oxford St. A3
Park Crescent Terr. . . .A3
Phoenix Art Gallery 🏛.B3
Phoenix Rise. A3
Police Station 🏢. . .B2/C2
Post Office 🏤
  . . . .A1/A2/A3/B1/B2/C3
Preston Rd. A2
Preston St. B1
Prestonville Rd. A1
Queen's Rd. B2
Regency Sq. C1
Regent St. B2
Richmomd Pl. B3
Richmond St. B3
Richmond Terr. A3
Rose Hill Terr. A3
Royal Alexandra
  Hospital H. B1
Royal Pavilion 🏛. B2
St Bartholomew's 🏛. .B2
St James's St. C3
St Nicholas Rd. B2

St Nicholas' ♥. B2
St Peter's ✝. A3
Sea Life Centre ✦. . . .C3
Shaftesbury Rd. A3
Ship St. C2
Sillwood Rd. B1
Sillwood St. B1
Southover St. A3
Spring Gdns. B2
Stanford Rd. A1
Stanley Rd. A3
Surrey St. B2
Sussex St. B3
Sussex Terr. B3
Swimming Pool. B3
Sydney St. B3
Temple Gdns. A1
Terminus Rd. A2
The Lanes. C2
Theatre Royal 🎭. B2
Tidy St. B3
Town Hall. C2
Toy & Model Mus 🏛. .A2
Trafalgar St. A2
Union Rd. A3
University of Brighton.A3
Upper Lewes Rd. A3
Upper North St. B1
Viaduct Rd. A3
Victoria Gdns. B3
Victoria Rd. B1
Volk's Electric
  Railway ✦. C3
West Pier (derelict). . .C1
West St. C2
Western Rd. B1
Whitecross St. B2
York Ave. B1
York Pl. B3

Bristol 332

Acramans Rd. C4
Albert Rd. C6
Alfred Hill. A4
All Saint's St. A4
All Saints' ♥. B4
Allington Rd. C4
Alpha Rd. C5
Ambra Vale. B1
Ambra Vale East. B2
Ambrose Rd. B1
Amphitheatre. C3
Anchor Rd. B3
Anvil St. B6
Architecture Ctr ✦. . . .A3
Argyle Pl. B1
Arlington Villas,
  The ✦. A2
Arnolfini Arts Centre,
  The ✦. B4
Art Gallery 🏛. A3
Ashton Gate Rd. C1
Ashton Rd. C1
at-Bristol ✦. B3
Avon Bridge. C1
Avon Cr. C1
Avon St. B5
Baldwin St. B4
Baltic Wharf. C2
Baltic Wharf L Ctr &
  Caravan Pk ♣. C2
Baltic Wharf Marina . .C2
Barossa Pl. C3
Barton Manor. B6
Barton Rd. B6
Barton Vale. B6
Bath Rd. C6
Bathurst Basin. C4
Bathurst Parade. C4
Beauley Rd. C3
Bedminster Bridge. . . .C5
Bedminster Parade. . . .C4
Bellevue. B2
Bellevue Cr. B2
Bellevue Rd. C6
Berkeley Pl. A2
Berkeley Sq. A3
Birch Rd. C3
Blackfriars. A4
Bond St. A5
Braggs La. B6
Brandon Hill. B3
Brandon Steep. B3
Bristol Bridge. B5
Bristol Cath (CE) ✝. . .B3
Bristol Eye Hospital
  (A&E) H. A4
Bristol Grammar
  School. A3
Bristol Harbour
  Railway ✦. C3
Bristol Royal Children's
  Hospital H. A4
Bristol Royal Infirmary
  (A&E) H. A4
Bristol Temple Meads
  Station ≥. B6
Broad Plain. B6
Broad Quay. B4
Broad St. A4
Broad Weir. A5
Broadcasting House . .A3
Broadmead. A5
Brunel Way. C1
Brunswick Sq. A5
Burton Cl. C5
Bus Station. A4
Butts Rd. B3
Cabot Circus. A5
Cabot Tower ✦. B3
Caledonia Pl. A1
Callowhill Ct. A5
Cambridge St. C6
Camden Rd. C2
Camp Rd. A1
Canada Way. C2
Cannon St. A4
Canon's Rd. B3/B4
Canon's Way. B3
Cantock's Cl. A3

Canynge Rd A1
Canynge Sq A1
Castle Park A5
Castle St A5
Catherine Meade St C4
Cattle Market Rd C6
Central Library B3
Charles Pl B1
Charlotte St B3
Charlotte St South B3
Chatterton House B5
Chatterton Sq C5
Chatterton St C5
Cheese La B5
Christchurch A4
Christchurch Rd A1
Christmas Steps ✦ A4
Church La B2/B5
Church St B5
City Museum A3
City of Bristol College B3
Clare St B4
Clarence Rd C5
Cliff Rd C1
Clift House Rd C1
Clifton Cath (RC) † A2
Clifton Down A1
Clifton Down Rd A1
Clifton Hill B2
Clifton Park A1/A2
Clifton Park Rd A1
Clifton Rd A2
Cliftonwood Cr B2
Cliftonwood Rd B2
Cliftonwood Terr B2
Clifton Vale B1
Cobblestone Mews A1
College Green B3
College Rd A1
College St B3
Colston Almshouses A4
Colston Ave B4
Colston Hall B4
Colston Parade C5
Colston St A4
Commercial Rd C4
Constitution Hill B2
Cooperage La C2
Corn St B4
Cornwallis Ave B1
Cornwallis Cr B1
Coronation Rd C2/C4
Council House B3
Counterslip B5
Courts A4
Create Centre, The ✦ C1
Crosby Row B2
Culver St B3
Cumberland Basin C1
Cumberland Cl C2
Cumberland Rd C2/C3
David St A6
Dean La C4
Deanery Rd B3
Denmark St B4
Dowry Sq B1
Eaton Cr A2
Elmdale Rd A3
Elton Rd A3
Eugene St A4/A6
Exchange, The and St Nicholas' Mkts B4
Fairfax St A4
Fire Station B5
Floating Harbour C3
Foster Almshouses A4
Frayne Rd C1
Frederick Pl A2
Freeland Pl B1
Frogmore St B3
Fry's Hill B2
Gas La B6
Gasferry Rd C3
General Hospital C4
Georgian House B3
Glendale B1
Glentworth Rd B2
Gloucester St A1
Goldney Hall B2
Goldney Rd B1
Gordon Rd A2
Granby Hill B1
Grange Rd A1
Great Ann St A6
Great George St A6/B3
Great George Rd B3
Great Western Way B6
Green St North B1
Green St South B1
Greenay Bush La C2
Greenbank Rd C2
Greville Smyth Park C1
Guildhall A4
Guinea St C4
Hamilton Rd C3
Hanbury Rd A2
Hanover Pl C2
Harbour Way B3
Harley Pl A1
Haymarket A5
Hensman's Hill B1
High St B4
Highbury Villas A3
Hill St B3
Hill St C6
Hippodrome B4
Hopechapel Hill B1
Horfield Rd A4
Horton St B6
Host St A4
Hotwell Rd B1/B2
Houlton St A6
Howard Rd C3
IMAX Cinema B4
Information Ctr B4
Islington Rd C3
Jacob St A5/A6
Jacob's Wells Rd B2
John Carr's Terr B2
John Wesley's Chapel A5
Joy Hill B1
Jubilee St B6
Kensington Pl A2
Kilkenny St B6
King St B4
Kingsland Rd B6
Kingston Rd C3
Lamb St A6
Lansdown Rd A2
Lawford St A6
Lawfords Gate A6
Leighton Rd C3
Lewins Mead A4
Lime Rd C2
Little Ann St A6
Little Caroline Pl B1
Little George St A6
Little King St B4
Litfield Rd A1
Llandoger Trow B4
Lloyds' Building, The C3
Lodge St A4
Lord Mayor's Chapel, The B4
Lower Castle St A5
Lower Church La A4
Lower Clifton Hill B2
Lower Guinea St C4
Lower Lamb St B3
Lower Maudlin St A4
Lower Park Rd A4
Lower Sidney St C2
Lucky La C4
Lydstep Terr C3
Mall (Galleries Shopping Centre), The A5
Manilla Rd A1
Mardyke Ferry Rd C2
Maritime Heritage Centre B3
Marlborough Hill A4
Marlborough St A4
Marsh St B4
Mead St C5
Merchant Dock B2
Merchant Seamen's Almshouses B4
Merchant St A5
Merchants Rd A1
Merchants Rd C1
Meridian Pl A2
Meridian Vale A2
Merrywood Rd C3
Midland Rd A6
Milford St C3
Millennium Sq B3
Mitchell La B5
Mortimer Rd A1
M Shed C4
Murray Rd C4
Myrtle Rd A3
Narrow Plain B5
Narrow Quay B4
Nelson St A4
New Charlotte St C4
New Kingsley Rd B6
New Queen St C5
New St A6
Newgate A5
Newton St A6
Norland Rd A1
North St C2
O2 Academy B3
Oakfield Gr A2
Oakfield Pl A2
Oakfield Rd A2
Old Bread St B6
Old Market St A6
Old Park Hill A4
Oldfield Rd B1
Orchard Ave B4
Orchard La B4
Orchard St B4
Osbourne Rd C3
Oxford St B6
Park Pl A2
Park Rd C3
Park Row A3
Park St A3
Passage St B5
Pembroke Gr A2
Pembroke Rd A2
Pembroke Rd C3
Pembroke St A5
Penn St A5
Pennywell Rd A6
Percival Rd A1
Pero's Bridge B4
Perry Rd A4
Pip & Jay A5
Plimsoll Bridge B1
Police Sta A4/A6
Polygon Rd B1
Portland St A1
Portwall La B5
Post Office A1/A3/A4/A5/A6/B1/B4/C4/C5
Prewett St C5
Prince St B4
Prince St Bridge C4
Princess St C5
Princess Victoria St B1
Priory Rd A3
Pump La C5
QEH Theatre A2
Queen Charlotte St B4
Quakers Friars A5
Quay St A4
Queen Elizabeth Hospital School B2
Queen Sq B4
Queen St A5
Queen's Ave A3
Queen's Parade B3
Queen's Rd A2/A3
Raleigh Rd C2
Randall Rd B2
Redcliffe Backs B5
Redcliffe Bridge B4
Redcliffe Hill C5
Redcliffe Parade C4
Redcliffe St B5
Redcliffe Way B5
Redcross St A6
Redgrave Theatre A1
Red Lodge A4
Regent St B1
Richmond Hill A2
Richmond Hill Ave A2
Richmond La A2
Richmond Park Rd A2
Richmond St C6
Richmond Terr A2
River St A6
Rownham Mead B2
Royal Fort Rd A3
Royal Park A2
Royal West of England Academy A3
Royal York Cr B1
Royal York Villas B1
Rupert St A4
Russ St B6
St Andrew's Walk B2
St George's B3
St George's Rd B3
St James A4
St John's A4
St John's Rd C4
St Luke's Rd C5
St Mary Redcliffe C5
St Mary's Hospital A3
St Matthias Park A6
St Michael's Hill A3
St Michael's Hospl A4
St Michael's Park A3
St Nicholas St B4
St Paul St A5
St Paul's Rd A2
St Peter's (ruin) A5
St Philip's Bridge B5
St Philips Rd A6
St Stephen's B4
St Stephen's St B4
St Thomas St B5
St Thomas the Martyr B5
Sandford Rd B1
Sargent St C5
Saville Pl B1
Ship La C5
Showcase Cinema de Lux A5
Silver St A4
Sion Hill A1
Small St A4
Smeaton Rd C1
Somerset Sq C5
Somerset St C5
Southernhay Ave B2
Southville Rd C4
Spike Island Artspace C2
Spring St C5
SS Great Britain and The Matthew B2
Stackpool Rd C3
Staight St B6
Stillhouse La C4
Stracey Rd C2
Sydney Row C2
Tankard's Cl A3
Temple Back B5
Temple Boulevard B5
Temple Bridge B5
Temple Church B5
Temple Circus B5
Temple Gate C5
Temple St B5
Temple Way B5
Terrell St A4
The Arcade A5
The Fosseway A2
The Grove B4
The Horsefair A5
The Mall A1
Theatre Royal B4
Thekla The B4
Thomas La B5
Three Kings of Cologne A4
Three Queens La B5
Tobacco Factory, The C2
Tower Hill B5
Tower La A4
Trenchard St A4
Triangle South A3
Triangle West A3
Trinity Rd A6
Trinity St A6
Tyndall Ave A3
Union St A5
Union St B6
Unity St A6
Unity St B3
University of Bristol A3
University Rd A3
Upper Maudlin St A4
Upper Perry Hill C3
Upper Byron Pl A3
Upton Rd C2
Valentine Bridge B6
Victoria Gr C5
Victoria Rd C6
Victoria Rooms A2
Victoria Sq A2
Victoria St B5
Vyvyan Rd A1
Vyvyan Terr A1
Wade St A6
Walter St C2
Wapping Rd C4
Water La B5
Waterloo Rd A6
Waterloo St A1
Waterloo St A6
Watershed Media Centre ✦ B4
Welling Terr B1
Welsh Back B4
West Mall A1
West St A6
Westfield Pl A1
Wetherell Pl A2
Whitehouse Pl C5
Whitehouse St C5
Whiteladies Rd A2
Whitson St A4
William St C5
Willway St C5
Windsor Pl B1
Windsor Terr B1
Wine St A4
Woodland Rise A3
Woodland Rd A3
Worcester Rd A1
Worcester Terr A1
YHA B4
York Gdns B1
York Pl A2
York Rd C5

Bury St Edmunds 332

Abbey Gardens B3
Abbey Gate B3
Abbeygate St B2
Albert Cr B1
Albert St B1
Ambulance Sta C1
Angel Hill B2
Angel La B2
Anglian Lane A1
Arc Shopping Centre B2
Athenaeum C2
Baker's La C3
Barwell Rd B3
Beetons Way A1
Bishops Rd B2
Bloomfield St B2
Bridewell La C2
Bullen Cl C1
Bury St Edmunds ≷ A2
Bury St Edmunds County Upper School A1
Bury St Edmunds L Ctr B1
Bury Town FC B3
Bus Station B2
Butter Mkt B2
Cannon St B2
Castle Rd C1
Cemetery C1
Chalk Rd (N) B1
Chalk Rd (S) B1
Church Row B2
Churchgate St C2
Cineworld B1
Citizens Advice Bureau B2
College St C2
Compiegne Way A3
Corn Exchange, The B2
Cornfield Rd B1
Cotton Lane B3
Courts B2
Covent Garden C2
Crown St C3
Cullum Rd C2
Eastern Way A3
Eastgate St B3
Enterprise Bsns Park A2
Etna Rd A2
Eyre Cl C2
Fire Station B1
Friar's Lane C2
Gage Cl A1
Garland St B2
Greene King Brewery C3
Grove Park B1
Grove Rd B1
Guildhall C2
Guildhall St C2
Hatter St C2
High Baxter St B2
Honey Hill C3
Hospital Rd C1/C2
Ickworth Dr C1
Information Ctr B2
Ipswich St A2
King Edward VI Sch A1
King's Rd C1/B2
Library B2
Long Brackland A2
Looms La B2
Lower Baxter St B2
Malthouse La A2
Maynewater La C3
Mill Rd C1
Mill Rd (South) C1
Minden Close B3
Moyses Hall B2
Mustow St B3
Norman Tower C3
Northgate Ave A2
Northgate St B2
Nutshell, The B2
Osier Rd A2
Out Northgate A2
Out Risbygate B1
Out Westgate C2
Parkway B1/C2
Peckham St B2
Petticoat La C1
Phoenix Day Hospl C1
Pinners Way C1
Police Station C3
Post Office B2/B3
Pump La B2
Queen's Rd B1
Raingate St C3
Raynham Rd A1
Retail Park C2
Risbygate St B1/B2
Robert Boby Way C2
St Andrew's St North B2
St Andrew's St South B2
St Botolph's La C3
St Edmunds Hospital (private) C3
St Edmund's C2
St Edmund's Abbey (Remains) ✦ B3
St Edmundsbury † C3
St John's St B2
St Marys C3
School Hall La B2
Shillitoe Cl C1
Shire Halls & Magistrates Ct C3
South Cl C1
Southgate St C3
Sparhawk St C3
Spring Lane B1
Springfield Rd B1
Station Hill A2
Swan La C3
Tayfen Rd B2
The Vinefields B3
Theatre Royal C3
Thingoe Hill A2
Victoria St B1
War Memorial ✦ C1
Well St B2
West Suffolk College B1
Westgarth Gdns C1
Westgate St C2
Whiting St C2
York Rd B1
York Terr B1

Cambridge 333

Abbey Rd A3
ADC A2
Anglia Ruskin Univ B3
Archaeology & Anthropology B2
Art Gallery A1
Arts Picture House B2
Arts Theatre B1
Auckland Rd A3
Bateman St C2
BBC C3
Benet St B1
Bradmore St B3
Bridge St A1
Broad St B3
Brookside C2
Brunswick Terr A3
Burleigh St B3
Bus Station B2
Butt Green A2
Cambridge Contemporary Art Gallery B1
Castle Mound A1
Castle St A1
Cemetery B3
Chesterton La A1
Christ's (Coll) B2
Christ's Lane B2
Christ's Pieces B2
City Rd B3
Clare (Coll) B1
Clarendon St B2
Coe Fen C2
Coronation St C2
Corpus Christi (Coll) B1
Council Offices C3
Cross St C3
Crusoe Bridge C1
Darwin (Coll) C1
Devonshire Rd C3
Downing (Coll) C2
Downing St B2
Earl St B2
East Rd B3
Eden St B3
Elizabeth Way A3
Elm St B2
Emery St B3
Emmanuel (Coll) B2
Emmanuel Rd B2
Emmanuel St B2
Fair St A3
Fenners Physical Education Centre C3
Fire Station B3
Fitzroy St A3
Fitzwilliam Mus C2
Fitzwilliam St C2
Folk Museum A1
Glisson Rd C3
Gonville & Caius (Coll) B1
Gonville Place C2
Grafton Centre A3
Grand Arcade B2
Gresham Rd C3
Green St B1
Guest Rd B3
Guildhall B2
Harvey Rd C3
Hills Rd C3
Hobson St B2
Hughes Hall (Coll) B3
Information Ctr B2
James St A3
Jesus (Coll) A2
Jesus Green A2
Jesus La A2
Jesus Terr B3
John St B3
Kelsey Kerridge Sports Centre B3
King St A2
King's (Coll) B1
King's Coll Chapel B1
King's Parade B1
Lammas Land Rec Gd C1
Lensfield Rd C2
Library B2
Lion Yard B2
Little St Mary's La B1
Lyndewod Rd C3
Magdalene (Coll) A1
Magdalene St A1
Maid's Causeway A3
Malcolm St A2
Market Hill B1
Market St B1
Mathematical Bridge B1
Mawson Rd C3
Midsummer Common A3
Mill La B1
Mill Rd B3
Mill St C3
Mumford B3
Napier St A3
New Square A2
Newmarket Rd A3
Newnham Rd C1
Norfolk St B3
Northampton St A1
Norwich St C2
Orchard St B2
Panton St C2
Paradise Nature Reserve C1
Paradise St B3
Park Parade A1
Park St A2
Park Terr B2
Parker St B2
Parker's Piece B2
Parkside B3
Parkside Pools B3
Parsonage St A3
Pemberton Terr C2
Pembroke (Coll) B2
Pembroke St B1
Perowne St B3
Peterhouse (Coll) C1
Petty Cury B2
Police Station B3
Post Office A1/A3/B2/B3/C1/C2/C3
Queens' (Coll) B1
Queen's La B1
Queen's Rd B1
Regent St B2
Regent Terr B2
Ridley Hall (Coll) C1
Riverside A3
Round Church, The A1
Russell St C2
St Andrew's St B2
St Benet's B1
St Catharine's (Coll) B1
St Eligius St C2
St John's (Coll) A1
St Mary's B1
St Paul's Rd C3
Saxon St C2
Scott Polar Institute & Museum C2
Sedgwick Museum B2
Sheep's Green C1
Shire Hall A1
Sidgwick Ave C1
Sidney St A2
Sidney Sussex (Coll) A2
Silver St B1
Station Rd C3
Tenison Ave C3
Tenison Rd C3
Tennis Court Rd B2
The Backs B1
The Fen Causeway C1
Thompson's La A1
Trinity (Coll) A1
Trinity Hall (Coll) B1
Trinity St B1
Trumpington Rd C2
Trumpington St B1
Union Rd C2
University Botanic Gardens C2
Victoria Ave A2
Victoria St B2
Warkworth St B3
Warkworth Terr B3
Wesley House (Coll) A2
West Rd B1
Westcott House (Coll) A2
Westminster (Coll) A1
Whipple B2
Willis Rd B3
Willow Walk A2

Canterbury 333

Artillery St B2
Barton Mill Rd A3
Beaconsfield Rd A1
Beaney The B2
Beverley Rd A1
Bingley's Island B1
Black Griffin La B1
Broad Oak Rd A2
Broad St B2
Brymore Rd A3
Burgate B2
Bus Station C2
Canterbury College C3
Canterbury East ≷ C1
Canterbury Tales, The ✦ B2
Canterbury West ≷ A1
Castle C1
Castle Row C1
Castle St C1
Cathedral † B2
Chaucer Rd A3
Christ Church Univ B3
Christchurch Gate ✦ B2
City Council Offices A3
City Wall B2
Coach Park A2
College Rd B3
Cossington Rd C2
Court B2
Craddock Rd A3
Crown & County Courts B3
Dane John Gdns C2
Dane John Mound ✦ C1
Deanery B2
Dover St C2
Duck La B2
Eastbridge Hospl B1
Edgar Rd B3
Ersham Rd C3
Ethelbert Rd C3
Fire Station C2
Forty Acres Rd A1
Gordon Rd C1
Greyfriars ✦ B1
Guildford Rd C1
Havelock St B2
Heaton Rd C1
High St B2
HM Prison B3
Information Ctr A2/B2
Ivy La B2
Ivy Pl C1
King St B2
King's School B2/B3
King's School Leisure Facilities A2
Kingsmead Leisure Centre A2
Kingsmead Rd A2
Kirby's La B1
Lansdown Rd C2
Lime Kiln Rd C1
Longport B3
Lower Chantry La C3
Mandeville Rd A1
Market Way A2
Marlowe Arcade B2
Marlowe Ave C2
Marlowe Theatre B2
Martyrs Field Rd C1
Mead Way B1
Military Rd B2
Monastery St B2
Mus of Canterbury (Rupert Bear Mus) B1
New Dover Rd C3
Norman Rd C2
North Holmes Rd B3
North La B1
Northgate A2
Nunnery Fields C2
Nunnery Rd C2
Oaten Hill C2
Odeon Cinema C2
Old Dover Rd C2
Old Palace B2
Old Ruttington La B2
Old Weavers B2
Orchard St B1
Oxford Rd C1
Palace St B2
Pilgrims Way C3
Pin Hill C1
Pine Tree Ave A1
Police Station C2
Post Office B2/C1/C2
Pound La B1
Puckle La C2
Raymond Ave C2
Registry Office A2
Rheims Way B1
Rhodaus Cl C2
Rhodaus Town C2
Roman Museum B2
Roper Gateway A1
Roper Rd A1
Rose La B2
St Augustine's Abbey (remains) † B3
St Augustine's Rd C3
St Dunstan's A1
St Dunstan's St A1
St George's Pl C2
St George's St B2
St George's Tower ✦ B2
St Gregory's Rd B3
St John's Hospital A2
St Margaret's St B2
St Martin's B3
St Martin's Ave B3
St Martin's Rd B3
St Michael's Rd A1
St Mildred's C1
St Peter's Gr B1
St Peter's La B2
St Peter's Pl B1
St Peter's St B1
St Radigunds St B2
St Stephen's Ct A1
St Stephen's Path A1
St Stephen's Rd A2
Salisbury Rd A1
Simmonds Rd C1
Spring La C3
Station Rd West B1
Stour St B1
Sturry Rd A3
The Causeway A2
The Friars B2
Tourtel Rd A3
Tudor Rd C1
Union St B2
University for the Creative Arts C3
Vernon Pl C2
Victoria Rd C1
Watling St B2
Westgate Gdns B1
Westgate Towers B1
Whitefriars B2
Whitehall Gdns B1
Whitehall Rd B1
Wincheap C1
York Rd C1
Zealand Rd C2

Cardiff Caerdydd 333

Adam St B3
Alexandra Gdns A2
Allerton St C1
Arran St A3
ATRiuM (Univ of Glamorgan) C3
Beauchamp St C1
Bedford St A3
Blackfriars Priory (rems) † B1
Boulevard De Nantes B2
Brains Brewery C2
Brook St B1
Bus Station C2
Bute Park B1
Bute St C2
Bute Terr C3
Callaghan Sq C2/C3
Capitol Sh Ctr, The B3
Cardiff Arms Park (Cardiff RFC) B1
Cardiff Bridge B1
Cardiff Castle B2
Cardiff Central Sta ≷ C2
Cardiff Ctr Trading Est C3
Cardiff Univ A1/A2/B3
Cardiff University Student's Union A2
Caroline St C2
Castle Green B2
Castle Mews A1
Castle St (Heol y Castell) B1
Cathays Station ≷ A2
Celerity Drive C3
Central Library C2
Central Sq C2
Charles St (Heol Siarl) B3
Churchill Way B3
City Hall A2
City Rd A3
Clare Rd C1
Clare St C1
Coburn St A3
Coldstream Terr B1
College Rd A1
Colum Rd A1
Court C2
Court Rd C1
Craiglee Drive C3
Cranbrook St A3
Customhouse St C2
Cyfartha St A3
Despenser Place C1
Despenser St C1
Dinas St C1
Duke St (Heol y Dug) B2
Dumfries Place B3
East Grove A3
Ellen St C3
Fire Station B3
Fitzalan Place B3
Fitzhamon Emb C1
Fitzhamon La C1
g39 B2
Gloucester St C1
Glynrhondda St A2
Gordon Rd A3
Gorsedd Gdns B2
Green St B1
Greyfriars Rd B2
HM Prison B3
Hafod St C1
Herbert St C3
High St B2
Industrial Estate C3
John St C3
Jubilee St C1
King Edward VII Ave A1
Kingsway (Ffordd y Brenin) B2
Knox Rd B3
Law Courts B2
Llanbleddian Gdns A2
Llantwit St A2
Lloyd George Ave C3
Lower Cathedral Rd B1
Lowther Rd A3
Magistrates Court B3
Mansion House A3
Mardy St C1
Mark St B1
Market B2
Mary Ann St C3
Merches Gdns C1
Mill La C2
Millennium Bridge B1
Miskin St A2
Monmouth St C1
Motorpoint Arena Cardiff ✦ C3
Museum Ave A2
Museum Place A2
National Museum of Wales A2
National War Meml ✦ A2
Neville Place C1
New Theatre B2
Newport Rd B3
Northcote La A3
Northcote St A3
Park Grove A4
Park Place A2
Park St C2
Penarth Rd C2
Pendyris St C1
Plantaganet St C1
Principality Stadium C1
Principality Stadium Tours (Gate 3) ✦ B2
Quay St B2
Queen Anne Sq A1
Queen St (Heol y Frenhines) B2
Queen St Station ≷ B3
Regimental Museums B2
Rhymney St A3
Richmond Rd A3
Royal Welsh College of Music and Drama A1
Russell St A3
Ruthin Gdns A2
St Andrews Place A2
St David's † B2
St David's 2 C2
St David's Centre B2
St David's Hall ✦ B2
St John The Baptist B2
St Mary St (Heol Eglwys Fair) B2
St Peter's St A3
Salisbury Rd A3
Sandon St B3
Schooner Way C3
Scott Rd C2
Scott St C2
Senghennydd Rd A2
Sherman Theatre A2
Sophia Gardens A1
South Wales Baptist College A3
Stadium Plaza Leisure Complex C1
Stafford Rd C1
Station Terr B3
Stuttgarter Strasse B2
Sussex St C1
Taffs Mead Emb C1
Talworth St A3
Temple of Peace & Health ✦ A1
The Cardiff Story B2
The Friary B2
The Hayes B2
The Parade A3
The Walk A3
Treharris St A3
Trinity St B2
Tudor La C1
Tudor St C1
Welsh Assembly Offices A1
Welsh Inst of Sport ✦ A1
West Grove A3
Westgate St (Heol y Porth) B2
Windsor Place B3
Womanby St B2
Wood St C2
Working St B2
Wyeverne Rd A2

Carlisle 333

Abbey St A1
Aglionby St B3
Albion St C3
Alexander St C3
AMF Bowl ✦ C2
Annetwell St A1
Bank St B2
Bitts Park A1
Blackfriars St B2
Blencome St C1
Blunt St C1
Botchergate B2
Boustead's Grassing C2
Bowman St B3
Broad St B3
Bridge St A1
Brook St C3
Brunswick St B2
Bus Station B2
Caldew Bridge A1
Caldew St C1
Carlisle (Citadel) Station ≷ B2
Carlisle College A2
Castle A1
Castle St A1
Castle Way A1
Cathedral † A1
Cecil St B2
Chapel St A2
Charles St B3
Charlotte St B1
Chatsworth Square A2
Chiswick St B2
Citadel, The ✦ B2
City Walls A1
Civic Centre A2
Clifton St C1
Close St B3
Collingwood St C1
Colville St C1
Colville Terr C1
Court B2
Court St B2
Crosby St B2
Crown St C2
Currock Rd C2
Dacre Rd A1
Dale St C1
Denton St C1
Devonshire Walk A1
Duke's Rd A2
East Dale St C1
East Norfolk St C1
Eden Bridge A2
Edward St B3
Elm St B1
English St B2
Fire Station A2
Fisher St A1
Flower St B3
Freer St C1
Fusehill St B3
Georgian Way A2
Gloucester Rd C3
Golf Course A2
Graham St C1
Grey St B3
Guildhall Museum A2
Halfey's La B3
Hardwicke Circus A2
Hart St B3
Hewson St C2
Howard Pl A3
Howe St B3
Information Ctr A2
James St B2
Junction St B1
King St B2

Earl of Inverness Rd...A3
Fassifern Rd...........B1
Fire Station..........A2
Fort William ≥........B2
Fort William
  (Remains) ✦......B2
Glasdrum Rd..........C1
Glen Nevis Pl.........B3
Gordon Sq............B1
Grange Rd............C1
Heather Croft Rd.....C1
Henderson Row.......C2
High St...............A2
Highland Visitor Ctr..B3
Hill Rd................B2
Hospital Belhaven
  Annexe.............
Information Ctr ℹ.....A3
Inverlochy Ct.........A3
Kennedy Rd.........B2/C2
Library................C1
Lime Tree Gallery ✦..C1
Linnhe Rd............B1
Lochaber Leisure Ctr..B3
Lochiel Rd............C1
Lochy Rd..............A3
Lundavra Cres........C1
Lundavra Rd..........C1
Lundy Rd.............A3
Mamore Cr...........B2
Mary St...............B1
Middle St.............B1
Montrose Ave........A3
Moray Pl.............C1
Morven Pl............C2
Moss Rd...............B2
Nairn Cres...........C1
Nevis Bridge.........B3
Nevis Rd..............A3
Nevis Sports Centre..A2
Nevis Terr............A3
North Rd..............B3
Obelisk...............B2
Parade Rd............B2
Police Station 🏛...A3/C1
Post Office 🏤.......A3/B2
Ross Pl................C1
St Andrews ᵻ.........B2
Shaw Pl...............B1
Station Brae.........B1
Studio 🎭.............B1
Treig Rd..............A3
Underwater Centre...A1
Union Rd.............A2
Victoria Rd...........A2
Wades Rd.............A3
West Highland
West Highland Collge
  UHI..................A2
Young Pl..............B2

Glasgow   335

Admiral St............C2
Albert Bridge.........C5
Albion St..............B5
Anderston ≥..........B3
Anderston Centre....B3
Anderston Quay......B3
Arches 🎭.............B4
Argyle
  St....A1/A2/B3/B4/B5
Argyle Street ≥.......B5
Argyll Arcade.........B5
Arlington St..........A3
Arts Centre 🏛........B3
Ashley St..............A3
Bain St................C6
Baird St...............A6
Baliol St...............A3
Ballater St.............C5
Barras, The (Market)..C6
Bath St................A3
BBC Scotland/SMG....B1
Bell St.................C6
Bell's Bridge..........B1
Bentinck St...........A2
Berkeley St...........A3
Bishop La..............B3
Black St................A6
Blackburn St..........C2
Blackfriars St.........B6
Blantyre St............A1
Blythswood Sq.......A4
Blythswood St........B4
Bothwell St...........B4
Brand St...............C1
Breadalbane St.......A2
Bridge St..............C4
Bridge St Ⓜ...........C4
Bridgegate............C5
Briggait...............C5
Broomhill Park.......A6
Broomielaw...........B4
Broomielaw Quay
  Gdns................B3
Brown St..............B4
Brunswick St..........B5
Buccleuch St.........A3
Buchanan Bus Station..A5
Buchanan Galleries...A5
Buchanan St...........B5
Buchanan St Ⓜ.......B5
Cadogan St............B4
Caledonian University..A5
Calgary St.............A5
Cambridge St.........A4
Canal St................A5
Candleriggs..........B5
Carlton Pl.............C4
Carnarvon St.........A3
Carrick St.............B4
Castle St...............B6
Cathedral Sq.........B6
Cathedral St..........B5
Central College of
  Commerce..........B5
Ctr for Contemporary
  Arts 🎭.............A4
Centre St..............C4

Cessnock Ⓜ..........C1
Cessnock St...........C1
Charing Cross ≥......A3
Charlotte St...........C6
Cheapside St..........B3
Cineworld 🎬..........A5
Citizens' Theatre 🎭..C5
City Chambers
  Complex............B5
City Halls 🎭..........B5
Clairmont Gdns......A2
Claremont St..........A2
Claremont Terr.......A2
Claythorne St.........C6
Cleveland St..........A3
Clifford La............C1
Clifford St............C1
Clifton Pl.............A2
Clifton St.............A2
Clutha St..............C1
Clyde Arc.............B2
Clyde Auditorium....B2
Clyde Pl...............C4
Clyde Place Quay....C5
Clyde St...............C5
Clyde Walkway......C4
Clydeside Expressway..B2
Coburg St.............C4
Cochrane St...........B5
College of Nautical
  Studies.............C5
College St.............B5
Collins St.............B6
Commerce St..........C4
Cook St...............C4
Cornwall St...........C1
Couper St.............A5
Cowcaddens Ⓜ.......A4
Cowcaddens Rd......A4
Crimea St.............B3
Custom House 🎭.....C5
Custom Ho Quay Gdns..C4
Dalhousie St..........A4
Derby St...............A1
Dobbie's Loan.....A4/A5
Dobbie's Loan Pl......A5
Dorset St..............A3
Douglas St.............B4
Doulton Fountain ✦..C6
Dover St...............B3
Drury St...............B4
Drygate...............B6
Duke St................B6
Dunaskin St...........A1
Dunblane St...........A5
Dundas St.............B5
Dunlop St.............C5
East Campbell St.....C6
Eastvale Pl...........A1
Eglinton St...........C4
Elderslie St...........A3
Elliot St...............B2
Elmbank St............A3
Esmond St.............A1
Exhibition Centre ≥..B2
Exhibition Way.......B2
Eye Infirmary 🏥.....A4
Festival Park.........C1
Film Theatre 🎬......A4
Finnieston Quay......B2
Finnieston St..........B2
Finnieston St..........B2
Fitzroy Pl..............A2
Florence St............C5
Fox St.................C5
Gallowgate............C6
Garnet St.............A3
Garnethill St..........A4
Garscube Rd..........A4
George Sq.............B5
George St..............B5
George V Bridge......C4
Gilbert St.............A1
Glasgow Bridge......C4
Glasgow Cathedral ✝..B6
Glasgow Central ≥...B4
Glasgow Green........C6
Glasgow Metropolitan
  College..........B5/C5
Glasgow Tower ✦.....B1
Glasgow Science
  Centre 🏛............B1
Glasgow Science Centre
  Footbridge.........B1
Glassford St...........B5
Glebe St................A6
Gorbals Cross.........C5
Gorbals St..............C5
Gordon St..............B4
Govan Rd......B1/C1/C2
Grace St...............B3
Grand Ole Opry ✦....C2
Grafton Pl.............A5
Grant St................A3
Granville St...........A3
Gray St................A2
Greendyke St.........C6
Grey Eagle St.........B7
Harley St..............C1
Harvie St..............C2
Haugh Rd.............A1
Heliport................C2
Henry Wood Hall 🎭..A2
High Court.............C5
High St................B6
High Street ≥.........B6
Hill St.................A3
Holland St.............A3
Holm St...............B4
Hope St................B4
Houldsworth St.......B2
Houston Pl............C2
Houston St............C3
Howard St.............C5
Hunter St..............C6
Hutcheson St..........B5
Hutchesons Hall 🏛..B5
Hydepark St..........B3
Hydro The 🎭..........B2

Imax Cinema 🎬......B1
India St.................A3
Information Ctr ℹ.....B5
Ingram St..............B5
Jamaica St.............B4
James Watt St........B4
John Knox St.........B6
John St.................B5
Kelvin Hall ✦..........A1
Kelvin Statue ✦......A1
Kelvin Way...........A1
Kelvingrove Art Gallery
  & Museum 🏛........A1
Kelvingrove Park.....A1
Kelvingrove St........A1
Kelvinhaugh St.......A1
Kennedy St...........A6
Kent Rd................A2
Killermont St.........A5
King St................C5
King's 🎭..............A3
Kingston Bridge......C3
Kingston St............C4
Kinning Park Ⓜ.......C2
Kyle St.................A5
Lancefield Quay......B2
Lancefield St..........B3
Langshot St............C1
Lendel Pl..............C1
Lighthouse ✦.........B4
Lister St................A6
Little St................B3
London Rd.............C6
Lorne St...............C1
Lower Harbour........A1
Lumsden St...........A1
Lymburn St...........A1
Lyndoch Cr...........A3
Lyndoch Pl...........A3
Maclellan St..........C1
Mair St................C1
Maitland St...........A4
Mansell St............C7
Mavisbank Gdns.....C2
Mcalpine St............B3
Mcaslin St.............A6
McLean Sq...........C1
McLellan Gallery 🏛..A4
McPhater St...........A4
Merchants' House 🏛..B5
Middlesex St..........C1
Middleton St..........C1
Midland St.............B4
Miller St...............B5
Millroad St............C7
Milnpark St...........C2
Milton St...............A4
Minerva St.............B2
Mitchell Library......A3
Mitchell St West......B4
Mitchell Theatre 🎭..A3
Modern Art Gallery 🏛..B5
Moir St.................C6
Molendinar St........C6
Moncur St.............C6
Montieth Row.........C6
Montrose St...........B5
Morrison St...........C3
Mosque................C5
Nairn St...............A1
Nelson Mandela Sq..B5
Nelson St...............C4
Nelson's Monument...C6
New City Rd..........A4
Newton St.............A3
Newton Pl.............A3
Nicholson St..........C4
Nile St.................B5
Norfolk Court.........C5
Norfolk St.............C5
North Frederick St....B5
North Hanover St.....B5
North Portland St.....B6
North St...............A3
North Wallace St.....A5
O2 Academy ✦........C4
Odeon 🎬..............A4
Old Dumbarton Rd...A1
Osborne St...........B5/C5
Oswald St..............B4
Overnewton St........A1
Oxford St...............C4
Pacific Dr..............B1
Paisley Rd.............C3
Paisley Rd West......C1
Park Circus...........A2
Park Gdns.............A2
Park St South.........A2
Park Terr...............A2
Parkgrove Terr.......A2
Parnie St...............C5
Partick Bridge.........A1
Passport Office.......B3
Pavilion Theatre 🎭..A4
Pembroke St..........A2
People's Palace 🏛...C6
Pinkston Rd...........A6
Piping Centre, The
  National ✦..........A5
Pitt St................A4/B4
Plantation Park.......C1
Plantation Quay......B1
Police Sta 🏛...A4/A6/B5
Port Dundas Rd......A5
Port St................B2
Portman St............C2
Prince's Dock.........B1
Princes Sq............B5
Provand's Lordship 🏛..B6
Queen St...............B5
Queen Street ≥.......B5
Renfrew St..........A3/A4
Renton St..............A5
Richmond St..........B5
Robertson St..........B4
Rose St................A4
Rottenrow.............B6
Royal Concert Hall 🎭..A5

Royal Cr...............A2
Royal Exchange Sq...B5
Royal Highland Fusiliers
  Museum 🏛...........A3
Royal Hospital For Sick
  Children 🏥.........A1
Royal Infirmary 🏥...B6
Royal Scottish Academy
  of Music & Drama...A4
Royal Terr............A1
Rutland Cr.............C2
St Kent St.............C6
St Andrew's (RC) ✝..C6
St Andrew's ✝........C6
St Andrew's St........C5
St Enoch Ⓜ...........B5
St Enoch Shopping Ctr..B5
St Enoch Sq...........B4
St George's Rd.......A3
St James Rd...........B6
St Mungo Ave.....A5/A6
St Mungo Museum of
  Religious Life........B6
St Mungo Pl...........A6
St Vincent Cr.........A2
St Vincent Pl.........B5
St Vincent St......B3/B4
St Vincent Street
  Church 🎭...........B4
St Vincent Terr.......B3
Saltmarket............C5
Sandyford Pl..........A3
Sauchiehall St.....A2/A4
School of Art.........A4
Sclater St..............B7
Scotland St...........C2
Scott St................A4
Scottish Exhibition &
  Conference Centre..B1
Seaward St............C2
Shaftesbury St.......B3
Sheriff Court.........C5
Shields Rd Ⓜ.........C2
Shuttle St..............B6
Somerset Pl..........A2
South Portland St....C4
Springburn Rd.......A6
Springfield Quay.....C3
Stanley St..............C2
Stevenson St..........C6
Stewart St............A4
Stirling Rd............B6
Stirling's Library......B5
Stobcross Quay......B1
Stobcross St..........B1
Stock Exchange 🏛...B5
Stockwell Pl..........C5
Stockwell St..........C5
Stow College.........A4
Strathclyde Univ......B6
Sussex St..............C2
Synagogues........A3/C4
Taylor Pl..............A6
Tenement House 🏛..A3
Teviot St...............A1
Theatre Royal 🎭.....A4
Tolbooth Steeple &
  Mercat Cross ✦.....C6
Tower St...............C2
Trades House 🏛......B5
Tradeston St..........C4
Transport Museum 🏛..C1
Tron 🎭................C5
Trongate...............B5
Tunnel St..............B2
Turnbull St............C5
Union St...............B4
Victoria Bridge........C5
Virginia St............B5
West Greenhill Pl.....B2
West Regent St.......A4
Wallace St.............C3
Walls St...............B6
Walmer Cr.............C1
Warrock St............B3
Washington St........B4
Waterloo St...........B4
Watson St.............B6
Watt St................C2
Wellington St.........B4
West Campbell St....B4
West George St.......B4
West Graham St......A4
West Regent St.......A4
West St................C4
West St Ⓜ............C4
Westminster Terr.....A2
Whitehall St...........B3
Wilkes St...............C7
Wilson St...............B5
Woodlands Gate......A3
Woodlands Rd........A3
Woodlands Terr......A2
Woodside Cr...........A3
Woodside Pl...........A3
Woodside Terr........A3
York St................B4
Yorkhill Pde..........A1
Yorkhill St.............A1

Gloucester   335

Albion St..............C1
Alexandra Rd.........B3
Alfred St...............C3
All Saints Rd..........C2
Alvin St................B2
Arthur St...............C2
Barton St..............C2
Barrack Square.......C2
Blackfriars 🏛.........B1
Blenheim Rd..........C3
Bristol Rd..............C1
Brunswick Rd.........C2
Bruton Way............B2
Bus Station............B2
City Council Offices...B1
City Mus, Art Gall &
  Library 🏛...........B2
Clarence St............B2

Commercial Rd.......B1
Cromwell St...........C2
Deans Way............A2
Denmark Rd..........A3
Derby Rd..............C3
Docks ✦...............C1
Eastgate Shopping Ctr..B1
Eastgate St............B2
Edwy Pde.............A3
Estcourt Cl............A3
Estcourt Rd...........A3
Falkner St..............C2
GL1 Leisure Centre..B2
Gloucester Cath ✝...B1
Gloucester Quays
  Outlet Shopping....C1
Gloucester Station ≥..B2
Gloucestershire Royal
  Hospital (A&E) 🏥...A3
Gloucester Waterways
  Mus 🏛..............C1
Goodyere St...........C2
Gouda Way...........A2
Great Western Rd....B3
Guildhall 🏛...........B2
Heathville Rd.........A3
Henry Rd...............A3
Henry St...............B3
Hinton Rd.............A2
HM Prison.............B1
India Rd................C1
Information Ctr ℹ.....B1
Jersey Rd..............B3
King's 🎭..............C2
King's Sq..............B2
Kingsholm
  (Gloucester RFC)....A2
Kingsholm Rd.........A2
Lansdown Rd.........A3
Library.................C2
Llanthony Rd.........C1
London Rd.............B2
Longhorn Ave........A1
Longsmith St..........B1
Malvern Rd............A3
Market Pde...........A1
Mercia Rd.............A1
Metz Way.............C2
Midland Rd............C2
Millbrook St...........C2
Montpellier............C1
Napier St...............C3
Nettleton Rd..........B2
New Inn 🏛............B1
New Olympus 🎭.....C3
North Rd...............A3
Northgate St..........B2
Oxford Rd.............C3
Oxford St..............B3
Pk & Ride Gloucester..A1
Park Rd................C2
Park St.................B2
Parliament St.........C1
Pitt St.................A1
Police Station 🏛.....B1
Post Office 🏤........B2
Quay St................B1
Recreation Gd....A1/A2
Regent St..............C2
Robert Raikes Ho 🏛..B1
Royal Oak Rd.........B1
Russell St..............B2
Ryecroft St............C2
St Aldate St............B2
St Ann Way...........C1
St Catherine St.......A2
St Mark St.............A2
St Mary de Crypt ᵻ..B1
St Mary de Lode ᵻ...B1
St Nicholas's ᵻ.......B1
St Oswald's Rd.......A1
St Oswald's Retail Pk..A1
St Peter's ᵻ...........B2
Seabroke Rd..........A3
Sebert St..............A3
Severn Rd.............C1
Sherborne St.........B2
Shire Hall 🏛..........B1
Sidney St...............C3
Soldiers of
  Gloucestershire 🏛..B1
Southgate St.......B1/C1
Spa Field..............C1
Spa Rd.................C1
Sports Ground....A2/B2
Station Rd.............B2
Stratton Rd............C3
Stroud Rd..............C1
Superstore............A1
Swan Rd...............A2
The Park...............C2
The Quay..............B1
Trier Way...........C1/C2
Union St................A2
Vauxhall Rd...........C3
Victoria St.............C2
Walham Lane.........A1
Wellington St..........C2
Westgate Retail Park..B1
Westgate St...........B1
Widden St..............C2
Worcester St...........B2

Grimsby   335

Abbey Drive East.....C2
Abbey Drive West....C2
Abbey Park Rd........C2
Abbey Rd..............C2
Abbey Walk...........C2
Abbeygate Sh Ctr....C2
Abbotsway.............C2
Adam Smith St....A1/A2
Ainslie St...............C1
Albert St...............A3
Alexandra Dock........B2
Alexandra Retail Park..A2
Alexandra Rd......A2/B2

Annesley St............A2
Armstrong St..........A1
Arthur St...............A1
Augusta St.............C1
Bargate...............C1
Beeson St..............A1
Bethlehem St.........C2
Bodiam Way..........B3
Bradley St..............B3
Brighowgate......C1/C2
Bus Station.........B2/C2
Canterbury Dr........C1
Cartergate........B1/C1
Catherine St..........C1
Caxton St.............C3
Chantry La............A1
Charlton St.............A1
Church La.............C1
Church St..............A1
Cleethorpe Rd........C1
College.................C1
College St..............C1
Compton Dr..........A1
Corporation Bridge...A2
Corporation Rd.......A1
Court...................B3
Crescent St...........A1
Deansgate.............C1
Doughty Rd...........C2
Dover St...............A1
Duchess St.............C2
Dudley St...............C1
Duke of York Gardens..C1
Duncombe St.........B3
Earl La.................C1
East Marsh St.........B2
East St..................C1
Eastgate...............B3
Eastside Rd...........A1
Eaton Ct...............C1
Eleanor St..............C1
Ellis Way...............A2
Fisherman's Chapel 🏛..B2
Fisherman's Wharf...B2
Fishing Heritage
  Centre 🏛...........B2
Flour Sq...............A3
Frederick St...........C1
Frederick Ward Way..A2
Freeman St........A3/B3
Freshney Dr...........B1
Freshney Pl...........B2
Garden St..............C2
Garibaldi St...........C1
Garth La...............B2
Grime St...............A3
Hainton Ave..........C1
Har Way...............B3
Hare St.................B1
Harrison St............A1
Haven Ave............A1
Hay Croft Ave........B1
Hay Croft St...........B1
Heneage Rd.......B3/C3
Henry St................A1
Holme St...............B3
Hume St...............C1
James St...............B3
Joseph St..............B1
Kent St.................A3
King Edward St........A2
Lambert Rd............C2
Library.................B2
Lime St................B2
Lister St................B2
Littlefield La..........C1
Lockhill................A2
Lord St.................A1
Ludford St.............B3
Macaulay St...........C1
Mallard Mews........C3
Manor Ave............A3
Market.................B2
Market Hall...........B2
Market St..............B3
Moss Rd...............A3
Nelson St...............A3
New St.................B2
Osbourne St..........B2
Pasture St.............B3
Peaks Parkway.......C2
Pelham Rd.............A1
Police Station 🏛.....A3
Post Office 🏤...B1/B2/C2
PS Lincoln Castle ᵻ..B2
Pyewipe Rd...........A1
Railway St.............A1
Railway St.............B2
Recreation Ground..A2
Rendel St...............A2
Retail Park............B3
Richard St.............B1
Ripon St................B1
Robinson St East.....B3
Royal St................A1
St Hilda's Ave.........C1
St James St...........C1
Sheepfold St.......B3/C3
Sixhills St..............B3
South Park.............B2
Spring St...............A3
Superstore............B3
Tasburgh St...........B2
Tennyson St..........C1
The Close..............C1
Thesiger St...........A3
Time Trap 🏛..........B2
Town Hall 🏛..........B2
Veal St.................B1
Victoria Retail Park..A2
Victoria St North.....B3
Victoria St South.....B3
Victoria St West......B3
Watkin St..............A1
Welholme Ave........C1
Welholme Rd.........C1
Wellington St..........B3
Wellowgate............C2

Werneth Rd...........B3
West Coates Rd......A1
Westgate...............B1
Westminster Dr......C1
Willingham St.........C1
Wintringham Rd......B1
Wood St...............B3
Yarborough Dr.......B1
Yarborough Hotel 🏛..C2

Hanley   335

Acton St...............A3
Albion St...............A2
Argyle St...............C2
Ashbourne Gr.........C1
Avoca St................A3
Baskerville Rd.........B3
Bedford Rd............C1
Bedford St.............C1
Bethesda St...........B1
Bexley St...............A2
Birches Head Rd......A2
Botteslow St...........C2
Boundary St...........C1
Broad St...............C2
Broom St...............A3
Bryan St...............A2
Bucknall New Rd.....C2
Bucknall Old Rd......C2
Bus Station............B2
Cannon St..............C2
Castlefield St..........C1
Cleveland Rd..........C2
Clifford St..............C3
Clough St..............B1
Clyde St................A3
College Rd.............C2
Cooper St..............C1
Corbridge Rd..........A3
Cutts St................C2
Davis St................C2
Denbigh St............A1
Derby St................C2
Dilke St.................A3
Dundas St.............C1
Dundee Rd............C1
Dyke St................B3
Eastwood Rd..........C3
Eaton St................B3
Etruria Park...........B1
Etruria Rd.............B1
Etruria Vale Rd.......B1
Festing St..............A3
Fire Station...........A3
Foundry St............A2
Franklyn St...........C3
Garnet St...............A1
Garth St................B2
George St...............A3
Gilman St.............A2
Glass St................A3
Goodson St...........A3
Greyhound Way......C1
Grove Pl...............C1
Hampton St............A3
Hanley Park...........C2
Harding Rd............A2
Hassall St..............A1
Havelock Pl...........A1
Hazlehurst St.........C3
Hinde St................C2
Hope St................A3
Houghton St..........A1
Hulton St...............A3
Information Ctr ℹ.....B2
Jasper St................C2
Jervis St...............A3
John Bright St........A3
John St.................B2
Keelings Rd...........A3
Kimberley Rd.........C1
Ladysmith Rd.........A1
Lawrence St...........C2
Leek Rd................C2
Lichfield St............B2
Lindfield Rd...........A3
Loftus St...............C2
Lower Bedford St.....C1
Lower Bryan St.......A1
Lower Mayer St......A3
Lowther St............A1
Magistrates Court....B2
Malham St.............A2
Marsh St...............B2
Matlock St.............A1
Mayer St...............A3
Milton St...............C3
Mitchell Memorial
  Theatre 🎭..........B2
Morley St..............C3
Moston St.............A3
Mount Pleasant......C1
Mulgrave St...........A1
Mynors St.............B3
Nelson Pl.............A3
New Century St.......B1
Octagon Retail Park..B1
Ogden Rd.............C2
Old Hall St.............B3
Old Town Rd..........A2
Pall Mall..............B2
Palmerston St.........C1
Park and Ride..........B3
Parker St..............B2
Pavilion Dr............A1
Pelham St.............C3
Percy St................B2
Piccadilly..............B2
Picton St...............B3
Plough St..............A3

Police Station 🏛.....C2
Portland St............B3
Post Office 🏤...A3/B3/C3
Potteries Museum & Art
  Gallery 🏛...........B2
Potteries Sh Ctr......B2
Potteries Way.........C2
Powell St...............A1
Pretoria Rd............A1
Quadrant Rd...........B2
Ranelagh St...........A2
Rectory Rd............C1
Regent Rd.............C3
Regent Theatre 🎭...B2
Richmond Terr.......C1
Ridgehouse Dr.......A1
Robson St.............A1
St Ann St..............B3
St Luke St..............B3
Sampson St...........C2
Shaw St................A1
Sheaf St...............C2
Shearer St.............C1
Shelton New Rd.......C1
Shirley Rd.............C2
Slippery La............A2
Snow Hill..............C2
Spur St................C3
Stafford St.............B2
Statham St.............B2
Stubbs La..............C3
Sun St.................C1
Supermarket.......A1/B2
Talbot St...............C2
The Parkway.........A3
The Regent 🎭........B2
Town Hall 🏛..........A3
Town Rd...............A3
Trinity St...............B2
Union St...............A2
Upper Hillchurch St..A3
Upper Huntbach St..B3
Victoria Hall
  Theatre 🎭...........B3
Warner St..............C1
Warwick St............C1
Waterloo Rd...........A1
Waterloo St...........B3
Well St.................C3
Wellesley St...........C2
Wellington Rd.........B3
Wellington St.........B3
Whitehaven Dr......A2
Whitmore St...........C1
Windermere St.......A1
Woodall St.............A1
Yates St.................C2
York St.................A1

Harrogate   335

Albert St...............B2
Alexandra Rd.........B2
Arthington Ave.......B2
Ashfield Rd............A2
Back Cheltenham
  Mount...............A2
Beech Grove..........C1
Belmont Rd...........C1
Bilton Dr..............A2
Bower Rd.............B2
Bower St...............B2
Bus Station............B2
Cambridge Rd.......B2
Cambridge St.........B2
Cemetery..............A2
Chatsworth Pl........A2
Chatsworth Grove....A2
Chatsworth Rd.......A2
Chelmsford Rd.......B3
Cheltenham Cr.......B2
Cheltenham Mt.......A2
Cheltenham Pde......B2
Christ Church.........B3
Christ Church Oval...B3
Chudleigh Rd.........B3
Clarence Dr...........B1
Claro Rd...............A3
Claro Way.............A3
Coach Park...........B2
Coach Rd.............B3
Cold Bath Rd.........C1
Commercial St.......B2
Coppice Ave...........A2
Coppice Dr...........A1
Coppice Gate..........A1
Cornwall Rd...........B1
Council Offices.......B2
Court..................C3
Crescent Gdns.......B1
Crescent Rd...........B1
Dawson Terr..........A3
Devonshire Pl........B3
Diamond Mews.......C1
Dixon Rd..............A2
Dixon Terr.............A2
Dragon Ave...........A3
Dragon Parade.......A2
Dragon Rd.............A2
Duchy Rd..............B1
East Parade...........B2
East Park Rd...........C3
Esplanade.............B1
Fire Station...........A2
Franklin Mount.......A2
Franklin Rd............A2
Franklin Square......A2
Glebe Rd..............C1
Grove Park Ct.........A3
Grove Park Terr......A3
Grove Rd..............A2
Hampswaite Rd.......A1
Harcourt Dr...........B3
Harcourt Rd...........B3
Harrogate 🏛.........B2
Harrogate Int Ctr.....B1
Harrogate Ladies Coll..B1
Harrogate Theatre 🎭..B2
Heywood Rd.........C1
Hollins Cr.............A1

Hollins Mews.........A1
Hollins Rd.............A1
Homestead Rd.......A1
Hydro Leisure Ctr, The..A1
Information Ctr ℹ.....B1
James St...............B2
Jenny Field Dr........A1
John St.................B2
Kent Dr................A1
Kent Rd...............A1
Kings Rd...............B2
Kingsway.............A3
Kingsway Dr..........A3
Lancaster Rd..........C1
Leeds Rd...............C2
Lime Grove............A3
Lime St................A2
Mayfield Grove.......B2
Mayfield Pl...........A2
Mercer 🏛.............B1
Montpellier Hill......B1
Mornington Cr.......A3
Mornington Terr......A3
Mowbray Sq..........B3
North Park Rd.........B3
Nydd Vale Rd.........B2
Oakdale Ave..........A1
Oatlands Dr..........C3
Odeon 🎬..............B2
Osborne Rd...........A2
Otley Rd...............C2
Oxford St..............B2
Park Chase............B3
Park Parade...........B3
Park View.............B2
Parliament St.........B1
Police Station 🏛.....B2
Post Office 🏤.....B2/C1
Providence Terr.......A2
Queen Parade.......B3
Queen's Rd............C1
Raglan St.............B2
Regent Ave...........A3
Regent Grove.........A3
Regent Parade........A3
Regent St..............A3
Regent Terr...........A3
Rippon Rd.............A1
Robert St..............C2
Royal Baths &
  Turkish Baths ᵻ.....B1
Royal Pump Room 🏛..B1
St Luke's Mount.....A2
St Mary's Ave.........C1
St Mary's Walk.......C1
Scargill Rd.............A1
Skipton Rd............A3
Skipton St.............A2
Slingsby Walk........C3
South Park Rd.........C2
Spring Grove..........A1
Springfield Ave.......B1
Station Ave............B2
Station Parade........B2
Strawberry Dale......A2
Stray Rein.............C2
Studley Rd............A2
Superstore............B2
Swan Rd...............B1
The Parade............B2
The Stray..........C2/C3
Tower St...............C2
Trinity Rd.............C2
Union St...............B3
Valley Dr..............C1
Valley Gardens.......C1
Valley Mount.........C1
Victoria Ave..........C2
Victoria Rd.............C1
Victoria Shopping Ctr..B2
Waterloo St...........C2
West Park.............C2
West Park St...........C2
Wood View...........A1
Woodfield Ave........A3
Woodfield Dr..........A3
Woodfield Grove.....A3
Woodfield Rd.........A3
Woodfield Square....A3
Woodside...............B3
York Pl................C3
York Rd................B1

Holyhead   Caergybi   335

Armenia St.............A2
Arthur St...............C2
Beach Rd..............A1
Boston St...............C2
Bowling Green.......C3
Bryn Erw Rd...........C2
Bryn Glas Cl..........C3
Bryn Glas Rd..........C3
Bryn Gwyn Rd........C1
Bryn Marchog........C1
Bryn Mor Terr.........A2
Bryngoleu Ave.......C2
Cae Braenar...........C3
Cambria St.............C1
Captain Skinner's
  Obelisk ✦...........B2
Cecil St.................C2
Celtic Gateway
  Footbridge..........B2
Cemetery...........C1/C2
Cleveland Ave........C1
Coastguard Lookout..A2
Court..................C2
Customs House.......A2
Cybi St.................C2
Cyttir Rd...............C3
Edmund St.............C1
Empire 🎬.............B2
Ferry Terminals.......B2
Ffordd Beibio.........B3
Ffordd Feurig.........C3
Ffordd Hirnos........C3
Ffordd Jasper........C3
Ffordd Tudur.........C3
Fire Station...........C2

Hull • Inverness • Ipswich • Kendal • King's Lynn • Lancaster • Leeds 351

Garreglwyd Rd B1
Gilbert St C2
Gorsedd Circle B1
Gwelfor Ave A1
Harbour View B3
Henry St C2
High Terr C1
Hill St B2
Holborn Rd C2
Holland Park Ind Est C3
Holyhead Park B1
Holyhead Station ⇌ B2
Information Ctr B2
King's Rd C2
Kingsland Rd C2
Lewascote C3
Library B2
Lifeboat Station A1
Llanfawr Cl C3
Llanfawr Rd C3
Lligwy St C2
Lon Deg C3
London Rd C3
Longford Rd B1
Longford Terr B1
Maes Cybi B1
Maes Hedd A1
Maes-Hyfryd Rd C1
Maes-y-Dref B1
Maes-yr-Haf A2/B1
Maes-yr-Ysgol C3
Marchog C3
Marina A1
Maritime Museum A1
Market B2
Market St B2
Mill Bank B1
Min-y-Mor Rd A1
Morawelon Ind Est B3
Morawelon Rd B3
Moreton Rd C1
New Park Rd B1
Newry St A2
Old Harbour Lighthouse A3
Plas Rd C1
Police Station B2
Porth-y-Felin Rd A1
Post Office A1/B1/B2/B3/C2/C3
Prince of Wales Rd A2
Priory La B3
Pump St C1
Queens Park B1
Reseifion Rd C1
Rock St B1
Roman Fort B2
St Cybi St B2
St Cybi's Church B2
St Seiriol's Cl B1
Salt Island Bridge A2
Seabourne Rd A1
South Stack Rd B1
Sports Ground B1
Stanley St B2
Station St B2
Tan-y-Bryn Rd A1
Tan-yr-Efail C2
Tara St C1
Thomas St B1
Town Hall A2
Treseifion Estate C2
Turkey Shore Rd B2
Ucheldre Arts Ctr ✦ B1
Ucheldre Ave B1
Upper Baptist St B1
Victoria Rd B2
Victoria Terr B2
Vulcan St B1
Walthew Ave A1
Walthew La A1
Wian St C2

Hull 335

Adelaide St C1
Albert Dock C1
Albion St B2
Alfred Gelder St B2
Anlaby Rd B1
Arctic Corsair ✦ B3
Beverley Rd A1
Blanket Row C2
Bond St B2
Bridlington Ave A2
Brook St B1
Brunswick Ave A1
Bus Station B1
Camilla Cl C3
Cannon St A2
Cannon's C1
Caroline St A2
Carr La B2
Castle St C2
Central Library B1
Charles St A2
Citadel Way B3
City Hall B2
City Hall Theatre B2
Clarence St B3
Cleveland St A3
Clifton St A1
Club Culture C2
Colonial St B1
Court B2
Deep, The C3
Dock Office Row B3
Dock St B2
Dinostar C2
Drypool Bridge B3
Egton St A3
English St C1
Ferens Gallery B2
Ferensway B1
Francis St A2
Francis St West A2
Freehold St A1
Freetown Way A2
Fruit Theatre C2
Garrison Rd B3
George St B2
Gibson St A2
Great Thornton St B1
Great Union St A3
Green La A2
Grey St A1
Grimston St B2
Grosvenor St A1
Guildhall B2
Guildhall Rd B2
Hands-on History B2
Harley St A1
Hessle Rd C1
High St B3
Holy Trinity B2
Hull & East Riding Museum B3
Hull Arena C1
Hull College B3
Hull History Centre A2
Hull (Paragon) Sta ⇌ B1
Hull Truck Theatre B1
Humber Dock Marina C2
Humber Dock St C2
Humber St C2
Hyperion St A3
Information Ctr B2
Jameson St B1
Jarratt St B2
Jenning St A3
King Billy Statue ✦ C2
King Edward St B2
King St A2
Kingston Retail Park C1
Kingston St C2
Liddell St A1
Lime St A3
Lister St C1
Lockwood St A2
Maister House B3
Maritime Museum B2
Market B2
Market Place B2
Minerva Pier C2
Mulgrave St A3
Myton Bridge C3
Myton St B1
NAPA (Northern Acad of Performing Arts) B1
Nelson St C2
New Cleveland St A3
New George St A2
New Theatre A2
Norfolk St A1
North Bridge A3
North St B1
Odeon C1
Old Harbour C3
Osborne St B1
Paragon St B2
Park St B1
Percy St A2
Pier St C2
Police Station B1
Post Office A1/B1/B2
Porter St C1
Portland St B1
Posterngate B2
Prince's Quay B2
Prospect Centre B1
Prospect St B1
Queen's Gdns B2
Railway Dock Marina C2
Railway St C2
Real B1
Red Gallery B1
Reform St A2
Retail Park B1
River Hull Footbridge B3
Riverside Quay C2
Roper St B2
St James St C1
St Luke's St B1
St Mark St A3
St Mary the Virgin B3
St Stephens Sh Ctr B1
Scott St A2
South Bridge Rd B3
Spring Bank A1
Spring St B1
Spurn Lightship C2
Spyvee St A3
Streetlife Transport Museum B3
Sykes St A2
Tidal Surge Barrier ✦ C3
Tower St B3
Trinity House B2
University B2
Vane St A1
Victoria Pier ✦ C2
Waterhouse La B2
Waterloo St A1
Waverley St C1
Wellington St C2
Wellington St West C2
West St B1
Whitefriargate B2
Wilberforce Dr B2
Wilberforce House B3
Wilberforce Monument ✦ B3
William St C1
Wincolmlee A3
Witham A3
Wright St A1

Inverness 336

Abban St A1
Academy St B2
Alexander Pl B2
Anderson St A2
Annfield Rd C3
Ardconnel St B3
Ardconnel Terr B3
Ardross Pl B2
Ardross St B2
Argyle St B3
Argyle Terr B3
Attadale Rd B1
Ballifeary La C2
Ballifeary Rd C1/C2
Balnacraig La A1
Balnain House ✦ B2
Balnain St B2
Bank St B2
Bellfield Park C2
Bellfield Terr C3
Benula Rd A1
Birnie Terr A1
Bishop's Rd C2
Bowling Green A2
Bowling Green B2
Bowling Green C2
Bridge St B2
Brown St A2
Bruce Ave C1
Bruce Gdns C1
Bruce Pk C1
Burial Ground A2
Burnett Rd A3
Bus Station B3
Caledonian Rd B1
Cameron Rd A1
Cameron Sq A1
Carse Rd A1
Carsegate Rd Sth A1
Castle Garrison Encounter ✦ B2
Castle Rd B2
Castle St B3
Celt St B2
Chapel St A2
Charles St B3
Church St B2
Clachnacuddin Football Ground A1
Columba Rd B1/C1
Crown Ave B3
Crown Circus B3
Crown Dr B3
Crown Rd B3
Crown St B3
Culduthel Rd C3
Dalneigh Cres C1
Dalneigh Rd C1
Denny St B3
Dochfour Dr B1/C1
Douglas Row B2
Duffy Dr C3
Dunabban Rd A1
Dunain Rd B1
Duncraig St B2
Eastgate Shopping Ctr B3
Eden Court C2
Fairfield Rd B1
Falcon Sq B3
Fire Station A3
Fraser St B2
Fraser St C2
Friars' Bridge A2
Friars' La B2
Friars' St A2
George St A2
Gilbert St A2
Glebe St A2
Glendoe Terr A1
Glenurquhart Rd C1
Gordon Terr B3
Gordonville Rd C2
Grant St A2
Greig St B2
HM Prison B3
Harbour Rd A3
Harrowden Rd B1
Haugh Rd C2
Heatherley Cres C3
High St B3
Highland Council HQ, The C2
Hill Park C3
Hill St B3
Huntly Pl A2
Huntly St B2
India St A2
Industrial Estate A3
Information Ctr B2
Innes St A2
Inverness ⇌ B3
Inverness College (Midmills Campus) B3
Inverness College UHI A3
Inverness High School B1
Inverness Museum B2
Jamaica St A2
Kenneth St B2
Kilmuir Rd A1
King St B2
Kingsmills Rd B3
Laurel Ave B1/C1
Library A3
Lilac Gr B1
Lindsay Ave C1
Lochalsh Rd A1/B1
Longman Rd A3
Lotland Pl A2
Lower Kessock St A1
Madras St A2
Market Hall B3
Maxwell Dr C1
Mayfield Rd C3
Millburn Rd B3
Mitchell's La C3
Montague Row B2
Muirfield Rd C3
Muirtown St B1
Nelson St A2
Ness Bank C2
Ness Bridge B2
Ness Walk B2/C2
Old Edinburgh Rd C3
Old High Church B2
Park Rd C1
Paton St C2
Perceval Rd B1
Planefield Rd B2
Police Station A3
Porterfield Bank C3
Porterfield Rd C3
Portland Pl A2
Post Office A2/B1/B2/B3
Queen St B2
Queensgate B2
Railway Terr A3
Rangemore Rd B1
Reay St B3
Riverside St A2
Rose St A2
Ross Ave B1
Rowan Rd B1
Royal Northern Infirmary C2
St Andrew's Cath † C2
St Columba B2
St John's Ave C1
St Mary's Ave C1
Sheriff Court B3
Shore St A2
Smith Ave C1
Southside Pl C3
Southside Rd C3
Spectrum Centre B2
Strothers La B3
Superstore A1
TA Centre C2
Telford Gdns B1
Telford Rd A1
Telford St A1
Tomnahurich Cemetery C1
Tomnahurich St B2
Town Hall B3
Union Rd B3
Union St B3
Walker Pl A2
Walker Rd A3
War Memorial ✦ C2
Waterloo Bridge A2
Wells St B1
Young St B2

Ipswich 336

Alderman Rd B2
All Saints' Rd A1
Alpe St B2
Ancaster Rd C1
Ancient House B3
Anglesea Rd B2
Ann St B2
Arboretum A2
Austin St C2
Belstead Rd C2
Berners St B2
Bibb Way B1
Birkfield Dr C1
Black Horse La B2
Bolton La B3
Bond St C3
Bowthorpe Cl B2
Bramford La A1
Bramford Rd A1
Bridge St C2
Brookfield Rd A1
Brooks Hall Rd A1
Broomhill A2
Broomhill Rd A1
Broughton Rd A2
Bulwer Rd B1
Burrell Rd C2
Butter Market B2
Buttermarket Shopping Centre, The B3
Cardinal Park L Park C2
Carr St B3
Cecil Rd B2
Cecilia St C2
Chancery Rd C2
Charles St B2
Chevallier St A1
Christchurch Mansion & Wolsey Art Gallery B3
Christchurch Park A3
Christchurch St B3
Cineworld C2
Civic Centre B2
Civic Dr B2
Clarkson St B1
Cobbold St B3
Commercial Rd C2
Constable Rd A3
Constantine Rd C1
Constitution Hill A2
Corder Rd A3
Corn Exchange B2
Cotswold Ave A2
Council Offices C2
County Hall B3
Crown Court C2
Crown St B2
Cullingham Rd B1
Cumberland St B2
Curriers La B2
Dale Hall La A2
Dales View Rd A1
Dalton Rd B2
Dillwyn St B1
Elliot St B1
Elm St B2
Elsmere Rd A3
Falcon St C2
Felaw St C3
Flint Wharf C3
Fonnereau Rd B2
Fore St C3
Foundation St C3
Franciscan Way C2
Friars St C2
Gainsborough Rd A3
Gatacre Rd B1
Geneva Rd B2
Gippeswyk Ave C1
Gippeswyk Park C1
Grafton Way C2
Graham Rd A1
Grimwade St C3
Great Whip St C3
Handford Cut B1
Handford Rd B1
Henley Rd A2
Hervey St B3
High St B2
Holly Rd A2
Information Ctr B3
Ipswich Haven Marina ✦ C3
Ipswich School A2
Ipswich Station ⇌ C2
Ipswich Town FC (Portman Road) C2
Ivry St A2
Kensington Rd A1
Kesteven Rd C1
Key St C3
Kingsfield Ave A3
Kitchener Rd A1
Magistrates Court B2
Little's Cr C2
London Rd B1
Low Brook St C3
Lower Orwell St C3
Luther Rd C2
Manor Rd A3
Mornington Ave A1
Mus & Art Gallery B2
Museum St B2
Neale St B3
New Cardinal St C2
New Cut East C3
New Cut West C3
New Wolsey B2
Newson St B2
Norwich Rd A1/B1
Oban St B2
Old Customs House C3
Old Foundry Rd B3
Old Merchant's Ho C3
Orford St B2
Paget Rd A2
Park Rd A3
Park View Rd A2
Peter's St C2
Philip Rd C2
Pine Ave A2
Pine View Rd A2
Police Station B2
Portman Rd B2
Portman Walk C1
Post Office B2/B3
Princes St C2
Prospect St B1
Queen St B2
Ranelagh Rd C1
Recreation Ground B1
Rectory Rd C2
Regent Theatre B3
Retail Park C1
Retail Park C2
Richmond Rd A1
Rope Walk C3
Rose La C2
Russell Rd C2
St Edmund's Rd A2
St George's St B2
St Helen's St B3
Sherrington Rd A1
Silent St C2
Sir Alf Ramsey Way C1
Sirdar Rd B1
Soane St B3
Springfield La A1
Star La C3
Stevenson Rd B1
Suffolk College C3
Suffolk Retail Park B1
Superstore B1
Surrey Rd B1
Tacket St C3
Tavern St B3
The Avenue A3
Tolly Cobbold Mus C3
Tower Ramparts B2
Tower Ramparts Shopping Centre B2
Tower St B3
Town Hall B2
Tuddenham Rd A3
Upper Brook St B3
Upper Orwell St B3
University C3
Valley Rd A2
Vermont Cr B3
Vermont Rd B3
Vernon St C3
Warrington Rd A2
Waterloo Rd A1
Waterworks St C3
Wellington St B1
West End Rd B1
Westerfield Rd A3
Westgate St B2
Westholme Rd A1
Westwood Ave A1
Willoughby Rd C2
Withipoll St B3
Woodbridge Rd B3
Woodstone Ave A3
Yarmouth Rd B1

Kendal 336

Abbot Hall Art Gallery & Museum of Lakeland Life C2
Ambulance Station A2
Anchorite Fields C2
Anchorite Rd C2
Ann St A3
Appleby Rd A3
Archers Meadow C3
Ashleigh Rd A2
Aynam Rd B2
Bankfield Rd B1
Beast Banks B2
Beezon Fields A2
Beezon Rd A2
Beezon Trad Est A3
Belmont B2
Birchwood Cl C1
Blackhall Rd B2
Brewery Arts Ctr B2
Bridge St B2
Brigsteer Rd C1
Burneside Rd A2
Bus Station B2
Buttery Well La C2
Canal Head North B3
Captain French La C2
Caroline St A2
Castle Hill B3
Castle Howe B2
Castle Rd B3
Castle St A3/B3
Cedar Gr C1
Council Offices B2
County Council Offices A2
Cricket Ground A3
Cricket Ground C3
Cross La C2
Dockray Hall Ind Est A2
Dowker's La B2
Dry Ski Slope ✦ B3
East View B1
Echo Barn Hill C1
Elephant Yard Sh Ctr B2
Fairfield La A1
Finkle St B2
Fire Station A2
Fletcher Square C3
Football Ground C3
Fowling La A3
Gillinggate C2
Glebe Rd C2
Golf Course B1
Goose Holme B3
Gooseholme Bridge B3
Green St A1
Greengate C2
Greengate La C1/C2
Greenside B1
Greenwood C1
Gulfs Rd B2
High Tenterfell B1
Highgate B2
Hillswood Ave C1
Horncop La A2
Information Ctr B2
K Village and Heritage Centre ✦ C2
Kendal Business Park A3
Kendal Castle (Remains) ✦ B3
Kendal Fell B1
Kendal Green A1
Kendal A3
Kendal Station ⇌ A3
Kent Pl B2
Kirkbarrow C2
Kirkland C2
Library B2
Library Rd B2
Little Aynam B3
Little Wood B1
Long Cl C1
Longpool A3
Lound Rd C3
Lound St C3
Low Fellside B2
Lowther St B2
Maple Dr C1
Market Pl B2
Maude St B2
Miller Bridge B2
Milnthorpe Rd C2
Mint St A3
Mintsfeet Rd A2
Mintsfeet Rd South A2
New Rd B2
Noble's Rest B2
Parish Church C2
Park Side Rd C3
Parkside Bsns Park C3
Parr St B3
Police Station A2
Post Office A3/B2/C2
Quaker Tapestry ✦ B2
Queen's Rd B1
Riverside Walk C2
Rydal Mount A2
Sandes Ave A2
Sandgate A3
Sandylands Rd A3
Serpentine Rd B1
Serpentine Wood B1
Shap Rd A3
South Rd C2
Stainbank Rd C1
Station Rd A3
Stramongate B2
Stramongate Bridge B2
Stricklandgate A2/B2
Sunnyside C3
Thorny Hills B3
Town Hall B2
Undercliff Rd B1
Underwood C1
Union St A2
Vicar's Fields C2
Vicarage Dr C1/C2
Wainwright Yd Sh Ctr B2
Wasdale Cl C3
Well Ings C2
Westmorland Shopping Centre & Market Hall B2
Westwood Ave C1
Wildman St A3
Windermere Rd A1
YHA B2
YWCA B2

King's Lynn 336

Albert St A2
Albion St B2
All Saints B2
All Saints St B2
Austin Fields A2
Austin St A2
Avenue Rd B3
Bank Side B1
Beech Rd C2
Birch Tree Cl B2
Birchwood St A2
Blackfriars Rd B2
Blackfriars St B2
Boal St B1
Bridge St B2
Broad St B2
Broad Walk B3
Burkitt St A2
Bus Station A2
Carmelite Terr C2
Chapel St A2
Chase Ave C3
Checker St C2
Church St B2
Clough La B2
Coburg St B2
College of West Anglia A3
Columbia Way A3
Corn Exchange A1
County Court Rd B2
Cresswell St A2
Custom House A1
Eastgate St A2
Edma St A2
Exton's Rd C3
Ferry La B1
Ferry St A1
Framingham's Almshouses B2
Friars St C2
Friars Walk C2
Gaywood Rd A3
George St A2
Gladstone Rd C2
Goodwin's Rd C3
Green Quay ✦ B1
Greyfriars' Tower ✦ B2
Guanock Terr C2
Guildhall A1
Hansa Rd C3
Hardwick Rd C2
Hextable Rd A2
High St B1
Holcombe Ave C3
Hospital Walk C2
Information Ctr B1
John Kennedy Rd A2
Kettlewell Lane A2
King George V Ave B3
King's Lynn Art Ctr A1
King's Lynn FC B3
King's Lynn Station ⇌ B2
King St B1
Library B2
Littleport St A2
Loke Rd A2
London Rd B2
Lynn Museum B2
Majestic B2
Magistrates Court B1
Market La A1
Millfleet B2
Milton Ave A3
Nar Valley Walk C2
Nelson St B1
New Conduit St B2
Norfolk St A2
North Lynn Discovery Centre ✦ A3
North St A2
Oldsunway B2
Ouse Ave C1
Page Stair Lane A1
Park Ave B3
Police Station B2
Portland Pl C1
Portland St B2
Post Office A3/C2
Purfleet B1
Queen St B1
Raby Ave A3
Railway Rd A2
Red Mount Chapel B3
Regent Way B2
River Walk A1
Robert St C2
Saddlebow Rd C2
St Ann's St A1
St James' Rd B2
St JamesÆ Swimming Pool B2
St James St B2
St John's Walk B3
St Margaret's B1
St Nicholas A2
St Nicholas St A1
St Peter's Rd B1
Sir Lewis St A2
Smith Ave A3
South Everard St C2
South Gate ✦ C2
South Quay B1
South St B2
Southgate St C2
Stonegate St B2
Surrey St A1
Sydney St C3
Tennyson Ave B3
Tennyson Rd B3
Tower St B2
Town Hall B1
Town Ho & Tales of The Old Gaol Ho B1
Town Wall (Remains) ✦ B3
True's Yard Mus A2
Valingers Rd C2
Vancouver Ave C2
Vancouver Quarter B2
Waterloo St B2
Wellesley St B2
White Friars Rd C2
Windsor Rd C2
Winfarthing St C2
Wyatt St A2
York Rd C3

Lancaster 336

Aberdeen Rd C3
Adult College, The C3
Aldcliffe Rd C2
Alfred St B3
Ambleside Rd A3
Ambulance Sta A3
Ashfield Ave B1
Ashton Rd C2
Assembly Rooms, The B2
Balmoral Rd B3
Bath House B2
Bath Mill La B3
Bath St B3
Blades St B1
Borrowdale Rd B3
Bowerham Rd C3
Brewery La B2
Bridge La B2
Brook St C1
Bulk Rd A3
Bulk St B2
Bus Station B2
Cable St B2
Canal Cruises & Waterbus ✦ C2
Carlisle Bridge A1
Carr House La C2
Castle B1
Castle Park B1
Caton Rd A3
China St B2
Church St B2
City Museum B2
Clarence St C3
Common Gdn St B2
Coniston Rd A3
Cottage Museum B2
Council Offices B2
Court B2
Cromwell Rd C1
Crown Court B1
Dale St C3
Dallas Rd B1/C1
Dalton Rd B3
Dalton Sq B2
Damside St B2
De Vitre St B3
Dee Rd A1
Denny Ave A1
Derby Rd A2
Dukes B2
Earl St A2
East Rd B3
Eastham St C3
Edward St B3
Fairfield Rd B1
Fenton St B2
Firbank Rd A3
Fire Station B2
Friend's Meeting Ho B1
Garnet St B3
George St B2
Giant Axe Field B1
Grand, The B2
Grasmere Rd B3
Greaves Rd C2
Green St A3
Gregson Centre, The B3
Gregson Rd C3
Greyhound Bridge A2
Greyhound Bridge Rd A2
High St B2
Hill Side B1
Hope St C3
Hubert Pl B1
Information Ctr B2
Judges Lodgings B2
Kelsy St B1
Kentmere Rd B3
King St B2
Kingsway A3
Kirkes Rd C3
Lancaster & Lakeland C3
Lancaster City Football Club B1
Lancaster Station ⇌ B1
Langdale Rd A3
Ley Ct B1
Library B2
Lincoln Rd B1
Lindow St C2
Lodge St B2
Long Marsh La B1
Lune Rd A1
Lune St A2
Lune Valley Ramble A3
Mainway A2
Maritime Museum A1
Market St B2
Mkt Gate Shopping Ctr B2
Meadowside C2
Meeting House La B1
Millennium Bridge A2
Moor La B2
Moorgate B3
Morecambe Rd A1/A2
Nelson St B2
North Rd B2
Orchard La C1
Owen Rd A2
Park Rd B3
Parliament St A3
Patterdale Rd A3
Penny St B2
Police Station B2
Portland St C2
Post Office A3/B1/B2/B3/C3
Primrose St C3
Priory B1
Prospect St C3
Quarry Rd B3
Queen St C2
Regent St C2
Ridge La A3
Ridge St A3
Royal Lancaster Infirmary (A&E) C2
Rydal Rd B3
Ryelands Park A1
St Georges Quay A1
St John's B2
St Leonard's Gate B2
St Martin's Rd C3
St Nicholas Arcades Shopping Centre B2
St Oswald St C3
St Peter's † B3
St Peter's Rd B3
Salisbury Rd B1
Scotch Quarry Urban Park C3
Shire Hall/HM Prison B1
Sibsey St B1
Skerton Bridge A2
South Rd C2
Station Rd B1
Stirling Rd C3
Storey Ave B1
Sunnyside La C1
Sylvester St C1
Tarnsyke Rd A1
Thurnham St C2
Town Hall B2
Troutbeck Rd B3
Ulleswater Rd B3
University of Cumbria C3
Vicarage Field B1
Vue B2
West Rd B1
Westbourne Dr C1
Westbourne Rd B1
Westham St C3
White Cross Bsns Park C2
Wheatfield St B1
Williamson Rd B3
Willow La B1
Windermere Rd B3
Wingate-Saul Rd B1
Wolseley St B3
Woodville St B3
Wyresdale Rd C3

Leeds 336

Aire St B3
Aireside Centre B2
Albion Pl B4
Albion St B4
Albion Way B1
Alma St A6
Arcades B4
Armley Rd B1
Back Burley Lodge Rd A1
Back Hyde Terr A2
Back Row C3
Bath Rd C3
Beckett St A6
Bedford St B3
Belgrave St A4
Belle View Rd A2
Benson St A5
Black Bull St C5
Blenheim Walk A3
Boar La B4
Bond St B4
Bow St C5
Bowman La C4
Brewery ✦ C4
Bridge St A5/B5
Briggate B4
Bruce Gdns C1
Burley Rd A1
Burley St B1
Burmantofs St B6
Bus & Coach Station B5
Butterly St C4
Butts Cr B4
Brewery Wharf C5
Byron St A5
Call La B4
Calverley St A3/B3
Canal St B1
Canal Wharf C3
Carlisle Rd C5
Cavendish Rd A1
Cavendish St A2
Chadwick St C5
Cherry Pl A6
Cherry Row A5
City Museum A4
City Palace of Varieties B4
City Sq B3
Civic Hall A3
Clarence Road C5
Clarendon Rd A2
Clarendon Way A3
Clark La C6
Clay Pit La A4
Cloberry St A2
Clyde Approach C1
Clyde Gdns C1
Coleman St C2
Commercial St B4
Concord St A5
Cookridge St A4
Copley Hill C1
Corn Exchange B4
Cromer Terr A2
Cromwell St A5
Cross Catherine St B6
Cross Green La C6
Cross Stamford St A5
Crown & County Courts A3
Crown Point Bridge C5
Crown Point Retail Pk C4
Crown Point Rd C4
David St C3
Dent St C6
Derwent Pl C3
Dial St C6

352 Leicester • Lewes • Lincoln • Liverpool • Llandudno

Dock St C4
Dolly La A6
Domestic St C2
Duke St B5
Duncan St B4
Dyer St B5
East Field St B6
East Pde B3
East St C5
Eastgate B5
Easy Rd C6
Edward St B4
Ellerby La C6
Ellerby Rd C6
Fenton St A3
Fire Station B2
First Direct Arena A4
Fish St B4
Flax Pl B5
Gelderd Rd C1
George St B4
Globe Rd C2
Gloucester Cr B1
Gower St A5
Grafton St A4
Grand Theatre B4
Granville Rd A6
Great George St A3
Great Wilson St C4
Greek St B3
Green La C1
Hanover Ave A2
Hanover La A2
Hanover Sq A2
Hanover Way A2
Harewood St B4
Harrison St B4
Haslewood Cl B6
Haslewood Drive B6
High Court B5
Holbeck La C2
Holdforth Cl C1
Holdforth Gdns B1
Holdforth Gr C1
Holdforth Pl C1
Holy Trinity B4
Hope Rd A5
Hunslet La C4
Hunslet Rd C4
Hyde Terr A2
Infirmary St B3
Information Ctr B3
Ingram Row C3
Junction St C4
Kelso Gdns A2
Kelso Rd A2
Kelso St A2
Kendal La A2
Kendell St C4
Kidacre St C4
King Edward St B4
King St B3
Kippax Pl C6
Kirkgate B4
Kirkgate Market B4
Kirkstall Rd A1
Kitson St C6
Lady La B4
Lands La B4
Lavender Walk B6
Leeds Art Gallery B3
Leeds Bridge C4
Leeds Coll of Music B5
Leeds General Infirmary (A&E) A3
Leeds Metropolitan University A3/A4
Leeds Museum Discovery Centre C5
Leeds Shopping Plaza B4
Leeds Station B3
Leeds University A3
Library B3
Lincoln Green Rd A6
Lincoln Rd A6
Lindsey Gdns A6
Lindsey Rd A6
Lisbon St B3
Little Queen St B3
Long Close La C6
Lord St C2
Lovell Park A4
Lovell Park Rd A4
Lovell Rd A5
Lower Brunswick St A5
Mabgate A5
Macauly St A5
Magistrates Court A3
Manor Rd C3
Mark La B4
Marlborough St B2
Marsh La B5
Marshall St C3
Meadow La C4
Meadow Rd C4
Melbourne St A5
Merrion Centre A4
Merrion St A4
Merrion Way A4
Mill St B5
Millennium Sq A3
Mount Preston St A2
Mushroom St A5
Neville St C4
New Briggate A4/B4
New Market St B4
New Station St B4
New York Rd A5
New York St B5
Nile St A5
Nippet La A6
North St A4
Northern St B3
Oak Rd B1
Oxford Pl B3
Oxford Row A3
Park Cross St B3
Park La A2
Park Pl B3
Park Row B4
Park Sq B3
Park Sq East B3
Park Sq West B3
Park St B3
Police Station B5
Pontefract La B6
Portland Cr A3
Portland Way A3
Post Office B4/B5
Project Space Leeds C2
Quarry House (NHS/DSS Headquarters) B5
Quebec St B3
Queen St B3
Railway St B5
Rectory St A6
Regent St A5
Richmond St C5
Rigton Approach B6
Rigton Dr B6
Rillbank La A1
Rosebank Rd A1
Royal Armouries C5
Russell St B3
Rutland St B2
St Anne's Cath (RC) A4
St Anne's St B4
St James' Hospital A6
St Johns Centre B4
St John's Rd A2
St Mary's St B5
St Pauls St B3
St Peter's B5
Saxton La B5
Sayner La C5
Shakespeare Ave A6
Shannon St B6
Sheepscar St South A5
Siddall St C3
Skinner La A5
South Pde B3
Sovereign St C4
Spence La C2
Springfield Mount A2
Springwell Ct C2
Springwell Rd C2
Springwell St C2
Stoney Rock La A6
Studio Rd A1
Sutton St C2
Sweet St C3
Sweet St West C3
Swinegate B4
Templar St B5
The Calls B5
The Close B6
The Core B4
The Drive B6
The Garth B5
The Headrow B3/B4
The Lane B5
The Light B4
The Parade B6
The Tetley C4
Thoresby Pl A3
Torre Rd A6
Town Hall A3
Union Pl C3
Union St B5
Upper Accomodation Rd B6
Upper Basinghall St B4
Vicar La B4
Victoria Bridge C4
Victoria Quarter B4
Victoria Rd C4
Vue B4
Wade La A4
Washington St A1
Water La C3
Waterloo Rd C4
Wellington Rd B2/C1
Wellington St B3
West St B2
West Yorkshire Playhouse B5
Westfield Rd A1
Westgate B3
Whitehall Rd B3/C2
Whitelock St A5
Willis St C6
Willow Approach A1
Willow Ave A1
Willow Terrace Rd A3
Wintoun St A5
Woodhouse La A3/A4
Woodsley Rd A1
York Pl B3
York Rd B6
Yorkshire Television Studios A1

Leicester 336

Abbey St A2
All Saints' A1
Aylestone Rd C2
Bath La A1
Bede Park C1
Bedford St A3
Bedford St South A3
Belgrave Gate A2
Belle Vue A2
Belvoir St B2
Braunstone Gate B1
Burleys Way A2
Burnmoor St C2
Bus Station A2
Canning St A2
Carlton St C2
Castle B1
Castle Gardens B1
Cathedral B2
Causeway La A2
Charles St B3
Chatham St B2
Christow St A3
Church Gate A2
City Gallery B3
Civic Centre B2
Clank St B2
Clock Tower B2
Clyde St A3
Colton St B3
Conduit St B3
Crafton St A3
Craven St A1
Crown Courts B3
Curve B3
De Lux A2
De Montfort Hall C3
De Montfort St C3
De Montfort Univ C1
Deacon St C2
Dover St B3
Duns La B1
Dunton St A1
East St B3
Eastern Boulevard C1
Edmonton Rd A3
Erskine St A3
Filbert St C1
Filbert St East C2
Fire Station C3
Fleet St A3
Friar La B2
Friday St A2
Gateway St C2
Glebe St B3
Granby St B3
Grange La C2
Grasmere St C1
Great Central St A1
Guildhall B2
Guru Nanak Sikh Museum B1
Halford St B2
Havelock St C2
Haymarket Sh Ctr A2
High St A2
Highcross St A1
Highcross Sh Ctr A2
HM Prison C2
Horsefair St B2
Humberstone Gate B2
Humberstone Rd A3
Infirmary St C2
Information Ctr B2
Jarrom St C2
Jewry Wall B1
Kamloops Cr A3
King Richards Rd B1
King St B2
Lancaster Rd C3
LCB Depot B3
Lee St A3
Leicester Royal Infirmary (A&E) C2
Leicester Station B3
Library B2
Little Theatre, The B3
London Rd C3
Lower Brown St B2
Magistrates Court B2
Manitoba Rd A3
Mansfield St A2
Market A2
Market St B2
Mill La C2
Montreal Rd A3
Narborough Rd North B1
Nelson Mandela Park C2
New Park St B1
New St B2
New Walk C3
New Walk Museum & Art Gallery C3
Newarke Houses B2
Newarke St B2
Northgate St A1
Orchard St A2
Ottawa Rd A3
Oxford St C2
Upper Brown St B2
Phoenix Square B3
Police Station A3
Post Office A1/B2/C2/C3
Prebend St C3
Princess Rd East C3
Princess Rd West C3
Queen St B3
Regent College C3
Regent Rd C2/C3
Repton St A1
Rutland St B3
St George St B3
St Georges Way B3
St John St A2
St Margaret's A2
St Margaret's Way A2
St Martins B2
St Mary de Castro B1
St Matthew's Way A3
St Nicholas B1
St Nicholas Circle B1
Sanvey Gate A2
Silver St B2
Slater St A1
Soar La A1
South Albion St B3
Southampton St B3
Swain St B3
Swan St A1
The Gateway C2
The Newarke B1
The Rally Com Park A2
Tigers Way C3
Tower St C3
Town Hall B2
Tudor Rd B1
University of Leicester C3
University Rd C3
Upperton Rd C1
Vaughan Way A2
Walnut St C2
Watling St A2
Welford Rd B2
Welford Rd Stadium C2
Wellington St B2
West Bridge B1
West St C3
West Walk C3
Western Boulevard C1
Western Rd C1
Wharf St North A3
Wharf St South A3
Y' Theatre, The B3
Yeoman St B3
York Rd B2

Lewes 336

Abinger Pl B1
All Saints Centre B2
Ambulance Station B2
Anne of Cleves Ho C1
Barbican Ho Mus B1
Brewery B2
Brook St A2
Brooks Rd A2
Bus Station B2
Castle Ditch La B1
Castle Precincts B1
Chapel Hill B3
Church La A1/A2
Cliffe High St B2
Cliffe Industrial Est C3
Cluny St C1
Cockshut Rd C1
Convent Field C2
Coombe Rd A2
County Hall B1
County Records Office B1
Court B2
Court Rd B2
Crown Court B2
Cuilfail Tunnel B3
Davey's La A3
East St B2
Eastport La C1
Fire Station A2
Fisher St B2
Friars Walk B2
Garden St B1
Government Offices C2
Grange Rd B1
Ham La C2
Harveys Way B2
Hereward Way A2
High St B1/B2
Hop Gallery B2
Information Ctr B2
Keere St B1
King Henry's Rd B1
Lancaster St B2
Landport Rd A1
Leisure Centre C3
Lewes Bridge B2
Lewes Castle B1
Lewes Football Gd C2
Lewes Golf Course B3
Lewes Southern By-Pass C2
Lewes Station B2
Library B2
Malling Ind Est A2
Malling Brook Ind Est A3
Malling Hill A3
Malling St A3/B3
Market St B2
Martyr's Monument B3
Mayhew Way A2
Morris Rd B3
Mountfield Rd C2
New Rd B1
Newton Rd A1
North St A2/B2
Offham Rd B1
Old Malling Way A1
Orchard Rd A3
Paddock La B1
Paddock Rd B1
Paddock Sports Gd B1
Park Rd B1
Pelham Terr A1
Pells Open Air Swimming Pool A1
Phoenix Causeway B2
Phoenix Ind Est B2
Phoenix Pl B2
Pinwell Rd B2
Police Station B1
Post Office A2/B1/B2/C1
Prince Edward's Rd B1
Priory St C1
Priory of St Pancras (remains of) C1
Railway La B2
Railway Land Nature Reserve B3
Rotten Row B1
Rufus Cl B1
St Pancras Rd C1
St John St B2
St John's Terr B1
St Nicholas La B2
Sewage Works C3
South Downs Bsns Pk A3
South St B3/C3
Southdowns Rd A2
Southerham Junction C3
Southover Grange Gdns B1
Southover High St C1
Southover Rd B1
Spences Field A3
Spences La A2
Stansfield Rd A1
Station Rd B2
Station St B2
Sun St B1
Sussex Downs College C2
Sussex Police HQ A2
Talbot Terr B1
The Avenue B1
The Course C1
The Martlets A2
The Needlemakers B2
The Pells A1
Thebes Gallery B2
Toronto Terr B1
Town Hall B2
West St B2
White Hill B1
Willeys Bridge A1

Lincoln 337

Alexandra Terr B1
Anchor St C1
Arboretum B3
Arboretum Ave B3
Baggholme Rd B3
Bailgate A2
Beaumont Fee B1
Brayford Way C1
Brayford Wharf East C1
Brayford Wharf North B1
Bruce Rd A2
Burton Rd A1
Bus Station (City) C2
Canwick Rd C2
Cardinal's Hat B2
Carline Rd B1
Castle B1
Castle St A1
Cathedral B2
Cathedral St B2
Cecil St A2
Chapel La A2
Cheviot St B3
Church La A2
City Hall B1
Clasketgate B2
Clayton Sports Gd A3
Coach Park C2
Collection, The B2
County Hospl (A&E) B3
County Office B1
Courts C1
Croft St B2
Cross St C2
Crown Courts B1
Curle Ave A3
Danesgate B2
Drill Hall B2
Drury La B1
East Bight A2
East Gate A2
Eastcliff Rd B3
Eastgate B2
Egerton Rd A3
Ellis Windmill A1
Engine Shed, The C1
Environment Agency C2
Exchequer Gate B2
Firth Rd C1
Flaxengate B2
Florence St B3
George St C3
Good La A2
Gray St A1
Great Northern Terr C3
Great Northern Terrace Industrial Estate C3
Greetwell Rd B3
Greetwellgate B3
Haffenden Rd A2
High St B2/C1
HM Prison A3
Hospital (Private) A2
Hungate B2
James St A2
Jews House & Ct B2
Kesteven St C2
Langworthgate A2
Lawn Visitor Centre, The B1
Lee Rd A3
Library B2
Lincoln College B2
Lincoln Central Sta C2
Lincolnshire Life/Royal Lincolnshire Regiment Museum A1
Lindum Rd B2
Lindum Sports Ground A3
Lindum Terr B3
Mainwaring Rd A3
Manor Rd A2
Market C2
Massey Rd A3
Medieval Bishop's Palace B2
Mildmay St A1
Mill Rd A1
Millman Rd B3
Minster Yard B2
Monks Rd B3
Montague St B2
Mount St A1
Nettleham Rd A2
Newland B1
Newport A2
Newport Arch A2
Newport Cemetery A2
Northgate A2
Odeon C1
Orchard St B1
Oxford St C2
Park St B1
Pelham Bridge C2
Pelham St C2
Police Station B1
Portland St C2
Post Office A1/A2/B1/B3/C2
Potter Gate B2
Priory Gate B2
Queensway A3
Rasen La A1
Ropewalk C1
Rosemary La B2
St Anne's Rd B3
St Benedict's C1
St Giles Ave A3
St John's Rd A2
St Marks St C1
St Mark's Sh Ctr C1
St Mary-Le-Wigford C1
St Mary's St C2
St Nicholas St A2
St Swithin's B2
Saltergate C1
Saxon St A1
Sch of Art & Design B2
Sewell Rd B3
Silver St B2
Sincil St C2
Spital St A2
Spring Hill B1
Stamp End C3
Steep Hill B2
Stonebow & Guildhall C2
Stonefield Ave A2
Tentercroft St C1
The Avenue B1
The Grove A3
Theatre Royal B2
Tritton Retail Park C1
Tritton Rd C1
Union Rd B1
University of Lincoln C1
Upper Lindum St B3
Upper Long Leys Rd A1
Usher B2
Vere St A2
Victoria St B1
Victoria Terr B1
Vine St B3
Wake St A1
Waldeck St A1
Waterside Sh Ctr C2
Waterside North C2
Waterside South C2
West Pde B1
Westgate A2
Wigford Way C1
Williamson St A2
Wilson St A1
Winn St B3
Wragby Rd A3
Yarborough Rd A1

Liverpool 337

Abercromby Sq C5
Acc Liverpool C2
Addison St A3
Adelaide Rd B6
Ainsworth St B4
Albany Rd B6
Albert Dock C2
Albert Edward Rd B6
Angela St C6
Anson St B4
Archbishop Blanche High School B6
Argyle St C3
Arrad St C4
Ashton St B5
Audley St A4
Back Leeds St A2
Basnett St B3
Bath St A1
Beatles Story C2
Beckwith St C3
Bedford Close C5
Bedford St North C5
Bedford St South C5
Benson St C4
Berry St C4
Birkett St A4
Bixteth St B2
Blackburne Place C4
Bluecoat B3
Bold Place C4
Bold St C4
Bolton St B3
Bridport St B4
Bronte St B4
Brook St A1
Brownlow Hill B4/B5
Brownlow St B5
Brunswick Rd A5
Brunswick St B1
Bus Station C2
Butler Cr A6
Byrom St A3
Caledonia St C4
Cambridge St C5
Camden St A4
Canada Blvd B1
Canning Dock C2
Canterbury St A4
Cardwell St C6
Carver St A4
Cases St B3
Castle St B2
Catherine St C5
Cavern Club B3
Central Library A3
Central Station B3
Chapel St B2
Charlotte St B3
Chatham Place C6
Chatham St C5
Cheapside B2
Chestnut St C5
Christian St A3
Church St B3
Churchill Way North A3
Churchill Way South B3
Clarence St B4
Coach Station A4
Cobden St A5
Cockspur St A2
College St C3
College St North A5
College St South A5
Colquitt St C4
Comus St A3
Concert St C3
Connaught Rd B6
Cook St B2
Copperas Hill B4
Cornwallis St C3
Covent Garden B2
Craven St A4
Cropper St B3
Crown St B5/C6
Cumberland St B2
Cunard Building B1
Dale St B2
Dansie St B4
Daulby St B5
Dawson St B3
Derby Sq B2
Drury La B2
Duckinfield St B4
Duke St C3
Earle St A2
East St A2
Eaton St A2
Echo Arena C2
Edgar St A3
Edge La B6
Edinburgh Rd A6
Edmund St B2
Elizabeth St B5
Elliot St B3
Empire Theatre B4
Empress Rd B6
Epworth St A5
Erskine St A5
Everyman Theatre C5
Exchange St East B2
Fact Centre, The C4
Falkland St A5
Falkner St C5/C6
Farnworth St A6
Fenwick St B2
Fielding St A6
Fleet St C3
Fraser St A4
Freemasons Row A2
Gardner Row A3
Gascoyne St A2
George Pier Head C1
George St B2
Gibraltar Road A1
Gilbert St C3
Gildart St A4
Gill St B4
Goree B2
Gower St C2
Gradwell St C3
Great Crosshall St A3
Great George St C4
Great Howard St A1
Great Newton St B4
Greek St B4
Green La B4
Greenside A5
Greetham St C3
Gregson St A5
Grenville St C3
Grinfield St C6
Grove St C5
Guelph St A6
Hackins Hey B2
Haigh St A4
Hall La B6
Hanover St B3
Harbord St C6
Hardman St C4
Harker St A4
Hart St B4
Hatton Garden A2
Hawke St B4
Helsby St B6
Henry St C3
HM Customs & Excise National Museum C2
Highfield St A2
Highgate St B6
Hilbre St B4
Hope Place C4
Hope St C4
Houghton St B3
Hunter St A3
Hutchinson St A6
Information Ctr C2
Institute For The Performing Arts C4
Irvine St B6
Irwell St B2
Islington A4
James St B2
James St Station B2
Jenkinson St A4
Johnson St A3
Jubilee Drive B6
Kempston St A4
Kensington A6
Kensington Gdns B6
Kensington St A6
Kent St C3
King Edward St A1
Kinglake St B6
Knight St C4
Lace St A3
Langsdale St A4
Law Courts C2
Leece St C4
Leeds St A2
Leopold Rd B6
Lime St B3
Lime St Station B4
Little Woolton St B5
Liver St C2
Liverpool John Moores University A3/B4/C4
Liverpool Landing Stage B1
Liverpool One C2
London Rd A4/B4
Lord Nelson St B4
Lord St B2
Lovat St C6
Low Hill A5
Low Wood St A6
Lydia Ann St C3
Mansfield St A4
Marmaduke St B6
Marsden St A6
Martensen St B6
Marybone A3
Maryland St C4
Mason St B6
Mathew St B2
May St B4
Melville Place C6
Merseyside Maritime Museum C2
Metquarter B3
Metropolitan Cathedral (RC) B5
Midghall St A2
Molyneux Rd A6
Moor Place B4
Moorfields B2
Moorfields Station B2
Moss St A5
Mount Pleasant B4/B5
Mount St C4
Mount Vernon B6
Mulberry St C5
Municipal Buildings A2
Mus of Liverpool C2
Myrtle Gdns C6
Myrtle St C5
Naylor St A2
Nelson St C4
Neptune Theatre B3
New Islington A4
New Quay B1
Newington St C3
North John St B2
North St A3
North View B6
Norton St A4
Oakes St B5
O2 Academy
Odeon B4
Old Hall St A1
Old Leeds St A2
Oldham Place C4
Oldham St C4
Olive St C6
Open Eye Gallery C3
Oriel St A2
Ormond St B2
Orphan St C6
Overbury St C6
Overton St B6
Oxford St C5
Paisley St A1
Pall Mall A2
Paradise St C3
Park La C3
Parker St B3
Parr St C3
Peach St B5
Pembroke Place B4
Pembroke St B5
Philharmonic Hall C5
Pickop St A2
Pilgrim St C4
Pitt St C3
Playhouse Theatre B3
Pleasant St B4
Police HQ C2
Police Station A4/B4
Pomona St B4
Port of Liverpool Building B2
Post Office A2/A4/A5/A6/B2/B3/B4/C4
Pownall St C2
Prescot St A5
Preston St B3
Princes Dock A1
Princes Gdns A2
Princes Jetty A1
Princes Pde B1
Princes St B2
Pythian St A6
Queen Sq Bus Station B3
Queensland St C6
Queensway Tunnel (Docks exit) B1
Queensway Tunnel (Entrance) B3
Radio City B2
Ranelagh St B3
Redcross St B2
Renfrew St B6
Renshaw St B4
Richmond Row A4
Richmond St B3
Rigby St A2
Roberts St A1
Rock St B4
Rodney St C4
Rokeby St A4
Romily St A6
Roscoe La C4
Roscoe St C4
Rose Hill A3
Royal Court Theatre B3
Royal Liver Building B1
Royal Liverpool Hospital (A&E) B5
Royal Mail St B4
Rumford Place B2
Rumford St B2
Russell St B4
St Andrew St B4
St Anne St A4
St Georges Hall B3
St John's Centre B3
St John's Gdns B3
St John's La B3
St Joseph's Cr A4
St Minishull St B5
St Nicholas Place B1
St Paul's Sq A2
St Vincent Way B4
Salisbury St A4
Salthouse Dock C2
Salthouse Quay C2
Sandon St C5
Saxony Rd B6
Schomberg St A6
School La B2
Seel St C3
Seymour St B4
Shaw St A5
Sidney Place C6
Sir Thomas St B3
Skelhorne St B4
Slater St C3
Slavery Museum C2
Smithdown La B6
Soho Sq A4
Soho St A4
South John St B2
Springfield A4
Stafford St A4
Standish St A3
Stanley St B2
Strand St C2
Suffolk St C3
Tabley St C3
Tarleton St B3
Tate Gallery C2
Teck St B6
Temple St B2
The Beacon B3
The Strand B2
Tithebarn St B2
Town Hall B2
Traffic Police HQ C6
Trowbridge St B4
Trueman St A3
Union St B2
Unity Theatre C4
University C5
Univ of Liverpool B5
Upper Duke St C4
Upper Frederick St C3
Upper Baker St A6
Vauxhall Rd A2
Vernon St B2
Victoria Gallery & Museum B5
Victoria St B2
Vine St C5
Wakefield St A4
Walker Art Gallery A3
Walker St A6
Wapping C2
Water St B1/B2
Waterloo Rd A1
Wavertree Rd B6
West Derby Rd A6
West Derby St B5
Whitechapel B3
Western Approaches War Museum B2
Whitley Gdns A5
William Brown St B3
William Henry St A4
Williamson Sq B3
Williamson St B3
Williamson's Tunnels Heritage Centre C6
Women's Hospital C6
Wood St B3
World Museum, Liverpool A3
York St C3

Llandudno 337

Abbey Pl B1
Abbey Rd B1
Adelphi St B3
Alexandra Rd C2
Anglesey Rd A1
Argyll Rd B3
Arvon Ave A2
Atlee Cl C3
Augusta St B3
Back Madoc St B2
Bodafon St B3
Bodhyfryd Rd A2
Bodnant Cr C3
Bodnant Rd C3
Bridge Rd C2
Bryniau Rd C1
Builder St B3
Builder St West C2
Cabin Lift A2
Camera Obscura A3
Caroline Rd B2
Chapel St A2
Charlton St B3
Church Cr C1
Church Walks A2
Claremont Rd B2
Clement Ave A2
Clifton Rd B2
Clonmel St B3
Coach Station B3
Conway Rd B3
Council St West C3
Cricket and Rec Gd B2
Cwlach Rd A2
Cwlach St A1
Cwm Howard La C3
Cwm Pl C3
Cwm Rd C3
Dale Rd C1
Deganwy Ave B2
Denness Pl C2
Dinas Rd C2
Dolydd B1
Erol Pl B2
Ewloe Dr C3
Fairways C2
Ffordd Dewi C3
Ffordd Dulyn C2
Ffordd Dwyfor C3
Ffordd Elisabeth C3
Ffordd Gwynedd C3
Ffordd Las C3
Ffordd Morfa C3
Ffordd Penrhyn C3
Ffordd Tudno C3
Ffordd yr Orsedd C3
Ffordd Ysbyty C2

Pritchard St C4
Quay St A2
Quay St B2
Queen St B3
Radium St A5
Redhill St A5
Regent Rd B1
Renold Theatre A2
Retail Park A5
Rice St B2
Richmond St B4
River St C3
Roby St B5
Rodney St A6
Roman Fort B2
Rosamond St A2
Royal Exchange A3
Sackville St B4
St Andrew's St B6
St Ann St A3
St Ann's A3
St George's Ave C1
St James St B4
St John St B3
St John's Cath (RC) A2
St Mary's B3
St Mary's Gate A3
St Mary's Parsonage A3
St Peter's Sq B3
St Stephen St A2
Salford Approach A3
Salford Central A2
Sheffield St B5
Shepley St B5
Sherratt St A5
Shudehill A4
Shudehill A4
Sidney St C4
Silk St A5
Silver St B4
Skerry Cl C5
Snell St B6
South King St B3
Sparkle St B5
Spear St A4
Spring Gdns A4
Stanley St A2/B2
Station Approach B5
Store St B5
Swan St A4
Tariff St B5
Tatton St C1
Temperance St B6/C6
The Triangle A4
Thirsk St C6
Thomas St A4
Thompson St A5
Tib La B3
Tib St A4
Town Hall (Manchester) B3
Town Hall (Salford) A2
Trafford St C3
Travis St B5
Trinity Way A2
Turner St A4
Union St C6
University of Manchester (Sackville Street Campus) C5
Upper Brook St C5
Upper Cleminson St A1
Upper Wharf St A1
Vesta St B6
Victoria A4
Victoria Station A4
Victoria St A3
Wadesdon Rd C5
Water St B2
Watson St B3
West Fleet St B1
West King St A2
West Mosley St B4
West Union St B1
Weybridge Rd A6
Whitworth St B4
Whitworth St West C3
Wilburn St B1
William St A2
William St C6
Wilmott St C3
Windmill St B3
Windsor Cr A1
Withy Gr A4
Woden St C1
Wood St B3
Woodward St A6
Worrall St C1
Worsley St C2
York St B4
York St C2
York St C4

Merthyr Tydfil
Merthyr Tudful 340

Aberdare Rd B2
Abermorlais Terr B2
Alexandra Rd A3
Alma St C3
Arfryn Pl C3
Argyle St C3
Avenue De Clichy C2
Bethesda St B2
Bishops Gr A3
Brecon Rd A1/B2
Briarmead A3
Bryn St C3
Bryntirion Rd B3/C3
Bus Station B2
Caedraw Rd C2
Cae Mari Dwn B3
Castle Sq A1
Castle St B2
Chapel C2
Chapel Bank A1
Church St B3
Civic Centre B2
Coedcae'r Ct C3
Court B3
Courts B2
Court St C3
Cromwell St B2
Cyfarthfa Castle School and Museum A1
Cyfarthfa Ind Est A1
Cyfarthfa Park A1
Cyfarthfa Rd A1
Dane St A2
Dane Terr A2
Danyparc B3
Darren View A3
Dixon St B2
Dyke St C3
Dynevor St B2
Elwyn Dr C3
Fire Station B2
Fothergill St B3
Galonuchaf Rd A3
Garth St B2
Georgetown B2
Grawen Terr A2
Grove Pk A2
Gurnos Rd A2
Gwaelodygarth Rd A2/A3
Gwaunfarren Gr A3
Gwaunfarren Rd A3
Gwendoline St A3
Hampton St C3
Hanover St A2
Heol S O Davies B1
Heol-Gerrig B1
Highland View C3
High St A3/B2/B3/C2
Howell Cl B1
Information Ctr B2
Jackson's Bridge B2
James St C3
John St B3
Joseph Parry's Cottage B2
Lancaster St A2
Library B2
Llewellyn St A2
Llwyfen St B2
Llwyn Berry B1
Llwyn Dic Penderyn B1
Llwyn-y-Gelynen C1
Lower Thomas St B3
Market C2
Mary St C3
Masonic St C2
Merthyr RFC C2
Merthyr College B2
Merthyr Town FC B3
Merthyr Tydfil Leisure Village C3
Merthyr Tydfil Sta C3
Meyrick Villas A2
Miniature Railway A1
Mount St A2
Nantygwenith St B1
Norman Terr B2
Oak Rd A2
Old Cemetery B3
Pandy Cl A1
Pantycelynen B1
Park Terr B2
Penlan View C2
Penry St B2
Pentwyn Villas A2
Penyard Rd B3
Penydarren Park A3
Penydarren Rd B3
Plymouth St C3
Police Station C2
Pont Marlais West B2
Post Office A3/B2/C3
Quarry Row B2
Queen's Rd B3
Rees St C3
Rhydycar Link C2
Riverside Park A1
St David's B3
St Tydfil's C2
St Tydfil's Ave C3
St Tydfil's Hospital (No A+E) B3
St Tydfil's Sq Sh Ctr C2
Saxon St A2
School of Nursing A2
Seward St A3
Shiloh La B3
Stone Circles B3
Stuart St A2
Summerhill Pl B3
Superstore B3
Swan St C2
Swansea Rd B1
Taff Glen View C3
Taff Vale Ct B3
Theatre Soar B2
The Grove A2
The Parade B3
The Walk B2
Thomastown Park B3
Tramroad La A3
Tramroad Side B2
Tramroad Side North B3
Tramroad Side South C3
Trevithick Gdns C3
Trevithick St A3
Tudor Terr B2
Twynyrodyn Rd C3
Union St B3
Upper Colliers Row B1
Upper Thomas St B3
Victoria St B2
Vue C3
Vulcan Rd B2
Warlow St C3
Well St A2
Welsh Assembly Government Offices C2
Wern La C1
West Gr A2
William St C3
Yew St C3
Ynysfach Engine Ho C2
Ynysfach Rd C2

Middlesbrough
340

Abingdon Rd C3
Acklam Rd C1
Albert Park C2
Albert Rd B2
Albert Terr C2
Aubrey St C3
Ayresome Gdns C2
Ayresome Green La C1
Ayresome St C2
Barton Rd A1
Bilsdale Rd C3
Bishopton Rd C3
Borough Rd B2/B3
Bowes Rd A2
Breckon Hill Rd B3
Bridge St East B3
Bridge St West B2
Brighouse Rd A1
Burlam Rd C1
Bus Station B2
Cannon Park B1
Cannon Park Way B2
Cannon St B1
Captain Cook Sq B2
Carlow St C1
Castle Way C3
Chipchase Rd C2
Cineworld B3
Clairville Sports Stadium C3
Cleveland Centre B2
Clive Rd C2
Commercial St A2
Corporation Rd B2
Costa St C2
Council Offices B3
Crescent Rd C2
Cumberland Rd C2
Depot Rd A2
Derwent St B2
Devonshire Rd C2
Diamond Rd B2
Disabled Driver Test Circuit B1
Dorman Museum C2
Douglas St B3
Eastbourne Rd C2
Eden Rd C3
Enterprise Centre A2
Forty Foot Rd A2
Gilkes St B2
Gosford St A2
Grange Rd B2
Gresham Rd B2
Harehills Rd C1
Harford St C2
Hartington Rd B2
Haverton Hill Rd A1
Hey Wood St B1
Highfield Rd C3
Hill St Centre B2
Holwick Rd B1
Hutton Rd C3
ICI Works A1
Information Ctr B2
Lambton Rd C3
Lancaster Rd C2
Lansdowne Rd C3
Latham Rd C2
Law Courts B2/B3
Lees Rd B2
Leeway B3
Linthorpe Cemetery C1
Linthorpe Rd B2
Lloyd St B2
Longford St C2
Longlands Rd C3
Lower East St A3
Lower Lake C3
Maldon Rd C1
Manor St B2
Marsh St B2
Marton Rd B3
Middlehaven B3
Middlesbrough By-Pass B2/C1
Middlesbrough Coll B3
Middlesbrough L Park B3
Middlesbrough Sta B2
Middlesbrough Theatre C2
Middletown Park C2
MIMA B3
Mosque B2
Mosque C3
Mulgrave Rd C2
North Ormesby Rd B3
Newport Bridge B1
Newport Bridge Approach Rd B1
Newport Rd B2
North Rd B2
Northern Rd C1
Outram St B2
Oxford Rd C2
Park La C2
Park Rd North C2
Park Rd South C2
Park Vale Rd C3
Parliament Rd B1
Police Station A2
Port Clarence Rd A3
Portman St B2
Post Office B2/B3/C1/C2/C3
Princes Rd B2
Python A2
Riverside Bsns Park A2
Riverside Park Rd A1
Riverside Stadium (Middlesbrough FC) B3
Rockliffe Rd C2
Romaldkirk Rd B1
Roman Rd C2
Roseberry Rd C3
St Barnabas' Rd C2
St Paul's Rd B2
Saltwells Rd B3
Scott's Rd A3
Seaton Carew Rd A3
Shepherdson Way B3
Sikh Temple B2
Snowdon Rd A2
South West Ironmasters Park B1
Southfield Rd B2
Southwell Rd C2
Springfield Rd C1
Startforth Rd A2
Stockton Rd C1
Stockton St A2
Surrey St C2
Sycamore Rd C2
Synagogue C2
Tax Offices B3
Tees Viaduct C1
Teessaurus Park A2
Teesside Tertiary Coll C3
Temenos B3
The Avenue C2
The Crescent C2
Thornfield Rd C1
Town Hall B2
Transporter Bridge (Toll) A3
Union St B2
University of Teesside B2
Upper Lake C2
Valley Rd C3
Ventnor Rd C2
Victoria Rd B2
Visitor Centre A3
Vulcan St A2
Warwick St C2
Wellesley Rd B3
West Lane Hospital C1
Westminster Rd C2
Wilson St B2
Windward Way B3
Woodlands Rd B2
York Rd C3

Milton Keynes
340

Abbey Way A1
Arbrook Ave B1
Armourer Dr A3
Arncliffe Dr A1
Avebury C2
Avebury Blvd C2
Bankfield B3
Bayard Ave A2
Belvedere A2
Bishopstone A1
Blundells Rd A1
Boycott Ave C2
Bradwell Comm Blvd B1
Bradwell Rd C1
Bramble Ave A2
Brearley Ave C2
Breckland A1
Brill Place B1
Burnham Dr B1
Bus Station C1
Campbell Park B3
Cantle Ave A3
Central Milton Keynes Shopping Area B2
Century Ave C2
Chaffron Way C3
Childs Way C1
Christ the Cornerstone B2
Cineworld B2
Civic Offices B2
Cleavers Ave B2
Colesbourne Dr A3
Conniburrow Blvd B2
County Court B2
Currier Dr A2
Dansteed Way A2/A3/B1
Deltic Ave B1
Downs Barn A2
Downs Barn Blvd A3
Eaglestone C3
Eelbrook Ave B1
Elder Gate B1
Evans Gate C2
Fairford Cr A3
Falcon Ave B3
Fennel Dr A2
Fishermead Blvd C3
Food Centre B3
Fulwoods Dr C3
Glazier Dr A2
Glovers La A1
Grafton Gate C1
Grafton St A1/C2
Gurnards Ave B3
Harrier Dr C3
Ibstone Ave B1
Langcliffe Dr A1
Leisure Plaza C1
Leys Rd C1
Library B2
Linford Wood A2
Marlborough Gate B3
Marlborough St A2/B3
Mercers Dr A1
Midsummer C2
Midsummer Blvd B2
Milton Keynes Central C1
Monks Way A1
Mullen Ave A3
Mullion Pl C3
National Hockey Stadium B1
Neath Hill A3
North Elder C1
North Grafton B1
North Overgate A3
North Row B2
North Saxon B2
North Secklow B2
North Skeldon A3
North Witan B1
Oakley Gdns A3
Oldbrook Blvd C2
Open-Air Theatre B3
Overgate A3
Overstreet A3
Patriot Dr B1
Pencarrow Pl B3
Penryn Ave B3
Perran Ave C3
Pitcher La C1
Place Retail Park, The C1
Point Centre, The B2
Police Station B2
Portway B2
Post Office A2/B2/C3
Precedent Dr B1
Quinton Dr B1
Ramsons Ave B2
Rockingham Dr A2
Rooksley B1
Rooksley Retail Park C1
Saxon Gate B2
Saxon St A1/C3
Secklow Gate B2
Shackleton Pl C2
Silbury Blvd B2
Skeldon A3
South Grafton C2
South Row C2
South Saxon C2
South Secklow B3
South Witan C2
Springfield B3
Stanton Wood A1
Stantonbury A1
Stantonbury L Ctr A1
Strudwick Dr C2
Sunrise Parkway A2
Telephone Exchange C3
The Boundary C3
Theatre & Art Gallery B3
Tolcarne Ave C3
Towan Ave C3
Trueman Pl C2
Vauxhall A1
Winterhill Retail Park C2
Witan Gate B2
X-Scape B3

Newcastle upon Tyne
340

Albert St B3
Argyle St B3
Back New Bridge St B3
BALTIC Centre for Contemporary Art C3
Barker St A3
Barrack Rd B1
Bath La B1
Bell's Court B2
Bessie Surtees Ho C2
Bigg Market C2
Biscuit Factory B3
Black Gate C2
Blackett St B2
Blandford Sq C1
Boating Lake A1
Boyd St B3
Brandling Park A2
Bus Station B2
Buxton St B3
Byron St A3
Camden St B2
Castle Keep C2
Central C1
Central Library B2
Central Motorway B2
Chester St A3
City Hall B2
City Rd B3/C3
City Walls C1
Civic Centre A2
Claremont Rd A1
Clarence St B3
Clarence Walk B3
Clayton St C1/B1
Clayton St West C1
Coach Station C1
College St B2
Collingwood St C2
Copland Terr B3
Coppice Way B3
Corporation St B1
Courts C3
Crawhall Rd B3
Dean St C2
Discovery C1
Dinsdale Pl A3
Dinsdale Rd A3
Doncaster Rd A3
Durant Rd B2
Eldon Sq B1
Eldon Sq Shopping Ctr B2
Ellison Pl B2
Empire B1
Eskdale Terr A2
Eslington Terr A1
Exhibition Park A1
Falconar St B3
Fenkle St C1
Forth Banks C1
Forth St C1
Gallowgate B1
Gateshead Heritage @ St Mary's C3
Gateshead Millennium Bridge C3
Gibson St B3
Goldspink La A3
Grainger Market B2
Grainger St B2
Grantham Rd A3
Granville Rd A3
Great North Mus: Hancock A2
Grey St B2
Groat Market C2
Guildhall C2
Hancock St A2
Hanover St C2
Hatton Gallery A1
Hawks Rd C3
Haymarket B2
Heber St B1
Helmsley Rd A3
High Bridge B2
High Level Bridge C2
Hillgate C3
Howard St B3
Hutton Terr A3
Information Ctr C3
Jesmond A2
Jesmond Rd A2/A3
John Dobson St B2
John George Joicey Museum C2
Jubilee Rd B3
Kelvin Gr A3
Kensington Terr A2
Laing Gallery B2
Lambton Rd A2
Leazes Cr B1
Leazes La B1
Leazes Park B1
Leazes Park Rd B1
Leazes Terr B1
Live C2
Low Friar St C1
Manor Chare C2
Manors B2
Manors Station B2
Market St B2
Melbourne St B2
Mill Rd C3
Mill Volvo Tyne C1
Monument B2
Monument Mall Sh Ctr B2
Morpeth St A2
Mosley St C2
Napier St A3
Nazareth House A3
New Bridge St B2/B3
Newcastle Central Station C1
Newcastle University A1
Newgate Shopping Ctr C1
Newgate St B1
Newington Rd A3
Northern Stage Theatre A2
Northumberland Rd B2
Northumberland St B2
Northumbria Univ A2
Northwest Radial Rd A1
O2 Academy C1
Oakwellgate C3
Orchard St C2
Osborne Rd A2
Osborne Terr A3
Pandon C3
Pandon Bank B3
Park Terr A1
Percy St B1
Pilgrim St B2
Pipewellgate C2
Pitt St B1
Plummer Tower A2
Police Station B1
Portland Rd A3/B3
Portland Terr A3
Post Office A3/B1/B2/B3
Pottery La C1
Prudhoe Pl B1
Prudhoe St B1
Quayside C2
Queen Elizabeth II Bridge C2
Queen Victoria Rd A1
Richardson Rd A1
Ridley Pl B2
Rock Terr B3
Rosedale Terr A3
Royal Victoria Infirmary A1
Sage Gateshead, The C3
St Andrew's St B1
St James B1
St James' Blvd C1
St James' Park (Newcastle Utd FC) B1
St Mary's (RC) C1
St Mary's Place B2
St Nicholas C2
St Nicholas St C2
St Thomas' St B1
Sandyford Rd A2/A3
Science Park B2
Shield St B3
Shieldfield B3
Simpson Terr B3
South Shore Rd C3
South St C1
Starbeck Ave A3
Stepney Rd B3
Stoddart St B3
Stowell St B1
Strawberry Pl B1
Swing Bridge C2
Temple St C1
Terrace Pl B1
The Close C2
The Gate B1
The Side C2
Theatre Royal B2
Times Sq C1
Tower St B3
Trinity House C2
Tyne Bridge C2
Tyne Bridges C2
Tyneside B2
Victoria Sq A2
Warwick St A3
Waterloo St C1
Wellington St B1
Westgate Rd C1/C2
Windsor Terr A2
Worswick St B2
Wretham Pl B3

Newport
Casnewydd 340

Albert Terr B1
Allt-yr-Yn Ave A1
Alma St C2
Ambulance Station C3
Bailey St B2
Barrack Hill A2
Bath St A3
Bedford Rd B3
Belle Vue La C1
Belle Vue Park C1
Bishop St A3
Blewitt St B1
Bolt Cl C3
Bolt St C3
Bond St A2
Bosworth Dr A1
Bridge St B1
Bristol St A3
Bryngwyn Rd B1
Brynhyfryd Ave C1
Brynhyfryd Rd C1
Bus Station B2
Caerau Cres C1
Caerau Rd B1
Caerleon Rd A3
Capel Cres C2
Cardiff Rd C2
Caroline St B3
Castle (Remains) A2
Cedar Rd B3
Charles St B2
Charlotte Dr C2
Chepstow Rd A3
Church Rd A3
City Cinema B1
Civic Centre B1
Clarence Pl A2
Clifton Pl B1
Clifton Rd C1
Clyffard Cres B1
Clytha Park Rd B1
Clytha Sq C2
Coldra Rd C1
Collier St A3
Colne St B3
Comfrey Cl A1
Commercial Rd C3
Commercial St B2
Corelli St A3
Corn St B2
Corporation Rd B3
Coulson Cl C2
County Court A2
Courts A1
Courts B1
Crawford St A3
Cyril St B3
Dean St A3
Devon Pl B1
Dewsland Park Rd C2
Dolman B2
Dolphin St C3
East Dock Rd C3
East St B1
East Usk Rd A3
Ebbw Vale Wharf B3
Emlyn St B2
Enterprise Way C3
Eton Rd B3
Evans St A2
Factory Rd A2
Fields Rd B1
Francis Dr C2
Frederick St C3
Friars Rd C1
Gaer La C1
George St C3
George Street Bridge C3
Godfrey Rd B1
Gold Tops B1
Gore St A3
Gorsedd Circle C1
Grafton Rd A3
Graham St B1
Granville St C3
Harlequin Dr A1
Harrow Rd B3
Herbert Rd A3
Herbert Walk C2
Hereford St A3
High St B2
Hill St B2
Hoskins St A2
Information Ctr B2
Ivor Sq B2
Jones St B1
Junction Rd A3
Keynshaw Ave C2
King St C2
Kingsway B2
Kingsway Centre B2
Ledbury Dr A2
Library A3
Library, Museum & Art Gallery B2
Liverpool Wharf B3
Llanthewy Rd B1
Llanvair Rd A3
Locke St A2
Lower Dock St C3
Lucas St A2
Manchester St A3
Market B2
Marlborough Rd B3
Mellon St C3
Mill St A2
Morgan St A3
Mountjoy Rd C2
Newport Bridge A2
Newport Ctr B2
Newport RFC B3
Newport Station B2
North St B2
Oakfield Rd B1
Park Sq C2
Police Station A3/C2
Post Office B1/B2/C1/C3
Power St A1
Prince St A3
Pugsley St A2
Queen St C2
Queen's Cl A1
Queen's Hill A1
Queen's Hill Cres A1
Queensway B2
Railway St B2
Riverfront Arts Centre B2
Riverside A3
Rodney Rd B2
Royal Gwent (A&E) C2
Rudry St A3
Rugby Rd B3
Ruperra La C3
Ruperra St C3
St Edmund St B1
St Mark's Cres A1
St Mary St B1
St Vincent Rd A3
St Woolos C2
St Woolos General (no A+E) C1
St Woolos Rd B1
School La B2
Serpentine Rd B1
Shaftesbury Park A2
Sheaf La A3
Skinner St B2
Sorrel Dr A1
South Market St C3
Spencer Rd B1
Stow Hill B2/C1/C2
Stow Park Ave C1
Stow Park Dr C1
TA Centre A1
Talbot St B2
Tennis Club A1
Tregare St A3
Trostrey St A3
Tunnel Terr B1
Turner St A3
Upper Dock St B2
Usk St A3
Usk Way B3/C3
Victoria Cr B1
War Memorial A3
Waterloo Rd C1
West St B1
Wharves B2
Wheeler St A2
Whitby Pl A3
Windsor Terr B1
York Pl C1

Newquay
340

Agar Rd B2
Alma Pl B1
Ambulance Station B2
Anthony Rd C1
Atlantic Hotel A1
Bank St B1
Barrowfields A3
Bay View Terr B2
Beachfield Ave B1
Beach Rd B1
Beacon Rd A1
Belmont Pl A1
Berry Rd B2
Blue Reef Aquarium B1
Boating Lake C2
Bus Station B1
Chapel Hill B1
Chester Rd A3
Cheviot Rd C1/C2
Chichester Cres C2
Chynance Dr C1
Chyverton Cl C1
Cliff Rd B2
Coach Park B2
Colvreath Rd A3
Council Offices B1
Crantock St B1
Criggar Rocks A3
Dale Cl C3
Dale Rd C3
Dane Rd A1
East St B2
Edgcumbe Ave B3
Edgcumbe Gdns B3
Eliot Gdns B3
Elm Cl C3
Ennor's Rd B1
Fernhill Rd B1
Fire Station B1
Fore St B1
Gannel Rd C2
Golf Driving Range B3
Gover La B1
Great Western Beach A2
Grosvenor Ave B2
Harbour A1
Hawkins Rd C2
Headleigh Rd B2
Hilgrove Rd A3/B3
Holywell Rd B3
Hope Terr B1
Huer's House, The A1
Information Ctr B1
Island Cres B2
Jubilee St B1
Kew Cl C3
Killacourt Cove A2
King Edward Cres A1
Lanhenvor Ave B2
Library B1
Lifeboat Station A1
Linden Ave C2
Listry Rd C2
Lusty Glaze Beach A3
Lusty Glaze Rd A3
Manor Rd B1
Marcus Hill B2
Mayfield Rd B2
Meadowside C3
Mellanvrane La C2
Michell Ave B2
Miniature Golf Course C3
Miniature Railway B3
Mount Wise B1
Mowhay Cl C3
Narrowcliff A3
Newquay B2
Newquay Hospital (no A&E) B2
Newquay Town Football Ground B1
Newquay Zoo B3
North Pier A1
North Quay Hill A1
Oakleigh Terr B2
Pargolla Rd B2
Pendragon Cres C3
Pengannel Cl C1
Penina Ave C3
Police Sta & Courts B2
Post Office B1/B2
Quarry Park Rd B3
Rawley La C2
Reeds Way B1
Robartes Rd B2
St Anne's Rd A3
St Aubyn Cres B3
St George's Rd B1
St John's Rd B1
St Mary's Rd B1
St Michael's B1
St Michael's Rd B1
St Thomas' Rd B2
Seymour Ave B2
South Pier A1
South Quay Hill A1
Sweet Briar Cres C3
Sydney Rd A1
The Crescent B1
Tolcarne Beach A2
Tolcarne Point A2
Tolcarne Rd B2
Tor Rd B2
Towan Beach A1
Towan Blystra Rd B3
Tower Rd A1
Trebarwith Cres B2
Tredour Rd C2
Treforda Rd C3
Tregoss Rd B3
Tregunnel Hill B1/C1
Tregunnel Saltings C1
Trelawney Rd B2
Treloggan La C3
Treloggan Rd C3
Trembath Cres C1
Trenance Ave B2
Trenance Gardens B2
Trenance La C2
Trenance Leisure Park B3
Trenance Rd B2
Trenarth Rd B2
Treninnick Hill C3
Tretherras Rd B3
Trethewey Way C1
Trevemper Rd C2
Tunnels Through Time B1
Ulalia Rd B3
Vivian Cl B2
Waterworld B3
Whitegate Rd B3
Wych Hazel Way C3

Newtown
Y Drenewydd 340

Ash Cl A3
Back La B2
Baptist Chapel B2
Barn La A2
Bear Lanes Sh Ctr B2
Beech Cl A2
Beechwood Dr A2
Brimmon Cl C2
Brimmon Rd C2
Broad St B2
Bryn Bank A1
Bryn Cl A2
Bryn Gdns A1
Bryn House A1
Bryn La A1/A2
Bryn Meadows A2
Bryn St A2
Brynglais Ave A2
Brynglais Cl A2
Bus Station B2
Byrnwood Dr A1
Cambrian Bridge B3
Cambrian Gdns B2
Cambrian Way B2
Canal Rd A3
Castle Mound B2
Cedewain C1
Cefnaire C2
Cefnaire Coppice C2
Ceiriog C2
Cemetery A3
Church (Remains of) B2
Churchill Dr A3
Cledan B3
Colwyn B3
Commercial St A2
Council Offices B1
Crescent St A1
Cwm Llanfair A2
Davies Memorial Gallery B2
Dinas B2
Dolafon Rd B3
Dolerw Park B1
Dolfor Rd C1
Eirianell C1
Fairfield Dr A2
Ffordd Croesawdy B2

Castlegate A5
Cathedral (RC) B4
Cathedral B4
Cavendish St B5
Charles St C4
Charter Row C4
Children's Hospital (A&E) B2
Church St B4
City Hall B4
City Hall B4
City Rd C6
Claremont Cr B2
Claremont Pl B2
Clarke St C3
Clarkegrove Rd C2
Clarkehouse Rd C1
Clarkson St B2
Cobden View Rd A1
Collegiate Cr C2
Commercial St B5
Commonside A1
Conduit Rd B1
Cornish St A3
Corporation St A4
Court B4
Cricket Inn Rd B6
Cromwell St A1
Crookes Rd B1
Crookes Valley Park B2
Crookes Valley Rd B2
Crookesmoor Rd A2
Crown Court A4
Crucible Theatre B5
Cutlers Gate A6
Cutler's Hall B4
Daniel Hill A2
Dental Hospital B2
Dept for Education & Employment C4
Devonshire Green B3
Devonshire St B3
Division St B4
Dorset St C2
Dover St A3
Duchess Rd C5
Duke St B5
Duncombe St A1
Durham Rd B2
Earl St C4
Earl Way C4
Ecclesall Rd C3
Edward St B3
Effingham Rd A6
Effingham St A6
Egerton St C3
Eldon St B3
Elmore Rd B1
Exchange St B5
Eyre St C4
Fargate B4
Farm Rd C5
Fawcett St A3
Filey St B3
Fire & Police Mus A4
Fire Station C4
Fir St A1
Fitzalan Sq/ Ponds Forge B5
Fitzwater Rd C6
Fitzwilliam Gate C4
Fitzwilliam St B3
Flat St B5
Foley St A6
Foundry Climbing Ctr A4
Fulton Rd A1
Furnace Hill A4
Furnival Rd A5
Furnival Sq C4
Furnival St C4
Garden St B3
Gell St B3
Gibraltar St A4
Glebe Rd B1
Glencoe Rd C6
Glossop Rd B2/B3/C1
Gloucester St C2
Granville Rd C6
Granville Rd/ Sheffield College C5
Graves Gallery B5
Greave Rd B3
Green La A4
Hadfield St A1
Hanover St C3
Hanover Way C3
Harcourt Rd B1
Harmer La B5
Havelock St C2
Hawley St B4
Haymarket B5
Headford St C3
Heavygate Rd A1
Henry St A3
High St B4
Hodgson St C3
Holberry Gdns C2
Hollis Croft B4
Holly St B4
Hounsfield Rd B3
Howard Rd A1
Hoyle St A3
Hyde Park A6
Infirmary Rd A3
Infirmary Rd A3
Information Ctr B4
Jericho St A3
Johnson St A5
Kelham Island Industrial Museum A4
Lawson Rd C1
Leadmill Rd C5
Leadmill St C5
Leadmill, The C5
Leamington St A1
Leavy Rd B3
Lee Croft B4
Leopold St B4
Leveson St A6
Library A2
Library B5
Library C1
Lyceum Theatre B5
Malinda St A3
Maltravers St A5
Manor Oaks Rd B6
Mappin St B3
Marlborough Rd B1
Mary St C4
Matilda St C4
Matlock Rd A1
Meadow St A3
Melbourn Rd A1
Melbourne Ave C1
Millennium Galleries B5
Milton St C3
Mitchell St B3
Mona Ave A1
Mona Rd A1
Montgomery Terr Rd A3
Montgomery Theatre B4
Monument Gdns C6
Moor Oaks Rd B1
Moore St C3
Mowbray St A4
Mushroom La B2
Netherthorpe Rd B3
Netherthorpe Rd B3
Newbould La C1
Nile St C1
Norfolk Park Rd C6
Norfolk Rd C6
Norfolk St B4
North Church St B4
Northfield Rd A1
Northumberland Rd B1
Nursery St A5
O2 Academy B5
Oakholme Rd C1
Octagon B2
Odeon B5
Old St B6
Orchard Square B4
Oxford St A2
Paradise St B4
Park La C2
Park Sq B5
Parker's Rd B1
Pearson Building (Univ) C2
Penistone Rd A3
Pinstone St B4
Pitt St B3
Police Station A4/B5
Pond Hill B5
Pond St B5
Ponds Forge Int Sports Ctr B5
Portobello St B3
Post Office A1/A2/B3/B4/B5/B6/C1/C3/C4/C6
Powell St A2
Queen St B4
Queen's Rd C5
Ramsey Rd B1
Red Hill B3
Redcar Rd B1
Regent St B3
Rockingham St B4
Roebuck Rd A2
Royal Hallamshire Hospital C2
Russell St A4
Rutland Park C1
St George's Cl B3
St Mary's Gate C3
St Mary's Rd C4/C5
St Peter & St Paul Cathedral B4
St Philip's Rd A3
Savile St A5
School Rd B1
Scotland St A4
Severn Rd B1
Shalesmoor A4
Shalesmoor A3
Sheaf St B5
Sheffield Hallam Univ B5
Sheffield Ice Sports Ctr – Skate Central C5
Sheffield Interchange B5
Sheffield Parkway A6
Sheffield Station C5
Sheffield Station/ Sheffield Hallam Univ B5
Sheffield University B2
Shepherd St A3
Shipton St A2
Shoreham St C4
Showroom, The C5
Shrewsbury Rd C5
Sidney St C4
Site Gallery C5
Slinn St A1
Smithfield A4
Snig Hill A5
Snow La A4
Solly St B3
Southbourne Rd C1
South La C4
South Street Park B5
Spital Hill A5
Spital St A5
Spring Hill B1
Spring Hill Rd B1
Springvale Rd A1
Stafford Rd C6
Stafford St B6
Stanley St A5
Suffolk Rd C5
Summer St B2
Sunny Bank C3
Surrey St B4
Sussex St A6
Sutton St B3
Sydney Rd A2
Sylvester St C4
Talbot St B5
Taptonville Rd B1
Tax Office C4
Tenter St B4
The Moor C4
Town Hall B4
Townend St A1
Townhead St B4
Trafalgar St B4
Tree Root Walk B2
Trinity St A4
Trippet La B4
Turner Mus of Glass B3
Union St B4
Univ Drama Studio B2
Univ of Sheffield B3
Upper Allen St A3
Upper Hanover St B3
Upperthorpe Rd A2/A3
Verdon St A5
Victoria Quays B5
Victoria Rd C2
Victoria St B3
Waingate B5
Watery St A3
Watson Rd C1
Wellesley Rd B2
Wellington St C3
West Bar A4
West Bar Green A4
West One Plaza B3
West St B3
West St B4
Westbourne Rd C1
Western Bank B2
Western Rd A1
Weston Park B2
Weston Park Hospl B2
Weston Park Mus B2
Weston St B2
Wharncliffe Rd C3
Whitham Rd B1
Wicker A5
Wilkinson St B2
William St C3
Winter Garden B4
Winter St B2
York St B4
Yorkshire Artspace C5
Young St C4

Shrewsbury 342

Abbey Church B3
Abbey Foregate B3
Abbey Lawn Bsns Park B3
Abbots House B2
Agricultural Show Gd A1
Albert St A2
Alma St B1
Ashley St A3
Ashton Rd C1
Avondale Dr A3
Bage Way C3
Barker St B1
Beacall's La A2
Beeches La C2
Beehive La C1
Belle Vue Gdns C2
Belle Vue Rd C2
Belmont Bank C1
Berwick Ave A1
Berwick Rd A1
Betton St C2
Bishop St C3
Bradford St B3
Bridge St B1
Bus Station B2
Butcher Row B2
Burton St A3
Butler Rd C1
Bynner St C2
Canon St B3
Canonbury C1
Castle Bsns Park, The A2
Castle Foregate A2
Castle Gates B2
Castle Museum B2
Castle St B2
Cathedral (RC) C1
Chester St A2
Cineworld C3
Claremont Bank B1
Claremont Hill B1
Cleveland St B3
Coleham Head B2
Coleham Pumping Station C2
College Hill B1
Corporation La A1
Coton Cres A1
Coton Hill A2
Coton Mount A1
Crescent La C1
Crewe St A2
Cross Hill B1
Darwin Centre B2
Dingle, The B1
Dogpole B2
Draper's Hall B2
English Bridge B2
Fish St B2
Frankwell B1
Gateway Ctr, The A2
Gravel Hill La A1
Greyfriars Rd C2
Guildhall B1
Hampton Rd A3
Haycock Way C3
HM Prison B2
High St B1
Hills La B1
Holywell St B3
Hunter St A1
Information Ctr B1
Ireland's Mansion & Bear Steps B1
John St A3
Kennedy Rd C1
King St B3
Kingsland Bridge C1
Kingsland Bridge (toll) C1
Kingsland Rd C1
Library B2
Lime St C2
Longden Coleham C2
Longden Rd C1
Longner St B1
Luciefelde Rd C1
Mardol B1
Market B1
Marine Terr C2
Monkmoor Rd B3
Moreton Cr C2
Mount St A1
New Park Cl A3
New Park Rd A2
New Park St A3
North St A2
Oakley St C1
Old Coleham C2
Old Market Hall B1
Old Potts Way C3
Parade Centre B2
Police Station B1
Post Office A2/B1/B2/B3
Pride Hill B1
Pride Hill Centre B1
Priory Rd B1
Pritchard Way C3
Queen St A3
Raby Cr C2
Rad Brook C1
Rea Brook C3
Riverside B1
Roundhill La A1
St Alkmund's B2
St Chad's B1
St Chad's Terr B1
St John's Hill B1
St Julians Friars C2
St Mary's B2
St Mary's St B2
Salters La C2
Scott St C3
Severn Bank A3
Severn St A2
Shrewsbury B2
Shrewsbury High School for Girls C1
Shrewsbury Museum & Art Gallery B1
Shrewsbury School C1
Shropshire Wildlife Trust B3
Smithfield Rd B1
South Hermitage C1
Swan Hill B1
Sydney Ave A3
Tankerville St B3
The Dana B2
The Quarry B1
The Square B1
Tilbrook Dr A3
Town Walls C1
Trinity St C2
Underdale Rd B3
Victoria Ave B1
Victoria Quay B1
Victoria St B2
Welsh Bridge B1
Whitehall St B3
Wood St A2
Wyle Cop B2

Southampton 342

Above Bar St A2
Albert Rd North B3
Albert Rd South C3
Anderson's Rd B3
Archaeology Mus (God's Ho Tower) C2
Argyle Rd A2
Arundel Tower B1
Bargate, The B2
BBC Regional Centre A1
Bedford Pl A1
Belvidere Rd A3
Bernard St C2
Blechynden Terr A1
Brazil Rd C3
Brinton's Rd A2
Britannia Rd A3
Briton St C2
Brunswick Pl A2
Bugle St C1
Canute Rd C3
Castle Way C2
Catchcold Tower B1
Central Bridge C3
Central Rd C2
Channel Way C3
Chapel Rd B3
Cineworld C3
City Art Gallery A1
City College B3
Civic Centre A1
Civic Centre Rd A1
Coach Station B1
Commercial Rd A1
Cumberland Pl A1
Cunard Rd C2
Derby Rd A3
Devonshire Rd A1
Dock Gate 4 C2
Dock Gate 8 B1
East Park A2
East Park Terr A2
East St B2
Endle St B3
European Way C2
Fire Station A2
Floating Bridge Rd C3
Golden Gr A3
Graham Rd A2
Guildhall A1
Hanover Bldgs B2
Harbour Lights C3
Harbour Pde B1
Hartington Rd A3
Havelock Rd A1
Henstead Rd A1
Herbert Walker Ave B1
High St B2
Hoglands Park B2
Holy Rood (Rems), Merchant Navy Memorial B2
Houndwell Park B2
Houndwell Pl B2
Hythe Ferry C2
Information Ctr A1
Isle of Wight Ferry Terminal C1
James St B3
Java Rd C3
Kingsway A2
Leisure World B1
Library A1
Lime St B2
London Rd A2
Marine Pde B3
Marsh La B2
Mayflower Meml C1
Mayflower Park C1
Mayflower Theatre, The A1
Medieval Merchant's House C1
Melbourne St B3
Millais A2
Morris Rd A1
National Oceanography Centre C3
Neptune Way C3
New Rd A2
Nichols Rd A3
North Front A2
Northam Rd A3
Ocean Dock C2
Ocean Village Marina C3
Ocean Way C3
Odeon B1
Ogle Rd B1
Old Northam Rd A2
Orchard La B2
Oxford Ave A2
Oxford St C2
Palmerston Park A2
Palmerston Rd A2
Parsonage Rd A3
Peel St A3
Platform Rd C2
Police Station A1
Portland Terr B1
Post Office A2/A3/B2
Pound Tree Rd B2
Quays Swimming & Diving Complex, The B1
Queen's Park C2
Queen's Peace Fountain A2
Queen's Terr C2
Queen's Way B2
Radcliffe Rd A3
Rochester St A3
Royal Pier C1
Royal South Hants Hospital A2
Sea City Mus A1
St Andrew's Rd A2
St Mary St A2
St Mary's B3
St Mary's Leisure Ctr A2
St Mary's Pl B2
St Mary's Rd A2
St Mary's Stadium (Southampton FC) A3
St Michael's C1
Solent Sky C3
South Front B2
Southampton Central Station A1
Southampton Solent University A2
SS Shieldhall C2
Terminus Terr C2
The Mall, Marlands A1
The Polygon A1
Threefield La B2
Titanic Engineers' Memorial A2
Town Quay C1
Town Walls B2
Tudor House C1
Vincent's Walk B2
West Gate Hall C1
West Marlands Rd A1
West Park A1
West Park Rd A1
West Quay Rd B1
West Quay Retail Park B1
West Quay Sh Ctr B1
West Rd C2
Western Esplanade B1
Winton St A2

Southend-on-Sea 343

Adventure Island C3
Albany Ave A1
Albert Rd C3
Alexandra Rd C2
Alexandra St C2
Alexandra Yacht Club C2
Ashburnham Rd B2
Ave Rd B1
Avenue Terr B1
Balmoral Rd B1
Baltic Ave B3
Baxter Ave A2/B2
Beecroft Art Gallery C1
Bircham Rd A2
Boscombe Rd B3
Boston Ave A1/B2
Bournemouth Park Rd A3
Browning Ave A3
Bus Station C3
Byron Ave A3
Cambridge Rd C1/C2
Canewdon Rd B1
Carnarvon Rd A2
Central Ave A3
Chelmsford Ave A1
Chichester Rd B2
Church Rd C3
Civic Centre A2
Clarence Rd C2
Clarence St C2
Cliff Ave B1
Cliffs Pavilion C1
Clifftown Parade C2
Clifftown Rd C2
Colchester Rd A1
College Way B2
Coleman St B3
County Court B3
Cromer Rd B3
Crowborough Rd A2
Dryden Ave A3
East St A2
Elmer App B2
Elmer Ave B2
Gainsborough Dr A1
Gayton Rd A2
Glenhurst Rd A2
Gordon Pl B2
Gordon Rd B2
Grainger Rd A2
Greyhound Way A3
Guildford Rd B3
Hamlet Ct Rd B1
Hamlet Rd C1
Harcourt Ave A1
Hartington Rd C3
Hastings Rd B3
Herbert Gr C3
Heygate Ave C3
High St B2/C2
Information Ctr C3
Kenway A2
Kilworth Ave B3
Lancaster Gdns B3
Library B2
London Rd B1
Lucy Rd C3
MacDonald Ave A1
Magistrates Court A2
Maldon Rd A2
Maine Ave C1
Marine Rd C1
Marine Parade C2
Milton Rd B1
Milton St B2
Napier Ave B2
North Ave A3
North Rd A1/B1
Odeon B2
Osborne Rd B1
Park Cres B1
Park Rd B1
Park St B1
Park Terr B1
Pier Hill C3
Pleasant Rd C3
Police Station A2
Post Office B2/B3
Princes St B2
Queens Rd B2
Queensway B2/B3/C3
Rayleigh Ave A1
Redstock Rd A2
Rochford Ave A1
Royal Mews C2
Royal Terr C2
Royals Sh Ctr, The C3
Ruskin Ave A3
St Ann's Rd B3
St Helen's Rd B1
St John's Rd B1
St Leonard's Rd C3
St Lukes Rd A3
St Vincent's Rd C1
Salisbury Ave A1/B1
Scratton Rd C2
Shakespeare Dr A1
Short St A2
South Ave A3
Southchurch Rd B3
South Essex College B2
Southend Central B2
Southend Pier Railway C3
Southend Radio C2
Southend United FC A1
Southend Victoria B2
Stadium Rd A2
Stanfield Rd A2
Stanley Rd C3
Sutton Rd A3/B3
Swanage Rd B3
Sweyne Ave A1
Sycamore Gr A3
Tennyson Ave A3
The Grove A3
Tickfield Ave A2
Tudor Rd A1
Tunbridge Rd A2
Tylers Ave B3
Tyrrel Dr B3
Univ of Essex B2/C2
Vale Ave A2
Victoria Ave A2
Victoria Sh Ctr, The B2
Warrior Sq B3
Wesley Rd C3
West Rd A1
West St A1
Westcliff Ave C1
Westcliff Parade C1
Western Esplanade C1
Weston Rd C2
Whitegate Rd B3
Wilson Rd C1
Wimborne Rd B3
York Rd C3

Stirling 343

Abbey Rd A3
Abbotsford Pl A3
Abercromby Pl C1
Albert Halls B1
Albert Pl B1
Alexandra Pl A3
Allan Park C2
Ambulance Station A2
AMF Ten Pin Bowling B2
Argyll Ave A3
Argyll's Lodging B1
Back O' Hill Ind Est A1
Back O' Hill Rd A1
Baker St B2
Ballengeich Pass A1
Balmoral Pl B1
Barn Rd B1
Barnton St B2
Bow St B1
Bruce St A2
Burghmuir Ind Est C2
Burghmuir Rd A2/B2/C2
Bus Station B2
Cambuskenneth Bridge A3
Carlton C2
Castle Ct B1
Causewayhead Rd A2
Cemetery A1
Church of the Holy Rude B1
Clarendon Pl C1
Club House B1
Colquhoun St C3
Corn Exchange B2
Council Offices C2
Court B2
Cowane A2
Cowane St A2
Cowane's Hospital B1
Crawford Sh Arc B2
Crofthead Rd A1
Dean Cres A3
Douglas St A2
Drip Rd A1
Drummond La C1
Drummond Pl C1
Drummond Pl La C1
Dumbarton Rd C2
Eastern Access Rd B2
Edward Ave A3
Edward Rd A2
Forrest Rd A2
Fort A1
Forth Cres B2
Forth St A2
Gladstone Pl C1
Glebe Ave C1
Glebe Cres C1
Golf Course C1
Goosecroft Rd B2
Gowanhill A1
Greenwood Ave B1
Harvey Wynd A1
Information Ctr B1
Irvine Pl B2
James St A2
John St B1
Kerse Rd C3
King's Knot B1
King's Park C1
King's Park Rd C1
Laurencecroft Rd A2
Leisure Pool B2
Library B2
Linden Ave C2
Lovers Wk A2
Lower Back Walk B1
Lower Bridge St A2
Lower Castlehill A1
Mar Pl B1
Meadow Pl A3
Meadowforth Rd C3
Middlemuir Rd C3
Millar Pl A3
Morris Terr B2
Mote Hill A1
Murray Pl B2
Nelson Pl C2
Old Town Cemetery B1
Old Town Jail B1
Orchard House Hospital (No A+E) A2
Park Terr C1
Phoenix Industrial Est C3
Players Rd C3
Port St C2
Princes St B2
Queen St B2
Queen's Rd B1
Queenshaugh Dr A3
Rainbow Slides B2
Ramsay Pl A2
Riverside Dr A3
Ronald Pl A1
Rosebery Pl A2
Royal Gardens B1
Royal Gdns B1
St Mary's Wynd B1
St Ninian's Rd C2
Scott St A2
Seaforth Pl B2
Shore Rd B2
Smith Art Gallery & Museum B1
Snowdon Pl C1
Snowdon Pl La C1
Spittal St B2
Springkerse Ind Est C3
Springkerse Rd C3
Stirling Bsns Centre C2
Stirling Castle A1
Stirling County Rugby Football Club A3
Stirling Enterprise Pk B3
Stirling Old Bridge A2
Stirling Station B2
Superstore A2
Sutherland Ave A3
TA Centre C3
Tannery La A2
The Bastion C2
The Changing Room B1
Thistle Industrial Est C3
Thistles Sh Ctr, The B2
Tollbooth, The B1
Town Wall B1
Union St A2
Upper Back Walk B1
Upper Bridge St A1
Upper Castlehill B1
Upper Craigs C2
Victoria Pl C1
Victoria Rd B1
Victoria Sq B1/C1
Vue B2
Wallace St A2
Waverley Cres A3
Wellgreen Rd C2
Windsor Pl C1
YHA B1

Stoke 343

Ashford St A3
Avenue Rd A3
Aynsley Rd A2
Barnfield C1
Bath St C2
Beresford St A3
Bilton St C2
Boon Ave C2
Booth St C2
Boothen Rd C2/C3
Boughey St C2
Boughley Rd B3
Brighton St B1
Campbell Rd C2
Carlton Rd B2
Cauldon Rd A3
Cemetery A2
Cemetery Rd A2
Church (RC) B2
Church St C2
City Rd C3
Civic Centre & King's Hall B3
Cliff Vale Pk A1
College Rd A2
Convent Cl B2
Copeland St B2
Cornwallis St C3
Corporation St C2
Crowther St A3
Dominic St B1
Elenora St B2
Elgin St B2
Epworth St A3
Etruscan St A1
Film Theatre B3
Fleming Rd C2
Fletcher Rd C2
Floyd St B2
Foden St C2
Frank St C2
Franklin Rd C1
Frederick Ave B1
Garden St C1
Garner St A1
Gerrard St B2
Glebe St B3
Greatbach Ave B1
Hanley Park A3
Harris St B1
Hartshill Rd B1
Hayward St A2
Hide St B2
Higson Ave B2
Hill St B2
Honeywall B2
Hunters Dr C1
Hunters Way C1
Keary St C2
Kingsway B2
Leek Rd B3
Library C2
Lime St C2
Liverpool Rd B2
London Rd C2
Lonsdale St C2
Lovatt St B2
Lytton St B3
Market C1
Newcastle La C1
Newlands St A2
Norfolk St A2
North St A1/B2
North Staffordshire Royal Infirmary (A&E) B1
Northcote Ave B2
Oldmill St C3
Oriel St B1
Oxford St B1
Penkhull New Rd C1
Penkhull St C1
Police Station C2
Portmeirion Pottery C2
Post Office A3/B1/B3/C1/C2
Prince's Rd B1
Pump St B2
Quarry Ave B1
Quarry Rd B1
Queen Anne St A3
Queen's Rd C1
Queensway A1/B2/C3
Richmond St B1
Rothwell St C1
St Peter's B3
St Thomas Pl C1
Scrivenor Rd A1
Seaford St A3
Selwyn St C3
Shelton New Rd A1
Shelton Old Rd B2
Sheppard St C2
Spark St C2
Spencer Rd B3
Spode St C2
Squires View B3
Staffordshire Univ B3
Stanley Matthews Sports Centre B3
Station Rd B3
Stoke Business Park C3
Stoke Recreation Ctr C2
Stoke Rd A2
Stoke-on-Trent Coll A3
Stoke-on-Trent Sta B3
Sturgess St C2
The Villas C1
Thistley Hough C1
Thornton Rd B3
Tolkien Way B1
Trent Valley Rd C1
Vale St B2
Watford St A3
Wellesley St A3
West Ave B1
Westland St B1
Yeaman St C2
Yoxall Ave B1

Stratford-upon-Avon 343

Albany Rd B1
Alcester Rd B1
Ambulance Station B1
Arden St B2
Avenue Farm A1
Ave Farm Ind Est A1
Avenue Rd A3
Avon Industrial Estate A2
Baker Ave A1
Bandstand C3
Benson Rd A3
Birmingham Rd A2
Boat Club B3
Borden Pl C1
Brass Rubbing Ctr C2
Bridge St B2
Bridgetown Rd C3
Bridgeway B3
Broad St C2
Broad Walk C2
Brookvale Rd C1
Bull St C2
Bus Station B2
Butterfly Farm C3
Cemetery C1
Chapel La B2
Cherry Orchard C1
Chestnut Walk B2
Children's Playground C3
Church St C2
Civic Hall B2
Clarence Rd B1
Clopton Bridge B3
Clopton Rd A2
Coach Terminal & Park B3
College B1
College La C2
College St C2
Com Sports Centre B1
Council Offices (District) B2
Courtyard C2
Cox's Yard B3
Cricket Ground C3
Ely Gdns B2
Ely St B2
Evesham Rd C1
Fire Station B1
Foot Ferry C3
Fordham Ave A2
Gallery, The B3
Garrick Way C1
Gower Memorial B3
Great William St B2
Greenhill St B2
Grove Rd B2
Guild St B2
Guildhall & School B2
Hall's Croft C2
Hartford Rd C1
Harvard House B2
Henley St B2
High St B2
Holton St C2
Holy Trinity C2
Information Ctr B3
Jolyffe Park Rd A2
Kipling Rd C3
Leisure & Visitor Ctr B3
Library B2
Lodge Rd B1
Maidenhead Rd A3
Mansell St B2
Masons Court B2
Masons Rd A1
Maybird Shopping Pk A2
Maybrook Rd A1
Mayfield Ave A2
Meer St B2
Mill La C2
Moat House Hotel B3
Narrow La C2
Nash's Ho & New Pl B2
New St C2
Old Town C2
Orchard Way C1
Paddock La C1
Park Rd B1
Payton St B2
Percy St A2
Police Station B2
Post Office B2/B3
Recreation Ground C2
Regal Road A2
Rother St B2
Rowley Cr A3

Royal Shakespeare Theatre....B3
Ryland St....C2
Saffron Meadow....C2
St Andrew's Cr....B1
St Gregory's....A3
St Gregory's Rd....A3
St Mary's Rd....A2
Sanctus Dr....C2
Sanctus St....C1
Sandfield Rd....C2
Scholars La....B2
Seven Meadows Rd....C2
Shakespeare Ctr ✦....B2
Shakespeare Institute..C2
Shakespeare St....B2
Shakespeare's Birthplace ✦....B2
Sheep St....B2
Shelley Rd....C3
Shipston Rd....C3
Shottery Rd....C1
Slingates Rd....A2
Southern La....C2
Station Rd....B1
Stratford Healthcare [H]....B2
Stratford Hospital [H]....B2
Stratford Sports Club..B1
Stratford-upon-Avon Station....B3
Swan's Nest La....B3
Swan Theatre 🏛....B3
Talbot Rd....A2
The Greenway....C2
The Willows....B1
The Willows North....B1
Tiddington Rd....B3
Timothy's Bridge Industrial Estate....A1
Timothy's Bridge Rd....A1
Town Hall & Council Offices....B2
Town Sq....B2
Trinity St....C2
Tyler St....B2
War Memorial Gdns...B3
Warwick Rd....B3
Waterside....B3
Welcombe Rd....A3
West St....C2
Western Rd....A2
Wharf Rd....A2
Wood St....B2

Sunderland 343

Albion Pl....C2
Alliance Pl....B1
Argyle St....C2
Ashwood St....C1
Athenaeum St....B2
Azalea Terr....C2
Beach St....A1
Bede Theatre 🏛....C3
Bedford St....B2
Beechwood Terr....C1
Belvedere Rd....C1
Blandford St....B2
Borough Rd....B3
Bridge Cr....B2
Bridge St....B2
Brooke St....A2
Brougham St....B2
Burdon Rd....C2
Burn Park....C1
Burn Park Rd....C1
Burn Park Tech Park..C1
Carol St....B1
Charles St....A3
Chester Rd....C1
Chester Terr....B1
Church St....A3
Civic Centre....C2
Cork St....B3
Coronation St....C3
Cowan Terr....C2
Crowtree Rd....B2
Dame Dorothy St....A2
Deptford Rd....B1
Deptford Terr....A1
Derby St....C2
Derwent St....C2
Dock St....A3
Dundas St....A2
Durham Rd....C1
Easington St....A2
Egerton St....C3
Empire 🏛....B2
Empire Theatre 🏛....B2
Farringdon Row....B1
Fawcett St....C2
Fox St....C1
Foyle St....B3
Frederick St....B3
Gill Rd....B2
Hanover Pl....A1
Havelock Terr....C1
Hay St....A2
Headworth Sq....B3
Hendon Rd....B3
High St East....B3
High St West....B2/B3
Holmeside....B2
Hylton Rd....B1
Information Ctr [i]....B2
John St....B2
Kier Hardie Way....A2
Lambton St....B2
Laura St....C3
Lawrence St....B3
Leisure Centre....B2
Library & Arts Centre..B2
Lily St....B1
Lime St....B1
Livingstone Rd....B2
Low Row....B2
Matamba Terr....B1
Millburn St....B1
Millennium Way....A2

Minster ♦....B2
Monkwearmouth Station Museum 🏛....A2
Mowbray Park....C3
Mowbray Rd....C3
Murton St....C2
National Glass Ctr ✦..A3
New Durham Rd....C1
Newcastle Rd....A2
Nile St....B3
Norfolk St....B3
North Bridge St....A2
Northern Gallery for Contemporary Art 🏛..B3
Otto Terr....C1
Park La....C2
Park Lane Ⓜ....C2
Park Rd....C2
Paul's St....B3
Peel St....C3
Police Station 🚓....B2
Post Office ⊠....B2
Priestly Cr....A1
Queen St....B3
Railway Row....B1
Retail Park....B1
Richmond St....A2
Roker Ave....B1
Royalty Theatre 🏛....C1
Ryhope Rd....C1
St Mary's Way....B2
St Michael's Way....C2
St Peter's....A3
St Peter's Ⓜ....A3
St Peter's Way....A3
St Vincent St....C3
Salem Rd....C3
Salem St....C3
Salisbury St....C3
Sans St....B3
Silkworth Row....B1
Southwick Rd....A1
Stadium of Light (Sunderland AFC)..A2
Stadium Way....A2
Stobart St....A2
Stockton Rd....C2
Suffolk St....C3
Sunderland Aquatic Centre....A2
Sunderland Ⓜ....B3
Sunderland Mus 🏛....B3
Sunderland Station ≥..B2
Sunderland St....B3
Tatham St....C3
Tavistock Pl....B3
The Bridges....B2
The Place....B3
The Royalty....C1
Thelma St....C1
Thomas St North....A2
Thornholme Rd....C1
Toward Rd....C3
Transport Interchange....C2
Trimdon St Way....B1
Tunstall Rd....C2
University Ⓜ....C1
University Library....C1
University of Sunderland (City Campus)....B1
University of Sunderland (Sir Tom Cowle at St Peter's Campus)..A3
Vaux Brewery Way....A1
Villiers St....B3
Villiers St South....B3
Vine Pl....C2
Violet St....B1
Walton La....C3
Waterworks Rd....C1
Wearmouth Bridge....B2
Wellington La....A1
West Sunniside....B3
West Wear St....B3
Westbourne Rd....C1
Western Hill....C1
Wharncliffe....B1
Whickham St....B1
White House Rd....C3
Wilson St North....A1
Winter Gdns....C3
Wreath Quay....A1
Post Office ⊠....A1/A2/B2/C1

Swansea Abertawe 343

Adelaide St....C3
Albert Row....C1
Alexandra Rd....B3
Argyle St....C1
Baptist Well Pl....A2
Beach St....C1
Belle Vue Way....B3
Berw Rd....A2
Berwick Terr....A1
Bond St....C1
Brangwyn Concert Hall 🏛....C1
Bridge St....A3
Brookands Terr....B1
Brunswick St....C1
Bryn-Syfi Terr....A2
Bryn-y-Mor Rd....C1
Bullins La....B1
Burrows Rd....C1
Bus/Rail link....A3
Bus Station....B2
Cadfan Rd....A1
Cadrawd Rd....A1
Caer St....B3
Carig Cr....A1
Carlton Terr....B2
Carmarthen Rd....A2
Castle Square....B3
Castle St....B3
Catherine St....C1
Cinema 🎬....C3
Civic Centre & Library..C2
Clarence St....C2
Colbourne Terr....A2

Constitution Hill....B1
Court....A2
Creidiol Rd....A2
Cromwell St....B2
Duke St....B2
Dunvant Pl....C2
Dyfatty Park....A3
Dyfatty St....A3
Dyfed Ave....A1
Dylan Thomas Ctr ✦..B3
Dylan Thomas Theatre 🏛....B3
Eaton Cr....A1
Eigen Cr....A1
Elfed Rd....A1
Emlyn Rd....A1
Evans Terr....A3
Fairfield Terr....B1
Ffynone Dr....C1
Ffynone Rd....C1
Fire Station....B3
Firm St....A2
Fleet St....C1
Francis St....C1
Fullers Row....B2
George St....C1
Glamorgan St....C2
Glyndŵr Pl....A1
Graig Terr....A3
Grand Theatre 🏛....C2
Granogwen Rd....A2
Guildhall....C1
Guildhall Rd South...C1
Gwent Rd....A1
Gwynedd Ave....A1
Hafod St....A3
Hanover St....C1
Harcourt St....B2
Harries St....A2
Heathfield....B2
Henrietta St....C1
Hewson St....A2
High St....A3/B3
High View....A1
Hill St....C1
Historic Ships Berth ⚓....C3
HM Prison....C2
Information Ctr [i]....C2
Islwyn Rd....A1
King Edward's Rd....C1
Law Courts....B2
Long Ridge....A2
Madoc St....C2
Mansel St....B2
Maritime Quarter....C3
Market....B3
Mayhill Gdns....A1
Mayhill Rd....A1
Mega Bowl ✦🎳....B1
Milton Terr....A2
Mission Gallery 🏛....C3
Montpellier Terr....B1
Morfa Rd....C1
Mount Pleasant....B2
National Waterfront Museum 🏛....C3
Nelson St....C2
New Cut Rd....A3
New St....A3
Nicander Pde....A2
Nicander Pl....A2
Nicholl St....B2
Norfolk St....B2
North Hill Rd....A2
Northampton La....B2
Orchard St....B3
Oxford St....C1
Oystermouth Rd....C1
Page St....B2
Pant-y-Celyn Rd....C1
Parc Tawe Link....B3
Parc Tawe North....B3
Parc Tawe Sh & L Ctr..B3
Patti Pavilion 🏛....C1
Paxton St....C1
Penmaen Terr....A1
Pen-y-Graig Rd....A1
Phillips Pde....C1
Picton Terr....B2
Plantasia ❀....B3
Police Station 🚓....B2
Post Office ⊠....A1/A2/B2/C1
Powys Ave....A1
Primrose St....A1
Princess Way....B3
Promenade....B1
Pryder Gdns....A1
Quadrant Centre....C2
Quay Park....B3
Rhianfa La....B1
Rhondda St....B2
Richardson St....C2
Rodney St....C1
Rose Hill....B1
Rosehill Terr....B1
Russell St....B1
St Helen's Ave....C1
St Helen's Cr....C1
St Helen's Rd....C1
St James Gdns....B1
St James's Cr....B1
St Mary's....B3
Sea View Terr....A3
Singleton St....C2
South Dock....C3
Stanley Pl....B1
Strand....B3
Swansea Castle 🏰....B3
Swansea Coll Arts Ctr..C1
Swansea Metropolitan University....B2
Swansea Museum 🏛....C3
Swansea Station ≥....A3
Taliesyn Rd....A1
Tan y Marian Rd....A1
Tegid Rd....A1
Teilo Cr....A1
Terrace Rd....B1/B2

The Kingsway....B2
The LC....C3
Tontine St....A3
Tower of Eclipse ✦....A3
Townhill Rd....A1
Tramshed The 🏛....C3
Trawler Rd....C3
Union St....B2
Upper Strand....A3
Vernon St....A3
Victoria Quay....C3
Victoria Rd....C3
Vincent St....C1
Walter Rd....B1
Watkin St....A2
Waun-Wen Rd....A2
Wellington St....C2
Westbury St....C1
Western St....C1
Westway....C2
William St....C2
Wind St....B3
Woodlands Terr....B1
YMCA....B2
York St....C3

Swindon 343

Albert St....C3
Albion St....C1
Alfred St....C1
Alvescot Rd....C1
Art Gallery & Mus 🏛....B2
Ashford Rd....C1
Aylesbury St....A2
Bath Rd....C2
Bathampton St....C1
Bathurst Rd....B3
Beatrice St....A2
Beckhampton St....B3
Bowood Rd....C1
Bristol St....A1
Broad St....A3
Brunel Arcade....B2
Brunel Plaza....B2
Brunswick St....C2
Bus Station....B2
Cambria Bridge Rd....C1
Cambria Place....C1
Canal Walk....B2
Carfax St....B2
Carr St....B1
Cemetery....C1/C3
Chandler Cl....C1
Chapel....A1
Chester St....B1
Christ Church ⛪....C3
Church Place....B1
Cirencester Way....A3
Clarence St....B2
Clifton St....C1
Cockleberry ⚘....A2
Colbourne ⚘....A3
Colbourne St....A3
College St....B2
Commercial Rd....B2
Corporation St....A2
Council Offices....B3
County Rd....A3
Courts....B2
Cricket Ground....A3
Cricklade Street....A3
Crombey St....B1/C2
Cross St....C2
Curtis St....B1
Deacon St....C1
Designer Outlet (Great Western)....C1
Dixon St....C2
Dover St....C2
Dowling St....A3
Drove Rd....C3
Dryden St....C1
Durham St....C3
East St....B1
Eastcott Hill....C2
Eastcott Rd....C2
Edgeware Rd....B2
Edmund St....C2
Elmina Rd....A3
Emlyn Square....B1
Euclid St....B2
Exeter St....A1
Fairview....C1
Faringdon Rd....B1
Farnsby St....B1
Fire Station....B3
Fleet St....B2
Fleming Way....B2/B3
Florence St....A2
Gladstone St....A2
Gooch St....A2
Graham St....A2
Great Western Way....A1/A3
Groundwell Rd....B3
Hawksworth Way....A1
Haydon St....A2
Henry St....B2
Hillside Ave....C1
Holbrook Way....A2
Hunt St....C1
Hydro....B1
Hythe Rd....C2
Information Ctr [i]....B2
Joseph St....C1
Kent Rd....C2
King William St....C1
Kingshill Rd....C1
Lansdown Rd....C2
Leicester St....B3
Library....B2
Lincoln St....B3
Little London....C3
London St....B1
Magic 🎭....B3
Maidstone Rd....C1
Manchester Rd....A3
Maxwell St....B1
Milford St....B2

Milton Rd....B1
Morse St....C2
National Monuments Record Centre....B3
Newcastle St....B3
Newcombe Drive....A1
Newcombe Trading Estate....A1
Newhall St....C2
North St....C2
North Star Ave....A1
North Star ⚘....A1
Northampton St....B3
Oasis Leisure Centre..A1
Ocotal Way....A3
Okus Rd....C1
Old Town....B3
Oxford St....B1
Park Lane....B1
Park Lane ⚘....B1
Pembroke St....C2
Plymouth St....B3
Polaris House....A1
Polaris Way....A2
Police Station 🚓....A2
Ponting St....A2
Post Office ⊠....B1/B2/C1/C3
Poulton St....B3
Princes St....B2
Prospect Hill....C2
Prospect Place....C2
Queen St....B2
Queen's Park....C3
Radnor St....C1
Read St....C1
Reading St....B1
Regent St....B2
Retail Park....A2/A3/B3
Rosebery St....A3
St Mark's....B1
Salisbury St....A3
Savernake St....C2
Shelley St....C1
Sheppard St....B1
South St....C2
Southampton St....A3
Spring Gardens....B3
Stafford Street....C2
Stanier St....C2
Station Road....B1
STEAM 🏛....B1
Swindon College....A2
Swindon Rd....C2
Swindon Station ≥....B2
Swindon Town Football Club....A3
T A Centre....B1
Tennyson St....B1
The Lawn....C3
The Nurseries....C1
The Parade....B2
The Park....B3
Theobald St....A1
Town Hall....B2
Transfer Bridges ⚘....A3
Union St....C2
Upham Rd....C3
Victoria Rd....C3
Walcot Rd....C3
War Memorial ✦....B2
Wells St....B2
Western St....C1
Westmorland Rd....B3
Whalebridge ⚘....B2
Whitehead St....C1
Whitehouse Rd....A2
William St....C2
Wood St....C3
Wyvern Theatre & Arts Centre 🏛....B2
York Rd....B3

Taunton 343

Addison Gr....A1
Albemarle Rd....A1
Alfred St....B3
Alma St....C3
Bath Pl....C1
Belvedere Rd....A1
Billet St....B2
Billetfield....C2
Birch Gr....A1
Brewhouse Theatre 🏛....B2
Bridge St....B1
Bridgwater & Taunton Canal....A3
Broadlands Rd....C1
Burton Pl....C1
Bus Station....B1
Canal Rd....C1
Cann St....C1
Canon St....B2
Castle 🏰....B1
Castle St....B1
Cheddon Rd....A2
Chip Lane....A1
Clarence St....B3
Cleveland St....B1
Clifton Terr....A2
Coleridge Cres....A3
Compass Hill....C1
Compton Cl....A2
Corporation St....B1
Council Offices....A1
County Walk Sh Ctr....C2
Courtyard....B2
Cranmer Rd....B2
Critchard Way....B3
Cyril St....A2
Deller's Wharf....B1
Duke St....B2
East Reach....B3
East St....B3
Eastbourne Rd....B3
Eastleigh Rd....C3
Eaton Cres....A2
Elm Gr....A2
Elms Cl....A1

Fons George....C1
Fore St....B2
Fowler St....A1
French Weir Rec Grd..B1
Geoffrey Farrant Wk..B2
Gray's Almshouses....B2
Grays Rd....C3
Greenway Ave....A1
Guildford Pl....A1
Hammet St....B2
Haydon Rd....C3
Heavitree Way....A2
Herbert St....A1
High St....C2
Holway Ave....C3
Hugo St....B3
Huish's Almshouses....B2
Hurdle Way....C2
Information Ctr [i]....B2
Jubilee St....A1
King's College....B3
Kings Cl....C3
Laburnum St....C2
Lambrook St....C3
Lansdowne Rd....A3
Leslie Ave....B3
Leycroft Rd....B3
Library....C2
Linden St....A3
Magdalene St....B2
Magistrates Court....B1
Malvern Terr....A2
Market House 🏛....B2
Mary St....C2
Middle St....B2
Midford Rd....B3
Mitre Court....A3
Mount Nebo....C1
Mount St....C2
Mountway....C1
Mus of Somerset 🏛....B1
North St....B2
Northfield Ave....A1
Northfield Rd....A1
Northleigh Rd....C3
Obridge Allotments....A3
Obridge Lane....A3
Obridge Rd....A3
Obridge Viaduct....A3
Old Mkt Shopping Ctr..C2
Osborne Way....C1
Park St....C1
Paul St....C2
Plais St....C2
Playing Field....C3
Police Station 🚓....B1
Portland St....B1
Post Office ⊠....B1/B2/C1
Priorswood Ind Est....A3
Priorswood Rd....A3
Priory Ave....A3
Priory Bridge Rd....A2
Priory Fields Retail Pk..A3
Priory Park....A2
Priory Way....A2
Queen St....B3
Railway St....A1
Records Office....A2
Recreation Grd....A1
Riverside Place....B2
St Augustine St....B2
St George's....C2
St Georges Sq....C2
St James....B2
St James St....B2
St John's....C1
St John's Rd....C1
St Josephs Field....C1
St Mary Magdalene's 🏛....B2
Samuels Ct....A1
Shire Hall & Law Courts....C1
Somerset County Cricket Ground....A2
Somerset County Hall..C1
Somerset Cricket 🏛....A2
South Rd....C2
South St....C2
Staplegrove Rd....A1
Station Rd....A2
Stephen St....B2
Swimming Pool....A1
Tancred St....B2
Tauntfield Cl....C3
Taunton Dean Cricket Club....A2
Taunton Station ≥....A2
The Avenue....A1
The Crescent....C1
The Mount....C1
Thomas St....A1
Toneway....A3
Tower St....B1
Trevor Smith Pl....C3
Trinity Bsns Centre....C3
Trinity Rd....B3
Trinity St....B3
Trull Rd....C1
Tudor House 🏛....B2
Upper High St....C2
Venture Way....A3
Victoria Gate....B3
Victoria Park....B3
Victoria St....B3
Viney St....C3
Vivary Park....C1
Vivary Rd....C1
War Memorial ✦....C1
Wellesley St....A2
Wheatley Cres....A3
Whitehall....A1
Wilfred Rd....B3
William St....A1
Wilton Church....C1
Wilton Cl....C1
Wilton Gr....C1
Wilton St....C1
Winchester St....B2

Winters Field....B2
Wood St....B1
Yarde Pl....B1

Telford 343

Alma Ave....C2
Amphitheatre....C2
Bowling Alley....C3
Brandsfarm Way....C3
Brunel Rd....B1
Bus Station....B2
Buxton Rd....C1
Central Park....A2
Civic Offices....B2
Coach Central....B2
Coachwell Cl....B1
Colliers Way....A1
Courts....B2
Dale Acre Way....B3
Darliston....C3
Deepdale....B3
Deercote....B2
Dinthill....C3
Doddington....C3
Dodmoor Grange....C3
Downemead....B3
Duffryn....B3
Dunsheath....B3
Euston Way....A3
Eyton Mound....C1
Eyton Rd....C1
Forgegate....B2
Grange Central....B2
Hall Park Way....B1
Hinkshay Rd....C2
Hollinsworth Rd....A2
Holyhead Rd....A3
Housing Trust....A1
Ice Rink....B2
Information Ctr [i]....B2
Ironmasters Way....A2
Job Centre....B2
Land Registry....B1
Lawn Central....B2
Lawnswood....C3
Library....B2
Malinsgate....B2
Matlock Ave....C1
Moor Rd....C1
Mount Rd....C1
NFU Offices....B1
Odeon 🎬....B2
Park Lane....A1
Police Station 🚓....B2
Portland St....B1
Post Office ⊠....B1/B2/C1
Priorslee Ave....A3
Queen Elizabeth Ave..C3
Queen Elizabeth Way..B1
Queensway....A2/B3
Rampart Way....A3
Randlay Ave....C3
Randlay Wood....C3
Rhodes Ave....C1
Royal Way....A2
St Leonards Rd....B1
St Quentin Gate....B2
Shifnal Rd....C1
Sixth Ave....A1
Southwater One (SW1)....A2
Southwater Way....A1
Spout Lane....C1
Spout Mound....C1
Spout Way....C1
Stafford Court....B3
Stafford Park....B3
Stirchley Ave....C3
Stone Row....C1
Telford Bridge Ret Pk..A1
Telford Central Sta ≥..A3
Telford Centre, The....B2
Telford Forge Sh Pk...A1
Telford Hornets RFC....C1
Telford Int Ctr....C2
Telford Way....A2
Third Ave....A2
Town Park....C2
Town Park Visitor Ctr..B2
Walker House....B2
Wellswood Ave....B1
West Centre Way....B1
Withywood Drive....C1
Woodhouse Central....A1
Yates Way....A1

Torquay 344

Abbey Rd....B2
Alexandra Rd....A2
Alpine Rd....A2
Ash Hill Rd....A2
Babbacombe Rd....B3
Bampfylde Rd....B1
Barton Rd....A1
Beacon Quay....C2
Belgrave Rd....A1/B1
Belmont Rd....A3
Berea Rd....A3
Braddons Hill Rd East..B3
Brewery Park....A3
Bronshill Rd....A3
Castle Circus....A2
Castle Rd....A2
Cavern Rd....A3
Central ⚘....B2
Chatsworth Rd....A2
Chestnut Ave....B1
Church St....A2
Civic Offices....A1
Coach Station....A1
Corbyn Head....C1
Croft Hill....B1
Croft Rd....B1
Daddyhole Plain....C3
East St....A1
Egerton Rd....A3
Ellacombe Church Rd..A3
Ellacombe Rd....A3
Falkland Rd....B1
Fleet St....B2

Fleet Walk Sh Ctr....B2
Grafton Rd....B3
Haldon Pier....C2
Hatfield Rd....A2
Highbury Rd....A2
Higher Warberry Rd...A3
Hillesdon Rd....A3
Hollywood Bowl ⚘....B2
Hoxton Rd....A2
Hunsdon Rd....B3
Information Ctr [i]....C2
Inner Harbour....C2
Kenwyn Rd....A3
Laburnum St....A1
Law Courts....A1
Library....A1
Lime Ave....A1
Living Coasts 🐧....C3
Lower Warberry Rd....B3
Lucius St....B1
Lymington Rd....A1
Magdalene Rd....A1
Marina....C2
Market Forum The....B2
Market St....B2
Meadfoot Lane....C3
Meadfoot Rd....C3
Melville St....B2
Middle Warberry Rd...B3
Mill Lane....A1
Montpellier Rd....B3
Morgan Ave....C1
Museum Rd....B3
Newton Rd....A1
Oakhill Rd....A1
Outer Harbour....C2
Parkhill Rd....C3
Pavilion Shopping Ctr..C2
Pimlico....B2
Police Station 🚓....A1
Post Office ⊠....A1/B2
Princes Rd....A3
Princes Rd East....A3
Princes Rd West....A3
Princess Gdns....C2
Princess Pier....C2
Princess Theatre 🏛....C2
Rathmore Rd....B1
Recreation Grd....A2
Riviera Int Ctr....B1
Rock End Ave....C3
Rock Rd....B1
Rock Walk....B1
Rosehill Rd....A3
St Efride's Rd....A1
St John's....B3
St Luke's Rd....B2
St Luke's Rd North....B2
St Luke's Rd South....B2
St Marychurch Rd....A2
Scarborough Rd....B1
Shedden Hill....B2
South Pier....C2
South St....A1
Spanish Barn....B1
Stitchill Rd....B3
Strand....C2
Sutherland Rd....B3
Teignmouth Rd....A1
Temperance St....B2
The King's Drive....B1
The Terrace....B3
Thurlow Rd....A1
Tor Bay....C2
Tor Church Rd....A1
Tor Hill Rd....A1
Torbay Rd....B2
Torquay Museum 🏛....B3
Torquay Station ≥....C1
Torre Abbey Mansion 🏛....B1
Torre Abbey Meadows..B1
Torre Abbey Sands....B1
Torwood Gdns....B3
Torwood St....C3
Town Hall....A2
Union Square....A1
Union St....A1
Upton Hill....A2
Upton Park....A1
Upton Rd....A1
Vanehill Rd....C3
Vansittart Rd....A1
Vaughan Parade....C2
Victoria Parade....C2
Victoria Rd....A2
Warberry Rd West....A2
Warren Rd....B2
Windsor Rd....A2/A3
Woodville Rd....A3

Truro 344

Adelaide Ter....B1
Agar Rd....B3
Arch Hill....C2
Arundell Pl....C2
Avondale Rd....B1
Back Quay....B3
Barrack La....C2
Barton Meadow....A1
Benson Rd....C2
Bishops Cl....A3
Bosvean Gdns....B1
Bosvigo Gardens ❀....B1
Bosvigo La....A1
Bosvigo Rd....A1
Broad St....A3
Burley Cl....C2
Bus Station....B3
Calenick St....C3
Campfield Hill....B3
Carclew St....B3
Carew Rd....A2
Carey Park....B2
Carlyon Rd....A3
Carvoza Rd....A3
Castle St....B2
Cathedral View....A3
Chainwalk Dr....A2

Chapel Hill....B1
Charles St....B3
City Hall....B3
City Rd....B3
Coinage Hall 🏛....B3
Comprigney Hill....A1
Coosebean La....A1
Copes Gdns....B1
County Hall....B1
Courtney Rd....A2
Crescent Rd....C2
Crescent Rise....B1
Daniell Court....C2
Daniell Rd....C2
Daniell St....C2
Daubuz Cl....A2
Dobbs La....A1
Edward St....B1
Eliot Rd....A3
Elm Court....A3
Enys Cl....A1
Enys Rd....A1
Fairmantle St....C3
Falmouth Rd....C2
Ferris Town....B2
Fire Station....B1
Frances St....B2
George St....B2
Green Cl....C2
Green La....C1
Grenville Rd....A2
Hall For Cornwall 🏛....B3
Hendra Rd....C1
Hendra Vean....A1
High Cross....B3
Higher Newham La...C3
Higher Trehaverne....A2
Hillcrest Ave....A1
Hospital [H]....B2
Hunkin Cl....C2
Hurland Rd....C3
Infirmary Hill....B2
James Pl....B3
Kenwyn Church Rd....A1
Kenwyn Hill....A1
Kenwyn Rd....A2
Kenwyn St....B2
Kerris Gdns....A1
King St....B3
Lemon Quay....B3
Lemon St Gallery 🏛....B3
Library....B1/B3
Malpas Rd....B3
Market....B3
Memorial Gdns....B2
Merrifield Close....B1
Mitchell Hill....A3
Moresk Cl....A3
Moresk Rd....A3
Morlaix Ave....C3
Nancemere Rd....A3
Newham Bsns Park....C3
Newham Industrial Est..C3
Newham Rd....C3
Northfield Dr....C2
Oak Way....A3
Old County Hall 🏛....B1
Pal's Terr....C3
Park View....C2
Pendarves Rd....A2
Plaza Cinema 🎬....B3
Police Station 🚓....B3
Post Office ⊠....B2/B3
Prince's St....B3
Pydar St....B2
Quay St....B3
Redannick Cres....C2
Redannick La....C2
Richard Lander Monument ✦....C2
Richmond Hill....B1
River St....B2
Rosedale Rd....A2
Royal Cornwall Mus 🏛....B2
St Aubyn Rd....C2
St Clement St....B3
St George's Rd....C2
School La....C2
Station Rd....B2
Stokes Rd....A2
Strangways Terr....C3
Tabernacle St....B3
The Avenue....A3
The Crescent....B2
The Leats....B2
The Spires....A2
Trehaverne La....A2
Tremayne Rd....C2
Treseder's Gdns....A3
Treworder Rd....B1
Treyew Rd....C1
Truro Cathedral ✝....B3
Truro Harbour Office...C3
Truro Station ≥....B3
Union St....B2
Upper School La....C2
Victoria Gdns....B2
Waterfall Gdns....B2

Wick 344

Ackergill Cres....A2
Ackergill St....A2
Albert St....A2
Ambulance Station....A2
Argyle Sq....C2
Assembly Rooms....C2
Bank Row....C3
Bankhead....A1
Barons Well....B2
Barrogill St....C2
Bay View....B3
Bexley Terr....C1
Bignold Park....C2
Bowling Green....C2
Breadalbane Terr....C2
Bridge of Wick....C1
Bridge St....B2
Brown Pl....B1
Burn St....B2

360 Winchester • Windsor • Wolverhampton • Worcester • Wrexham • York

Bus Station B1
Caithness General Hospital (A&E) B1
Cliff Rd B1
Coach Rd B2
Coastguard Station C3
Corner Cres B3
Coronation St C1
Council Offices B2
Court B2
Crane Rock C3
Dempster St C2
Dunnet Ave A2
Fire Station B2
Fish Market C3
Francis St C1
George St A1
Girnigoe St B2
Glamis Rd B2
Gowrie Pl B1
Grant St C2
Green Rd B2
Gunns Terr B3
Harbour Quay B2
Harbour Rd C3
Harbour Terr C2
Harrow Hill C2
Henrietta St A2/B2
Heritage Museum C2
High St B2
Hill Ave A2
Hillhead Rd B3
Hood St C1
Huddart St C2
Information Ctr B2
Kenneth St C1
Kinnaird St C2
Kirk Hill B1
Langwell Cres B3
Leishman Ave B3
Leith Walk A2
Library B2
Lifeboat Station C3
Lighthouse C3
Lindsay Dr B3
Lindsay Pl B3
Loch St C2
Louisburgh St B2
Lower Dunbar St C2
Macleay La B1
Macleod Rd B3
MacRae St C2
Martha Terr B2
Miller Ave B1
Miller La B1
Moray St C2
Mowat Pl B3
Murchison St C3
Newton Ave C1
Newton Rd C1
Nicolson St C3
North Highland Coll B2
North River Pier B3
Northcote St C2
Owen Pl A2
Police Station B1
Port Dunbar B3
Post Office B2/C2
Pulteney Distillery ✦ C2
River St B2
Robert St A1
Rutherford St C2
St John's Episcopal C2
Sandigoe Rd B3
Scalesburn B3
Seaforth Ave C1
Shore La B2
Sinclair Dr B3
Sinclair Terr C2
Smith Terr C3
South Pier C3
South Quay C3
South Rd C1
South River Pier B3
Station Rd B1
Swimming Pool B2
TA Centre C2
Telford St B2
The Shore B2
Thurso Rd B1
Thurso St B1
Town Hall B2
Union St B2
Upper Dunbar St C2
Vansittart St C3
Victoria Pl B2
War Memorial A1
Well of Cairndhuna ✦ C3
Wellington Ave C3
Wellington St C3
West Banks Ave C1
West Banks Terr C1
West Park C1
Whitehorse Park B2
Wick Harbour Bridge B2
Wick Industrial Estate A2
Wick Parish Church B1
Wick Station B1
Williamson St B2
Willowbank B2

Winchester 344

Andover Rd A2
Andover Rd Retail Pk A2
Archery La C2
Arthur Rd A2
Bar End Rd C3
Beaufort Rd C2
Beggar's La B3
Bereweeke Ave A1
Bereweeke Rd A1
Boscobel Rd A2
Brassey Rd A2
Broadway B3
Brooks Sh Ctr, The B3
Bus Station B3
Butter Cross ✦ B2
Canon St C2
Castle Wall C2/C3
Castle, King Arthur's Round Table B2
Cathedral C2
Cheriton Rd A1
Chesil St C3
Chesil Theatre C3
Christchurch Rd C1
City Mill ✦ B3
City Museum B2
City Offices C3
City Rd B2
Clifton Rd B1
Clifton Terr B2
Close Wall C2/C3
Coach Park A2
Colebrook St C3
College St C2
College Walk C3
Compton Rd C2
County Council Offices B2
Cranworth Rd A2
Cromwell Rd C1
Culver Rd C2
Domum Rd C3
Durngate Pl B3
Eastgate St B3
Edgar Rd C2
Egbert Rd A2
Elm Rd B1
Everyman C2
Fairfield Rd A1
Fire Station B3
Fordington Ave B1
Fordington Rd A1
Friarsgate B3
Gordon Rd B3
Greenhill Rd B1
Guildhall B3
HM Prison B1
Hatherley Rd A1
High St B2
Hillier Way A3
Hyde Abbey (Remains) A2
Hyde Abbey Rd B2
Hyde Cl A2
Hyde St A2
Information Ctr B3
Jane Austen's Ho C2
Jewry St B2
John Stripe Theatre C1
King Alfred Pl A2
Kingsgate Arch C2
Kingsgate Park C2
Kingsgate Rd C2
Kingsgate St C2
Lankhills Rd A2
Library B2
Lower Brook St B3
Magdalen Hill B3
Market La B2
Mews La B1
Middle Brook St B3
Middle Rd B1
Military Museums B2
Milland Rd C3
Milverton Rd B1
Monks Rd A3
North Hill Cl A2
North Walls B2
North Walls Rec Gnd A3
Nuns Rd A3
Oram's Arbour B1
Owen's Rd A2
Parchment St B2
Park & Ride C3
Park Ave B3
Playing Field A1
Police HQ B1
Police Station B3
Portal Rd C3
Post Office B2/C1
Quarry Rd C3
Ranelagh Rd C1
Regiment Museum B2
River Park Leisure Ctr B3
Romans' Rd C2
Romsey Rd B1
Royal Hampshire County Hospital (A&E) B1
St Cross Rd C2
St George's St B2
St Giles Hill C3
St James' La B1
St James' Terr B1
St James Villas C2
St John's B3
St John's St B3
St Michael's Rd C2
St Paul's Hill B1
St Peter St B2
St Swithun St C2
St Thomas St C2
Saxon Rd A2
School of Art B3
Sleepers Hill Rd C1
Southgate St B2
Sparkford Rd C1
Staple Gdns B2
Station Rd B2
Step Terr B1
Stockbridge Rd A1
Stuart Cres C1
Sussex St B2
Swan Lane B2
Tanner St B3
The Square B2
The Weirs C3
The Winchester Gallery B3
Theatre Royal B2
Tower St B2
Town Hall C3
Union St B3
Univ of Southampton (Winchester School of Art) B3
Univ of Winchester (King Alfred Campus) C1
Upper Brook St B2
Wales St B3
Water Lane B3
West End Terr B1
West Gate B1
Western Rd B1
Wharf Hill C3
Winchester College C2
Winchester Sta A2
Winnall Moors Wildlife Reserve A3
Wolvesey Castle C3
Worthy Lane A2
Worthy Rd A2

Windsor 344

Adelaide Sq C3
Albany Rd C2
Albert St B1
Alexandra Gdns B2
Alexandra Rd C2
Alma Rd B2
Ambulance Station B1
Arthur Rd B2
Bachelors Acre B3
Barry Ave B2
Beaumont Rd C2
Bexley St B1
Boat House B2
Brocas St B2
Brook St C3
Bulkeley Ave C1
Castle Hill B3
Charles St B2
Claremont Rd C2
Clarence Cr B2
Clarence Rd B1
Clewer Court Rd B1
Coach Park B2
College Cr C1
Courts C2
Cricket Ground C3
Dagmar Rd C2
Datchet Rd B3
Devereux Rd C2
Dorset Rd C2
Duke St B1
Elm Rd C1
Eton College ✦ A3
Eton Ct A2
Eton Sq A2
Eton Wick Rd A2
Fire Station C2
Farm Yard B3
Frances Rd C2
Frogmore Dr B3
Gloucester Pl C3
Goslar Way C1
Goswell Hill B2
Goswell Rd B2
Green La C1
Grove Rd C2
Guildhall B3
Helena Rd C2
Helston La B1
High St A2/B3
Holy Trinity C2
Hospital (Private) C2
Household Cavalry C2
Imperial Rd C1
Information Ctr B2/B3
Keats La A2
King Edward Ct B2
King Edward VII Ave A3
King Edward VII Hospital C2
King George V Meml B3
King's Rd C3
King Stable St A2
Library C2
Maidenhead Rd B1
Meadow La A2
Municipal Offices C3
Nell Gwynne's Ho B3
Osborne Rd C2
Oxford Rd B1
Park St B3
Peascod St B2
Police Station C2
Post Office A2
Princess Margaret Hospital C2
Queen Victoria's Walk B3
Queen's Rd C2
River St B2
Romney Island A3
Romney Lock A3
Romney Lock Rd A3
Russell St C2
St John's B3
St John's Chapel A2
St Leonards Rd C2
St Mark's Rd C2
Sheet St C3
South Meadow A2
South Meadow La A2
Springfield Rd C1
Stovell Rd B1
Sunbury Rd A2
Tangier La A2
Tangier St A3
Temple Rd C2
Thames St B3
The Brocas A2
The Home Park A3/C3
The Long Walk C3
Theatre Royal B3
Trinity Pl C2
Vansittart Rd B1/C1
Vansittart Rd Gdns C1
Victoria Barracks C2
Victoria St C2
Ward Royal B2
Westmead C1
White Lilies Island A1
William St B2
Windsor Arts Ctr C2
Windsor Castle B3
Windsor & Eton Central B2
Windsor & Eton Riverside A3
Windsor Bridge B3
Windsor Great Park C3
Windsor Leisure Ctr B1
Windsor Relief Rd A1
Windsor Royal Sh B2
York Ave C1
York Rd C1

Wolverhampton 344

Albion St B3
Alexandra St C1
Arena B2
Arts Gallery B2
Ashland St C1
Austin St A1
Badger Dr A3
Bailey St B3
Bath Ave B1
Bath Rd B1
Bell St C2
Berry St B3
Bilston Rd C3
Bilston St C3
Birmingham Canal A3
Bone Mill La A2
Brewery Rd B1
Bright St A1
Burton Cres B3
Bus Station B3
Cambridge St A3
Camp St B2
Cannock Rd A3
Castle St C2
Chapel Ash C1
Cherry St C1
Chester St A1
Church La C2
Church St C2
Civic Centre B2
Clarence Rd B2
Cleveland St C2
Clifton St C1
Coach Station B2
Compton Rd B1
Corn Hill B3
Coven St A3
Craddock St A1
Cross St North A2
Crown & County Courts C3
Crown St A2
Culwell St B3
Dale St C1
Darlington St C1
Dartmouth St C3
Devon Rd A1
Drummond St B2
Dudley Rd C2
Dudley St B2
Duke St C3
Dunkley St B1
Dunstall Ave A2
Dunstall Hill A2
Dunstall Rd A1/A2
Evans St A1
Fawdry St A1
Field St B3
Fire Station C1
Fiveways A2
Fowler Playing Fields A3
Fox's La A2
Francis St A2
Fryer St B3
Gloucester St A1
Gordon St C3
Graiseley St C1
Grand B3
Granville St C3
Great Brickkiln St C1
Great Hampton St A1
Great Western St A2
Grimstone St B3
Harrow St A1
Hilton St A3
Horseley Fields C3
Humber Rd C1
Jack Hayward Way A2
Jameson St A1
Jenner St C3
Kennedy Rd B3
Kimberley St C1
King St B2
Laburnum St C1
Lansdowne Rd B1
Leicester St A1
Lever St C3
Library C3
Lichfield St B2
Light House B3
Little's La B3
Lock St B3
Lord St C1
Lowe St A1
Lower Stafford St A2
Magistrates Court B2
Mander Centre C2
Mander St C1
Market St B2
Market C2
Melbourne St C3
Merridale St C1
Middlecross C3
Molineux St B2
Mostyn St A1
New Hampton Rd East A1
Nine Elms La A3
North Rd A2
Oaks Cres C1
Oxley St A2
Paget St A1
Park Ave B1
Park Road East A1
Park Road West B1
Paul St C2
Pelham St C1
Penn Rd C2
Piper's Row B3
Pitt St C2
Police Station C3
Pool St C2
Poole St A3
Post Office A1/A2/B2/B2
Powlett St C3
Queen St B2
Raby St C3
Raglan St C1
Railway Dr B3
Red Hill St A2
Red Lion St B2
Retreat St C1
Ring Rd B2
Rugby St A1
Russell St C1
St Andrew's B1
St David's B3
St George's C3
St George's Parade C2
St James St C3
St John's C2
St John's C2
St John's Retail Park C2
St John's Square C2
St Mark's C1
St Marks Rd C1
St Marks St C1
St Patrick's B2
St Peter's B2
St Peter's B2
Salisbury St C1
Salop St C2
School St C2
Sherwood St A2
Smestow St A3
Snowhill C2
Springfield Rd A3
Stafford St B2
Staveley Rd A1
Steelhouse La C3
Stephenson St C1
Stewart St C2
Sun St B3
Sutherland Pl C3
Tempest St C2
Temple St C2
Tettenhall Rd B1
The Maltings B2
The Royal C3
Thomas St C2
Thornley St B2
Tower St C2
University B2
Upper Zoar St C1
Vicarage Rd C3
Victoria St C2
Walpole St A1
Walsall St C3
Ward St C3
Warwick St C3
Water St A3
Waterloo Rd B2
Wednesfield Rd B3
West Pk (not A&E) B1
West Park Swimming Pool B1
Wharf St C3
Whitmore Hill B2
Wolverhampton B3
Wolverhampton St George's C2
Wolverhampton Wanderers Football Gnd (Molineux) B2
Worcester St C2
Wulfrun Centre C2
Yarwell Cl A3
York St C3
Zoar St C1

Worcester 344

Albany Terr A1
Alice Otley School A2
Angel Pl B2
Angel St B2
Ashcroft Rd A2
Athelstan Rd C3
Back Lane North A1
Back Lane South A1
Barbourne Rd A2
Bath Rd C2
Battenhall Rd C3
Bridge St B2
Britannia Sq A1
Broad St B2
Bromwich La C1
Bromwich Rd C1
Bromyard Rd C1
Bus Station B2
Carden St B3
Castle St A2
Cathedral C2
Cathedral Plaza B2
Charles St B3
Chequers La B1
Chestnut St A2
Chestnut Walk A2
Citizens' Advice Bureau B2
City Walls Rd B2
Cole Hill C3
College of Technology B2
College St C2
Commandery C3
Cripplegate Park B1
Croft Rd B1
Cromwell St B3
CrownGate Centre B2
Deansway B2
Diglis Pde C2
Diglis Rd C2
Edgar Tower ✦ C2
Farrier St A2
Fire Station B2
Foregate St B2
Foregate Street B2
Fort Royal Hill C3
Fort Royal Park C3
Foundry St B3
Friar St C2
George St B3
Grand Stand Rd B1
Greenhill C3
Greyfriars B2
Guildhall B2
Henwick Rd B1
High St B2
Hill St B3
Huntingdon Hall B2
Hylton Rd B1
Information Ctr B2
King Charles Pl Shopping Centre C1
King's School C2
King's School Playing Field C2
Kleve Walk C2
Lansdowne Cr A3
Lansdowne Rd A3
Lansdowne Walk A3
Laslett St A3
Leisure Centre A3
Library, Museum & Art Gallery A2
Little Chestnut St A2
Little London A2
London Rd C3
Lowell St A3
Lowesmoor B2
Lowesmoor Terr A3
Lowesmoor Wharf A3
Magistrates Court A2
Midland Rd B3
Mill St C2
Moors Severn Terr A1
New Rd C1
New St B2
Northfield St A2
Odeon B2
Padmore St B3
Park St C3
Pheasant St B3
Pitchcroft Racecourse A1
Police Station A2
Portland St C2
Post Office B2
Quay St B2
Queen St B2
Rainbow Hill A3
Recreation Ground A2
Reindeer Court B2
Rogers Hill A3
Sabrina Rd A1
St Dunstan's Cr C3
St John's C1
St Martin's Gate B3
St Oswald's Rd A2
St Paul's St B3
St Swithin's Church B2
St Wulstans Cr C3
Sansome Walk A2
Severn St C2
Shaw St B2
Shire Hall Crown Ct A2
Shrub Hill B3
Shrub Hill Retail Park B3
Shrub Hill Rd B3
Slingpool Walk C1
South Quay B2
Southfield St A2
Sports Ground A2/C1
Stanley Rd B3
Swan, The A1
Swimming Pool A2
Tallow Hill B3
Tennis Walk A2
The Avenue C1
The Butts B2
The Cross B2
The Shambles B2
The Tything A2
Tolladine Rd B3
Tudor House ✦ B2
Tybridge St B1
Univ of Worcester B2
Vincent Rd B3
Vue C2
Washington St A3
Woolhope Rd C3
Worcester Bridge B2
Worcester County Cricket Ground C1
Worcester Library & History Centre B3
Worcester Porcelain Museum C2
Worcester Royal Grammar School A2
Wylds La C3

Wrexham Wrecsam 344

Abbot St B2
Acton Rd A3
Albert St C3
Alexandra Rd C1
Aran Rd A3
Barnfield C3
Bath Rd C2
Beechley Rd C3
Belgrave Rd C2
Belle Vue Park C2
Belle Vue Rd C2
Belvedere Dr A1
Bennion's Rd C3
Berse Rd A1
Bersham Rd C1
Birch St C3
Bodhyfryd B3
Border Retail Park B3
Bradley Rd C2
Bright St B1
Bron-y-Nant B1
Brook St C2
Bryn-y-Cabanau Rd C3
Bury St C3
Bus Station B2
Butchers Market B3
Caia Rd C3
Cambrian Ind Est C3
Caxton Pl B2
Cemetery C1
Centenary Rd C1
Chapel St C2
Charles St B3
Chester Rd A3
Chester St B3
Cilcen Gr A3
Citizens Advice Bureau B2
Cobden Rd B1
Council Offices B3
County B2
Crescent Rd B3
Crispin La A2
Croesnewyth Rd B1
Cross St A2
Cunliffe St A2
Derby Rd C3
Dolydd Rd B1
Duke St B2
Eagles Meadow C3
Earle St C2
East Ave A2
Edward St C2
Egerton St B2
Empress Rd C1
Erddig Rd C2
Fairy Rd C2
Fire Station B2
Foster Rd A3
Foxwood Dr C1
Garden Rd A2
General Market B3
Gerald St B2
Gibson St C1
Glyndŵr University Plas Coch Campus A1
Greenbank St C3
Greenfield A2
Grosvenor Rd B2
Grove Park B3
Grove Park Rd B3
Grove Rd A3
Guildhall B2
Haig Rd C3
Hampden Rd C2
Hazel Gr A3
Henblas St B3
High St B3
Hightown Rd C3
Hill St B2
Holt Rd B3
Holt St B3
Hope St B2
Huntroyde Ave C3
Information Ctr B3
Island Gn Sh Ctr B2
Job Centre B2
Jubilee Rd B2
King St B2
Kingsmills Rd C3
Lambpit St B3
Law Courts B3
Lawson Cl A3
Lawson Rd A3
Lea Rd C2
Library & Arts Centre B2
Lilac Way B1
Llys David Lord B1
Lorne St A2
Maesgwyn Rd B1
Maesydre Rd A3
Manley Rd B3
Market St B3
Mawddy Ave A2
Mayville Ave A2
Memorial Gallery B2
Memorial Hall B3
Mold Rd A1
Mount St C3
Neville Cres A3
New Rd A2
North Wales Regional Tennis Centre A1
North Wales School of Art & Design B2
Oak Dr A3
Park Ave A3
Park St A2
Peel St C1
Pentre Felin C2
Pen y Bryn C2
Penymaes Ave A3
Peoples Market B3
Percy St C2
Plas Coch Retail Park A1
Plas Coch Rd A1
Police Station B3
Poplar Rd C2
Post Office A2/B2/C2/C3
Powell Rd B3
Poyser St C2
Price's La A2
Primose Way B1
Princess St C1
Queen St B3
Queens Sq B2
Regent St B2
Rhosddu Rd A2/B2
Rhosnesni La A3
Rivulet Rd C3
Ruabon Rd C2
Ruthin Rd C1/C2
St Giles C3
St Giles Way C3
St James Ct A2
St Mary's B2
Salisbury Rd C3
Salop Rd C3
Sontley Rd C2
Spring Rd A2
Stanley St C3
Stansty Rd A2
Station Approach B2
Studio B2
Talbot Rd C2
Techniquest Glyndŵr ✦ A2
The Beeches A3
The Pines A3
Town Hill C2
Trevor St C2
Trinity St B2
Tuttle St C3
Vale Park A1
Vernon St B2
Vicarage Hill B2
Victoria Rd C2
Walnut St A2
War Memorial B3
Waterworld L Ctr ✦ B3
Watery Rd B1/B2
Wellington Rd C2
Westminster Dr A3
William Aston Hall A1
Windsor Rd A1
Wrexham AFC A1
Wrexham Central B2
Wrexham General B2
Wrexham Maelor Hospital (A&E) B1
Wrexham Technology Park B1
Wynn Ave A2
Yale College B3
Yale Gr A3
Yorke St C3

York 344

Aldwark B2
Ambulance Station B3
Barbican Rd C3
Barley Hall B2
Bishopgate St C2
Bishopthorpe Rd C2
Blossom St C1
Bootham A1
Bootham Cr A1
Bootham Terr A1
Bridge St B2
Brook St A2
Brownlow St A2
Burton Stone La A1
Castle Museum C2
Castlegate B2
Cemetery Rd C3
Cherry St C2
City Screen B2
City Wall A2/B1/C3
Clarence St A2
Clementhorpe C2
Clifford St B2
Clifford's Tower B2
Clifton A1
Coach park A2
Coney St B2
Cromwell Rd C2
Crown Court C2
Davygate B2
Deanery Gdns A2
DIG ✦ B2
Ebor Industrial Estate B3
Fairfax House B2
Fishergate C3
Foss Islands Retail Pk B3
Foss Islands Rd B3
Fossbank A3
Garden St A2
George St C3
Gillygate A2
Goodramgate B2
Grand Opera House B2
Grosvenor Terr A1
Guildhall B2
Hallfield Rd A3
Heslington Rd C3
Heworth Green A3
Holy Trinity B2
Hope St C3
Huntington Rd A3
Information Ctr B2
James St B3
Jorvik Viking Ctr B2
Kent St C3
Lawrence St C3
Layerthorpe A3
Leeman Rd B1
Lendal B2
Lendal Bridge B1
Library B1
Longfield Terr A1
Lord Mayor's Walk A2
Lower Eldon St A2
Lowther St A2
Mansion House B2
Margaret St C3
Marygate A1
Melbourne St C3
Merchant Adventurer's Hall B2
Merchant Taylors' Hall B2
Micklegate B1
Micklegate Bar C1
Minster, The A2
Monkgate A2
Moss St C1
Museum Gdns B1
Museum St B1
National Railway Museum B1
Navigation Rd B3
Newton Terr C2
North Parade A1
North St B2
Nunnery La C1
Nunthorpe Rd C1
Ouse Bridge B2
Paragon St C3
Park Gr A3
Park St C1
Parliament St B2
Peasholme Green B3
Penley's Grove St A2
Piccadilly B2
Police Station B2
Post Office B1/B2/C3
Priory St B1
Purey Cust Nuffield Hospital, The A2
Queen Anne's Rd A1
Quilt Museum B3
Reel C1
Regimental Museum B2
Richard III Museum A2
Roman Bath B2
Rowntree Park C2
St Andrewgate B2
St Benedict Rd C1
St John St A2
St Olave's Rd A1
St Peter's Gr A1
St Saviourgate B2
Scarcroft Hill C1
Scarcroft Rd C1
Skeldergate C2
Skeldergate Bridge C2
Station Rd B1
Stonegate B2
Sycamore Terr A1
Terry Ave C2
The Shambles B2
The Stonebow B2
Theatre Royal B2
Thorpe St C1
Toft Green B1
Tower St C2
Townend St A2
Treasurer's House A2
Trinity La B1
Undercroft Mus A2
Union Terr A2
Victor St C2
Vine St C2
Walmgate B3
Wellington St C3
York Art Gallery A1
York Barbican C3
York Brewery ✦ B1
York Dungeon, The B2
York Station B1

361

Abbreviations used in the index

Abbreviation	
Aberdeen	Aberdeen City
Aberds	Aberdeenshire
Ald	Alderney
Anglesey	Isle of Anglesey
Angus	Angus
Argyll	Argyll and Bute
Bath	Bath and North East Somerset
Bedford	Bedford
Bl Gwent	Blaenau Gwent
Blackburn	Blackburn with Darwen
Blackpool	Blackpool
Bmouth	Bournemouth
Borders	Scottish Borders
Brack	Bracknell
Bridgend	Bridgend
Brighton	City of Brighton and Hove
Bristol	City and County of Bristol
Bucks	Buckinghamshire
C Beds	Central Bedfordshire
Caerph	Caerphilly
Cambs	Cambridgeshire
Cardiff	Cardiff
Carms	Carmarthenshire
Ceredig	Ceredigion
Ches E	Cheshire East
Ches W	Cheshire West and Chester
Clack	Clackmannanshire
Conwy	Conwy
Corn	Cornwall
Cumb	Cumbria
Darl	Darlington
Denb	Denbighshire
Derby	City of Derby
Derbys	Derbyshire
Devon	Devon
Dorset	Dorset
Dumfries	Dumfries and Galloway
Dundee	Dundee City
Durham	Durham
E Ayrs	East Ayrshire
E Dunb	East Dunbartonshire
E Loth	East Lothian
E Renf	East Renfrewshire
E Sus	East Sussex
E Yorks	East Riding of Yorkshire
Edin	City of Edinburgh
Essex	Essex
Falk	Falkirk
Fife	Fife
Flint	Flintshire
Glasgow	City of Glasgow
Glos	Gloucestershire
Gtr Man	Greater Manchester
Guern	Guernsey
Gwyn	Gwynedd
Halton	Halton
Hants	Hampshire
Hereford	Herefordshire
Herts	Hertfordshire
Highld	Highland
Hrtlpl	Hartlepool
Hull	Hull
IoM	Isle of Man
IoW	Isle of Wight
Invclyd	Inverclyde
Jersey	Jersey
Kent	Kent
Lancs	Lancashire
Leicester	City of Leicester
Leics	Leicestershire
Lincs	Lincolnshire
London	Greater London
Luton	Luton
M Keynes	Milton Keynes
M Tydf	Merthyr Tydfil
Mbro	Middlesbrough
Medway	Medway
Mers	Merseyside
Midloth	Midlothian
Mon	Monmouthshire
Moray	Moray
N Ayrs	North Ayrshire
N Lincs	North Lincolnshire
N Lanark	North Lanarkshire
N Som	North Somerset
N Yorks	North Yorkshire
NE Lincs	North East Lincolnshire
Neath	Neath Port Talbot
Newport	City and County of Newport
Norf	Norfolk
Northants	Northamptonshire
Northumb	Northumberland
Nottingham	City of Nottingham
Notts	Nottinghamshire
Orkney	Orkney
Oxon	Oxfordshire
Pboro	Peterborough
Pembs	Pembrokeshire
Perth	Perth and Kinross
Plym	Plymouth
Poole	Poole
Powys	Powys
Ptsmth	Portsmouth
Reading	Reading
Redcar	Redcar and Cleveland
Renfs	Renfrewshire
Rhondda	Rhondda Cynon Taff
Rutland	Rutland
S Ayrs	South Ayrshire
S Glos	South Gloucestershire
S Lanark	South Lanarkshire
S Yorks	South Yorkshire
Scilly	Scilly
Shetland	Shetland
Shrops	Shropshire
Slough	Slough
Som	Somerset
Soton	Southampton
Staffs	Staffordshire
Southend	Southend-on-Sea
Stirling	Stirling
Stockton	Stockton-on-Tees
Stoke	Stoke-on-Trent
Suff	Suffolk
Sur	Surrey
Swansea	Swansea
Swindon	Swindon
T&W	Tyne and Wear
Telford	Telford & Wrekin
Thurrock	Thurrock
Torbay	Torbay
Torf	Torfaen
V Glam	The Vale of Glamorgan
W Berks	West Berkshire
W Dunb	West Dunbartonshire
W Isles	Western Isles
W Loth	West Lothian
W Mid	West Midlands
W Sus	West Sussex
W Yorks	West Yorkshire
Warks	Warwickshire
Warr	Warrington
Wilts	Wiltshire
Windsor	Windsor and Maidenhead
Wokingham	Wokingham
Worcs	Worcestershire
Wrex	Wrexham
York	City of York

Index to road maps of Britain

How to use the index

Example **Blatherwycke** Northants **137** D9

- grid square
- page number
- county or unitary authority

A

Aar–Alm

Aaron's Hill Sur 50 E3
Aaron's Town Cumb 240 E2
Abbas Combe Som 30 C2
Abberley Worcs 116 D5
Abberton Essex 89 B8
Worcs 117 G9
Abberwick Northumb 264 G4
Abbess End Essex 87 C9
Abbess Roding Essex 87 C9
Abbey Devon 27 E10
Abbeycwmhir Powys 113 C11
Abbey-cwm-hir Powys 113 C11
Abbeydale Glos 80 B5
S Yorks 186 E4
Abbeydale Park S Yorks 186 E4
Abbey Dore Hereford 97 E7
Abbey Field Essex 107 G9
Abbey Gate Kent 53 B9
Abbey Green Shrops 149 C10
Staffs 169 D7
Abbey Hey Gtr Man 184 B5
Abbeyhill Edin 280 G5
Abbey Hulton Stoke 168 F6
Abbey Mead Sur 66 F4
Abbey St Bathans
Borders 272 C5
Abbeystead Lancs 203 C7
Abbey Town Cumb 238 G5
Abbey Village Lancs 194 C6
Abbey Wood London 68 D3
Abbots Bickington Devon 24 E5
Abbots Bromley Staffs 151 E11
Abbotsbury Dorset 17 D7
Abbotsford W Sus 36 C4
Abbotsham Devon 24 B6
Abbotskerswell Devon 9 B7
Abbots Langley Herts 85 E9
Abbotsleigh Devon 8 F6
Abbots Leigh N Som 60 E4
Abbotsley Cambs 122 F4
Abbot's Meads Ches W 166 B5
Abbots Morton Worcs 117 F10
Abbots Ripton Cambs 122 B4
Abbots Salford Warks 117 G11
Abbotstone Hants 48 G5
Abbotswood Hants 32 C5
Sur 50 C4
Abbots Worthy Hants 48 G3
Abbotts Ann Hants 47 E10
Abcott Shrops 115 B7
Abdon Shrops 131 F11
Abdy S Yorks 186 B6
Aber Ceredig 93 B9
Aberaeron Ceredig 111 E9
Aberaman Rhondda 77 E8
Aberangell Gwyn 146 G6
Aber-Arad Carms 92 D6
Aberarder Highld 290 E6
Aberarder House Highld 300 G6
Aberarder Lodge Highld 291 E7
Aberargie Perth 286 F5
Aberarth Ceredig 111 E9
Aberavon Neath 57 C8
Aber-banc Ceredig 93 C7
Aberbargoed Caerph 77 E11
Aberbechan Powys 130 E2
Aberbeeg Bl Gwent 78 E2
Aberbran Powys 95 F9
Abercanaid M Tydf 77 E9
Abercarn Caerph 78 G2
Abercastle Pembs 91 E7
Abercegir Powys 128 C6
Aberchalder Highld 290 C5
Aberchirder Aberds 302 D6
Abercorn W Loth 279 F11
Aber Cowarch Gwyn 147 F7
Abercraf Powys 76 C4
Abercregan Neath 57 B11
Abercrombie Fife 287 G9
Abercwmboi Rhondda 77 F8
Abercych Pembs 92 C4
Abercynafon Powys 77 B9
Abercynffig / Aberkenfig
Bridgend 57 E11
Abercynon Rhondda 77 F9
Aberdalgie Perth 286 E4
Aberdâr / Aberdare
Rhondda 77 E7
Aberdare / Aberdâr
Rhondda 77 E7
Aberdaron Gwyn 144 D3
Aberdeen Aberdeen 293 C11
Aberdesach Gwyn 162 E6
Aberdour Fife 280 D3
Aberdovey / Aberdyfi
Gwyn 128 D2
Aberdulais Neath 76 E3
Aberdyfi / Aberdovey
Gwyn 128 D2
Aberedw Powys 95 B11
Abereiddy Pembs 90 E5
Abererch Gwyn 145 B7
Aberfan M Tydf 77 E9
Aberfeldy Perth 286 C2
Aberffraw Anglesey 162 B5
Aberffrwd Ceredig 112 B3
Mon 78 D5
Aberford W Yorks 206 F4
Aberfoyle Stirl 285 G9
Abergarw Bridgend 58 C2
Abergarwed Neath 76 E4
Abergavenny Mon 78 C3
Abergele Conwy 180 F6
Aber-Giâr Carms 93 C10
Abergorlech Carms 93 E11
Abergwaun / Fishguard
Pembs 91 D9
Abergwesyn Powys 113 G7
Abergwili Carms 93 G8
Abergwynant Gwyn 146 F3
Abergwynfi Neath 57 B11
Aber-gwynfi Neath 57 B11
Abergwyngregyn Gwyn 179 G11
Abergynolwyn Gwyn 128 B3
Aber-Hirnant Gwyn 147 C9
Aberhosan Powys 128 D6
Aberkenfig / Abercynffig
Bridgend 57 E11
Aberlady E Loth 281 E9
Aberlemno Angus 287 B9
Aberllerry Ceredig 128 E2
Aberllefenni Gwyn 128 B5
Aberllydan / Broad Haven
Pembs 72 C5
Aberllynfi / Three Cocks
Powys 96 D3
Abermagwr Ceredig 112 C3
Abermaw / Barmouth
Gwyn 146 F2
Abermeurig Ceredig 111 F11
Aber miwl / Abermule
Powys 130 E3
Abermorddu Flint 166 D4
Abermule / Aber-miwl
Powys 130 E3
Abernaint Powys 148 E2
Abernant Carms 92 G6
Powys 130 D3
Aber-nant Rhondda 77 E8
Abernethy Perth 286 F5
Abernyte Perth 286 D6
Aber-oer Wrex 166 F3
Aberogwr / Ogmore by Sea
V Glam 57 F11
Aberpennar / Mountain Ash
Rhondda 77 F8
Aberporth Ceredig 110 G5
Aber-Rhiwlech Gwyn 147 E8
Aberriw / Berriew
Powys 130 C3
Abersoch Gwyn 144 D6
Abersychan Torf 78 E3
Abertawe / Swansea
Swansea 56 C6
Aberteifi / Cardigan
Ceredig 92 B3
Aberthin V Glam 58 D4
Abertillery Bl Gwent 78 E2
Abertridwr Caerph 58 B6
Powys 147 F10
Abertrinant Gwyn 128 B2
Abertysswg Caerph 77 D10
Aberuchill Castle
Perth 285 E11
Aberuthven Perth 286 F3
Aber-Village Powys 96 G2
Aberyscir Powys 95 F9
Aberystwyth Ceredig 111 A11
Abhainn Suidhe
W Isles 305 H2
Abingdon-on-Thames
Oxon 83 F7
Abinger Common Sur 50 D6
Abinger Hammer Sur 50 D5
Abington Northants 120 E5
S Lnrk 259 E10
Abington Pigotts Cambs 104 C6
Abington Vale Northants 120 E5
Abingworth W Sus 35 D10
Ab Kettleby Leics 154 E4
Ab Lench Worcs 117 G10
Ablington Glos 81 D10
Wilts 47 D7
Abney Derbys 185 F11
Aboyne Aberds 293 D7
Abraham Heights Lancs 211 G9
Abram Gtr Man 194 G6
Abriachan Highld 300 F5
Abridge Essex 87 F7
Abronhill N Lnrk 278 F5
Abshot Hants 33 F8
Abson S Glos 61 E8
Abthorpe Northants 102 B2
Abune-the-Hill Orkney 314 D2
Aby Lincs 190 F6
Acaster Malbis York 207 D7
Acaster Selby N Yorks 207 E7
Accrington Lancs 195 B9
Acha Argyll 275 B8
Argyll 288 D3
Achabraid Argyll 275 E9
Achachork Highld 298 E4
Achadh an Eas Highld 308 F6
Achad nan Darach
Highld 284 B4
Achadunan Argyll 284 F5
Achafolla Argyll 275 B8
Achagary Highld 308 D7
Achaglass Argyll 255 C8
Achahoish Argyll 275 F8
Achalader Perth 286 C5
Achallader Argyll 285 C7
Achalone Highld 310 D5
Acha Mor W Isles 304 F5
Achanalt Highld 300 C2
Achanamara Argyll 275 E8
Achandunie Highld 300 B6
Achanelid Argyll 275 E11
Ach'an Todhair Highld 290 F2
Achany Highld 309 J5
Achaphubuil Highld 290 F2
Acharacle Highld 289 C8
Acharn Highld 289 D9
Perth 285 C11
Acharole Highld 310 D6
Acharossan Argyll 275 F10
Acharry Muir Highld 309 K6
Achath Aberds 293 B9
Achavanich Highld 310 E5
Achavelgin Highld 301 D9
Achavraat Highld 301 E9
Achddu Carms 74 E6
Achdregnie Moray 302 G2
Achduart Highld 307 J5
Achentoul Highld 310 F2
Achfary Highld 306 F7
Achfrish Highld 309 H5
Achgarve Highld 307 K3
Achiemore Highld 308 C3
Highld 310 D2
A'Chill Highld 294 E4
Achiltibuie Highld 307 J5
Achina Highld 308 C7
Achinahuagh Highld 308 C5
Achindaul Highld 290 E3
Achindown Highld 301 E8
Achinduich Highld 309 J5
Achinduin Argyll 289 F10
Achingills Highld 310 C5
Achininver Highld 308 C5
Achintee Highld 290 F3
Highld 299 E9
Achintraid Highld 295 B10
Achlaven Argyll 289 F11
Achlean Highld 291 D10
Achleck Argyll 288 E6
Achlorachan Highld 300 D3
Achluachrach Highld 290 E4
Achlyness Highld 306 D7
Achmelvich Highld 307 G5
Achmore Highld 295 B10
Stirl 285 D9
Achnaba Argyll 275 E10
Argyll 289 F11
Achnabat Highld 300 F5
Achnabreck Argyll 275 D9
Achnacarnin Highld 306 F5
Achnacarry Highld 290 E3
Achnacloich Argyll 289 F11
Highld 295 E7
Achnaconeran Highld 290 B6
Achnacraig Argyll 288 E6
Achnacree Argyll 289 F11
Achnacree Bay Argyll 289 F11
Achnacroish Argyll 289 E10
Achnadrish Argyll 288 D6
Achnafalnich Argyll 284 E6
Achnagarron Highld 300 C6
Achnaha Highld 288 C6
Achnahanat Highld 309 K5
Achnahannet Highld 301 G9
Achnahard Argyll 288 G5
Achnairn Highld 309 H5
Achnaluachrach Highld 309 J6
Achnandarach Highld 295 B10
Achnanellan Highld 290 E2
Achnasaul Highld 290 E3
Achnasheen Highld 299 D11
Achnashelloch Argyll 275 D9
Achnavast Highld 310 C4
Achneigie Highld 299 B10
Achormlarie Highld 309 K6
Achorn Highld 310 F5
Achosnich Highld 288 C6
Achranich Highld 289 E9
Achreamie Highld 310 C4
Achriabhach Highld 290 G3
Achriesgill Highld 306 D7
Achrimsdale Highld 311 J3
Achtoty Highld 308 C6
Achurch Northants 137 G10
Achuvoldrach Highld 308 D5
Achvaich Highld 309 K7
Achvarasdal Highld 310 C3
Ackenthwaite Cumb 211 C10
Ackergill Highld 310 D7
Acklam Mbro 225 B9
N Yorks 216 G5
Ackleton Shrops 132 D5
Acklington Northumb 252 C6
Ackton W Yorks 198 C2
Ackworth Moor Top
W Yorks 198 D2
Acle Norf 161 G8
Acock's Green W Mid 134 G2
Acol Kent 71 F10
Acomb Northumb 241 D10
York 207 C7
Acre Gtr Man 196 F2
Lancs 195 C9
Acrefair Wrex 166 G3
Acres Nook Staffs 168 E4
Acre Street W Sus 21 B11
Acton Ches E 167 E10
Dorset 18 F5
London 67 C8
Shrops 130 G6
Staffs 168 G4
Suff 107 C7
Worcs 116 D6
Wrex 166 E4
Acton Beauchamp
Hereford 116 G3
Acton Bridge Ches W 183 F9
Acton Burnell Shrops 131 C10
Acton Green Hereford 116 G3
London 67 D8
Acton Pigott Shrops 131 C10
Acton Place Suff 107 B7
Acton Reynald Shrops 149 E10
Acton Round Shrops 132 D2
Acton Scott Shrops 131 F9
Acton Trussell Staffs 151 F8
Acton Turville S Glos 61 C10
Adabroc W Isles 304 B7
Adambrae W Loth 269 A10
Adam's Green Dorset 29 F8
Adbaston Staffs 150 D5
Adber Dorset 29 C9
Adbolton Notts 154 B2
Adderbury Oxon 101 D9
Adderley Shrops 150 B3
Adderley Green Stoke 168 G6
Adderstone Northumb 264 C4
Addiewell W Loth 269 C9
Addingham W Yorks 205 D7
Addingham Moorside
W Yorks 205 D7
Addington Bucks 102 F4
Corn 6 B5
Kent 53 B7
London 67 G11
Addinston Borders 271 E10
Addiscombe London 67 F10
Addlestone Sur 66 G5
Addlestonemoor Sur 66 F4
Addlethorpe Lincs 175 B8
Adel W Yorks 205 F11
Adeney Telford 150 F4
Adeyfield Herts 85 D9
Adfa Powys 129 C11
Adforton Hereford 115 C8
Adgestone IoW 21 D7
Adisham Kent 55 C8
Adlestrop Glos 100 F4
Adlingfleet E Yorks 199 C10
Adlington Ches E 184 E6
Lancs 194 E6
Adlington Park Lancs 194 E5
Admaston Staffs 151 E10
Telford 150 G2
Admington Warks 100 B4
Adpar Ceredig 92 C6
Adsborough Som 28 B3
Adscombe Som 43 F7
Adstock Bucks 102 E4
Adstone Northants 119 G11
Adswood Gtr Man 184 D5
Adversane W Sus 35 C9
Advie Highld 301 F11
Adwalton W Yorks 197 B8
Adwell Oxon 83 F11
Adwick le Street
S Yorks 198 F4
Adwick upon Dearne
S Yorks 198 G3
Adziel Aberds 303 D9
Ae Dumfries 247 F11
Ae Village Dumfries 247 F11
Affetside Gtr Man 195 E9
Affleck Aberds 303 G8
Affpuddle Dorset 18 C2
Affric Lodge Highld 299 G11
Afon Eitha Wrex 166 F3
Afon-wen Flint 181 G10
Afon Wen Gwyn 145 B8
Afton IoW 20 D2
Agar Nook Leics 153 G9
Agbrigg W Yorks 197 D10
Aggborough Worcs 116 B6
Agglethorpe N Yorks 213 B11
Aglionby Cumb 239 F10
Agneash IoM 192 D5
Aifft Denb 165 B10
Aigburth Mers 182 D5
Aiginis W Isles 304 E6
Aike E Yorks 209 D7
Aikenway Moray 302 E2
Aikerness Orkney 314 A4
Aikers Orkney 314 G4
Aiketgate Cumb 230 B5
Aikton Cumb 239 G7
Ailby Lincs 190 F6
Ailey Hereford 96 B6
Ailstone Warks 118 G4
Ailsworth Pboro 138 D2
Aimes Green Essex 86 E5
Ainderby Quernhow
N Yorks 215 C7
Ainderby Steeple
N Yorks 224 G6
Aingers Green Essex 108 G2
Ainley Top W Yorks 196 D6
Ainsdale Mers 193 E10
Ainsdale-on-Sea Mers 193 E9
Ainstable Cumb 230 B6
Ainsworth Gtr Man 195 E9
Ainthorpe N Yorks 226 D4
Aintree Mers 182 B5
Aird Argyll 275 C8
Dumfries 236 C2
Highld 299 B7
W Isles 296 F3
W Isles 304 E7
Airdachuilinn Highld 306 E7
Aird a Mhachair
W Isles 297 G3
Aird a' Mhulaidh
W Isles 305 G3
Aird Asaig W Isles 305 H3
Aird Dhail W Isles 304 B6
Airdens Highld 309 K6
Airdeny Argyll 289 G11
Aird Mhidhinis W Isles 297 L3
Aird Mhighe W Isles 296 C6
W Isles 305 J3
Aird Mhòr W Isles 297 G4
Aird Mhor W Isles 297 L3
Aird of Sleat Highld 295 E7
Airdrie N Lnrk 268 B5
Airds of Kells Dumfries 237 B8
Aird Thunga W Isles 304 E6
Airdtorrisdale Highld 308 C6
Aird Uig W Isles 304 E2
Airedale W Yorks 198 B3
Aire View N Yorks 204 D5
Airidh a Bhruaich
W Isles 305 G4
Airieland Dumfries 237 D9
Airinis W Isles 304 E6
Airlie Angus 287 B7
Airlies Dumfries 236 D5
Airmyn E Yorks 199 B8
Airntully Perth 286 D4
Airor Highld 295 E9
Airth Falk 279 D7
Airthrey Castle Stirl 278 B6
Airton N Yorks 204 B4
Airyhassen Dumfries 236 E5
Airy Hill N Yorks 227 D7
Airyligg Dumfries 236 C4
Aisby Lincs 155 B10
Lincs 188 C5
Aisgernis W Isles 297 J3
Aish Devon 8 C3
Devon 8 D6
Aisholt Som 43 F7
Aiskew N Yorks 214 B5
Aislaby N Yorks 216 B5
N Yorks 227 D7
Stockton 225 C8
Aisthorpe Lincs 188 E6
Aith Orkney 314 E2
Shetland 312 D8
Shetland 313 H5
Aithnen Powys 148 E4
Aithsetter Shetland 313 K6
Aitkenhead S Ayrs 245 B8
Aitnoch Highld 301 F9
Akeld Northumb 263 D11
Akeley Bucks 102 D4
Akenham Suff 108 B2
Albany T&W 243 F7
Albaston Corn 12 G4
Alberbury Shrops 149 G7
Albert Town Pembs 72 B6
Albert Village Leics 152 F6
Albourne W Sus 36 D3
Albourne Green W Sus 36 D3
Albrighton Shrops 132 C6
Shrops 149 F9
Albro Castle Ceredig 92 B3
Alburgh Norf 142 F5
Albury Herts 105 G8
Sur 50 D5
Albury End Herts 105 G8
Albury Heath Sur 50 D5
Albyfield Cumb 240 G2
Alby Hill Norf 160 C3
Alcaig Highld 300 D5
Alcaston Shrops 131 F9
Alcester Dorset 30 C5
Warks 117 F11
Alcester Lane's End
W Mid 133 G11
Alciston E Sus 23 D8
Alcombe Som 42 D3
Wilts 61 F10
Alconbury Cambs 122 B3
Alconbury Weston
Cambs 122 B3
Aldbar Castle Angus 287 B9
Aldborough Norf 160 C3
N Yorks 215 F8
Aldborough Hatch
London 68 B3
Aldbourne Wilts 63 D9
Aldbrough E Yorks 209 F10
Aldbrough St John
N Yorks 224 C4
Aldbury Herts 85 C7
Aldcliffe Lancs 211 G9
Aldclune Perth 291 G11
Aldeburgh Suff 127 F9
Aldeby Norf 143 E8
Aldenham Herts 85 F10
Alderbrook E Sus 37 B8
Alderbury Wilts 31 B11
Aldercar Derbys 170 F6
Alderford Norf 160 F2
Alder Forest Gtr Man 184 B3
Alderholt Dorset 31 E10
Alderley Glos 80 G3
Alderley Edge Ches E 184 F4
Alderman's Green
W Mid 135 G7
Aldermaston W Berks 64 F5
Aldermaston Soke
W Berks 64 G6
Aldermaston Wharf
W Berks 64 F6
Alderminster Warks 100 B4
Aldermoor Soton 32 D5
Alder Moor Staffs 152 D4
Alderney Poole 18 C6
Alder Row Som 45 E9
Aldersbrook London 68 B2
Alder's End Hereford 98 C2
Aldersey Green
Ches W 167 D7
Aldershawe Staffs 134 B2
Aldershot Hants 49 C11
Alderton Glos 99 E10
Northants 102 B4
Shrops 149 E9
Suff 108 C6
Wilts 61 C10
Alderton Fields Glos 99 E10
Alderwasley Derbys 170 E4
Aldfield N Yorks 214 F5
Aldford Ches W 166 D6
Aldgate Rutland 137 C9
Aldham Essex 107 F8
Suff 107 B10
Aldie Highld 309 L7
Aldingbourne W Sus 22 B6
Aldingham Cumb 210 E5
Aldington Kent 54 F5
Worcs 99 C11
Aldington Frith Kent 54 F4
Aldivalloch Moray 302 G3
Aldochlay Argyll 277 C7
Aldon Shrops 115 B8
Aldoth Cumb 229 B8
Aldourie Castle Highld 300 F6
Aldreth Cambs 123 C8
Aldridge W Mid 133 C11
Aldringham Suff 127 E8
Aldrington Brighton 36 F3
Aldsworth Glos 81 C11
Aldunie Moray 302 G3
Aldwark Derbys 170 D2
N Yorks 215 G9
Aldwarke S Yorks 186 C6
Aldwick W Sus 22 D6
Aldwincle Northants 137 G10
Aldworth W Berks 64 D5
Alehouseburn Aberds 302 C6
Alehousehill Aberds 303 G10
Ale Oak Shrops 130 G4
Alexandria W Dunb 277 F7
Aley Som 43 F7
Aley Green C Beds 85 B9
Alfardisworthy Devon 24 E3
Alfington Devon 15 B8
Alfold Sur 50 G4
Alfold Bars W Sus 50 G4
Alfold Crossways Sur 50 F4
Alford Aberds 293 B7
Lincs 191 F7
Som 44 G6
Alfred's Well Worcs 117 C8
Alfreton Derbys 170 D6
Alfrick Worcs 116 G4
Alfrick Pound Worcs 116 G4
Alfriston E Sus 23 E8
Algakirk Lincs 156 B5
Algaltraig Argyll 275 F11
Algarkirk Lincs 156 B5
Alhampton Som 44 G6
Aline Lodge W Isles 305 G3
Alisary Highld 289 B9
Alkborough N Lincs 199 C11
Alkerton Glos 80 D3
Oxon 101 C7
Alkham Kent 55 E9
Alkington Shrops 149 B10
Alkmonton Derbys 152 B3
Alkrington Garden Village
Gtr Man 195 G11
Alladale Lodge Highld 309 L4
Allaleigh Devon 8 E6
Allanaquoich Aberds 292 D3
Allanbank Borders 271 F10
N Lnrk 268 D6
Allangrange Mains
Highld 300 D6
Allanshaugh Borders 271 F8
Allanshaws Borders 271 G9
Allanton Borders 273 E7
N Lnrk 269 D7
S Lnrk 268 E4
Allaston Glos 79 E10
Allathasdal W Isles 297 L2
Allbrook Hants 33 C7
All Cannings Wilts 62 G5
Allendale Town
Northumb 241 F8
Allen End Warks 134 D3
Allenheads Northumb 232 B3
Allensford Durham 242 G3
Allens Green Herts 87 B7
Allensmore Hereford 97 D9
Allenton Derby 153 C7
Allenwood Cumb 239 F11
Aller Devon 9 B7
Devon 27 F9
Dorset 30 G3
Som 28 B6
Allerby Cumb 229 D7
Allerford Som 27 B11
Som 42 D2
Aller Park Devon 9 B7
Allerston N Yorks 217 C7
Allerthorpe E Yorks 207 D11
Allerton Mers 182 D6
W Yorks 205 G8
Allerton Bywater
W Yorks 198 B2
Allerton Mauleverer
N Yorks 206 B4
Allesley W Mid 134 G6
Allestree Derby 152 B6
Allet Corn 4 F5
Allexton Leics 136 C6
Allgreave Ches E 169 B7
Allhallows Medway 69 D10
Allhallows-on-Sea
Medway 69 D10
Alligin Shuas Highld 299 D8
Allimore Green Staffs 151 F7
Allington Kent 53 B8
Lincs 172 G5
Wilts 47 F8
Wilts 61 D11
Wilts 62 G5
Allington Bar Wilts 61 E11
Allithwaite Cumb 211 D7
Alloa Clack 279 C7
Allonby Cumb 229 C7
Allostock Ches W 184 G2
Alloway S Ayrs 257 F8
Allowenshay Som 28 E5
All Saints Devon 28 G4
All Saints South Elmham
Suff 142 G6
Allscot Shrops 132 D4
Allscott Telford 150 G2
All Stretton Shrops 131 D9
Allt Carms 75 E9
Alltami Flint 166 B3
Alltbeithe Highld 290 C2
Alltchaorunn Highld 284 B5
Alltforgan Powys 147 E9
Alltmawr Powys 95 B11
Alltnacaillich Highld 308 E4
Allt-na-giubhsaich
Aberds 292 E4
Allt na h-Airbhe
Highld 307 K6
Allt-nan-sùgh Highld 295 C11
Alltrech Argyll 289 F8
Alltsigh Highld 290 B6
Alltwalis Carms 93 E8
Alltwen Neath 76 E2
Alltyblaca Ceredig 93 B10
Allt-yr-yn Newport 59 B9
Allwood Green Suff 125 C10
Alma Notts 171 E7

Bedlam N Yorks 214 G5
Som 45 D9
Bedlam Street W Sus 36 D3
Bedlar's Green Essex 105 G10
Bedlington Northumb 253 G7
Bedlington Station
Northumb 253 G7
Bedlinog M Tydf 77 E9
Bedminster Bristol 60 E5
Bedminster Down Bristol 60 F5
Bedmond Herts 85 E9
Bednall Staffs 151 F9
Bednall Head Staffs 151 F9
Bedrule Borders 262 F4
Bedstone Shrops 115 B7
Bedwas Caerph 59 B7
Bedwell Herts 104 G4
Wrex 166 F5
Bedwellty Caerph 77 E11
Bedwellty Pits Bl Gwent 77 D11
Bedwlwyn Wrex 148 B4
Bedworth Warks 135 F7
Bedworth Heath Warks 134 F6
Bedworth Woodlands
Warks 134 F6
Bed-y-coedwr Gwyn 146 D4
Beeby Leics 136 B3
Beech Hants 49 F7
Staffs 151 B7
Beechcliff Staffs 151 B7
Beechcliffe W Yorks 205 E7
Beechen Cliff Bath 61 G9
Beech Hill Gtr Man 194 F5
W Berks 65 G7
Beechingstoke Wilts 46 B5
Beech Lanes W Mid 133 F10
Beechwood Halton 183 E8
Newport 59 B10
W Mid 118 B5
W Yorks 206 F2
Beecroft C Beds 103 G10
Beedon W Berks 64 D3
Beedon Hill W Berks 64 D3
Beeford E Yorks 209 C8
Beeley Derbys 170 B3
Beelsby NE Lincs 201 G8
Beenham W Berks 64 F5
Beenham's Heath
Windsor 65 D10
Beenham Stocks
W Berks 64 F5
Beeny Corn 11 C8
Beer Devon 15 D10
Som 44 G2
Beercrocombe Som 28 C4
Beer Hackett Dorset 29 E9
Beesands Devon 8 G6
Beesby Lincs 191 E7
Beeslack Midloth 270 C4
Beeson Devon 8 G6
Beeston C Beds 104 B3
Ches W 167 D8
Norf 159 F8
Notts 153 B10
W Yorks 205 G11
Beeston Hill W Yorks 205 G11
Beeston Park Side
W Yorks 197 B9
Beeston Regis Norf 177 E11
Beeston Royds
W Yorks 205 G11
Beeston St Lawrence
Norf 160 E6
Beeswing Dumfries 237 C10
Beetham Cumb 211 D9
Som 28 E3
Beetley Norf 159 F9
Beffcote Staffs 150 F6
Began Cardiff 59 C8
Begbroke Oxon 83 C7
Begdale Cambs 139 B9
Begelly Pembs 73 D10
Beggar Hill Essex 87 E10
Beggarington Hill
W Yorks 197 C9
Beggars Ash Hereford 98 D4
Beggars Bush W Sus 35 F11
Beggar's Bush Powys 114 E5
Beggars Pound V Glam 58 F4
Beggearn Huish Som 42 F4
Beguildy Powys 114 B3
Beighton Norf 143 B7
S Yorks 186 E6
Beighton Hill Derbys 170 E3
Beili-glas Mon 78 C4
Beitearsaig W Isles 305 G1
Beith N Ayrs 266 E6
Bekesbourne Kent 55 B7
Bekesbourne Hill Kent 55 B7
Belah Cumb 239 F9
Belan Powys 130 C4
Belaugh Norf 160 F5
Belbins Hants 32 C5
Belbroughton Worcs 117 B8
Belchalwell Dorset 30 F3
Belchalwell Street Dorset 30 F3
Belchamp Otten Essex 106 C6
Belchamp St Paul Essex 106 C5
Belchamp Walter Essex 106 C6
Belcher's Bar Leics 135 B8
Belchford Lincs 190 F3
Beleybridge Fife 287 F9
Belfield Gtr Man 196 E2
Belford Northumb 264 C4
Belgrano Conwy 181 F7
Belgrave Ches W 166 C5
Leicester 135 B11
Staffs 134 C4
Belgravia London 67 D9
Belhaven E Loth 282 F3
Belhelvie Aberds 293 B11
Belhinnie Aberds 302 G4
Bellabeg Aberds 292 B5
Bellamore S Ayrs 244 F6
Bellanoch Argyll 275 D8
Bellanrigg Borders 260 B6
Bellasize E Yorks 199 B10
Bellaty Angus 286 B6
Bell Bar Herts 86 D3
Bell Busk N Yorks 204 B4
Bell Common Essex 86 E6
Belleau Lincs 190 F6
Belle Eau Park Notts 171 D11
Belle Green S Yorks 197 F11
Bellehiglash Moray 301 F11
Belle Isle W Yorks 197 B10
Bell End Worcs 117 B8
Bellerby N Yorks 224 G2
Belle Vale Mers 182 D6
W Mid 133 G9
Bellever Devon 13 F9
Bellevue Worcs 117 C9
Belle Vue Cumb 229 E8
Cumb 239 F9
Gtr Man 184 B5
Shrops 149 G9
S Yorks 198 G5
W Yorks 197 D10
Bellfield E Ayrs 257 B10
Bellfields Sur 50 C3
Bell Green London 67 E11
W Mid 135 G7
Bell Heath Worcs 117 B9
Bell Hill Hants 34 C2
Belliehill Angus 293 G7
Bellingdon Bucks 84 D6
Bellingham London 67 E11
Northumb 251 G8
Bellmount Norf 157 E10
Belloch Argyll 255 D7
Bellochantuy Argyll 255 D7
Bell o' th' Hill Ches W 167 F8
Bellsbank E Ayrs 245 C11
Bell's Close T&W 242 E5
Bell's Corner Suff 107 D9
Bellshill N Lnrk 268 C4
Northumb 264 C4
Bellside N Lnrk 268 D6
Bellsmyre W Dunb 277 F8
Bellspool Borders 260 B5
Bellsquarry W Loth 269 C10
Bells Yew Green E Sus 52 F6
Belluton Bath 60 G6
Bellyeoman Fife 280 D2
Belmaduthy Highld 300 D6
Belmesthorpe Rutland 155 G10
Belmont Blkburn 195 D7
Durham 234 C2
E Sus 38 E4
Harrow 67 G9
Oxon 63 B11
S Ayrs 257 E8
Shetland 312 C7
Sutton 85 G11
Belnacraig Aberds 292 B5
Belnagarrow Moray 302 E3
Belnie Lincs 156 C5
Belowda Corn 5 C9
Belper Derbys 170 F4
Belper Lane End Derbys 170 F4
Belph Derbys 187 F8
Belsay Northumb 242 B4
Belses Borders 262 D3
Belsford Devon 8 D5
Belsize Herts 85 E8
Belstead Suff 108 C2
Belston S Ayrs 257 E9
Belstone Devon 13 C8
Belstone Corner Devon 13 B8
Belthorn Blkburn 195 C8
Beltinge Kent 71 F7
Beltingham Northumb 241 E7
Beltoft N Lincs 199 F10
Belton Leics 153 E8
Lincs 155 B8
N Lincs 199 F9
Norf 143 C9
Belton in Rutland
Rutland 136 C6
Beltring Kent 53 D7
Belts of Collonach
Aberds 293 D8
Belvedere London 68 D3
W Loth 269 B9
Belvoir Leics 154 C6
Bembridge IoW 21 D8
Bemersyde Borders 262 C3
Bemerton Wilts 46 G6
Bemerton Heath Wilts 46 G6
Bempton E Yorks 218 E3
Benacre Suff 143 G10
Ben Alder Lodge Highld 291 F7
Ben Armine Lodge
Highld 309 H7
Benbuie Dumfries 246 D6
Ben Casgro W Isles 304 F6
Benchill Gtr Man 184 D4
Bencombe Glos 80 F3
Benderloch Argyll 289 F11
Bendish Herts 104 G3
Bendronaig Lodge
Highld 299 F10
Benenden Kent 53 G10
Benfield Dumfries 236 C5
Benfieldside Durham 242 G3
Bengal Pembs 91 E9
Bengate Norf 160 D6
Bengeo Herts 86 C4
Bengeworth Worcs 99 C10
Bengrove Glos 99 E9
Benhall Glos 99 G8
Benhall Green Suff 127 E7
Benhall Street Suff 127 E7
Benhilton London 67 F9
Benholm Aberds 293 G10
Beningbrough N Yorks 206 B6
Benington Herts 104 G5
Lincs 174 F5
Benington Sea End
Lincs 174 F6
Benllech Anglesey 179 E8
Benmore Argyll 276 E2
Stirl 285 E8
Benmore Lodge Argyll 289 F7
Highld 309 H3
Bennacott Corn 11 C11
Bennah Devon 14 E2
Bennan N Ayrs 255 E10
Bennane Lea S Ayrs 244 F3
Bennetland E Yorks 199 B10
Bennetsfield Highld 300 D6
Bennett End Bucks 84 F3
Bennetts End Herts 85 D9
Benniworth Lincs 190 E2
Benover Kent 53 D8
Ben Rhydding W Yorks 205 D8
Bensham T&W 242 E6
Benslie N Ayrs 266 G6
Benson Oxon 83 G10
Benston Shetland 313 H6
Bent Aberds 293 F8
Benter Som 44 D6
Bentfield Bury Essex 105 F9
Bentfield Green Essex 105 F10
Bentgate Gtr Man 196 E2
Bent Gate Lancs 195 C9
Benthall Northumb 264 D6
Shrops 132 C3
Bentham Glos 80 B6
Benthoul Aberdeen 293 C10
Bentilee Stoke 168 F6
Bentlass Pembs 73 E7
Bentlawnt Shrops 130 C6
Bentley Essex 87 F9
E Yorks 208 F6
Hants 49 E9
Suff 108 D2
S Yorks 198 F5
Warks 134 D5
W Mid 133 D9
Worcs 117 D9
Bentley Common Warks 134 D5
Bentley Heath Herts 86 F2
W Mid 118 B3
Bentley Rise S Yorks 198 G5
Benton Devon 41 F7
Benton Green W Mid 118 B5
Bentpath Dumfries 249 E8
Bents W Loth 269 C9
Bents Head W Yorks 205 F7
Bentwichen Devon 41 G8
Bentworth Hants 49 E7
Benvie Dundee 287 D7
Benville Dorset 29 G8
Benwell T&W 242 E6
Benwick Cambs 138 E6
Beobridge Shrops 132 E5
Beoley Worcs 117 D11
Beoraidbeg Highld 295 F8
Bepton W Sus 34 D5
Berden Essex 105 F9
Bere Alston Devon 7 B8
Berechurch Essex 107 G9
Bere Ferrers Devon 7 C9
Berefold Aberds 303 F9
Berepper Corn 2 E5
Bere Regis Dorset 18 C2
Bergh Apton Norf 142 C6
Berghers Hill Bucks 66 B2
Berhill Som 44 F2
Berinsfield Oxon 83 F9
Berkeley Glos 79 F11
Berkeley Heath Glos 79 F11
Berkeley Road Glos 80 E2
Berkeley Towers
Ches E 167 E11
Berkhamsted Herts 85 D7
Berkley Som 45 D10
Berkley Down Som 45 D9
Berkley Marsh Som 45 D10
Berkswell W Mid 118 B4
Bermondsey London 67 D10
Bermuda Warks 135 F7
Bernards Heath Herts 85 D11
Bernera Highld 295 C10
Berner's Cross Devon 25 F10
Berner's Hill E Sus 53 G8
Berners Roding Essex 87 D10
Bernice Argyll 276 C2
Bernisdale Highld 298 D4
Berrick Salome Oxon 83 G10
Berriedale Highld 311 G5
Berrier Cumb 230 F3
Berriew / Aberriw
Powys 130 C3
Berrington Northumb 273 G10
Shrops 131 B10
Worcs 115 D11
Berrington Green
Worcs 115 D11
Berriowbridge Corn 11 F11
Berrow Som 43 C10
Worcs 98 E5
Berrow Green Worcs 116 F4
Berry Swansea 56 D3
Berry Brow W Yorks 196 E6
Berry Cross Devon 25 E7
Berry Down Cross Devon 40 E5
Berryfield Wilts 61 G11
Berrygate Hill E Yorks 201 C8
Berry Hill Glos 79 C9
Pembs 91 C11
Stoke 168 F6
Worcs 117 E7
Berryhillock Moray 302 C5
Berrylands London 67 F7
Berry Moor S Yorks 197 G9
Berrynarbor Devon 40 D5
Berry Pomeroy Devon 8 C6
Berrysbridge Devon 26 G6
Berry's Green London 52 B2
Bersham Wrex 166 F4
Berstane Orkney 314 E4
Berth-ddu Flint 166 B2
Berthengam Flint 181 F10
Berwick E Sus 23 D8
Kent 54 F6
S Glos 60 C5
Berwick Bassett Wilts 62 E5
Berwick Hill Northumb 242 B5
Berwick Hills Mbro 225 B10
Berwick St James Wilts 46 F5
Berwick St John Wilts 30 C6
Berwick St Leonard
Wilts 46 G2
Berwick-upon-Tweed
Northumb 273 E9
Berwick Wharf Shrops 149 G10
Berwyn Denb 165 G11
Bescaby Leics 154 D6
Bescar Lancs 193 E11
Bescot W Mid 133 D10
Besford Shrops 149 E11
Worcs 99 C8
Bessacarr S Yorks 198 G6
Bessels Green Kent 52 B4
Bessels Leigh Oxon 83 E7
Besses o' th' Barn
Gtr Man 195 F10
Bessingby E Yorks 218 F3
Bessingham Norf 160 B3
Best Beech Hill E Sus 52 G6
Besthorpe Norf 141 D11
Notts 172 C4
Bestwood Nottingham 171 G9
Bestwood Village Notts 171 F9
Beswick E Yorks 208 D6
Gtr Man 184 B5
Betchcott Shrops 131 D8
Betchton Heath Ches E 168 C3
Betchworth Sur 51 D8
Bethania Ceredig 111 E11
Gwyn 163 E10
Gwyn 164 F2
Bethany Corn 6 D6
Bethel Anglesey 178 G5
Corn 5 E10
Gwyn 147 B9
Gwyn 163 B8
Bethelnie Aberds 303 F7
Bethersden Kent 54 E2
Bethesda Gwyn 163 B10
Pembs 73 B9
Bethlehem Carms 94 F3
Bethnal Green London 67 C10
Betley Staffs 168 F3
Betley Common Staffs 168 F2
Betsham Kent 68 E6
Betteshanger Kent 55 C10
Bettiscombe Dorset 16 B3
Bettisfield Wrex 149 B9
Betton Shrops 130 C6
Shrops 150 B3
Betton Strange Shrops 131 B10
Bettws Bridgend 58 B2
Mon 78 B3
Newport 78 G3
Bettws Cedewain Powys 130 D2
Bettws Gwerfil Goch
Denb 165 F8
Bettws Ifan Ceredig 92 B6
Bettws Newydd Mon 78 D5
Bettws-y-crwyn Shrops 130 G4
Bettyhill Highld 308 C7
Betws Bridgend 57 D11
Carms 75 C10
Betws Bledrws Ceredig 111 G11
Betws-Garmon Gwyn 163 D8
Betws Ifan Ceredig 92 B6
Betws-y-Coed Conwy 164 D4
Betws-yn-Rhos Conwy 180 G6
Beulah Ceredig 92 B5
Powys 113 G8
Bevendean Brighton 36 F4
Bevercotes Notts 187 G11
Beverley E Yorks 208 F6
Beverston Glos 80 G5
Bevington Glos 79 F11
Bewaldeth Cumb 229 E10
Bewbush W Sus 51 F8
Bewcastle Cumb 240 C3
Bewdley Worcs 116 B5
Bewerley N Yorks 214 G3
Bewholme E Yorks 209 C9
Bewley Common Wilts 62 F2
Bewlie Borders 262 D3
Bewlie Mains Borders 262 D3
Bewsey Warr 183 D9
Bexfield Norf 159 D10
Bexhill E Sus 38 F2
Bexley London 68 E3
Bexleyheath London 68 D3
Bexleyhill W Sus 34 B6
Bexon Kent 53 B11
Bexwell Norf 140 C2
Beyton Suff 125 E8
Beyton Green Suff 125 E8
Bhalasaigh W Isles 304 E3
Bhaltos W Isles 304 E2
Bhatarsaigh W Isles 297 M2
Bhlàraidh Highld 290 B5
Bibstone S Glos 79 G11
Bibury Glos 81 D10
Bicester Oxon 101 G11
Bickenhall Som 28 D3
Bickenhill W Mid 134 G3
Bicker Lincs 156 B4
Bicker Bar Lincs 156 B4
Bicker Gauntlet Lincs 156 B4
Bickershaw Gtr Man 194 G6
Bickerstaffe Lancs 194 G2
Bickerton Ches E 167 E8
Devon 9 G11
N Yorks 206 C5
Bickford Staffs 151 G7
Bickham Som 42 E3
Bickingcott Devon 26 B3
Bickington Devon 13 G11
Devon 40 G4
Bickleigh Devon 7 C10
Devon 26 F6
Bickleton Devon 40 G4
Bickley Ches W 167 F8
London 68 F2
Worcs 116 C2
Bickley Moss Ches W 167 F8
Bickley Town Ches W 167 F8
Bickleywood Ches W 167 F8
Bickmarsh Warks 100 B2
Bicknacre Essex 88 E3
Bicknoller Som 42 F6
Bicknor Kent 53 B11
Bickton Hants 31 E11
Bicton Hereford 115 E9
Pembs 72 D4
Shrops 130 G5
Shrops 149 F8
Bicton Heath Shrops 149 G9
Bidborough Kent 52 E5
Bidden Hants 49 D8
Biddenden Kent 53 F11
Biddenden Green Kent 53 E11
Biddenham Beds 103 B10
Biddestone Wilts 61 E11
Biddick T&W 243 F8
Biddick Hall T&W 243 E9
Biddisham Som 43 C11
Biddlesden Bucks 102 C2
Biddlestone Northumb 251 B11
Biddulph Staffs 168 D5
Biddulph Moor Staffs 168 D6
Bideford Devon 25 B7
Bidford-on-Avon Warks 118 G2
Bidlake Devon 12 D5
Bidston Mers 182 C3
Bidston Hill Mers 182 D3
Bidwell C Beds 103 G10
Bielby E Yorks 207 E11
Bieldside Aberdeen 293 C10
Bierley IoW 20 F6
W Yorks 205 G9
Bierton Bucks 84 B4
Bigbury Devon 8 F3
Bigbury-on-Sea Devon 8 G3
Bigby Lincs 200 F5
Bigfrith Windsor 65 C11
Biggar Cumb 210 F3
S Lnrk 260 B2
Biggar Road N Lnrk 268 C5
Biggin Derbys 169 D11
Derbys 170 F3
N Yorks 206 F6
Thurrock 69 D7
Biggings Shetland 313 G3
Biggin Hill London 52 B2
Biggleswade C Beds 104 C3
Bighouse Highld 310 C2
Bighton Hants 48 G6
Biglands Cumb 239 G7
Big Mancot Flint 166 B4
Bignall End Staffs 168 E4
Bignor W Sus 35 E7
Bigods Essex 106 G2
Bigram Stirl 285 G10
Bigrigg Cumb 219 C10
Big Sand Highld 299 B7
Bigswell Orkney 314 E3
Bigton Shetland 313 L5
Bilberry Corn 5 C10
Bilborough Nottingham 171 G8
Bilbrook Som 42 E4
Staffs 133 C7
Bilbrough N Yorks 206 D6
Bilbster Highld 310 D6
Bilby Notts 187 E10
Bildershaw Durham 233 G10
Bildeston Suff 107 B9
Billacombe Plym 7 E10
Billacott Corn 11 C11
Billericay Essex 87 G11
Billesdon Leics 136 C4
Billesley Warks 118 F2
W Mid 133 G11
Billesley Common
W Mid 133 G11
Billingborough Lincs 156 C2
Billinge Mers 194 G4
Billingford Norf 126 B3
Norf 159 E10
Billingham Stockton 234 G5
Billinghay Lincs 173 E11
Billingley S Yorks 198 G2
Billingshurst W Sus 35 B9
Billingsley Shrops 132 F4
Billington C Beds 103 G8
Lancs 203 F10
Staffs 151 E7
Billockby Norf 161 G8
Bill Quay T&W 243 E7
Billy Mill T&W 243 D8
Billy Row Durham 233 D9
Bilmarsh Shrops 149 D9
Bilsborrow Lancs 202 F6
Bilsby Lincs 191 F7
Bilsby Field Lincs 191 F7
Bilsdon Devon 14 C2
Bilsham W Sus 35 G7
Bilsington Kent 54 G4
Bilson Green Glos 79 C11
Bilsthorpe Notts 171 C10
Bilsthorpe Moor Notts 171 D11
Bilston Midloth 270 C5
W Mid 133 D9
Bilstone Leics 135 B7
Bilting Kent 54 D5
Bilton E Yorks 209 G9
Northumb 264 G6
N Yorks 206 B2
Warks 119 C9
Bilton Haggs N Yorks 206 D5
Bilton in Ainsty N Yorks 206 D5
Bimbister Orkney 314 E3
Binbrook Lincs 190 C2
Binchester Blocks
Durham 233 E10
Bincombe Dorset 17 E9
Som 43 F7
Bindal Highld 311 L3
Bindon Som 27 C10
Binegar Som 44 D6
Bines Green W Sus 35 D11
Binfield Brack 65 E10
Binfield Heath Oxon 65 D8
Bingfield Northumb 241 C11
Bingham Edin 280 G6
Notts 154 B4
Bingley W Yorks 205 F8
Bings Heath Shrops 149 F10
Binham Norf 159 B9
Binley Hants 48 C2
W Mid 119 B7
Binley Woods Warks 119 B7
Binnegar Dorset 18 D3
Binniehill Falk 279 G7
Binscombe Sur 50 D3
Binsey Oxon 83 D7
Binsoe N Yorks 214 D4
Binstead Hants 49 E9
IoW 21 C7
Binsted Hants 49 E9
W Sus 35 F7
Binton Warks 118 G2
Bintree Norf 159 E10
Binweston Shrops 130 C6
Birch Essex 88 B6
Gtr Man 195 F11
Birch Acre Worcs 117 C11
Birchall Hereford 98 D3
Staffs 169 E7
Bircham Newton Norf 158 C5
Bircham Tofts Norf 158 C5
Birchan Coppice Worcs 116 C6
Birchanger Essex 105 G10
Birch Berrow Worcs 116 E4
Birchburn N Ayrs 255 E10
Birch Cross Staffs 152 C2
Birchden E Sus 52 F4
Birchencliffe W Yorks 196 D6
Birchend Hereford 98 C3
Birchendale Staffs 151 B11
Bircher Hereford 115 D9
Birches Green W Mid 134 E2
Birches Head Stoke 168 F5
Birchett's Green E Sus 53 G7
Birchfield Highld 301 G9
W Mid 133 E11
Birch Green Essex 88 B6
Herts 86 C3
Lancs 194 F3
Worcs 99 B7
Birchgrove Cardiff 59 D7
E Sus 36 B2
Swansea 57 B8
Birchhall Corner Essex 107 E10
Birch Heath Ches W 167 C8
Birch Hill Brack 65 F11
Ches W 183 G8
Birchill Devon 28 G4
Birchills W Mid 133 D10
Birchington Kent 71 F9
Birchley Heath Warks 134 E5
Birchmoor Warks 134 C5
Birchmoor Green
C Beds 103 E8
Bircholt Forstal Kent 54 E5
Birchover Derbys 170 C2
Birch Vale Derbys 185 D8
Birchwood Herts 86 D2
Lincs 172 B6
Som 28 E2
Warr 183 C10
Birchy Hill Hants 19 B11
Bircotes Notts 187 C10
Birdbrook Essex 106 C4
Birdbush Wilts 30 C6
Birdfield Argyll 275 D10
Birdforth N Yorks 215 D9
Birdham W Sus 22 D4
Birdholme Derbys 170 B5
Birdingbury Warks 119 D8
Birdlip Glos 80 C6
Birdsall N Yorks 216 F6
Birds Edge W Yorks 197 F8
Birds End Suff 124 E5
Birdsgreen Shrops 132 F5
Birds Green Essex 87 D9
Birdsmoorgate Dorset 28 G5
Birdston E Dunb 278 F3
Bird Street Suff 125 G10
Birdwell S Yorks 197 G10
Birdwood Glos 80 B2
Birgham Borders 263 B7
Birichen Highld 309 K7
Birkacre Lancs 194 D5
Birkby Cumb 229 D7
N Yorks 224 E6
W Yorks 196 D6
Birkdale Mers 193 D10
Birkenbog Aberds 302 C5
Birkenhead Mers 182 D4
Birkenhills Aberds 303 E7
Birkenshaw N Lnrk 268 C3
S Lnrk 268 F5
W Yorks 197 B8
Birkenshaw Bottoms
W Yorks 197 B8
Birkenside Borders 271 G11
Birkett Mire Cumb 230 G2
Birkhall Aberds 292 D5
Birkhill Angus 287 D7
Borders 260 F6
Borders 271 G11
Birkholme Lincs 155 E9
Birkhouse W Yorks 197 C7
Birkin N Yorks 198 B4
Birks Cumb 222 G3
W Yorks 197 B9
Birkshaw Northumb 241 D7
Birley Hereford 115 G9
Birley Carr S Yorks 186 C4
Birley Edge S Yorks 186 C4
Birleyhay Derbys 186 E5
Birling Kent 69 G7
Northumb 252 B6
Birling Gap E Sus 23 F9
Birlingham Worcs 99 C8
Birmingham W Mid 133 F11
Birnam Perth 286 C4
Birniehill S Lnrk 268 E2
Birse Aberds 293 D7
Birsemore Aberds 293 D7
Birstall Leics 135 B11
W Yorks 197 B8
Birstall Smithies
W Yorks 197 B8
Birstwith N Yorks 205 B10
Birthorpe Lincs 156 C2
Birtle Gtr Man 195 E10
Birtley Hereford 115 D7
Northumb 241 B9
Shrops 131 E9
T&W 243 F7
Birtley Green Sur 50 E4
Birtsmorton Worcs 98 D6
Birts Street Worcs 98 D5
Bisbrooke Rutland 137 D7
Biscathorpe Lincs 190 D2
Biscombe Som 27 E11
Biscot Luton 103 G11
Biscovey Corn 5 E11
Bisham Windsor 65 C10
Bishampton Worcs 117 G9
Bish Mill Devon 26 B2
Bishon Common Hereford 97 C8
Bishop Auckland
Durham 233 F10
Bishopbridge Lincs 189 C8
Bishopbriggs E Dunb 278 G2
Bishop Burton E Yorks 208 F5
Bishopdown Wilts 47 G7
Bishop Kinkell Highld 300 D5
Bishop Middleham
Durham 234 E2
Bishopmill Moray 302 C2
Bishop Monkton
N Yorks 214 F6
Bishop Norton Lincs 189 C7
Bishopsbourne Kent 55 C7
Bishops Cannings Wilts 62 G4
Bishop's Castle Shrops 130 F6
Bishop's Caundle Dorset 29 E11
Bishop's Cleeve Glos 99 F9
Bishop's Down Dorset 29 E11
Bishops Frome Hereford 98 B3
Bishopsgarth Stockton 234 G4
Bishopsgate Sur 66 E3
Bishops Green Essex 87 B10
Bishop's Green W Berks 64 G4
Bishop's Hull Som 28 C2
Bishop's Itchington
Warks 119 F7
Bishops Lydeard Som 27 B11
Bishop's Norton Glos 98 G6
Bishops Nympton Devon 26 C3
Bishop's Offley Staffs 150 D5
Bishop's Quay Corn 2 D6
Bishop's Stortford
Herts 105 G9
Bishop's Sutton Hants 48 G6
Bishop's Tachbrook
Warks 118 E6
Bishops Tawton Devon 40 G5
Bishopsteignton Devon 14 G4
Bishopstoke Hants 33 D7
Bishopston Bristol 60 D5
Swansea 56 D5
Bishopstone Bucks 84 C4
E Sus 23 E7
Hereford 97 C8
Kent 71 F8
Swindon 63 C8
Wilts 31 B9
Bishopstrow Wilts 45 E11
Bishop Sutton Bath 44 B5
Bishop's Waltham Hants 33 D9
Bishopswood Som 28 E3
Bishop's Wood Staffs 132 B6
Bishopsworth Bristol 60 F5
Bishop Thornton
N Yorks 214 G5
Bishopthorpe York 207 D7
Bishopton Darl 234 G3
Dumfries 236 E6
N Yorks 214 E6
Renfs 277 G8
Warks 118 F3
Bishopwearmouth T&W 243 F9
Bishop Wilton E Yorks 207 B11
Bishpool Newport 59 B10
Bishton Newport 59 B11
Staffs 151 E10
Bisley Glos 80 D6
Sur 50 B3
Bisley Camp Sur 50 B2
Bispham Blkpool 202 E2
Bispham Green Lancs 194 E3
Bissoe Corn 4 G5
Bissom Corn 3 C7
Bisterne Hants 31 G10
Bisterne Close Hants 32 G2
Bitchet Green Kent 52 C5
Bitchfield Lincs 155 D9
Bittadon Devon 40 E4
Bittaford Devon 8 D3
Bittering Norf 159 F8
Bitterley Shrops 115 B11
Bitterne Soton 33 E7
Bitterne Park Soton 32 E6
Bitterscote Staffs 134 C4
Bitteswell Leics 135 F10
Bittles Green Dorset 30 C5
Bitton S Glos 61 F7
Bix Oxon 65 B8
Bixter Shetland 313 H5
Blaby Leics 135 D11
Blackacre Dumfries 248 E2
Blackadder West
Borders 272 E6
Blackawton Devon 8 E6
Black Bank Cambs 139 F10
Warks 135 F7
Black Banks Darl 224 C5
Black Barn Lincs 157 D8
Blackbeck Cumb 219 D10
Blackbird Leys Oxon 83 E9
Blackborough Devon 27 F9
Norf 158 G3
Blackborough End Norf 158 G3
Black Bourton Oxon 82 E3
Blackboys E Sus 37 C8
Blackbraes Aberds 293 B10
Blackbrook Derbys 170 F4
Derbys 185 E9
Mers 183 B8
Staffs 150 B5
Sur 51 D7
Blackburn Aberds 293 B10
Aberds 302 F5
Blkburn 195 B7
S Yorks 186 C5
W Loth 269 B9
Black Callerton T&W 242 D5
Black Carr Norf 141 D11
Blackcastle Midloth 271 D8
Blackchambers Aberds 293 B9
Black Clauchrie S Ayrs 245 G7
Black Corner W Sus 51 F9
Black Corries Lodge
Highld 284 B6
Blackcraig Dumfries 246 G6
Blackcraigs Angus 293 E7
Black Crofts Argyll 289 F11
Black Cross Corn 5 C8
Black Dam Hants 48 C6
Blackden Heath Ches E 184 G3
Blackditch Oxon 82 D6
Blackdog Aberds 293 B11
Black Dog Devon 26 F4
Blackdown Dorset 28 G5
Hants 33 C8
Warks 118 D6
Blackdyke Cumb 238 G4
Blackdykes E Loth 281 E11
Blacker Hill S Yorks 197 G11
Blacketts Kent 70 F2
Blackfell T&W 243 F7
Blackfen London 68 E3
Blackfield Hants 32 G6
Blackford Cumb 239 E9
Dumfries 248 G4
Perth 286 G2
Shrops 131 G11
Som 29 B11
Som 42 D2
Som 44 D2
Blackford Bridge
Gtr Man 195 F10
Blackfordby Leics 152 F6
Blackfords Staffs 151 G9
Blackgang IoW 20 F5
Blackgate Angus 287 B8
Blackhall Aberds 293 D8
Edin 280 G4
Renfs 267 C9
Blackhall Colliery
Durham 234 D5
Blackhall Mill T&W 242 F4
Blackhall Rocks Durham 234 D5
Blackham E Sus 52 F3
Blackhaugh Borders 261 B10
Blackheath Essex 107 G10
London 67 D11
Suff 127 C8
Sur 50 D4
W Mid 133 F9
Blackheath Park London 68 D2
Black Heddon Northumb 242 B3
Blackhill Aberds 303 D10
Aberds 303 E10
Aberds 303 F10
Durham 242 G3
Hants 32 D4
Highld 298 D3
Black Hill W Yorks 204 E6
Blackhillock Moray 302 E4
Blackhills Highld 301 D9
Moray 302 D2
Swansea 56 C5
Blackhorse Devon 14 C5
S Glos 61 D7
Black Horse Drove
Cambs 139 E11
Blackjack Lincs 156 B5
Black Lake W Mid 133 E9
Blackland Wilts 62 F4
Blacklands E Sus 38 E4
Hereford 98 C2
Black Lane Gtr Man 195 F9
Blacklaw Aberds 302 D6
Blackleach Lancs 202 G5
Blackley Gtr Man 195 G11
W Yorks 196 D6
Blacklunans Perth 292 G3
Black Marsh Shrops 130 D6
Blackmarstone Hereford 97 D10
Blackmill Bridgend 58 B2
Blackminster Worcs 99 C11
Blackmoor Bath 60 G5
Gtr Man 195 G7
Hants 49 G9
N Som 60 G3
Som 27 D11
Black Moor Lancs 194 E3
W Yorks 205 F11
Blackmoorfoot W Yorks 196 E5
Blackmoor Gate Devon 41 E7
Blackmore Essex 87 E10
Shrops 130 B6
Blackmore End Essex 106 E4
Herts 85 B11
Worcs 98 C6
Black Mount Argyll 284 C6
Blackness Aberds 293 D8
E Sus 52 G4
Falk 279 F11
Blacknest Hants 49 E9
Windsor 66 F3
Blacknoll Dorset 18 D2
Black Notley Essex 106 G5
Blacko Lancs 204 E3
Blackoe Shrops 149 B10
Black Park Dumfries 236 C5
Black Park Wrex 166 G4
Black Pill Swansea 56 C6
Blackpole Worcs 117 F7
Black Pole Lancs 202 F5
Blackpool Blkpool 202 F2
Devon 7 E11
Devon 9 F7
Devon 14 G2
Pembs 73 C9
Blackpool Gate Cumb 240 B2
Blackridge W Loth 269 B7
Blackrock Argyll 274 G4
Bath 60 F6
Mon 78 C2
Black Rock Brighton 36 G4
Corn 2 C5
Blackrod Gtr Man 194 E6
Blackshaw Dumfries 238 D2
Blackshaw Head
W Yorks 196 B3
Blackshaw Moor Staffs 169 D8
Blacksmith's Corner
Suff 108 C2
Blacksmith's Green Suff 126 D2
Blacksnape Blkburn 195 C8
Blackstone Worcs 116 C5
W Sus 36 D2
Black Street Suff 143 F10
Black Tar Pembs 73 D7
Blackthorn Oxon 83 B10
Blackthorpe Suff 125 E8
Blacktoft E Yorks 199 C10
Blacktop Aberdeen 293 C10
Black Torrington Devon 25 F7
Blacktown Newport 59 C9
Black Vein Caerph 78 G2
Blackwall Derbys 170 F3
London 67 C11
Blackwall Tunnel
London 67 C11
Blackwater Corn 4 F4
Dorset 19 B8
Hants 49 B11
IoW 20 D6
Norf 159 E11
Som 28 D3
Blackwaterfoot N Ayrs 255 E9
Blackwater Lodge
Moray 302 G3
Blackweir Cardiff 59 D7
Blackwell Cumb 239 G10
Darl 224 C5
Derbys 170 D6
Derbys 185 G10
Devon 27 B8
Warks 100 C4
Worcs 117 C9
W Sus 51 F11
Blackwood Caerph 77 F11
S Lnrk 268 G5
Warr 183 C10
Blackwood Hill Staffs 168 D6
Blacon Ches W 166 B5
Bladbean Kent 55 D7
Blades N Yorks 223 F9
Bladnoch Dumfries 236 D6
Bladon Oxon 82 C6
Blaenannerch Ceredig 92 B4
Blaenau Carms 75 C10
Flint 166 D2
Blaenau Dolwyddelan
Conwy 164 E2
Blaenau Ffestiniog
Gwyn 164 F2
Blaenau-Gwent Bl Gwent 78 E2
Blaenavon Torf 78 D3
Blaenbedw Fawr
Ceredig 111 G7
Blaencaerau Bridgend 57 C11
Blaencelyn Ceredig 111 G7
Blaen-Cil-Llech Ceredig 92 C6
Blaen Clydach Rhondda 77 G7
Blaencwm Rhondda 76 F6
Blaendulais / Seven Sisters
Neath 76 D4
Blaendyryn Powys 95 D8
Blaenffos Pembs 92 D3
Blaengarw Bridgend 76 G6
Blaengwrach Neath 76 E5
Blaengwynfi Neath 57 B11
Blaen-gwynfi Neath 57 B11
Blaenllechau Rhondda 77 F8
Blaen-pant Ceredig 92 C5
Blaenpennal Ceredig 112 E2
Blaenplwyf Ceredig 111 B11
Blaenporth Ceredig 92 B5
Blaenrhondda Rhondda 76 E6
Blaenwaun Carms 92 F4
Blaen-waun Carms 92 F4
Ceredig 111 G7
Blaen-y-coed Carms 92 F6
Blaenycwm Ceredig 112 B6
Blaen-y-cwm Bl Gwent 77 C10
Denb 147 C10
Gwyn 146 E4
Powys 147 E11
Blagdon N Som 44 B4
Torbay 9 C7
Blagdon Hill Som 28 D2
Blagill Cumb 231 B10
Blaguegate Lancs 194 F3
Blaich Highld 290 F2
Blain Highld 289 C8
Blaina Bl Gwent 78 D2
Blainacraig Ho Aberds 293 D7
Blair Fife 280 C6
Blair Atholl Perth 291 G10
Blairbeg N Ayrs 256 C2
Blairburn Fife 279 D9
Blairdaff Aberds 293 B8
Blair Drummond Stirl 278 B4
Blairdryne Aberds 293 D9
Blairglas Argyll 276 D6
Blairgorm Highld 301 G10
Blairgowrie Perth 286 C5
Blairhall Fife 279 D10
Blairhill N Lnrk 268 B4
Blairingone Perth 279 B9
Blairland N Ayrs 266 F6
Blairlinn N Lnrk 278 G5
Blairlogie Stirl 278 B6
Blairlomond Argyll 276 B3
Blairmore Argyll 276 E3
Highld 306 D6
Blairnamarrow Moray 292 B4
Blairquhosh Stirl 277 E10
Blair's Ferry Argyll 275 G10
Blairskaith E Dunb 277 F11
Blaisdon Glos 80 B2
Blaise Hamlet Bristol 60 D5
Blakebrook Worcs 116 B6
Blakedown Worcs 117 B7
Blake End Essex 106 G4
Blakelands M Keynes 103 C7
Blakelaw Borders 263 C7
T&W 242 D6
Blakeley Staffs 133 E7
Blakeley Lane Staffs 169 F7
Blakelow Ches E 167 E11
Blakemere Hereford 97 C7
Blakenall Heath
W Mid 133 C10
Blakeney Glos 79 D11
Norf 177 E8
Blakenhall Ches E 168 F2
W Mid 133 D8
Blakeshall Worcs 132 G6
Blakesley Northants 120 G2
Blanchland Northumb 241 G11
Blandford Camp Dorset 30 F6
Blandford Forum Dorset 30 F5
Blandford St Mary Dorset 30 F5
Bland Hill N Yorks 205 C10
Blandy Highld 308 D6
Blanefield Stirl 277 F11
Blanerne Borders 272 D6
Blank Bank Staffs 168 F4
Blankney Lincs 173 C9
Blantyre S Lnrk 268 D3
Blar a'Chaorainn Highld 290 G3
Blaran Argyll 275 B9
Blarghour Argyll 275 B10
Blarmachfoldach Highld 290 G2
Blarnalearoch Highld 307 K6
Blasford Hill Essex 88 C2
Blashford Hants 31 F11
Blaston Leics 136 D6
Blatchbridge Som 45 D9
Blatherwycke Northants 137 D9
Blawith Cumb 210 B5
Blaxhall Suff 127 F7
Blaxton S Yorks 199 G7
Blaydon T&W 242 E5
Blaydon Burn T&W 242 E5
Blaydon Haughs T&W 242 E5
Bleach Green Cumb 219 B9
Suff 126 B4
Bleadney Som 44 D3
Bleadon N Som 43 B10
Bleak Acre Hereford 98 B2
Bleak Hall M Keynes 103 D7
Bleak Hey Nook
Gtr Man 196 F4

Bressingham Common Norf. 141 G11
Bretby Derbys 152 E5
Bretford Warks 119 B8
Bretforton Worcs 99 C11
Bretherdale Head Cumb. 221 E11
Bretherton Lancs 194 C3
Brettabister Shetland 313 H6
Brettenham Norf 141 G8
Suff 125 G9
Bretton Derbys 186 F2
Flint 166 C5
Pboro. 138 C3
Brewer's End Essex 105 G11
Brewers Green Norf 142 G2
Brewer Street Sur 51 C10
Brewlands Bridge Angus 292 G3
Brewood Staffs 133 B7
Briach Moray 301 D10
Briants Puddle Dorset 18 C2
Briar Hill Northants 120 F4
Brick End Essex 105 F11
Brickendon Herts. 86 D4
Bricket Wood Herts 85 E10
Brickfields Worcs. 117 F7
Brickhill Beds 121 G11
Brick Hill Sur 66 G3
Brick House End Essex 105 F9
Brickhouses Ches E 168 C3
Brick Houses S Yorks 186 E4
Brick-kiln End Notts 171 D9
Bricklehampton Worcs 99 C9
Bride IoM 192 B5
Bridekirk Cumb. 229 E8
Bridell Pembs. 92 C3
Bridestowe Devon 12 D6
Brideswell Aberds 302 F5
Bridford Devon 14 D2
Bridfordmills Devon 14 D2
Bridge Corn 4 G3
Kent. 55 C7
Som 28 F5
Bridge Ball Devon 41 D8
Bridge End Beds 121 G10
Cumb. 230 B3
Devon 8 F3
Durham 232 D6
Essex 106 E3
Flint 166 D4
Hereford 98 B2
Lincs 156 B2
Northumb 241 D10
Northumb 241 E10
Oxon 83 G9
Bridge-End Shetland 313 K5
Bridge End Sur 50 B5
Warks 118 E5
Worcs 98 E6
Bridgefoot Aberds 292 C6
Angus 287 D7
Cumb 229 F7
Bridge Green Essex 105 D9
Norf 142 G2
Bridgehampton Som 29 C9
Bridge Hewick N Yorks 214 E6
Bridgehill Durham 242 G3
Bridge Ho Argyll 254 B4
Bridgeholm Green Derbys 185 E8
Bridgehouse Gate N Yorks 214 F3
Bridgelands Borders 261 C11
Bridgemary Hants 33 G9
Bridgemere Ches E 168 F2
Bridgemont Derbys 185 E8
Bridgend Aberds 293 B7
Aberds 302 F5
Angus 293 G7
Argyll 255 D8
Argyll 274 G4
Argyll 275 D9
Corn 0 D2
Cumb 221 C7
Devon 7 F11
Fife 287 F7
Glos 80 E4
Highld 300 D3
Invclyd 276 F5
Moray 302 F3
N Lnrk 278 G3
Pembs 92 B3
W Loth 279 F10
Bridgend of Lintrathen Angus 286 B6
Bridgend / Pen-y-Bont ar-ogwr Bridgend 58 C2
Bridgeness Falk 279 E10
Bridge of Alford Aberds 293 B7
Bridge of Allan Stirl 278 E5
Bridge of Avon Moray 301 F11
Moray 301 G11
Bridge of Awe Argyll 284 E4
Bridge of Balgie Perth 285 C9
Bridge of Cally Perth 286 B5
Bridge of Canny Aberds 293 D8
Bridge of Craigisla Angus 286 B6
Bridge of Dee Dumfries 237 D9
Bridge of Don Aberdeen 293 B11
Bridge of Dun Angus 287 B10
Bridge of Dye Aberds 293 E8
Bridge of Earn Perth 286 F5
Bridge of Ericht Perth 285 B9
Bridge of Feugh Aberds 293 D9
Bridge of Forss Highld 310 C4
Bridge of Gairn Aberds 292 D5
Bridge of Gaur Perth 285 B9
Bridge of Lyon Perth 285 C11
Bridge of Muchalls Aberds 293 D10
Bridge of Muick Aberds 292 D5
Bridge of Oich Highld 290 C5
Bridge of Orchy Argyll 284 D6
Bridge of Waith Orkney 314 E2
Bridge of Walls Shetland 313 H4
Bridge Reeve Devon 25 E11
Bridgerule Devon 24 G3
Bridges Corn 5 D10
Shrops 131 D7
Bridge Sollers Hereford 97 C8
Bridge Street Suff 107 B7
Bridgeton Glasgow 268 C2
Bridgetown Corn 11 D10
Devon 8 C6
Som 42 G2
Staffs 133 B9
Bridge Town Warks 118 G4
Bridge Trafford Ches W 183 G7
Bridgham Norf 141 F9
Bridgnorth Shrops 132 E4

Bridgtown Staffs 133 B9
Bridgwater Som 43 F10
Bridlington E Yorks 218 F3
Bridport Dorset 16 C5
Bridstow Hereford 97 G11
Brierfield Lancs 204 F2
Brierholme Carr S Yorks 199 E7
Brierley Glos 79 B10
Hereford 115 F9
S Yorks 198 E2
Brierley Hill W Mid 133 F8
Brierton Hrtlpl. 234 E5
Briestfield W Yorks 197 D8
Brigflatts Cumb. 222 G2
Brigg N Lincs 200 F3
N Lincs 200 F4
Briggate Norf 160 D6
Briggswath N Yorks 227 D7
Brigham Cumb. 229 G11
Cumb 229 G11
E Yorks 209 C7
Brighouse W Yorks 196 C6
Brighstone IoW 20 E4
Brightgate Derbys 170 D3
Brighthampton Oxon 82 E5
Brightholmlee S Yorks 186 B3
Brightley Devon 13 B7
Brightling E Sus 37 C11
Brightlingsea Essex 89 B9
Brighton Brighton 36 G4
Corn 5 E8
Brighton Hill Hants 48 D6
Brightons Falk 279 F8
Brightside S Yorks 186 D5
Brightwalton W Berks 64 D2
Brightwalton Green W Berks 64 D2
Brightwalton Holt W Berks 64 D2
Brightwell Suff 108 C4
Brightwell Baldwin Oxon 83 F11
Brightwell cum Sotwell Oxon 83 G9
Brigmerston Wilts 47 D7
Brignall Durham 223 C11
Brig o'Turk Stirl 285 G9
Brigsley NE Lincs 201 G9
Brigsteer Cumb 211 B9
Brigstock Northants 137 F7
Brill Bucks 83 C11
Corn 2 D6
Brilley Hereford 96 B5
Brilley Mountain Powys 114 E5
Brimaston Pembs 91 G8
Brimfield Hereford 115 D10
Brimington Derbys 186 G6
Brimington Common Derbys 186 G6
Brimley Devon 13 F11
Devon 28 G4
Brimpsfield Glos 80 C6
Brimps Hill Glos 79 B11
Brimpton W Berks 64 G5
Brimpton Common W Berks 64 G5
Brims Orkney 314 H2
Brims Castle Highld 310 B4
Brimscombe Glos 80 E5
Brimsdown London 86 F5
Brimstage Mers 182 E4
Brinacory Highld 295 F9
Brincliffe S Yorks 186 D4
Brind E Yorks 207 G10
Brindham Som 44 E4
Brindister Shetland 313 H4
Shetland 313 K6
Brindle Lancs 194 C6
Brindle Heath Gtr Man 195 G10
Brindley Ches E 167 E9
Brindley Ford Stoke 168 E5
Brindwoodgate Derbys 186 F4
Brineton Staffs 150 G6
Bringewood Forge Hereford 115 C9
Bringhurst Leics 136 E6
Bringsty Common Hereford 116 F4
Brington Cambs 121 B11
Brinian Orkney 314 D4
Briningham Norf 159 C10
Brinkhill Lincs 190 G5
Brinkley Cambs 124 G2
Notts 172 E2
Brinkley Hill Hereford 97 E11
Brinklow M Keynes 103 D8
Warks 119 B8
Brinkworth Wilts 62 C4
Brinmore Highld 300 H5
Brinnington Gtr Man 184 C6
Brinscall Lancs 194 C6
Brinsea N Som 60 G2
Brinsford Staffs 133 B8
Brinsley Notts 171 E6
Brinsop Hereford 97 C8
Brinsop Common Hereford 97 C8
Brinsworth S Yorks 186 D6
Brinsworthy Devon 41 G9
Brinton Norf 159 B10
Brisco Cumb. 239 G10
Briscoe Cumb 219 C10
Briscoerigg N Yorks 205 C11
Brisley Norf 159 E8
Brislington Bristol 60 E6
Brissenden Green Kent 54 F2
Bristnall Fields W Mid 133 F10
Bristol Bristol 60 E5
Briston Norf 159 C11
Britain Bottom S Glos 61 B9
Britannia Lancs 195 C11
Britford Wilts 31 B11
Brithdir Caerph 77 E11
Ceredig 92 B6
Gwyn 146 G5
Brithem Bottom Devon 27 E8
British Torf 78 E3
Briton Ferry / Llansawel Neath 57 C8
Britten's Bath 45 B7
Brittwell Slough 66 C3
Britwell Salome Oxon 83 G11
Brixham Torbay 9 D8
Brixton Devon 7 E11
London 67 D10
Brixton Deverill Wilts 45 E11
Brixworth Northants 120 C4
Brize Norton Oxon 82 D4
Broad Alley Worcs 117 D7
Broad Blunsdon Swindon 81 G11
Broadbottom Gtr Man 185 C7
Broadbridge W Sus 22 B4
Broadbridge Heath W Sus 50 G6
Broadbury Devon 12 B5
Broadbush Swindon 81 G11

Broad Campden Glos 100 D3
Broad Carr W Yorks 196 D5
Broad Chalke Wilts 31 B8
Broadclyst Devon 14 B5
Broad Colney Herts. 85 E11
Broad Common Worcs 117 D7
Broadfield Gtr Man 195 E10
Inclyd 276 G6
Lancs 194 C4
Lancs 195 B8
Pembs 73 E10
W Sus. 51 G9
Broadford Highld 295 C8
Sur 50 D3
Broad Ford Kent 53 F8
Broad Ford Bridge W Sus 35 C8
Broadgate Hants 32 C5
Broadgrass Green Suff 125 E9
Broad Green Cambs 124 F3
C Beds 103 C9
Essex 105 D8
Essex 107 G7
Mers 182 C6
Suff 124 F5
Suff 125 F11
Worcs 116 F5
Worcs 117 C9
Broadgreen Wood Herts. 86 D4
Broadhalgh Gtr Man 195 E11
Broadham Green Sur 51 C11
Broadhaugh Borders 249 B10
Broadhaven Highld 310 D7
Broad Haven / Aberllydan Pembs. 72 C5
Broadheath Gtr Man 184 D3
Broad Heath Powys 114 E6
Staffs 151 D7
Worcs 116 D3
Broadhembury Devon 27 G10
Broadhempston Devon 8 B6
Broad Hill Cambs 123 B11
Broad Hinton Wilts 62 D6
Broadholm Derbys 170 F4
Broadholme Derbys 170 F4
Lincs 188 G5
Broad Ings E Yorks 208 C2
Broadland Row E Sus 38 D4
Broadlands Devon 14 G3
Broadlane Corn 2 C4
Broad Lane Corn 4 G3
Broad Lanes Shrops 132 F5
Broadlay Carms 74 D5
Broad Laying Hants 64 G2
Broad Layings Hants 64 G2
Broadley Lancs 195 D11
Moray 302 C3
Broadley Common Essex 86 D6
Broadleys Aberds 303 C8
Broad Marston Worcs 100 B2
Broadmayne Dorset 17 D10
Broad Meadow Staffs 168 F4
Broadmeadows Borders 261 C10
Broadmere Hants 48 D6
Broadmoor Pembs 73 D9
Sur 50 D6
Broadmoor Common Hereford 98 D2
Broadmore Green Worcs 116 G6
Broadoak Dorset 16 B4
Glos 80 C2
Hants 33 E8
Shrops 149 F9
Wrex 166 D5
Broad Oak Carms 93 G11
Cumb 220 G2
Dorset 30 E3
E Sus 37 C10
E Sus 38 D4
Hants 49 C9
Hereford 97 G9
Kent 54 F4
Kent 71 G7
Mers 183 B8
Shrops 132 F5
Broadoak End Herts 86 C4
Broadoak Park Gtr Man 195 G9
Broad Parkham Devon 24 C5
Broadplat Oxon 65 C8
Broadrashes Moray 302 D4
Broadrock Glos 79 E8
Broadsands Torbay 9 D7
Broadsea Aberds 303 C9
Broad's Green Essex 87 C11
Wilts 62 F3
Broadshard Som 28 E6
Broadstairs Kent 71 F11
Broadstone Hants 53 D11
Mon 79 B8
Poole 18 B6
Shrops 131 F10
Broad Street E Sus 38 D5
Kent 53 B10
Kent 54 E4
Kent 55 E7
Medway 69 E9
Suff 107 C9
Wilts 46 B5
Broad Street Green Essex 88 C4
Broad Tenterden Kent 53 G11
Broad Town Wilts 62 D5
Broadwas Worcs 116 F5
Broadwater Herts 104 G4
W Sus. 35 G11
Broadwater Down Kent 52 F5
Broadwaters Worcs 116 B6
Broadwath Cumb 239 F11
Broadway Carms 74 D3
Carms 74 D5
Pembs 72 C5
Som 28 D4
Suff 127 B7
Worcs 99 D11
Broadway Lands Hereford 97 E11
Broadwell Glos 79 C9
Glos 100 F4
Oxon 82 E3
Warks 119 D9
Broadwell Ho Northumb 241 F10
Broadwey Dorset 17 E9
Broadwindsor Dorset 28 G6
Broadwood Kelly Devon 25 F10
Broadwoodwidger Devon 12 D4
Brobury Hereford 96 C6
Brochel Highld 298 E5
Brochroy Argyll 284 D4
Brock Lancs 202 E6
Brockamin Worcs 116 G5
Brockbridge Hants 33 D10
Brockdish Norf 126 B4
Brockencote Worcs 117 C7
Brockenhurst Hants 32 G4
Brocketsbrae S Lnrk 259 B8
Brockfield Devon 28 E4
Brockford Green Suff 126 D2

Brockford Street Suff 126 D2
Brockhall Northants 120 E2
Brockhall Village Lancs 203 F10
Brockhampton Glos 99 G9
Glos 99 B10
Hants 22 B2
Hereford 97 E11
Brockhampton Green Dorset 30 F2
Brockhill Borders 261 E9
Brock Hill Essex 88 F2
Brockholes N Yorks 197 E7
Brockhollands Glos 79 D10
Brockhurst Derbys 170 C5
Hants 33 G10
Warks 135 G9
Brocklebank Cumb 230 C2
Brocklehirst Dumfries 238 C3
Brocklesby Lincs 200 E6
Brockley London 67 E11
N Som 60 F3
Brockley Corner Suff 124 C6
Brockley Green Suff 106 B4
Suff 124 G6
Brockleymoor Cumb 230 D5
Brockloch Dumfries 246 D2
Brockmanton Hereford 115 F10
Brockmoor W Mid 133 F8
Brocks Green Hants 64 G4
Brock's Watering Norf 142 G2
Brockton Shrops 130 C6
Shrops 130 F6
Shrops 131 E11
Shrops 132 C6
Staffs 150 C6
Telford 150 F4
Brockweir Glos 79 E8
Brockwell Som 42 E2
Brockwood Hants 33 B10
Brockworth Glos 80 B5
Brocton Corn 5 D9
Staffs 151 F9
Brodick N Ayrs 256 B2
Brodie Moray 301 D9
Brodiesord Aberds 302 C5
Brodsworth S Yorks 198 F4
Brogaig Highld 298 C4
Brogborough C Beds 103 D9
Broke Hall Suff 108 C3
Brokenborough Wilts 62 B2
Broken Cross Ches E 184 G5
Ches W 183 G11
Broken Green Herts 105 G8
Brokerswood Wilts 45 C10
Brokes N Yorks 224 F3
Brombil Neath 57 D9
Bromborough Mers 182 E4
Bromborough Pool Mers 182 E4
Bromdon Shrops 132 G2
Brome Suff 126 B2
Brome Street Suff 126 B3
Bromeswell Suff 126 F6
Bromfield Cumb 229 B9
Shrops 115 B9
Bromford W Mid 134 E2
Bromham Beds 121 G10
Wilts 62 G3
Bromley Herts. 105 G8
London 67 C11
S Yorks 132 D4
W Mid 133 F8
Bromley Common London 68 F3
Bromley Cross Essex 107 F11
Gtr Man 195 E8
Bromley Green Kent 54 F3
Bromley Hall Staffs 150 C5
Bromley Heath S Glos 61 D7
Bromley Park London 67 F11
Bromley Wood Staffs 152 E2
Bromlow Shrops 130 C6
Brompton London 67 D9
Medway 69 E9
N Yorks 217 G8
N Yorks 225 F7
Shrops 131 B10
Brompton-by-Sawdon N Yorks 217 C10
Brompton-on-Swale N Yorks 224 F4
Brompton Ralph Som 42 G5
Brompton Regis Som 42 G3
Bromsash Hereford 98 G2
Bromsberrow Heath Glos 98 E4
Bromsgrove Worcs 117 C9
Bromstead Common Staffs 150 F5
Bromstead Heath Staffs 150 F6
Bromstone Kent 71 F11
Bromyard Hereford 116 G3
Bromyard Downs Hereford 116 F3
Bronaber Gwyn 146 C4
Broncroft Shrops 131 F10
Brondesbury London 67 C8
Brondesbury Park London 67 C8
Brongest Ceredig 92 B6
Bronington Wrex 149 B9
Bronllys Powys 96 D2
Bronnant Ceredig 112 D2
Bronwydd Ceredig 93 C7
Bronwydd Arms Carms 93 G8
Bronydd Powys 96 C4
Bronygarth Shrops 148 B5
Brook Carms 74 D3
Hants 32 D4
Hants 48 F3
IoW 20 E3
Kent 54 E5
Sur 50 E2
Brook Bottom Gtr Man 185 D7
Brooke Norf 142 D6
Rutland 136 B6
Brookenby Lincs 190 B2
Brookend Glos 79 E11
Glos 79 F9
Oxon 100 G6
Brook End Beds 121 E11
Cambs 121 C11
C Beds 103 B9
M Keynes 103 C8
Bucks 84 C4
Cambs 121 D10
Worcs 117 E8

Worcs 99 B11
Brookfield Derbys 185 B8
Lancs 203 G7
Mbro. 225 B9
Renfs 267 C8
Brookfoot W Yorks 196 C6
Brookgreen IoW 20 E3
Brook Green London 67 D8
Suff 125 F7
Brookhampton Oxon 83 F10
Shrops 131 E11
Som 29 B10
Brook Hill Hants 32 E3
Notts 153 C11
Brookhouse Blkburn 195 B7
Ches E 184 F6
Lancs 211 G10
S Yorks 187 D8
W Yorks 196 B5
Brookhouse Green Ches E 168 C4
Brookhouses Derbys 185 D8
Staffs 169 G7
Brookhurst Mers 182 E4
Brookland Kent 39 B7
Brooklands Dumfries 237 B10
Gtr Man 184 C3
Shrops 167 G8
Brookleigh Devon 14 B5
Brookmans Park Herts 86 E2
Brookpits W Sus 35 G8
Brook Place Sur 66 G3
Brookrow Shrops 116 C2
Brooks Corn 6 C3
Powys 130 D2
Brooksbottoms Gtr Man 195 D9
Brooksby Leics 154 F3
Brooks End Kent 71 F9
Brooks Green W Sus 35 C11
Brookside Brack 66 E2
Derbys 186 G5
Telford 132 B3
Brookthorpe Glos 80 C4
Brookvale Halton 183 E8
Brookvile Norf 140 D4
Brook Waters Wilts 30 C6
Brookwood Sur 50 B2
Broom C Beds 104 C3
Cumb 231 G9
Devon 28 G4
E Renf 267 D10
Fife 287 F7
Pembs 73 D10
S Yorks 186 C6
Warks 118 F2
Worcs 117 G11
Broombank Worcs 116 C3
Broome Norf 143 E7
Shrops 131 D10
Shrops 131 G8
Worcs 117 B8
Broomedge Warr 184 D2
Broome Park Northumb 264 G4
Broomer's Corner W Sus 35 C10
Broomershill W Sus 35 D9
Broomfield Aberds 303 F9
Cumb 230 B2
Essex 88 D2
Kent 53 C10
Kent 71 G7
Som 43 G8
Wilts 61 D11
Broomfields Shrops 149 F8
Broomfleet E Yorks 199 B11
Broom Green Norf 159 E8
Broomhall Ches E 167 F10
Windsor 66 F3
Broomhall Green Ches E 167 F10
Broomham E Sus 23 C8
Broomhaugh Northumb 242 E2
Broomhill Borders 261 D11
Bristol 60 D6
Ches W 167 B7
Highld 301 G9
Kent 55 B8
Norf 140 C2
N Yorks 217 B8
Northumb 252 C6
Notts 171 F8
S Yorks 186 C4
Broom Hill Bristol 60 E6
Dorset 31 G8
Durham 242 G4
London 68 F3
Suff 108 B5
Worcs 117 B8
Broomhill Bank Kent 52 E5
Broomholm Norf 160 C6
Broomlands Borders 261 D11
Broomley Northumb 242 E2
Broompark Durham 233 C10
Broom's Barn Suff 124 D5
Broom's Green Glos 98 E4
Broomsthorpe Norf 158 D6
Broom Street Kent 70 G4
Broomton Highld 301 B8
Broomy Hill Hereford 97 D9
Broomy Lodge Hants 32 E2
Broomyshaw Staffs 169 F9
Brora Highld 311 J3
Broseley Shrops 132 C3
Brotherhouse Bar Lincs 156 G6
Brotheridge Green Worcs 98 C6
Brotherlee Durham 232 D4
Brothertoft Lincs 174 F3
Brotherton N Yorks 198 B3
Brothybeck Cumb 230 C2
Brotton Redcar 226 B3
Broubster Highld 310 C4
Brough Cumb 222 C5
Derbys 185 E11
E Yorks 200 B2
Highld 310 B6
Notts 172 D4
Orkney 314 F4
Shetland 312 C7
Shetland 312 F7
Shetland 313 G7
Shetland 313 H6
Shetland 313 J7
Broughall Shrops 167 G9
Brough Lodge Shetland 312 D7
Brough Sowerby Cumb 222 C5
Broughton Borders 260 B4
Bucks 84 C4
Cambs 122 B4
Flint 166 B4

Flint 166 C5
Hants 47 G10
Lancs 202 F6
M Keynes 103 C7
N Lincs 200 F3
Northants 120 B6
N Yorks 204 C4
N Yorks 216 E5
Orkney 314 B4
Oxon 101 D8
Staffs 150 C5
V Glam 58 E3
Broughton Astley Leics 135 E10
Broughton Beck Cumb 210 C5
Broughton Common Cumb. 210 B4
Wilts 61 G11
Broughton Cross Cumb 229 E7
Broughton Gifford Wilts 61 G11
Broughton Green Worcs 117 E9
Broughton Hackett Worcs 117 G8
Broughton in Furness Cumb. 210 B4
Broughton Lodges Leics 154 E4
Broughton Mills Cumb 220 G4
Broughton Moor Cumb 228 E6
Broughton Park Gtr Man 195 G10
Broughton Poggs Oxon 82 E2
Broughtown Orkney 314 B6
Broughty Ferry Dundee 287 D8
Brow Edge Cumb. 211 C7
Browhouses Dumfries 239 D7
Browland Shetland 313 H4
Brown Bank N Yorks 205 C10
Brownber Cumb 222 D4
Brownbread Street E Sus 23 B11
Brown Candover Hants 48 F5
Brown Edge Lancs 193 E11
Mers 183 C8
Staffs 168 E6
Brownheath Devon 27 D10
Ches W 167 B7
Hants 33 D8
Brownheath Common Worcs 117 E7
Brownhill Aberds 302 E6
Aberds 303 E8
Blkburn 203 G9
Shrops 149 E8
Brownhills Fife 287 F9
W Mid 133 B10
Brownieside Northumb 264 E5
Browninghill Green Hants 48 B5
Brown Knowl Ches W 167 E7
Brown Lees Staffs 168 D5
Brownlow Ches E 168 C4
Brownlow Fold Gtr Man 195 E8
Brownlow Heath Ches E 168 C4
Brown Moor W Yorks 206 G3
Brownmuir Aberds 293 F9
Brownrigg Cumb 229 G7
Brownshill Glos 80 E5
Brownshill Green W Mid 134 G4
Brownside Lancs 204 G3
Brownsover Warks 119 B10
Brownston Devon 8 E4
Brown Street Suff 125 E11
Browns Wood M Keynes 103 D8
Browston Green Norf 143 D9
Browtop Cumb 229 G7
Broxa N Yorks 227 G9
Broxbourne Herts 86 D5
Broxburn E Loth 282 F3
W Loth 279 G11
Broxfield Northumb 264 F6
Broxholme Lincs 188 F6
Broxted Essex 105 F11
Broxton Ches W 167 E7
Broxtowe Nottingham 171 G8
Broxwood Hereford 115 G7
Broyle Side E Sus 23 C7
Brù W Isles 304 D5
Bruairnis W Isles 297 L3
Bruan Highld 310 F7
Bruar Lodge Perth 291 F10
Brucefield Fife 280 D2
Brucehill W Dunb 277 F7
Bruche Warr 183 D10
Brucklebog Aberds 293 D9
Bruera Ches W 166 C6
Bruern Abbey Oxon 100 G5
Bruichladdich Argyll 274 G3
Bruisyard Suff 126 D6
Brumby N Lincs 199 F11
Brund Staffs 169 C10
Brundall Norf 142 A6
Brundish Norf 143 D7
Suff 126 D5
Brundish Street Suff 126 C5
Brunery Highld 289 B9
Brunnion Corn 2 B2
Brunshaw Lancs 204 G3
Brunstane Edin 280 G6
Brunstock Cumb 239 F10
Brunswick Gtr Man 184 B4
Brunswick Park London 86 F3
Brunswick Village T&W 242 C6
Bruntcliffe W Yorks 197 B9
Brunthwaite W Yorks 205 D7
Bruntingthorpe Leics 136 F2
Bruntland Aberds 302 G5
Brunton Fife 287 E7
Northumb 264 E6
Wilts 47 B8
Brushes Gtr Man 185 B7
Brushford Devon 25 F11
Som 26 B3
Bruton Som 45 G7
Bryanston Dorset 30 F5
Bryan's Green Worcs 117 D7
Bryant's Bottom Bucks 84 F4
Brydekirk Dumfries 238 C5
Bryher Scilly 1 G3
Brymbo Conwy 180 G4
Wrex 166 E3
Brympton Som 29 D8
Brympton D'Evercy Som 29 D8
Bryn Caerph 77 E11

Neath 57 C10
Powys 130 C3
Rhondda 76 E6
Shrops 130 F5
Swansea 56 C4
Brynamman Carms 76 C2
Brynawel Caerph 77 G11
Bryn Bwbach Gwyn 146 B2
Bryncae Rhondda 58 C3
Bryncethin Bridgend 58 C2
Bryncir Gwyn 163 G7
Bryn-coch Neath 57 B8
Bryncroes Gwyn 144 C4
Bryncrug Gwyn 128 C2
Bryn Du Anglesey 178 G4
Bryn Dulas Conwy 180 F6
Bryneglwys Denb 165 F10
Bryn Eglwys Gwyn 163 B10
Brynford Flint 181 G11
Bryn Gates Gtr Man 194 G5
Bryn Golau Rhondda 58 B3
Bryngwran Anglesey 178 F4
Bryn-glas Conwy 164 B4
Brynglas Sta Gwyn 128 C2
Bryngwyn Ceredig 92 B5
Mon 78 D5
Powys 96 B3
Brynhenllan Pembs 91 D10
Brynhoffnant Ceredig 110 G6
Bryniau Denb 181 E9
Bryn-Iwan Carms 92 G6
Brynithel BI Gwent 78 E2
Brynllywarch Powys 130 E2
Brynmawr BI Gwent 77 C11
Bryn-mawr Gwyn 144 C4
Brynmenyn Bridgend 58 C2
Brynmill Swansea 56 C6
Brynmorfudd Conwy 164 C4
Bryn Myrddin Carms 93 G8
Brynna Rhondda 58 C3
Bryn-nantllech Conwy 165 C7
Bryn-newydd Denb 165 G11
Bryn Offa Wrex 166 F4
Brynore Shrops 149 B7
Bryn-penarth Powys 130 C2
Bryn Pen-y-lan Wrex 166 F4
Bryn Pydew Conwy 180 F4
Brynrefail Anglesey 179 D7
Gwyn 163 C9
Bryn Rhyd-yr-Arian Conwy 165 B7
Bryn-rhys Conwy 180 F4
Brynsadler Rhondda 58 C4
Bryn Saith Marchog Denb 165 E9
Brynsiencyn Anglesey 163 B7
Bryn Sion Gwyn 147 F7
Brynsworthy Devon 40 G4
Bryn Tanat Powys 148 E4
Brynteg Anglesey 179 E7
Ceredig 93 C9
Wrex 166 E4
Bryntirion Bridgend 57 E11
Bryn-y-cochin Shrops 149 B7
Bryn-y-gwenin Mon 78 B4
Bryn-y-maen Conwy 180 F4
Bryn-yr-eryr Gwyn 162 F5
Bryn-yr-ogof Denb 165 D11
Buaile nam Bodach W Isles 297 L3
Bualintur Highld 294 C6
Bualnaluib Highld 307 K3
Buarthmeini Gwyn 147 B8
Bubbenhall Warks 119 C7
Bubblewell Glos 80 E5
Bubnell Derbys 186 G2
Bubwith E Yorks 207 F10
Buccleuch Borders 261 G10
Buchanan Smithy Stirl 277 D7
Buchanhaven Aberds 303 E11
Buchan Hill W Sus 51 G9
Buchanty Perth 286 E3
Buchley E Dunb 277 G11
Buchlyvie Stirl 277 D9
Buckabank Cumb 230 B3
Buckden Cambs 122 D3
N Yorks 213 D9
Buckenham Norf 143 B7
Buckerell Devon 27 G10
Buckfast Devon 8 B4
Buckfastleigh Devon 8 B4
Buckhaven Fife 281 B7
Buck Hill Wilts 62 E3
Buckholm Borders 261 B11
Buckholt Mon 79 B8
Buckhorn Devon 12 B3
Buckhorn Weston Dorset 30 C3
Buckhurst Kent 53 E10
Buckhurst Hill Essex 86 G5
Buckie Moray 302 C4
Buckies Highld 310 C5
Buckingham Bucks 102 D3
Buckland Bucks 84 C5
Devon 8 G4
Glos 99 D11
Hants 20 B2
Herts 105 E7
Kent 55 E10
Oxon 82 G4
Sur 51 D8
Buckland Brewer Devon 24 C6
Buckland Common Bucks 84 D6
Buckland Dinham Som 45 C8
Buckland Down Som 45 D8
Buckland End W Mid 134 F2
Buckland Filleigh Devon 25 F7
Buckland in the Moor Devon 13 G11
Buckland Monachorum Devon 7 B8
Buckland Newton Dorset 29 F11
Buckland Ripers Dorset 17 E8
Buckland St Mary Som 28 E3
Buckland Valley Kent 55 E10

Bucklandwharf Bucks 84 C5
Bucklebury W Berks 64 E5
Bucklebury Alley W Berks 64 E4
Bucklegate Lincs 156 B6
Buckleigh Devon 24 B6
Bucklerheads Angus 287 D8
Bucklers Hard Hants 20 B5
Bucklesham Suff 108 C5
Buckley / Bwcle Flint 166 C3
Buckley Green Warks 118 D3
Buckley Hill Mers 182 B4
Bucklow Hill Ches E 184 E2
Buckminster Leics 155 E7
Bucknall Lincs 173 B11
Stoke. 168 F6
Bucknell Oxon 101 F11
Shrops 114 B6
Buckoak Ches W 183 G8
Buckover S Glos 79 G10
Buckpool Moray 302 C4
W Mid 133 F7
Buckridge Worcs 116 C4
Bucksburn Aberdeen 293 C10
Buck's Cross Devon 24 C4
Bucks Green W Sus 50 G5
Buckshaw Village Lancs 194 C5
Bucks Hill Herts 85 E9
Bucks Horn Oak Hants 49 E10
Buckskin Hants 48 C6
Buck's Mills Devon 24 C5
Buckton E Yorks 218 E3
Hereford 115 C7
Northumb 264 B3
Buckton Vale Gtr Man 196 G3
Buckworth Cambs 122 B2
Budbrooke Warks 118 D5
Budby Notts 171 B10
Buddbrake Shetland 312 B8
Buddileigh Staffs 168 F3
Budd's Titson Corn 24 G2
Bude Corn 24 F2
Budge's Shop Corn 6 D6
Budlake Devon 14 B5
Budle Northumb 264 B5
Budleigh Som 27 D11
Budleigh Salterton Devon 15 E7
Budlett's Common E Sus 37 C7
Budock Water Corn 3 C7
Budworth Heath Ches W 183 F11
Buersil Head Gtr Man 196 E2
Buerton Ches E 167 G11
Buffler's Holt Bucks 102 D3
Bufton Leics 135 B8
Bugbrooke Northants 120 F3
Bugford Devon 40 E6
Bughtlin Edin 280 G3
Buglawton Ches E 168 C5
Bugle Corn 5 D10
Bugle Gate Worcs 116 C6
Bugley Dorset 30 C3
Wilts 45 E11
Bugthorpe E Yorks 207 B11
Building End Essex 105 D8
Buildwas Shrops 132 C2
Builth Road Powys 113 G10
Builth Wells Powys 113 G10
Buirgh W Isles 305 J2
Bulbourne Herts 85 C7
Bulby Lincs 155 D11
Bulcote Notts 171 G11
Buldoo Highld 310 C3
Bulford Wilts 47 E7
Bulford Camp Wilts 47 E7
Bulkeley Ches E 167 E8
Bulkeley Hall Shrops 167 F11
Bulkington Warks 135 F7
Wilts 46 B2
Bulkworthy Devon 24 D5
Bullamoor N Yorks 225 G7
Bull Bay / Porthllechog Anglesey 178 C6
Bullbridge Derbys 170 E5
Bullbrook Brack 65 F11
Bulleign Kent 53 G11
Bullenhill Wilts 45 B11
Bullen's Green Herts 86 D2
Bulley Glos 80 B3
Bullgill Cumb 228 D6
Bull Hill Hants 20 B2
Bullinghope Hereford 97 D10
Bullington Hants 48 E3
Lincs 189 F8
Bull's Green Herts 86 C3
Norf 143 E8
Bull's Hill Hereford 97 G11
Bullwood Argyll 276 F2
Bullyhole Bottom Mon 79 F7
Bulmer Essex 106 C6
N Yorks 216 F2
Bulmer Tye Essex 106 D6
Bulphan Thurrock 68 B6
Bulstrode Herts 85 E8
Bulthy Shrops 148 G6
Bulverhythe E Sus 38 F2
Bulwark Aberds 303 E9
Mon 79 G8
Bulwell Nottingham 171 F8
Bulwell Forest Nottingham 171 F8
Bulwick Northants 137 E8
Bumble's Green Essex 86 D6
Bun Abhainn Eadarra W Isles 305 H3

Bunacaimb Highld 295 G8
Bun a'Mhuilinn W Isles 297 K3
Bunarkaig Highld 290 E3
Bunbury Ches E 167 D9
Bunbury Heath Ches E 167 D9
Bunchrew Highld 300 E5
Bundalloch Highld 295 C10
Buness Shetland 312 C8
Bunessan Argyll 288 G5
Bungay Suff 142 F6
Bunker's Hill Cambs 139 B8
Lincs 174 E3
Bunkers Hill Lincs 189 G7
Norf 142 B3
Oxon 83 B7
Bunloit Highld 300 G5
Bun Loyne Highld 290 C4
Bunnahabhain Argyll 274 F5
Bunny Notts 153 D11
Bunree Highld 290 G2
Bunroy Highld 290 E4
Bunsley Bank Ches E 167 G11
Bunwell Norf 142 E2
Bunwell Hill Norf 142 E2

Carrutherstown Dumfries 238 C4
Carr Vale Derbys 171 B7
Carrville Durham 234 C2
Carry Argyll 275 G10
Carsaig Argyll 275 E8
Argyll 289 G7
Carscreugh Dumfries 236 D4
Carsegowan Dumfries 236 D6
Carse Gray Angus 287 B8
Carse Ho Argyll 275 G8
Carseriggan Dumfries 236 C5
Carsethorn Dumfries 237 D11
Carshalton London 67 G9
Carshalton Beeches London 67 G9
Carshalton on the Hill London 67 G9
Carsington Derbys 170 E3
Carskiey Argyll 255 G7
Carsluith Dumfries 236 D6
Carsphairn Dumfries 246 E3
Carstairs S Lnrk 269 F8
Carstairs Junction S Lnrk 269 F9
Carswell Marsh Oxon 82 F4
Cartbridge Sur 50 B4
Carterhaugh Borders 261 D10
Carter Knowle S Yorks 186 E4
Carter's Clay Hants 32 C4
Carter's Green Essex 87 C8
Carter's Hill Wokingham 65 F9
Carterspiece Glos 79 C9
Carterton Oxon 82 D3
Carterway Heads Northumb 242 G2
Carthamartha Corn 12 F3
Carthew Corn 2 B5
Corn 5 D10
Carthorpe N Yorks 214 C6
Cartington Northumb 252 C2
Cartland S Lnrk 269 F7
Cartledge Derbys 186 F4
Cartmel Cumb 211 D7
Cartmel Fell Cumb 211 B8
Cartsdyke Invclyd 276 F5
Cartworth W Yorks 196 F6
Carty Port Dumfries 236 C6
Carway Carms 75 D7
Carwinley Cumb 239 C10
Carwynnen Corn 2 B5
Cary Fitzpaine Som 29 B9
Carzantic Corn 12 E3
Carzield Dumfries 247 G11
Carzise Corn 2 C3
Cascob Powys 114 D4
Cashes Green Glos 80 D4
Cashlie Perth 285 C8
Cashmoor Dorset 31 E7
Cas Mael / Puncheston Pembs 91 F10
Cassey Compton Glos 81 C9
Cassington Oxon 83 C7
Cassop Durham 234 D2
Castallack Corn 1 D5
Castell Conwy 164 B3
Denb 165 B10
Castellau Rhondda 58 B5
Castell-Howell Ceredig 93 B8
Castell nedd / Neath Neath 57 B8
Castell Newydd Emlyn / Newcastle Emlyn Carms 92 C6
Castell-y-bwch Torf 78 G3
Castell-y-rhingyll Carms 75 C9
Casterton Cumb 212 D2
Castle Devon 28 G4
Som 27 B9
Castle Acre Norf 158 F6
Castle Ashby Northants 121 F7
Castle Bolton N Yorks 223 G10
Castle Bromwich W Mid 134 F2
Castle Bytham Lincs 155 F9
Castlebythe Pembs 91 F10
Castle Caereinion Powys 130 B3
Castle Camps Cambs 106 C2
Castle Carlton Lincs 190 E5
Castle Carrock Cumb 240 F2
Castlecary N Lnrk 278 F5
Castle Cary Som 44 G6
Castle Combe Wilts 61 D10
Castlecraig Highld 301 C8
Castle Craig Borders 270 G2
Castlecroft Staffs 133 D7
Castle Donington Leics 153 D8
Castle Douglas Dumfries 237 C9
Castle Eaton Swindon 81 F10
Castle Eden Durham 234 D4
Castle End Pboro 138 B2
Castlefairn Dumfries 246 F6
Castlefields Halton 183 E8
Castle Fields Shrops 149 G10
Castle Forbes Aberds 293 B8
Castleford W Yorks 198 B2
Castle Frome Hereford 98 B3
Castle Gate Corn 1 C5
Castlegreen Shrops 130 F6
Castle Green London 68 C3
Sur 66 G3
S Yorks 197 G9
Castle Gresley Derbys 152 F5
Castlehead Renfs 267 C9
Castle Heaton Northumb 273 G8
Castle Hedingham Essex 106 D5
Castlehill Argyll 254 B4
Borders 260 B6
Highld 310 C5
S Ayrs 257 E9
W Dunb 277 F7
Castle Hill E Sus 37 B9
Gtr Man 184 C6
Kent 53 E7
Suff 108 B3
Worcs 116 F5
Castle Huntly Perth 287 E7
Castle Kennedy Dumfries 236 D3
Castlemaddy Dumfries 246 F3
Castlemartin Pembs 72 F6
Castlemilk Dumfries 238 B5
Glasgow 268 D2
Castlemorris Pembs 91 E8
Castlemorton Worcs 98 D5
Castle O'er Dumfries 248 E6
Castlerigg Cumb 229 G11
Castle Rising Norf 158 E3
Castleside Durham 233 B7
Castle Street W Yorks 196 C3
Castle Stuart Highld 301 E7
Castlethorpe M Keynes 102 C6
N Lincs 200 F3
Castleton Angus 287 C7
Argyll 275 E9
Derbys 185 E11
Gtr Man 195 E11
Moray 301 G11
Newport 59 C9
N Yorks 226 D3
Castleton Village Highld 300 E6
Castle Toward Argyll 266 B2
Castletown Ches W 166 E6
Cumb 230 E6
Dorset 17 G9
Highld 301 E7
Highld 310 C5
IoM 192 F3
Staffs 151 E8
T&W 243 F9
Castle Town W Sus 36 E2
Castletump Glos 98 F4
Castle-upon-Alun V Glam 58 E2
Castle Vale W Mid 134 E2
Castleweary Borders 249 C10
Castlewigg Dumfries 236 E6
Castley N Yorks 205 D11
Castling's Heath Suff 107 C9
Caston Norf 141 D9
Castor Pboro 138 D2
Caswell Swansea 56 D5
Catacol N Ayrs 255 C10
Cat Bank Cumb 220 F6
Catbrain S Glos 60 C5
Catbrook Mon 79 E8
Catch Flint 182 G2
Catchall Corn 1 D4
Catchems Corner W Mid 118 B4
Catchems End Worcs 116 B5
Catchgate Durham 242 G5
Catchory Highld 310 D6
Catcleugh Northumb 250 C6
Catcliffe S Yorks 186 D6
Catcomb Wilts 62 D4
Catcott Som 43 F11
Caterham Sur 51 B10
Catfield Norf 161 E7
Catfirth Shetland 313 H6
Catford London 67 E11
Catforth Lancs 202 F5
Cathays Cardiff 59 D7
Cathays Park Cardiff 59 D7
Cathcart Glasgow 267 C11
Cathedine Powys 96 F2
Catherine-de-Barnes W Mid 134 G3
Catherine Slack W Yorks 196 B5
Catherington Hants 33 E11
Catherton Shrops 116 B3
Cat Hill S Yorks 197 F8
Cathiron Warks 119 B9
Catholes Cumb 222 G3
Cathpair Borders 271 F9
Catisfield Hants 33 F8
Catley Lane Head Gtr Man 195 D11
Catley Southfield Hereford 98 C3
Catlodge Highld 291 D8
Catlowdy Cumb 239 B11
Catmere End Essex 105 D9
Catmore W Berks 64 C3
Caton Devon 13 G11
Lancs 211 G10
Caton Green Lancs 211 F10
Catrine E Ayrs 258 D2
Cat's Ash Newport 78 G5
Cat's Common Norf 160 E6
Cats Edge Staffs 169 E7
Catsfield E Sus 38 E2
Catsfield Stream E Sus 38 E2
Catsgore Som 29 B8
Catsham Som 44 G5
Catshaw S Yorks 197 G8
Catshill W Mid 133 B11
Worcs 117 C9
Cat's Hill Cross Staffs 150 C6
Catslackburn Borders 261 D8
Catslip Oxon 65 B8
Catstree Shrops 132 D4
Cattadale Argyll 274 G4
Cattal N Yorks 206 C4
Cattawade Suff 108 E2
Cattedown Plym 7 E9
Catterall Lancs 202 E5
Catterick N Yorks 224 F4
Catterick Bridge N Yorks 224 F4
Catterick Garrison N Yorks 224 F3
Catterlen Cumb 230 E5
Catterline Aberds 293 F10
Catterton N Yorks 206 D6
Catteshall Sur 50 E3
Catthorpe Leics 119 B11
Cattistock Dorset 17 B7
Cattle End Northants 102 C3
Catton Northumb 241 F8
N Yorks 215 D7
Catwick E Yorks 209 D8
Catworth Cambs 121 C11
Caudle Green Glos 80 C6
Caudlesprings Norf 141 C8
Caulcott C Beds 103 C9
Oxon 101 G10
Cauld Borders 261 G11
Cauldcoats Holdings Falk 279 F10
Cauldcots Angus 287 C10
Cauldhame Stirl 278 C2
Cauldmill Borders 262 G2
Cauldon Staffs 169 F9
Cauldon Lowe Staffs 169 F9
Cauldwells Aberds 303 D7
Caulkerbush Dumfries 237 D11
Caulside Dumfries 249 G10
Caundle Marsh Dorset 29 E11
Caunsall Worcs 132 G6
Caunton Notts 172 D2
Causeway Hants 33 E11
Hants 34 C2
Mon 60 B2
Causewayend S Lnrk 260 B2
Causeway End Cumb 210 C6
Cumb 211 B9
Dumfries 236 C6
Essex 87 B11
Wilts 62 C4
Causeway Foot W Yorks 197 E7
W Yorks 205 G7
Causeway Green W Mid 133 F9
Causewayhead Cumb 238 G4
Stirl 278 B6
Causewaywood Shrops 131 D10
Causey Durham 242 F6
Causeyend Aberds 293 B11
Causey Park Bridge Northumb 252 E5
Causeyton Aberds 293 B8
Caute Devon 24 E6
Cautley Cumb 222 G3
Cavendish Suff 106 B6
Cavendish Bridge Leics 153 D8
Cavenham Suff 124 D5
Cavers Carre Borders 262 D3
Caversfield Oxon 101 F11
Caversham Reading 65 E8
Caversham Heights Reading 65 D8
Caverswall Staffs 169 G7
Cavil E Yorks 207 G11
Cawdor Highld 301 D8
Cawkeld E Yorks 208 C5
Cawkwell Lincs 190 F3
Cawood N Yorks 207 F7
Cawsand Corn 7 E8
Cawston Norf 160 E2
Warks 119 C9
Cawthorne N Yorks 216 B5
S Yorks 197 F9
Cawthorpe Lincs 155 E11
Cawton N Yorks 216 D2
Caxton Cambs 122 F6
Caynham Shrops 115 C11
Caythorpe Lincs 172 F6
Notts 171 F11
Cayton N Yorks 217 C11
Ceallan W Isles 296 F4
Ceann a Bhaigh W Isles 296 E3
Ceann a Bhàigh W Isles 305 J4
Ceannacroc Lodge Highld 290 B4
Ceann a Deas Loch Baghasdail W Isles 297 K3
Ceann Shiphoirt W Isles 305 G4
Ceann Tarabhaigh W Isles 305 G4
Cearsiadair W Isles 304 F5
Ceathramh Meadhanach W Isles 296 D4
Cefn Newport 59 B9
Powys 148 G5
Cefn Berain Conwy 165 B7
Cefn-brith Conwy 164 E6
Cefn-bryn-brain Carms 76 C2
Cefn-bychan Swansea 56 B4
Wrex 166 G3
Cefncaeau Carms 56 B4
Cefn Canol Powys 148 C4
Cefn-coch Conwy 164 B5
Cefn Coch Powys 129 C10
Powys 148 D2
Cefn-coed-y-cymmer M Tydf 77 D9f
Cefn Cribbwr Bridgend 57 E11
Cefn Cross Bridgend 57 E11
Cefn-ddwysarn Gwyn 147 B9
Cefn Einion Shrops 130 F5
Cefneithin Carms 75 C9
Cefn-eurgain Flint 166 B2
Cefn Fforest Caerph 77 F11
Cefn Glas Bridgend 57 E11
Cefn Golau Bl Gwent 77 D10
Cefn-gorwydd Powys 95 B8
Cefn Hengoed Caerph 77 F10
Cefn-hengoed Swansea 57 B7
Cefn Llwyd Ceredig 128 G2
Cefn-mawr Wrex 166 G3
Cefnpennar Rhondda 77 E8
Cefn Rhigos Rhondda 76 D6
Cefn-y-bedd Flint 166 D4
Cefn-y-Crib Torf 78 F2
Cefn-y-Garth Swansea 76 E2
Cefn-y-pant Carms 92 F3
Cegidfa / Guilsfield Powys 148 G4
Cei-bach Ceredig 111 F8
Ceinewydd / New Quay Ceredig 111 F7
Ceint Anglesey 179 F7
Ceinws Powys 128 B5
Cellan Ceredig 94 B2
Cellarhead Staffs 169 F7
Cellarhill Kent 70 G3
Celyn-Mali Flint 165 B11
Cemaes Anglesey 178 C5
Cemmaes Powys 128 B6
Cemmaes Road / Glantwymyn Powys 128 C6
Cenarth Carms 92 C5
Cenin Gwyn 163 F7
Central Invclyd 276 F5
Central Milton Keynes M Keynes 102 D6
Ceos W Isles 304 F5
Ceres Fife 287 F8
Ceri / Kerry Powys 130 F2
Cerne Abbas Dorset 29 G11
Cerney Wick Glos 81 F9
Cerrigceinwen Anglesey 178 G6
Cerrig Llwydion Neath 57 C9
Cerrig-mân Anglesey 179 C7
Cerrigydrudion Conwy 165 F7
Cess Norf 161 F8
Cessford Borders 262 E6
Ceunant Gwyn 163 C8
Chaceley Glos 99 E7
Chaceley Hole Glos 98 E6
Chaceley Stock Glos 99 F7
Chacewater Corn 4 G4
Chackmore Bucks 102 D3
Chacombe Northants 101 C9
Chadbury Worcs 99 B10
Chadderton Gtr Man 196 F2
Chadderton Fold Gtr Man 195 F11
Chaddesden Derby 153 B7
Chaddesley Corbett Worcs 117 C7
Chaddlehanger Devon 12 F5
Chaddlewood Plym 7 D11
Chaddleworth W Berks 64 D2
Chadkirk Gtr Man 184 D6
Chadlington Oxon 100 G6
Chadshunt Warks 118 G6
Chadsmoor Staffs 151 G9
Chadstone Northants 121 F7
Chad Valley W Mid 133 F10
Chadwell Leics 154 E5
Shrops 150 G5
Chadwell End Beds 121 D11
Chadwell Heath London 68 B3
Chadwell St Mary Thurrock 68 D6
Chadwick Worcs 116 D6
Chadwick End W Mid 118 C4
Chadwick Green Mers 183 B8
Chaffcombe Som 28 E5
Chafford Hundred Thurrock 68 D5
Chagford Devon 13 D10
Chailey E Sus 36 D5
Chainbridge Cambs 139 C8
Chain Bridge Lincs 174 G4
Chainhurst Kent 53 D8
Chalbury Dorset 31 F8
Chalbury Common Dorset 31 F8
Chaldon Sur 51 B10
Chaldon Herring or East Chaldon Dorset 17 E11
Chale IoW 20 F5
Chale Green IoW 20 F5
Chalfont Common Bucks 85 G8
Chalfont Grove Bucks 85 G7
Chalfont St Giles Bucks 85 G7
Chalfont St Peter Bucks 85 G8
Chalford Glos 80 E5
Oxon 84 E2
Wilts 45 C11
Chalford Hill Glos 80 E5
Chalgrave C Beds 103 F10
Chalgrove Oxon 83 F10
Chalk Kent 69 E7
Chalk End Essex 87 C10
Chalkfoot Cumb 230 B2
Chalkhill Norf 141 C7
Chalkhouse Green Oxon 65 D8
Chalkshire Bucks 84 D4
Chalksole Kent 55 E9
Chalkway Som 28 F5
Chalkwell Kent 69 G11
Sthend 69 B11
Challaborough Devon 8 G3
Challacombe Devon 41 E7
Challister Shetland 312 G7
Challoch Dumfries 236 C5
Challock Kent 54 C4
Chalmington Dorset 29 G9
Chalton C Beds 103 F10
Hants 34 D2
Chalvedon Essex 69 B8
Chalvey Slough 66 D3
Chalvington E Sus 23 D8
Chambercombe Devon 40 D4
Chamber's Green Kent 54 E2
Champson Devon 26 B4
Chance Inn Fife 287 F7
Chancery / Rhydgaled Ceredig 111 B11
Chance's Pitch Hereford 98 C4
Chandler's Cross Herts 85 F9
Worcs 98 D5
Chandler's Ford Hants 32 C6
Chandlers Green Hants 49 B8
Channel's End Beds 122 F2
Channel Tunnel Kent 55 F7
Channerwick Shetland 313 L6
Chantry Devon 25 C9
Som 45 D8
Suff 108 C2
Chapel Corn 4 C6
Cumb 229 E10
Fife 280 C5
Chapel Allerton Som 44 C2
W Yorks 206 F2
Chapel Amble Corn 10 F5
Chapel Brampton Northants 120 D4
Chapel Chorlton Staffs 150 B6
Chapel Cleeve Som 42 E4
Chapel Cross E Sus 37 C10
Chapel End Beds 103 B11
Beds 122 F2
Cambs 138 G2
C Beds 103 C11
Ches E 167 G11
Essex 105 G11
Northants 138 F2
Warks 134 E6
Chapel-en-le-Frith Derbys 185 E9
Chapel Field Gtr Man 195 F9
Norf 161 E7
Chapel Fields W Mid 118 B6
York 207 C7
Chapelgate Lincs 157 E8
Chapel Green Herts 104 D6
Warks 119 E9
Warks 134 F5
Chapel Haddlesey N Yorks 198 B5
Chapelhall N Lnrk 268 C5
Chapel Head Cambs 138 G6
Chapelhill Dumfries 248 E3
Highld 301 B8
N Ayrs 266 G4
Perth 286 D4
Perth 286 E3
Perth 286 E6
Chapel Hill Aberds 303 F10
Glos 79 E10
Lincs 174 E2
Mon 79 F8
N Yorks 206 D2
Chapel House Lancs 194 F3
Chapel Knapp Wilts 61 F11
Chapelknowe Dumfries 239 C8
Chapel Lawn Shrops 114 B6
Chapel-le-Dale N Yorks 212 D4
Chapel Leigh Som 27 B10
Chapel Mains Borders 271 G11
Chapel Milton Derbys 185 E9
Chapel of Garioch Aberds 303 G7
Chapel of Stoneywood Aberdeen 293 B10
Chapel on Leader Borders 271 G11
Chapel Outon Dumfries 236 E6
Chapel Plaister Wilts 61 F10
Chapel Row Essex 88 E3
E Sus 23 C10
W Berks 64 F5
Chapels Blkburn 195 C7
Cumb 210 C4
Chapel St Leonards Lincs 191 G9
Chapel Stile Cumb 220 D6
Chapelthorpe W Yorks 197 D10
Chapelton Angus 287 C10
Devon 25 B9
Highld 291 B11
S Lnrk 268 F3
Chapelton Row Dumfries 237 E8
Chapeltown Blkburn 195 D8
Moray 302 G2
S Yorks 186 B5
W Yorks 206 F2
Chapel Town Corn 5 D7
Chapman's Hill Worcs 117 B9
Chapmanslade Wilts 45 D10
Chapman's Town E Sus 23 B10
Chapmans Well Devon 12 C3
Chapmore End Herts 86 B4
Chappel Essex 107 F7
Charaton Cross Corn 6 B6
Charcott Kent 52 D4
Chard Som 28 F4
Chard Junction Dorset 28 G4
Chardleigh Green Som 28 E4
Chardstock Devon 28 G4
Charfield S Glos 80 G2
Charfield Green S Glos 80 G2
Charfield Hill S Glos 80 G2
Charford Worcs 117 D9
Chargrove Glos 80 B6
Charing Kent 54 D3
Charing Cross Dorset 31 E10
Charing Heath Kent 54 D2
Charing Hill Kent 54 C3
Charingworth Glos 100 D4
Charlbury Oxon 82 B5
Charlcombe Bath 61 F8
Charlcutt Wilts 62 D3
Charlecote Warks 118 F5
Charlemont W Mid 133 E10
Charles Devon 41 G7
Charles Bottom Devon 41 G7
Charlesfield Borders 262 D3
Dumfries 238 D5
Charleshill Sur 49 E11
Charleston Angus 287 C7
Renfs 267 C9
Charlestown Aberdeen 293 C11
Corn 5 E10
Derbys 185 C8
Dorset 17 F9
Fife 279 E11
Gtr Man 195 G10
Gtr Man 195 G11
Highld 299 B8
Highld 300 E6
W Yorks 196 B3
W Yorks 205 F9
Charlestown of Aberlour Moray 302 E2
Charles Tye Suff 125 G10
Charlesworth Derbys 185 C8
Charleton Devon 8 G5
Charlinch Som 43 F8
Charlottetown Fife 286 F6
Charlton Hants 47 D11
Herts 104 F3
London 68 D2
Northants 101 D10
Northumb 251 F8
Oxon 64 B2
Redcar 226 B2
Som 28 B3
Som 44 E6
Som 45 C7
Sur 66 F5
Telford 149 G11
Wilts 30 C6
Wilts 46 B6
Wilts 62 B3
Worcs 99 B10
Worcs 116 C6
W Sus 34 E5
Charlton Abbots Glos 99 G10
Charlton Adam Som 29 B8
Charlton-All-Saints Wilts 31 C11
Charltonbrook S Yorks 186 B4
Charlton Down Dorset 17 C9
Charlton Horethorne Som 29 C11
Charlton Kings Glos 99 G9
Charlton Mackrell Som 29 B8
Charlton Marshall Dorset 30 G5
Charlton Musgrove Som 30 B2
Charlton on Otmoor Oxon 83 B9
Charlton on the Hill Dorset 30 G5
Charlton Park Glos 99 G9
Charlton St Peter Wilts 46 B6
Charlwood E Sus 51 G11
Hants 49 G7
Sur 51 E8
Charlynch Som 43 F8
Charminster Bmouth 19 C8
Dorset 17 C9
Charmouth Dorset 16 C3
Charnage Wilts 45 G10
Charndon Bucks 102 G3
Charnes Staffs 150 C5
Charney Bassett Oxon 82 G5
Charnock Green Lancs 194 D5
Charnock Hall S Yorks 186 E5
Charnock Richard Lancs 194 D5
Charsfield Suff 126 F5
Chart Corner Kent 53 C9
Charter Alley Hants 48 B5
Charterhouse Som 44 B3
Chartershall Stirl 278 C6
Charterville Allotments Oxon 82 C4
Chartham Kent 54 C6
Chartham Hatch Kent 54 B6
Chart Hill Kent 53 D9
Chartridge Bucks 84 E6
Chart Sutton Kent 53 D10
Charvil Wokingham 65 D9
Charwelton Northants 119 F10
Chase Cross London 87 G8
Chase End Street Worcs 98 D5
Chase Hill S Glos 61 B8
Chase Terrace Staffs 133 B10
Chasetown Staffs 133 B10
Chastleton Oxon 100 F4
Chasty Devon 24 G4
Chatburn Lancs 203 E11
Chatcull Staffs 150 C5
Chatford Shrops 131 B9
Chatham Caerph 59 B8
Medway 69 F9
Chatham Green Essex 88 B2
Chathill Northumb 264 D5
Chat Hill W Yorks 205 G8
Chatley Worcs 117 E7
Chattenden Medway 69 E9
Chatter End Essex 105 F9
Chatteris Cambs 139 F7
Chatterley Staffs 168 E4
Chattern Hill Sur 66 E5
Chatterton Lancs 195 D9
Chattisham Suff 107 C11
Chattle Hill Warks 134 E3
Chatto Borders 263 F7
Chatton Northumb 264 D3
Chaulden Herts 85 D8
Chaul End C Beds 103 G11
Chavel Shrops 149 G8
Chavenage Green Glos 80 F5
Chavey Down Brack 65 F11
Chawleigh Devon 26 E2
Chawley Oxon 83 E7
Chawson Worcs 117 E7
Chawston Beds 122 F3
Chawton Hants 49 F8
Chaxhill Glos 80 C2
Chazey Heath Oxon 65 D7
Cheadle Gtr Man 184 D5
Staffs 169 G8
Cheadle Heath Gtr Man 184 D5
Cheadle Hulme Gtr Man 184 D5
Cheadle Park Staffs 169 G8
Cheam London 67 G8
Cheapside Herts 105 E8
Sur 50 B4
Windsor 66 F2
Chearsley Bucks 84 C2
Chebsey Staffs 151 D7
Checkendon Oxon 65 C7
Checkley Ches E 168 F2
Hereford 97 D11
Staffs 151 B10
Checkley Green Ches E 168 F2
Chedburgh Suff 124 F5
Cheddar Som 44 C3
Cheddington Bucks 84 B6
Cheddleton Staffs 169 E7
Cheddleton Heath Staffs 169 E7
Cheddon Fitzpaine Som 28 B2
Chedglow Wilts 80 G6
Chedgrave Norf 143 D7
Chedington Dorset 29 F7
Chediston Suff 127 B7
Chediston Green Suff 127 B7
Chedworth Glos 81 C9
Chedworth Laines Glos 81 C8
Chedzoy Som 43 F10
Cheeklaw Borders 272 E5
Cheeseman's Green Kent 54 F4
Cheetam Hill Gtr Man 195 G10
Cheglinch Devon 40 E4
Chegworth Kent 53 C10
Cheldon Devon 26 E2
Chelfham Devon 40 F6
Chelford Ches E 184 G4
Chellaston Derby 153 C7
Chell Heath Stoke 168 E5
Chellington Beds 121 F9
Chells Herts 104 F5
Chelmarsh Shrops 132 F4
Chelmer Village Essex 88 D2
Chelmick Shrops 131 E9
Chelmondiston Suff 108 D4
Chelmorton Derbys 169 B10
Chelmsford Essex 88 D2
Chelmsine Som 27 D11
Chelmsley Wood W Mid 134 F3
Chelsea London 67 D9
Chelsfield London 68 G3
Chelsham Sur 51 B11
Chelston Som 27 C11
Torbay 9 C7
Chelston Heathfield Som 27 C11
Chelsworth Suff 107 B9
Chelsworth Common Suff 107 B9
Cheltenham Glos 99 G8
Chelveston Northants 121 D9
Chelvey N Som 60 F3
Chelvey Batch N Som 60 F3
Chelwood Bath 60 G6
Chelwood Common E Sus 36 B6
Chelwood Gate E Sus 36 B6
Chelworth Wilts 81 G7
Chelworth Lower Green Wilts 81 G9
Chelworth Upper Green Wilts 81 G9
Chelynch Som 45 E7
Chemistry Shrops 167 G8
Cheney Longville Shrops 131 G8
Chenhalls Corn 2 B3
Chenies Bucks 85 F8
Cheny Longville Shrops 131 G8
Chepstow Mon 79 G8
Chequerbent Gtr Man 195 F7
Chequerfield W Yorks 198 C3
Chequers Corner Norf 139 B9
Chequertree Kent 54 F4
Cherhill Wilts 62 E4
Cherington Glos 80 F6
Warks 100 D5
Cheristow Devon 24 B3
Cheriton Devon 41 D8
Hants 33 B9
Kent 55 F7
Swansea 56 C3
Cheriton Bishop Devon 13 C11
Cheriton Cross Devon 13 C11
Cheriton Fitzpaine Devon 26 F5
Cheriton or Stackpole Elidor Pembs 73 F7
Cherrington Telford 150 E3
Cherrybank Perth 286 E5
Cherry Burton E Yorks 208 E5
Cherry Green Essex 105 F11
Herts 105 F7
Cherry Hinton Cambs 123 F9
Cherry Orchard Shrops 149 G9
Worcs 117 G7
Cherry Tree Blkburn 195 B7
Gtr Man 185 C7
Cherrytree Hill Derby 153 B7
Cherry Willingham Lincs 189 G8
Chertsey Sur 66 F4
Chertsey Meads Sur 66 F5
Cheselbourne Dorset 17 B11
Chesham Bucks 85 E7
Gtr Man 195 E10
Chesham Bois Bucks 85 F7
Cheshunt Herts 86 E5
Chesley Kent 69 G11
Cheslyn Hay Staffs 133 B9
Chessetts Wood Warks 118 C3
Chessington London 67 G7
Chessmount Bucks 85 E7
Chestall Staffs 151 G11
Chester Ches W 166 B6
Chesterblade Som 45 E7
Chesterfield Derbys 186 G5
Staffs 134 B2
Chesterhill Midloth 271 B7
Chesterhope Northumb 251 F9
Chesterknowes Borders 262 D2
Chester-le-Street Durham 243 G7
Chester Moor Durham 233 B11
Chesters Borders 262 E4
Borders 262 G4
Chesterton Cambs 123 E9
Cambs 138 D2
Glos 81 E8
Oxon 101 G11
Shrops 132 D5
Staffs 168 F4
Warks 118 F6
Chesterton Green Warks 118 F6
Chesterwood Northumb 241 D8
Chestfield Kent 70 F6
Chestnut Hill Cumb 229 G11
Chestnut Street Kent 69 G11
Cheston Devon 8 D3
Cheswardine Shrops 150 D4
Cheswell Telford 150 F4
Cheswick Northumb 273 F10
Cheswick Buildings Northumb 273 F10
Cheswick Green W Mid 118 B2
Chetnole Dorset 29 F10
Chettiscombe Devon 27 E7
Chettisham Cambs 139 G10
Chettle Dorset 31 E7
Chetton Shrops 132 E3
Chetwode Bucks 102 F2
Chetwynd Aston Telford 150 F5
Cheveley Cambs 124 E3
Chevening Kent 52 B3
Cheverell's Green Herts 85 B9
Chevin End W Yorks 205 E9
Chevington Suff 124 F5
Chevithorne Devon 27 D7
Chew Magna Bath 60 G5
Chew Moor Gtr Man 195 F7
Chew Stoke Bath 60 G5
Chewton Keynsham Bath 61 F7
Chewton Mendip Som 44 C5
Cheylesmore W Mid 118 B6
Chichacott Devon 13 B8
Chicheley M Keynes 103 B8
Chichester W Sus 22 C5
Chickenley W Yorks 197 C9
Chickerell Dorset 17 E8
Chicklade Wilts 46 G2
Chickney Essex 105 F11
Chicksands C Beds 104 D2
Chicksgrove Wilts 46 G3
Chickward Hereford 114 G5
Chidden Hants 33 D11
Chiddingfold Sur 50 F3
Chiddingly E Sus 23 C8
Chiddingstone Kent 52 D3
Chiddingstone Causeway Kent 52 D4
Chiddingstone Hoath Kent 52 E3
Chideock Dorset 16 C4
Chidgley Som 42 F4
Chidham W Sus 22 C3
Chidswell W Yorks 197 C9
Chieveley W Berks 64 E3
Chignall St James Essex 87 D11
Chignall Smealy Essex 87 C11
Chigwell Essex 86 G6
Chigwell Row Essex 87 G7
Chilbolton Hants 47 F11
Chilbolton Down Hants 48 F2
Chilbridge Dorset 31 G7
Chilcomb Hants 33 B8
Chilcombe Dorset 16 C6
Som 42 F6
Chilcompton Som 44 C6
Chilcote Leics 152 G5
Childerditch Essex 68 B6
Childerley Gate Cambs 123 F7
Childer Thornton Ches W 182 F5
Child Okeford Dorset 30 E4
Childrey Oxon 63 B11
Childsbridge Kent 52 B5
Child's Ercall Shrops 150 E3
Child's Hill London 67 B8
Childswickham Worcs 99 D11
Childwall Mers 182 D6
Childwick Bury Herts 85 C10
Childwick Green Herts 85 C10
Chilfrome Dorset 17 B7
Chilgrove W Sus 34 E4
Chilham Kent 54 C5
Chilhampton Wilts 46 G5
Chilla Devon 24 G6
Chillaton Devon 12 E4
Chillenden Kent 55 C9
Chillerton IoW 20 E5
Chillesford Suff 127 G7
Chillingham Northumb 264 D3
Chillington Devon 8 G5
Som 28 E5
Chillmill Kent 53 E7
Chilmark Wilts 46 G3
Chilmington Green Kent 54 E3
Chilsham E Sus 23 C10
Chilson Oxon 82 B4
Som 28 G4
Chilson Common Som 28 G4
Chilsworthy Corn 12 G4
Devon 24 F4
Chiltern Green Beds 85 B10
Chilthorne Domer Som 29 D8
Chiltington E Sus 36 D5
Chilton Bucks 83 C11
Durham 233 F11
Kent 71 G11
Oxon 64 B3
Suff 107 C7
Chilton Candover Hants 48 E5
Chilton Cantelo Som 29 C9
Chilton Foliat Wilts 63 E10
Chilton Lane Durham 234 E2
Chilton Moor T&W 234 B2
Chilton Polden Som 43 F11
Chilton Street Suff 106 B5
Chilton Trinity Som 43 F9
Chilvers Coton Warks 135 E7
Chilwell Notts 153 B10
Chilworth Hants 32 D6
Sur 50 D4
Chilworth Old Village Hants 32 D6
Chimney Oxon 82 E5
Chimney-end Oxon 82 B4
Chimney Street Suff 106 B4
Chineham Hants 49 C7
Chingford London 86 G5
Chingford Green London 86 G5
Chingford Hatch London 86 G5
Chinley Derbys 185 E8
Chinley Head Derbys 185 E9
Chinnor Oxon 84 E3
Chipley Som 27 C10
Chipmans Platt Glos 80 D3
Chipnall Shrops 150 C4
Chippenhall Green Suff 126 B5
Chippenham Cambs 124 D3
Wilts 62 E2
Chipperfield Herts 85 E8
Chipping Herts 105 E7
Lancs 203 E8
Chipping Barnet London 86 F2
Chipping Campden Glos 100 D3
Chipping Hill Essex 88 B4
Chipping Norton Oxon 100 F6
Chipping Ongar Essex 87 E8
Chipping Sodbury S Glos 61 C8
Chipping Warden Northants 101 B9
Chipstable Som 27 B8
Chipstead Kent 52 B3
Sur 51 B9
Chirbury Shrops 130 D5
Chirk Bank Shrops 148 B5
Chirk Green Wrex 148 B5
Chirk / Y Waun Wrex 148 B5
Chirmorrie S Ayrs 236 B4
Chirnside Borders 273 D7
Chirnsidebridge Borders 273 D7
Chirton T&W 243 D8
Wilts 46 B5
Chisbridge Cross Bucks 65 B10
Chisbury Wilts 63 F9
Chiselborough Som 29 E7
Chiseldon Swindon 63 D7
Chiserley W Yorks 196 B4
Chislehampton Oxon 83 F9
Chislehurst London 68 E2
Chislehurst West London 68 E2
Chislet Kent 71 G8
Chislet Forstal Kent 71 G8
Chiswell Dorset 17 G9
Chiswell Green Herts 85 E10
Chiswick London 67 D8
Chiswick End Cambs 105 B7
Chisworth Derbys 185 C7
Chitcombe E Sus 38 C4
Chithurst W Sus 34 C4
Chittering Cambs 123 C9
Chitterley Devon 26 G6
Chitterne Wilts 46 E3
Chittlehamholt Devon 25 C11
Chittlehampton Devon 25 B10
Chittoe Wilts 62 F3
Chitts Hills Essex 107 F9
Chitty Kent 71 G8
Chivelstone Devon 9 G10
Chivenor Devon 40 G4
Chivery Bucks 84 D6
Chobham Sur 66 G3
Choicelee Borders 272 E4
Cholderton Wilts 47 E8
Cholesbury Bucks 84 D6
Chollerford Northumb 241 C10
Chollerton Northumb 241 C10
Cholmondeston Ches E 167 C10
Cholsey Oxon 64 B5
Cholstrey Hereford 115 F9
Cholwell Bath 44 B6
Chop Gate N Yorks 225 F11
Choppington Northumb 253 G7
Chopwell T&W 242 F4
Chorley Ches E 167 E9
Lancs 194 D5
Shrops 132 G3
Staffs 151 G11
Chorley Common W Sus 34 B4
Chorleywood Herts 85 F8
Chorleywood Bottom Herts 85 F8
Chorleywood West Herts 85 F8
Chorlton Ches E 168 E2
Chorlton-cum-Hardy Gtr Man 184 C4
Chorlton Lane Ches W 167 F7
Choulton Shrops 131 F7
Chowdene T&W 243 F7
Chowley Ches W 167 D7
Chownes Mead W Sus 36 C4
Chreagain Highld 289 C10
Chrishall Essex 105 D8
Christchurch Cambs 139 D9
Dorset 19 C9
Glos 79 C9
Newport 59 B10
Christian Malford Wilts 62 D3
Christleton Ches W 166 B6
Christmas Common Oxon 84 G2
Christon N Som 43 B11
Christon Bank Northumb 264 E6
Christow Devon 14 D2
Chryston N Lnrk 278 G3
Chub Tor Devon 7 B10
Chuck Hatch E Sus 52 G3
Chudleigh Devon 14 F3
Chudleigh Knighton Devon 14 F2
Chulmleigh Devon 25 E11
Chunal Derbys 185 C8
Church Lancs 195 B8
Churcham Glos 80 B3
Church Aston Telford 150 F4
Churchbank Shrops 114 B6
Church Brampton Northants 120 D4
Churchbridge Corn 6 D4
Staffs 133 B9
Church Brough Cumb 222 C5
Church Broughton Derbys 152 C4
Church Charwelton Northants 119 F10
Church Clough Lancs 204 F3
Church Common Hants 34 B2
Church Coombe Corn 4 G3
Church Cove Corn 2 G6
Church Crookham Hants 49 C10
Churchdown Glos 80 B5
Church Eaton Staffs 150 F6
Churchend Essex 89 G8
Essex 106 G2
Glos 80 D3
Reading 65 E7
S Glos 80 G2
Church End Barnet 86 G2
Beds 121 G12
Beds 122 F2
Brent 67 C8
Bucks 84 B6
Bucks 84 D2
Cambs 121 C11
Cambs 123 C7
Cambs 123 D7
Cambs 138 G4
Cambs 139 B7
C Beds 85 B8
C Beds 103 E9
C Beds 103 G9
C Beds 104 D3
C Beds 122 G3
Essex 88 B2
Essex 105 C11
Essex 105 F11
Essex 106 F4
E Yorks 209 C7
Glos 80 D2
Glos 99 D7
Hants 49 B7
Herts 85 C10
Herts 85 F8
Herts 104 E5
Herts 105 G8
Lincs 156 C4
Lincs 190 B6
Norf 157 F10
Oxon 82 D5
Oxon 100 E6
Suff 108 D4
Sur 50 B5
Warks 134 E4
Warks 134 E5
Wilts 62 D4
W Mid 119 B7
Worcs 98 C6
Church Enstone Oxon 101 G7
Churches Green E Sus 23 B10
Church Fenton N Yorks 206 F6
Churchfield Hereford 98 B4
W Mid 133 E10
Churchfields Wilts 31 B10
Churchgate Herts 86 E4
Churchgate Street Essex 87 C7
Church Green Devon 15 B9
Norf 141 E11
Church Gresley Derbys 152 F5
Church Hanborough Oxon 82 C6
Church Hill Ches W 167 C10
Pembs 73 C7
Staffs 151 G10
W Mid 133 D9
Worcs 117 D11
Church Hougham Kent 55 E9
Church Houses N Yorks 226 F3
Churchill Devon 28 G4

Devon 40 E5
N Som 44 B2
Oxon 100 G5
Worcs 117 B7
Worcs 117 G8
Churchill Green N Som 60 G2
Churchinford Som 28 E2
Church Knowle Dorset . . .18 E4
Church Laneham Notts . . .188 F4
Church Langton Leics 136 E4
Church Lawford Warks . . .119 B8
Church Lawton ChesE . . .168 D4
Church Leigh Staffs 151 B10
Church Lench Worcs 117 G10
Church Mayfield Staffs 169 G11
Church Minshull
ChesE 167 C11
Churchmoor Rough
Shrops 131 F8
Church Norton WSus 22 D5
Church Oakley Hants 48 C5
Churchover Warks 135 G8
Churchtown Corn 11 F7
Cumb 230 C3
Derbys 170 C3
Devon 24 G3
Devon 41 E7
IoM 192 C5
Lancs 202 E6
Mers 193 D11
Shrops 130 F5
Som 42 F3
Church Town Corn 4 G3
Leics 153 F7
N Lincs 199 F9
Sur 51 C11
Church Village Rhondda . .58 B5
Church Warsop Notts 171 B9
Church Westcote Glos . . .100 G5
Church Whitfield Kent 55 D10
Church Wilne Derbys 153 C8
Churchwood WSus 35 D8
Churnet Grange Staffs 169 E7
Churnsike Lodge
Northumb 240 B5
Churscombe Torbay 9 C7
Churston Ferrers Torbay . . .9 C8
Churt Sur 49 F11
Churton ChesW 166 D6
Churwell W Yorks 197 B9
Chute Cadley Wilts 47 C10
Chute Standen Wilts 47 C10
Chweffordd Conwy 180 G4
Chwilog Gwyn 145 B8
Chwitffordd / Whitford
Flint 181 F10
Chyandour Corn 1 C5
Chyanvounder Corn 2 E5
Chycoose Corn 3 B8
Chynhale Corn 2 C4
Chynoweth Corn 2 C2
Chyvarloe Corn 2 E5
Cicelyford Mon 79 E8
Cilan Uchaf Gwyn 144 E5
Cilcain Flint 165 B11
Cilcennin Ceredig 111 E10
Cilcewydd Powys 130 C4
Cilfor Gwyn 146 B2
Cilfrew Neath 76 E3
Cilfynydd Rhondda 77 G9
Cilgerran Pembs 92 C3
Cilgwyn Carms 94 E2
Ceredig 92 C6
Gwyn 163 E7
Pembs 91 D11
Ciliau Aeron Ceredig 111 F9
Cill Amhlaidh WIsles 297 G3
Cill Donnain WIsles 297 J3
Cille Bhrighde WIsles . . .297 K3
Cille Eireabhagh WIsles 297 G4
Cille Pheadair WIsles . . .297 K3
Cilmaengwyn Neath 76 D2
Cilmery Powys 113 G10
Cilsan Carms 93 G11
Ciltalgarth Gwyn 164 G5
Ciltwrch Powys 96 C3
Cilybebyll Neath 76 E2
Cil y coed / Caldicot
Mon 60 B3
Cilycwm Carms 94 D5
Cimla Neath 57 B9
Cinderford Glos 79 C11
Cinderhill Derbys 170 F5
Nottingham 171 G8
Cinder Hill GtrMan 195 F9
Kent 52 D4
WMid 133 E8
WSus 36 B5
Cinnamon Brow Warr. .183 C10
Cippenham Slough 66 C2
Cippyn Pembs 92 B2
Circebost WIsles 304 E3
Cirencester Glos 81 E8
Ciribhig WIsles 304 D3
City London 67 C10
Powys 130 F4
VGlam 58 D3
City Dulas Anglesey 179 D7
Clabhach Argyll 288 D3
Clachaig Argyll 276 E2
Highld 292 B2
N Ayrs 255 D10
Clachan Argyll 255 B8
Argyll 275 B8
Argyll 284 F5
Argyll 289 E10
Highld 295 B4
Highld 298 C4
Highld 307 L6
WIsles 297 G3
Clachaneasy Dumfries . . .236 B5
Clachanmore Dumfries. . .236 E2
Clachan na Luib
WIsles 296 E4
Clachan of Campsie
EDunb 278 F2
Clachan of Glendaruel
Argyll 275 E10
Clachan-Seil Argyll 275 B8
Clachan Strachur Argyll 284 G4
Clachbrain Angus 292 G5
Clachtoll Highld. 307 G5
Clackmannan Clack 279 C8
Clackmarras Moray 302 D2
Clacton-on-Sea Essex . . .89 B11
Cladach NArs 256 B2
Cladach Chairinis
WIsles 296 F4

Cladach Chireboist
WIsles 296 E3
Claddach Argyll 254 B2
Claddach-knockline
WIsles 296 E3
Cladich Argyll 284 E4
Cladich Steading Argyll 284 E4
Cladswell Worcs 117 F10
Claggan Highld 289 E8
Highld 290 F3
Claigan Highld 298 D2
Claines Worcs 117 F7
Clandown Bath 45 B7
Clanfield Hants 33 D11
Oxon 82 E3
Clanking Bath 84 D4
Clanville Hants 47 D10
Som 44 G6
Wilts 62 D2
Claonaig Argyll 255 B9
Claonel Highld 309 J5
Clapgate Dorset 31 G8
Herts 105 G8
Clapham Beds 121 G10
Devon 14 D3
London 67 D9
N Yorks 212 F4
WSus 35 F9
Clapham Green Beds . .121 G10
N Yorks 205 B10
Clapham Hill Kent 70 G6
Clapham Park London . . .67 D9
Clap Hill Kent 54 F5
Clapper Corn 10 G6
Clapper Hill Kent 53 F10
Clappers Borders 273 D8
Clappersgate Cumb 221 E7
Clapton Som 28 E6
Som 44 C6
WBerks 63 E11
Clapton in Gordano
N Som 60 E3
Clapton-on-the-Hill
Glos 81 B11
Clapton Park London 67 B11
Clapworthy Devon 25 C11
Clarach Ceredig 128 G2
Clarack Aberds 292 D6
Clarborough Notts. 188 E2
Clardon Highld. 310 C5
Clare Oxon 83 F11
Suff 106 B5
Clarebrand Dumfries 237 C9
Claregate W Mid 133 C7
Claremont Park Sur 66 G6
Claremount W Yorks 196 B5
Clarencefield Dumfries. . .238 D3
Clarence Park N Som 59 G10
Clarendon Park
Leicester 135 C11
Clareston Pembs. 73 C7
Clarilaw Borders 262 D3
Borders 262 F2
Clarken Green Hants. 48 C5
Clark Green ChesE 184 F6
Clarksfield GtrMan 196 G2
Clark's Green Sur. 51 F7
Clarkston ERenf 267 D11
N Lanrk 268 B5
Clase Swansea 57 B7
Clashandorran Highld. . . .300 E5
Clashcoig Highld. 309 K6
Clashedy Highld 308 C6
Clashgour Argyll 284 C6
Clashindarroch Aberds . . .302 F4
Clashmore Highld. 306 F5
Highld 309 L7
Clashnessie Highld. 306 F5
Clashnoir Moray 302 G2
Clate Shetland 313 G7
Clatford Wilts 63 F7
Clatford Oakcuts Hants . .47 F10
Clathy Perth 286 F3
Clatt Aberds 302 G5
Clatter Powys. 129 D9
Clatterford IoW 20 D5
Clatterford End Essex 87 C10
Essex 87 D9
Essex 87 E8
Clatterin Bridge Aberds . .293 F8
Clatto Fife 287 F8
Clatworthy Som 42 G5
Claughton Lancs 202 E6
Lancs 211 F11
Mers 182 D4
Clavelshay Som 43 G9
Claverdon Warks 118 E3
Claverham N Som 60 F2
Claverhambury Essex. 86 E6
Clavering Essex 105 E9
Claverley Shrops 132 E5
Claverton Bath 61 G9
Claverton Down Bath 61 G9
Clawdd-côch VGlam 58 D5
Clawdd-newydd Denb . . .165 E9
Clawdd Poncen Denb 165 G10
Clawthorpe Cumb 211 D10
Clawton Devon 12 B3
Claxby Lincs 189 C10
Lincs 191 G7
Claxby St Andrew Lincs .191 G7
Claxton Norf 142 C4
NYorks 216 G3
Claybokie Aberds 292 D2
Claybrooke Magna Leics 135 F9
Claybrooke Parva Leics . .135 F9
Clay Common Suff 143 G9
Clay Coton Northants 119 B11
Clay Cross Derbys. 170 C5
Claydon Glos 99 E8
Oxon 119 G9
Suff 126 G2
Clay End Herts 104 F6
Claygate Dumfries 239 B9
Kent 52 C6
Kent 53 E8
Sur. 67 G7
Claygate Cross Kent 52 B6
Clayhall Hants 21 B8
London 86 G6
Clayhanger Devon 27 C8
WMid 133 C10
Worcs 98 B6
York 197 C7
Clayhidon Devon 27 D11
Clayhill ESus 38 C4
Hants 32 F4
Clay Hill Bristol 60 E6
London 86 F4
WBerks 64 E5
Clayhithe Cambs 123 E10
Clayholes Angus 287 D9
Clay Lake Lincs 156 E5
Clayland Stirl 277 D11
Clay Mills Derbys. 152 D5

Clayock Highld 310 D5
Claypit Hill Cambs 123 G7
Claypits Devon 27 B7
Glos 80 D3
Kent 55 B8
Suff 140 G4
Claypole Lincs 172 F5
Clayton GtrMan 184 B5
Staffs 168 G5
SYorks 198 F3
WSus 36 E3
WYorks 205 G8
Clayton Brook Lancs 194 C5
Clayton Green Lancs 194 C5
Clayton Heights
WYorks 205 G8
Clayton-le-Dale Lancs . .203 G9
Clayton-le-Moors
Lancs 203 G10
Clayton-le-Woods
Lancs 194 C5
Clayton West W Yorks . . .197 E9
Clayworth Notts 188 D2
Cleadale Highld 294 G6
Cleadon T&W 243 E9
Cleadon Park T&W 243 E9
Cleat Orkney 314 H4
Orkney 314 H4
Cleatlam Durham 224 B2
Cleator Cumb 219 C10
Cleator Moor Cumb 219 B10
Cleave Devon 28 G2
Clebrig Highld 308 F5
Cleckheaton W Yorks 197 B7
Cleddon Mon 79 E8
Cleddon Shrops 131 G11
Cleedownton Shrops 131 G11
Cleehill Shrops 115 B11
Cleekhimin N Lanrk 268 D5
Cleemarsh Shrops 131 G11
Clee St Margaret
Shrops 131 G11
Cleestanton Shrops 115 B11
Cleethorpes NELincs. . . .201 F10
Cleeton St Mary Shrops . .116 B2
Suff 125 E9
Cleeve N Som 60 F3
Oxon 64 C6
Cleeve Hill Glos 99 F9
Cleeve Prior Worcs 99 B11
Cleghorn SLanrk 269 F8
Clegyrnant Powys 129 B8
Clehonger Hereford 97 D9
Cleirwy / Clyro Powys . . .96 C4
Cleish Perth 279 B11
Cleland N Lanrk 268 D5
Clements End Glos 79 D9
Clement's End CBeds 85 B8
Clement Street Kent 68 E4
Clench Wilts 63 G7
Clench Common Wilts . . .63 F7
Clenchwarton Norf 157 E11
Clennell Northumb 251 B10
Clent Worcs 117 B8
Cleobury Mortimer
Shrops 116 B3
Cleobury North Shrops . .132 F2
Cleongart Argyll 255 D7
Clephanton Highld. 301 D8
Clerkenwater Corn 5 B11
Clerkenwell London 67 C10
Clerk Green W Yorks 197 C8
Clerklands Borders 262 E2
Clermiston Edin 280 G3
Clestrain Orkney 314 F3
Cleuch Head Borders 262 G3
Cleughbrae Dumfries 238 C3
Clevancy Wilts 62 D5
Clevans Renfs 267 B7
Clevedon N Som 60 E2
Cleveley Oxon 101 G7
Cleveleys Lancs 202 E2
Cleverton Wilts 62 B3
Clevis Bridgend 57 F11
Clewer Som 44 C2
Clewer Green Windsor . . .66 D2
Clewer New Town
Windsor 66 D3
Clewer Village Windsor . . .66 D3
Cley next the Sea Norf . . .177 E8
Cliaid WIsles 297 L2
Cliasmol WIsles 305 H2
Cliburn Cumb 231 G7
Click Mill Orkney. 314 D3
Cliddesden Hants 48 C6
Cliff Derbys 185 D8
Warks 134 D4
Cliffburn Angus. 287 C10
Cliffe Lancs. 203 G10
Medway 69 D8
NYorks 207 G9
NYorks 224 B4
Cliff End ESus 38 E5
WYorks 196 B6
Cliffe Woods Medway 69 E8
Clifford Devon 24 C4
Hereford 96 B4
WYorks 206 E4
Clifford Chambers
Warks 118 G3
Clifford's Mesne Glos . . .98 G4
Cliffs End Kent 71 G10
Cliffstown Sthend. 69 B11
Clifton Bristol 60 E5
CBeds 104 D2
ChesW 183 F8
Cumb 230 F6
Derbys 169 G11
Devon 40 E5
GtrMan 195 G9
Lancs 202 G5
Nmbld 252 G6
Nottingham 153 C11
Oxon 101 D9
Stirl 285 D7
SYorks 186 C6
Worcs 98 B6
Worcs 117 C7
York 207 C7
Clifton Campville Staffs 152 G5
Cliftoncote Borders 263 E8
Clifton Green GtrMan . . .195 G9
Clifton Hampden Oxon . . .83 F8
Clifton Junction
GtrMan 195 G9
Clifton Manor CBeds . . .104 D3
Clifton Maybank Dorset . .29 E9
Clifton Moor York. 207 B7
Clifton Reynes
MKeynes 121 G8
Clifton upon Dunsmore
Warks 119 B10

Clifton upon Teme
Worcs 116 E4
Cliftonville Kent 71 E11
N Lnrk 268 B4
Clint N Yorks 205 B11
Climping WSus 35 G8
Climpy S Lnrk 269 D8
Clink Som 45 D9
Clinkham Wood Mers 183 B8
Clint N Yorks 205 B11
Clint Green Norf 159 G10
Clintmains Borders 262 C4
Cliobh WIsles 304 E2
Clipiau Gwyn 146 G6
Clippesby Norf 161 G8
Clippings Green Norf 159 G10
Clipsham Rutland 155 F9
Clipston Northants 136 G4
Notts 154 C2
Clipstone C Beds 103 F8
Clitheroe Lancs 203 E10
Cliuthar WIsles 305 J3
Clive Ches W 167 B11
Shrops 149 E10
Clive Green ChesW 167 C11
Clive Vale ESus. 38 E4
Clivocast Shetland 312 C8
Clixby Lincs 200 G6
Cloatley Wilts 81 G7
Cloatley End Wilts 81 G7
Clocaenog Denb 165 E9
Clochan Aberds 303 E9
Moray 302 C4
Clock Face Mers. 183 C8
Clock House London 67 G9
Clockmill Borders 272 E5
Clock Mills Hereford 96 B5
Cloddiau Powys 130 B4
Cloddymoss Moray 301 D9
Clodock Hereford 96 F6
Cloford Som 45 E8
Cloford Common Som . . .45 E8
Cloigyn Carms 74 C6
Clola Aberds 303 E10
Clophill CBeds 103 D11
Clopton Northants 137 G11
Suff 126 G4
Clopton Corner Suff 126 G4
Clopton Green Suff 124 G5
Suff 125 E9
Closeburn Dumfries 247 E9
Close Clark IoM 192 E3
Close House Durham 233 F10
Closworth Som 29 E9
Clothall Herts 104 E5
Clothall Common Herts . .104 E5
Clotton ChesW 167 C8
Clotton Common
Ches W 167 C8
Cloudesley Bush Warks . .135 F9
Clouds Hereford 97 D11
Cloud Side Staffs 168 C6
Clough GtrMan 196 D2
GtrMan 196 E2
WYorks 196 E5
Clough Dene Durham 242 F5
Cloughfold Lancs 195 C10
Clough Foot W Yorks 196 C2
Clough Hall Staffs 168 E4
Clough Head W Yorks . . .196 C5
Cloughton N Yorks 227 G10
Cloughton Newlands
N Yorks 227 F10
Clounlaid Highld 289 D9
Clousta Shetland 313 H5
Clouston Orkney 314 E2
Clova Aberds 302 G4
Angus 292 F5
Clovelly Devon 24 C4
Clove Lodge Durham 223 B8
Clovenfords Borders 261 B10
Clovenstone Aberds 293 B9
Cloves Moray 301 C11
Clovullin Highld 290 G2
Clowance Wood Corn. 2 C4
Clow Bridge Lancs 195 B10
Clowne Derbys 187 F7
Clows Top Worcs 116 C4
Cloy Wrex 166 G5
Cluanie Inn Highld 290 B2
Cluanie Lodge Highld 290 B2
Clubmoor Mers. 182 C5
Clubworthy Corn 11 C11
Cluddley Telford 150 G2
Clun Shrops. 130 G6
Clunbury Shrops 131 G7
Clunderwen Carms 73 B10
Clune Highld 301 G7
Highld 301 G7
Clunes Aberds 302 D6
Highld 290 E4
Clungunford Shrops 115 B7
Clunie Aberds 302 D6
Perth 286 C5
Clunton Shrops 130 G6
Cluny Fife 280 B4
Cluny Castle Aberds 293 B8
Highld 291 D10
Clutton Bath 44 B6
ChesW 166 E6
Clutton Hill Bath 44 B6
Clwt-grugoer Conwy 165 C7
Clwt-y-bont Gwyn 163 C9
Clwydyfagwyr MTydf . . .77 D8
Clydach Mon 78 C2
Swansea 76 D2
Clydach Terrace Powys . .77 C11
Clydach Vale Rhondda . . .77 G7
Clydebank WDunb 277 G10
Clyffe Pypard Wilts 62 D5
Clynder Argyll 276 E4
Clyne Neath 76 E4
Clynelish Highld 311 J2
Clynnog-fawr Gwyn 162 F6
Clyro / Cleirwy Powys . . .96 C4
Clyst Honiton Devon 14 C5
Clyst Hydon Devon 27 G8
Clyst St George Devon . . .14 D5
Clyst St Lawrence Devon .27 G8
Clyst St Mary Devon 14 C5
Cnip WIsles 304 E2
Cnoc Amhlaigh WIsles . .304 E7
Cnoc an t-Solais
WIsles 304 D6
Cnocbreac Argyll 274 F5
Cnoc Fhionn Highld 295 D10
Cnoc Màiri WIsles 304 E6
Cnoc Rolum WIsles 296 F3
Cnwch-coch Ceredig 112 B3
Coachford Aberds 302 E4
Coad's Green Corn 11 F11
Coal Aston Derbys 186 F5
Coalbank Darl 234 G3
Coal Bank Darl 234 G3
Coalbrookdale Telford . . .132 C3
Coalbrookvale BlGwent . .77 D11
Coalburn S Lanrk 259 C8
Coalburns T&W 242 E4
Coalcleugh Northumb 232 B2
Coaley Glos 80 E3
Coaley Peak Glos. 80 D3
Coalford Aberds 293 D10

Coalhall EAyrs 257 F10
Coalhill Essex 88 F3
Coalmoor Telford 132 B3
Coalpit Field Warks 135 F7
Coalpit Heath SGlos 61 C7
Coalpit Hill Staffs 168 E4
Coal Pool W Mid 133 C10
Coalport Telford 132 C3
Coalsnaughton Clack 279 B8
Coaltown of Balgonie
Fife 280 B6
Coaltown of Wemyss
Fife 280 B6
Coalville Leics 153 G8
Coanwood Northumb 240 F5
Coarsewell Devon 8 E4
Coatbridge N Lnrk 268 C4
Coatdyke N Lnrk 268 C5
Coate Swindon 63 C7
Wilts 62 G4
Coates Cambs 138 D6
Glos 81 E7
Lancs 204 D3
Lincs 188 E6
Midloth 270 C4
Notts 188 E4
WSus 35 D7
Coatham Redcar 235 F7
Coatham Mundeville
Darl 233 G11
Coatsgate Dumfries 248 B3
Cobairdy Aberds 302 E5
Cobbaton Devon 25 B10
Cobbler's Corner Worcs .116 F5
Cobbler's Green Norf . . .142 E5
Cobbler's Plain Mon 79 E7
Cobbs Warr. 183 D10
Cobb's Cross Glos 98 E5
Cobbs Fenn Essex 106 E5
Cobby Syke N Yorks 205 B9
Coberley Glos 81 B7
Cobhall Common
Hereford 97 D9
Cobham Kent 69 F7
Sur 66 G6
Coble Dean T&W 243 D8
Cobleland Stirl 277 B10
Cobler's Green Essex 87 B11
Cobley Dorset 31 C8
Cobley Hill Worcs 117 C10
Cobnash Hereford 115 E9
Cobridge Stoke 168 F5
Coburty Aberds 303 C9
Cockayne N Yorks 226 F2
Cock Alley Derbys 186 G6
Cock and End Suff 124 G4
Cockayne N Yorks 226 F2
Cock Bank Wrex 166 F5
Cock Bevington Warks . .117 G11
Cock Bridge Aberds 292 C4
Cockburnspath Borders . .282 G5
Cock Clarks Essex 88 E4
Cockden Lancs 204 G3
Cockenzie and Port Seton
E Loth 281 F8
Cocker Bar Lancs 194 C4
Cockerham Lancs 202 C5
Cockermouth Cumb 229 E8
Cockernhoe Herts 104 G2
Cockernhoe Green
Herts 104 G2
Cockersdale W Yorks 197 B8
Cockerton Darl 224 B5
Cockett Swansea 56 C6
Cockety Bottom N Yorks .293 F9
Cockfield Durham 233 G8
Suff 125 G8
Cockfosters London. 86 F3
Cock Gate Hereford 115 D9
Cock Green Essex 87 B11
Cockhill Som 44 G6
Cock Hill N Yorks 206 B6
Cocking WSus 34 D5
Cocking Causeway
WSus 34 D5
Cockington Torbay 9 C7
Cocklake Som 44 D2
Cocklaw Northumb 241 C10
Cockleford Glos 81 C7
Cockley Beck Cumb 220 E4
Cockley Cley Norf 140 C5
Cockley Hill W Yorks 197 D7
Cocknowle Dorset 18 E4
Cockpole Green
Wokingham 65 C9
Cocks Corn 4 E5
Cocks Green Suff 125 F7
Cockshead Ceredig 112 F2
Cockshoot Hereford 97 D11
Cockshutford Shrops 131 G11
Cockshutt Shrops 149 D8
Cock Street Kent 53 C9
Cockthorpe Norf 177 E7
Cockwells Corn 2 C2
Cockwood Devon 14 E5
Som 43 E8
Cockyard Derbys 185 F8
Hereford 97 E8
Codda Corn. 11 F9
Coddenham Suff 126 G2
Coddington ChesW 167 D7
Hereford 98 C4
Notts 172 E4
Codford St Mary Wilts . . .46 F3
Codford St Peter Wilts . . .46 F3
Codicote Herts 86 B2
Codicote Bottom Herts . . .86 B2
Codmore Hill WSus 35 C10
Codnor Derbys 170 F6
Codnor Breach Derbys . . .170 F6
Codnor Gate Derbys 170 E6
Codnor Park Derbys 170 E6
Codrington SGlos 61 D8
Codsall Staffs 133 C7
Codsall Wood Staffs 132 B6
Codsend Som 41 F11
Coedcae Bl Gwent 77 D11
Coed Cwnwr Mon 78 F6
Coedely Rhondda 58 B4
Coed Eva Torf 78 G3
Coedkernew Newport 59 C9
Coed Llai / Leeswood
Flint 166 D3
Coed Morgan Mon 78 C5
Coedpoeth Wrex 166 E3
Coed-Talon Flint 166 D3
Coedway Powys 148 G6
Coed-y-bryn Ceredig 93 C7
Coed-y-caerau Newport . .78 G5
Coed-y-fedw Mon 78 D6
Coed y garth Ceredig 128 E3
Coed y go Shrops 148 D5

Coed-y-paen Mon 78 F4
Coed-yr-ynys Powys 96 G3
Coed Ystumgwern
Gwyn 145 E11
Coed-y-wlad Powys 130 B4
Coelbren Powys 76 C4
Coffee Hall MKeynes 103 D7
Coffinswell Devon 9 B7
Cofton Devon 14 E5
Cofton Common
W Mid 117 B10
Cofton Hackett Worcs . . .117 B10
Cog V Glam 59 F7
Cogan V Glam 59 E7
Cogenhoe Northants 120 E6
Cogges Oxon 82 D5
Coggeshall Essex 106 G6
Coggeshall Hamlet
Essex 107 G7
Coggins Mill ESus 37 B9
Coignafearn Lodge
Highld 291 B9
Coignascallan Highld 291 B9
Coig Peighinnean
WIsles 304 C7
Coig Peighinnean Bhuirgh
WIsles 304 C7
Coilacriech Aberds 292 D5
Coilantogle Stirl 285 G9
Coilessan Argyll 284 G6
Coilleag WIsles 297 K3
Coillemore Highld 300 B6
Coillore Highld 294 B5
Coirea-chrombe Stirl. 285 G9
Coisley Hill SYorks 186 E6
Coity Bridgend 58 C2
Cokenach Herts 105 D7
Cokhay Green Derbys . . .152 D5
Col WIsles 304 D6
Colaboll Highld 309 H5
Colan Corn 5 C7
Colaton Raleigh Devon . . .15 D7
Colburn N Yorks 224 F3
Colby Cumb 231 G9
IoM 192 E3
Norf 160 C4
Colchester Essex 107 F10
Colchester Green Suff . . .125 F8
Colcot V Glam 58 F6
Cold Ash W Berks 64 F4
Cold Ashby Northants . . .120 B3
Cold Ash Hill Hants 49 G10
Cold Ashton SGlos 61 E9
Cold Aston Glos 81 B10
Coldbackie Highld 308 C6
Coldbeck Cumb 222 E4
Coldblow London 68 E4
Cold Blow Pembs 73 C10
Cold Brayfield
MKeynes 121 G8
Coldbrook Powys 96 D3
Cold Christmas Herts 86 B5
Cold Cotes N Yorks 212 E4
Coldean Brighton 36 F4
Coldeast Devon 14 G2
Colden W Yorks 196 B3
Colden Common Hants . . .33 C7
Coldfair Green Suff 127 E8
Coldham Cambs 139 C8
Staffs 133 B7
Coldham's Common
Cambs 123 F9
Cold Hanworth Lincs 189 E8
Coldharbour Corn 4 F5
Devon 27 E9
Glos 79 E9
Kent 52 C5
London 68 D4
Sur 50 E6
Cold Harbour Dorset. 18 D4
Herts 85 B10
Kent 69 G11
Lincs 155 C9
Oxon 64 D6
Wilts 45 D11
Windsor 65 D11
Cold Hatton Telford 150 E2
Cold Hatton Heath
Telford 150 E2
Cold Hesledon Durham . .234 B4
Cold Hiendley W Yorks . .197 E11
Cold Higham Northants . .120 G3
Coldingham Borders 273 B8
Cold Inn Pembs 73 D10
Cold Kirby N Yorks 215 C10
Coldmeece Staffs 151 C7
Cold Newton Leics 136 B4
Cold Northcott Corn 11 D10
Cold Norton Essex 88 E4
Coldoch Stirl 278 B3
Cold Overton Leics 154 G6
Coldra Newport 59 B11
Coldrain Perth 286 G4
Coldred Kent 55 D9
Coldridge Devon 25 F11
Cold Row Lancs 202 E3
Coldstream Angus 287 D8
Borders 263 B8
Colt's Green SGlos 61 C8
Colt's Hill Kent 52 E6
Col Uarach WIsles 304 E6
Columbia T&W 243 F8
Coldwaltham WSus 35 D8
Coldwells Aberds 303 E11
Coldwells Croft Aberds . .302 G6
Cole Som 45 G7
Colebatch Shrops 130 F6
Colebrook Devon 27 F8
Colebrooke Devon 13 B11
Coleburn Moray 302 D2
Coleby Lincs 173 C7
N Lincs 199 D11
Cole End Essex 105 D11
Warks 134 F3
Coleford Devon 26 G3
Glos 79 C9
Som 45 D7
Coleford Water Som 42 G6
Cole Green Herts 86 C3
Herts 105 G8
Cole Henley Hants 48 C3
Colehill Dorset 31 G8
Coleman Green Herts 85 C11
Coleman's Hatch ESus . .52 G3
Colemere Shrops 149 C8
Colemore Hants 49 G8
Colemore Green Shrops .132 D4
Coleorton Leics 153 F7
Coleorton Moor Leics . . .153 F7
Cole Park London 67 D7
Colerne Wilts 61 E10
Colesbourne Glos 81 C7
Colesden Beds 122 F2
Cole's Green Suff 126 E5
Coleshill Bucks 85 F7
Oxon 82 G2
Warks 134 F4
Coles Meads Sur 51 C9
Colestocks Devon 27 G9
Colethrop Glos 80 C4
Coley Bath 44 B5
Reading 65 E8
W Yorks 196 B6
Colfin Dumfries 236 D2
Colgate WSus 51 G8
Colgrain Argyll 276 E6
Colham Green London. . . .66 C5
Colinburn Fife 287 G8
Colinton Edin 270 B4
Colintraive Argyll 275 F11
Colkirk Norf 159 D8
Collace Perth 286 D6
Collafield Glos 79 C11
Collafirth Shetland 312 G6
Collam WIsles 305 J3
Collamoor Head Corn 11 C9
Collaton Devon 9 G9
Collaton St Mary Torbay. . .9 D7
College Milton SLnrk . . .268 D2
College of Roseisle
Moray 301 C11
College Park London 67 C8
College Town Brack. 65 G11
Collennan S Ayrs 257 C8
Collessie Fife 286 F6
Colleton Mills Devon 25 D11
Collett's Br Norf 139 B9
Collett's End Herts 105 G7
Collier's End ESus 53 F9
Colliers Hatch Essex 87 E8
Collier Street Kent. 53 D8
Colliery Row T&W 234 B2
Collieston Aberds 303 G10
Collin Dumfries 238 B2
Collingbourne Ducis
Wilts 47 D8
Collingbourne Kingston
Wilts 47 D8
Collingham Notts 172 C4
W Yorks 206 D3
Collington Hereford 116 E2
Collingtree Northants 120 F5
Collingwood Northumb . .243 B7
Collins Green Warr 183 C9
Worcs 116 F4
Collipriest Devon 27 E7
Colliston Angus 287 C10
Colliton Devon 27 G9
Collycroft Warks 135 F7
Collyhurst GtrMan 195 G11
Collynie Aberds 303 F8
Collyweston Northants . . .137 C9
Colmonell S Ayrs 244 F4
Colmslie Borders 262 B2
Colmsliehill Borders 271 G10
Colmworth Beds. 122 F2
Colnabaichin Aberds 292 C4
Colnbrook Slough 66 D4
Colne Cambs 123 B7
Lancs 204 E3
Colne Bridge W Yorks . . .197 C7
Colne Edge Lancs 204 E3
Colne Engaine Essex. 107 E7
Colnefields Cambs 123 B7
Colney Norf 142 B3
Colney Hatch London. 86 G3
Colney Heath Herts 86 D2
Colney Street Herts 85 E11
Coln Rogers Glos 81 D9
Coln St Aldwyns Glos . . .81 D10
Coln St Dennis Glos 81 C9
Cologin Argyll 289 G10
Colpitts Grange
Northumb 241 F11
Colpy Aberds 302 F6
Colquhar Borders 270 G6
Colscott Devon 24 E5
Colshaw Staffs 169 B8
Colsterdale N Yorks 214 C2
Colsterworth Lincs 155 E8
Colston EDunb 268 B2
Colston Bassett Notts . . .154 C3
Colstrope Bucks 65 B9
Coltfield Moray 301 C11
Colt Hill Hants 49 C8
Colthouse Cumb 221 F7
Coltishall Norf 160 F5
Coltness N Lnrk 268 D6
Colton Cumb 210 B6
Norf 142 B2
N Yorks 206 D6
Staffs 151 E11
Suff 125 D7
W Yorks 206 G3
Colton Hills Staffs 133 D8
Colt Park Cumb 210 D5
Cold Row Lancs 202 E3
Coldstream Angus 287 D8

Cole's Cross Dorset 28 G5
Colesden Beds 122 F2
Coles Green Suff 107 C11
Combe Fishacre Devon . . .8 C6
Combe Florey Som 43 G7
Combe Hay Bath 45 B8
Combeinteignhead
Devon 14 G4
Combe Martin Devon 40 E5
Combe Moor Hereford . . .115 E7
Combe Pafford Torbay 9 B8
Combe Raleigh Devon . . .27 G11
Comberbach ChesW 183 E11
Comberford Staffs 134 B3
Comberton Cambs 123 F7
Hereford 115 D9
Combe St Nicholas Som . .28 E4
Combe Throop Som 30 C2
Combpyne Devon 28 G2
Combridge Staffs 151 B11
Combrook Warks 118 G6
Combs Derbys 185 F8
Suff 125 F11
W Yorks 197 D8
Combs Ford Suff. 125 F11
Combwich Som 43 E9
Comers Aberds 293 C8
Come-to-Good Corn 4 G6
Cometytrowe Som 28 C2
Comford Corn 2 B6
Comfort Corn 2 D6
Comhampton Worcs 116 D6
Comins Coch Ceredig . . .128 G2
Comins Coch Powys 128 C6
Comley Shrops 131 D9
Commercial End
Cambs 123 E11
Commins Denb 165 C10
Commins Capel Betws
Ceredig 112 F2
Commins Coch Powys . . .128 C6
Common Cefn-llwyn
Mon 78 G4
Commondale N Yorks . . .226 C3
Common Edge Blkpool . .202 G2
Common End Cumb 228 G6
Glos 170 G6
Common Hill Hereford . . .97 E11
Commonmoor Corn 6 B4
Common Moor Corn 6 B4
Common Platt Wilts 62 B6
Commonside ChesW 183 G8
Derbys 170 G3
Notts 171 D7
Common Side Derbys 167 B9
Derbys 170 F6
Derbys 186 F4
Commonwood Herts 85 E8
Shrops 149 D9
Wrex 166 E5
Common-y-coed Mon . . .60 B2
Comp Kent 52 B6
Compass Som 43 G9
Compstall GtrMan 185 C7
Compton Devon 169 F11
Devon 9 C7
Farnham, Sur 49 D11
Hants 32 B4
Hants 33 B7
Plym. 7 D9
Staffs 132 G6
Sur. 50 D3
W Berks 64 D4
Wilts 46 G6
W Sus 34 E3
W Yorks 206 E3
Compton Abbas Dorset . .30 D5
Compton Abdale Glos 81 B9
Compton Bassett Wilts . . .62 E4
Compton Beauchamp
Oxon 63 B9
Compton Bishop Som . . .43 B11
Compton Chamberlayne
Wilts 31 B8
Compton Common Bath . .60 G6
Compton Dando Bath 60 G6
Compton Dundon Som . . .44 G3
Compton Durville Som . . .28 D6
Compton End Hants 33 B7
Compton Green Glos 98 F4
Compton Greenfield
S Glos 60 C5
Compton Martin Bath 44 B4
Compton Pauncefoot
Som 29 B10
Compton Valence
Dorset 17 C7
Comrie Fife 279 D10
Highld 300 D4
Perth 285 E11
Perth 285 E11
Comrue Dumfries 248 F3
Conaglen House Highld . .290 G2
Conanby SYorks 187 B7
Conchra Argyll 275 E11
Highld 295 C11
Concord T&W 243 F8
Concraig Perth 286 F2
Concraigie Perth 286 C5
Conder Green Lancs 202 B5
Conderton Worcs 99 D9
Condicote Glos 100 F3
Condorrat N Lnrk 278 G5
Condover Shrops 131 B9
Coney Hill London 67 G11
Glos 80 B5
Coneyhurst WSus 35 C10
Coneysthorpe N Yorks. . .216 E4
Coneythorpe N Yorks . . .206 B3
Coney Weston Suff. 125 B9
Conford Hants 49 G10
Congash Highld 301 G10
Congdon's Shop Corn. . . .11 F11
Congeith Dumfries 237 C10
Congelow Kent 53 D7
Congerstone Leics 135 B7
Congham Norf 158 E4
Congleton ChesE 168 C5
Congleton Edge ChesE. . .168 C5
Congl-y-wal Gwyn 164 G2
Congresbury N Som 60 G2
Congreve Staffs 151 G8
Conham Bristol 60 E6
Conicavel Moray 301 D9
Coningsby Lincs 174 D2
Conington Cambs 122 D6
Cambs 138 F3
Conisbrough SYorks 187 B8
Conisby Argyll 274 G3
Conisholme Lincs 190 B6
Coniston Cumb 220 F6
E Yorks 209 F8
Coniston Cold N Yorks . .204 B4
Conistone N Yorks 213 F9
Conkwell Wilts 61 G9
Connage Moray 302 C4
Connah's Quay Flint 166 B3
Connel Argyll 289 F11
Connel Park EAyrs 258 G4
Conniburrow MKeynes . .103 D7

Crovie Aberds 303 C8
Crow Hants 31 G11
Crowan Corn 2 C4
Crowborough E Sus 52 G4
Staffs 168 D6
Crowborough Warren
E Sus 52 G4
Crowcombe Som 42 F6
Crowcroft Worcs 116 G5
Crowden Derbys 185 B9
Devon 12 B5
Crowder Park Devon 8 D4
Crowdhill Hants 33 C7
Crowdicote Derbys 169 B10
Crowdleham Kent 52 B5
Crowdon N Yorks 227 F9
Crow Edge S Yorks 197 G7
Crowell Oxon 84 F2
Crowell Hill Oxon 84 F3
Crowfield Northants 102 C2
Suff 126 F2
Crowgate Street Norf 160 E6
Crowgreaves Shrops 132 D4
Crow Green Essex 87 F9
Crowhill Gtr Man 184 B6
M Keynes 102 D6
Crow Hill Hereford 98 F2
Crowhole Derbys 186 F4
Crowhurst E Sus 38 E3
Sur 51 D11
Crowhurst Lane End
Sur 51 D11
Crowland Lincs 156 G4
Crowlas Corn 2 C2
Crowle N Lincs 199 E9
Worcs 117 F8
Crowle Green Worcs 117 F8
Crowle Hill N Lincs 199 E9
Crowle Park N Lincs 199 E9
Crowmarsh Gifford Oxon 64 B6
Crown Corner Suff 126 C5
Crown East Worcs 116 G6
Crown Nest W Yorks 205 F8
Crownfield Bucks 84 F4
Crownhill Plym 7 D9
Crown Hills Leicester 136 C2
Crownland Suff 125 D10
Crownpits Sur 50 E3
Crownthorpe Norf 141 C11
Crowntown Corn 2 C4
Crown Wood Brack 65 F11
Crows-an-wra Corn 1 D3
Crow's Green Essex 106 F3
Crowshill Norf 141 B8
Crowsley Oxon 65 D8
Crowsnest Shrops 131 C7
Crow's Nest Corn 6 B5
Crowther's Pool Powys 96 B4
Crowthorne Brack 65 G10
Crowton Ches W 183 G9
Crow Wood Halton 183 D8
Croxall Staffs 152 G3
Croxby Lincs 189 B11
Croxby Top Lincs 189 B11
Croxdale Durham 233 D11
Croxden Staffs 151 B11
Croxley Green Herts 85 F9
Croxteth Mers 182 B6
Croxton Cambs 122 E4
N Lincs 200 E5
Norf 141 F7
Norf 159 C9
Staffs 150 C5
Croxtonbank Staffs 150 C5
Croxton Green Ches E 167 E8
Croxton Kerrial Leics 154 D6
Croy Highld 301 E7
N Lnrk 278 F4
Croyde Devon 40 F2
Croyde Bay Devon 40 F2
Croydon Cambs 104 B6
London 67 F10
Crozen Hereford 97 B11
Crubenbeg Highld 291 D8
Crubenmore Lodge
Highld 291 D8
Cruckmeole Shrops 131 B8
Cruckton Shrops 149 G8
Cruden Bay Aberds 303 F10
Crudgington Telford 150 F2
Crudie Aberds 303 D7
Crudwell Wilts 81 G7
Crug Powys 114 C3
Crugmeer Corn 10 F4
Crugybar Carms 94 D3
Cruise Hill Worcs 117 E10
Crulabhig W Isles 304 E3
Crumlin Caerph 78 F2
Crumplehorn Corn 6 E4
Crumpsall Gtr Man 195 G10
Crumpsbrook Shrops 116 B2
Crumpton Hill Worcs 98 B5
Crundale Kent 54 D5
Pembs 73 B7
Cruwys Morchard Devon 26 E5
Crux Easton Hants 48 B2
Cruxton Dorset 17 B8
Crwbin Carms 75 C7
Crya Orkney 314 F3
Cryers Hill Bucks 84 F5
Crymlyn Gwyn 179 G10
Crymych Pembs 92 E3
Crynant / Creunant
Neath 76 E3
Crynfryn Ceredig 111 E11
Cuaich Highld 291 E8
Cuaig Highld 299 D7
Cuan Argyll 275 B8
Cubbington Warks 118 D6
Cubeck N Yorks 213 B9
Cubert Corn 4 D5
Cubitt Town London 67 D11
Cubley S Yorks 197 G8
Cubley Common Derbys 152 B3
Cublington Bucks 102 G6
Hereford 97 D8
Cuckfield W Sus 36 B4
Cucklington Som 30 B3
Cuckney Notts 187 G9
Cuckold's Green Suff 143 G9
Wilts 46 B3
Cuckoo Green Suff 143 D10
Cuckoo Hill Notts 188 C2
Cuckoo's Corner Hants 49 E8
Wilts 46 B4
Cuckoo's Knob Wilts 63 G7
Cuckoo Tye Suff 107 C7
Cuckron Shetland 313 H6
Cucumber Corner Norf 143 B7
Cuddesdon Oxon 83 E10
Cuddington Bucks 84 C2
Ches W 183 G10
Cuddington Heath
Ches W 167 F7
Cuddy Hill Lancs 202 F5
Cudham London 52 B2
Cudlipptown Devon 12 F6
Cudliptown Devon 12 F6
Cudworth Som 28 E5
Sur 51 E8
S Yorks 197 F11
Cudworth Common
S Yorks 197 F11
Cuerden Green Lancs 194 C5
Cuerdley Cross Warr 183 D8
Cufaude Hants 48 B6
Cuffern Pembs 91 G7
Cuffley Herts 86 E4
Cuiashader W Isles 304 C7
Cuidhir W Isles 297 L2
Cuidhtinis W Isles 296 C6
Cuiken Midloth 270 C4
Cuilcheanna Ho Highld 290 G2
Cuin Argyll 288 D6
Culbo Highld 300 C6
Culbokie Highld 300 D6
Culburnie Highld 300 E4
Culcabock Highld 300 E6
Culcairn Highld 300 C6
Culcharry Highld 301 D8
Culcheth Warr 183 B11
Culcronchie Dumfries 237 C7
Cùl Doirlinn Highld 289 B8
Culdrain Aberds 302 F5
Culduie Highld 299 E7
Culeave Highld 309 K5
Culford Suff 124 D6
Culfordheath Suff 125 C7
Culfosie Aberds 293 C9
Culgaith Cumb 231 F8
Culham Oxon 83 F8
Culkein Highld 306 F5
Culkein Drumbeg Highld 306 F6
Culkerton Glos 80 F6
Cullachie Highld 301 G9
Cullen Moray 302 C5
Cullercoats T&W 243 C9
Cullicudden Highld 300 C6
Cullingworth W Yorks 205 F7
Cullipool Argyll 275 B8
Cullivoe Shetland 312 C7
Culloch Perth 285 F11
Culloden Highld 301 E7
Cullompton Devon 27 F8
Culmaily Highld 311 K2
Culmazie Dumfries 236 D5
Culm Davy Devon 27 D10
Culmer Sur 50 F2
Culmers Kent 70 G5
Culmington Shrops 131 G9
Culmore Stirl 278 B3
Culmstock Devon 27 E10
Culnacraig Highld 307 J5
Cul na h-Aird W Isles 305 H3
Culnaightrie Dumfries 237 D9
Culnaknock Highld 298 C5
Culnaneam Highld 294 C6
Culpho Suff 108 B4
Culrain Highld 309 K5
Culra Lodge Highld 291 F7
Culross Fife 279 D9
Culroy S Ayrs 257 G8
Culscadden Dumfries 236 E6
Culsh Aberds 292 D5
Aberds 303 E8
Culshabbin Dumfries 236 D5
Culswick Shetland 313 J4
Cultercullen Aberds 303 G9
Cults Aberdeen 293 C10
Aberds 302 F5
Dumfries 236 E6
Fife 287 G7
Culverlane Devon 8 C4
Culverstone Green Kent 68 G6
Culverthorpe Lincs 173 G8
Culworth Northants 101 B10
Culzie Lodge Highld 300 B5
Cumberlow Green Herts 104 E6
Cumbernauld N Lnrk 278 G5
Cumbernauld Village N
Lnrk 278 F5
Cumber's Bank Wrex 149 B8
Cumberworth Lincs 191 G8
Cumdivock Cumb 230 B2
Cumeragh Village Lancs 203 F7
Cuminestown Aberds 303 D8
Cumledge Borders 272 D5
Cumlewick Shetland 313 L6
Cumlodden Argyll 275 D11
Cumloden Dumfries 236 C6
Cummersdale Cumb 239 G9
Cummerton Aberds 303 C8
Cummertrees Dumfries 238 D4
Cummingston Moray 301 C11
Cumnock E Ayrs 258 E3
Cumnor Oxon 83 E7
Cumnor Hill Oxon 83 D7
Cumrew Cumb 240 G2
Cumwhinton Cumb 239 G10
Cumwhitton Cumb 240 G2
Cundall N Yorks 215 E8
Cundy Cross S Yorks 197 F11
Cundy Hos S Yorks 186 B4
Cunninghamhead
N Ayrs 267 G7
Cunnister Shetland 312 D7
Cupar Fife 287 F7
Cupar Muir Fife 287 F7
Cupernham Hants 32 C5
Cupid Green Herts 85 D9
Cupid's Hill Mon 97 F8
Curbar Derbys 186 G3
Curborough Staffs 152 G2
Curbridge Hants 33 E8
Oxon 82 D4
Curdridge Hants 33 E8
Curdworth Warks 134 E3
Curgurrell Corn 3 B9
Curin Highld 300 D3
Curland Som 28 D3
Curland Common Som 28 D3
Curlew Green Suff 127 D7
Curling Tye Green Essex 88 D4
Curload Som 28 B4
Currarie S Ayrs 244 E5
Currian Vale Corn 5 D9
Curridge W Berks 64 E3
Currie Edin 270 B3
Currock Cumb 239 G10
Curry Lane Corn 11 C11
Curry Mallet Som 28 C4
Curry Rivel Som 28 B5
Cursiter Orkney 314 E3
Curteis' Corner Kent 53 F11
Curtisden Green Kent 53 E8
Curtisknowle Devon 8 E4
Curtismill Green Essex 87 F8
Cury Corn 2 E5
Cusbay Orkney 314 C5
Cusgarne Corn 4 G5
Cushnie Aberds 303 C7
Cushuish Som 43 G7
Cusop Hereford 96 C4
Custards Hants 32 F3
Custom House London 68 C2
Cusveorth Coombe Corn 4 G5
Cusworth S Yorks 198 G4
Cutcloy Dumfries 236 F6
Cutcombe Som 42 F2
Cutgate Gtr Man 195 E11
Cuthill E Loth 281 G7
Cutiau Gwyn 146 F2
Cutlers Green Essex 105 E11
Cutler's Green Som 44 C5
Cutmadoc Corn 5 C11
Cutmere Corn 6 C6
Cutnall Green Worcs 117 D7
Cutsdean Glos 99 E11
Cutsyke W Yorks 198 C2
Cutteslowe Oxon 83 C8
Cutthorpe Derbys 186 G4
Cuttiford's Door Som 28 E4
Cutts Shetland 313 K6
Cuttybridge Pembs 72 B6
Cuttyhill Aberds 303 D10
Cuxham Oxon 83 F11
Cuxton Medway 69 F8
Cuxwold Lincs 201 G7
Cwm Bl Gwent 77 D11
Denb 181 F9
Neath 57 C10
Powys 129 D11
Powys 130 E5
Shrops 114 B6
Swansea 57 B7
Cwmafan Neath 57 C9
Cwmaman Rhondda 77 F8
Cwmann Carms 93 B11
Cwmavon Torf 78 D3
Cwmbach Carms 75 E7
Carms 92 F5
Powys 96 D3
Rhondda 77 E8
Cwmbâch Rhondda 77 E8
Cwmbach Llechrhyd
Powys 113 G10
Cwmbelan Powys 129 G8
Cwmbran Torf 78 G3
Cwmbrwyno Ceredig 128 G4
Cwm-byr Carms 94 E2
Cwm Capel Carms 75 E7
Cwmcarn Caerph 78 G2
Cwmcarvan Mon 79 D7
Cwm-celyn Bl Gwent 78 D2
Cwm-Cewydd Gwyn 147 G7
Cwmcoednerth Ceredig 92 B6
Cwm-cou Ceredig 92 C5
Cwmcrawnon Powys 77 B10
Cwmcych Carms 92 D5
Cwmdare Rhondda 77 E7
Cwm Dows Caerph 78 F2
Cwmdu Carms 94 E2
Powys 96 G3
Swansea 56 C6
Cwmduad Carms 93 E7
Cwm-Dulais Swansea 75 E10
Cwmdwr Carms 94 E4
Cwmerfyn Ceredig 128 G3
Cwmfelin Bridgend 57 D11
M Tydf 77 E9
Cwmfelin Boeth Carms 73 B11
Cwm felin fach Caerph 77 G11
Cwmfelin Mynach Carms 92 G4
Cwmffrwd Carms 74 B6
Cwm Ffrwd-oer Torf 78 E3
Cwm-Fields Torf 78 E3
Cwm Gelli Caerph 77 F11
Cwmgiedd Powys 76 C3
Cwmgors Neath 76 C2
Cwmgwili Carms 75 C9
Cwmgwrach Neath 76 E5
Cwm Gwyn Swansea 56 C6
Cwm Head Shrops 131 F8
Cwm-hesgen Gwyn 146 D5
Cwmhiraeth Carms 92 D6
Cwm-hwnt Rhondda 76 D6
Cwmifor Carms 94 F3
Cwm Irfon Powys 95 B7
Cwmisfael Carms 75 B7
Cwm-Llinau Powys 128 B6
Cwmllynfell Neath 76 C2
Cwm-mawr Carms 75 C8
Cwm-miles Carms 92 G3
Cwm Nant-gam Bl Gwent 78 C2
Cwmnantyrodyn Caerph 77 F11
Cwmorgan Pembs 92 E5
Cwmparc Rhondda 77 F7
Cwm-parc Rhondda 77 F7
Cwmpengraig Carms 92 D6
Cwm Penmachno Conwy 164 F3
Cwmpennar Rhondda 77 E8
Cwm Plysgog Ceredig 92 C3
Cwmrhos Powys 96 G3
Cwmrhydyceirw Swansea 57 B7
Cwmsychpant Ceredig 93 B9
Cwmsyfiog Caerph 77 E11
Cwmsymlog Ceredig 128 G4
Cwmtillery Bl Gwent 78 D2
Cwm-twrch Isaf Powys 76 C3
Cwm-twrch Uchaf Powys 76 C3
Cwmwdig Water Pembs 90 E6
Cwmwysg Powys 95 F7
Cwm-y-glo Carms 75 C9
Gwyn 163 C8
Cwmynyscoy Torf 78 F3
Cwmyoy Mon 96 G5
Cwmystwyth Ceredig 112 C5
Cwrt Gwyn 128 C3
Cwrt-newydd Ceredig 93 B9
Cwrt-y-cadno Carms 94 C3
Cwrt-y-gollen Powys 78 B2
Cydweli / Kidwelly
Carms 74 D6
Cyffordd Llandudno /
Llandudno Junction
Conwy 180 F3
Cyffylliog Denb 165 D9
Cyfronydd Powys 130 B2
Cymau Flint 166 D3
Cymdda Bridgend 58 C2
Cymer Neath 57 B11
Cymmer Rhondda 77 G8
Cyncoed Cardiff 59 C7
Cynghordy Carms 94 C6
Cynheidre Carms 75 D7
Cynonville Neath 57 B10
Cyntwell Cardiff 58 D6
Cynwyd Denb 165 G9
Cynwyl Elfed Carms 93 F7
Cywarch Gwyn 147 F7

D

Daccombe Devon 9 B8
Dacre Cumb 230 F5
N Yorks 214 G3
Dacre Banks N Yorks 214 G3
Daddry Shield Durham 232 D3
Dadford Bucks 102 D3
Dadlington Leics 135 D8
Dafarn Faig Gwyn 163 F7
Dafen Carms 75 E8
Daffy Green Norf 141 B9
Dagdale Staffs 151 C11
Dagenham London 68 C3
Daggons Dorset 31 E10
Daglingworth Glos 81 D7
Dagnall Bucks 85 B7
Dagtail End Worcs 117 E10
Dagworth Suff 125 E10
Dail Beag W Isles 304 D4
Dail bho Dheas W Isles 304 B6
Dail bho Thuath
W Isles 304 B6
Daill Argyll 274 G4
Dailly S Ayrs 245 C7
Dail Mor W Isles 304 D4
Dainton Devon 9 B7
Dairsie or Osnaburgh
Fife 287 F8
Daisy Green Suff 125 D10
Suff 125 D11
Daisy Hill Gtr Man 195 G7
W Yorks 197 B9
W Yorks 205 G8
Daisy Nook Gtr Man 196 G2
Dalabrog W Isles 297 J3
Dalavich Argyll 275 B10
Dalbeattie Dumfries 237 C10
Dalbeg Highld 291 B8
Dalblair E Ayrs 258 F4
Dalbog Angus 293 F7
Dalbrack Stirl 285 G11
Dalbury Derbys 152 C5
Dalby IoM 192 E3
Lincs 190 G6
N Yorks 216 E2
Dalchalloch Perth 291 G9
Dalchalm Highld 311 J3
Dalchenna Argyll 284 G4
Dalchirach Moray 301 F11
Dalchonzie Perth 285 E11
Dalchork Highld 309 H5
Dalchreichart Highld 290 B4
Dalchruin Perth 285 F11
Dalderby Lincs 174 B2
Dale Cumb 230 C6
Gtr Man 196 F3
Pembs 72 D4
Shetland 312 G6
Dale Abbey Derbys 153 B8
Dalebank Derbys 170 C5
Dale Bottom Cumb 229 G11
Dale Brow Ches E 184 F6
Dale End Derbys 170 C2
N Yorks 204 D5
Dale Head Cumb 221 B8
Dale Hill E Sus 53 G7
E Sus 53 G8
Dalelia Highld 289 C9
Dale Moor Derbys 153 B8
Dale of Walls Shetland 313 H3
Dales Brow Gtr Man 195 G9
Dales Green Staffs 168 D5
Daless Highld 301 F8
Dalestie Moray 292 B3
Dalestorth Notts 171 C8
Dalfaber Highld 291 B11
Dalfoil Stirl 277 D11
Dalganachan Highld 310 E4
Dalgarven N Ayrs 266 F5
Dalgety Bay Fife 280 E3
Dalginross Perth 285 E11
Dalguise Perth 286 C3
Dalhalvaig Highld 310 D2
Dalham Suff 124 E4
Dalhastnie Angus 293 F7
Dalhenzean Perth 292 G3
Dalinlongart Argyll 276 E2
Dalkeith Midloth 270 B6
Dallam Warr 183 C9
Dallas Moray 301 D11
Dallas Lodge Moray 301 D11
Dallcharn Highld 308 D6
Dalleagles E Ayrs 258 G3
Dallicott Shrops 132 E5
Dallimores IoW 20 C6
Dallinghoo Suff 126 G5
Dallington E Sus 23 B11
Northants 120 E4
Dallow N Yorks 214 E3
Dalmadilly Aberds 293 B9
Dalmally Argyll 284 E5
Dalmarnock Glasgow 268 C2
Perth 286 C3
Dalmary Stirl 277 B10
Dalmellington E Ayrs 245 B11
Dalmeny Edin 280 F2
Dalmigavie Highld 291 B9
Dalmigavie Lodge
Highld 301 G7
Dalmilling S Ayrs 257 E9
Dalmore Highld 300 C6
Dalmuir W Dunb 277 G9
Dalnabreck Highld 289 C8
Dalnacardoch Lodge
Perth 291 F9
Dalnacroich Highld 300 D3
Dalnaglar Castle Perth 292 G3
Dalnahaitnach Highld 301 G8
Dalnamein Lodge Perth 291 G9
Dalnarrow Argyll 289 F9
Dalnaspidal Lodge
Perth 291 F8
Dalnavaid Perth 292 G2
Dalnavie Highld 300 B6
Dalnaw Dumfries 236 B5
Dalnawillan Lodge
Highld 310 E4
Dalness Highld 284 B5
Dalnessie Highld 309 H6
Dalphaid Highld 309 H3
Dalqueich Perth 286 G4
Dalrannoch Argyll 289 E11
Dalreavoch Highld 309 J7
Dalriach Highld 301 F10
Dalrigh Stirl 285 E7
Dalry Edin 280 G4
N Ayrs 266 F5
Dalrymple E Ayrs 257 G9
Dalscote Northants 120 G3
Dalserf S Lnrk 268 E6
Dalshannon N Lnrk 278 G4
Dalston Cumb 239 G9
London 67 C10
Dalswinton Dumfries 247 F10
Dalton Cumb 211 D10
Dumfries 238 C4
Lancs 194 F3
Northumb 241 F10
Northumb 242 C4
N Yorks 215 D8
N Yorks 224 D2
S Lnrk 268 D3
S Yorks 187 C7
W Yorks 197 D7
Dalton-in-Furness
Cumb 210 E4
Dalton-le-Dale Durham 234 B4
Dalton Magna S Yorks 187 C7
Dalton-on-Tees
N Yorks 224 D5
Dalton Parva S Yorks 187 C7
Dalton Piercy Hrtlpl 234 E5
Dalveallan Highld 300 F6
Dalveich Stirl 285 E10
Dalvina Lo Highld 308 E6
Dalwey Telford 132 B3
Dalwhinnie Highld 291 E8
Dalwood Devon 28 G3
Dalwyne S Ayrs 245 D8
Damask Green Herts 104 F5
Damems W Yorks 204 F6
Damerham Hants 31 D10
Damery Glos 80 G2
Damgate Norf 143 B8
Norf 161 F9
Dam Green Norf 141 F11
Damhead Moray 301 D10
Dam Head W Yorks 196 B6
Damhead Holdings
Midloth 270 B5
Dam Mill Staffs 133 C7
Damnaglaur Dumfries 236 F3
Dam of Quoiggs Perth 286 G2
Damside Borders 270 F3
Dam Side Lancs 202 D4
Danaway Kent 69 G11
Danbury Essex 88 E3
Danbury Common Essex 88 E3
Danby N Yorks 226 D4
Danby Wiske N Yorks 224 F6
Dan Caerlan Rhondda 58 C5
Dancers Hill Herts 86 F2
Dancing Green Hereford 98 G2
Dandaleith Moray 302 E2
Danderhall Midloth 270 B6
Dandy Corner Suff 125 D11
Danebank Ches E 185 E7
Dane Bank Gtr Man 184 B6
Danebridge Ches E 169 B7
Dane End Herts 104 G6
Danegate E Sus 52 G5
Danehill E Sus 36 B6
Dane in Shaw Ches E 168 C5
Danemoor Green Norf 141 B11
Danesbury Herts 86 B2
Danesfield Bucks 65 C10
Danesford Shrops 132 E4
Daneshill Hants 49 C7
Danesmoor Derbys 170 C6
Danes Moss Ches E 184 G6
Dane Street Kent 54 C5
Daneway Glos 80 E6
Dangerous Corner
Gtr Man 195 G7
Lancs 194 E4
Daniel's Water Kent 54 E3
Danna na Cloiche Argyll 275 F7
Dannonchapel Corn 10 E6
Danskine E Loth 271 B11
Danthorpe E Yorks 209 G10
Danygraig Caerph 78 G2
Danzey Green Warks 118 D2
Dapple Heath Staffs 151 D10
Darby End W Mid 133 F9
Darby Green Hants 65 G10
Darbys Green Worcs 116 F4
Darby's Hill W Mid 133 F9
Darcy Lever Gtr Man 195 F8
Dardy Powys 78 B2
Darenth Kent 68 E5
Daresbury Halton 183 E9
Daresbury Delph Halton 183 E9
Darfield S Yorks 198 G2
Darfoulds Notts 187 F9
Dargate Kent 70 G5
Dargate Common Kent 70 G5
Darite Corn 6 B5
Darkland Moray 302 C2
Darland Wrex 166 D5
Darlaston W Mid 133 D9
Darlaston Green W Mid 133 D9
Darley N Yorks 205 B10
Shrops 132 D3
Darley Abbey Derby 153 B7
Darley Bridge Derbys 170 C3
Darley Dale Derbys 170 C3
Darleyford Corn 11 G11
Darley Green Warks 118 C3
Darleyhall Herts 104 G2
Darley Head N Yorks 205 B9
Darley Hillside Derbys 170 C3
Darlingscott Warks 100 C4
Darlington Darl 224 C5
Darliston Shrops 149 C11
Darlton Notts 188 G3
Darmsden Suff 125 G11
Darnall S Yorks 186 D5
Darnaway Castle Moray 301 D9
Darnford Staffs 134 B2
Darnhall Ches W 167 C10
Darnhall Mains Borders 270 F4
Darn Hill Gtr Man 195 E10
Darnick Borders 262 C2
Darowen Powys 128 C6
Darra Aberds 303 E7
Darracott Devon 24 D2
Devon 40 F3
Darras Hall Northumb 242 C5
Darrington W Yorks 198 D3
Darrow Green Norf 142 F5
Darsham Suff 127 D8
Darshill Som 44 E6
Dartford Kent 68 E4
Dartford Crossing Kent 68 D5
Dartington Devon 8 C5
Dartmeet Devon 13 G9
Dartmouth Devon 9 E7
Dartmouth Park London 67 B9
Darton S Yorks 197 F10
Darvel E Ayrs 258 B3
Darvillshill Bucks 84 F4
Darwell Hole E Sus 23 B11
Darwen Blkburn 195 C7
Dassels Herts 105 F7
Datchet Windsor 66 D3
Datchet Common
Windsor 66 D3
Datchworth Herts 86 B3
Datchworth Green Herts 86 B3
Daubhill Gtr Man 195 F8
Daugh of Kinermony
Moray 302 E2
Dauntsey Wilts 62 C3
Dauntsey Lock Wilts 62 C3
Dava Moray 301 F10
Davenham Ches W 183 G11
Davenport Ches E 168 B4
Gtr Man 184 D5
Davenport Green
Ches E 184 F4
Gtr Man 184 D4
Daventry Northants 119 E11
Davidson's Mains Edin 280 F4
Davidston Highld 301 C7
Davidstow Corn 11 D9
David Street Kent 68 G6
David's Well Powys 113 B11
Davington Dumfries 248 C6
Kent 70 G4
Daviot Aberds 303 G7
Highld 301 F7
Davis's Town E Sus 23 B8
Davoch of Grange
Moray 302 D4
Davo Mains Aberds 293 F9
Davyhulme Gtr Man 184 B3
Daw Cross N Yorks 205 C11
Dawdon Durham 234 B4
Daw End W Mid 133 C10
Dawesgreen Sur 51 D8
Dawker Hill N Yorks 207 F7
Dawley Telford 132 B3
Dawley Bank Telford 132 B3
Dawlish Devon 14 F5
Dawlish Warren Devon 14 F5
Dawn Conwy 180 G5
Daw's Cross Essex 107 E7
Daw's Green Som 27 C11
Daws Heath Essex 69 B10
Dawshill Worcs 116 G6
Daw's House Corn 12 E2
Dawsmere Lincs 157 C8
Daybrook Notts 171 F9
Day Green Ches E 168 D3
Dayhills Staffs 151 C9
Dayhouse Bank Worcs 117 B9
Daylesford Glos 100 F4
Daywall Shrops 148 C5
Ddol Flint 181 G10
Ddôl Cownwy Powys 147 F10
Ddrydwy Anglesey 178 G5
Deacons Hill Herts 85 F11
Deadman's Cross
C Beds 104 C2
Deadman's Green
Staffs 151 B10
Deadwater Hants 49 F10
Northumb 250 D4
Deaf Hill Durham 234 D3
Deal Kent 55 C11
Deal Hall Essex 89 F8
Dean Cumb 229 F7
Devon 8 C4
Devon 40 D6
Devon 40 E4
Devon 41 D8
Dorset 31 D7
Edin 280 G4
Hants 33 D9
Hants 48 G2
Lancs 195 B11
Oxon 100 G6
Som 45 E7
Dean Bank Durham 233 E11
Deanburnhaugh
Borders 261 G9
Dean Court Oxon 83 D7
Dean Cross Devon 40 E4
Deane Gtr Man 195 F7
Hants 48 C4
Deanend Dorset 31 D7
Dean Head S Yorks 197 G9
Deanich Lodge Highld 309 L3
Deanland Dorset 31 D7
Deanlane End W Sus 34 E2
Dean Lane Head
W Yorks 205 G7
Dean Park Renfs 267 B10
Dean Prior Devon 8 C4
Dean Row Ches E 184 E5
Deans W Loth 269 B10
Deans Bottom Kent 69 G11
Deanscales Cumb 229 F7
Deansgreen Ches E 183 D11
Dean's Green Warks 118 D2
Deanshanger Northants 102 D5
Deans Hill Kent 69 G11
Deanston Stirl 285 G11
Dean Street Kent 53 C8
Dearham Cumb 229 D7
Dearnley Gtr Man 196 D2
Debach Suff 126 G4
Debdale Gtr Man 184 B5
Debden Essex 86 F6
Essex 105 E11
Debden Cross Essex 105 E11
Debden Green Essex 86 F6
Essex 105 E11
De Beauvoir Town
London 67 C10
Debenham Suff 126 E3
Deblin's Green Worcs 98 B6
Dechmont W Loth 279 G10
Deckham T&W 243 E7
Deddington Oxon 101 E9
Dedham Essex 107 E11
Dedham Heath Essex 107 E11
Dedridge W Loth 269 B11
Dedworth Windsor 66 D2
Deebank Aberds 293 D8
Deecastle Aberds 292 D6
Deene Northants 137 E8
Deenethorpe Northants 137 E9
Deepcar S Yorks 186 B3
Deepclough Derbys 185 B8
Deepcut Sur 50 B2
Deepdale C Beds 104 B4
Cumb 212 C4
N Yorks 213 D7
Deepdene Sur 51 D7
Deepfields W Mid 133 E8
Deeping Gate Lincs 138 B2
Deeping St James Lincs 138 B3
Deeping St Nicholas
Lincs 156 F4
Deepthwaite Cumb 211 C10
Deepweir Mon 60 B3
Deerhill Moray 302 D4
Deerhurst Glos 99 F7
Deerhurst Walton Glos 99 F7
Deerland Pembs 73 C7
Deerness Orkney 314 F5
Deer's Green Essex 105 E9
Deerstones N Yorks 205 C7
Deerton Street Kent 70 G3
Defford Worcs 99 C8
Defynnog Powys 95 F8
Deganwy Conwy 180 F3
Degar V Glam 58 D4
Degibna Corn 2 D5
Deighton N Yorks 225 E7
W Yorks 197 D7
York 207 E8
Deiniolen Gwyn 163 C9
Deishar Highld 291 B11
Delabole Corn 11 E7
Delamere Ches W 167 B9
Delfour Highld 291 C10
Delfrigs Aberds 303 G9
Delliefure Highld 301 F10
Dell Lodge Highld 292 B2
Dell Quay W Sus 22 C4
Delly End Oxon 82 C5
Delnabo Moray 292 B3
Delnadamph Aberds 292 C4
Delnamer Angus 292 G3
Delph Gtr Man 196 F3
Delves Durham 233 B8
Delvine Perth 286 C5
Delvin End Essex 106 D5
Dembleby Lincs 155 B10
Demelza Corn 5 C9
Denaby Main S Yorks 187 B7
Denbeath Fife 281 B7
Denbigh Denb 165 B9
Denbury Devon 8 B6
Denby Derbys 170 F5
Denby Bottles Derbys 170 F5
Denby Common Derbys 170 F6
Denby Dale W Yorks 197 F8
Dendron Cumb 210 E4
Denel End C Beds 103 D10
Denend Aberds 302 F6
Dene Park Kent 52 C5
Deneside Durham 234 B4
Denford Northants 121 B9
Staffs 169 E7
Dengie Essex 89 E7
Denham Bucks 66 B4
Bucks 102 G5
Suff 124 E5
Suff 126 C3
Denham Corner Suff 126 C3
Denham End Suff 124 E5
Denham Green Bucks 66 B4
Denham Street Suff 126 C3
Denhead Aberds 303 D9
Fife 287 F8
Denhead of Arbilot
Angus 287 C9
Denhead of Gray
Dundee 287 D7
Denholm Borders 262 F3
Denholme W Yorks 205 G7
Denholme Clough
W Yorks 205 G7
Denholme Edge
W Yorks 205 G7
Denholme Gate
W Yorks 205 G7
Denholmhill Borders 262 F3
Denio Gwyn 145 B7
Denmead Hants 33 E11
Denmore Aberdeen 293 B11
Denmoss Aberds 302 E6
Dennington Suff 126 D5
Dennington Corner Suff 126 D5
Dennington Hall Suff 126 D5
Denny Falk 278 E6
Denny Bottom Kent 52 F5
Denny End Cambs 123 D9
Dennyloanhead Falk 278 E6
Denny Lodge Hants 32 F4
Dennystown W Dunb 277 F7
Denshaw Gtr Man 196 E3
Denside Aberds 293 D10
Densole Kent 55 E8
Denston Suff 124 G5
Denstone Staffs 169 G9
Denstroude Kent 70 G6
Dent Cumb 212 B4
Dent Bank Durham 232 F4
Denton Cambs 138 F2
Darl 224 B4
E Sus 23 E7
Gtr Man 184 B6
Kent 55 D8
Kent 69 E7
Lincs 155 C7
Norf 142 F5
Northants 120 F6
N Yorks 205 D8
Oxon 83 E9
Denton Burn T&W 242 D5
Denton Holme Cumb 239 G10
Denton's Green Mers 183 B7
Denver Norf 140 C2
Denvilles Hants 22 B2
Denwick Northumb 264 G6
Deopham Norf 141 C11
Deopham Green Norf 141 D10
Deopham Stalland
Norf 141 D10
Depden Suff 124 F5
Depden Green Suff 124 F5
Deppers Bridge Warks 119 F7
Deptford London 67 D11
T&W 243 F9
Wilts 46 F4
Derby Derbys 153 B7
Devon 40 G5
Derbyhaven IoM 192 F3
Derbyshire Hill Mers 183 C8
Dereham Norf 159 G9
Dergoals Dumfries 236 D4
Deri Caerph 77 E10
Derriford Plym 7 D9
Derril Devon 24 G4
Derringstone Kent 55 D8
Derrington Shrops 132 E2
Staffs 151 E7
Derriton Devon 24 G4
Derry Stirl 285 E10
Derrydaroch Stirl 285 E7
Derry Downs London 68 F3
Derry Fields Wilts 81 G8
Derryguaig Argyll 288 F6
Derry Hill Wilts 62 E3
Derry Lodge Aberds 292 D2
Derrythorpe N Lincs 199 F10
Dersingham Norf 158 C3
Dertfords Wilts 45 D10
Dervaig Argyll 288 D6
Derwen Bridgend 58 C2
Denb 165 E9
Derwenlas Powys 128 D4
Desborough Northants 136 G6
Desford Leics 135 C9
Deskryshiel Aberds 292 B6
Detchant Northumb 264 B3
Detling Kent 53 B9
Deuchar Angus 292 G6
Deuddwr Powys 148 F4
Deuxhill Shrops 132 F3
Devauden Mon 79 F7
Deveral Corn 2 B3
Devil's Bridge /
Pontarfynach Ceredig 112 B4
Devitts Green Warks 134 E5
Devizes Wilts 62 G4
Devol Invclyd 276 G6
Devonport Plym 7 E9
Devonside Clack 279 B8
Devon Village Clack 279 B8
Devoran Corn 3 B7
Dewar Borders 270 F6
Dewartown Midloth 271 C7
Dewes Green Essex 105 E9
Dewlands Common
Dorset 31 F9
Dewlish Dorset 17 B11
Dewsbury W Yorks 197 C8
Dewsbury Moor
W Yorks 197 C8
Dewshall Court Hereford 97 E9
Dhoon IoM 192 D5
Dhoor IoM 192 C5
Dhowin IoM 192 B5
Dhustone Shrops 115 B11
Dial Green W Sus 34 B6
Dial Post W Sus 35 D11
Dibberford Dorset 29 G7
Dibden Hants 32 F6
Dibden Purlieu Hants 32 F6
Dickens Heath W Mid 118 B2
Dickleburgh Norf 142 G3
Dickleburgh Moor Norf 142 G3
Dickon Hills Lincs 174 D6
Didbrook Glos 99 E11
Didcot Oxon 64 B4
Diddington Cambs 122 D3
Diddlebury Shrops 131 F10
Diddywell Devon 25 B7
Didley Hereford 97 E9
Didling W Sus 34 D4
Didlington Norf 140 D5
Didmarton Glos 61 B10
Didsbury Gtr Man 184 C4
Didworthy Devon 8 C3
Diebidale Highld 309 L4
Digbeth W Mid 133 F11
Digby Lincs 173 E9
Digg Highld 298 C4
Diggle Gtr Man 196 F4
Diglis Worcs 116 G6
Digmoor Lancs 194 F3
Digswell Herts 86 B3
Digswell Park Herts 86 C2
Digswell Water Herts 86 C3
Dihewyd Ceredig 111 F9
Dilham Norf 160 D6
Dilhorne Staffs 169 G7
Dillarburn S Lnrk 268 G6
Dill Hall Lancs 195 B8
Dillington Cambs 122 D2
Som 28 D5
Dilston Northumb 241 E11
Dilton Marsh Wilts 45 D11
Dilwyn Hereford 115 G8
Dimlands V Glam 58 F3
Dimmer Som 44 G6
Dimple Derbys 170 C3
Gtr Man 195 D8
Dimsdale Staffs 168 F4
Dimson Corn 12 G4
Dinas Carms 92 E5
Corn 10 G4
Gwyn 144 B5
Gwyn 163 D7
Dinas Cross Pembs 91 D10
Dinas Dinlle Gwyn 162 D6
Dinas-Mawddwy Gwyn 147 G7
Dinas Mawr Conwy 164 E4
Dinas Powys V Glam 59 E7
Dinbych y Pysgod / Tenby
Pembs 73 E10
Dinckley Lancs 203 F9
Dinder Som 44 E5
Dinedor Hereford 97 D10
Dinedor Cross Hereford 97 D10
Dines Green Worcs 116 F6
Dingestow Mon 79 C7
Dinghurst N Som 44 B2
Dingle Mers 182 D5
Dingleden Kent 53 G10
Dingleton Borders 262 C2
Dingley Northants 136 F5
Dingwall Highld 300 D5
Dinlabyre Borders 250 E2
Dinmael Conwy 165 G8
Dinnet Aberds 292 D6
Dinnington Som 28 E6
S Yorks 187 D8
T&W 242 C6
Dinorwic Gwyn 163 C9
Dinton Bucks 84 C3
Wilts 46 G4
Dinwoodie Mains
Dumfries 248 E4
Dinworthy Devon 24 D4
Dipford Som 28 C2
Dipley Hants 49 B8
Dippenhall Sur 49 D10
Dippertown Devon 12 E4
Dippin N Ayrs 256 E2
Dipple Devon 24 D4
Moray 302 D3
S Ayrs 244 C6
Diptford Devon 8 D4
Dipton Durham 242 G5
Diptonmill Northumb 241 E10
Dirdhu Highld 301 G10
Direcleit W Isles 305 J3
Dirleton E Loth 281 E10
Dirt Pot Northumb 232 B3
Discoed Powys 114 E5
Discove Som 45 G7
Diseworth Leics 153 E9
Dishes Orkney 314 D6
Dishforth N Yorks 215 E7
Dishley Leics 153 E10
Disley Ches E 185 E7
Diss Norf 126 B2
Disserth Powys 113 F10
Distington Cumb 228 G6
Ditchampton Wilts 46 G5
Ditcheat Som 44 F6
Ditchfield Bucks 84 G4
Ditchford Hill Worcs 100 D4
Ditchingham Norf 142 E6
Ditchling E Sus 36 D4
Ditherington Shrops 149 G10
Ditteridge Wilts 61 F10
Dittisham Devon 9 E7
Ditton Halton 183 D7
Kent 53 B8
Ditton Green Cambs 124 F3
Ditton Priors Shrops 132 F2
Dittons E Sus 23 E10
Divach Highld 300 G4
Divlyn Carms 94 D5
Dixton Glos 99 E9
Mon 79 C8
Dizzard Corn 11 B9
Dobcross Gtr Man 196 F3
Dobs Hill Flint 166 C4
Dobson's Bridge Shrops 149 C9
Dobwalls Corn 6 C4
Doccombe Devon 13 D11
Dochfour Ho Highld 300 F6
Dochgarroch Highld 300 E6
Dockeney Norf 143 E7
Dockenfield Sur 49 E10
Docker Lancs 211 E11
Docking Norf 158 B5
Docklow Hereford 115 F11
Dockray Cumb 230 G3
Dockroyd W Yorks 204 F6
Doc Penfro / Pembroke
Dock Pembs 73 E7
Docton Devon 24 C2
Dodbrooke Devon 8 G4
Dodburn Borders 249 B11
Doddenham Worcs 116 F5
Doddinghurst Essex 87 F9
Doddington Cambs 139 E7
Kent 54 B2
Lincs 188 G6
Northumb 263 C11
Shrops 116 B2
Doddiscombsleigh
Devon 14 D3
Doddshill Norf 158 C3
Doddycross Corn 6 C6
Dodford Northants 120 E2
Worcs 117 C8
Dodington S Glos 61 C9
Som 43 E7
Dodleston Ches W 166 C5
Dodmarsh Hereford 97 C11
Dodscott Devon 25 D8
Dods Leigh Staffs 151 C10

East Hartford Northumb. 243 B7
East Harting W Sus 34 D3
East Hatch Wilts 30 B6
East Hatley Cambs 122 G5
Easthaugh Norf 159 F11
East Hauxwell N Yorks 224 G3
East Haven Angus 287 D9
Eastheath Wokingham 65 F10
East Heckington Lincs 173 G11
East Hedleyhope
Durham 233 C9
East Helmsdale Highld 311 H4
East Hendred Oxon 64 B3
East Herringthorpe
S Yorks 187 C7
East Herrington T&W 243 G9
East Heslerton N Yorks 217 D8
East Hewish N Som 59 G11
East Hill Kent 68 G5
East Hoathly E Sus 23 B8
East Hogaland Shetland 313 K5
East Holme Dorset 18 D3
East Holton Dorset 18 C5
East Holywell Northumb 243 C8
Easthope Shrops 131 D11
Easthopewood Shrops 131 D11
East Horndon Essex 68 B6
Easthorpe Essex 107 G8
Leics 154 B6
Notts 172 E2
East Horrington Som 44 D5
East Horsley Sur 50 C5
East Horton Northumb 264 C2
Easthouse Shetland 313 J5
Easthouses Midloth 270 B6
East Howdon T&W 243 D8
East Howe Bmouth 19 B7
East Huntspill Som 43 E10
East Hyde C Beds 85 B10
East Ilkerton Devon 41 D8
East Ilsley W Berks 64 C3
Easting Orkney 314 A7
Eastington Devon 26 F2
Glos 80 D3
Glos 81 C10
East Keal Lincs 174 C5
East Kennett Wilts 62 F6
East Keswick W Yorks 206 E3
East Kilbride S Lnrk 268 E2
East Kimber Devon 12 B5
East Kingston W Sus 35 G9
East Kirkby Lincs 174 C4
East Knapton N Yorks 217 D7
East Knighton Dorset 18 D2
East Knowstone Devon 26 C4
East Knoyle Wilts 45 G11
East Kyloe Northumb 264 B3
East Kyo Durham 242 G5
East Lambrook Som 28 D6
East Lamington Highld 301 B7
Eastland Gate Hants 33 E11
East Langdon Kent 55 D10
East Langton Leics 136 E4
East Langwell Highld 309 J7
East Lavant W Sus 22 B5
East Lavington W Sus 34 D6
East Law Northumb 242 G3
East Layton N Yorks 224 D3
Eastleach Martin Glos 82 D2
Eastleach Turville Glos 81 D11
East Leake Notts 153 D11
East Learmouth
Northumb 263 B9
Eastleigh Devon 25 B7
Hants 32 D6
East Leigh Devon 8 E3
Devon 25 F11
East Lexham Norf 159 F7
East Lilburn Northumb 264 E2
Eastling Kent 54 B3
East Linton E Loth 281 F11
East Liss Hants 34 B3
East Lockinge Oxon 64 B2
East Loftus Redcar 226 B4
East Looe Corn 6 E5
East Lound N Lincs 188 B3
East Lulworth Dorset 18 E3
East Lutton N Yorks 217 F8
East Lydeard Som 27 B11
East Lydford Som 44 G5
East Lyng Som 28 B4
East Mains Aberds 293 D8
Borders 271 F11
S Lnrk 268 E2
East Malling Kent 53 B8
East Malling Heath Kent 53 B7
East March Angus 287 D8
East Marden W Sus 34 E4
East Markham Notts 188 G2
East Marsh NE Lincs 201 E9
East Martin Hants 31 D9
East Marton N Yorks 204 C4
East Melbury Dorset 30 C5
East Meon Hants 33 C11
East Mere Devon 27 D7
East Mersea Essex 89 C9
East Mey Highld 310 B7
East Molesey Sur 67 F7
Eastmoor Derbys 186 G4
Norf 140 C4
East Moor W Yorks 197 C10
East Moors Cardiff 59 D8
East Morden Dorset 18 B4
East Morton W Yorks 205 E7
East Moulsecoomb
Brighton 36 F4
East Ness N Yorks 216 D3
East Newton E Yorks 209 F11
N Yorks 216 D2
Eastney Ptsmth 21 B9
Eastnor Hereford 98 D4
East Norton Leics 136 C5
East Nynehead Som 27 C11
East Oakley Hants 48 C5
Eastoft N Lincs 199 D10
East Ogwell Devon 14 G2
Eastoke Hants 21 B10
Easton Bristol 60 E6
Cambs 122 C2
Cumb 239 C10
Cumb 239 F7
Devon 8 F3
Devon 13 D10
Dorset 17 G9
Hants 48 G4
IoW 20 D2
Lincs 155 D8
Norf 160 G2
Som 44 D4
Suff 126 F5
W Berks 64 E2
Wilts 61 E11
Easton Grey Wilts 61 B11
Easton in Gordano
N Som 60 D4
Easton Maudit Northants 121 F7
Easton on the Hill
Northants 137 C10
Easton Royal Wilts 63 G8
Easton Town Som 44 G5
Wilts 61 B11
East Orchard Dorset 30 D4
East Ord Northumb 273 E9
Eastover Som 43 F10
East Panson Devon 12 C3
Eastpark Dumfries 238 D2
East Parley Dorset 19 B8
East Peckham Kent 53 D7
East Pennard Som 44 F5
East Perry Cambs 122 D3
East Portholland Corn 5 G9
East Portlemouth Devon 9 G9
East Prawle Devon 9 G10
East Preston W Sus 35 G9
East Pulham Dorset 30 F2
East Putford Devon 24 D5
East Quantoxhead Som 42 E6
East Rainton T&W 234 B2
East Ravendale NE Lincs 190 B2
East Raynham Norf 159 D7
Eastrea Cambs 138 D5
East Rhidorroch Lodge
Highld 307 K7
Eastriggs Dumfries 238 D6
East Rigton W Yorks 206 E3
Eastrington E Yorks 199 B9
Eastrip Wilts 61 E10
East Rolstone N Som 59 G11
Eastrop Hants 48 C6
East Rounton N Yorks 225 E8
East Row N Yorks 227 C7
East Rudham Norf 158 D6
East Runton Norf 177 E11
East Ruston Norf 160 D6
Eastry Kent 55 C10
East Saltoun E Loth 271 B9
East Sheen London 67 D8
East Skelston Dumfries 247 F8
East Sleekburn
Northumb 253 G7
East Somerton Norf 161 F9
East Stanley Durham 242 G6
East Stockwith Lincs 188 C3
East Stoke Dorset 18 D3
Notts 172 F3
Som 29 D7
East Stour Dorset 30 C4
East Stour Common
Dorset 30 C4
East Stourmouth Kent 71 G9
East Stowford Devon 25 B10
East Stratton Hants 48 F4
East Street Kent 55 B10
Som 44 F4
East Studdal Kent 55 D10
East Suisnish Highld 295 B7
East Taphouse Corn 6 C3
East-the-Water Devon 25 B7
East Third Borders 262 B4
East Thirston Northumb 252 D5
East Tilbury Thurrock 69 D7
East Tisted Hants 49 G8
East Torrington Lincs 189 E10
East Town Som 42 G6
Som 44 E6
Wilts 45 B11
East Trewent Pembs 73 F8
East Tuddenham Norf 159 G11
East Tuelmenna Corn 6 B4
East Tytherley Hants 32 B3
East Tytherton Wilts 62 E3
East Village Devon 26 F4
V Glam 58 E3
Eastville Bristol 60 E6
Lincs 174 D6
East Wall Shrops 131 E10
East Walton Norf 158 F4
East Water Som 44 C4
East Week Devon 13 C9
Eastwell Leics 154 D5
East Wellow Hants 32 C4
Eastwell Park Kent 54 D4
East Wemyss Fife 280 B6
East Whitburn W Loth 269 B9
Eastwick Herts 86 C6
Shetland 312 F5
East Wickham London 68 D3
East Williamston Pembs 73 E9
East Winch Norf 158 F3
East Winterslow Wilts 47 G8
East Wittering W Sus 21 B11
East Witton N Yorks 214 B2
Eastwood Hereford 98 C2
Notts 171 F7
S'thend 69 B10
S Yorks 186 C6
W Yorks 196 B3
East Woodburn
Northumb 251 F10
Eastwood End Cambs 139 E8
Eastwood Hall Notts 171 F7
East Woodhay Hants 64 G2
East Woodlands Som 45 E9
East Worldham Hants 49 F8
East Worlington Devon 26 E3
East Worthing W Sus 35 G11
East Wretham Norf 141 E8
East Youlstone Devon 24 D3
Eathorpe Warks 119 D7
Eaton Ches E 168 B5
Ches W 167 C9
Hereford 115 F10
Leics 154 D5
Norf 142 B4
Notts 188 F2
Oxon 82 E6
Shrops 131 F7
Shrops 131 F10
Eaton Bishop Hereford 97 D8
Eaton Bray C Beds 103 G9
Eaton Constantine
Shrops 131 B11
Eaton Ford Cambs 122 E3
Eaton Green C Beds 103 G9
Eaton Hastings Oxon 82 F3
Eaton Mascott Shrops 131 B10
Eaton on Tern Shrops 150 E3
Eaton Socon Cambs 122 F3
Eaton upon Tern Shrops 150 E3
Eau Brink Norf 157 F11
Eau Withington
Hereford 97 C10
Eaves Green W Mid 134 G5
Eavestone N Yorks 214 F4
Ebberly Hill Devon 25 D9
Ebberston N Yorks 217 C7
Ebbesbourne Wake Wilts 31 C7
Ebblake Hants 31 F10
Ebbw Vale Bl Gwent 77 D11
Ebchester Durham 242 F4
Ebdon N Som 59 G11
Ebernoe W Sus 35 B7
Ebford Devon 14 D5
Ebley Glos 80 D4
Ebnal Ches W 167 F7
Ebnall Hereford 115 F9
Ebreywood Shrops 149 F10
Ebrington Glos 100 C3
Ecchinswell Hants 48 B4
Ecclaw Borders 272 B5
Ecclefechan Dumfries 238 C5
Eccle Riggs Cumb 210 B4
Eccles Borders 272 G5
Gtr Man 184 B3
Kent 69 G8
Ecclesall S Yorks 186 E4
Ecclesfield S Yorks 186 C5
Ecclesgreig Aberds 293 G9
Eccleshall Staffs 150 D6
Eccleshill W Yorks 205 F9
Ecclesmachan W Loth 279 G11
Eccles on Sea Norf 161 D8
Eccles Road Norf 141 E10
Eccleston Ches W 166 C6
Lancs 194 D4
Mers 183 B7
Eccleston Park Mers 183 C7
Eccliffe Dorset 30 B3
Eccup W Yorks 205 E11
Echt Aberds 293 C9
Eckford Borders 262 D6
Eckfordmoss Borders 262 D6
Eckington Derbys 186 F6
Worcs 99 C8
Eckington Corner E Sus 23 D8
Ecton Northants 120 E6
Staffs 169 D9
Ecton Brook Northants 120 E6
Edale Derbys 185 D10
Edale End Derbys 185 D11
Edbrook Som 43 E8
Edburton W Sus 36 E2
Edderside Cumb 229 B7
Edderton Highld 309 L7
Eddington Kent 71 F7
W Berks 63 F10
Eddistone Devon 24 C3
Eddleston Borders 270 F4
Eddlewood S Lnrk 268 E4
Edenbridge Kent 52 D2
Edenfield Lancs 195 D9
Edenhall Cumb 231 E7
Edenham Lincs 155 E11
Eden Mount Cumb 211 D8
Eden Park London 67 F11
Edensor Derbys 170 B2
Edentaggart Argyll 276 C6
Edenthorpe S Yorks 198 F6
Edentown Cumb 239 F9
Eden Vale Durham 234 D4
Wilts 45 C11
Ederline Argyll 275 C9
Edern Gwyn 144 B5
Edford Som 45 D7
Edgarley Som 44 F4
Edgbaston W Mid 133 G11
Edgcote Northants 101 B10
Edgcott Bucks 102 G3
Som 41 F10
Edgcumbe Corn 2 C6
Edge Glos 80 D4
Shrops 131 B7
Edgebolton Shrops 149 E11
Edge End Glos 79 C9
Lancs 203 G10
Edgefield Norf 159 C11
Edgefield Street Norf 159 C11
Edge Fold Blkburn 195 D8
Gtr Man 195 F8
Edge Green Ches W 167 E7
Gtr Man 183 B9
Norf 141 F10
Edgehill Warks 101 B7
Edge Hill Mers 182 C5
Warks 134 D4
Edgeley Gtr Man 184 D5
Edge Mount S Yorks 186 C3
Edgerley Shrops 148 F6
Edgerston Borders 262 G5
Edgerton W Yorks 196 D6
Edgeside Lancs 195 C10
Edgeworth Glos 80 D6
Edginswell Devon 9 B7
Edgiock Worcs 117 E10
Edgmond Telford 150 F4
Edgmond Marsh Telford 150 E4
Edgton Shrops 131 F7
Edgware London 85 G11
Edgwick W Mid 134 G6
Edgworth Blkburn 195 D8
Edham Borders 262 B6
Edial Staffs 133 B11
Edinample Stirl 285 E9
Edinbane Highld 298 D3
Edinburgh Edin 280 G5
Edinchip Stirl 285 E9
Edingale Staffs 152 G4
Edingight Ho Moray 302 D5
Edingley Notts 171 D11
Edingthorpe Norf 160 C6
Edingthorpe Green Norf 160 C6
Edington Som 43 E11
Wilts 46 C2
Edingworth Som 43 C11
Edintore Moray 302 E4
Edistone Devon 24 C2
Edithmead Som 43 D10
Edith Weston Rutland 137 B8
Edlaston Derbys 169 G11
Edlesborough Bucks 85 B7
Edlingham Northumb 252 B4
Edlington Lincs 190 G2
Edmondsham Dorset 31 E9
Edmondsley Durham 233 B10
Edmondstown Rhondda 77 G8
Edmondthorpe Leics 155 F7
Edmonston S Lnrk 269 G11
Edmonstone Orkney 314 D5
Edmonton Corn 10 G5
London 86 G4
Edmundbyers Durham 242 G2
Ednam Borders 262 B6
Ednaston Derbys 170 G2
Edney Common Essex 87 E11
Edradynate Perth 286 B2
Edrom Borders 272 D6
Edstaston Shrops 149 C10
Edstone Warks 118 E3
Edvin Loach Hereford 116 F3
Edwalton Notts 153 B11
Edwardstone Suff 107 C8
Edwardsville M Tydf 77 F9
Edwinsford Carms 94 E2
Edwinstowe Notts 171 B10
Edworth C Beds 104 C4
Edwyn Ralph Hereford 116 F2
Edzell Angus 293 G7
Efail-fâch Neath 57 B9
Efail Isaf Rhondda 58 C5
Efailnewydd Gwyn 145 B7
Efailwen Carms 92 F2
Efenechtyd Denb 165 D10
Effingham Sur 50 C6
Effirth Shetland 313 H5
Efflinch Staffs 152 F3
Efford Devon 26 G5
Plym 7 D10
Egbury Hants 48 C2
Egdon Worcs 117 G8
Egerton Gtr Man 195 E8
Kent 54 D2
Egerton Forstal Kent 53 D11
Egerton Green Ches E 167 E8
Egford Som 45 D9
Eggbeare Corn 12 D2
Eggborough N Yorks 198 C5
Eggbuckland Plym 7 D10
Eggesford Station
Devon 25 E11
Eggington C Beds 103 F9
Egginton Derbys 152 D5
Egginton Common
Derbys 152 D5
Egglesburn Durham 232 G5
Egglescliffe Stockton 225 C8
Eggleston Durham 232 G5
Egham Sur 66 E4
Egham Hythe Sur 66 E4
Egham Wick Sur 66 E3
Egleton Rutland 137 B7
Eglingham Northumb 264 F4
Egloshayle Corn 10 G5
Egloskerry Corn 11 D11
Eglwysbach Conwy 180 G4
Eglwys-Brewis V Glam 58 F4
Eglwys Cross Wrex 167 G7
Eglwys Fach Ceredig 128 D3
Eglwyswen Pembs 92 D3
Eglwyswrw Pembs 92 D2
Egmanton Notts 172 B2
Egmere Norf 159 B8
Egremont Cumb 219 C10
Mers 182 C4
Egton N Yorks 226 D6
Egton Bridge N Yorks 226 D6
Egypt Bucks 66 B3
Hants 48 E3
W Berks 64 D2
W Yorks 205 G7
Eiden Highld 309 J7
Eight Ash Green Essex 107 F8
Eighton Banks T&W 243 F7
Eignaig Highld 289 E9
Eign Hill Hereford 97 D10
Eil Highld 291 B10
Eilanreach Highld 295 D10
Eildon Borders 262 C3
Eileanach Lodge Highld 300 C5
Eilean Anabaich
W Isles 305 H4
Eilean Darach Highld 307 L6
Eilean Shona Ho Highld 289 B8
Einacleite W Isles 304 F3
Einsiob / Evenjobb
Powys 114 E5
Eisgean W Isles 305 G5
Eisingrug Gwyn 146 C2
Eland Green Northumb 242 C5
Elan Village Powys 113 D8
Elberton S Glos 60 B6
Elborough N Som 43 B11
Elbridge Shrops 149 E7
W Sus 22 C6
Elburton Plym 7 E10
Elcho Perth 286 E5
Elcock's Brook Worcs 117 E10
Elcombe Glos 80 F3
Swindon 62 C6
Elcot W Berks 63 F11
Eldene Swindon 63 C7
Eldernell Cambs 138 D6
Eldersfield Worcs 98 E6
Elderslie Renfs 267 C8
Elder Street Essex 105 E11
Eldon Durham 233 F10
Eldon Lane Durham 233 F10
Eldrick S Ayrs 245 G7
Eldroth N Yorks 212 F5
Eldwick W Yorks 205 E8
Elemore Vale T&W 234 B3
Elerch / Bont-goch
Ceredig 128 F3
Elfhowe Cumb 221 F9
Elford Northumb 264 C5
Staffs 152 G3
Elford Closes Cambs 123 C10
Elgin Moray 302 C2
Elgol Highld 295 D7
Elham Kent 55 E7
Eliburn W Loth 269 B10
Elie Fife 287 G8
Elim Anglesey 178 D5
Eling Hants 32 E5
W Berks 64 D4
Elishader Highld 298 C5
Elishaw Northumb 251 D9
Elizafield Dumfries 238 C2
Elkesley Notts 187 F11
Elkington Northants 120 B2
Elkins Green Essex 87 E10
Elkstone Glos 81 C7
Ellacombe Torbay 9 C8
Ellan Highld 301 G8
Elland W Yorks 196 C6
Elland Lower Edge
W Yorks 196 C6
Elland Upper Edge
W Yorks 196 C6
Ellary Argyll 275 F8
Ellastone Staffs 169 G10
Ellel Lancs 202 B5
Ellemford Borders 272 C4
Ellenborough Cumb 228 D6
Ellenbrook Herts 86 D2
IoM 192 E4
Ellenglaze Corn 4 D5
Ellenhall Staffs 150 D6
Ellen's Green Sur 50 F5
Ellerbeck N Yorks 225 F8
Ellerburn N Yorks 216 C6
Ellerby N Yorks 226 C5
Ellerdine Telford 150 E2
Ellerdine Heath Telford 150 E2
Ellerhayes Devon 27 G7
Elleric Argyll 284 C4
Ellerker E Yorks 200 B2
Ellerton E Yorks 207 F10
N Yorks 224 F5
Shrops 150 D4
Ellesborough Bucks 84 D4
Ellesmere Shrops 149 C8
Ellesmere Park Gtr Man 184 B3
Ellesmere Port Ches W 182 F6
Ellicombe Som 42 E3
Ellingham Hants 31 F10
Norf 143 E7
Northumb 264 D5
Ellingstring N Yorks 214 C3
Ellington Cambs 122 C3
Northumb 253 E7
Ellington Thorpe Cambs 122 C3
Elliot Angus 287 D10
Elliots Green Som 45 D9
Elliot's Town Caerph 77 E10
Ellisfield Hants 48 D6
Elliston Borders 262 D3
Ellistown Leics 153 G8
Ellon Aberds 303 F9
Ellonby Cumb 230 D4
Ellough Suff 143 F8
Elloughton E Yorks 200 B2
Ellwood Glos 79 D9
Elm Cambs 139 B9
Elmbridge Glos 80 B5
Worcs 117 D8
Elm Corner Sur 50 B5
Elm Cross Wilts 62 D6
Elmdon Essex 105 D9
W Mid 134 G3
Elmdon Heath W Mid 134 G3
Elmer W Sus 35 G7
Elmers End London 67 F11
Elmers Green Lancs 194 F3
Elmers Marsh W Sus 34 B5
Elmesthorpe Leics 135 D9
Elmfield IoW 21 C8
Elm Hill Dorset 30 B4
Elmhurst Bucks 84 B4
Staffs 152 G2
Elmley Castle Worcs 99 C9
Elmley Lovett Worcs 117 D7
Elmore Glos 80 B3
Elmore Back Glos 80 B3
Elm Park London 68 B4
Elmscott Devon 24 C2
Elmsett Suff 107 B11
Elms Green Hereford 115 F10
Worcs 116 D4
Elmslack Lancs 211 D9
Elmstead Essex 107 F11
London 68 E2
Elmstead Heath Essex 107 G11
Elmstead Market
Essex 107 G11
Elmsted Kent 54 E6
Elmsthorpe Leics 135 D9
Elmstone Kent 71 G9
Elmstone Hardwicke
Glos 99 F8
Elmswell E Yorks 208 B5
Suff 125 E9
Elmton Derbys 187 G8
Elness Orkney 314 C6
Elphin Highld 307 H7
Elphinstone E Loth 281 G7
Elrick Aberds 293 C10
Elrig Dumfries 236 E5
Elrigbeag Argyll 284 F5
Elrington Northumb 241 E9
Elscar S Yorks 197 G11
Elsdon Hereford 114 G6
Northumb 251 E10
Elsecar S Yorks 186 B5
S Yorks 197 G11
Elsenham Essex 105 F10
Elsenham Sta Essex 105 F10
Elsfield Oxon 83 C8
Elsham N Lincs 200 E4
Elsing Norf 159 F11
Elslack N Yorks 204 D4
Elson Hants 33 G10
Shrops 149 B7
Elsrickle S Lnrk 269 G11
Elstead Sur 50 E2
Elsted W Sus 34 D4
Elsthorpe Lincs 155 E11
Elstob Durham 234 G2
Elston Devon 26 G3
Notts 172 F3
Wilts 46 E5
Elstone Devon 25 D11
Elstow Beds 103 B11
Elstree Herts 85 F11
Elstronwick E Yorks 209 G10
Elswick Lancs 202 F4
T&W 242 E6
Elswick Leys Lancs 202 F4
Elsworth Cambs 122 E6
Elterwater Cumb 220 E6
Eltham London 68 E2
Eltisley Cambs 122 F5
Elton Cambs 137 E11
Ches W 183 F7
Derbys 170 C2
Glos 80 C2
Gtr Man 195 E9
Hereford 115 C9
Notts 154 B5
Stockton 225 B8
Elton Green Ches W 183 G7
Elton's Marsh Hereford 97 C9
Eltringham Northumb 242 E3
Elvanfoot S Lnrk 259 F11
Elvaston Derbys 153 C8
Elveden Suff 124 B6
Elvet Hill Durham 233 C11
Elvingston E Loth 281 G9
Elvington Kent 55 C9
York 207 D9
Elwell Devon 41 G7
Dorset 17 E9
Elwick Hrtlpl 234 E5
Northumb 264 B4
Elworth Ches E 168 C2
Elworthy Som 42 G5
Ely Cambs 139 G10
Cardiff 58 D6
Emberton M Keynes 103 B7
Embleton Cumb 229 E9
Durham 234 F4
Northumb 264 E6
Embo Highld 311 K2
Emborough Som 44 C6
Embo Street Highld 311 K2
Embsay N Yorks 204 C6
Emerson Park London 68 B4
Emerson's Green S Glos 61 D7
Emerson Valley
M Keynes 102 E6
Emery Down Hants 32 F3
Emley W Yorks 197 E8
Emmbrook Wokingham 65 F9
Emmer Green Reading 65 D8
Emmett Carr Derbys 187 F7
Emmington Oxon 84 E2
Emneth Norf 139 B9
Emneth Hungate Norf 139 B10
Emorsgate Norf 157 E10
Empingham Rutland 137 B8
Empshott Hants 49 G9
Empshott Green Hants 49 G8
Emscote Warks 118 D5
Emstrey Shrops 149 G10
Emsworth Hants 22 B2
Enborne W Berks 64 F2
Enborne Row W Berks 64 G2
Enchmarsh Shrops 131 D10
Enderby Leics 135 D10
Endmoor Cumb 211 C10
Endon Staffs 168 E6
Endon Bank Staffs 168 E6
Energlyn Caerph 58 B6
Enfield London 86 F4
Worcs 117 D10
Enfield Highway London 86 F5
Enfield Lock London 86 F5
Enfield Town London 86 F4
Enfield Wash London 86 F5
Enford Wilts 46 C6
Engamoor Shetland 313 H4
Engedi Anglesey 178 F5
Engine Common S Glos 61 C7
Englefield W Berks 64 E6
Englefield Green Sur 66 E3
Englesea-brook Ches E 168 E3
English Bicknor Glos 79 B9
Englishcombe Bath 61 G8
English Frankton
Shrops 149 D9
Engollan Corn 10 G3
Enham Alamein Hants 47 D11
Enis Devon 25 B9
Enisfirth Shetland 312 F5
Enmore Som 43 G8
Enmore Field Hereford 115 E9
Enmore Green Dorset 30 C5
Ennerdale Bridge
Cumb 219 B11
Enniscaven Corn 5 D9
Enoch Dumfries 247 C9
Enochdhu Perth 292 G2
Ensay Argyll 288 E5
Ensbury Bmouth 19 B7
Ensbury Park Bmouth 19 C7
Ensdon Shrops 149 F8
Ensis Devon 25 B9
Enslow Oxon 83 B7
Enstone Oxon 101 G7
Enterkinfoot Dumfries 247 C9
Enterpen N Yorks 225 D9
Enton Green Sur 50 E3
Enville Staffs 132 F6
Eolaigearraidh W Isles 297 L3
Eorabus Argyll 288 G5
Eòropaidh W Isles 304 B7
Epney Glos 80 C3
Epperstone Notts 171 F11
Epping Essex 87 E7
Epping Green Essex 86 D6
Herts 86 D3
Epping Upland Essex 86 E6
Eppleby N Yorks 224 C3
Eppleworth E Yorks 208 G6
Epsom Sur 67 G8
Epwell Oxon 101 C7
Epworth N Lincs 199 G9
Epworth Turbary
N Lincs 199 G9
Erbistock Wrex 166 G5
Erbusaig Highld 295 C9
Erchless Castle Highld 300 E4
Erdington W Mid 134 E2
Eredine Argyll 275 C10
Eriboll Highld 308 D4
Ericstane Dumfries 260 G3
Eridge Green E Sus 52 F5
Erines Argyll 275 F9
Eriswell Suff 124 B4
Erith London 68 D4
Erlestoke Wilts 46 C3
Ermine Lincs 189 G7
Ermington Devon 8 E2
Ernesettle Plym 7 D8
Erpingham Norf 160 C3
Erriottwood Kent 54 B2
Errogie Highld 300 G5
Errol Perth 286 E6
Errol Station Perth 286 E6
Erskine Renfs 277 G9
Erskine Bridge Renfs 277 G9
Ervie Dumfries 236 C2
Erwarton Suff 108 E4
Erwood Powys 95 C11
Eryholme N Yorks 224 D6
Eryrys Denb 166 D2
Escomb Durham 233 E9
Escott Som 42 F5
Escrick N Yorks 207 E8
Esgairdawe Carms 94 C2
Esgairgeiliog Powys 128 B5
Esgyryn Conwy 180 F4
Esh Durham 233 C9
Esher Sur 66 G6
Eshiels Borders 261 B7
Esholt W Yorks 205 E9
Eshott Northumb 252 D6
Eshton N Yorks 204 B4
Esh Winning Durham 233 C9
Eskadale Highld 300 F4
Eskbank Midloth 270 B6
Eskdale Green Cumb 220 E2
Eskdalemuir Dumfries 249 D7
Eske E Yorks 209 E7
Eskham Lincs 190 B5
Eskholme S Yorks 198 D6
Esknish Argyll 274 G4
Esk Valley N Yorks 226 E6
Eslington Park
Northumb 264 G2
Esperley Lane Ends
Durham 233 G8
Esprick Lancs 202 F4
Essendine Rutland 155 G10
Essendon Herts 86 D3
Essich Highld 300 F6
Essington Staffs 133 C9
Esslemont Aberds 303 G9
Eston Redcar 225 B11
Estover Plym 7 D10
Eswick Shetland 313 H6
Etal Northumb 263 B10
Etchilhampton Wilts 62 G4
Etchingham E Sus 38 B2
Etchinghill Kent 55 F7
Staffs 151 F10
Etchingwood E Sus 37 C8
Etherley Dene Durham 233 F9
Ethie Castle Angus 287 C10
Ethie Mains Angus 287 C10
Etling Green Norf 159 G10
Etloe Glos 79 D11
Eton Windsor 66 D3
Eton Wick Windsor 66 D2
Etruria Stoke 168 F5
Etsell Shrops 131 C7
Etterby Cumb 239 F9
Etteridge Highld 291 D8
Ettersgill Durham 232 F3
Ettiley Heath Ches E 168 C2
Ettingshall W Mid 133 D8
Ettingshall Park W Mid 133 D8
Ettington Warks 100 B5
Etton E Yorks 208 E5
Pboro 138 B2
Ettrick Borders 261 G7
Ettrickbridge Borders 261 E9
Ettrickdale Argyll 275 G11
Ettrickhill Borders 261 G7
Etwall Derbys 152 C5
Etwall Common Derbys 152 C5
Eudon Burnell Shrops 132 F3
Eudon George Shrops 132 F3
Euston Suff 125 B7
Euximoor Drove
Cambs 139 D9
Euxton Lancs 194 D5
Evanstown Bridgend 58 B3
Evanton Highld 300 C6
Evedon Lincs 173 F9
Eve Hill W Mid 133 E8
Evelix Highld 309 K7
Evendine Hereford 98 C5
Evenjobb / Einsiob
Powys 114 E5
Evenley Northants 101 E11
Evenlode Glos 100 F4
Even Pits Hereford 97 D11
Even Swindon Swindon 62 B6
Evenwood Durham 233 G9
Evenwood Gate Durham 233 G9
Everbay Orkney 314 D6
Evercreech Som 44 F6
Everdon Northants 119 F11
Everingham E Yorks 208 E2
Everland Shetland 312 D8
Everleigh Wilts 47 C8
Everley N Yorks 217 B9
Eversholt C Beds 103 E9
Evershot Dorset 29 G9
Eversley Essex 69 B8
Hants 65 G9
Eversley Centre Hants 65 G9
Eversley Cross Hants 65 G9
Everthorpe E Yorks 208 G4
Everton C Beds 122 G4
Hants 19 C11
Mers 182 C5
Notts 187 C11
Evertown Dumfries 239 B9
Evesbatch Hereford 98 B3
Evesham Worcs 99 C10
Evington Kent 54 D6
Leicester 136 C2
Ewanrigg Cumb 228 D6
Ewden Village S Yorks 186 B3
Ewell Sur 67 G8
Ewell Minnis Kent 55 E9
Ewelme Oxon 83 G10
Ewen Glos 81 F8
Ewenny V Glam 58 D2
Ewerby Lincs 173 F10
Ewerby Thorpe Lincs 173 F10
Ewes Dumfries 249 E9
Ewesley Northumb 252 E3
Ewhurst Sur 50 E5
Ewhurst Green E Sus 38 C3
Sur 50 F5
Ewloe Flint 166 B4
Ewloe Green Flint 166 B3
Ewood Blkburn 195 B7
Ewood Bridge Lancs 195 C9
Eworthy Devon 12 C5
Ewshot Hants 49 D10
Ewyas Harold Hereford 97 F7
Exbourne Devon 25 G10
Exbury Hants 20 B4
Exceat E Sus 23 F8
Exebridge Devon 26 C6
Exelby N Yorks 214 B5
Exeter Devon 14 C4
Exford Som 41 F11
Exfords Green Shrops 131 B9
Exhall Warks 118 F2
Warks 135 F7
Exlade Street Oxon 65 C7
Exley W Yorks 196 C5
Exley Head W Yorks 204 F6
Exminster Devon 14 D4
Exmouth Devon 14 E6
Exnaboe Shetland 313 M5
Exning Suff 124 D2
Exted Kent 55 E7
Exton Devon 14 D5
Hants 33 C10
Rutland 155 G8
Som 42 G2
Exwick Devon 14 C4
Eyam Derbys 186 F2
Eydon Northants 119 G10
Eye Hereford 115 E9
Pboro 138 C4
Suff 126 C2
Eye Green Pboro 138 C4
Eyemouth Borders 273 C8
Eyeworth C Beds 104 B4
Eyhorne Street Kent 53 C10
Eyke Suff 126 G6
Eynesbury Cambs 122 F3
Eynort Highld 294 C5
Eynsford Kent 68 F4
Eynsham Oxon 82 D6
Eype Dorset 16 C5
Eyre Highld 295 B7
Highld 298 D4
Eyres Monsell
Leicester 135 D11
Eythorne Kent 55 D9
Eyton Hereford 115 E9
Shrops 131 F7
Shrops 149 G7
Wrex 166 G4
Eyton on Severn
Shrops 131 B11
Eyton upon the Weald
Moors Telford 150 G3

F

Faberstown Wilts 47 C9
Faccombe Hants 47 B11
Faceby N Yorks 225 E9
Fachell Gwyn 163 B8
Fachwen Gwyn 163 C9
Facit Lancs 195 D11
Fackley Notts 171 C7
Faddiley Ches E 167 E9
Faddonch Highld 295 C11
Fadmoor N Yorks 216 B3
Faerdre Swansea 75 E11
Fagley W Yorks 205 G9
Fagwyr Swansea 75 E11
Faichem Highld 290 C4
Faifley W Dunb 277 G10
Failand N Som 60 E4
Failford S Ayrs 257 D11
Failsworth Gtr Man 195 G11
Fain Highld 299 B11
Faindouran Lodge
Moray 292 C2
Fairbourne Gwyn 146 G2
Fairbourne Heath Kent 53 C11
Fairburn N Yorks 198 B3
Fairburn House Highld 300 D4
Fair Cross London 68 B3
Fairfield Clack 279 C7
Derbys 185 G9
Gtr Man 184 B6
Gtr Man 195 E10
Kent 39 B7
Mers 182 C5
Stockton 225 B8
Worcs 99 C10
Worcs 117 B8
Fairfield Park Bath 61 F9
Fairfields Glos 98 E4
Fairford Glos 81 E11
Fair Green Norf 158 F3
Fairhaven Lancs 193 B10
N Ayrs 255 C10
Fairhill S Lnrk 268 E4
Fair Hill Cumb 230 E6
Fairlands Sur 50 C3
Fairlee IoW 20 C6
Fairlie N Ayrs 266 D4
Fairlight E Sus 38 E5
Fairlight Cove E Sus 38 E5
Fairlop London 87 G7
Fairmile Devon 15 B7
Dorset 19 C9
Sur 66 G6
Fairmilehead Edin 270 B4
Fair Moor Northumb 252 F5
Fairoak Caerph 77 F11
Staffs 150 C5
Fair Oak Hants 33 D7
Hants 64 G5
Lancs 203 D8
Fair Oak Green Hants 65 G7
Fairseat Kent 68 G6
Fairstead Essex 88 B3
Norf 158 F2
Fairview Glos 99 G9
Fairwarp E Sus 37 B7
Fairwater Cardiff 58 D6
Torf 78 G3
Fairwood Wilts 45 C10
Fairy Cottage IoM 192 D5
Fairy Cross Devon 24 C6
Fakenham Norf 159 D8
Fakenham Magna Suff 125 B8
Fala Midloth 271 C8
Fala Dam Midloth 271 C8
Falahill Borders 271 D7
Falcon Hereford 98 E2
Falcon Lodge W Mid 134 D2
Falconwood London 68 D3
Falcutt Northants 101 C11
Faldingworth Lincs 189 E9
Faldonside Borders 262 C2
Falfield Fife 287 G8
S Glos 79 G11
Falkenham Suff 108 D5
Falkenham Sink Suff 108 D5
Falkirk Falk 279 F7
Falkland Fife 286 G6
Falla Borders 262 G6
Fallgate Derbys 170 C5
Fallin Stirl 278 C6
Fallinge Derbys 170 B3
Fallings Heath W Mid 133 D9
Fallowfield Gtr Man 184 C5
Fallside N Lnrk 268 C4
Falmer E Sus 36 F5
Falmouth Corn 3 C8
Falnash Borders 249 B9
Falsgrave N Yorks 217 B10
Falside W Loth 269 B9
Falsidehill Borders 272 G3
Falstone Northumb 250 F6
Fanagmore Highld 306 E6
Fancott C Beds 103 F10
Fangdale Beck
N Yorks 225 G11
Fangfoss E Yorks 207 C11
Fanich Highld 311 J2
Fankerton Falk 278 E5
Fanmore Argyll 288 E6
Fanner's Green Essex 87 C11
Fannich Lodge Highld 300 C2
Fans Borders 272 G2
Fanshowe Ches E 184 G5
Fant Kent 53 B8
Faoilean Highld 295 C7
Far Arnside Cumb 211 D8
Far Bank S Yorks 198 E6
Far Banks Lancs 194 C2
Far Bletchley M Keynes 103 E7
Farcet Cambs 138 E4
Far Coton Leics 135 C7
Far Cotton Northants 120 F4
Farden Shrops 115 B11
Fareham Hants 33 F9
Far End Cumb 220 F6
Farewell Staffs 151 G11
Far Forest Worcs 116 C4
Farforth Lincs 190 F4
Far Green Glos 80 E3
Farhill Derbys 170 C5
Far Hoarcross Staffs 152 E2
Faringdon Oxon 82 F3
Farington Lancs 194 B4
Farington Moss Lancs 194 C4
Farlam Cumb 240 F3
Farlands Booth Derbys 185 D9
Farlary Highld 309 J7
Far Laund Derbys 170 F5
Farleigh N Som 60 F3
Sur 67 G11
Farleigh Court Sur 67 G11
Farleigh Green Kent 53 C8
Farleigh Hungerford
Som 45 B10
Farleigh Wallop Hants 48 D6
Farleigh Wick Wilts 61 G10
Farlesthorpe Lincs 191 G7
Farleton Cumb 211 C10
Lancs 211 F11
Farley Bristol 60 E2
Derbys 170 C3
Shrops 131 B7
Shrops 132 C2
Staffs 169 G9
Wilts 32 B2
Far Ley Staffs 132 D5
Farley Green Suff 124 G4
Sur 50 D5
Farley Hill Luton 103 G11
Wokingham 65 G8
Farleys End Glos 80 B3
Farlington N Yorks 216 F2
Ptsmth 33 F11
Farlow Shrops 132 G2
Farmborough Bath 61 G7
Farmbridge End
Essex 87 C10
Farmcote Glos 99 F11
Shrops 132 E5
Farmington Glos 81 B10
Farmoor Oxon 82 D6
Far Moor Gtr Man 194 G4
Farms Common Corn 2 C5
Farmtown Moray 302 D5
Farm Town Leics 153 F7
Farnah Green Derbys 170 F4
Farnborough Hants 49 C11
London 68 G2
Warks 101 B8
W Berks 64 C2
Farnborough Green
Hants 49 B11
Farnborough Park
Hants 49 B11
Farnborough Street
Hants 49 B11
Farncombe Sur 50 E3
Farndish Beds 121 E8
Farndon Ches W 166 E6
Notts 172 E3
Farnell Angus 287 B10
Farnham Dorset 31 D7
Essex 105 G9

Farnham *continued*
N Yorks 215 G7
Suff 127 E7
Sur 49 D10
Farnham Common Bucks 66 C3
Farnham Green Essex . 105 F9
Farnham Park Bucks . . 66 C3
Farnham Royal Bucks . . 66 C3
Farnhill N Yorks 204 D6
Farningham Kent 68 F4
Farnley N Yorks 205 D10
    W Yorks 205 G11
Farnley Bank W Yorks . 197 E7
Farnley Tyas W Yorks . 197 E7
Farnsfield Notts 171 D10
Farnworth Gtr Man 195 F8
    Halton 183 D8
Far Oakridge Glos 80 E6
Farr Highld 291 C10
    Highld 300 F6
    Highld 308 C7
Farraline Highld 300 G5
Farr House Highld 300 E5
Farrington Dorset 14 C6
    T&W 243 G9
Farrington Dorset 30 D4
Farrington Gurney Bath . 44 B6
Far Royds W Yorks . . . 205 G11
Far Sawrey Cumb 221 F7
Farsley W Yorks 205 F10
Farsley Beck Bottom
    W Yorks 205 F10
Farther Howegreen
    Essex 88 E4
Farthing Corner
    Medway 69 G10
Farthing Green Kent . . . 53 D10
Farthinghoe Northants . 101 D10
Farthingloe Kent 55 E9
Farthingstone Northants 120 F2
Far Thrupp Glos 80 E5
Fartown W Yorks 196 D6
Farway Devon 15 B9
Farway Marsh Devon . . 28 G4
Fasach Highld 297 G7
Fasag Highld 299 D8
Fascadale Highld 289 B7
Faslane Port Argyll . . . 276 D4
Fasnacloich Argyll 284 C4
Fasnakyle Ho Highld . . 300 G3
Fassfern Highld 290 F2
Fatfield T&W 243 G8
Fattahead Aberds 302 D6
Fauldclean W Loth . . . 279 G11
Faugh Cumb 240 G2
Faughill Borders 262 C2
Fauld Staffs 152 D3
Fauldhouse W Loth . . . 269 C8
Fauldiehill Angus 287 D9
Fauldshope Borders . . . 261 D10
Faulkbourne Essex 88 B3
Faulkland Som 45 C8
Fauls Shrops 149 C11
Faverdale Darl 224 B5
Faversham Kent 70 G4
Favillar Moray 302 F2
Fawdington N Yorks . . 215 E8
Fawdon Northumb 264 F2
    T&W 242 D6
Fawfieldhead Staffs . . . 169 C9
Fawkham Green Kent . . 68 F5
Fawler Oxon 63 B10
    Oxon 82 B5
Fawley Bucks 65 B9
    Hants 33 G7
    W Berks 63 C11
Fawley Bottom Bucks . . 65 B8
Fawley Chapel Hereford . 97 F11
Faxfleet E Yorks 199 C11
Faygate W Sus 51 G8
Fazakerley Mers 182 B5
Fazeley Staffs 134 C4
Feagour Highld 291 D7
Fearby N Yorks 214 C3
Fearn Highld 301 B8
Fearnan Perth 285 C11
Fearnbeg Highld 299 D7
Fearn Lodge Highld . . . 309 L6
Fearnmore Highld 299 C7
Fearn Station Highld . . 301 B8
Fearnville W Yorks . . . 206 F2
Featherstone Staffs . . . 133 B8
    W Yorks 198 C2
Featherwood Northumb 251 C8
Feckenham Worcs 117 E10
Fedw Fawr Anglesey . . 179 E10
Feering Essex 107 G7
Feetham N Yorks 223 F9
Fegg Hayes Stoke 168 E5
Fèith Mhor Highld 301 G8
Feizor N Yorks 212 F5
Felbridge Sur 51 F11
Felbrigg Norf 160 B4
Felcourt Sur 51 E11
Felden Herts 85 E8
Felderland Kent 55 B10
Feldy Ches E 183 F11
Felhampton Shrops . . . 131 F8
Felin-Crai Powys 95 G7
Felindre Carms 75 B7
    Carms 93 D7
    Carms 93 G11
    Carms 94 E3
    Carms 94 F4
    Ceredig 111 F10
    Powys 96 B3
    Powys 96 G3
    Powys 130 C3
    Powys 130 G3
    Rhondda 58 C3
    Swansea 75 E10
Felindre Farchog Pembs . 92 D2
Felinfach Ceredig 111 F10
    Powys 95 E11
Felinfoel Carms 75 E8
Felingwmisaf Carms . . 93 G10
Felingwmuchaf Carms . 93 G10
Felin Newydd Carms . . . 94 D3
Felin-newydd Powys . . . 96 D2
Felin Newydd / New Mills
    Powys 129 C10
Felin Puleston Wrex . . 166 F4
Felin-Wnda Ceredig . . . 92 B6
Felinwynt Ceredig 110 G4
Felixkirk N Yorks 215 C9
Felixstowe Suff 108 E5
Felixstowe Ferry Suff . 108 E5
Felkington Northumb . . 273 G8
Felkirk W Yorks 197 E11
Felldyke Cumb 219 B11
Fell End Cumb 222 F4
Fellgate T&W 243 E8
Felling T&W 243 E7
Felling Shore T&W . . . 243 E7
Fell Lane W Yorks 204 E6
Fellside T&W 242 E5
Fell Side Cumb 230 D2
Felmersham Beds 121 F9

Felmingham Norf 160 D5
Felmore Essex 69 B8
Felpham W Sus 35 H7
Felsham Suff 125 F8
Felsted Essex 106 G3
Feltham London 66 E6
    Som 28 D2
Felthamhill London 66 E5
Felthorpe Norf 160 F3
Felton Hereford 97 B11
    Northumb 252 C5
    N Som 60 F4
Felton Butler Shrops . . 149 F7
Feltwell Norf 140 E4
Fenay Bridge W Yorks . 197 D7
Fence Lancs 204 F2
Fence Houses T&W . . . 243 G8
Fencott Oxon 83 B9
Fen Ditton Cambs 123 E9
Fen Drayton Cambs . . . 122 D6
Fen End Lincs 156 E4
    W Mid 118 B4
Fengate Norf 160 E3
    Pboro 138 D4
Fenham Northumb 273 G11
    T&W 242 D6
Fenhouses Lincs 174 G3
Feniscliffe Blkburn . . . 195 B7
Feniscowles Blkburn . . 194 B6
Feniton Devon 15 B8
Fenlake Beds 103 B11
Fenn Green Shrops . . . 132 G5
Fennington Som 27 B11
Fenn's Bank Wrex 149 B10
Fenn Street Medway . . . 69 D9
Fenny Bentley Derbys . 169 E11
Fenny Bridges Devon . . 15 B8
Fenny Castle Som 44 E4
Fenny Compton Warks . 119 G8
Fenny Drayton Leics . . 134 D6
Fenny Stratford
    M Keynes 103 E7
Fenrother Northumb . . 252 E5
Fen Side Lincs 174 D4
Fenstanton Cambs 122 D6
Fenstead End Suff 124 G6
Fen Street Norf 141 G11
    Suff 125 B9
    Suff 125 B11
Fenton Cambs 122 B6
    Cumb 240 F2
    Lincs 172 E5
    Lincs 188 F4
    Northumb 263 C11
    Stoke 168 G5
Fenton Barns E Loth . . 281 E10
Fenton Low Stoke 168 F5
Fenton Pits Corn 6 B2
Fenton Town Northumb 263 C11
Fenwick E Ayrs 267 G9
    Northumb 242 C3
    Northumb 273 G11
    S Yorks 198 D5
Feochaig Argyll 255 F8
Feock Corn 3 B8
Feolin Ferry Argyll . . . 274 G5
Fergushie Park Renfs . . 267 C9
Ferindonald Highld . . . 295 E8
Feriniquarrie Highld . . 296 F7
Ferlochan Argyll 289 E11
Fern Angus 292 G6
Fern Bank Gtr Man . . . 185 B7
Ferndale Kent 52 E5
    Rhondda 77 F7
Ferndown Dorset 31 G9
Ferne Wilts 30 C6
Ferness Highld 301 E10
Ferney Green Cumb . . . 221 F8
Fernham Oxon 82 G3
Fernhill Gtr Man 195 E10
    Rhondda 77 F8
    W Sus 51 E10
Fern Hill Suff 108 B6
Fernhill Gate Gtr Man . 195 F7
Fernhill Heath Worcs . 117 F7
Fernhurst W Sus 34 B5
Fernie Fife 287 F7
Ferniebrae Aberds 303 D9
Ferniegair S Lnrk 268 E4
Ferniehirst Borders . . . 271 G8
Fernilea Highld 294 B5
Fernilee Derbys 185 F8
Fernsplatt Corn 4 G5
Ferrensby N Yorks 215 G7
Ferring W Sus 35 G9
Ferrybridge W Yorks . . 198 C3
Ferryden Angus 287 B11
Ferryhill Aberdeen . . . 293 C11
    Durham 233 E11
Ferry Hill Cambs 139 G7
Ferryhill Station Durham 234 E2
Ferry Point Highld 309 L7
Ferryside / Glan-y-Ffer
    Carms 74 C5
Ferryton Highld 300 C6
Fersfield Norf 141 G11
Fersit Highld 290 F5
Feshiebridge Highld . . 291 C10
Fetcham Sur 50 B6
Fetterangus Aberds . . . 303 D9
Fettercairn Aberds . . . 293 F8
Fetterdale Fife 287 E8
Fettes Highld 300 D5
Fewcott Oxon 101 F10
Fewston N Yorks 205 D9
Fewston Bents N Yorks 205 C9
Ffairfach Carms 94 G2
Ffair-Rhos Ceredig . . . 112 D4
Ffaldybrenin Carms . . . 94 C3
Ffarmers Carms 94 C3
Ffawyddog Powys 78 B2
Ffodun / Forden Powys 130 C4
Ffont y gari / Font y gary
    V Glam 58 F5
Fforddlas Powys 96 D4
Ffordd-las Denb 165 C10
Ffordd-y-Gyfraith
    Bridgend 57 E11
Fforest Carms 75 E9
Fforest-fach Swansea . . 56 B6
Fforest Gôch Neath 76 E2
Ffostrasol Ceredig 93 B7
Ffos-y-ffin Ceredig . . . 111 E8
Ffos-y-go Wrex 166 E4
Ffridd Powys 130 D3
Ffrith Wrex 166 D3
Ffrwd Gwyn 163 D7
Ffwl y mwn / Fonmon
    V Glam 58 F4
Ffynnon Carms 74 C4
Ffynnon ddrain Carms . 93 G8
Ffynnongroes / Crosswell
    Pembs 92 D2
Ffynnon Gron Pembs . . 91 F8
Ffynnongroyw Flint . . 181 E10
Ffynnon Gynydd Powys 96 C3
Ffynnon-oer Ceredig . . 111 G10
Fickleshole Sur 67 G11
Fidden Argyll 288 G5

Fiddes Aberds 293 E10
Fiddington Glos 99 E8
    Som 43 E8
Fiddington Sands Wilts . 46 C4
Fiddleford Dorset 30 E4
Fiddler' Green Norf . . . 141 D10
Fiddler's Ferry Mers . . 193 C11
    Warr 183 D9
Fiddler's Green Glos . . . 99 G8
    Hereford 97 D11
Fiddlers Hamlet Essex . . 87 E7
Field Hereford 114 G6
    Som 44 E6
    Staffs 151 C10
Field Assarts Oxon 82 C4
Field Broughton Cumb . 211 C7
Field Common Sur 66 F6
Field Dalling Norf 159 B10
Field Green Kent 38 B3
Field Head Leics 135 B9
Fields End Herts 85 D8
Field's Place Hereford . 115 G8
Fifehead Magdalen
    Dorset 30 C3
Fifehead Neville Dorset . 30 E3
Fifehead St Quintin
    Dorset 30 E3
Fife Keith Moray 302 D4
Fifield Oxon 82 B2
    Wilts 46 C6
    Windsor 66 D2
Fifield Bavant Wilts . . . 31 B8
Figheldean Wilts 47 D7
Filands Wilts 62 B2
Filby Norf 161 G9
Filby Heath Norf 161 G9
Filchampstead Oxon . . . 83 D7
Filey N Yorks 218 C2
Filgrave M Keynes 103 B7
Filham Devon 8 D2
Filkins Oxon 82 E2
Filleigh Devon 25 B11
    Devon 26 E2
Fillingham Lincs 188 D6
Fillongley Warks 134 F5
Filmore Hill Hants 33 B11
Filton S Glos 60 D6
Fimber E Yorks 217 G7
Finavon Angus 287 B8
Fincastle Ho Perth 291 G10
Finchairn Argyll 275 C10
Fincham Mers 182 C6
    Norf 140 B3
Finchampstead
    Wokingham 65 G9
Finchdean Hants 34 E2
Finchingfield Essex . . . 106 E3
Finchley London 86 G3
Findern Derbys 152 C6
Findhorn Moray 301 C10
Findhorn Bridge Highld 301 G8
Findochty Moray 302 C4
Findo Gask Perth 286 E4
Findon Aberds 293 D11
    W Sus 35 F10
Findon Mains Highld . . 300 C6
Findon Valley W Sus . . 35 F10
Findrack Ho Aberds . . . 293 C8
Finedon Northants 121 C8
Fineglen Argyll 275 B10
Fine Street Hereford . . . 96 D6
Fingal Street Suff 126 D4
Fingask Aberds 303 G7
Fingerpost Worcs 116 C4
Fingest Bucks 84 G3
Finghall N Yorks 214 B3
Fingland Cumb 239 F7
    Dumfries 259 F7
Finglesham Kent 55 C10
Fingringhoe Essex 107 G10
Finham W Mid 118 B6
Finkle Street S Yorks . . 186 B4
Finlarig Stirl 285 D9
Finmere Oxon 102 E2
Finnart Perth 285 B8
Finney Green Ches E . . 184 E5
    Staffs 168 F3
Finningham Suff 125 D11
Finningley S Yorks . . . 187 B11
Finnygaud Aberds 302 D5
Finsbury London 67 C10
Finsbury Park London . . 67 B10
Finstall Worcs 117 D9
Finsthwaite Cumb 211 B7
Finstock Oxon 82 B5
Finstown Orkney 314 E3
Fintry Aberds 303 D7
    Dundee 287 D8
    Stirl 278 C3
Finwood Warks 118 D3
Finzean Aberds 293 D8
Finzean Ho Aberds . . . 293 D7
Fionnphort Argyll 288 G5
Fionnsbhagh W Isles . . 296 C6
Firbank Cumb 222 G2
Firbeck S Yorks 187 D9
Firby N Yorks 214 B5
    N Yorks 216 F4
Firemore Highld 307 L3
Firgrove Gtr Man 196 E2
Firkin Argyll 285 G7
Firle E Sus 23 D7
Firsby Lincs 175 C7
Firsdown Wilts 47 G8
Firs Lane Gtr Man 194 G6
First Coast Highld 307 K4
Firswood Gtr Man 184 B4
Firth Shetland 312 F6
Firth Moor Darl 224 C6
Firth Park S Yorks 186 C5
Fir Toll Kent 54 E2
Fir Tree Durham 233 E8
Fir Vale S Yorks 186 C5
Firwood Fold Gtr Man . 195 E8
Fishbourne IoW 21 C7
    W Sus 22 C4
Fishburn Durham 234 E3
    N Yorks 217 D10
Fisherdark Ches E 279 B7
Fisherford Aberds 302 F6
Fishermead M Keynes . 103 D7
Fisher Place Cumb 220 B6
Fisherrow E Loth 280 G6
Fishersgate Brighton . . . 36 F3
Fishers Green Herts . . . 104 F4
Fisher's Pond Hants . . . 33 C7
Fisherstreet W Sus 50 G3
Fisherton Highld 301 D7
    S Ayrs 257 F7
Fisherton de la Mere
    Wilts 46 F4
Fishguard / Abergwaun
    Pembs 91 D9
Fishlake S Yorks 199 E7
Fishleigh Devon 25 F8
Fishleigh Barton Devon . 25 C9
Fishley Norf 161 G8
Fishmere End Lincs . . . 156 B5
Fishponds Bristol 60 D6
Fishpool Glos 98 F3
    Gtr Man 195 F10
    N Yorks 205 D10
Fishpools Powys 114 D3
Fishtoft Lincs 174 G5
Fishtoft Drove Lincs . . 174 F4
Fishtown of Usan
    Angus 287 B11
Fishwick Borders 273 E8
    Lancs 194 B5
Fiskavaig Highld 294 B5
Fiskerton Lincs 189 G8
    Notts 172 E2
Fitling E Yorks 209 G11
Fittleton Wilts 46 D6
Fittleworth W Sus 35 D8
Fitton End Cambs 157 G8
Fitz Shrops 149 F8
Fitzhead Som 27 B10
Fitzwilliam W Yorks . . 198 D2
Fiunary Highld 289 E8
Five Acres Glos 79 C9
Five Ash Down E Sus . . 37 C7
Five Ashes E Sus 37 C9
Five Bells Som 42 E5
Five Bridges Hereford . . 98 B3
Fivecrosses Ches W . . . 183 F8
Fivehead Som 28 C5
Five Houses IoW 20 D4
Five Lane Ends Lancs . . 202 C6
Five Lanes Mon 78 G6
Five Oak Green Kent . . . 52 D6
Five Oaks W Sus 35 B9
Five Roads Carms 75 D7
Five Ways Warks 118 D4
Five Wents Kent 53 C10
Flackley Ash E Sus 38 C5
Flack's Green Essex 88 B3
Flackwell Heath Bucks . 65 B11
Fladbury Worcs 99 B9
Fladbury Cross Worcs . . 99 B9
Fladda Shetland 312 E5
Fladdabister Shetland . 313 K6
Flagg Derbys 169 B10
Flaggoners Green
    Hereford 116 G2
Flamborough E Yorks . 218 E4
Flamstead Herts 85 C9
Flamstead End Herts . . 86 E4
Flansham W Sus 35 G7
Flanshaw W Yorks . . . 197 C10
Flappit Spring W Yorks 205 F7
Flasby N Yorks 204 B4
Flash Staffs 169 B8
Flashader Highld 298 D3
Flask Inn N Yorks 227 D8
Flathurst W Sus 35 C7
Flaunden Herts 85 E8
Flawborough Notts . . . 172 G3
Flawith N Yorks 215 F9
Flax Bourton N Som . . . 60 F4
Flaxby N Yorks 206 B3
Flaxholme Derbys 170 G4
Flaxlands Norf 142 E2
Flaxley Glos 79 B11
Flax Moss Lancs 195 C9
Flaxpool Som 42 F6
Flaxton N Yorks 216 G3
Fleckney Leics 136 E2
Flecknoe Warks 119 E10
Fledborough Notts 188 G4
Fleet Dorset 17 E8
    Hants 22 C2
    Hants 49 C10
    Lincs 157 E7
Fleet Downs Kent 68 E5
Fleetend Hants 33 F8
Fleet Hargate Lincs . . . 157 E7
Fleetlands Hants 33 G9
Fleets N Yorks 213 G9
Fleetville Herts 85 D11
Fleetwood Lancs 202 D2
Fleggburgh / Burgh St
    Margaret Norf 161 G8
Fleming Field Durham . 234 C3
Flemings Corn 5 B9
Flemingston V Glam . . . 58 E4
Flemington S Lnrk 268 D3
    S Lnrk 268 G4
Flempton Suff 124 D6
Fleoideabhagh W Isles . 296 C6
Fletchersbridge Corn . . 6 B2
Fletcher's Green Kent . . 52 C4
Fletchertown Cumb . . . 229 C10
Fletching E Sus 36 C6
Fletching Common
    E Sus 36 C6
Fleuchary Highld 309 K7
Fleuchlang Dumfries . . 237 D8
Fleur-de-lis Caerph 77 F11
Flexbury Corn 24 F2
Flexford Hants 32 C6
    Sur 50 D2
Flimby Cumb 228 E6
Flimwell E Sus 53 G8
Flint Flint 182 G2
Flint Cross Cambs 105 C8
Flintham Notts 172 F2
Flint Hill Durham 242 G5
Flinton E Yorks 209 F11
Flint's Green W Mid . . 134 G5
Flintsham Hereford . . . 114 F6
Flishinghurst Kent 53 F9
Flitcham Norf 158 D4
Flitholme Cumb 222 B5
Flitton C Beds 103 D11
Flitwick C Beds 103 D10
Flixborough N Lincs . . 199 D11
Flixborough Stather
    N Lincs 199 D11
Flixton Gtr Man 184 C2
    N Yorks 217 D10
    Suff 142 F6
Flockton W Yorks 197 E8
Flockton Green
    W Yorks 197 D8
Flodaigh W Isles 296 F4
Floddan Northumb . . . 263 B10
Flodigarry Highld 298 B4
Floodgates Hereford . . 114 F6
Flood's Ferry Cambs . . 139 E7
Flookburgh Cumb 211 D7
Flordon Norf 142 D3
Flore Northants 120 E2
Florence Stoke 168 G6
Flotterton Northumb . . 251 C11
Flowers Bottom Bucks . 84 F4
Flowers Green E Sus . . . 23 C10
Flowery Field Gtr Man . 184 B6
Flowton Suff 107 B11
Flowton Suff 107 B11
Fluchter E Dunb 277 G11
Flugarth Shetland 313 G6

Flushdyke W Yorks . . . 197 C9
Flush House W Yorks . 196 F6
Flushing Aberds 303 E10
    Corn 3 C8
    Corn 3 D7
Flushing Glos 98 F3
Flyford Flavell Worcs . 117 G9
Foals Green Suff 126 C5
Fobbing Thurrock 69 C8
Fochabers Moray 302 D3
Fochriw Caerph 77 D10
Fockerby N Lincs 199 D10
Fodderletter Moray . . . 301 G11
Forfar Angus 287 B8
Fodderty Highld 300 D5
Foddington Som 29 B9
Foel Powys 147 G9
Foel-gastell Carms 75 C8
Foffarty Angus 287 C8
Foggathorpe E Yorks . . 207 F11
Foggbrook Gtr Man . . . 184 C6
Fogo Borders 272 F5
Fogorig Borders 272 F5
Foindle Highld 306 E6
Folda Angus 292 G3
Fold Head Lancs 195 D11
Fold Hill Lincs 175 E7
Foldrings S Yorks 186 C3
Foleshill W Mid 135 G7
Foley Park Worcs 116 B6
Folke Dorset 29 E11
Folkestone Kent 55 F8
Folkingham Lincs 155 C11
Folkington E Sus 23 E9
Folksworth Cambs 138 F2
Folkton N Yorks 217 D11
Folla Rule Aberds 303 F7
Follifoot N Yorks 206 C2
Follingsby T&W 243 E8
Folly Dorset 30 G2
    Pembs 91 G8
Folly Cross Devon 25 F7
Folly Gate Devon 13 B7
Folly Green Essex 106 F6
Fonmon / Ffwl-y-mwn
    V Glam 58 F4
Fonston Corn 11 C10
Fonthill Bishop Wilts . . 46 G2
Fonthill Gifford Wilts . . 46 G2
Fontmell Magna Dorset . 30 D5
Fontmell Parva Dorset . 30 E4
Fontwell W Sus 35 F7
Font-y-gary / Font-y-gari
    V Glam 58 F5
Foodieash Fife 287 F7
Foolow Derbys 185 F11
Foots Green Glos 99 F10
Footherley Staffs 134 C2
Footrid Worcs 116 C3
Foots Cray London 68 E3
Forbestown Aberds . . . 292 B5
Force Forge Cumb 220 G6
Force Green Kent 52 B2
Force Mills Cumb 220 G6
Forcett N Yorks 224 C3
Ford Argyll 275 C9
    Bucks 84 D3
    Derbys 186 E6
    Devon 8 E2
    Devon 8 F3
    Devon 24 C6
    Devon 28 G2
    Glos 99 F11
    Hereford 115 F10
    Kent 71 F8
    Mers 182 B4
    Northumb 263 B10
    Pembs 91 F9
    Plym 7 D9
    Shrops 149 G8
    Som 44 C5
    Som 42 F5
    Staffs 169 E9
    Wilts 47 G2
    Wilts 61 E10
    W Sus 35 G7
Forda Devon 12 C6
    Devon 40 F3
Fordbridge W Mid 134 F3
Fordcombe Kent 52 E4
Fordell Fife 280 D3
Forden / Ffodun Powys 130 C4
Forder Corn 7 D8
Forder Green Devon . . . 8 B5
Fordgate Som 43 G10
Ford Green Lancs 202 D5
Fordham Cambs 124 C2
    Essex 107 F8
    Norf 140 D2
Fordham Heath Essex . 107 F8
Ford Heath Shrops 149 G8
Fordhouses W Mid . . . 133 C8
Fordingbridge Hants . . . 31 E10
Fordington Lincs 190 G6
Fordley T&W 243 C7
Fordon E Yorks 217 D10
Fordoun Aberds 293 F9
Ford's Green Suff 125 D11
    Suff 125 D11
Fordstreet Essex 107 F8
Ford Street Som 27 D11
Ford Devon 14 B2
Fordwater Devon 28 F3
Fordwells Oxon 82 C4
Fordwich Kent 55 B7
Fordyce Aberds 302 C5
Forebridge Staffs 151 E8
Foredale N Yorks 212 F6
Forehill S Ayrs 257 E8
Foreland Fields IoW . . . 21 D9
Foreland Ho Argyll . . . 274 G3
Foremark Derbys 152 D6
Forest Becks Lancs . . . 203 C11
Forest Coal Pit Mon . . . 96 G5
Forestdale London 67 G11
Forest Gate London 67 G11
Foresterseat Moray . . . 301 D11
Forest Gate Hants 33 E10
Forest Green Glos 80 E4
    Sur 50 E6
Forest Hall Cumb 221 E10
    T&W 243 D7
Forest Head Cumb 240 F3
Forest Hill London 67 E11
    Oxon 83 D9
Forest Holme Lancs . . . 195 B10
Forest-in-Teesdale
    Durham 232 F3
Forest Lane Head
    N Yorks 206 B2

Forest Lodge Argyll . . . 284 C6
    Highld 292 B2
    Perth 291 F11
Forest Mill Clack 279 C9
Forest Moor N Yorks . . 206 B2
Forestreet Devon 24 E5
Forest Row W Sus 52 F2
Forestside W Sus 34 E3
Forest Side IoW 20 D5
Forest Town Notts 171 C9
Forewoods Common
    Wilts 61 G10
Forgandenny Perth . . . 286 F4
Forge Corn 4 F3
    Powys 128 D3
Forge Hammer Torf . . . 78 F3
Forge Side Torf 78 D2
Forgewood N Lnrk 268 D5
Forgie Moray 302 D3
Forglen Ho Aberds . . . 302 D6
Forgrigarth Shetland . . 313 H4
Forgue Aberds 302 E6
Forhill Worcs 117 B11
Formby Mers 193 F10
Forncett End Norf 142 E2
Forncett St Mary Norf . 142 E3
Forncett St Peter Norf . 142 E3
Forneth Perth 286 C5
Fornham All Saints Suff 124 D6
Fornham St Martin
    Suff 124 D6
Fornham St Genevieve
    Suff 124 D6
Fornighty Highld 301 D9
Forrabury Corn 11 C7
Forres Moray 301 D10
Forrestfield N Lnrk . . . 269 B7
Forrest Lodge Dumfries 246 F3
Forry's Green Essex . . . 106 E5
Forsbrook Staffs 169 G7
Forse Highld 310 F6
Forsinain Highld 310 E3
Forsinard Highld 310 E2
Forsinard Station Highld 310 E2
Forstal Kent 53 E8
Forston Dorset 17 B9
Fort Augustus Highld . 290 C5
Forteviot Perth 286 F4
Fort George Highld . . . 301 D7
Forth S Lnrk 269 E8
Forthampton Glos 99 E7
Forthay Glos 80 F2
Forth Road Bridge Edin . 280 F2
Fortingall Perth 285 C11
Fortis Green London . . . 67 B9
Fort Matilda Invclyd . . 276 F5
Forton Hants 48 E2
    Lancs 202 C5
    Shrops 149 F8
    Som 28 F4
    Staffs 150 E5
Forton Heath Shrops . . 149 F8
Fortrie Aberds 302 E6
    Aberds 303 D7
Fortrose Highld 301 D7
Fortuneswell Dorset . . . 17 G9
Fort William Highld . . . 290 F3
Forty Green Bucks 84 G3
    Bucks 84 G6
Forty Hill London 86 F4
Forward Green Suff . . . 125 F11
Forwood Glos 80 E5
Fosbury Wilts 47 B10
Foscot Oxon 100 G4
Foscote Bucks 102 E4
    Wilts 61 D11
Fosdyke Lincs 156 C6
Fosdyke Bridge Lincs . 156 C6
Foss Perth 285 B11
Foss Cross Glos 81 D9
Fossebridge Glos 81 C9
Fosterhouses S Yorks . 199 E7
Foster's Booth
    Northants 120 G3
Foster's Green Worcs . 117 D9
Foster Street Essex 87 D7
Foston Derbys 152 C3
    Leics 136 D2
    Lincs 172 G5
    N Yorks 216 F3
Foston on the Wolds
    E Yorks 209 B8
Fotherby Lincs 190 C4
Fothergill Cumb 228 E6
Fotheringhay Northants 137 E11
Foubister Orkney 314 F5
Foul Anchor Cambs . . . 157 F8
Foulbridge Cumb 230 B4
Foulby W Yorks 197 D11
Foulden Borders 273 D8
    Norf 140 D5
Foul End Warks 134 E4
Foulford Hants 31 F11
Foulis Castle Highld . . 300 C5
Foul Mile E Sus 23 B10
Foulridge Green E Sus . 23 E9
Foulridge Lancs 204 E3
Foulsham Norf 159 E10
Foundry Corn 2 C2
Foundry Hill Norf 159 D11
Fountain Bridgend 57 E11
Fountainhall Borders . . 271 F8
Four Ashes Bucks 84 F6
    Staffs 132 F6
    Staffs 133 B8
    Suff 125 C10
    W Mid 118 B3
Four Crosses Powys . . 129 B11
    Powys 148 G5
    Staffs 133 B9
    Wrex 166 G3
Four Elms Devon 28 D3
    Kent 52 D3
Four Foot Som 44 G5
Four Forks Som 43 F8
Four Gates Gtr Man . . . 194 F6
Four Gotes Cambs 157 F9
Four Houses Corner
    W Berks 64 F6
Four Lane End S Yorks . 197 G9
Four Lane Ends Blkburn 195 B7
    Ches W 167 C9
    Gtr Man 195 F9
    N Yorks 205 B8
Four Lanes Corn 2 B5
Four Marks Hants 49 G7
Four Mile Bridge
    Anglesey 178 F3
Four Mile Elm Glos . . . 80 C4
Four Oaks E Sus 38 C5
    Glos 98 F3
    Kent 70 G3
    W Mid 134 D2
    W Mid 134 G4

Four Oaks Park W Mid . 134 D2
Fourpenny Highld 311 K2
Four Points W Berks . . . 64 D5
Four Pools Worcs 99 C10
Four Roads Carms 74 D6
    IoM 192 F3
Fourstones Northumb . 241 D9
Four Throws Kent 38 B3
Four Wantz Essex 87 C10
Four Wents Kent 53 F9
Fovant Wilts 31 B8
Foveran Aberds 303 G9
Fowey Corn 6 E2
Fowler's Plot Som 43 F10
Fowley Common Warr . 183 B11
Fowlis Angus 287 D7
Fowlis Wester Perth . . 286 E3
Fowlmere Cambs 105 B8
Fownhope Hereford . . . 97 E11
Foxash Estate Essex . . 107 E11
Foxbar Renfs 267 C9
Foxbury London 68 E2
Foxcombe Hill Oxon . . . 83 E7
Fox Corner C Beds 103 F8
    Sur 50 C3
Foxcote Glos 81 B8
    Som 45 B8
Foxcotte Hants 47 D10
Foxdale IoM 192 E3
Foxdown Hants 48 C4
Foxearth Essex 106 C6
Foxendown Kent 69 G7
Foxfield Cumb 210 B4
Foxford W Mid 135 G7
Foxham Wilts 62 D3
Fox Hatch Essex 87 F9
Fox Hill Bath 61 G9
    Hereford 98 B3
Foxhills Hants 32 E4
Foxhole Corn 5 E9
    Swansea 57 C7
Foxcotte Hants 47 D10
Foxholes N Yorks 217 E10
Fox Holes Wilts 45 E11
Foxhunt Green E Sus . . 23 B8
Fox Lane Hants 49 B11
Foxley Hereford 97 B8
    Norf 159 E10
    Norf 161 F8
    Staffs 168 F4
    Wilts 61 B11
Fox Royd W Yorks . . . 197 D8
Fox Street Essex 107 F10
Foxt Staffs 169 F8
Foxton Cambs 105 B8
    Durham 234 F3
    Leics 136 F4
    N Yorks 225 G8
Foxup N Yorks 213 D7
Foxwist Green Ches W . 167 B11
Foxwood Shrops 116 B2
Foy Hereford 97 F11
Foyers Highld 300 G4
Foynesfield Highld . . . 301 D8
Fraddam Corn 2 C3
Fraddon Corn 5 D8
Fradley Staffs 152 F3
Fradley Junction Staffs 152 F3
Fradswell Staffs 151 C9
Fraisthorpe E Yorks . . 218 G3
Framfield E Sus 37 C7
Framingham Earl Norf . 142 C5
Framingham Pigot Norf 142 C5
Framlingham Suff 126 E5
Frampton Dorset 17 B8
    Lincs 156 B6
Frampton Cotterell
    S Glos 61 C7
Frampton Court Glos . . 99 E10
Frampton End S Glos . . 61 C7
Frampton Mansell Glos . 80 E6
Frampton on Severn
    Glos 80 D2
Frampton West End
    Lincs 174 G4
Framsden Suff 126 F3
Framwellgate Moor
    Durham 233 C11
    Hants 33 C11
    Hants 49 B10
    Herts 85 E11
France Lynch Glos 80 E6
Franche Worcs 116 B6
Frandley Ches W 183 F10
Frankby Mers 182 D2
Frankfort Norf 160 E6
Franklands Gate
    Hereford 97 B10
Frankley Worcs 133 G9
Frankley Green Worcs . 133 G9
Frankley Hill Worcs . . 117 B9
Frank's Bridge Powys . 114 F2
Frankton Warks 119 C8
Frankwell Shrops 149 G9
Frans Green Norf 160 G2
Fraserburgh Aberds . . 303 C9
Frating Essex 107 G11
Frating Green Essex . . 107 G11
Fratton Ptsmth 21 B9
Freasley Warks 134 D4
Freathy Corn 7 E8
Frecheville S Yorks . . . 186 E5
Freckenham Suff 124 C3
Freckleton Lancs 194 B2
Fredley Sur 51 C7
Freebirch Derbys 186 G4
Freeby Leics 154 E6
Freefolk Hants 48 D3
Freehay Staffs 169 G8
Freeland Oxon 82 C6
    Renfs 267 B9
Freeland Corner Norf . 160 F3
Freeport Village Durham 232 G6
Freester Shetland 313 H6
Freethorpe Norf 143 B8
Free Town London 195 E10
Freezy Water London . . 86 F5
Freiston Lincs 174 G5
Freiston Shore Lincs . . 174 G5
Fremington Devon 40 G4
    N Yorks 223 F10
Frenchay S Glos 60 D6
Frenchbeer Devon 13 D9
Frenches Green Essex . 106 G4
Frenchmoor Hants 32 B3
Frenich Stirl 285 G8
Frensham Sur 49 E10
Frenze Norf 142 G2
Fresgoe Highld 310 C3
Freshbrook Swindon . . . 62 C6
Freshfield Mers 193 F9
Freshford Bath 61 G9
Freshwater IoW 20 D2
Freshwater Bay IoW . . . 20 D2
Freshwater East Pembs . 73 F8
Fressingfield Suff 126 B5
Freston Suff 108 D3
Freswick Highld 310 C7
Frethern Glos 80 D2
Fretherne Glos 80 D2
Frettenham Norf 160 F4

Freuchie Fife 286 G6
Freuchies Angus 292 G4
Freystrop Pembs 73 C7
Friarton Som 29 D7
Friar Park W Mid 133 E10
Friars' Gate E Sus 52 G2
Friar's Hill E Sus 38 E5
Friarton Perth 286 E5
Friday Bridge Cambs . . 139 C8
Friday Hill London 86 G5
Friday Street E Sus 23 E9
    Suff 126 G6
    Suff 127 E7
    Sur 50 D6
Fridaythorpe E Yorks . 208 B3
Friendly W Yorks 196 C5
Frien Barnet London . . 86 G3
Friesland Argyll 288 D3
Friesthorpe Lincs 189 E9
Frieston Lincs 172 F6
Frieth Bucks 84 G3
Friezeland Notts 171 E7
Frilford Oxon 82 F6
Frilford Heath Oxon . . . 82 F6
Frilsham W Berks 64 E4
Frimley Sur 49 B11
Frimley Green Sur 49 B11
Frimley Ridge Sur 49 B11
Frindsbury Medway . . . 69 E8
Fring Norf 158 C4
Fringford Oxon 102 F2
Friningham Kent 53 B10
Frinkle Green Essex . . 106 C4
Frinsted Kent 53 B11
Frinton-on-Sea Essex . 108 G4
Friockheim Angus 287 C9
Friog Gwyn 146 G2
Frisby Leics 136 C4
Frisby on the Wreake
    Leics 154 F3
Friskney Lincs 175 D7
Friskney Eaudyke Lincs 175 D7
Friskney Tofts Lincs . . 175 D7
Friston E Sus 23 F8
    Suff 127 E8
Fritchley Derbys 170 E5
Frith Kent 54 B2
Fritham Hants 32 E2
Frith Bank Lincs 174 F4
Frith Common Worcs . . 116 D3
Frithelstock Devon 25 D7
Frithelstock Stone Devon 25 D7
Frithend Hants 49 F10
Frith-hill Bucks 84 E6
Frith Hill Sur 50 E3
Frithsden Herts 85 D8
Frithville Lincs 174 E4
Frittenden Kent 53 E10
Frittiscombe Devon . . . 8 G6
Fritton Norf 142 E4
    Norf 143 D9
    Norf 161 F8
Fritwell Oxon 101 F10
Frizinghall W Yorks . . 205 F9
Frizington Cumb 219 B11
Frizzeler's Green Suff . 124 E5
Frobost W Isles 297 J3
Frocester Glos 80 E3
Frochas Powys 148 G5
Frodesley Shrops 131 C10
Frodingham N Lincs . . 199 E11
Frodsham Ches W 183 F8
Frogden Borders 263 D7
Frog End Cambs 123 G9
    Cambs 123 G8
Froggatt Derbys 186 F2
Froghall Staffs 169 F8
Frogham Hants 31 E11
    Kent 55 C9
Froghole Kent 52 C2
Frogland Cross S Glos . 61 C7
Frog Moor Swansea . . . 56 C3
Frogmore Devon 8 G5
    Hants 33 C11
    Hants 49 B10
    Herts 85 E11
Frognall Lincs 156 G4
Frogpool Corn 4 G5
Frogs' Green Essex . . . 105 D11
Frogshail Norf 160 B5
Frogwell Corn 6 B6
Frolesworth Leics 135 E10
Frome Som 45 D9
Frombridge Glos 80 D3
Fromefield Som 45 D9
Frome St Quintin Dorset . 29 G9
Frome Whitfield Dorset . 17 B9
Fromington Hereford . . 97 B10
Fromton Denb 9 B7
    Gwyn 145 F7
    Gwyn 163 B8
    Powys 113 D11
    Powys 129 C8
    Powys 130 C4
    Shrops 148 B5
Fron-Bache Denb 166 G2
Froncysyllte Wrex . . . 166 G3
Fron-deg Wrex 166 G3
Frongoch Gwyn 147 B8
Fron Isaf Wrex 166 G3
Frost Devon 26 E6
Frostenden Suff 143 G9
Frostenden Corner Suff 143 G9
Frosterley Durham . . . 232 D6
Frostlane Hants 32 F6
Frost Row Norf 141 C10
Frotoft Orkney 314 D4
Froxfield C Beds 103 E8
    Wilts 63 F9
Froxfield Green Hants . 34 B2
Froyle Hants 49 E9
Fryern Hill Hants 32 C6
Fryerning Essex 87 E10
Fryerns Essex 69 B8
Fryton N Yorks 216 E3

Fugglestone St Peter
    Wilts 46 F6
Fulbeck Lincs 172 E6
    Northumb 252 G6
Fulbrook Oxon 82 C3
Fulford Som 28 B2
    Staffs 151 B8
    York 207 D8
Fulham London 67 D8
Fulking W Sus 36 F2
Fullabrook Devon 40 E4
Fullarton Glasgow . . . 268 C2
    N Ayrs 257 B8
Fuller's Moor Ches W . 167 E7
Fuller Street Essex 88 B2
    Kent 52 B5
Fullerton Hants 47 F11

Fulletby Lincs....190 G3
Fullshaw S Yorks....197 G8
Full Sutton E Yorks....207 B10
Fullwell Cross London....86 G6
Fullwood E Ayrs....267 E8
  Gtr Man....196 F2
Fulmer Bucks....66 B3
Fulmodeston Norf....159 C9
Fulneck W Yorks....205 G10
Fulnetby Lincs....189 F9
Fulney Lincs....156 E5
Fulready Warks....100 B5
Fulstone Park W Yorks....184 E4
Fulstone S Yorks....197 F7
Fulstow Lincs....190 B4
Fulthorpe Stockton....234 G4
Fulwell Oxon....101 G7
  T&W....243 F9
Fulwood Lancs....202 G6
  Som....28 C2
  S Yorks....186 D4
Fundenhall Norf....142 D2
Fundenhall Street Norf....142 D2
Funtington W Sus....22 B3
Funtley Hants....33 F9
Funtullich Perth....285 E11
Funzie Shetland....312 D8
Furley Devon....28 G3
Furnace Argyll....284 G4
  Carms....74 E6
  Carms....75 E8
  Ceredig....128 D3
  Highld....299 B9
Furnace End Warks....134 E4
Furnace Green W Sus....51 F7
Furnace Wood W Sus....51 F11
Furneaux Pelham Herts....105 F8
Furness Vale Derbys....185 E8
Furneux Pelham Herts....105 F8
Furnham Som....28 F4
Further Ford End Essex....105 E9
Further Quarter Kent....53 F11
Furtho Northants....102 C5
Furze Devon....25 B10
Furzebrook Dorset....18 E4
Furzedown Hants....32 B5
  London....67 F9
Furzehill Devon....41 D8
  Dorset....31 G8
Furze Hill Hants....31 E11
Furzeley Corner Hants....33 E11
Furze Platt Windsor....65 C11
Furzey Lodge Hants....32 G5
Furzley Hants....32 D3
Furzton M Keynes....102 D6
Fyfett Som....28 E2
Fyfield Essex....87 D9
  Glos....82 E2
  Hants....47 D9
  Oxon....82 F6
  Wilts....63 F7
  Wilts....63 G11
Fylingthorpe N Yorks....227 D8
Fyning W Sus....34 C4
Fyvie Aberds....303 F7

G

Gabalfa Cardiff....59 D7
Gabhsann bho Dheas W Isles....304 C6
Gabhsann bho Thuath W Isles....304 C6
Gable Head Hants....21 B10
Gablon Highld....309 K7
Gabroc Hill E Ayrs....267 E9
Gadbrook Sur....51 D8
Gaddesby Leics....154 G3
Gadebridge Herts....85 D8
Gadfa Anglesey....179 D7
Gadfield Elm Worcs....98 E5
Gadlas Shrops....149 B7
Gadlys Rhondda....77 E7
Gadshill Kent....69 E8
Gaer Newport....59 B9
  Powys....96 G3
Gaer-fawr Mon....78 F6
Gaerllwyd Mon....78 F6
Gaerwen Anglesey....179 G7
Gagingwell Oxon....101 F8
Gaick Lodge Highld....291 E9
Gailey Staffs....151 G8
Gailey Wharf Staffs....151 G8
Gainford Durham....224 B3
Gain Hill Kent....53 D8
Gainsborough Lincs....188 C4
  Suff....108 C3
Gainsford End Essex....106 D4
Gairletter Argyll....276 E3
Gairloch Highld....299 B8
Gairlochy Highld....290 E3
Gairney Bank Perth....280 B2
Gairnshiel Lodge Aberds....292 C4
Gaisgill Cumb....222 D2
Gaitsgill Cumb....230 B3
Galadean Borders....271 G11
Galashiels Borders....261 B11
Galdlys Flint....182 G2
Gale Gtr Man....196 D2
Galgate Lancs....202 B5
Gallaberry Dumfries....247 G11
Gallachoille Argyll....275 E8
Gallanach Argyll....288 C4
  Argyll....289 G10
  Highld....294 E4
Gallantry Bank Ches E....167 E8
Gallatown Fife....280 C5
Galley Common Warks....134 E6
Galleyend Essex....88 E2
Galley Hill Cambs....122 D6
  Lincs....190 F6
Galleywood Essex....88 E2
Gallin Perth....285 C9
Gallovie Highld....291 E7
Gallowfauld Angus....287 C8
Gallowhill Glasgow....267 D11
  Renfs....267 B9
Gallowhills Aberds....303 D10
Gallows Corner London....87 G8
Gallowsgreen Torf....78 D3
Gallows Green Essex....106 F2
  Essex....107 F8
  Staffs....169 G9
  Worcs....117 E8
Gallows Inn Derbys....171 G7
Gallowstree Common Oxon....65 C7
Galltair Highld....295 C10
Galltegfa Denb....165 D10
Gallt Melyd / Meliden Denb....181 E9
Gallt-y-foel Gwyn....163 C9
Gallypot Street E Sus....52 F3
Galmington Som....28 C2
Galmisdale Highld....294 G6

Galmpton Devon....8 G3
  Torbay....9 D7
Galon Uchaf M Tydf....77 D9
Galphay N Yorks....214 E5
Galston E Ayrs....258 B2
Galtrigill Highld....296 F7
Gam Corn....11 F7
Gamble Hill W Yorks....205 G11
Gamblesby Cumb....231 D8
Gamble's Green Essex....88 C3
Gamelsby Cumb....239 G7
Gamesley Derbys....185 C8
Gamlingay Cambs....122 G4
Gamlingay Cinques Cambs....122 G4
Gamlingay Great Heath Cambs....122 G4
Gammaton Devon....25 B7
Gammaton Moor Devon....25 C7
Gammersgill N Yorks....213 C11
Gamston Notts....154 B2
  Notts....188 F2
Ganarew Hereford....79 B8
Ganavan Argyll....289 F10
Ganders Green Glos....98 G4
Gang Corn....6 B6
Ganllwyd Gwyn....146 E4
Gannetts Dorset....30 D3
Gannochy Angus....293 F7
  Perth....286 E5
Ganstead E Yorks....209 G8
Ganthorpe N Yorks....216 E3
Ganton N Yorks....217 D9
Gants Hill London....68 B2
Ganwick Corner Herts....86 F3
Gaodhail Argyll....289 F8
Gappah Devon....14 F3
Garafad Highld....298 C4
Garamor Highld....295 F8
Garbat Highld....300 C4
Garbhallt Argyll....275 D11
Garboldisham Norf....141 G10
Garbole Highld....301 G7
Garden City Bl Gwent....77 D11
  Flint....166 B4
Gardeners Green Wokingham....65 F10
Gardenstown Aberds....303 C7
Garden Village Swansea....56 B5
  S Yorks....186 B3
  Wrex....166 E4
  W Yorks....206 G4
Garderhouse Shetland....313 J5
Gardham E Yorks....208 E5
Gardie Shetland....312 D7
Gardin Shetland....312 G6
Gare Hill Som....45 E9
Garelochhead Argyll....276 C4
Garford Oxon....82 F6
Garforth W Yorks....206 G4
Gargrave N Yorks....204 C4
Gargunnock Stirl....278 C4
Garizim Conwy....179 F11
Garker Corn....5 E10
Garlandhayes Devon....27 D11
Garlands Cumb....239 G10
Garleffin S Ayrs....244 G3
Garlieston Dumfries....236 E6
Garlinge Kent....71 F10
Garlinge Green Kent....54 C6
Garlogie Aberds....293 C9
Garmelow Staffs....150 D5
Garmond Aberds....303 D8
Garmondsway Durham....234 E2
Garmony Argyll....289 E8
Garmouth Moray....302 C3
Garmston Shrops....132 B2
Garn Powys....130 G2
Garnant Carms....75 C11
Garndiffaith Torf....78 E3
Garndolbenmaen Gwyn....163 G7
Garnedd Conwy....164 E2
Garnett Bridge Cumb....221 F10
Garnetts Essex....87 B10
Garnfadryn Gwyn....144 C5
Garnkirk N Lnrk....268 B3
Garnlydan Bl Gwent....77 C11
Garnsgate Lincs....157 E8
Garnswllt Swansea....75 D10
Garn-swllt Swansea....75 D10
Garn-yr-erw Torf....78 C2
Garrabost W Isles....304 E7
Garrachra Argyll....275 E11
Garras Corn....2 E6
Garreg Flint....181 F10
  Gwyn....163 G10
Garrets Green W Mid....134 F2
Garrick Perth....286 F2
Garrigill Cumb....231 C10
Garrison Stirl....285 G7
Garriston N Yorks....224 G3
Garroch Dumfries....246 G3
Garrogie Lodge Highld....291 B9
Garros Highld....298 C4
Garrow Perth....286 C2
Garrowhill Glasgow....268 C3
Garryguaich Highld....290 C3
Garryhorn Dumfries....246 E2
Garsdale Cumb....212 B4
Garsdale Head Cumb....222 G5
Garsdon Wilts....62 B3
Garshall Green Staffs....151 C9
Garsington Oxon....83 E9
Garstang Lancs....202 D5
Garston Herts....85 F10
  Mers....182 E6
Garswood Mers....183 B9
Gartachoil Stirl....277 C10
Gartbreck Argyll....254 B3
Gartcosh N Lnrk....268 B3
Garth Bridgend....57 C11
  Ceredig....128 G2
  Flint....181 E10
  Gwyn....179 G9
  Newport....59 B9
  Newport....78 G4
  Perth....285 B11
  Powys....95 B9
  Powys....114 C5
  Shetland....313 H4
  Shetland....313 H6
  Wrex....166 G3
Garthamlock Glasgow....268 B3
Garthbeg Highld....291 B7
Garthbrengy Powys....95 E10
Garthdee Aberdeen....293 C11
Gartheli Ceredig....111 F11
Garthmyl Powys....130 D3
Garthorpe Leics....154 E6
  N Lincs....199 D11
Garth Owen Powys....130 E2
Garth Row Cumb....221 F10
Garth Trevor Wrex....166 G3
Gartlea N Lnrk....268 C5
Gartloch Glasgow....268 B3

Gartly Aberds....302 F5
Gartmore Stirl....277 B10
Gartnagrenach Argyll....255 B8
Gartness N Lnrk....268 C5
  Stirl....277 D10
Gartocharn W Dunb....277 D8
Garton E Yorks....209 F11
Garton-on-the-Wolds E Yorks....208 B5
Gartsherrie N Lnrk....268 B4
Gartur Stirl....277 B11
Gartymore Highld....311 H4
Garvald E Loth....281 G11
Garvamore Highld....291 D7
Garvard Argyll....274 D4
Garvault Hotel Highld....308 F7
Garvault Argyll....300 C3
Garvestone Norf....141 B10
Garvock Aberds....293 F9
  Invclyd....276 G5
Garwick Fife....280 D2
Garway Hereford....97 G9
Garway Hill Hereford....97 F8
Gaskan Highld....289 B9
Gastard Wilts....61 F11
Gasthorpe Norf....141 G9
Gaston Green Essex....87 B7
Gatacre Park Shrops....132 F5
Gatcombe IoW....20 D5
Gateacre Mers....182 D6
Gatebeck Cumb....211 B10
Gate Burton Lincs....188 E4
Gateford Notts....187 E9
Gateford Common Notts....187 E9
Gateforth N Yorks....198 B5
Gatehead E Ayrs....257 B9
Gate Helmsley N Yorks....207 B9
Gatehouse Northumb....251 F7
Gatehouse of Fleet Dumfries....237 D8
Gatelawbridge Dumfries....247 D10
Gateley Norf....159 E9
Gatenby N Yorks....214 B6
Gatesgarth Cumb....220 B3
Gateshead T&W....243 E7
Gatesheath Ches W....167 C7
Gateside Aberds....293 B8
  Angus....287 C8
  Dumfries....248 E4
  E Renf....267 D9
  Fife....286 G5
  N Ayrs....267 E7
  Shetland....312 F4
Gatewen Wrex....166 E4
Gatherley Devon....12 E3
Gathurst Gtr Man....194 F4
Gatley Gtr Man....184 D4
Gatley End Cambs....104 C5
  Gtr Man....184 D4
Gatton Sur....51 C9
Gattonside Borders....262 B2
Gatwick Glos....80 C2
Gatwick Airport W Sus....51 F8
Gaufron Powys....113 D9
Gauldry Fife....287 E7
Gauldswick Leics....136 C3
Gauntons Bank Ches E....167 F9
Gaunt's Common Dorset....31 F8
Gaunt's Earthcott S Glos....60 C6
Gaunt's End Essex....105 F10
Gautby Lincs....189 G11
Gavinton Borders....272 E5
Gawber S Yorks....197 F10
Gawcott Bucks....102 E3
Gawsworth Ches E....168 B5
Gawthorpe W Yorks....197 C9
  W Yorks....197 D8
Gawthrop Cumb....212 B3
Gawthwaite Cumb....210 C5
Gay Bowers Essex....88 E3
Gaydon Warks....119 G7
Gayfield Orkney....314 A4
Gayhurst M Keynes....103 B7
Gayle N Yorks....213 B7
Gayles N Yorks....224 D2
Gay Street W Sus....35 C9
Gayton Mers....182 E3
  Norf....158 F4
  Northants....120 G4
  Staffs....151 D9
Gayton Engine Lincs....191 D7
Gayton le Marsh Lincs....190 E6
Gayton le Wold Lincs....190 D2
Gayton Thorpe Norf....158 F4
Gaywood Norf....158 E2
Gaza Shetland....312 F5
Gazeley Suff....124 E4
Geanies House Highld....301 B8
Gearraidh Bhailteas W Isles....297 J3
Gearraidh Bhaird W Isles....304 F5
Gearraidh Dubh W Isles....296 F4
Gearraidh na h-Aibhne W Isles....304 E4
Gearraidh na Monadh W Isles....297 K3
Geàrraidh Sheilidh W Isles....297 J3
Geary Highld....298 C2
Geat Wolford Warks....100 E4
Geddes House Highld....301 D8
Gedding Suff....125 F9
Geddington Northants....137 G2
Gedgrave Hall Suff....109 B8
Gedintailor Highld....295 B7
Gedling Notts....171 G10
Gedney Lincs....157 E8
Gedney Broadgate Lincs....157 E8
Gedney Drove End Lincs....157 D9
Gedney Dyke Lincs....157 D8
Gedney Hill Lincs....156 G6
Gee Cross Gtr Man....185 C7
Geeston Rutland....137 C9
Gegin Wrex....166 E3
Geilston Argyll....276 F6
Geirinis W Isles....297 G3
Geisiadar W Isles....304 E3
Geldeston Norf....143 E7
Gell Conwy....164 B5
Gelli Pembs....73 C7
  Rhondda....77 G7
Gellideg M Tydf....77 E8
Gellifor Denb....165 C10
Gelligaer Caerph....77 F10
Gelli-gaer Neath....57 C8
Gelligroes Caerph....77 G11
Gelli-hôf Caerph....77 G11
Gellilydan Gwyn....146 B3
Gellinudd Neath....76 D2
Gellyburn Perth....286 D4
Gellygron Neath....76 E2
Gellywen Carms....92 G3

Gelsmoor Leics....153 F8
Gelston Dumfries....237 D9
  Lincs....172 G6
Gembling E Yorks....209 B8
Gemini Warr....183 C9
Gendros Swansea....56 B6
Genesis Green Suff....124 F4
Gentleshaw Staffs....151 G11
Geocrab W Isles....305 J3
Georgefield Dumfries....249 E7
George Green Bucks....66 C4
Georgeham Devon....40 F3
George Nympton Devon....26 C2
Georgetown Bl Gwent....77 D10
Georgia Corn....2 B3
Georgracked Corn....3 B9
Gerlan Gwyn....163 B10
Germansweek Devon....12 C4
Germiston Glasgow....268 B2
Germoe Corn....2 C2
Gernon Bushes Essex....87 E7
Gerrans Corn....3 B9
Gerrard's Bromley Staffs....150 C5
Gerrards Cross Bucks....66 B4
Gerrick Redcar....226 C4
Geseiilfa Powys....129 E8
Gestingthorpe Essex....106 D6
Gesto Ho Highld....294 B5
Geuffordd Powys....148 G4
Geufron Denb....166 G2
Gibbet Hill Warks....135 G10
  Mid....118 C6
Gibb Hill Ches W....183 F10
Gibbshill Dumfries....237 B9
Gib Heath W Mid....133 F11
Gibraltar Beds....103 B10
  Bucks....84 C3
  Kent....55 F8
Gibralter Oxon....83 B7
Gibshill Invclyd....276 G6
Gidleigh Devon....13 D9
Gidea Park London....68 B4
Giddy Green Dorset....18 D2
Giffard Park M Keynes....103 C7
Giffnock E Renf....267 D11
Gifford E Loth....271 B10
Giffordland N Ayrs....266 F5
Giffordtown Fife....286 F6
Gigg Gtr Man....195 F10
Giggetty Staffs....133 E7
Giggleswick N Yorks....212 G6
Giggshill Sur....67 F7
Gignog Pembs....91 G7
Gilberdyke E Yorks....199 B10
Gilbert's Coombe Corn....4 G4
Gilbert's End Worcs....98 C6
Gilbert's Green Warks....118 D2
Gilbertstone W Mid....134 G2
Gilbert Street Hants....49 G7
Gilchriston E Loth....271 B9
Gilcrux Cumb....229 D8
Gildersome W Yorks....197 B8
Gildersome Street W Yorks....197 B8
Gildingwells S Yorks....187 D9
Gileston V Glam....58 F4
Gilfach Caerph....77 F11
Gilfach Goch Rhondda....58 B3
Gilfachreda Ceredig....111 F8
Gilgarran Cumb....228 G6
Gill N Yorks....204 E5
Gillamoor N Yorks....216 B3
Gillan Corn....3 E7
Gillar's Green Mers....183 B7
Gillbank Cumb....221 F7
Gillbent Gtr Man....184 E5
Gillen Highld....298 D2
Gillesbie Dumfries....248 E5
Gilling East N Yorks....216 D2
Gillingham Dorset....30 B4
  Medway....69 F9
  Norf....143 E8
Gilling West N Yorks....224 D3
Gillmoss Mers....182 B6
Gillow Heath Staffs....168 D5
Gills Highld....310 B7
Gill's Green Kent....53 G9
Gillway Staffs....134 C4
Gilmanscleuch Borders....261 E8
Gilmerton Edin....270 B5
  Perth....286 E2
Gilmonby Durham....223 C9
Gilmorton Leics....135 F11
Gilmourton S Lnrk....268 G3
Gilroyd S Yorks....197 G10
Gilsland Cumb....240 D4
Gilsland Spa Cumb....240 D4
Gilson Warks....134 E3
Gilstead W Yorks....205 F8
Gilston Borders....271 D11
  Herts....86 C6
Gilston Park Herts....86 C6
Gilwern Mon....78 C2
Gimingham Norf....160 B5
Giosla W Isles....304 F3
Gipping Suff....125 E11
Gipsey Bridge Lincs....174 E3
Gipsy Row Suff....107 D11
Gipsyville Hull....200 B5
Gipton Wood W Yorks....206 F2
Girdle Toll N Ayrs....266 G6
Girlington W Yorks....205 G8
Girlsta Shetland....313 H6
Girsby Lincs....190 D2
  N Yorks....225 D7
Girt Corn....29 C10
Girtford C Beds....104 B3
Girthon Dumfries....237 D8
Girton Cambs....123 E8
  Notts....172 B4
Girvan S Ayrs....244 D5
Gisburn Lancs....204 D2
Gisleham Suff....143 F10
Gislingham Suff....125 D11
Gissing Norf....142 F3
Gittisham Devon....27 G11
Givons Grove Sur....51 C7
Glachavoil Argyll....275 F11
Glackmore Highld....300 D6
Gladestry Powys....114 F4
Gladsmuir E Loth....281 G10
Glaichbea Highld....300 F5
Glais Swansea....76 E2
Glaisdale N Yorks....226 D5

Glame Highld....298 E5
Glamis Angus....287 C7
Glan Adda Gwyn....179 G9
Glanafon Pembs....73 B7
Glanaman Carms....75 C11
Glan-Conwy Conwy....164 E4
Glandford Norf....177 E8
Glan-Dwyfach Gwyn....163 G7
Glan-Duar Carms....93 C10
Glandwr Caerph....78 E2
  Pembs....92 F3
Glan-dwr Pembs....92 F3
Glandy Cross Carms....92 F2
Glandyfi Ceredig....128 D3
Glan Gors Anglesey....179 F7
Glangrwyney Powys....78 B2
Glanhanog Powys....129 D9
Glanmule Powys....130 E3
Glanrafon Carms....128 G2
Glanrhyd Gwyn....144 B5
  Pembs....92 C2
Glan-rhyd Gwyn....163 D7
  Powys....76 D3
Glanton Northumb....264 F3
Glanton Pike Northumb....264 G3
Glantwymyn / Cemmaes Road Powys....128 C6
Glanvilles Wootton Dorset....29 E11
Glanwern Ceredig....128 F2
Glanwydden Conwy....180 E4
Glan-y-don Flint....181 F11
Glan y Ffer / Ferryside Carms....74 C5
Glan-y-llyn Rhondda....58 C6
Glan-y-môr Carms....74 C4
Glan-y-nant Caerph....77 F10
Glan-yr-afon Anglesey....179 E10
  Gwyn....129 G8
  Gwyn....165 G8
  Shrops....148 E4
Glapthorn Northants....137 E10
Glapwell Derbys....171 B7
Glas-allt Shiel Aberds....292 E4
Glasbury Powys....96 D3
Glaschoil Highld....301 F10
Glascoed Denb....181 G7
  Mon....78 E4
  Powys....129 F11
Glascorrie Aberds....292 D5
  Perth....286 E2
Glascote Staffs....134 C4
Glascwm Powys....114 G3
Glasdrum Argyll....284 C4
Glasfryn Conwy....164 E6
Glasgoed Ceredig....92 B6
Glasgoforest Aberds....293 B10
Glasgow Glasgow....267 B11
Glashvin Highld....298 C4
Glasinfryn Gwyn....163 B9
Glasllwch Newport....59 B9
Glasnacardoch Highld....295 F8
Glasnakille Highld....295 D7
Glasphein Highld....297 G7
Glaspwll Powys....128 D4
Glassburn Highld....300 F3
Glassel Aberds....293 D8
Glassenbury Kent....53 F8
Glasserton Dumfries....236 F6
Glasshouse Glos....98 G4
Glasshouse Hill Glos....98 G4
Glasshouses N Yorks....214 G3
Glasslie Fife....286 G6
Glasson Cumb....239 E7
  Lancs....202 B4
Glassonby Cumb....231 D7
Glasterlaw Angus....287 B9
Glaston Rutland....137 C7
Glastonbury Som....44 F4
Glatton Cambs....138 F3
Glazebrook Warr....183 C11
Glazebury Warr....183 B11
Glazeley Shrops....132 F4
Gleadless S Yorks....186 E5
Gleadless Valley S Yorks....186 E5
Gleadmoss Ches E....168 B4
Gleadsmoss Ches E....168 B4
Gleanhead Dumfries....245 G10
Gleann Tholàstaidh W Isles....304 D7
Gleaston Cumb....210 E5
Glebe Hants....33 D9
  Shetland....313 J6
  T&W....243 F8
Glecknabae Argyll....275 G11
Gledhow W Yorks....206 F2
Gledrid Shrops....148 B5
Gleiniant Powys....129 E9
Glemsford Suff....106 B6
Glen Dumfries....237 B10
  Dumfries....237 D7
Glenamachrie Argyll....289 G11
Glenample Stirl....285 E9
Glenancross Highld....295 F8
Glenapp Castle S Ayrs....244 G3
Glenaros Ho Argyll....289 E7
Glen Auldyn IoM....192 C5
Glenbarr Argyll....255 D7
Glenbeg Highld....289 C7
  Highld....301 G10
Glen Bernisdale Highld....298 E4
Glenbervie Aberds....293 E9
Glenboig N Lnrk....268 B5
Glenborrodale Highld....289 C8
Glenbranter Argyll....276 B2
Glenbreck Borders....260 C3
Glenbrein Lodge Highld....290 B6
Glenbrittle House Highld....294 C6
Glenbrook Edin....270 B2
Glenbuchat Castle Aberds....292 B5
Glenbuck E Ayrs....259 D7
Glenburn Renfs....267 C9
Glenbyre Argyll....289 G7
Glencalvie Lodge Highld....309 L4
Glencanisp Lodge Highld....307 G6
Glencaple Dumfries....237 C11
Glencarron Lodge Highld....299 D10
Glencarse Perth....286 E6

Glencassley Castle Highld....309 J4
Glenceitlein Highld....284 C5
Glencoe Highld....284 B4
Glencraig Fife....280 B3
Glencripesdale Highld....289 D8
Glencrosh Dumfries....247 F9
Glendavan Ho Aberds....292 C6
Glendearg Borders....262 B2
  Perth....286 G3
Glendevon Perth....286 G3
Glendoe Lodge Highld....290 C6
Glendoebeg Highld....290 C6
Glendoick Perth....286 E6
Glendoll Lodge Angus....292 F4
Glenduckie Fife....286 F6
Glendye Lodge Aberds....293 E8
Gleneagles Hotel Perth....286 F3
Gleneagles House Perth....286 G3
Glenearn Perth....286 F5
Glenedegale Argyll....254 B4
Gleneig Highld....295 D10
Glenernie Moray....301 E10
Glenfarg Perth....286 F5
Glenfarquhar Lodge Aberds....293 E9
Glenferness House Highld....301 E9
Glenfeshie Lodge Highld....291 D10
Glenfiddich Lodge Moray....302 F3
Glenfield Leics....135 B10
Glenfinnan Highld....295 G10
Glenfintaig Ho Highld....290 E4
Glenfoot Perth....286 F5
Glenfyne Lodge Argyll....284 F6
Glengap Dumfries....237 D8
Glengarnock N Ayrs....266 E6
Glengolly Highld....310 C5
Glengorm Castle Argyll....288 D6
Glengoulandie Perth....285 B11
Glengrasco Highld....298 E4
Glenhead Farm Angus....292 G4
Glen Ho Borders....261 C7
Glenholt Plym....7 C10
Glenhoul Dumfries....246 F4
Glenhurich Highld....289 C10
Glenkerry Borders....261 G7
Glenkiln Dumfries....237 B10
Glenkindie Aberds....292 B6
Glenlair Dumfries....237 B9
Glenlatterach Moray....301 D11
Glenlee Dumfries....246 F4
Glenleigh Park E Sus....38 F2
Glenleraig Highld....306 F6
Glenlichorn Perth....285 F11
Glenlivet Moray....301 G11
Glenlochar Dumfries....237 C9
Glenlochsie Perth....292 F2
Glenlomond Perth....286 G5
Glenluce Dumfries....236 D4
Glenlussa Ho Argyll....255 E8
Glenmallan Argyll....276 B5
Glenmanna Argyll....292 F6
Glenmark Angus....292 F6
Glenmarkie Lodge Angus....292 G4
Glenmarksie Highld....300 D3
Glenmavis N Lnrk....268 B5
  W Loth....269 B9
Glenmaye IoM....192 E3
Glenmeanie Highld....300 D2
Glenmidge Dumfries....247 G10
Glenmoidart Ho Highld....289 B9
Glen Mona IoM....192 D5
Glen Mor Highld....295 B10
Glenmore Argyll....275 G11
  Argyll....289 G8
  Highld....298 E4
Glenmore Lodge Highld....291 C11
Glenmoy Angus....292 G6
Glennembie Highld....300 D2
Glen Nevis House Highld....290 F4
Glennoe Argyll....284 D4
Glen of Newmill Moray....302 D4
Glenogil Angus....292 G6
Glenowen Pembs....73 D7
Glenprosen Lodge Angus....292 G4
Glenprosen Village Angus....292 G4
Glenquaich Lodge Perth....286 D2
Glenquiech Angus....292 G6
Glenquithlie Aberds....303 C8
Glenrath Borders....260 B6
Glenrazie Dumfries....236 C5
Glenreasdell Mains Argyll....255 B9
Glenree N Ayrs....255 E10
Glenridding Cumb....221 B7
Glenrossal Highld....309 J4
Glenrothes Fife....286 G6
Glensanda Highld....289 E10
Glensaugh Aberds....293 F8
Glenshero Lodge Highld....291 D7
Glenstockadale Dumfries....236 C2
Glenstriven Argyll....275 F11
Glentaggart S Lnrk....259 D8
Glen Tanar House Aberds....292 D6
Glentarkie Perth....286 F5
Glenternie Borders....260 B6
Glentham Lincs....189 C8
Glentirranmuir Stirl....278 C3
Glenton Aberds....302 G6
Glentress Borders....261 B7
Glentromie Lodge Highld....291 D10
Glen Trool Lodge Dumfries....245 G10
Glentrool Village Dumfries....236 B5
Glentruim House Highld....291 D8
Glentworth Lincs....188 D6
Glenuig Highld....289 B8
Glenurquhart Highld....301 C7
Glen Vic Askil Highld....298 E3
Glenview Argyll....284 D4
Glen Village Falk....279 F7
Glen Vine IoM....192 E4
Glespin S Lnrk....259 D8
Gletness Shetland....313 H6
Glewstone Hereford....97 G11

Gonfirth Shetland....313 G5
Good Easter Essex....87 C10
Gooderstone Norf....140 C5
Goodleigh Devon....40 G6
Goodley Stock Kent....52 C2
Goodmanham E Yorks....208 E3
Goodmayes London....68 B3
Goodnestone Kent....55 C9
  Kent....70 G4
Goodrich Hereford....79 B9
Goodrington Torbay....9 D7
Good's Green Worcs....132 G5
Goodshaw Lancs....195 B10
Goodshaw Chapel Lancs....195 B10
Goodshaw Fold Lancs....195 B10
Goodstone Devon....13 G11
Goodwick / Wdig Pembs....91 D8
Goodworth Clatford Hants....47 E11
Goodyers End Warks....134 F6
Goodyhills Cumb....229 B8
Goole E Yorks....199 C8
Goom's Hill Worcs....117 G10
Goonabarn Corn....5 E9
Goonbell Corn....4 F4
Goonhavern Corn....4 E5
Goonhusband Corn....2 D5
Goonlaze Corn....4 G4
Goonown Corn....4 E4
Goonpiper Corn....3 B8
Goonvrea Corn....4 F4
Gooseberry Green Essex....87 E11
Goosecruives Aberds....293 E9
Gooseford Devon....13 C9
Goose Green Cumb....211 C10
  Essex....108 F2
  Gtr Man....194 G5
  Hants....32 F4
  Herts....86 D5
  Kent....52 C6
  Kent....53 F10
  Lancs....194 C3
  Norf....142 F2
  S Glos....61 C8
  W Sus....34 G3
  W Sus....35 D10
Gooseham Mill Devon....24 D2
Goosehill W Yorks....197 C10
Goose Hill Hants....64 G4
Goosehill Green Worcs....117 E8
Goosemoor Staffs....150 F6
Goosemoor Green Staffs....151 G11
Gooseford Som....28 E2
Goose Pool Hereford....97 D9
Goosewell Devon....40 D5
Goosey Oxon....82 G5
Goosnargh Lancs....203 F7
Goostrey Ches E....184 G3
Gorbals Glasgow....267 C11
Gorcott Hill Warks....117 D11
Gord Shetland....313 L6
Gorddinog Conwy....179 G11
Gordon Borders....272 G2
Gordonbush Highld....311 J2
Gordonsburgh Moray....302 C4
Gordonstoun Moray....301 C11
Gordonstown Aberds....302 D5
  Aberds....303 E7
Gore Corn....29 C9
  Kent....55 B10
Gorebridge Midloth....270 C6
Gore Cross Wilts....46 C4
Gore End Hants....64 G2
Gorefield Cambs....157 G8
Gorehill W Sus....35 C7
Gore Pit Essex....88 B5
Gore Street Kent....71 F9
Gorgie Edin....280 G4
Gorhambury Herts....85 D10
Goring Oxon....64 D6
Goring-by-Sea W Sus....35 G10
Goring Heath Oxon....65 D7
Gorleston-on-Sea Norf....143 C10
Gornalwood W Mid....133 E8
Gorrachie Aberds....303 D7
Gorran Churchtown Corn....5 G9
Gorran Haven Corn....5 G10
Gorran High Lanes Corn....5 G9
Gorrenberry Borders....249 D11
Gorrig Ceredig....93 C8
Gorse Covert Warr....183 C11
Gorsedd Flint....181 F11
Gorse Hill Gtr Man....184 B4
  Swindon....63 B7
Gorseinon Swansea....56 B5
Gorseness Orkney....314 E4
Gorsethorpe Notts....171 B9
Gorseybank Derbys....170 E3
Gorsgoch Ceredig....111 G9
Gorslas Carms....75 C9
Gorsley Glos....98 F3
Gorsley Common Hereford....98 F3
Gorsley Ley Staffs....133 B11
Gorstage Ches W....183 G10
Gorstan Highld....300 C3
Gorstanvorran Highld....289 B10
Gorstella Ches W....166 C5
Gorsteyhill Ches E....168 E2
Gorst Hill Worcs....116 C4
Gorstyhill Staffs....151 D11
Gortan Argyll....274 F3
Gortantaoid Argyll....274 F4
Gortenacullish Highld....295 G8
Gorteneorn Highld....289 C8
Gortenfern Highld....289 C8
Gortinanane Argyll....255 C8
Gorton Gtr Man....184 B5
Gortonallister N Ayrs....256 D2
Gosbeck Suff....126 F3
Gosberton Lincs....156 C5
Gosberton Cheal Lincs....156 C5
Gosberton Clough Lincs....156 D3
Goscote W Mid....133 C10
Goseley Dale Derbys....152 E6
Gosfield Essex....106 F5
Gosford Hereford....115 D10
  Oxon....83 C8
Gosford Green W Mid....118 B6
Gosforth Cumb....219 E11
  T&W....242 D6
Gosland Green Suff....124 G5
Gosling Green Suff....107 C9
Gosmere Kent....54 C4
Gosmore Herts....104 F4
Gospel Ash Staffs....132 F6
Gospel End Village Staffs....133 E7
Gospel Green W Sus....50 G2
Gospel Oak London....67 B9
Gosport Hants....21 B8
  Som....32 C5

Gossabrough Shetland 312 E7
Gossard's Green C Beds 103 C9
Gossington Glos 80 E2
Gossops Green W Sus 51 F9
Goswick Northumb 273 F11
Gotham Dorset 31 E9
E Sus 38 F2
Notts 153 C10
Gothelney Green Som 43 F9
Gotherington Glos 99 F9
Gothers Corn 5 D9
Gott Argyll 288 E2
Shetland 313 J6
Gotton Som 28 B2
Goudhurst Kent 53 F8
Goukstone Moray 302 D4
Goulceby Lincs 190 F3
Goulton N Yorks 225 E9
Gourdas Aberds 303 E7
Gourdon Aberds 293 F10
Gourock Invclyd 276 F4
Govan Glasgow 267 B11
Govanhill Glasgow 267 C11
Gover Hill Kent 52 C6
Goverton Notts 172 E2
Goveton Devon 8 F5
Govilon Mon 78 C3
Gowanhill Aberds 303 C10
Gowanwell Aberds 303 E8
Gowdall E Yorks 198 C6
Gowerton / Tre-Gwyr
Swansea 56 B5
Gowhole Derbys 185 E8
Gowkhall Fife 279 D11
Gowkthrapple N Lnrk 268 E5
Gowthorpe E Yorks 207 C11
Goxhill E Yorks 209 E9
N Lincs 200 C6
Goxhill Haven N Lincs 200 B6
Goybre Neath 57 D9
Goytre Neath 57 D9
Gozzard's Ford Oxon 83 F7
Grabhair W Isles 305 G5
Graby Lincs 155 D11
Gracca Corn 5 D10
Gracemount Edin 270 B5
Grade Corn 2 G6
Graffham W Sus 34 D6
Grafham Cambs 122 D3
Sur 50 E4
Grafton Hereford 97 D9
N Yorks 215 G8
Oxon 82 E3
Shrops 149 F8
Worcs 99 D9
Worcs 115 E11
Grafton Flyford Worcs 117 F9
Grafton Regis Northants 102 B5
Grafton Underwood
Northants 137 G8
Grafty Green Kent 53 D11
Grahamston Falk 279 E7
Graianrhyd Denb 166 D2
Graig Carms 74 E6
Conwy 180 G4
Denb 181 G9
Rhondda 58 B5
Wrex 148 B4
Graig-Fawr Swansea 75 E10
Graig-fechan Denb 165 E10
Graig Felen Swansea 75 E11
Graig Penllyn V Glam 58 D3
Graig Trewyddfa Swansea 57 B7
Grain Medway 69 D11
Grains Bar Gtr Man 196 F3
Grainsby Lincs 190 B3
Grainthorpe Lincs 190 B5
Grainthorpe Fen Lincs 190 B5
Graiselound N Lincs 188 B3
Grampound Corn 5 F8
Grampound Road Corn 5 E8
Gramsdal W Isles 296 F4
Granborough Bucks 102 F5
Granby Notts 154 B5
Grandborough Warks 119 D9
Grandpont Oxon 83 D8
Grandtully Perth 286 B3
Grange Cumb 220 B5
Dorset 31 G8
E Ayrs 257 B10
Fife 287 G8
Halton 183 E8
Lancs 203 G7
Medway 69 F9
Mers 182 D2
NE Lincs 201 F9
N Yorks 223 G8
Perth 286 E6
Warr 183 C10
Grange Crossroads
Moray 302 D4
Grange Estate Dorset 31 G10
Grange Hall Moray 301 C10
Grange Hill Durham 233 F10
Essex 86 G6
Grangemill Derbys 170 D2
Grange Moor W Yorks 197 D8
Grangemouth Falk 279 E8
Grangemuir Fife 287 G9
Grange of Cree
Dumfries 236 D6
Grange of Lindores Fife 286 F6
Grange-over-Sands
Cumb 211 D8
Grangepans Falk 279 E10
Grange Park London 86 F4
Mers 183 C7
Northants 120 F5
Swindon 62 C6
Grangetown Cardiff 59 E7
Redcar 235 G7
T&W 243 G10
Grange Villa Durham 242 G6
Grange Village Glos 79 C11
Granish Highld 291 B11
Gransmoor E Yorks 209 B8
Gransmore Green
Essex 106 G3
Granston / Treopert
Pembs 91 E7
Grantchester Cambs 123 F8
Grantham Lincs 155 B8
Grantley N Yorks 214 F4
Grantley Hall N Yorks 214 F4
Grantlodge Aberds 293 B9
Granton Dumfries 248 B3
Edin 280 F4
Grantown Aberds 302 D5
Grantown-on-Spey
Highld 301 G10
Grantsfield Hereford 115 E10
Grantshouse Borders 272 B6
Grant Thorold NE Lincs 201 F9
Graplin Dumfries 237 E8
Grappenhall Warr 183 D10
Grasby Lincs 200 G5
Grasmere Cumb 220 D6
Grasscroft Gtr Man 196 G3
Grassendale Mers 182 D5
Grassgarth Cumb 221 F8
Cumb 230 C2
Grass Green Essex 106 D4
Grassholme Durham 232 G4
Grassington N Yorks 213 G10
Grassmoor Derbys 170 B6
Grassthorpe Notts 172 B3
Grasswell T&W 243 G8
Grateley Hants 47 E9
Gratton Devon 24 E5
Gratwich Staffs 151 C10
Gravel Ches W 167 B11
Gravel Castle Kent 55 D8
Graveley Cambs 122 E4
Herts 104 F4
Gravelhill Shrops 149 G9
Gravel Hill Bucks 85 G8
Gravel Hole Gtr Man 196 F2
Shrops 149 B7
Gravelly Hill W Mid 134 E2
Gravels Shrops 130 D6
Gravelsbank Shrops 130 C6
Graven Shetland 312 F6
Graveney Kent 70 G5
Gravenhunger Moss
Shrops 168 G2
Gravesend Herts 105 F8
Kent 68 E6
Grayingham Lincs 188 B6
Grayrigg Cumb 221 F11
Grays Thurrock 68 D6
Grayshott Hants 49 F11
Grayson Green Cumb 228 F5
Grayswood Sur 50 G2
Graythorp Hrtlpl 234 F6
Grazeley Wokingham 65 F7
Grazeley Green W Berks 65 F7
Greagdhubh Lodge
Highld 291 D8
Greamchary Highld 310 F2
Greasbrough S Yorks 186 B6
Greasby Mers 182 D3
Greasley Notts 171 F7
Great Abington Cambs 105 B10
Great Addington
Northants 121 B9
Great Alne Warks 118 F2
Great Altcar Lancs 193 F10
Great Amwell Herts 86 C5
Great Asby Cumb 222 C3
Great Ashfield Suff 125 D9
Great Ashley Wilts 61 G10
Great Ayton N Yorks 225 C11
Great Baddow Essex 88 E2
Great Bardfield Essex 106 E3
Great Barford Beds 122 G2
Great Barrington Glos 82 C2
Great Barrow Ches W 167 B7
Great Barton Suff 125 D7
Great Barugh N Yorks 216 D4
Great Bavington
Northumb 251 G11
Great Bealings Suff 108 B4
Great Bedwyn Wilts 63 G9
Great Bentley Essex 108 G2
Great Berry Essex 69 B7
Great Billing Northants 120 E6
Great Bircham Norf 158 C5
Great Blakenham Suff 126 G2
Great Blencow Cumb 230 E5
Great Bolas Telford 150 E2
Great Bookham Sur 50 C6
Great Bosullow Corn 1 C4
Great Bourton Oxon 101 B9
Great Bowden Leics 136 F4
Great Bower Kent 54 C4
Great Bradley Suff 124 G3
Great Braxted Essex 88 C5
Great Bricett Suff 125 G10
Great Brickhill Bucks 103 E8
Great Bridge W Mid 133 E9
Great Bridgeford Staffs 151 D7
Great Brington
Northants 120 D3
Great Bromley Essex 107 F11
Great Broughton Cumb 229 E7
N Yorks 225 D10
Great Buckland Kent 69 G7
Great Budworth
Ches W 183 F11
Great Burdon Darl 224 B6
Great Burgh Sur 51 B8
Great Burstead Essex 87 G11
Great Busby N Yorks 225 D10
Great Canfield Essex 87 B9
Great Carlton Lincs 190 D6
Great Casterton Rutland 137 B9
Rutland 137 B10
Great Cellws Powys 113 E11
Great Chalfield Wilts 61 G11
Great Chart Kent 54 E3
Great Chatwell Staffs 150 G5
Great Chell Stoke 168 E5
Great Chesterford
Essex 105 C10
Great Cheveney Kent 53 E8
Great Cheverell Wilts 46 C3
Great Chilton Durham 233 E11
Great Chishill Cambs 105 D8
Great Clacton Essex 89 B11
Great Claydons Essex 88 E3
Great Cliff W Yorks 197 D10
Great Clifton Cumb 228 F6
Great Coates NE Lincs 201 F8
Great Comberton Worcs 99 C9
Great Common Suff 143 F7
W Sus 35 B8
Great Corby Cumb 239 G11
Great Cornard Suff 107 C7
Great Cowden E Yorks 209 E10
Great Coxwell Oxon 82 G3
Great Crakehall
N Yorks 224 G4
Great Cransley
Northants 120 B6
Great Cressingham
Norf 141 C7
Great Crosby Mers 182 B4
Great Crosthwaite
Cumb 229 G11
Great Cubley Derbys 152 B3
Great Dalby Leics 154 G4
Great Denham Beds 103 B10
Great Doddington
Northants 121 E7
Great Doward Hereford 79 B9
Great Dunham Norf 159 G7
Great Dunmow Essex 106 G2
Great Durnford Wilts 46 F6
Great Easton Essex 106 F2
Leics 136 E6
Great Eccleston Lancs 202 E4
Great Edstone N Yorks 216 C4
Great Ellingham Norf 141 D10
Great Elm Som 45 D8
Great Eppleton T&W 234 B3
Greater Doward Hereford 79 B9
Great Eversden Cambs 123 G7
Great Fencote N Yorks 224 G5
Greatfield Wilts 62 B5
Great Finborough Suff 125 F10
Greatford Lincs 155 G11
Great Fransham Norf 159 G7
Great Gaddesden Herts 85 C8
Greatgap Bucks 84 B6
Great Gate Staffs 169 G9
Great Gidding Cambs 138 G2
Great Givendale
E Yorks 208 C2
Great Glemham Suff 126 E6
Great Glen Leics 136 D3
Great Gonerby Lincs 155 B7
Great Gransden Cambs 122 F5
Great Green Cambs 104 C5
Norf 142 F5
Suff 125 B11
Suff 125 F8
Suff 126 B2
Great Habton N Yorks 216 D5
Great Hale Lincs 173 G10
Great Hallingbury Essex 87 B8
Greatham Hants 49 G9
Hrtlpl 234 F5
W Sus 35 D8
Great Hampden Bucks 84 E4
Great Harrowden
Northants 121 C7
Great Harwood Lancs 203 G10
Great Haseley Oxon 83 E10
Great Hatfield E Yorks 209 E9
Great Haywood Staffs 151 E9
Staffs 151 E10
Great Heath W Mid 134 G6
Great Heck N Yorks 198 C5
Great Henny Essex 107 D7
Great Hinton Wilts 46 B2
Great Hivings Bucks 85 E7
Great Hockham Norf 141 E9
Great Holcombe Oxon 83 F10
Great Holland Essex 89 B12
Great Hollands Brack 65 F11
Great Holm M Keynes 102 D6
Great Honeyborough
Pembs 73 D7
Great Horkesley Essex 107 E9
Great Hormead Herts 105 F7
Great Horton W Yorks 205 G8
Great Horwood Bucks 102 E5
Great Houghton
Northants 120 F5
S Yorks 198 F2
Great Howarth Gtr Man 196 D2
Great Hucklow Derbys 185 F11
Great Job's Cross Kent 38 B4
Great Kelk E Yorks 209 B8
Great Kendale E Yorks 217 G10
Great Kimble Bucks 84 D4
Great Kingshill Bucks 84 F5
Great Langton N Yorks 224 F5
Great Lea Common
Reading 65 F8
Great Leighs Essex 88 B2
Great Lever Gtr Man 195 F8
Great Limber Lincs 200 F6
Great Linford M Keynes 103 C7
Great Livermere Suff 125 C7
Great Longstone Derbys 186 G2
Great Lumley Durham 233 B11
Great Lyth Shrops 131 B9
Great Malgraves Thurrock 69 C7
Great Malvern Worcs 98 B5
Great Maplestead Essex 106 E6
Great Marton Blkpool 202 F2
Great Marton Moss
Blkpool 202 G2
Great Massingham Norf 158 E5
Great Melton Norf 142 B2
Great Milton Oxon 83 E10
Great Missenden Bucks 84 E5
Great Mitton Lancs 203 F10
Great Mongeham Kent 55 C10
Greatmoor Bucks 102 G4
Great Moor Gtr Man 184 D6
Staffs 132 D6
Great Moulton Norf 142 E3
Great Munden Herts 105 G7
Great Musgrave Cumb 222 C5
Greatness Kent 52 B4
Great Ness Shrops 149 F7
Great Notley Essex 106 G4
Great Oak Mon 78 D5
Great Oakley Essex 108 F3
Northants 137 F7
Great Offley Herts 104 F2
Great Ormside Cumb 222 B4
Great Orton Cumb 239 G8
Great Ouseburn
N Yorks 215 G8
Great Oxendon
Northants 136 G4
Great Oxney Green
Essex 87 D11
Great Palgrave Norf 158 G6
Great Parndon Essex 86 D6
Great Pattenden Kent 53 E8
Great Paxton Cambs 122 E4
Great Plumpton Lancs 202 G3
Great Plumstead Norf 160 G6
Great Ponton Lincs 155 C8
Great Preston W Yorks 198 B2
Great Purston
Northants 101 D10
Great Raveley Cambs 138 G5
Great Rissington Glos 81 B11
Great Rollright Oxon 100 E6
Great Ryburgh Norf 159 D9
Great Ryle Northumb 264 G2
Great Ryton Shrops 131 C9
Great Saling Essex 106 F4
Great Salkeld Cumb 231 D7
Great Sampford Essex 106 D2
Great Sankey Warr 183 D9
Great Saredon Staffs 133 B9
Great Saxham Suff 124 E5
Great Shefford W Berks 63 E11
Great Shelford Cambs 123 G9
Great Shoddesden Hants 47 D9
Great Smeaton N Yorks 224 E6
Great Snoring Norf 159 C8
Great Somerford Wilts 62 C3
Great Stainton Darl 234 G2
Great Stambridge Essex 88 G5
Great Staughton Cambs 122 E2
Great Steeping Lincs 174 C6
Great Stoke S Glos 60 C6
Great Stonar Kent 55 B10
Greatstone-on-Sea Kent 39 C9
Great Stretton Leics 136 C3
Great Strickland Cumb 231 G7
Great Stukeley Cambs 122 C4
Great Sturton Lincs 190 F2
Great Sutton Ches W 182 F5
Shrops 131 G10
Great Swinburne
Northumb 241 B10
Great Tew Oxon 101 F7
Great Tey Essex 107 F7
Great Thirkleby N Yorks 215 D9
Great Thurlow Suff 124 G3
Great Torrington Devon 25 D7
Great Tosson Northumb 252 C2
Great Totham Essex 88 C5
Great Tows Lincs 190 C2
Great Tree Corn 6 D5
Great Urswick Cumb 210 E5
Great Wakering Essex 70 B2
Great Waldingfield Suff 107 C8
Great Walsingham Norf 159 B8
Great Waltham Essex 87 C11
Great Warley Essex 87 G9
Great Washbourne Glos 99 E9
Great Weeke Devon 13 D10
Great Weldon Northants 137 F8
Great Welnetham Suff 125 F7
Great Wenham Suff 107 D11
Great Whittington
Northumb 242 C2
Great Wigborough Essex 89 C7
Great Wilbraham
Cambs 123 F10
Great Wilne Derbys 153 C8
Great Wishford Wilts 46 F5
Great Witchingham
Norf 160 E2
Great Witcombe Glos 80 C6
Great Witley Worcs 116 D5
Great Wolford Warks 100 E4
Greatworth Northants 101 C11
Great Wratting Suff 106 B3
Great Wymondley Herts 104 F4
Great Wyrley Staffs 133 B9
Great Wytheford
Shrops 149 F11
Great Yarmouth Norf 143 B10
Great Yeldham Essex 106 D5
Greave Gtr Man 184 C6
Lancs 195 C11
Grebby Lincs 174 B6
Greeba IoM 192 D4
Green Denb 165 B9
Pembs 73 E7
Powys 130 E5
Greenacres Gtr Man 196 F2
Greenan Argyll 275 G11
Greenbank Ches W 183 G10
Falk 279 F7
Shetland 312 C7
Green Bank Cumb 211 C7
Green Bottom Corn 4 F5
Glos 79 B11
Greenburn W Loth 269 C8
Green Close N Yorks 212 F4
Green Clough W Yorks 205 G7
Green Crize Hereford 97 D10
Greencroft Durham 242 G5
Green Cross Sur 49 F11
Greendale Ches E 184 F5
Greendikes Northumb 264 D3
Greendown Som 44 C5
Green Down Devon 28 G3
Greendykes Northumb 264 D3
Greenend N Lnrk 268 C4
Oxon 100 G6
Green End Beds 103 B10
Beds 121 E11
Beds 122 E2
Beds 122 G2
Bucks 84 F4
Bucks 103 E8
Cambs 122 C4
Cambs 123 F7
C Beds 103 D11
Herts 85 D8
Herts 104 E5
Herts 104 E6
Herts 104 G6
Herts 105 F7
Lancs 204 D4
N Yorks 226 E6
Warks 134 F5
Greenfaulds N Lnrk 278 G5
Greenfield C Beds 103 E11
Glasgow 268 C2
Gtr Man 196 G3
Highld 289 D11
Highld 290 C4
Oxon 84 G2
Greenfield / Maes-Glas
Flint 181 F11
Greenfoot N Lnrk 268 B4
Greenford London 66 C6
Greengairs N Lnrk 278 G5
Greengarth Hall Cumb 219 E11
Greengate Gtr Man 196 D2
Norf 159 F10
Green Gate Devon 27 D8
Greengates W Yorks 205 F9
Greengill Cumb 229 D8
Green Hailey Bucks 84 E4
Greenhalgh Lancs 202 F4
Greenhall S Lnrk 268 D3
Greenham Dorset 28 G6
Som 27 C9
W Berks 64 F3
Green Hammerton
N Yorks 206 B5
Greenhaugh Northumb 251 F7
Green Haworth Lancs 195 B9
Greenhead Borders 261 D11
Dumfries 247 D9
N Lnrk 268 E6
Northumb 240 D5
Staffs 169 F7
Green Head Cumb 230 B3
Green Heath Staffs 151 G9
Greenheys Gtr Man 195 G8
Greenhill Dumfries 238 B4
Durham 234 B3
Falk 278 F6
Hereford 98 B4
Kent 71 F7
Leics 153 G8
London 67 B7
S Yorks 186 E4
Worcs 99 B10
Worcs 116 B6
Green Hill Kent 53 C9
Lincs 155 B8
Wilts 62 B5
W Yorks 206 F4
Greenhill Bank Shrops 149 B7
Greenhillocks Derbys 170 F6
Greenhills N Ayrs 267 E7
S Lnrk 268 E2
Greenhithe Kent 68 E5
Greenholm E Ayrs 258 B2
Greenholme Cumb 221 D11
Greenhouse Borders 262 E3
Greenhow N Yorks 214 G2
Greenhow Hill N Yorks 214 G2
Greenigoe Orkney 314 F4
Greenland Highld 310 C6
S Yorks 186 D5
Greenland Mains Highld 310 C6
Greenlands Bucks 65 B9
Worcs 117 D11
Green Lane Devon 13 F11
Hereford 98 B2
Powys 130 D3
Warks 117 E11
Warks 118 B6
Greenlaw Aberds 302 D6
Borders 272 F4
Greenlaw Mains Midloth 270 C4
Greenlea Dumfries 238 B2
Greenley M Keynes 102 C6
Greenloaning Perth 286 G2
Greenlooms Ches W 167 C7
Greenman's Lane Wilts 62 C3
Greenmeadow Swindon 62 B6
Torf 78 F3
Green Moor S Yorks 186 B3
Greenmount Gtr Man 195 E9
Greenmow Shetland 313 L6
Greenoak E Yorks 199 B10
Greenock Invclyd 276 F5
Greenock West Invclyd 276 F5
Greenodd Cumb 210 C6
Green Ore Som 44 C5
Green Parlour Bath 45 C8
Green Quarter Cumb 221 E9
Greenrigg W Loth 269 C8
Greenrow Cumb 238 G4
Greens Borders 249 F11
Green St Green London 68 G3
Greensforge Staffs 133 F7
Greensgate Norf 160 F2
Greenside Cumb 222 E4
Derbys 186 F5
Gtr Man 184 B6
T&W 242 E4
W Yorks 197 D7
Green Side W Yorks 197 E7
W Yorks 205 G11
Greensidehill Northumb 263 F11
Greens Norton
Northants 102 B3
Greensplat Corn 5 D9
Greenstead Essex 107 F10
Greenstead Green Essex 106 F6
Greensted Essex 87 E8
Greensted Green Essex 87 E8
Green Street Essex 87 F10
E Sus 38 E3
Glos 80 B5
Glos 80 E3
Herts 85 F11
Herts 105 G9
Worcs 99 B7
Worcs 99 C7
W Sus 35 C10
Greenstreet Green
Suff 107 B10
Green Street Green Kent 68 E5
London 68 G3
Green Tye Herts 86 B6
Greenway Hereford 98 E4
Pembs 91 E11
Som 27 B11
V Glam 58 E5
Worcs 116 C4
Greenwell Cumb 240 F2
Greenwells Borders 262 C3
Greenwich London 67 D11
Suff 108 C3
Wilts 46 G2
Greenwith Common Corn 4 G5
Greenwoods Essex 87 F11
Greeny Orkney 314 D2
Greep Highld 298 E2
Greet Glos 99 E10
Kent 54 B2
Greete Shrops 115 C11
Greetham Lincs 190 G4
Rutland 155 G8
Greetland W Yorks 196 C5
Greetland Wall Nook
W Yorks 196 C5
Greetwell N Lincs 200 G2
Gregg Hall Cumb 221 G9
Gregson Lane Lancs 194 B5
Gregynog Powys 129 D11
Grèin W Isles 297 L2
Greinetobht W Isles 296 D4
Greinton Som 44 F2
Gremista Shetland 313 J6
Grenaby IoM 192 E3
Grendon Northants 121 E7
Warks 134 C5
Grendon Bishop
Hereford 115 F11
Grendon Common
Warks 134 D5
Grendon Green
Hereford 115 F11
Grendon Underwood
Bucks 102 G3
Grenofen Devon 12 G5
Grenoside S Yorks 186 C4
Greosabhagh W Isles 305 J3
Gresford Wrex 166 E5
Gresham Norf 160 B3
Greshornish Highld 298 D3
Gressenhall Norf 159 F9
Gressingham Lancs 211 F11
Gresty Green Ches E 168 E2
Greta Bridge Durham 223 C11
Gretna Dumfries 239 D8
Gretna Green Dumfries 239 D8
Gretton Glos 99 E10
Northants 137 E7
Shrops 131 D10
Gretton Fields Glos 99 E10
Grewelthorpe N Yorks 214 D4
Greyfield Bath 44 B6
Greygarth N Yorks 214 E3
Grey Green N Lincs 199 F9
Greylake Som 43 G11
Greylake Fosse Som 44 F2
Greynor Carms 75 D9
Greynor-isaf Carms 75 D9
Greyrigg Dumfries 248 F3
Greys Green Oxon 65 C8
Greysouthen Cumb 229 F7
Greystead Northumb 251 F7
Greystoke Cumb 230 E4
Greystoke Gill Cumb 230 F4
Greystone Aberds 292 D6
Aberds 302 F6
Angus 287 C9
Cumb 211 D10
Dumfries 237 B11
Greystonegill N Yorks 212 F3
Greystones S Yorks 186 D4
Warks 99 B11
Greytree Hereford 97 F11
Greywell Hants 49 C8
Griais W Isles 304 D6
Grianan W Isles 304 E6
Gribb Dorset 28 G5
Gribthorpe E Yorks 207 F11
Gridley Corner Devon 12 C3
Griff Warks 135 F7
Griffins Hill W Mid 133 G10
Griffithstown Torf 78 F3
Griffydam Leics 153 F8
Griggs Green Hants 49 G10
Grillis Corn 2 B5
Grilstone Devon 26 C2
Grimbister Orkney 314 E3
Grimblethorpe Lincs 190 D2
Grimeford Village Lancs 194 E6
Grimes Hill Worcs 117 B11
Grimesthorpe S Yorks 186 C5
Grimethorpe S Yorks 198 F2
Griminis W Isles 296 D3
W Isles 296 F3
Grimister Shetland 312 D6
Grimley Worcs 116 E6
Grimness Orkney 314 G4
Grimoldby Lincs 190 D5
Grimpo Shrops 149 D7
Grimsargh Lancs 203 G7
Grimsbury Oxon 101 C9
Grimsby NE Lincs 201 E9
Grimscote Northants 120 G3
Grimscott Corn 24 F3
Grimshaw Blkburn 195 C8
Grimshaw Green Lancs 194 E3
Grimsthorpe Lincs 155 E10
Grimston E Yorks 209 F11
Leics 154 E3
Norf 158 E4
York 207 C8
Grimstone Dorset 17 C8
Grimstone End Suff 125 D8
Grinacombe Moor Devon 12 C4
Grindale E Yorks 218 E2
Grindigar Orkney 314 F5
Grindiscol Shetland 313 K6
Grindle Shrops 132 C5
Grindleford Derbys 186 F2
Grindleton Lancs 203 D11
Grindley Staffs 151 D10
Grindley Brook Shrops 167 G8
Grindlow Derbys 185 F11
Grindon Northumb 273 G8
Staffs 169 E9
Stockton 234 F3
T&W 243 G9
Grindonmoor Gate
Staffs 169 E9
Grindsbrook Booth
Derbys 185 D10
Gringley on the Hill
Notts 188 C2
Grinsdale Cumb 239 F9
Grinshill Shrops 149 E10
Grinstead Hill Suff 125 G11
Grinton N Yorks 223 F10
Griomasaigh W Isles 297 G4
Griomsidar W Isles 304 F5
Grisdale Cumb 222 G5
Grishipoll Argyll 288 D3
Grisling Common E Sus 36 C6
Gristhorpe N Yorks 217 C11
Griston Norf 141 D8
Gritley Orkney 314 F5
Grittenham Wilts 62 C4
Grittlesend Hereford 98 B4
Grittleton Wilts 61 C11
Grizebeck Cumb 210 C4
Grizedale Cumb 220 G6
Groam Highld 300 E5
Grobister Orkney 314 D6
Grobsness Shetland 313 G5
Groby Leics 135 B10
Groes Conwy 165 C8
Neath 57 D9
Groes Efa Denb 165 B10
Groes-faen Rhondda 58 C5
Groes-fawr Denb 165 B10
Groesffordd Gwyn 144 B5
Powys 95 F11
Groesffordd Marli Denb 181 G8
Groeslon Gwyn 163 C8
Gwyn 163 D7
Groes-lwyd Mon 96 G6
Powys 148 G4
Groespluan Powys 130 B4
Groes-wen Caerph 58 B6
Grogport Argyll 255 C9
Gromford Suff 127 F7
Gronant Flint 181 E9
Gronwen Shrops 148 D5
Groombridge E Sus 52 F4
Grosmont Mon 97 G8
N Yorks 226 D6
Gross Green Warks 119 F7
Grotaig Highld 300 G4
Groton Suff 107 C9
Grotton Gtr Man 196 G3
Grougfoot Falk 279 F10
Grove Bucks 103 G8
Dorset 17 G10
Hereford 98 C2
Kent 71 G8
Notts 188 F2
Oxon 82 G6
Pembs 73 E7
Grove End Kent 69 G11
Warks 100 D6
Warks 134 D3
Grove Green Kent 53 B9
Grovehill E Yorks 208 F6
Herts 85 D9
Grove Hill E Sus 23 C10
Kent 71 G8
Grove Park London 67 D8
London 68 E2
Groves Kent 55 B9
Grovesend Swansea 75 E9
Grove Town W Yorks 198 C3
Grove Vale W Mid 133 E10
Grubb Street Kent 68 F5
Grub Street Staffs 150 D5
Grudie Highld 300 C3
Gruids Highld 309 J5
Gruinard House Highld 307 K4
Gruinards Highld 309 K5
Grula Highld 294 C5
Gruline Argyll 289 E7
Gruline Ho Argyll 289 F7
Grumbeg Highld 308 F6
Grumbla Corn 1 D4
Grunasound Shetland 313 K5
Grundisburgh Suff 126 G4
Grunsagill Lancs 203 C11
Gruting Shetland 313 J4
Grutness Shetland 313 N6
Gryn Goch Gwyn 162 F6
Gualachulain Highld 284 C5
Gualin Ho Highld 308 D3
Guardbridge Fife 287 F8
Guard House W Yorks 204 E6
Guarlford Worcs 98 B6
Guay Perth 286 C4
Gubbion's Green Essex 88 B2
Gubblecote Herts 84 C6
Guesachan Highld 289 B10
Guestling Green E Sus 38 E5
Guestling Thorn E Sus 38 D4
Guestwick Norf 159 D11
Guestwick Green Norf 159 D11
Guide Blkburn 195 B8
Guide Bridge Gtr Man 184 B6
Guide Post Northumb 253 F7
Guilden Morden Cambs 104 C5
Guilden Sutton Ches W 166 B6
Guildford Sur 50 D3
Guildford Park Sur 50 D3
Guildiehaugh W Loth 269 B9
Guildtown Perth 286 D5
Guilford Pembs 73 D7
Guilsborough Northants 120 C3
Guilsfield / Cegidfa
Powys 148 G4
Guilthwaite S Yorks 187 D7
Guilton Kent 55 B9
Guineaford Devon 40 F5
Guisachan Highld 300 G3
Guisborough Redcar 226 B2
Guiseley W Yorks 205 E9
Guist Norf 159 D9
Guith Orkney 314 C5
Guiting Power Glos 99 G11
Gulberwick Shetland 313 K6
Gullane E Loth 281 E9
Guller's End Worcs 99 D7
Gulling Green Suff 124 F6
Gullom Holme Cumb 231 F9
Gulval Corn 1 C5
Gulworthy Devon 12 G4
Gumfreston Pembs 73 E10
Gumley Leics 136 E3
Gummow's Shop Corn 5 D7
Gunby E Yorks 207 F10
Lincs 155 E8
Lincs 175 B7
Gundenham Som 27 C10
Gundleton Hants 48 G6
Gun Green Kent 53 G9
Gun Hill E Sus 23 C9
Gunn Devon 40 G6
Gunnersbury London 67 D7
Gunnerside N Yorks 223 F9
Gunnerton Northumb 241 C10
Gunness N Lincs 199 E10
Gunnislake Corn 12 G4
Gunnista Shetland 313 J7
Gunstone Staffs 133 C7
Guns Village W Mid 133 E9
Gunter's Bridge W Sus 35 C7
Gunthorpe Lincs 188 B4
Norf 159 C10
Notts 171 G11
Pboro 138 C3
Rutland 137 B7
Gunton Suff 143 D10
Gunville IoW 20 D5
Gunwalloe Corn 2 E5
Gunwalloe Fishing Cove
Corn 2 E5
Gupworthy Som 42 F3
Gurnard IoW 20 B5
Gurnett Ches E 184 G6
Gurney Slade Som 44 D6
Gurnos M Tydf 77 D8
Powys 76 D3
Gushmere Kent 54 B4
Gussage All Saints Dorset 31 E8
Gussage St Andrew
Dorset 31 E7
Gussage St Michael
Dorset 31 E7
Gustard Wood Herts 85 B11
Guston Kent 55 E10
Gutcher Shetland 312 D7
Guthram Gowt Lincs 156 E3
Guthrie Angus 287 B9
Guyhirn Cambs 139 C7
Guyhirn Gull Cambs 139 C7
Guy's Cliffe Warks 118 D5
Guy's Head Lincs 157 D9
Guy's Marsh Dorset 30 C4
Guyzance Northumb 252 C6
Gwaelod-y-garth Cardiff 58 C6
Gwaenysgor Flint 181 E9
Gwalchmai Anglesey 178 F5
Gwalchmai Uchaf
Anglesey 178 F5
Gwallon Corn 2 C2
Gwastad Pembs 91 G10
Gwastadgoed Gwyn 145 G11
Gwastadnant Gwyn 163 D10
Gwaun-Cae-Gurwen
Neath 76 C2
Gwaun-Leision Neath 76 C2
Gwavas Corn 2 D5
Corn 2 G6
Gwbert Ceredig 92 B3
Gwedna Corn 2 C4
Gweek Corn 2 D6
Gwehelog Mon 78 E5
Gwenddwr Powys 95 C11
Gwennap Corn 2 B6
Gwenter Corn 2 F6
Gwernaffield-y-Waun
Flint 166 C2
Gwernafon Powys 129 E8
Gwerneirin Powys 129 F10
Powys 130 G3
Gwernesney Mon 78 E6
Gwernogle Carms 93 E10
Gwernol Denb 166 E2
Gwern y brenin Shrops 148 D6
Gwernydd Powys 129 C11
Gwernymynydd Flint 166 C2
Gwern-y-Steeple V Glam 58 D5
Gwersyllt Wrex 166 E4
Gwespyr Flint 181 E10
Gwills Corn 4 D6
Gwinear Corn 2 B3
Gwinear Downs Corn 2 C4
Gwithian Corn 2 A3
Gwredog Anglesey 178 D6
Gwrhay Caerph 77 F11
Gwyddelwern Denb 165 F9
Gwyddgrug Carms 93 D9
Gwynfryn Wrex 166 E3
Gwystre Powys 113 D11
Gwytherin Conwy 164 C5
Gyfelia Wrex 166 F4
Gyffin Conwy 180 F3
Gylen Park Argyll 289 G10
Gyre Orkney 314 F3
Gyrn Denb 165 D11
Gyrn-goch Gwyn 162 F6

H

Habberley Shrops 131 C7
Worcs 116 B6
Habergham Lancs 204 G2
Habertoft Lincs 175 B8
Habin W Sus 34 C4
Habrough NE Lincs 200 E6
Haccombe Devon 14 G3
Haceby Lincs 155 B10
Hacheston Suff 126 F6
Hackbridge London 67 F9
Hackenthorpe S Yorks 186 E6
Hackford Norf 141 C11
Hackforth N Yorks 224 G4
Hack Green Ches E 167 F10
Hackland Orkney 314 D3
Hackleton Northants 120 F6
Hacklinge Kent 55 C10
Hackman's Gate Worcs 117 B7
Hackness N Yorks 227 G9
Orkney 314 G3
Som 43 D10
Hackney London 67 C10
Hackney Wick London 67 C11
Hackthorn Lincs 189 E7
Wilts 47 D7
Hackthorpe Cumb 230 G6
Haclait W Isles 297 G4
Haconby Lincs 156 D2
Hacton London 68 B4
Haddacott Devon 25 C8
Hadden Borders 263 B7
Haddenham Bucks 84 D2
Cambs 123 B9
Haddenham End Field
Cambs 123 B9
Haddington E Loth 281 G10
Lincs 172 C6
Haddiscoe Norf 143 D8
Haddoch Aberds 302 E5
Haddon Cambs 138 E2
Ches E 169 B7
Hade Edge W Yorks 196 F6
Hademore Staffs 134 B3
Haden Cross W Mid 133 F9
Hadfield Derbys 185 B8
Hadham Cross Herts 86 B6
Hadham Ford Herts 105 G8
Hadleigh Essex 69 B10
Suff 107 C10
Hadleigh Heath Suff 107 C9
Hadley London 86 F2
Telford 150 G3
Worcs 117 E7
Hadley Castle Telford 150 G3
Hadley End Staffs 152 E2
Hadley Wood London 86 F3
Hadlow Kent 52 D6
Hadlow Down E Sus 37 C8
Hadlow Stair Kent 52 D6
Hadnall Shrops 149 F10
Hadspen Som 45 G7
Hadstock Essex 105 C11
Hadston Northumb 253 D7
Hady Derbys 186 G5
Hadzor Worcs 117 E8
Haffenden Quarter Kent 53 E11
Hafod Swansea 57 C7
Hafod-Dinbych Conwy 164 E5
Hafod Grove Pembs 92 C2
Hafodiwan Ceredig 111 G7
Hafod-lom Conwy 180 G5
Hafod-y-Green Denb 181 G8
Hafodyrynys Bl Gwent 78 F2
Hag Fold Gtr Man 195 G7
Haggate Gtr Man 196 F2
Lancs 204 F3
Haggbeck Cumb 239 C11
Haggersta Shetland 313 J5
Haggerston London 67 C10
Northumb 273 G10
Hagginton Hill Devon 40 D5
Haggrister Shetland 312 F5
Haggs Falk 278 F5
Haghill Glasgow 268 B2
Hagley Hereford 97 C11
Worcs 133 G8
Hagloe Glos 79 D11
Hagmore Green Suff 107 D9
Hagnaby Lincs 174 C4
Lincs 191 F7
Hagnaby Lock Lincs 174 D4
Hague Bar Derbys 185 D7
Hagworthingham Lincs 174 B4
Haigh Gtr Man 194 F6
S Yorks 197 E9
Haigh Moor W Yorks 197 C9
Haighton Green Lancs 203 G7
Haighton Top Lancs 203 G7
Haile Cumb 219 D10
Hailes Glos 99 E10
Hailey Herts 86 C5
Oxon 64 B6
Oxon 82 C5
Hailsham E Sus 23 D9
Hailstone Hill Wilts 81 G9
Hail Weston Cambs 122 E3
Haimer Highld 310 C5
Haimwood Powys 148 F6
Hainault London 87 G7
Haine Kent 71 F11
Hainford Norf 160 F4
Hains Dorset 30 D3
Hainton Lincs 189 E11
Hainworth W Yorks 205 F7
Hainworth Shaw
W Yorks 205 F7
Hairmyres S Lnrk 268 E2
Haisthorpe E Yorks 218 G2
Hakeford Devon 40 F6
Hakin Pembs 72 D5
Halabezack Corn 2 C6
Halam Notts 171 E11
Halamanning Corn 2 C3
Halbeath Fife 280 D2
Halberton Devon 27 E8
Halcon Som 28 B2
Halcro Highld 310 C6
Haldens Herts 86 C2
Hale Cumb 211 D10
Gtr Man 184 D3
Halton 183 E7
Hants 31 D11
Kent 71 F9
Medway 69 F9
Som 30 B3
Sur 49 D10
Hale Bank Halton 183 E7
Hale Barns Gtr Man 184 D3
Halecommon W Sus 34 C4
Hale Coombe N Som 44 B2
Hale End London 86 G5
Hale Green E Sus 23 C9
Hale Mills Corn 4 G5
Hale Nook Lancs 202 E3
Hales Norf 143 D7
Staffs 150 C4
Hales Bank Hereford 116 G2
Halesfield Telford 132 C4
Halesgate Lincs 156 D6
Hales Green Derbys 169 G11
Norf 143 D7
Halesowen W Mid 133 G9
Hales Park Worcs 116 B5
Hales Place Kent 54 B6
Hales Street Norf 142 F3
Hale Street Kent 53 D7
Hales Wood Hereford 98 E2
Halesworth Suff 127 B7
Halewood Mers 183 D7
Half Moon Village Devon 14 B3
Halford Shrops 131 G8
Warks 100 B5
Halfpenny Cumb 211 B10
Halfpenny Furze Carms 74 C3
Halfpenny Green Staffs 132 E6
Halfway Carms 75 E8
Carms 94 E2
Carms 94 E6
S Yorks 186 E6
W Berks 64 F2
Wilts 45 D11
Halfway Bridge W Sus 34 C6
Halfway House Shrops 148 G6

Halfway Houses
Gtr Man 195 F9
Kent 70 E2
Halfway Street Kent 55 D9
Halgabron Corn 11 D7
Halifax W Yorks 196 B5
Halkburn Borders 271 G9
Halket E Ayrs 267 E8
Halkirk Highld 310 D5
Halkyn / Helygain Flint 182 G2
Halkyn Mountain Flint 182 G2
Hallam Fields Derbys 153 B9
Halland E Sus 23 B8
Hallaton Leics 136 D5
Hallatrow Bath 44 B6
Hallbankgate Cumb 240 F3
Hall Bower W Yorks 196 E6
Hall Broom S Yorks 186 D3
Hall Cross Lancs 202 G4
Hall Dunnerdale Cumb 220 F4
Halleaths Dumfries 248 G3
Hallen S Glos 60 C5
Hallend Warks 118 D2
Hall End Beds 103 B10
C Beds 103 D11
Lincs 174 E6
S Glos 61 B8
Warks 134 C5
Hallew Corn 5 D10
Hallfield Gate Derbys 170 D5
Hall Flat Worcs 117 C9
Hallgarth Durham 234 C2
Hall Garth York 207 C9
Hallglen Falk 279 F7
Hall Green Ches E 168 D4
Essex 106 D5
Lancs 194 C3
Lancs 194 F4
W Mid 133 E10
W Mid 134 G2
W Mid 135 G7
Wrex 167 G7
W Yorks 197 D10
Hall Grove Herts 86 C3
Halliburton Borders 261 B11
Borders 272 F3
Hallin Highld 298 D2
Halling Medway 69 G8
Hallingbury Street Essex 87 B8
Hallington Lincs 190 D4
Northumb 241 B11
Hall i' th' Wood Gtr Man 195 E8
Halliwell Gtr Man 195 E8
Hall of Clestrain Orkney 314 F2
Hall of Tankerness
Orkney 314 F5
Hall of the Forest
Shrops 130 G4
Hallon Shrops 132 D5
Hallonsford Shrops 132 D5
Halloughton Notts 171 E11
Hallow Worcs 116 F6
Hallowes Derbys 186 F5
Hallow Heath Worcs 116 F6
Hallowsgate Ches W 167 B8
Hallrule Borders 262 G3
Halls E Loth 282 G3
Hallsands Devon 9 G11
Hall Santon Cumb 220 E2
Hall's Cross E Sus 23 D11
Hallsford Bridge Essex 87 E9
Halls Green Essex 86 D6
Hall's Green Herts 104 F5
Kent 52 D4
Hallspill Devon 25 C7
Hallthwaites Cumb 210 B3
Hall Waberthwaite
Cumb 220 F2
Hallwood Green Glos 98 E3
Hallworthy Corn 11 D9
Hallyards Borders 260 B6
Hallyburton House
Perth 286 D6
Hallyne Borders 270 G3
Halmer End Staffs 168 F3
Halmond's Frome
Hereford 98 B3
Halmore Glos 79 E11
Halmyre Mains Borders 270 F3
Halnaker W Sus 22 B6
Halsall Lancs 193 E11
Halse Northants 101 C11
Som 27 B10
Halsetown Corn 2 B2
Halsfordwood Devon 14 C3
Halsham E Yorks 201 B9
Halsinger Devon 40 F4
Halstead Essex 106 E6
Kent 68 G3
Leics 136 B4
Halstock Dorset 29 F8
Halsway Som 42 F6
Haltcliff Bridge Cumb 230 D3
Halterworth Hants 32 C5
Haltham Lincs 174 C2
Haltoft End Lincs 174 F5
Halton Bucks 84 C5
Halton 183 E8
Lancs 211 G10
Northumb 241 D11
Wrex 148 B6
W Yorks 206 G2
Halton Barton Corn 7 B8
Halton Brook Halton 183 E8
Halton East N Yorks 204 C6
Halton Fenside Lincs 174 C6
Halton Gill N Yorks 213 D7
Halton Green Lancs 211 F10
Halton Holegate Lincs 174 B6
Halton Lea Gate
Northumb 240 F5
Halton Moor W Yorks 206 G2
Halton Shields
Northumb 242 D2
Halton View Halton 183 D8
Halton West N Yorks 204 C2
Haltwhistle Northumb 240 E6
Halvergate Norf 143 B8
Halvosso Corn 2 C6
Halwell Devon 8 E5
Halwill Devon 12 B4
Halwill Junction Devon 24 G6
Halwin Corn 2 C5
Ham Devon 28 G2
Glos 79 F11
Glos 99 G9
Highld 310 B6
Kent 55 C10
London 67 E7
Plym 7 D9
Shetland 313 K1
Som 27 C11
Som 28 B3
Som 28 E3
Som 45 D7
Wilts 63 G10
Hamar Shetland 312 F5
Hamarhill Orkney 314 C5
Hamars Shetland 313 G6
Hambleden Bucks 65 B9
Hambledon Hants 33 E10
Sur 50 F3
Hamble-le-Rice Hants 33 F7
Hambleton Lancs 202 E3
N Yorks 205 C7
N Yorks 207 G7
Hambleton Moss Side
Lancs 202 E3
Hambridge Som 28 C5
Hambrook S Glos 60 D6
W Sus 22 B3
Ham Common Dorset 30 B4
Hameringham Lincs 174 B4
Hamerton Cambs 122 B2
Hametoun Shetland 313 K1
Ham Green Bucks 83 B11
Hants 48 G2
Hereford 98 C4
Kent 38 B5
Kent 69 F10
N Som 60 D4
Wilts 61 G11
Worcs 117 E10
Ham Hill Kent 69 G8
Hamilton S Lnrk 268 D3
Hamister Shetland 313 G7
Hamlet Dorset 29 F9
Hammer W Sus 49 G11
Hammer Bottom Hants 49 G11
Hammerfield Herts 85 D8
Hammerpot W Sus 35 F9
Hammersmith Derbys 170 E5
London 67 D8
Hammerwich Staffs 133 B11
Hammerwood E Sus 52 F2
Hammill Kent 55 B9
Hammond Street Herts 86 E4
Hammoon Dorset 30 E4
Ham Moor Sur 66 G5
Hamnavoe Shetland 312 E4
Shetland 312 E6
Shetland 312 F6
Shetland 313 K5
Hamnish Clifford
Hereford 115 F10
Hamp Som 43 F10
Hampden Park E Sus 23 E10
Hampen Glos 81 B9
Hamperden End Essex 105 E11
Hamperley Shrops 131 F8
Hampers Green W Sus 35 C7
Hampeth Northumb 252 B5
Hampnett Glos 81 B10
Hampole S Yorks 198 E4
Hampreston Dorset 19 B7
Hampsfield Cumb 211 C8
Hampson Green Lancs 202 C5
Hampstead London 67 B9
Hampstead Garden Suburb
London 67 B9
Hampstead Norreys
W Berks 64 D4
Hampsthwaite N Yorks 205 B11
Hampton Kent 71 F7
London 66 F6
Shrops 132 F4
Swindon 81 G11
Worcs 99 C10
Hampton Bank Shrops 149 C9
Hampton Beech Shrops 130 B6
Hampton Bishop
Hereford 97 D11
Hampton Fields Glos 80 F5
Hampton Gay Oxon 83 B7
Hampton Green Ches W 167 F8
Glos 80 E5
Hampton Hargate Pboro 138 E3
Hampton Heath Ches W 167 F7
Hampton Hill London 66 E6
Hampton in Arden
W Mid 134 G4
Hampton Loade Shrops 132 F5
Hampton Lovett Worcs 117 D7
Hampton Lucy Warks 118 F5
Hampton Magna Warks 118 D5
Hampton on the Hill
Warks 118 E5
Hampton Park Hereford 97 D10
Soton 32 D6
Hampton Poyle Oxon 83 B8
Hamptons Kent 52 C6
Hampton Wick London 67 F7
Hamptworth Wilts 32 D2
Hamrow Norf 159 E8
Hamsey E Sus 36 E6
Hamsey Green London 51 B10
Hamshill Glos 80 E3
Hamstall Ridware Staffs 152 F2
Hamstead IoW 20 C4
W Mid 133 E10
Hamstead Marshall
W Berks 64 F2
Hamsterley Durham 233 E8
Durham 242 F4
Hamstreet Kent 54 G4
Ham Street Som 44 G5
Hamworthy Poole 18 C5
Hanbury Staffs 152 D3
Worcs 117 E9
Hanbury Woodend
Staffs 152 D3
Hanby Lincs 155 C10
Hanchett Village Suff 106 B3
Hanchurch Staffs 168 G4
Handbridge Ches W 166 B6
Handcross W Sus 36 B3
Handforth Ches E 184 E5
Hand Green Ches W 167 C8
Handless Shrops 131 E7
Handley Ches W 167 D7
Derbys 170 C5
Handley Green Essex 87 E11
Handsacre Staffs 151 F11
Handside Herts 86 C2
Handsworth S Yorks 186 D6
W Mid 133 E10
Handsworth Wood
W Mid 133 E11
Handy Cross Bucks 84 G5
Devon 24 B6
Som 42 G6
Hanford Dorset 30 E4
Stoke 168 G5
Hangersley Hants 31 F11
Hanging Bank Kent 52 C3
Hanging Heaton
W Yorks 197 C9
Hanging Houghton
Northants 120 C5
Hanging Langford Wilts 46 F4
Hangingshaw Borders 261 C9
Dumfries 248 F4
Hangleton Brighton 36 F3
W Sus 35 G9
Hangsman Hill S Yorks 199 E7
Hanham S Glos 60 E6
Hanham Green S Glos 60 E6
Hankelow Ches E 167 F11
Hankerton Wilts 81 G7
Hankham E Sus 23 D10
Hanley Stoke 168 F5
Hanley Castle Worcs 98 C6
Hanley Child Worcs 116 E3
Hanley Swan Worcs 98 C6
Hanley William Worcs 116 D3
Hanlith N Yorks 213 G8
Hanmer Wrex 149 B9
Hannaford Devon 25 B10
Hannafore Corn 6 E5
Hannah Lincs 191 F8
Hanningfields Green
Suff 125 G7
Hannington Hants 48 B4
Northants 120 C6
Swindon 81 G11
Hannington Wick
Swindon 81 F11
Hanscombe End C Beds 104 E2
Hansel Devon 8 F6
Hansel Village S Ayrs 257 C9
Hansley Cross Staffs 169 G9
Hanslope M Keynes 102 B6
Hanthorpe Lincs 155 E11
Hanwell London 67 C7
Oxon 101 C8
Hanwood Shrops 131 B8
Hanwood Bank Shrops 149 G8
Hanworth Brack 65 F11
London 66 E6
Norf 160 B3
Happendon S Lnrk 259 C9
Happisburgh Norf 161 C7
Happisburgh Common
Norf 161 D7
Hapsford Ches W 183 G7
Som 45 D9
Hapton Lancs 203 G11
Norf 142 D3
Hararden / Penarlâg
Flint 166 B4
Harberton Devon 8 D5
Harbertonford Devon 8 D5
Harbledown Kent 54 B6
Harborne W Mid 133 G10
Harborough Magna
Warks 119 B9
Harborough Parva
Warks 119 B9
Harbottle Northumb 251 C10
Harbour Heights E Sus 36 G6
Harbourland Kent 53 B9
Harbourneford Devon 8 C4
Harbours Hill Worcs 117 D9
Harbour Village Pembs 91 D8
Harbridge Hants 31 E10
Harbridge Green Hants 31 E10
Harburn W Loth 269 C10
Harbury Warks 119 F7
Harby Leics 154 C4
Notts 188 G5
Harcombe Devon 14 E3
Devon 15 C9
Harcombe Bottom Devon 16 B2
Harcourt Corn 3 B8
Harcourt Hill Oxon 83 E7
Hardbreck Orkney 314 F4
Hardeicke Glos 80 C4
Harden S Yorks 197 G7
W Mid 133 C10
W Yorks 205 F7
Hardendale Cumb 221 C11
Hardenhuish Wilts 62 E2
Harden Park Ches E 184 F4
Hardgate Aberds 293 C9
Dumfries 237 C10
N Yorks 214 G5
W Dunb 277 G10
Hardham W Sus 35 D8
Hardhorn Lancs 202 F3
Hardingham Norf 141 C10
Hardings Booth Staffs 169 C9
Hardingstone Northants 120 F5
Hardings Wood Staffs 168 E4
Hardington Som 45 C8
Hardington Mandeville
Som 29 E8
Hardington Marsh Som 29 F8
Hardington Moor Som 29 E8
Hardiston Perth 279 B11
Hardisworthy Devon 24 C2
Hardley Hants 32 G6
Hardley Street Norf 143 C7
Hardmead M Keynes 103 B8
Hardrow N Yorks 223 G7
Hardstoft Derbys 170 C6
Hardstoft Common
Derbys 170 C6
Hardway Hants 33 G10
Som 45 G8
Hardwick Bucks 84 B4
Cambs 122 D3
Cambs 123 F7
Norf 142 F4
Norf 158 F2
Northants 121 D7
Oxon 82 D5
Oxon 101 G8
Oxon 101 F11
Shrops 131 E7
Stockton 234 G4
S Yorks 187 D7
W Mid 133 D11
Hardwicke Glos 80 C3
Glos 99 F8
Hereford 96 C5
Hardwick Green Worcs 98 E6
Hardwick Village Notts 187 F10
Hardy's Green Essex 107 G8
Hare Som 28 D3
Hare Appletree Lancs 202 B6
Hareby Lincs 174 B4
Harecroft W Yorks 205 F7
Hareden Lancs 203 C8
Hare Edge Derbys 186 G4
Harefield London 85 G9
Soton 33 E7
Harefield Grove London 85 G9
Haregate Staffs 169 D7
Hare Green Essex 107 G11
Hare Hatch Wokingham 65 D10
Harehill Derbys 152 B3
Harehills W Yorks 206 G2
Harehope Borders 270 G4
Northumb 264 E3
Harelaw Durham 242 G5
Hareleeshill S Lnrk 268 E5
Hareplain Kent 53 F10
Haresceugh Cumb 231 C8
Harescombe Glos 80 C4
Haresfield Glos 80 C4
Swindon 82 G2
Haresfinch Mers 183 B8
Hareshaw N Lnrk 268 C6
Hareshaw Head
Northumb 251 F9
Harestanes E Dunb 278 G3
Harestock Hants 48 G3
Hare Street Essex 86 D6
Herts 104 F6
Herts 105 F7
Harewood W Yorks 206 D2
Harewood End Hereford 97 F10
Harewood Hill W Yorks 204 F6
Harford Carms 94 C2
Devon 8 D2
Devon 40 G6
Hargate Norf 142 E2
Hargate Hill Derbys 185 C8
Hargatewall Derbys 185 F10
Hargrave Ches W 167 C7
Northants 121 C10
Suff 124 F5
Harker Cumb 239 E9
Harker Marsh Cumb 229 E7
Harkland Shetland 312 E6
Harknett's Gate Essex 86 D6
Harkstead Suff 108 E3
Harlaston Staffs 152 G4
Harlaw Ho Aberds 303 G7
Harlaxton Lincs 155 C7
Harlech Gwyn 145 C11
Harlequin Notts 154 B3
Harlescott Shrops 149 F10
Harlesden London 67 C8
Harlesthorpe Derbys 187 F7
Harleston Devon 8 F5
Norf 142 G4
Suff 125 F10
Harlestone Northants 120 E4
Harle Syke Lancs 204 F3
Harley Shrops 131 C11
S Yorks 186 B5
Harleyholm S Lnrk 259 B10
Harley Shute E Sus 38 F3
Harleywood Glos 80 F4
Harling Road Norf 141 F9
Harlington C Beds 103 E10
London 66 D5
S Yorks 198 G3
Harlosh Highld 298 E2
Harlow Essex 86 C6
Harlow Carr N Yorks 205 C11
Harlow Green T&W 243 F7
Harlow Hill Northumb 242 D3
N Yorks 205 C11
Harlthorpe E Yorks 207 F10
Harlton Cambs 123 G7
Harlyn Corn 10 F3
Harman's Corner Kent 69 G11
Harman's Cross Dorset 18 E5
Harmans Water Brack 65 F11
Harmby N Yorks 214 B2
Harmer Green Herts 86 B3
Harmer Hill Shrops 149 E9
Harmondsworth London 66 D5
Harmston Lincs 173 C7
Harnage Shrops 131 C11
Harnham Northumb 242 B3
Wilts 31 B10
Wilts 31 B11
Harnhill Glos 81 E9
Harold Hill London 87 G8
Harold Park London 87 G9
Haroldston West Pembs 72 B5
Haroldswick Shetland 312 B8
Harold Wood London 87 G8
Harome N Yorks 216 C2
Harpenden Herts 85 C10
Harpenden Common
Herts 85 C10
Harper Green Gtr Man 195 F8
Harperley Durham 242 G5
Harper's Gate Staffs 169 D7
Harper's Green Norf 159 E8
Harpford Devon 15 C7
Harpham E Yorks 217 G11
Harpley Norf 158 D5
Worcs 116 E3
Harpole Northants 120 E3
Harpsdale Highld 310 D5
Harpsden Oxon 65 C9
Harpsden Bottom Oxon 65 C9
Harpswell Lincs 188 D6
Harpton Powys 114 F4
Harpurhey Gtr Man 195 G11
Harpur Hill Derbys 185 G9
Harraby Cumb 239 G10
Harracott Devon 25 B9
Harrapool Highld 295 C8
Harras Cumb 219 B9
Harraton T&W 243 G7
Harrier Shetland 313 J1
Harrietfield Perth 286 E3
Harrietsham Kent 53 C11
Harringay London 67 B10
Harrington Cumb 228 F5
Lincs 190 G5
Northants 136 G5
Harringworth Northants 137 D8
Harris Highld 294 F5
Harriseahead Staffs 168 D5
Harriston Cumb 229 C9
Harrogate N Yorks 206 C2
Harrold Beds 121 F8
Harrop Dale Gtr Man 196 F4
Harrow Highld 310 B6
London 67 B7
Harrowbarrow Corn 7 B7
Harrowbeer Devon 7 B10
Harrowby Lincs 155 B8
Harrowden Beds 103 B11
Harrowgate Hill Darl 224 B5
Harrowgate Village
Darl 224 B5
Harrow Green Suff 125 G7
Harrow Hill Glos 79 B10
Harrow on the Hill
London 67 B7
Harrow Street Suff 107 D9
Harrow Weald London 85 G11
Harry Stoke S Glos 60 D6
Harston Cambs 123 G8
Leics 154 C6
Harswell E Yorks 208 E2
Hart Hrtlpl 234 E5
Hartbarrow Cumb 221 G8
Hartburn Northumb 252 F3
Stockton 225 B8
Hartcliffe Bristol 60 F5
Hart Common Gtr Man 194 F6
Hartest Suff 124 G6
Hartest Hill Suff 124 G6
Hartfield E Sus 52 F3
Highld 299 E7
Hartford Cambs 122 C5
Ches W 183 G10
Som 27 B7
Hartfordbeach
Ches W 183 G10
Hartfordbridge Hants 49 B9
Hartford End Essex 87 B11
Hartforth N Yorks 224 D3
Hartgrove Dorset 30 D4
Hartham Herts 86 C4
Harthill Ches W 167 D8
N Lnrk 269 C8
S Yorks 187 E7
Hart Hill Luton 104 G2
Hartington Derbys 169 C10
Hartland Devon 24 C3
Hartle Worcs 117 B8
Hartlebury Shrops 132 D4
Worcs 116 C6
Hartlebury Common
Worcs 116 C6
Hartlepool Hrtlpl 234 E6
Hartley Cumb 222 D5
Kent 53 G9
Kent 68 F6
Northumb 243 B8
Plym 7 D9
Hartley Green Kent 68 F6
Staffs 151 D9
Hartley Mauditt Hants 49 F8
Hartley Westpall Hants 49 B7
Hartley Wintney Hants 49 B9
Hartlington N Yorks 213 G10
Hartlip Kent 69 G10
Hartmoor Dorset 30 C3
Hartmount Highld 301 B7
Hartoft End N Yorks 226 G5
Harton N Yorks 216 G4
Shrops 131 F9
T&W 243 E9
Hartpury Glos 98 F5
Hartsgreen Shrops 132 G5
Hart's Green Suff 125 F7
Hartshead W Yorks 197 C7
Hartshead Green
Gtr Man 196 G3
Hartshead Moor Side
W Yorks 197 C7
Hartshead Moor Top
W Yorks 197 B7
Hartshead Pike
Gtr Man 196 G3
Hartshill Stoke 168 F5
Warks 134 E6
Hart's Hill W Mid 133 F8
Hartshill Green Warks 134 E6
Hartshorne Derbys 152 E6
Hartsop Cumb 221 C8
Hart Station Hrtlpl 234 D5
Hartswell Som 27 B9
Hartwell Northants 120 G5
Staffs 151 B8
Hartwith N Yorks 214 G4
Hartwood Lancs 194 D5
N Lnrk 268 D6
Hartwoodburn Borders 261 D11
Harvel Kent 68 G6
Harvest Hill W Mid 134 G5
Harvieston Stirl 277 D11
Harvills Hawthorn
W Mid 133 E9
Harvington Worcs 99 B11
Worcs 117 C7
Harvington Cross Worcs 99 B11
Harvington Hill Worcs 99 B10
Harwell Notts 187 C11
Oxon 64 B3
Harwich Essex 108 E5
Harwood Durham 232 E2
Gtr Man 195 E8
Harwood Dale N Yorks 227 F9
Harwood Lee Gtr Man 195 E8
Harwood on Teviot
Borders 249 B10
Harworth Notts 187 C10
Hasbury W Mid 133 G9
Hascombe Sur 50 E3
Haselbech Northants 120 B4
Haselbury Plucknett Som 29 E7
Haseley Warks 118 D4
Haseley Green Warks 118 D4
Haseley Knob Warks 118 C4
Haselor Warks 118 F2
Hasfield Glos 98 F6
Hasguard Pembs 72 D5
Haskayne Lancs 193 F11
Hasketon Suff 126 G4
Hasland Derbys 170 B5
Haslemere Sur 50 G2
Haslingbourne W Sus 35 C7
Haslingden Lancs 195 C9
Haslingfield Cambs 123 G8
Haslington Ches E 168 D2
Hasluck's Green W Mid 118 B2
Hassall Ches E 168 D3
Hassall Green Ches E 168 D3
Hassell Street Kent 54 D5
Hassendean Borders 262 E2
Hassingham Norf 143 B7
Hassocks W Sus 36 D3
Hassop Derbys 186 G2
Haster Highld 310 D7
Hasthorpe Lincs 175 B7
Hastigrow Highld 310 C6
Hasting Hill T&W 243 G9
Hastingleigh Kent 54 E5
Hastings E Sus 38 F4
Som 28 D4
Hastingwood Essex 87 D7
Hastoe Herts 84 D6
Haston Shrops 149 E10
Haswell Durham 234 C3
Haswell Moor Durham 234 C3
Haswell Plough Durham 234 C3
Haswellsykes Borders 260 B6
Hatch C Beds 104 B3
Devon 8 F4
Hants 49 C7
Wilts 30 B6
Hatch Beauchamp Som 28 C4
Hatch Bottom Hants 33 E7
Hatch End Beds 121 E11
London 85 G10
Hatchet Gate Hants 32 G5
Hatchet Green Hants 31 D11
Hatch Farm Hill W Sus 34 B6
Hatch Green Som 28 D4
Hatching Green Herts 85 C10
Hatchmere Ches W 183 G9
Hatch Warren Hants 48 D6
Hatcliffe NE Lincs 201 G8
Hateley Heath W Mid 133 E10
Hatfield Hereford 115 F11
Herts 86 D2
S Yorks 199 F7
Worcs 117 G7
Hatfield Broad Oak Essex 87 B8
Hatfield Chase S Yorks 199 E8
Hatfield Garden Village
Herts 86 D2
Hatfield Heath Essex 87 B8
Hatfield Hyde Herts 86 C2
Hatfield Peverel Essex 88 C3
Hatfield Woodhouse
S Yorks 199 F7
Hatford Oxon 82 G4
Hatherden Hants 47 C10
Hatherleigh Devon 25 G8
Hatherley Glos 99 G8
Hathern Leics 153 E9
Hatherop Glos 81 D11
Hathersage Derbys 186 E2
Hathersage Booths
Derbys 186 E2
Hathershaw Gtr Man 196 G2
Hatherton Ches E 167 F11
Staffs 151 G9
Hatley St George Cambs 122 G5
Hatston Orkney 314 E4
Hatt Corn 7 C7
Hattersett Aberds 303 G9
Hattersley Gtr Man 185 C7
Hatt Hill Hants 32 B4
Hattingley Hants 48 F6
Hatton Aberds 303 F10
Angus 287 D9
Derbys 152 D4
Lincs 189 F11
London 66 D5
Moray 301 D11
Shrops 131 E9
Warks 118 D4
Warr 183 E9
Hattonburn Aberds 293 C9
Hatton Castle Aberds 303 E7
Hattoncrook Aberds 303 G8
Hatton Grange Shrops 132 C5
Hatton Heath Ches W 167 C7
Hatton Hill Sur 66 G2
Hattonknowe Borders 270 F4
Hatton of Fintray
Aberds 293 B10
Hatton Park Northants 121 D7
Haugh E Ayrs 257 D11
Gtr Man 196 E2
Lincs 190 F6
Haugham Lincs 190 E4
Haugh-head Borders 261 B8
Haugh Head Northumb 264 D2
Haughland Orkney 314 E5
Haughley Suff 125 E10
Haughley Green Suff 125 E10
Haughley New Street
Suff 125 E10
Haugh of Glass Moray 302 F4
Haugh of Kilnmaichlie
Moray 301 F11
Haugh of Urr Dumfries 237 C10
Haughs of Clinterty
Aberdeen 293 B10
Haughton Ches E 167 D9
Notts 187 G11
Powys 148 F6
Shrops 132 B4
Shrops 132 D3
Shrops 149 D7
Shrops 149 F11
Staffs 151 E7
Haughton Castle
Northumb 241 C10
Haughton Green
Gtr Man 184 C6
Haughton Le Skerne
Darl 224 B6
Haughurst Hill W Berks 64 G5
Haulkerton Aberds 293 F9
Haultwick Herts 104 G6
Haunn Argyll 288 E5
W Isles 297 K3
Haunton Staffs 152 G4
Hauxton Cambs 123 G8
Havannah Ches E 168 C5
Havant Hants 22 B2
Haven Hereford 97 B11
Hereford 115 G8
Haven Bank Lincs 174 E2
Haven Side E Yorks 201 B7
Havenstreet IoW 21 C7
Havercroft W Yorks 197 E11
Haverfordwest / Hwlffordd
Pembs 73 B7
Haverhill Suff 106 B3
Haverigg Cumb 210 D3
Havering-atte-Bower
London 87 G8
Haveringland Norf 160 E3
Haversham M Keynes 102 C6
Haverthwaite Cumb 210 C6
Haverton Hill Stockton 234 G5
Haviker Street Kent 53 D8
Havyatt Som 44 F4
Havyatt Green N Som 60 G3
Hawarden / Penarlâg
Flint 166 B4
Hawbridge Worcs 99 B8
Hawbush Green Essex 106 G5
Hawcoat Cumb 210 E4
Hawcross Glos 98 E5
Hawddamor Gwyn 146 F3
Hawen Ceredig 92 B6
Hawes N Yorks 213 B7
Hawes' Green Norf 142 D4
Hawes Side Blkpool 202 G2
Hawford Worcs 116 E6
Hawgreen Shrops 150 D2
Hawick Borders 262 F2
Hawkchurch Devon 28 G4
Hawkcombe Som 41 D11
Hawkedon Suff 124 G5
Hawkenbury Kent 52 F5
Kent 53 E10
Hawkeridge Wilts 45 C11
Hawkerland Devon 15 D7
Hawkersland Cross
Hereford 97 B10
Hawkesbury S Glos 61 B9
Warks 135 G7
Hawkesbury Upton
S Glos 61 B9
Hawkes End W Mid 134 G6
Hawkesley W Mid 117 B10
Hawk Green Gtr Man 185 D7
Hawkhill Northumb 264 G6
Hawk Hill Cumb 228 F6
Hawkhope Northumb 250 F6
Hawkhurst Kent 53 G9
Hawkhurst Common
E Sus 23 B8
Hawkinge Kent 55 F8
Hawkin's Hill Essex 106 E3
Hawkley Gtr Man 194 G5
Hants 34 B2
Hawkridge Som 41 G11
Hawksdale Cumb 230 B3
Hawks Green Staffs 151 G9
Hawkshaw Blkburn 195 D9
Hawkshead Cumb 221 F7
Hawkshead Hill Cumb 220 F6
Hawks Hill Bucks 66 B2
Hawk's Hill Sur 51 B7
Hawksland S Lnrk 259 B8
Hawkspur Green Essex 106 E3
Hawks Stones W Yorks 196 B2
Hawkswick N Yorks 213 E9
Hawksworth Notts 172 G3
W Yorks 205 E9
W Yorks 205 F11
Hawkwell Essex 88 G4
Hawley Hants 49 B11
Kent 68 E4
Hawley Bottom Devon 28 G2
Hawley Lane Hants 49 B11
Hawling Glos 99 G11
Hawn Orkney 314 D4
Hawnby N Yorks 215 B10
Hawne W Mid 133 G9
Haworth W Yorks 204 F6
Haws Bank Cumb 220 F6
Hawstead Suff 125 F7
Hawstead Green Suff 125 F7
Hawthorn Durham 234 B4
Hants 49 G7
Rhondda 58 B6
Wilts 61 F11
Hawthorn Corner Kent 71 F8
Hawthorn Hill Brack 65 E11
Lincs 174 D2
Hawthorns Staffs 168 F4
Hawthorpe Lincs 155 D10
Hawton Notts 172 E3
Haxby York 207 B8
Haxey N Lincs 188 B3
Haxey Carr N Lincs 199 G9
Haxted Sur 52 D2
Haxton Wilts 46 D6
Hay Corn 10 G5
Haybridge Shrops 116 C2
Som 44 D4
Telford 150 G3
Haydock Mers 183 B9
Haydon Bath 45 C7
Dorset 29 D11
Som 28 C3
Som 44 D5
Swindon 62 B6
Haydon Bridge
Northumb 241 E8
Haydon Wick Swindon 62 B6
Haye Corn 7 B7
Haye Fm Corn 6 B6
Hayes Bromley 68 F2
Hillingdon 66 C6
Staffs 169 C9
Hayes End London 66 C5
Hayes Knoll Wilts 81 G10
Hayes Town London 66 C6
Hayfield Derbys 185 D8
Fife 280 C5
Hay Field S Yorks 187 B10
Hayfield Green
S Yorks 187 B11
Haygate Telford 150 G2
Haygrass Som 28 C2
Hay Green Essex 87 E10
Herts 104 D6
Norf 157 F10
Hayhill E Ayrs 257 F11
Hayhillock Angus 287 C9
Haylands IoW 21 C7
Hayle Corn 2 B3
Hayley Green W Mid 133 G8
Hay Mills W Mid 134 G2
Haymoor End Som 28 B4
Haymoor Green
Ches E 167 E11
Hayne Devon 26 F5
Haynes C Beds 103 C11
Haynes Church End
C Beds 103 C11
Haynes West End
C Beds 103 C11
Hay-on-Wye Powys 96 C4
Hayscastle Pembs 91 F7
Hayscastle Cross Pembs 91 G8
Haysford Pembs 91 G8
Hayshead Angus 287 C10
Hayston E Dunb 278 G2
Haystoun Borders 261 B7
Hay Street Herts 105 F7
Haythorne Dorset 31 F8
Hayton Aberdeen 293 C11
Cumb 229 C8
Cumb 240 F2
E Yorks 208 D2
Notts 188 E2
Hayton's Bent Shrops 131 G10
Haytor Vale Devon 13 F11
Haytown Devon 24 E5
Haywards Heath W Sus 36 C4
Haywood S Lnrk 269 E9
S Yorks 198 E5
Haywood Oaks Notts 171 D10
Hazard's Green E Sus 23 C11
Hazelbank S Lnrk 268 F6
Hazelbeach Pembs 72 E6
Hazelbury Bryan Dorset 30 F2
Hazeleigh Essex 88 E4
Hazel End Essex 105 G9
Hazeley Hants 49 B8
Hazeley Bottom Hants 49 B9
Hazeley Heath Hants 49 B9
Hazeley Lea Hants 49 B8
Hazelgrove Notts 171 F8
Hazel Grove Gtr Man 184 D6
Hazelhurst Gtr Man 195 D9
Gtr Man 195 G9
Gtr Man 196 G3
Hazelslack Cumb 211 D9
Hazelslade Staffs 151 G10
Hazel Street Kent 53 B11
Kent 53 F7
Hazel Stub Suff 106 C3
Hazelton Glos 81 B9
Hazelton Walls Fife 287 E7
Hazelwood Derbys 170 F4
Devon 8 E4
London 68 G2
Hazlehead S Yorks 197 G7
Hazlemere Bucks 84 F5
Hazler Shrops 131 E9
Hazlerigg T&W 242 C6
Hazles Staffs 169 F8
Hazlescross Staffs 169 F8
Hazleton Glos 81 B9
Hazlewood N Yorks 205 C7
Hazon Northumb 252 C5
Heacham Norf 158 B3
Headbourne Worthy
Hants 48 G3
Headbrook Hereford 114 F6
Headcorn Kent 53 E10
Headingley W Yorks 205 F11
Headington Oxon 83 D8
Headington Hill Oxon 83 D8
Headlam Durham 224 B3
Headless Cross Cumb 211 D7
Worcs 117 D10
Headley Hants 49 F10
Hants 64 G4
Sur 51 C8
Headley Down Hants 49 F10
Headley Heath Worcs 117 B11
Headley Park Bristol 60 F5
Head of Muir Falk 278 E6
Headon Devon 24 G5
Notts 188 F2
Heads S Lnrk 268 F4
Headshaw Borders 261 E11
Heads Nook Cumb 239 F11
Headstone London 66 B6
Headwell Fife 279 D11
Heady Hill Gtr Man 195 E10
Heage Derbys 170 E5
Healaugh N Yorks 206 D5
N Yorks 223 F10
Heald Green Gtr Man 184 D4
Healds Green Gtr Man 195 F11
Heale Devon 40 D6
Som 28 B5
Som 28 D2
Som 45 E7
Healey Gtr Man 195 D11
Northumb 242 F2
N Yorks 214 C3
W Yorks 197 C8
W Yorks 197 D9
Healey Cote Northumb 252 C4
Healeyfield Durham 233 B7
Healey Hall Northumb 242 F2
Healing NE Lincs 201 E8
Heamoor Corn 1 C5
Heaning Cumb 221 F8
Heanish Argyll 288 E2
Heanor Derbys 170 F6
Heanor Gate Derbys 170 F6
Heanton Punchardon
Devon 40 F4
Heap Bridge Gtr Man 195 E10
Heapham Lincs 188 D5
Hearn Hants 49 F10
Hearnden Green Kent 53 D10
Hearthstane Borders 260 D4
Hearthstone Derbys 170 D4
Hearts Delight Kent 69 G11
Heasley Mill Devon 41 G8
Heast Highld 295 D8
Heath Cardiff 59 D7
Derbys 170 B6
Halton 183 E8
Heath and Reach
C Beds 103 F8
Heath Charnock Lancs 194 E5
Heath Common W Sus 35 E10
W Yorks 197 D11
Heathcot Aberds 293 C10
Heathcote Derbys 169 C10
Shrops 150 D3
Warks 118 E6
Heath Cross Devon 13 B10
Devon 14 C2
Heath End Bucks 84 F5
Bucks 85 D7
Derbys 153 E7
Hants 64 G2
Hants 64 G5
S Glos 61 B7
Sur 49 D10
Warks 118 E4
W Mid 133 C10
W Sus 35 D7
Heather Leics 153 G7
Heathercombe Devon 13 E10
Heatherfield Highld 298 E4
Heather Row Hants 49 C8
Heatherside Sur 50 B2
Heatherwood Park
Highld 311 K2
Heatherybanks Aberds 303 E7
Heathfield Cambs 105 B9
Devon 14 F2
E Sus 37 C9
Glos 80 F2
Hants 33 F9
Lincs 189 C10
N Yorks 214 F2
S Ayrs 257 E9
Som 27 B11
Som 43 G7
Heathfield Village Oxon 83 B8
Heath Green Hants 48 F6
Worcs 117 C11
Heathhall Dumfries 237 B11
Heath Hayes Staffs 151 G10
Heath Hill Shrops 150 G5
Heath House Som 44 D2
Heathlands Wokingham 65 F10
Heath Lanes Telford 150 E2
Heath Park London 68 B4
Heathrow Airport
London 66 D5
Heath Side Kent 68 E4
Heathstock Devon 28 G2
Heathton Shrops 132 E6
Heathtop Derbys 152 C4
Heath Town W Mid 133 D8
Heathwaite Cumb 221 F8
N Yorks 225 E9
Heatley Staffs 151 D11
Warr 184 D2
Heaton Gtr Man 195 F7
Lancs 211 G8
Staffs 169 C7
T&W 243 D7
W Yorks 205 G8
Heaton Chapel Gtr Man 184 C5
Heaton Mersey Gtr Man 184 C5
Heaton Moor Gtr Man 184 C5
Heaton Norris Gtr Man 184 C5
Heaton Royds W Yorks 205 F8
Heaton's Bridge Lancs 194 E2
Heaton Shay W Yorks 205 F8
Heaven's Door Som 29 C10
Heaverham Kent 52 B5
Heaviley Gtr Man 184 D6
Heavitree Devon 14 C4
Hebburn T&W 243 E8
Hebburn Colliery T&W 243 D8
Hebburn New Town
T&W 243 E8
Hebden N Yorks 213 G10
Hebden Bridge W Yorks 196 B3
Hebden Green Ches W 167 B10
Hebing End Herts 104 G6
Hebron Anglesey 179 E7
Carms 92 F3
Northumb 252 F5
Heck Dumfries 248 G3
Heckdyke N Lincs 188 B3
Heckfield Hants 65 G8
Heckfield Green Suff 126 B3
Heckfordbridge Essex 107 G8
Heckingham Norf 143 D7
Heckington Lincs 173 G10
Heckmondwike
W Yorks 197 C8
Heddington Wilts 62 F3
Heddington Wick Wilts 62 F3
Heddle Orkney 314 E3
Heddon Devon 25 B11
Heddon-on-the-Wall
Northumb 242 D4
Hedenham Norf 142 E6
Hedge End Dorset 30 F4
Hants 33 E7
Hedgehog Bridge Lincs 174 F3
Hedgerley Bucks 66 B3
Hedgerley Green Bucks 66 B3
Hedgerley Hill Bucks 66 B3
Hedging Som 28 B4
Hedley Hill Durham 233 C9
Hedley on the Hill
Northumb 242 F3
Hednesford Staffs 151 G9
Hedon E Yorks 201 B7
Hedsor Bucks 66 B2
Hedworth T&W 243 E8
Heelands M Keynes 102 D6
Heeley S Yorks 186 E5
Hegdon Hill Hereford 115 G11
Heggerscales Cumb 222 C6
Heggle Lane Cumb 230 D3

Invercarron Mains
Highld 309 K5
Invercassley Highld 309 J4
Invercauld House
Aberds 292 D3
Inverchaolain Argyll 275 F11
Invercharnan Highld 284 C5
Inverchoran Highld 300 D2
Inverdruie Highld 291 B11
Inverebrie Aberds 303 F9
Invereck Argyll 276 E2
Inverernan Ho Aberds 292 B5
Invereshie House
Highld 291 C10
Inveresk E Loth 280 G6
Inverey Aberds 292 E2
Inverfarigaig Highld 300 G5
Invergarry Highld 290 C5
Invergelder Aberds 292 D4
Invergeldie Perth 285 E11
Invergordon Highld 301 C7
Invergowrie Perth 287 D7
Inverguseran Highld 295 E9
Inverhadden Perth 285 B10
Inverhaggernie Stirl 285 E7
Inverharroch Moray 302 F3
Inverherive Stirl 285 E7
Inverie Highld 295 F9
Inverinan Argyll 275 B10
Inverinate Highld 295 C11
Inverkeilor Angus 287 C10
Inverkeithing Fife 280 E2
Inverkeithny Aberds 302 E6
Inverkip Invclyd 276 G4
Inverkirkaig Highld 307 H5
Inverlael Highld 307 L6
Inverleith Edin 280 F4
Inverliever Lodge Argyll 275 C9
Inverliver Argyll 284 D4
Inverlochlarig Stirl 285 F8
Inverlochy Argyll 284 E5
Highld 290 F3
Moray 301 G11
Inverlounin Argyll 276 B4
Inverlussa Argyll 275 E7
Inver Mallie Highld 290 E3
Invermark Lodge Angus 292 E6
Invermoidart Highld 289 B8
Invermoriston Highld 290 B6
Invernaver Highld 308 C7
Inverneill Argyll 275 E9
Inverness Highld 300 E6
Invernettie Aberds 303 E11
Invernoaden Argyll 276 B2
Inveronich Argyll 284 G6
Inveroran Hotel Argyll 284 C6
Inverpolly Lodge Highld 307 H5
Inverquharity Angus 287 B8
Inverquhomery Aberds 303 E10
Inverroy Highld 290 E4
Inversanda Highld 289 D11
Invershiel Highld 295 D11
Invershore Highld 310 F6
Inversnaid Hotel Stirl 285 G7
Invertrossachs Stirl 285 G9
Inverugie Aberds 303 E11
Inveruglas Argyll 285 G7
Inveruglass Highld 291 C10
Inverurie Aberds 303 G7
Invervar Perth 285 C10
Inverythan Aberds 303 E7
Inwardleigh Devon 13 B7
Inwood Shrops 131 D9
Inworth Essex 88 B5
Iochdar W Isles 297 G3
Iping W Sus 34 C5
Ipplepen Devon 8 B6
Ipsden Oxon 64 B6
Ipsley Worcs 117 D11
Ipstones Staffs 169 F8
Ipswich Suff 108 C3
Irby Mers 182 E3
Irby in the Marsh Lincs 175 C7
Irby upon Humber
NE Lincs 201 G7
Irchester Northants 121 D8
Ireby Cumb 229 D10
Lancs 212 D3
Ireland C Beds 104 C2
Orkney 314 F3
Shetland 313 L5
Wilts 45 C10
Ireland's Cross Shrops 162 G2
Ireland Wood W Yorks 205 F11
Ireleth Cumb 210 D4
Ireshopeburn Durham 232 D3
Ireton Wood Derbys 170 F3
Irlam Gtr Man 184 C2
Irlams o' th' Height
Gtr Man 195 G9
Irnham Lincs 155 D10
Iron Acton S Glos 61 C7
Ironbridge Telford 132 C3
Iron Bridge Cambs 139 D9
Iron Cross Warks 117 G11
Irongray Dumfries 237 B11
Iron Lo Highld 299 G10
Ironmacannie Dumfries 237 B8
Irons Bottom Sur 51 D9
Ironside Aberds 303 D8
Ironville Derbys 170 E6
Irstead Norf 161 E7
Irstead Street Norf 161 F7
Irthington Cumb 239 E11
Irthlingborough
Northants 121 C8
Irton N Yorks 217 C10
Irvine N Ayrs 257 B8
Irwell Vale Lancs 195 C9
Isabella Pit Northumb 253 G8
Isallt Bach Anglesey 178 F3
Isauld Highld 310 C3
Isbister Orkney 314 D2
Orkney 314 E3
Shetland 312 D5
Shetland 313 G7
Isel Cumb 229 E9
Isfield E Sus 36 D6
Isham Northants 121 C7
Ishriff Argyll 289 F8
Isington Hants 49 E9
Island Carr N Lincs 200 F3
Islands Common
Cambs 122 E3
Islay Ho Argyll 274 G4
Isle Abbotts Som 28 C5
Isle Brewers Som 28 C5
Isleham Cambs 124 C2
Isle of Axholme N Lincs 199 F9
Isle of Dogs London 67 D11
Isle of Man Dumfries 238 B2
Isle of Whithorn
Dumfries 236 F6
Isleornsay Highld 295 D9
Islesburgh Shetland 312 G5
Islesteps Dumfries 237 B11
Isleworth London 67 D7
Isley Walton Leics 153 D8
Islibhig W Isles 304 F1
Islington London 67 C10
Telford 150 E4
Islip Northants 121 B9
Oxon 83 C8
Isombridge Telford 150 G2
Istead Rise Kent 68 F6
Isycoed Wrex 166 E6
Itchen Soton 32 E6
Itchen Abbas Hants 48 G4
Itchen Stoke Hants 48 G5
Itchingfield W Sus 35 B10
Itchington S Glos 61 B7
Itteringham Norf 160 C2
Itteringham Common
Norf 160 D3
Itton Devon 13 B9
Mon 79 F7
Itton Common Mon 79 F7
Ivegill Cumb 230 C4
Ivelet N Yorks 223 F8
Iver Bucks 66 C4
Iver Heath Bucks 66 C4
Iverley Staffs 133 G7
Iveston Durham 242 G4
Ivinghoe Bucks 84 B6
Ivinghoe Aston Bucks 85 B7
Ivington Hereford 115 F9
Ivington Green Hereford 115 F9
Ivybridge Devon 8 D2
Ivy Chimneys Essex 86 E6
Ivychurch Kent 39 B8
Ivy Cross Dorset 30 C5
Ivy Hatch Kent 52 C5
Ivy Todd Norf 141 B7
Iwade Kent 69 F11
Iwerne Courtney or Shroton
Dorset 30 E5
Iwerne Minster Dorset 30 E5
Iwood N Som 60 G3
Ixworth Suff 125 C8
Ixworth Thorpe Suff 125 C8

J

Jackfield Telford 132 C3
Jack Green Lancs 194 B5
Jack Hayes Staffs 168 F6
Jack Hill N Yorks 205 C10
Jack in the Green Devon 14 B6
Jacksdale Notts 170 E6
Jack's Green Essex 105 G11
Glos 80 D5
Jack's Hatch Essex 86 D6
Jackson Bridge
W Yorks 197 F7
Jackstown Aberds 303 F7
Jacobstow Corn 11 B9
Jacobstowe Devon 25 G9
Jacobs Well Sur 50 C3
Jagger Green W Yorks 196 D5
Jameston Pembs 73 F9
Jamestown Dumfries 249 D8
Highld 300 D4
W Dunb 277 E7
Jamphlars Fife 280 B4
Janetstown Highld 310 C4
Janke's Green Essex 107 F8
Jarrow T&W 243 D8
Jarvis Brook E Sus 37 B8
Jasper's Green Essex 106 F4
Java Argyll 289 F9
Jawcraig Falk 278 F6
Jaw Hill W Yorks 197 C9
Jaywick Essex 89 C11
Jealott's Hill Brack 65 E11
Jeaniefield Borders 271 G10
Jedburgh Borders 262 E5
Jedurgh Borders 262 F5
Jeffreyston Pembs 73 D9
Jellyhill E Dunb 278 G2
Jemimaville Highld 301 C7
Jennetts Hill W Berks 64 E5
Jennyfield N Yorks 205 B11
Jericho Gtr Man 195 E10
Jersey Farm Herts 85 D11
Jersey Marine Neath 57 C8
Jerviswood S Lnrk 269 F7
Jesmond T&W 243 D7
Jevington E Sus 23 E9
Jewell's Cross Corn 24 G3
Jingle Street Mon 79 C7
Jockey End Herts 85 C8
Jodrell Bank Ches E 184 G3
Johnby Cumb 230 E4
John O'Gaunt Leics 136 B4
John O'Gaunts
W Yorks 197 B11
John o'Groats Highld 310 B7
John's Cross E Sus 38 C2
Johnshaven Aberds 293 G9
Johnson Fold Gtr Man 195 E7
Johnson's Hillock Lancs 194 C5
Johnson Street Norf 161 F7
Johnston Pembs 72 C6
Johnstone Renfs 267 C8
Johnstonebridge
Dumfries 248 E3
Johnstone Mains
Aberds 293 F9
Johnstown Carms 74 B6
Wrex 166 F4
Jolly's Bottom Corn 4 F5
Joppa Corn 2 B3
Edin 280 G6
S Ayrs 257 F10
Jordan Green Norf 159 E11
Jordanhill Glasgow 267 B10
Jordans Bucks 85 G7
Jordanston Pembs 91 E8
Jordanthorpe S Yorks 186 E5
Jordon S Yorks 186 C6
Joyford Glos 79 C9
Joy's Green Glos 79 B10
Jubilee Gtr Man 196 E2
Notts 170 E6
Jugbank Staffs 150 B5
Jump S Yorks 197 G11
Jumpers Common Dorset 19 C8
Jumpers Green Dorset 19 C8
Jumper's Town E Sus 52 G3
Junction N Yorks 204 D6
Juniper Northumb 241 F10
Juniper Green Edin 270 B3
Jurby East IoM 192 C4
Jurby West IoM 192 C4
Jurston Devon 13 E9
Jury's Gap E Sus 39 D7

K

Kaber Cumb 222 C5
Kaimend S Lnrk 269 F9
Kaimes Edin 270 B5
Kaimrig End Borders 269 G11
Kalemouth Borders 262 D6
Kame Fife 287 G7
Kames Argyll 275 B9
Argyll 275 F10
E Ayrs 258 D5
Kates Hill W Mid 133 E9
Kea Corn 4 G6
Keadby N Lincs 199 E10
Keal Cotes Lincs 174 C5
Kearby Town End
N Yorks 206 D2
Kearnsey Kent 55 E9
Kearsley Gtr Man 195 F9
Kearstwick Cumb 212 C2
Kearton N Yorks 223 F9
Kearvaig Highld 306 B7
Keasden N Yorks 212 F4
Kebroyd W Yorks 196 C4
Keckwick Halton 183 E9
Keddington Lincs 190 D4
Keddington Corner
Lincs 190 D5
Kedington Suff 106 B4
Kedleston Derbys 170 G4
Kedslie Borders 271 G11
Keekle Cumb 219 B10
Keelars Tye Essex 107 G11
Keelby Lincs 201 E7
Keele Staffs 168 F4
Keeley Green Beds 103 B10
Keelham W Yorks 205 G7
Keenley Northumb 241 F7
Keenthorne Som 43 F8
Keeres Green Essex 87 C9
Keeston Pembs 72 B6
Keevil Wilts 46 B2
Kegworth Leics 153 D9
Kehelland Corn 4 G2
Keig Aberds 293 B8
Keighley W Yorks 205 E7
Keil Highld 289 D11
Keilarsbrae Clack 279 C7
Keilhill Aberds 303 D7
Keillmore Argyll 275 E7
Keillor Perth 286 C6
Keillour Perth 286 E3
Keills Argyll 274 G5
Keils Argyll 274 G6
Keinton Mandeville Som 44 G4
Keir Mill Dumfries 247 E9
Keisby Lincs 155 D10
Keiss Highld 310 C7
Keistle Highld 298 D4
Keith Moray 302 D4
Keith Hall Aberds 303 G7
Keith Inch Aberds 303 E11
Keithock Angus 293 G8
Kelbrook Lancs 204 E4
Kelby Lincs 173 G8
Kelcliffe W Yorks 205 E9
Keld Cumb 221 C11
N Yorks 223 E7
Keldholme N Yorks 216 B4
Keld Houses N Yorks 214 G2
Kelfield N Lincs 199 G10
N Yorks 207 F7
Kelham Notts 172 D3
Kelhurn Argyll 276 F6
Kellacott Devon 12 D4
Kellamergh Lancs 194 B2
Kellan Argyll 289 E7
Kellas Angus 287 D8
Moray 301 D11
Kellaton Devon 9 G11
Kellaways Wilts 62 D3
Kelleth Cumb 222 D3
Kelleythorpe E Yorks 208 B5
E Yorks 208 B6
Kelling Norf 177 E9
Kellingley N Yorks 198 C4
Kellington N Yorks 198 C5
Kelloe Durham 234 D2
Kelloholm Dumfries 258 G6
Kells Cumb 219 B9
Kelly Corn 10 G6
Devon 12 E3
Kelly Bray Corn 12 G3
Kelmarsh Northants 120 B4
Kelmscott Oxon 82 F3
Kelsale Suff 127 D7
Kelsall Ches W 167 B8
Kelsall Hill Ches W 167 B8
Kelsay Argyll 254 B2
Kelshall Herts 104 D6
Kelsick Cumb 238 G5
Kelso Borders 262 C6
Kelstedge Derbys 170 C4
Kelstern Lincs 190 C2
Kelsterton Flint 182 G3
Kelston Bath 61 F8
Keltneyburn Perth 285 C11
Kelton Dumfries 237 B11
Durham 232 G4
Kelty Fife 280 C2
Keltybridge Fife 280 B2
Kelvedon Essex 88 B5
Kelvedon Hatch Essex 87 F9
Kelvin S Lnrk 268 E2
Kelvindale Glasgow 267 B11
Kelvinside Glasgow 267 B11
Kelynack Corn 1 D3
Kemacott Devon 41 D7
Kemback Fife 287 F8
Kemberton Shrops 132 C4
Kemble Glos 81 F7
Kemble Wick Glos 81 F7
Kemerton Worcs 99 D8
Kemeys Commander
Mon 78 E4
Kemincham Ches E 168 B4
Kemnay Aberds 293 B9
Kempe's Corner Kent 54 D4
Kempie Highld 308 D4
Kempley Glos 98 F3
Kempley Green Glos 98 F3
Kempsey Worcs 99 B7
Kempsford Glos 81 F11
Kemps Green Warks 118 C2
Kempshott Hants 48 C6
Kempston Beds 103 B10
Kempston Church End
Beds 103 B10
Kempston Hardwick
Beds 103 C10
Kempston West End
Beds 103 B9
Kempton Shrops 131 G7
Kemp Town Brighton 36 G4
Kemsing Kent 52 B4
Kemsley Kent 70 F2
Kemsley Street Kent 69 G10
Kenardington Kent 54 G3
Kenchester Hereford 97 C8
Kencot Oxon 82 E3
Kendal Cumb 221 G10
Kendal End Worcs 117 C10
Kendleshire S Glos 61 D7
Kendon Caerph 77 F11
Kendoon Dumfries 246 F4
Kendray S Yorks 197 F11
Kenfig Bridgend 57 E10
Kenfig Hill Bridgend 57 E10
Kengharair Argyll 288 E6
Kenilworth Warks 118 C5
Kenknock Stirl 285 D8
Kenley London 51 B10
Shrops 131 C11
Kenmore Argyll 284 G4
Highld 299 D7
Perth 285 C11
Kenmure Dumfries 237 B8
Kenn Devon 14 D4
N Som 60 F2
Kennacley W Isles 305 J3
Kennacraig Argyll 275 G9
Kennards House Corn 11 E11
Kenneggy Corn 2 D3
Kenneggy Downs Corn 2 D3
Kennerleigh Devon 26 F4
Kennet Clack 279 C8
Kennet End Suff 124 D4
Kennethmont Aberds 302 G5
Kennett Cambs 124 D3
Kennford Devon 14 D4
Kenninghall Norf 141 F10
Kenninghall Heath
Norf 141 G10
Kennington Kent 54 E4
London 67 D10
Oxon 83 E8
Kenn Moor Gate N Som 60 F2
Kennoway Fife 287 G7
Kenny Som 28 D4
Kenny Hill Suff 124 B3
Kennythorpe N Yorks 216 F5
Kenovay Argyll 288 E1
Kensaleyre Highld 298 D4
Kensal Green London 67 C8
Kensal Rise London 67 C8
Kensal Town London 67 C8
Kensary Highld 310 E6
Kensington London 67 D9
Mers 182 C5
Kensworth C Beds 85 B8
Kentallen Highld 284 B4
Kentchurch Hereford 97 F8
Kentford Suff 124 D4
Kentisbeare Devon 27 F9
Kentisbury Devon 40 E6
Kentisbury Ford Devon 40 E6
Kentish Town London 67 C9
Kentmere Cumb 221 E9
Kenton Devon 14 E5
London 67 B7
Suff 126 D3
T&W 242 D6
Kenton Bankfoot T&W 242 D6
Kenton Bar T&W 242 D6
Kenton Corner Suff 126 D4
Kenton Green Glos 80 C3
Kentra Highld 289 C8
Kentrigg Cumb 221 G10
Kents Corn 11 B9
Kents Bank Cumb 211 D7
Kent's Green Glos 98 G4
Kents Hill M Keynes 103 D7
Kent's Oak Hants 32 C4
Kent Street E Sus 38 D3
Kent 53 C7
W Sus 36 C2
Kenwick Shrops 149 C8
Kenwick Park Shrops 149 D8
Kenwyn Corn 4 F6
Kenyon Warr 183 B10
Keoldale Highld 308 C3
Keonchulish Ho Highld 307 K6
Kepdowrie Stirl 277 C11
Kepnal Wilts 63 G7
Keppanach Highld 290 G2
Keppoch Highld 295 C11
Keprigan Argyll 255 F7
Kepwick N Yorks 225 G9
Kerchesters Borders 263 B7
Kerdiston Norf 159 E11
Keresforth Hill S Yorks 197 F10
Keresley W Mid 134 G6
Keresley Newlands
Warks 134 G6
Kerfield Borders 270 G5
Kerley Downs Corn 4 G5
Kernborough Devon 8 G5
Kerne Bridge Hereford 79 B9
Kernsary Highld 299 B8
Kerridge Ches E 184 F6
Kerridge-end Ches E 184 F6
Kerris Corn 1 D4
Kerry / Ceri Powys 130 F2
Kerrycroy Argyll 266 C2
Kerry Hill Staffs 168 F6
Kerrysdale Highld 299 B8
Kerry's Gate Hereford 97 E7
Kersal Gtr Man 195 G10
Kersall Notts 172 C2
Kersbrook Cross Corn 12 F2
Kerscott Devon 25 B10
Kersey Suff 107 C10
Kersey Tye Suff 107 C9
Kersey Upland Suff 107 C9
Kershopefoot Cumb 249 G11
Kersoe Worcs 99 D9
Kerswell Devon 27 F9
Kerswell Green Worcs 99 B7
Kerthen Wood Corn 2 C3
Kesgrave Suff 108 B4
Kessingland Suff 143 F10
Kessingland Beach
Suff 143 F10
Kessington E Dunb 277 G11
Kestle Corn 5 F9
Kestle Mill Corn 5 D7
Keston London 68 G2
Keston Mark London 68 F2
Keswick Cumb 229 G11
Norf 142 C4
Norf 161 C7
Kete Pembs 72 E4
Ketford Glos 98 E4
Ketley Telford 150 G3
Ketley Bank Telford 150 G3
Ketsby Lincs 190 F5
Kettering Northants 121 B7
Ketteringham Norf 142 C3
Kettins Perth 286 D6
Kettlebaston Suff 125 G9
Kettlebridge Fife 287 G7
Kettlebrook Staffs 134 C4
Kettleburgh Suff 126 E5
Kettle Corner Kent 53 C8
Kettle Green Herts 86 B6
Kettlehill Fife 287 G7
Kettleholm Dumfries 238 B4
Kettleness N Yorks 226 B6
Kettleshulme Ches E 185 F7
Kettleshume Ches E 185 F7
Kettlesing N Yorks 205 B10
Kettlesing Bottom
N Yorks 205 B10
Kettlesing Head
N Yorks 205 B10
Kettlestone Norf 159 C9
Kettlethorpe Lincs 188 F4
W Yorks 197 D10
Kettletoft Orkney 314 C6
Kettlewell N Yorks 213 E9
Ketton Rutland 137 C9
Kevingtown London 68 F3
Kew London 67 D7
Keward Som 44 E4
Kew Bridge London 67 D7
Kewstoke N Som 59 G10
Kexbrough S Yorks 197 F9
Kexby Lincs 188 D5
York 207 C10
Keybridge Corn 11 G7
Keycol Kent 69 G11
Keyford Som 45 D9
Key Green Ches E 168 C5
N Yorks 226 E6
Keyham Leics 136 B3
Keyhaven Hants 20 C2
Keyingham E Yorks 201 B8
Keymer W Sus 36 D4
Keynsham Bath 61 F7
Keysers Estate Essex 86 D5
Key's Green Kent 53 F7
Keysoe Beds 121 E11
Keysoe Row Beds 121 E11
Keyston Cambs 121 B10
Key Street Kent 69 G11
Keyworth Notts 154 C2
Khantore Aberds 292 D4
Kibbear Som 28 C2
Kibblesworth T&W 242 F6
Kibworth Beauchamp
Leics 136 E3
Kibworth Harcourt
Leics 136 E3
Kidbrooke London 68 D2
Kidburngill Cumb 229 G7
Kiddal Lane End
W Yorks 206 F4
Kiddemore Green Staffs 133 B7
Kidderminster Worcs 116 B6
Kiddington Oxon 101 G8
Kidd's Moor Norf 142 C2
Kidlington Oxon 83 C7
Kidmore End Oxon 65 D7
Kidnal Ches W 167 F7
Kidsdale Dumfries 236 F6
Kidsgrove Staffs 168 E4
Kidstones N Yorks 213 C9
Kidwelly / Cydweli
Carms 74 D6
Kiel Crofts Argyll 289 F11
Kielder Northumb 250 E4
Kierfiold Ho Orkney 314 E2
Kiff Green W Berks 64 F5
Kilbagie Fife 279 D8
Kilbarchan Renfs 267 C8
Kilbeg Highld 295 E8
Kilberry Argyll 275 G8
Kilbirnie N Ayrs 266 E6
Kilbowie W Dunb 277 G10
Kilbraur Highld 311 H2
Kilbride Argyll 254 C4
Argyll 275 D9
Argyll 289 G10
Argyll 289 G11
Highld 295 C7
Kilbridemore Argyll 275 D11
Kilbryde Castle Stirl 285 G11
Kilburn Angus 292 G5
Derbys 170 F5
London 67 C9
N Yorks 215 D10
Kilby Leics 136 D2
Kilby Bridge Leics 136 D2
Kilchamaig Argyll 275 G9
Kilchattan Argyll 274 D4
Kilchattan Bay Argyll 266 E2
Kilchenzie Argyll 255 E7
Kilcheran Argyll 289 F10
Kilchiaran Argyll 274 G3
Kilchoan Argyll 275 B8
Highld 288 C6
Kilchoman Argyll 274 G3
Kilchrenan Argyll 284 E4
Kilconquhar Fife 287 G8
Kilcot Glos 98 F3
Kilcoy Highld 300 D5
Kilcreggan Argyll 276 E4
Kildale N Yorks 226 D2
Kildalloig Argyll 255 F8
Kildary Highld 301 B7
Kildaton Ho Argyll 254 C5
Kildavanan Argyll 275 G11
Kildermorie Lodge
Highld 300 B5
Kildonan Dumfries 236 D2
Highld 298 D3
N Ayrs 256 E2
Kildonan Lodge Highld 311 G3
Kildonnan Highld 294 G6
Kildrum N Lnrk 278 F5
Kildrummy Aberds 292 B6
Kildwick N Yorks 204 D6
Kilfinan Argyll 275 F10
Kilfinnan Highld 290 D4
Kilgetty Pembs 73 D10
Kilgour Fife 286 G6
Kilgrammie S Ayrs 245 C7
Kilgwrrwg Common Mon 79 F7
Kilhallon Corn 5 E11
Kilham E Yorks 217 G11
Northumb 263 C9
Kilkeddan Argyll 255 E8
Kilkenneth Argyll 288 E1
Kilkenny Glos 81 B8
Kilkerran Argyll 255 F8
Kilkhampton Corn 24 E3
Killamarsh Derbys 187 E7
Killaworgey Corn 5 C8
Killay Swansea 56 C6
Killbeg Argyll 289 E8
Killean Argyll 255 C7
Killearn Stirl 277 D10
Killegruer Argyll 255 D7
Killen Highld 300 D6
Killerby Darl 224 B3
Killichonan Perth 285 B9
Killiechoinich Argyll 289 G10
Killiechonate Highld 290 E4
Killiechronan Argyll 289 E7
Killiecrankie Perth 291 G11
Killiemor Argyll 288 F6
Killiemore House Argyll 288 G6
Killilan Highld 295 B11
Killimster Highld 310 D7
Killin Stirl 285 D9
Killinallan Argyll 274 F4
Killingbeck W Yorks 206 G2
Killinghall N Yorks 205 B11
Killington Cumb 212 B2
Devon 41 D7
Killingworth T&W 243 C7
Killingworth Moor T&W 243 C7
Killingworth Village
T&W 243 C7
Killin Lodge Highld 291 C7
Killivose Corn 2 B4
Killmahumaig Argyll 275 D8
Killochyett Borders 271 F9
Killocraw Argyll 255 D7
Killundine Highld 289 E7
Killylung Dumfries 247 G11
Kilmacolm Invclyd 267 B7
Kilmaha Argyll 275 C10
Kilmahog Stirl 285 G10
Kilmalieu Highld 289 D10
Kilmaluag Highld 298 B4
Kilmany Fife 287 E7
Kilmarie Highld 295 D7
Kilmarnock E Ayrs 257 B10
Kilmaron Castle Fife 287 F7
Kilmartin Argyll 275 D9
Kilmaurs E Ayrs 267 G8
Kilmelford Argyll 275 B9
Kilmeny Argyll 274 G4
Kilmersdon Som 45 C7
Kilmeston Hants 33 B9
Kilmichael Argyll 255 E7
Argyll 275 F10
Kilmichael Glassary
Argyll 275 D9
Kilmichael of Inverlussa
Argyll 275 E8
Kilmington Devon 15 B11
Wilts 45 F9
Kilmington Common
Wilts 45 F9
Kilmoluaig Argyll 288 E1
Kilmonivaig Highld 290 E3
Kilmorack Highld 300 E4
Kilmore Argyll 289 G10
Highld 295 E8
Kilmory Argyll 275 F8
Highld 289 B7
Highld 294 E5
N Ayrs 255 E10
Kilmory Lodge Argyll 275 C8
Kilmote Highld 311 H3
Kilmuir Highld 298 B3
Highld 298 E2
Highld 300 E6
Highld 301 B7
Kilmun Argyll 275 B10
Argyll 276 E3
Kilnave Argyll 274 F3
Kilncadzow S Lnrk 269 F7
Kilndown Kent 53 G8
Kiln Green Hereford 79 B10
Wokingham 65 D10
Kilnhill Cumb 229 E10
Kilnhurst S Yorks 187 B7
Kilninian Argyll 288 E5
Kilninver Argyll 289 G10
Kiln Pit Hill Northumb 242 G2
Kilnsea E Yorks 201 D12
Kilnsey N Yorks 213 F9
Kilnwick E Yorks 208 D5
Kilnwick Percy E Yorks 208 C2
Kiloran Argyll 274 D4
Kilpatrick N Ayrs 255 E10
Kilpeck Hereford 97 E8
Kilphedir Highld 311 H3
Kilpin E Yorks 199 B9
Kilpin Pike E Yorks 199 B9
Kilrenny Fife 287 G9
Kilsby Northants 119 C11
Kilspindie Perth 286 E6
Kilsyth N Lnrk 278 F4
Kiltarlity Highld 300 E5
Kilton Notts 187 F9
Redcar 226 B4
Som 43 E7
Kilton Thorpe Redcar 226 B3
Kiltyrie Perth 285 D10
Kilvaxter Highld 298 C3
Kilve Som 43 E7
Kilvington Notts 172 G3
Kilwinning N Ayrs 266 G6
Kimberley Norf 141 C11
Notts 171 G8
Kimberworth S Yorks 186 C6
Kimberworth Park
S Yorks 186 C6
Kimblesworth Durham 233 B11
Kimble Wick Bucks 84 D4
Kimbolton Cambs 121 D11
Hereford 115 E10
Kimbridge Hants 32 B4
Kimcote Leics 135 F11
Kimmeridge Dorset 18 F4
Kimmerston Northumb 263 B11
Kimpton Hants 47 D9
Herts 85 B11
Kimworthy Devon 24 E4
Kinabus Argyll 254 C3
Kinbeachie Highld 300 C6
Kinbrace Highld 310 F2
Kinbuck Stirl 285 G11
Kincaidston S Ayrs 257 F9
Kincaple Fife 287 F8
Kincardine Fife 279 D8
Highld 309 L6
Kincardine Bridge Falk 279 D8
Kincardine O'Neil
Aberds 293 D7
Kinclaven Perth 286 D5
Kincorth Aberdeen 293 C11
Kincorth Ho Moray 301 C10
Kincraig Highld 291 C10
Kincraigie Perth 286 C3
Kindallachan Perth 286 C3
Kine Moor S Yorks 197 G9
Kineton Glos 99 F11
Warks 118 G6
Kineton Green W Mid 134 G2
Kinfauns Perth 286 E5
Kingairloch Highld 289 D10
Kingarth Argyll 255 B11
Kingates IoW 20 F6
Kingbeare Corn 11 G11
Kingcoed Mon 78 D6
Kingdown N Som 60 G4
King Edward Aberds 303 D7
Kingerby Lincs 189 C9
Kingfield Sur 50 B4
Kingford Devon 24 F3
Devon 25 D10
Kingham Oxon 100 G5
Kinghay Wilts 30 B5
Kingholm Quay
Dumfries 237 B11
Kinghorn Fife 280 D5
Kingie Highld 290 C3
Kinglassie Fife 280 B4
Kingledores Borders 260 D4
Kingoodie Perth 287 E7
King's Acre Hereford 97 C9
Kingsand Corn 7 E8
Kingsash Bucks 84 D5
Kingsbarns Fife 287 F9
Kingsbridge Devon 8 G4
Som 42 F3
King's Bromley Staffs 152 F2
Kingsburgh Highld 298 D3
Kingsbury London 67 B8
Warks 134 D4
Kingsbury Episcopi Som 28 C6
Kingsbury Regis Som 29 D11
King's Caple Hereford 97 F11
Kingscauseway Highld 301 B7
Kingscavil W Loth 279 F10
Kingsclere Hants 48 B4
Kingsclere Woodlands
Hants 64 G4
King's Cliffe Northants 137 D10
Kings Clipstone Notts 171 C10
Kingscote Glos 80 F4
Kingscott Devon 25 D8
King's Coughton Warks 117 F11
Kingscourt Glos 80 E4
Kingscross N Ayrs 256 D2
Kingsditch Glos 99 G8
Kingsdon Som 29 B8
Kingsdown Kent 54 B2
Kent 55 D11
Swindon 63 B7
Wilts 61 F10
King's Dyke Cambs 138 D4
Kingseat Fife 280 C2
Kingseathill Fife 280 D2
King's End Worcs 116 G6
Kingsett Devon 12 E6
Kingsey Bucks 84 D2
Kingsfield Hereford 97 B10
Kingsfold Lancs 194 B4
W Sus 51 F7
Kingsford Aberds 293 B7
E Ayrs 267 F8
Worcs 132 G6
Kingsforth N Lincs 200 D4
King's Furlong Hants 48 C6
Kingsgate Kent 71 E11
King's Green Glos 98 E5
Worcs 116 E5
Kingshall Green Suff 125 E8
Kingshall Street Suff 125 E8
Kingsheanton Devon 40 F5
King's Heath Northants 120 E4
W Mid 133 G11
Kings Hedges Cambs 123 E9
Kingshill Glos 80 F3
Swindon 62 C6
Kings Hill Glos 81 E8
King's Hill Kent 53 C7
W Mid 133 D9
Kingsholm Glos 80 B4
Kingshouse Hotel
Highld 284 B6
Kingshurst W Mid 134 F3
Kingside Hill Cumb 238 G5
Kingskerswell Devon 9 B7
Kingskettle Fife 287 G7
Kingsknowe Edin 280 G4
Kingsland Anglesey 178 E2
Hereford 115 E8
London 67 C10
Shrops 149 G9
Kings Langley Herts 85 E9
Kingsley Ches W 183 G9
Hants 49 F9
Staffs 169 F8
Kingsley Green W Sus 49 G11
Kingsley Holt Staffs 169 F8
Kingsley Moor Staffs 169 F7
Kingsley Park Northants 120 E5
Kingslow Shrops 132 D5
King's Lynn Norf 158 E2
King's Meaburn Cumb 231 G8
Kingsmead Hants 33 E9
Kingsmere Oxon 101 G11
King's Mills Derbys 153 D8
Wrex 166 F4
Kingsmoor Essex 86 D6
Kings Moss Mers 194 G4
Kingsmuir Angus 287 C8
Fife 287 G9
Kings Muir Borders 261 B7
King's Newnham Warks 119 B9
King's Newton Derbys 153 D7
Kingsnordley Shrops 132 F5
Kingsnorth Kent 54 F4
King's Norton Leics 136 C3
W Mid 117 B11
King's Nympton Devon 25 D11
King's Pyon Hereford 115 G8
Kings Ripton Cambs 122 B5
King's Somborne Hants 47 G11
King's Stag Dorset 30 E2
King's Stanley Glos 80 E4
King's Sutton Northants 101 D9
King's Tamerton Plym 7 D9
Kingstanding W Mid 133 E11
Kingsteignton Devon 14 G3
Kingsteps Highld 301 D9
King Sterndale Derbys 185 G9
King's Thorn Hereford 97 E10
Kingsthorpe Northants 120 E5
Kingsthorpe Hollow
Northants 120 E5
Kingston Cambs 122 F6
Devon 8 F2
Devon 9 E8
Dorset 18 F5
Dorset 30 F3
E Loth 281 E10
Gtr Man 184 B6
Hants 31 G11
IoW 20 E5
Kent 55 C7
M Keynes 103 D8
Moray 302 C3
Ptsmth 33 G11
Suff 108 B5
Kingston Bagpuize Oxon 82 F6
Kingston Blount Oxon 84 F2
Kingston by Sea W Sus 36 F2
Kingston Deverill Wilts 45 F10
Kingstone Hereford 97 D8
Hereford 98 G2
Som 28 E5
Staffs 151 D11
S Yorks 197 F10
Kingstone Winslow Oxon 63 B9
Kingston Gorse W Sus 35 G9
Kingston Lisle Oxon 63 B10
Kingston Maurward
Dorset 17 C10
Kingston near Lewes
E Sus 36 F5
Kingston on Soar
Notts 153 D10
Kingston Park T&W 242 D6
Kingston Russell Dorset 17 C7
Kingston St Mary Som 28 B2
Kingston Seymour
N Som 60 F2
Kingston Stert Oxon 84 E2
Kingston upon Hull Hull 200 B5
Kingston upon Thames
London 67 F7
Kingston Vale London 67 E8
Kingstown Cumb 239 F9
King Street Essex 87 E9
King's Walden Herts 104 G3
Kingsway Bath 61 G8
Halton 183 D8
Kingswear Devon 9 E7
Kingswells Aberdeen 293 C10
Kingswinford W Mid 133 F7
Kingswood Bucks 83 B11
Essex 69 B8
Glos 80 G2
Hereford 114 G5
Herts 85 E10
Kent 53 C10
Powys 130 C4
S Glos 60 E6
Som 42 F6
Sur 51 B8
Warks 118 C3
Warr 183 C9
Kingswood Brook
Warks 118 C3
Kingswood Common
Staffs 132 C6
Worcs 116 D4
Kings Worthy Hants 48 G3
Kingthorpe Lincs 189 F10
Kington Hereford 114 F5
S Glos 79 G10
Worcs 117 F9
Kington Langley Wilts 62 D2
Kington Magna Dorset 30 C3
Kington St Michael Wilts 62 D2
Kingussie Highld 291 C9
Kingweston Som 44 G4
Kinhrive Highld 301 B7
Kininvie Ho Moray 302 E3
Kinkell Bridge Perth 286 F3
Kinknockie Aberds 303 E10
Aberds 303 G9
Kinkry Hill Cumb 240 B2
Kinlet Shrops 132 G4
Kinloch Fife 286 F6
Highld 289 D8
Highld 294 F5
Highld 295 D8
Highld 308 F3
Perth 286 C5
Perth 286 C6
Kinlochan Highld 289 C10
Kinlochard Stirl 285 G8
Kinlochbeoraid Highld 295 G10
Kinlochbervie Highld 306 D7
Kinloch Damph Highld 299 E8
Kinlocheil Highld 289 B11
Kinlochewe Highld 299 C10
Kinloch Hourn Highld 295 E11
Kinloch Laggan Highld 291 E7
Kinlochleven Highld 290 G3
Kinloch Lodge Highld 308 D5
Kinlochmoidart Highld 289 B9
Kinlochmorar Highld 295 F10
Kinlochmore Highld 290 G3
Kinloch Rannoch Perth 285 B10
Kinlochspelve Argyll 289 G8
Kinloid Highld 295 G8
Kinloss Moray 301 C10
Kinmel Bay / Bae Cinmel
Conwy 181 E7
Kinmuck Aberds 293 B10
Kinmundy Aberds 293 B10
Kinnadie Aberds 303 E9
Kinnaird Perth 286 B3
Perth 286 E6
Kinnaird Castle Angus 287 B10
Kinnauld Highld 309 J7
Kinneff Aberds 293 F10
Kinneil Falk 279 E9
Kinnelhead Dumfries 248 C2
Kinnell Angus 287 B10
Kinnerley Shrops 148 E6
Kinnersley Hereford 96 B6
Worcs 99 C7
Kinnerton Powys 114 E4
Kinnerton Green Flint 166 C4
Kinnesswood Perth 286 G5
Kinninvie Durham 233 G7
Kinnordy Angus 287 B7
Kinoulton Notts 154 C3
Kinross Perth 286 G5
Kinrossie Perth 286 D5
Kinsbourne Green Herts 85 B10
Kinsey Heath Ches E 167 G11
Kinsham Hereford 115 E7
Worcs 99 D8
Kinsley W Yorks 198 E2
Kinson Bmouth 19 B7
Kintallan Argyll 275 E8
Kintbury W Berks 63 F11
Kintessack Moray 301 C9
Kintillo Perth 286 F5
Kintocher Aberds 293 C7
Kinton Hereford 115 C8
Shrops 149 F7
Kintore Aberds 293 B9
Kintour Argyll 254 B5
Kintra Argyll 254 C4
Argyll 288 G5
Kintradwell Highld 311 J3
Kintraw Argyll 275 C9
Kinuachdrachd Argyll 275 D8
Kinveachy Highld 291 B11
Kinver Staffs 132 G6
Kinwalsey Warks 134 F5
Kip Hill Durham 242 G6
Kiplin N Yorks 224 F5
Kippax W Yorks 206 G4
Kippen Stirl 278 C3
Kippford or Scaur
Dumfries 237 D10
Kippilaw Borders 262 D2
Kippilaw Mains Borders 262 D2
Kipping's Cross Kent 52 F6
Kippington Kent 52 C4
Kirbister Orkney 314 D6
Orkney 314 E2
Orkney 314 F3
Kirbuster Orkney 314 D2
Kirby Bedon Norf 142 B5
Kirby Bellars Leics 154 F4
Kirby Cane Norf 143 E7
Kirby Corner W Mid 118 B5
Kirby Cross Essex 108 G4
Kirby Fields Leics 135 C10
Kirby Green Norf 143 E7
Kirby Grindalythe
N Yorks 217 F8
Kirby Hill N Yorks 215 F7
N Yorks 224 D2
Kirby Knowle N Yorks 215 B9
Kirby-le-Soken Essex 108 G4
Kirby Misperton
N Yorks 216 D5
Kirby Moor Cumb 240 E2
Kirby Muxloe Leics 135 C10
Kirby Row Norf 143 E7
Kirby Sigston N Yorks 225 G8
Kirby Underdale
E Yorks 208 B2
Kirby Wiske N Yorks 215 C7
Kirdford W Sus 35 B8
Kirk Highld 310 D6
Kirkabister Shetland 312 G6
Shetland 313 K6
Kirkandrews Dumfries 237 E8
Kirkandrews-on-Eden
Cumb 239 F9
Kirkapol Argyll 288 E2
Kirkbampton Cumb 239 F8
Kirkbean Dumfries 237 D11
Kirkborough Cumb 229 D7
Kirkbrae Orkney 314 B4
Kirk Bramwith S Yorks 198 E6
Kirkbride Cumb 238 F6
Kirkbridge N Yorks 224 G5

Llanfair-Nant-Gwyn
Pembs 92 D3
Llanfairpwll-gwyngyll
Anglesey 179 G8
Llanfair Talhaiarn
Conwy 180 G6
Llanfair Waterdine
Shrops 114 B4
Llanfairyneubwll
Anglesey 178 F3
Llanfairynghornwy
Anglesey 178 C4
Llanfallteg Carms 73 B11
Llanfallteg West Carms 73 B10
Llanfaredd Powys 113 G11
Llanfarian Ceredig 111 B11
Llanfechain Powys 148 E3
Llanfechan Powys 113 G9
Llanfechell Anglesey 178 C5
Llanferres Denb 165 C11
Llan Ffestiniog Gwyn 164 G2
Llanfflewyn Anglesey 178 D5
Llanfigael Anglesey 178 E4
Llanfihangel-ar-arth
Carms 93 D9
Llanfihangel-Crucorney
Mon 96 G6
Llanfihangel Glyn Myfyr
Conwy 165 F7
Llanfihangel-helygen
Powys 113 E10
Llanfihangel Nant Bran
Powys 95 E8
Llanfihangel-nant-Melan
Powys 114 F3
Llanfihangel Rhydithon
Powys 114 D3
Llanfihangel Rogiet Mon 60 B2
Llanfihangel Tal-y-llyn
Powys 96 F2
Llanfihangel Tor y Mynydd
Mon 79 E7
Llanfihangel-uwch-Gwili
Carms 93 G9
Llanfihangel-y-Creuddyn
Ceredig 112 B3
Llanfihangel-yng-Ngwynfa
Powys 147 F11
Llanfihangel yn Nhowyn
Anglesey 178 F4
Llanfihangel-y-pennant
Gwyn 128 B3
Gwyn 163 F8
Llanfilo Powys 96 E2
Llanfleiddan / Llanblethian
V Glam 58 E3
Llanfoist Mon 78 C3
Llanfor Gwyn 147 B8
Llanfrechfa Torf 78 G4
Llanfrothen Gwyn 163 G10
Llanfrynach Powys 95 F11
Llanfwrog Anglesey 178 E4
Denb 165 D10
Llanfyllin Powys 148 F2
Llanfynydd Carms 93 F11
Flint 166 D3
Llanfyrnach Pembs 92 E4
Llangadfan Powys 147 G10
Llangadog Carms 74 D6
Carms 94 F4
Llangadwaladr Anglesey 162 B5
Powys 148 C3
Llangaffo Anglesey 162 B6
Llangain Carms 74 B5
Llangammarch Wells
Powys 95 B8
Llangan V Glam 58 D3
Llangarron Hereford 97 G10
Llangasty Talyllyn Powys 96 F2
Llangathen Carms 93 G11
Llangattock Powys 78 B2
Llangattock Lingoed
Mon 97 G7
Llangattock nigh Usk
Mon 78 D4
Llangattock-Vibon-Avel
Mon 79 B7
Llangedwyn Powys 148 E3
Llangefni Anglesey 179 F7
Llangeinor Bridgend 58 B2
Llangeitho Ceredig 112 F2
Llangeler Carms 93 D7
Llangendeirne Carms 75 C7
Llangennech Carms 75 E9
Llangennith Swansea 56 C2
Llangenny Powys 78 B3
Llangernyw Conwy 164 B5
Llangeview Mon 78 E5
Llangewydd Court
Bridgend 57 E11
Llangian Gwyn 144 D5
Llangloffan Pembs 91 E8
Llanglydwen Carms 92 F3
Llangoed Anglesey 179 F10
Llangoedmor Ceredig 92 B3
Llangollen Denb 166 G2
Llangolman Pembs 92 F2
Llangors Powys 96 F2
Llangorwen Ceredig 128 G2
Llangovan Mon 79 D7
Llangower Gwyn 147 C8
Llangrannog Ceredig 110 G6
Llangristiolus Anglesey 178 G6
Llangrove Hereford 79 B8
Llangua Mon 97 F7
Llangunllo Powys 114 C4
Llangunnor Carms 74 B6
Llangurig Powys 113 B8
Llangwm Conwy 165 G7
Mon 78 E6
Pembs 73 D7
Llangwnnadl Gwyn 144 C4
Llangwyfan Denb 165 B10
Llangwyfan-isaf
Anglesey 162 B4
Llangwyllog Anglesey 178 F6
Llangwyryfon Ceredig 111 C11
Llangybi Ceredig 112 G2
Gwyn 162 G6
Mon 78 F5
Llangyfelach Swansea 56 B6
Llangyndeyrn Carms 75 C7
Llangynhafal Denb 165 C10
Llangynidr Powys 77 B11
Llangyniew Powys 130 B2
Llangynin Carms 74 B2
Llangynog Carms 74 B4
Powys 147 D11
Llangynwyd Bridgend 57 D11
Llanhamlach Powys 95 F11
Llanharan Rhondda 58 C4
Llanharry Rhondda 58 C4
Llanhennock Mon 78 G5
Llanhilleth Bl Gwent 78 E2
Llanhowel Pembs 90 F6
Llanidloes Powys 129 G9
Llaniestyn Gwyn 144 C5
Llanifyny Powys 129 G7
Llanigon Powys 96 D4
Llanilar Ceredig 112 C2
Llanilid Rhondda 58 C3
Llanilltud Fawr / Llantwit
Major V Glam 58 F3
Llanio Ceredig 112 F2
Llanion Pembs 73 E7
Llanishen Cardiff 59 C7
Mon 79 E7
Llanllawddog Carms 93 F9
Llanllechid Gwyn 163 B10
Llanllowell Mon 78 F5
Llanllugan Powys 129 C11
Llanllwch Carms 74 B5
Llanllwchaiarn Powys 130 E2
Llanllwni Carms 93 D9
Llanllwyd Shrops 130 G3
Llanllyfni Gwyn 163 E7
Llanmadoc Swansea 56 C2
Llanmaes Cardiff 58 D6
V Glam 58 F3
Llanmartin Newport 59 B11
Llanmerwig Powys 130 E3
Llanmihangel V Glam 58 E3
Llan-mill Pembs 73 C10
Llanmiloe Carms 74 D3
Llanmorlais Swansea 56 C4
Llannefydd Conwy 181 G7
Llannerch-y-môr Flint 181 F11
Llannon Carms 75 D8
Llan-non / Llanon
Ceredig 111 D10
Llannor Gwyn 145 B7
Llanon Pembs 90 E6
Llanon / Llan-non
Ceredig 111 D10
Llanover Mon 78 D4
Llanpumsaint Carms 93 F8
Llanreath Pembs 73 E7
Llanreithan Pembs 91 F7
Llanrhaeadr Denb 165 C9
Llanrhaeadr-ym-Mochnant
Powys 148 D2
Llanrhian Pembs 90 E6
Llanrhidian Swansea 56 C3
Llanrhos Conwy 180 E3
Llanrhyddlad Anglesey 178 D4
Llanrhystud Ceredig 111 D10
Llanrosser Hereford 96 D5
Llanrothal Hereford 79 B7
Llanrug Gwyn 163 C8
Llanrumney Cardiff 59 C8
Llanrwst Conwy 164 C4
Llansadurnen Carms 74 C3
Llansadwrn Anglesey 179 F9
Carms 94 E3
Llansaint Carms 74 D5
Llansamlet Swansea 57 B7
Llansanffraid Glan Conwy
Conwy 180 F4
Llansannan Conwy 164 B6
Llansannor V Glam 58 D3
Llansantffraed Ceredig 111 D10
Powys 96 G2
Llansantffraed Cwmdeuddwr
Powys 113 D9
Llansantffraed-in-Elwel
Powys 113 G11
Llansantffraid-ym-Mechain
Powys 148 E4
Llansawel Carms 94 D2
Llansawel / Briton Ferry
Neath 57 C8
Llansilin Powys 148 D4
Llansoy Mon 78 E6
Llanspyddid Powys 95 F10
Llanstadwell Pembs 72 D6
Llansteffan Carms 74 C5
Llanstephan Powys 96 C2
Llantarnam Torf 78 G4
Llanteems Mon 96 G6
Llanteg Pembs 73 C11
Llanthony Mon 96 F5
Llantilio Crossenny Mon 78 C5
Llantilio Pertholey Mon 78 B4
Llantood Pembs 92 C3
Llantrisant Anglesey 178 E5
Mon 78 F5
Rhondda 58 C4
Llantrithyd V Glam 58 E4
Llantwit Neath 57 B9
Llantwit Fardre Rhondda 58 B5
Llantwit Major / Llanilltud
Fawr V Glam 58 F3
Llanuwchllyn Gwyn 147 C7
Llanvaches Newport 78 G6
Llanvair Discoed Mon 78 G6
Llanvapley Mon 78 C5
Llanvetherine Mon 78 B5
Llanveynoe Hereford 96 E6
Llanvihangel Crucorney
Mon 96 G6
Llanvihangel Gobion
Mon 78 D4
Llanvihangel-Ystern-
Llewern Mon 78 C6
Llanwarne Hereford 97 F10
Llanwddyn Powys 147 F10
Llanwenarth Mon 78 C3
Llanwenog Ceredig 93 B9
Llanwern Newport 59 B11
Llanwinio Carms 92 F5
Llanwnda Gwyn 163 D7
Pembs 91 D8
Llanwnnen Ceredig 93 B10
Llanwnog Powys 129 E10
Llanwrda Carms 94 E4
Llanwrin Powys 128 C5
Llanwrthwl Powys 113 E9
Llanwrtud / Llanwrtyd Wells
Powys 95 B7
Llanwrtyd Wells / Llanwrtud
Powys 95 B7
Llanwyddelan Powys 129 C11
Llanyblodwel Shrops 148 E4
Llanybri Carms 74 C4
Llanybydder Carms 93 C10
Llanycefn Pembs 91 G11
Llanychaer Pembs 91 D9
Llanycil Gwyn 147 C8
Llanycrwys Carms 94 B2
Llanymawddwy Gwyn 147 F8
Llanymddyfri / Llandovery
Carms 94 E5
Llanymynech Powys 148 E5
Llanynghenedl Anglesey 178 E4
Llanynys Denb 165 C10
Llan-y-pwll Wrex 166 E5
Llanyrafon Torf 78 G4
Llanyre Powys 113 E10
Llanystumdwy Gwyn 145 B9
Llanywern Powys 96 F2
Llawhaden Pembs 73 B9
Llawnt Shrops 148 C5
Llawrdref Bellaf Gwyn 144 D5
Llawr-y-glyn Powys 129 E8
Llay Wrex 166 D4
Llechcynfarwy Anglesey 178 E5
Llecheiddior Gwyn 163 G7
Llechfaen Powys 95 F11
Llechfraith Gwyn 146 F3
Llechryd Caerph 77 D10
Ceredig 92 C4
Llechrydau Powys 148 C4
Llechwedd Conwy 180 F3
Lledrod Ceredig 112 C2
Llenmerewig Powys 130 E3
Llethrid Swansea 56 C4
Llettyrychen Carms 75 E7
Llidiad Nenog Carms 93 D10
Llidiardau Gwyn 147 B7
Llidiart-y-parc Denb 165 G10
Llithfaen Gwyn 162 G5
Lloc Flint 181 F10
Llong Flint 166 C3
Llowes Powys 96 C3
Lloyney Powys 114 B4
Llugwy Powys 128 D4
Llundain-fach Ceredig 111 F11
Llwydarth Bridgend 57 C11
Llwydcoed Rhondda 77 E7
Llwyn Denb 165 C9
Shrops 130 G5
Llwyncelyn Ceredig 111 F8
Llwyndafydd Ceredig 111 F7
Llwynderw Powys 130 C4
Llwyn-derw Powys 129 G8
Llwyn-du Mon 78 B3
Llwynduris Ceredig 92 C4
Llwyndyrys Gwyn 162 G5
Llwyneinion Wrex 166 F3
Llwyngwril Gwyn 110 B2
Llwynhendy Carms 56 B4
Llwyn-hendy Carms 56 B4
Llwynmawr Wrex 148 B4
Llwyn-on Village M Tydf 77 C8
Llwyn-Têg Carms 75 D9
Llwyn-y-brain Carms 73 C11
Llwyn-y-go Shrops 148 E6
Llwynygog Powys 129 E7
Llwyn-y-groes Ceredig 111 F11
Llwynypia Rhondda 77 G7
Llwyn-yr-hwrdd Pembs 92 E4
Llynclys Shrops 148 E5
Llynfaes Anglesey 178 F6
Llysfaen Conwy 180 F5
Llyswen Powys 96 D2
Llysworney V Glam 58 E3
Llys-y-frôn Pembs 91 G10
Llywel Powys 95 E7
Llywernog Ceredig 128 G4
Load Brook S Yorks 186 D3
Loan Falk 279 F9
Loandhu Highld 301 B8
Loanend Northumb 273 E8
Loanhead Aberds 302 D6
Midloth 270 B5
Perth 286 D5
Loanreoch Highld 300 B6
Loans S Ayrs 257 C8
Loansdean Northumb 252 G5
Loans of Tullich Highld 301 B8
Lobb Devon 40 F3
Lobhillcross Devon 12 D5
Lobley Hill T&W 242 E6
Lobthorpe Lincs 155 E9
Loch a Charnain
W Isles 297 G4
Loch a' Ghainmhich
W Isles 304 F4
Lochailort Highld 295 G9
Lochaline Highld 289 E8
Lochanhully Highld 301 G9
Lochans Dumfries 236 D2
Locharbriggs Dumfries 247 G11
Lochassynt Lodge
Highld 307 G6
Lochavich Ho Argyll 275 B10
Lochawe Argyll 284 E5
Loch Baghasdail
W Isles 297 K3
Lochbuie Argyll 289 G8
Lochbuie Ho Argyll 289 G8
Lochcallater Lodge
Aberds 292 E3
Lochcarron Highld 295 B10
Loch Choire Lodge
Highld 308 F6
Lochdhu Highld 310 E4
Lochdochart House
Stirl 285 E8
Lochdon Argyll 289 F9
Lochdrum Highld 300 B2
Lochead Argyll 275 E11
Argyll 275 F8
Lochearnhead Stirl 285 E9
Lochee Dundee 287 D7
Loch Eil Highld 290 F2
Lochend Edin 280 G5
Highld 300 F5
Highld 310 C6
Lochend Ho Stirl 277 B11
Locherben Dumfries 247 D11
Lochetive Ho Highld 284 C5
Loch Euphoirt W Isles 296 E4
Lochfoot Dumfries 237 B10
Lochgair Argyll 275 D10
Lochgarthside Highld 291 B7
Lochgelly Fife 280 C3
Lochgilphead Argyll 275 E9
Lochgoilhead Argyll 284 G6
Loch Head Dumfries 236 E5
Dumfries 245 E11
Lochhill Moray 302 C2
Lochhussie Highld 300 D4
Lochinch Castle
Dumfries 236 C3
Lochindorb Lodge
Highld 301 F9
Lochinver Highld 307 G5
Lochlane Perth 286 E2
Lochletter Highld 300 G4
Loch Loyal Lodge Highld 308 E6
Lochluichart Highld 300 C3
Lochmaben Dumfries 248 G3
Lochmore Cottage
Highld 310 E4
Lochmore Lodge Highld 306 F7
Loch nam Madadh
W Isles 296 E5
Lochnell Ho Argyll 289 F10
Lochore Fife 280 B3
Lochorodale Argyll 255 F7
Lochportain W Isles 296 D5
Lochran Perth 280 B2
Lochranza N Ayrs 255 B10
Lochs Crofts Moray 302 C3
Loch Sgioport W Isles 297 H4
Lochside Aberds 293 G9
Highld 301 D8
Highld 308 D4
Highld 310 F2
S Ayrs 257 E8
Lochslin Highld 311 L2
Lochstack Lodge Highld 306 E7
Lochton Aberds 293 D9
Lochty Angus 293 G7
Fife 287 G9
Perth 286 E4
Lochuisge Highld 289 D9
Lochurr Dumfries 247 F7
Lochwinnoch Renfs 267 D7
Lochwood Dumfries 248 D3
Glasgow 268 B3
Lochyside Highld 290 F3
Lockengate Corn 5 C10
Lockerbie Dumfries 248 G4
Lockeridge Wilts 62 F6
Lockeridge Dene Wilts 62 F6
Lockerley Hants 32 B3
Lockhills Cumb 230 B6
Locking N Som 43 B11
Lockinge Oxon 64 B2
Locking Stumps Warr 183 C10
Lockington E Yorks 208 D5
Leics 153 D9
Lockleaze Bristol 60 D6
Lockleywood Shrops 150 D3
Locksbottom London 68 F2
Locksbrook Bath 61 G8
Locksgreen IoW 20 C4
Locks Heath Hants 33 F8
Lockton N Yorks 226 G6
Lockwood W Yorks 196 D6
Loddington Leics 136 C5
Northants 120 B6
Loddiswell Devon 8 F4
Loddon Norf 143 D7
Loddon Ingloss Norf 142 D6
Lode Cambs 123 E10
Lode Heath W Mid 134 G3
Loders Dorset 16 C5
Lodgebank Shrops 149 D11
Lodge Green N Yorks 223 F9
W Mid 134 G5
Lodge Hill Corn 6 C4
W Mid 133 G10
W Yorks 197 C9
Lodge Lees Kent 55 D8
Lodge Moor S Yorks 186 D3
Lodge Park Worcs 117 D10
Lodsworth W Sus 34 C6
Lodsworth Common
W Sus 34 C6
Lodway Bristol 60 D4
Lofthouse N Yorks 214 E2
W Yorks 197 B10
Lofthouse Gate
W Yorks 197 C10
Loftus Redcar 226 B4
Logan E Ayrs 258 E3
Loganlea W Loth 269 C9
Logan Mains Dumfries 236 E2
Loggerheads Denb 165 C11
Logie Angus 293 G8
Fife 287 E8
Moray 301 D10
Logiealmond Lodge
Perth 286 D3
Logie Coldstone Aberds 292 C6
Logie Hill Highld 301 B7
Logie Newton Aberds 302 F6
Logie Pert Angus 293 G8
Logierait Perth 286 B3
Login Carms 92 G3
Logmore Green Sur 50 D6
Loidse Mhorsgail
W Isles 304 F3
Lolworth Cambs 123 E7
Lomeshaye Lancs 204 F2
Lôn Gwyn 147 C7
Lonbain Highld 298 D6
Londesborough E Yorks 208 D3
London Apprentice Corn 5 E10
London Beach Kent 53 F11
London Colney Herts 85 E11
Londonderry N Yorks 214 B6
W Mid 133 F10
London End Cambs 121 D11
London Fields W Mid 133 E8
London Minstead Hants 32 E3
Londonthorpe Lincs 155 B9
Londubh Highld 307 L3
Lonemore Highld 299 B7
Highld 309 L7
Long Ashton N Som 60 E5
Long Bank Worcs 116 C5
Longbar N Ayrs 266 E6
Longbarn Warr 183 C10
Long Bennington Lincs 172 G4
Longbenton T&W 243 D7
Longborough Glos 100 F3
Long Bredy Dorset 17 C7
Longbridge Plym 7 D10
Warks 118 E5
W Mid 117 B10
Longbridge Deverill
Wilts 45 E11
Longbridge Hayes Stoke 168 E5
Longbridgemuir
Dumfries 238 D3
Long Buckby Northants 120 D2
Long Buckby Wharf
Northants 120 D2
Longburgh Cumb 239 F8
Longburton Dorset 29 E11
Longcause Devon 8 C5
Long Clawson Leics 154 D4
Longcliffe Derbys 170 D2
Long Common Hants 33 E8
Long Compton Staffs 151 E7
Warks 100 E5
Longcot Oxon 82 G3
Long Crendon Bucks 83 D11
Long Crichel Dorset 31 E7
Longcroft Cumb 238 F6
Falk 278 F5
Longcross Devon 12 F4
Sur 66 F3
Long Cross Wilts 45 G9
Longdale Cumb 222 D2
Longdales Cumb 230 C6
Long Dean Wilts 61 D11
Longden Shrops 131 B8
Longden Common
Shrops 131 C8
Long Ditton Sur 67 F7
Longdon Staffs 151 G11
Worcs 98 D6
Longdon Green Staffs 151 G11
Longdon Heath Worcs 98 D6
Longdon Hill End Worcs 98 D6
Longdon on Tern
Telford 150 F2
Longdown Devon 14 C3
Longdowns Corn 2 C6
Long Drax N Yorks 199 B7
Longdrum Angus 292 G4
Long Duckmanton
Derbys 186 G6
Long Eaton Derbys 153 C9
Longfield Kent 68 F6
Shetland 313 M5
Wilts 45 B11
Longfield Hill Kent 68 F6
Longfleet Poole 18 C6
Longford Derbys 152 B4
Glos 98 G6
Kent 52 B4
London 66 D4
Shrops 150 C2
Telford 150 F4
Warr 183 C10
W Mid 135 G7
Longfordlane Derbys 152 B4
Longforgan Perth 287 E7
Longformacus Borders 272 D3
Longframlington
Northumb 252 C4
Long Gardens Essex 106 D6
Long Green Ches W 183 G7
Suff 125 B11
Worcs 98 E6
Longham Dorset 19 B7
Norf 159 F8
Long Hanborough Oxon 82 C6
Longhaven Aberds 303 F11
Longhedge Wilts 45 E10
Longhill Aberds 303 D9
Longhirst Northumb 252 F6
Longhope Glos 79 B11
Orkney 314 G3
Longhorsley Northumb 252 E4
Longhoughton
Northumb 264 G6
Longhouse Bath 61 G8
Long Itchington Warks 119 D8
Long John's Hill Norf 142 B4
Longlands Cumb 229 D11
London 68 E2
Longlane Derbys 152 B5
W Berks 64 E3
Long Lane Telford 150 F2
Long Lawford Warks 119 B9
Long Lee W Yorks 205 E7
Longlevens Glos 99 G7
Longley W Yorks 196 C5
W Yorks 196 F6
Longley Estate S Yorks 186 C5
Longley Green Worcs 116 G4
Longleys Perth 286 C6
Long Load Som 29 C7
Longmanhill Aberds 303 C7
Long Marston Herts 84 B5
N Yorks 206 C6
Warks 100 B3
Long Marton Cumb 231 G9
Long Meadow Cambs 123 E10
Long Meadowend
Shrops 131 G8
Long Melford Suff 107 B7
Longmoor Camp Hants 49 G9
Longmorn Moray 302 D2
Longmoss Ches E 184 G5
Long Newnton Glos 80 G6
Longnewton Borders 262 D3
Stockton 225 B7
Long Newton E Loth 271 C10
Longney Glos 80 C3
Longniddry E Loth 281 F8
Longnor Shrops 131 C9
Staffs 151 G7
Staffs 169 C9
Longnor Park Shrops 131 C9
Long Oak Shrops 149 E7
Longparish Hants 48 E2
Longpark Cumb 239 E10
E Ayrs 257 B10
Long Park Hants 48 G2
Longport Stoke 168 F5
Long Preston N Yorks 204 B2
Longridge Glos 80 D5
Lancs 203 F8
Staffs 151 F8
W Loth 269 C9
Longridge End Glos 98 G6
Longrigg N Lnrk 278 G6
Longriggend N Lnrk 278 G6
Long Riston E Yorks 209 E8
Longrock Corn 1 C5
Long Sandall S Yorks 198 F6
Longscales N Yorks 205 B10
Longsdon Staffs 169 E7
Longshaw Gtr Man 194 G4
Staffs 169 F9
Longside Aberds 303 E10
Longsight Gtr Man 184 B5
Long Sight Gtr Man 196 F2
Longslow Shrops 150 B3
Longsowerby Cumb 239 G9
Longstanton Cambs 123 D7
Longstock Hants 47 F11
Longstone Corn 2 B2
Corn 11 G7
Edin 280 G4
Pembs 73 D10
Som 28 B5
Longstowe Cambs 122 G6
Long Stratton Norf 142 E3
Longstreet Wilts 46 C6
Long Street M Keynes 102 B5
Long Sutton Hants 49 D8
Lincs 157 E8
Som 29 B7
Longthorpe Pboro 138 D3
Long Thurlow Suff 125 D10
Longthwaite Cumb 230 G4
Longton Lancs 194 B3
Stoke 168 G6
Longtown Cumb 239 D9
Hereford 96 F6
Longtownmail Orkney 314 F4
Longview Mers 182 C6
Longville in the Dale
Shrops 131 E10
Longway Bank Derbys 170 E4
Longwell Green S Glos 61 E7
Long Whatton Leics 153 E9
Longwick Bucks 84 D3
Long Wittenham Oxon 83 G8
Longwitton Northumb 252 F3
Longwood Shrops 132 B2
W Yorks 196 D6
Longwood Edge
W Yorks 196 D6
Longworth Oxon 82 F5
Longyester E Loth 271 B10
Lon-las Swansea 57 B8
Lonmay Aberds 303 D10
Lonmore Highld 298 E2
Looe Corn 6 E5
Looe Mills Corn 6 C4
Loose Kent 53 C9
Loosegate Lincs 156 D6
Loose Hill Kent 53 C9
Loosley Row Bucks 84 E4
Lopcombe Corner Wilts 47 F9
Lopen Som 28 E6
Lopen Head Som 28 E6
Loppergarth Cumb 210 D5
Loppington Shrops 149 D9
Lopwell Devon 7 C9
Lorbottle Northumb 252 B2
Lorbottle Hall Northumb 252 B2
Lordsbridge Norf 157 G11
Lord's Hill Soton 32 D5
Lordshill Common Sur 50 E4
Lordswood Soton 32 D6
Lords Wood Medway 69 G9
Lornty Perth 286 C5
Loscoe Derbys 170 F6
W Yorks 198 C2
Loscombe Dorset 16 B6
Losgaintir W Isles 305 J2
Lossiemouth Moray 302 B2
Lossit Argyll 254 B2
Lossit Lodge Argyll 274 G5
Lostford Shrops 150 C2
Lostock Gtr Man 195 F7
Lostock Gralam
Ches W 183 F11
Lostock Green Ches W 183 G11
Lostock Hall Lancs 194 B4
Lostock Junction
Gtr Man 195 F7
Lostwithiel Corn 6 D2
Loth Orkney 314 C6
Lothbeg Highld 311 H3
Lothersdale N Yorks 204 D5
Lothianbridge Midloth 270 C6
Lothmore Highld 311 H3
Lottisham Som 44 G5
Loudwater Bucks 84 G6
Herts 85 F9
Loughborough Leics 153 F10
Loughor Swansea 56 B5
Loughton Essex 86 F6
M Keynes 102 D6
Shrops 132 G2
Lound Lincs 155 F11
Notts 187 D11
Suff 143 D10
Loundsley Green Derbys 186 G5
Lount Leics 153 F7
Lour Angus 287 C8
Louth Lincs 190 D4
Lovat Highld 300 E5
Lovaton Devon 7 B10
Love Clough Lancs 195 B10
Lovedean Hants 33 E11
Love Green Bucks 66 C4
Lover Wilts 32 C2
Loversall S Yorks 187 B9
Loves Green Essex 87 E10
Lovesome Hill N Yorks 225 F7
Loveston Pembs 73 D9
Lovington Som 44 G5
Low Ackworth W Yorks 198 D3
Low Alwinton
Northumb 251 B10
Low Angerton Northumb 252 G3
Lowbands Glos 98 E5
Low Barlings Lincs 189 G9
Low Barugh S Yorks 197 F10
Low Bentham N Yorks 212 F2
Low Biggins Cumb 212 D2
Low Blantyre S Lnrk 268 D3
Low Borrowbridge
Cumb 222 E2
Low Bradfield S Yorks 186 C3
Low Bradley N Yorks 204 D6
Low Braithwaite Cumb 230 C4
Low Bridge Wilts 62 E3
Lowbridge House
Cumb 221 E10
Low Brunton Northumb 241 C10
Low Burnham N Lincs 199 G9
Low Burton N Yorks 214 C4
Low Buston Northumb 252 B6
Lowca Cumb 228 G5
Low Catton E Yorks 207 C10
Low Clanyard Dumfries 236 F3
Low Common Norf 142 E2
Low Compton Gtr Man 196 F2
Low Coniscliffe Darl 224 C5
Low Cotehill Cumb 239 G11
Low Coylton S Ayrs 257 F10
Low Crosby Cumb 239 F10
Lowcross Hill Ches W 167 E7
Low Dalby N Yorks 217 B7
Lowdham Notts 171 F11
Low Dinsdale Darl 224 C6
Lowe Shrops 149 C10
Lowedges S Yorks 186 E4
Lowe Hill Staffs 169 D7
Low Eighton T&W 243 F7
Low Ellington N Yorks 214 C4
Lower Achachenna
Argyll 284 E4
Lower Aisholt Som 43 F8
Lower Allscot Shrops 132 D4
Lower Altofts W Yorks 197 C11
Lower Amble Corn 10 G5
Lower Ansty Dorset 30 G3
Lower Ardtun Argyll 288 G5
Lower Arncott Oxon 83 B10
Lower Ashtead Sur 51 B7
Lower Ashton Devon 14 E2
Lower Assendon Oxon 65 C8
Lower Badcall Highld 306 E6
Lower Ballam Lancs 202 G3
Lower Bartle Lancs 202 G5
Lower Basildon W Berks 64 D6
Lower Bassingthorpe
Lincs 155 D9
Lower Bearwood
Hereford 115 F7
Lower Bebington Mers 182 E4
Lower Beeding W Sus 36 B2
Lower Benefield
Northants 137 F9
Lower Bentley Worcs 117 D9
Lower Beobridge
Shrops 132 E5
Lower Berry Hill Glos 79 C9
Lower Binton Warks 118 G2
Lower Birchwood
Derbys 170 E6
Lower Bitchet Kent 52 C5
Lower Blandford St Mary
Dorset 30 F5
Lower Blunsdon
Swindon 81 G10
Lower Bobbingworth Green
Essex 87 D8
Lower Bockhampton
Dorset 17 C10
Lower Boddington
Northants 119 G9
Lower Bodham Norf 160 B2
Lower Bodinnar Corn 1 C4
Lower Bois Bucks 85 E7
Lower Bordean Hants 33 C11
Lower Boscaswell Corn 1 C3
Lower Bourne Sur 49 E10
Lower Bradley W Mid 133 D9
Lower Brailes Warks 100 D6
Lower Breakish Highld 295 C8
Lower Bredbury
Gtr Man 184 C6
Lower Breinton Hereford 97 D9
Lower Broadheath
Worcs 116 F6
Lower Brook Hants 32 B4
Lower Broughton
Gtr Man 184 B4
Lower Brynamman Neath 76 C2
Lower Brynn Corn 5 C9
Lower Buckenhill
Hereford 98 E2
Lower Buckland Hants 20 B2
Lower Bullingham
Hereford 97 D10
Lower Bullington Hants 48 E3
Lower Bunbury Ches E 167 D9
Lower Burgate Hants 31 D11
Lower Burrow Som 28 C6
Lower Burton Hereford 115 F8
Lower Bush Medway 69 F7
Lower Cadsden Bucks 84 E4
Lower Caldecote
C Beds 104 B3
Lower Cam Glos 80 E2
Lower Canada N Som 43 B11
Lower Carden Ches W 167 E7
Lower Catesby
Northants 119 F10
Lower Cator Devon 13 F9
Lower Caversham
Reading 65 E8
Lower Chapel Powys 95 D10
Lower Chedworth Glos 81 C9
Lower Cheriton Devon 27 G10
Lower Chicksgrove Wilts 46 G3
Lower Chute Wilts 47 C10
Lower Clapton London 67 B11
Lower Clent Worcs 117 B8
Lower Clicker Corn 6 C5
Lower Clopton Warks 118 F3
Lower Common Hants 48 E6
Hants 65 G9
Mon 78 B2
Mon 78 E4
Shrops 131 B9
Lower Copthurst Lancs 194 C5
Lower Cotburn Aberds 303 D7
Lower Cousley Wood
E Sus 53 G7
Lower Cox Street Kent 69 G10
Lower Cragabus Argyll 254 C4
Lower Creedy Devon 26 G4
Lower Croan Corn 10 G6
Lower Crossings Derbys 185 E8
Lower Cumberworth
W Yorks 197 F8
Lower Cwm-twrch Powys 76 C3
Lower Daggons Hants 31 E9
Lower Darwen Blkburn 195 B7
Lower Dean Beds 121 D11
Devon 8 C4
Lower Dell Highld 292 B2
Lower Denby W Yorks 197 F8
Lower Denzell Corn 5 B7
Lower Deuchries
Aberds 302 D6
Lower Diabaig Highld 299 C7
Lower Dicker E Sus 23 C9
Lower Dinchope Shrops 131 G9
Lower Dowdeswell Glos 81 B8
Lower Down Shrops 130 G6
Lower Drift Corn 1 D4
Lower Dunsforth
N Yorks 215 G8
Lower Durston Som 28 B3
Lower Earley Wokingham 65 E9
Lower East Carleton
Norf 142 C3
Lower Eastern Green
W Mid 118 B5
Lower Edmonton London 86 G4
Lower Egleton Hereford 98 B2
Lower Elkstone Staffs 169 D9
Lower Ellastone Staffs 169 G10
Lower End Bucks 83 D11
Bucks 102 E4
C Beds 103 D8
C Beds 103 G9
Glos 81 E7
Northants 120 F6
Northants 120 G5
Northants 121 E7
Oxon 82 B4
Lower Everleigh Wilts 47 C7
Lower Eythorne Kent 55 D9
Lower Failand N Som 60 E4
Lower Faintree Shrops 132 F3
Lower Falkenham Suff 108 D5
Lower Farringdon Hants 49 F8
Lower Feltham London 66 E5
Lower Fittleworth W Sus 35 D8
Lowerford Lancs 204 F3
Lower Forge Shrops 132 F4
Lower Foxdale IoM 192 E3
Lower Frankton Shrops 149 C7
Lower Freystrop Pembs 73 C7
Lower Froyle Hants 49 E9
Lower Gabwell Devon 9 B8
Lower Gledfield Highld 309 K5
Lower Godney Som 44 E3
Lower Goldstone Kent 71 G9
Lower Gornal W Mid 133 E8
Lower Grange W Yorks 205 G8
Lower Gravenhurst
C Beds 104 D2
Lower Green Essex 88 E2
Essex 105 E8
Essex 106 E4
Gtr Man 184 B2
Herts 104 E3
Kent 52 E5
Kent 52 E6
Norf 159 B9
Staffs 133 B8
Suff 124 D4
Sur 66 F6
Warks 119 D10
W Berks 63 G11
Lower Grove Common
Hereford 97 F11
Lower Hacheston Suff 126 F6
Lower Halistra Highld 298 D2
Lower Halliford Sur 66 F5
Lower Halstock Leigh
Dorset 29 F8
Lower Halstow Kent 69 F11
Lower Hamswell S Glos 61 E8
Lower Hamworthy Poole 18 C6
Lower Hardres Kent 55 C7
Lower Hardwick
Hereford 115 F8
Lower Harpton Powys 114 E5
Lower Hartlip Kent 69 G10
Lower Hartshay Derbys 170 E5
Lower Hartwell Bucks 84 C3
Lower Hatton Staffs 150 B6
Lower Hawthwaite
Cumb 210 B4
Lower Haysden Kent 52 D5
Lower Hayton Shrops 131 G10
Lower Hazel S Glos 60 B6
Lower Heath Ches E 168 C5
Lower Hempriggs
Moray 301 C11
Lower Heppington Kent 54 C6
Lower Hergest Hereford 114 F5
Lower Herne Kent 71 F7
Lower Heyford Oxon 101 G9
Lower Heysham Lancs 211 G8
Lower Higham Kent 69 E8
Lower Highmoor Oxon 65 B8
Lower Holbrook Suff 108 E3
Lower Holditch Dorset 28 G4
Lower Holloway London 67 B10
Lower Holwell Dorset 31 E9
Lower Hook Worcs 98 C6
Lower Hookner Devon 13 E10
Lower Hopton Shrops 149 E7
W Yorks 197 D7
Lower Hordley Shrops 149 D7
Lower Horncroft W Sus 35 D8
Lower Horsebridge
E Sus 23 C9
Lowerhouse Ches E 184 F6
Lancs 204 G2
Lower House Halton 183 D8
Lower Houses W Yorks 197 D7
Lower Howsell Worcs 98 B5
Lower Illey Worcs 133 G9
Lower Island Kent 70 F6
Lower Kersal Gtr Man 195 G10
Lower Kilburn Derbys 170 F5
Lower Kilcott Glos 61 B9
Lower Killeyan Argyll 254 C3
Lower Kingcombe Dorset 17 B7
Lower Kingswood Sur 51 C8
Lower Kinnerton
Ches W 166 C4
Lower Kinsham
Hereford 115 E7
Lower Knapp Som 28 B4
Lower Knightley Staffs 150 E6
Lower Knowle Bristol 60 E5
Lower Langford N Som 60 G3
Lower Largo Fife 287 G8
Lower Layham Suff 107 C10
Lower Ledwyche
Shrops 115 C10
Lower Leigh Staffs 151 B10
Lower Lemington Glos 100 E4
Lower Lenie Highld 300 G5
Lower Lode Glos 99 E7
Lower Lovacott Devon 25 B8
Lower Loxhore Devon 40 F6
Lower Lydbrook Glos 79 B9
Lower Lye Hereford 115 D8
Lower Machen Newport 59 B8
Lower Maes-coed
Hereford 96 E6
Lower Mains Clack 279 B9
Lower Mannington
Dorset 31 F9
Lower Marsh Som 30 C2
Lower Marston Som 45 E9
Lower Meend Glos 79 E9
Lower Menadue Corn 5 D10
Lower Merridge Som 43 G8
Lower Mickletown
W Yorks 198 B2
Lower Middleton Cheney
Northants 101 C10
Lower Midway Derbys 152 E6
Lower Mill Corn 3 B10
Lower Milovaig Highld 296 F7
Lower Milton Som 44 D4
Lower Moor Wilts 81 G8
Worcs 99 B9
Lower Morton S Glos 79 G10
Lower Mountain Flint 166 D4
Lower Nazeing Essex 86 D5
Lower Netchwood
Shrops 132 E2
Lower Netherton Devon 14 G3
Lower New Inn Torf 78 F4
Lower Ninnes Corn 1 C5
Lower Nobut Staffs 151 C10
Lower North Dean Bucks 84 F5
Lower Norton Warks 118 E4
Lower Nyland Dorset 30 C2
Lower Ochrwyth Caerph 59 B8
Lower Odcombe Som 29 D8
Lower Oddington Glos 100 F4
Lower Ollach Highld 295 B7
Lower Padworth W Berks 64 F6
Lower Penarth V Glam 59 F7
Lower Penn Staffs 133 D7
Lower Pennington Hants 20 C2
Lower Penwortham
Lancs 194 B4
Lower Peover Ches W 184 G2
Lower Pexhill Ches E 184 G5
Lower Pilsley Derbys 170 C6
Lower Pitkerrie Highld 311 L2
Lower Place Gtr Man 196 E2
London 67 C8
Lower Pollicot Bucks 84 C2
Lower Porthkerry V Glam 58 F5
Lower Porthpean Corn 5 E10
Lower Quinton Warks 100 B3
Lower Rabber Hereford 114 G5
Lower Race Torf 78 E3
Lower Radley Oxon 83 F8
Lower Rainham Medway 69 F10
Lower Ratley Hants 32 C4
Lower Raydon Suff 107 D10
Lower Rea Glos 80 B4
Lower Ridge Devon 28 G2
Shrops 148 C6
Lower Roadwater Som 42 F4
Lower Rochford Worcs 116 D2
Lower Rose Corn 4 E5
Lower Row Dorset 31 G8
Lower Sapey Worcs 116 E3
Lower Seagry Wilts 62 C3
Lower Sheering Essex 87 C7
Lower Shelton C Beds 103 C9
Lower Shiplake Oxon 65 D9
Lower Shuckburgh
Warks 119 E9
Lower Skelly Swansea 56 C6
Lower Slackstead Hants 32 B5
Lower Slade Devon 40 D4
Lower Slaughter Glos 100 G3
Lower Solva Pembs 87 G11
Lower Soothill W Yorks 197 C9
Lower Soudley Glos 79 D11
Lower Southfield
Hereford 98 C3
Lower Stanton St Quintin
Wilts 62 C2
Lower Stoke Medway 69 D10
W Mid 119 B7
Lower Stondon C Beds 104 D3
Lower Stone Glos 79 G11
Lower Stonnall Staffs 133 C11
Lower Stow Bedon
Norf 141 E9
Lower Stratton Som 28 D6
Swindon 63 B7
Lower Street E Sus 38 E2
Norf 160 B5
Norf 160 C3
Norf 160 F6
Suff 108 E3
Suff 124 G5
Lower Strensham Worcs 99 C8
Lower Stretton Warr 183 E10
Lower Studley Wilts 45 B11
Lower Sundon C Beds 103 F10
Lower Swainswick Bath 61 F9
Lower Swanwick Hants 33 F7
Lower Swell Glos 100 F3
Lower Sydenham
London 67 E11
Lower Tadmarton Oxon 101 D8
Lower Tale Devon 27 G9
Lower Tasburgh Norf 142 D3
Lower Tean Staffs 151 B10

Meadle Bucks. 84 D4
Meadowbank Ches W . . 167 B11
Edin 280 C5
Meadowend Essex 106 C4
Meadowfield Durham . . 233 D10
Meadowfoot N Ayrs 266 F4
Meadow Green Hereford 116 F4
Meadow Hall S Yorks . . 186 C5
Meadow Head S Yorks . . 186 E5
Meadowley Shrops 132 E3
Meadowmill E Loth 281 G8
Meadows Nottingham . . 153 B11
Meadowtown Shrops . . 130 C6
Meads E Sus 23 F10
Meadside Oxon 83 G9
Mead Vale Sur 51 D9
Meadwell Devon 12 E4
Meaford Staffs 151 B7
Meagill N Yorks 205 B9
Mealabost W Isles 304 E6
Mealabost Bhuirgh
 W Isles. 304 C6
Mealasta W Isles 304 F1
Meal Bank Cumb. 221 F10
Meal Hill W Yorks 197 F7
Mealrig Cumb 229 B8
Mealsgate Cumb. 229 C10
Meanwood W Yorks 205 F11
Mearbeck N Yorks 212 G6
Meare Som 44 E3
Meare Green Som 28 C3
 Som 28 C3
Mearns Bath. 45 B7
 E Renf. 267 D10
Mears Ashby Northants. . 120 D6
Measborough Dike
 S Yorks 197 F11
Measham Leics 152 G6
Meath Green Sur 51 E9
Meathop Cumb 211 C8
Meaux E Yorks 209 F7
Meaver Corn. 2 F5
Meavy Devon 7 B10
Medbourne Leics 136 E5
 M Keynes 102 D6
Medburn Northumb . . . 242 C4
Medomsley Durham . . . 242 G4
Medstead Hants. 49 F7
Meerbrook Staffs. 169 C7
Meer Common Hereford. 115 G7
Meer End W Mid 118 C4
Meerhay Dorset 29 G7
Meers Bridge Lincs . . . 191 D7
Meersbrook S Yorks. . . 186 E5
Meesden Herts 105 E8
Meeson Telford. 150 E3
Meeson Heath Telford. . 150 E3
Meeth Devon 25 F8
Meethe Devon 26 D4
Meeting Green Suff. . . . 124 F4
Meeting House Hill
 Norf. 160 D6
Meggernie Castle Perth 285 C9
Meggethead Borders . . 260 E5
Meidrim Carms 92 G5
Meifod Denb 165 D8
 Powys 148 G3
Meigle N Ayrs 266 B3
Meikle Earnock S Lnrk . 268 E4
Meikle Ferry Highld. . . . 309 L7
Meikle Forter Angus . . 292 G3
Meikle Gluich Highld. . . 309 L6
Meikle Obney Perth. . . . 286 D4
Meikleour Perth 286 D5
Meikle Pinkerton
 E Loth 282 F4
Meikle Strath Aberds . . 293 F8
Meikle Tarty Aberds . . . 303 G9
Meikle Wartle Aberds . . 303 F7
Meinciau Carms 75 C7
Meir Stoke 168 G6
Meir Heath Staffs 168 G6
Melbourn Cambs 105 C7
Melbourne Derbys 153 D7
 E Yorks. 207 E11
 S Lnrk 269 G11
Melbury Abbas Dorset . 30 D5
Melbury Bubb Dorset. . 29 F9
Melbury Osmond Dorset 29 F9
Melbury Sampford
 Dorset. 29 F9
Melby Shetland. 313 H3
Melchbourne Beds 121 D10
Melcombe Som. 43 G8
Melcombe Bingham
 Dorset. 30 G3
Melcombe Regis Dorset. . 17 E9
Meldon Devon 13 C2
 Northumb 252 G4
Meldreth Cambs 105 B7
Meldrum Ho Aberds. . . 303 G8
Melfort Argyll. 275 B9
Melgarve Highld. 290 D6
Meliden / Gallt Melyd
 Denb 181 E9
Melinbyrhedyn Powys . 128 D6
Melin Caiach Caerph. . . 77 F11
Melincourt Neath. 76 E4
Melincryddan Neath . . . 57 B8
Melinsey Corn 3 B10
Melin-y-coed Conwy . . 164 C4
Melin-y-ddol Powys . . 129 B11
Melin-y-grug Powys . . 129 B11
Melin-y-Wig Denb. 165 F8
Melkington Northumb . 273 G7
Melkinthorpe Cumb . . . 231 F7
Melkridge Northumb . . 241 E7
Melksham Wilts 62 G2
Melksham Forest Wilts. 62 G2
Mellangaun Highld . . . 307 L3
Mellangoose Corn 2 D5
Melldalloch Argyll 275 F10
Mell Green W Berks . . . 64 D3
Mellguards Cumb. 230 B4
Melling Lancs 211 E11
 Mers 193 G11
Mellingey Corn 10 G4
Mellis Suff. 126 C2
Mellis Green Suff. 125 C2
Mellon Charles Highld . 307 K3
Mellon Udrigle Highld. . 307 K3
Mellor Gtr Man 185 D7
 Lancs. 203 G8
Mellor Brook Lancs . . . 203 G8
 Som 127 B8
Mells Green Som 45 D8
Melmerby Cumb 231 D8
 N Yorks. 213 B11
 N Yorks. 214 D6
Melon Green Suff. 124 F6

Melplash Dorset 16 B5
Melrose Borders 262 C2
Melsetter Orkney 314 H2
Melsonby N Yorks 224 D3
Meltham W Yorks 196 E6
Meltham Mills W Yorks . 196 E6
Melton E Yorks. 200 B3
 Suff. 126 G5
Meltonby E Yorks. 207 C11
Melton Constable Norf 159 C10
Melton Mowbray Leics . 154 F5
Melton Ross N Lincs . . 200 D5
Melvaig Highld. 307 L2
Melverley Shrops 148 F6
Melverley Green Shrops 148 F6
Melvich Highld. 310 C2
Membland Devon 7 F11
Membury Devon 28 G3
Memsie Aberds 303 C9
Memus Angus 287 B8
Mena Corn. 5 C10
Menabilly Corn 5 E11
Menadarva Corn. 4 G2
Menagissey Corn 4 G2
Menai Bridge / Porthaethwy
 Anglesey 179 G9
Mendham Suff. 142 G5
Mendlesham Suff. 126 D2
Mendlesham Green
 Suff. 125 E11
Menethorpe N Yorks . . 216 F5
Mengham Hants 21 B10
Menheniot Corn 6 C5
Menherion Corn 2 C5
Menithwood Worcs . . . 116 D4
Menna Corn 5 E8
Mennock Dumfries 247 B8
Menston W Yorks 205 E9
Menstrie Clack 278 B6
Mentmore Bucks 84 B6
Menzion Borders. 260 E3
Meoble Highld 295 G9
Meole Brace Shrops . . 149 G9
Meols Mers. 182 C2
Meon Hants 33 G8
Meonstoke Hants 33 D10
Meopham Kent 68 F6
Meopham Green Kent . 68 F6
Meopham Station Kent. 68 F6
Mepal Cambs 139 G8
Meppershall C Beds . . 104 D2
Merbach Hereford 96 B6
Mercaton Derbys 170 G3
Merchant Fields
 W Yorks 197 B7
Merchiston Edin. 280 G4
Mere Ches E 184 E2
 Wilts. 45 G10
Mere Brow Lancs 194 D2
Mereclough Lancs 204 G3
Mere Green W Mid 134 D2
 Worcs 117 E9
Merehead Wrex 149 B9
Mere Heath Ches W . . . 183 G11
Meresborough Medway . 69 G10
Mereside Blkpool 202 G2
Meretown Staffs 150 E5
Mereworth Kent 53 C7
Mergie Aberds. 293 E9
Meriden Herts 85 F10
 W Mid 134 G4
Merkadale Highld 294 B5
Merkland Dumfries . . . 237 B9
 N Ayrs 256 B2
 S Ayrs 244 E6
Merkland Lodge Highld 309 G4
Merle Common Sur 52 D2
Merley Poole 18 B5
Merlin's Bridge Pembs . 72 C6
Merlin's Cross Pembs. . 73 E7
Merridale W Mid 133 D7
Merridge Som 43 G8
Merrie Gardens IoW . . . 21 E7
Merrifield Devon 8 F6
 Devon 24 G3
Merrington Shrops. . . . 149 E9
Merrion Pembs 72 F6
Merriott Dorset. 16 B6
 Som 28 E6
Merrittsford Som 28 E6
Merritown Dorset 19 B8
Merrivale Devon 12 F6
 Hereford 98 G2
Merrow Sur 50 C4
Merrybent Durl 224 C4
Merry Field Hill Dorset . 31 G8
Merry Hill Herts 85 G10
 W Mid 133 D7
Merryhill Green
 Wokingham 65 E9
Merrylee E Renf. 267 D11
Merry Lees Leics. 135 B9
Merrymeet Corn. 6 B5
Merry Meeting Corn . . . 11 G7
Merry Oak Soton. 32 E6
Mersham Kent. 54 F5
Merstham Sur 51 C9
Merston W Sus. 22 C5
Merstone IoW 21 E7
Merther Corn. 5 G7
Merther Lane Corn 5 G7
Merthyr Carms 93 G7
Merthyr Cynog Powys . . 95 D9
Merthyr-Dyfan V Glam . 58 F6
Merthyr Mawr Bridgend . 57 F11
Merthyr Tydfil M Tydf . . 77 D8
Merthyr Vale M Tydf . . . 77 F9
Merton Devon 25 E8
 London 67 E9
 Norf 141 D8
 Oxon 83 B9
Merton Park London. . . 67 F9
Mervinslaw Borders. . . 262 G5
Meshaw Devon 26 D3
Messing Essex. 88 B5
Messingham N Lincs . . 199 G11
Mesty Croft W Mid 133 E9
Messur-y-porth Pembs . 87 E11
Metal Bridge Durham . . 233 E11
Metfield Suff. 142 G5
Metherell Corn 7 B8
Metheringham Lincs . . 173 C9
Methersgate Suff. 108 B5
Methil Fife 281 B7
Methilhill Fife 281 B7
Methley W Yorks 197 B11
Methley Junction
 W Yorks 197 B11
Methlick Aberds 303 F8
 Methven Perth. 286 E4
Methwold Norf 140 E4
Methwold Hythe Norf. . 140 E4
Mettingham Suff. 143 F7
Metton Norf 160 B3
Mevagissey Corn 5 G10
Mewith Head N Yorks. . 212 F4
 N Yorks. 214 D6
Mexborough S Yorks . . 187 B7
Mey Highld. 310 B6

Meyrick Park Bmouth . . 19 C7
Meysey Hampton Glos. . 81 F10
 W Isles 305 H2
 W Isles 305 J3
Miabhag W Isles. 304 E2
Mial Highld. 299 B7
Michaelchurch
 Hereford. 97 F10
Michaelchurch Escley
 Hereford. 96 E6
Michaelchurch on Arrow
 Powys. 114 G4
Michaelston-le-Pit
 V Glam. 59 E7
Michaelstow Corn 11 F7
Michaelston-super-Ely
 Cardiff. 58 D6
Michelcombe Devon . . . 8 B3
Micheldever Hants 48 F4
Michelmersh Hants . . . 32 B4
Mickfield Suff. 126 E2
Micklebring S Yorks . . . 187 C8
Mickleby N Yorks. 226 C6
Micklefield Bucks 84 G5
Micklefield Green Herts . 85 F8
Micklehurst Gtr Man . . 196 G3
Mickleover Derbys 152 C6
Micklethwaite Cumb. . . 239 G7
 W Yorks 205 E8
Mickleton Durham 232 G5
 Glos. 100 C3
Mickletown W Yorks . . . 197 B11
Mickle Trafford Ches W. 166 B6
 N Yorks. 186 F4
 N Yorks. 214 D5
 Shrops 150 C2
Mickley Green Suff. . . . 124 F6
Mickley Square
 Northumb 242 E3
Midanbury Hants 33 E7
Mid Ardlaw Aberds . . . 303 C9
Mid Auchinleck Inyclyd . 276 G6
Midbea Orkney. 314 B4
Mid Beltie Aberds 293 C8
Mid Calder W Loth 269 B11
 Glos. 80 C3
Mickletown N Yorks . . . 197 B11
Middleton Tyas N Yorks 224 D4
Middletown Cumb 219 D9
 N Som 60 E3
 Powys 148 G6
 Warks 117 F11
Middle Town Scilly 1 F4
Middle Tysoe Warks . . . 100 C6
Middle Wallop Hants. . . 47 F9
Middle Weald M Keynes . 102 D5
Middlewich Ches E. . . . 167 B11
Middle Wick Glos. 80 F2
Middle Winterslow Wilts 47 G8
Middlewood Ches E . . . 184 E6
 Corn 11 F11
 S Yorks 186 C4
Middle Woodford Wilts . 46 F6
Middlewood Green
 Suff. 125 E11
 Hants 64 G4
 S Yorks 197 G11
 Worcs 99 E8
Middridge Durham. . . . 233 F11
Midelney Som 28 C6
Midfield Highld 308 C5
Midford Bath 61 G9
Midge Hall Lancs 194 C4
Midgeholme Cumb. . . . 240 F4
Midgham W Berks 64 F5
Midgley W Yorks 196 B4
 W Yorks 197 E9
Mid Holmwood Sur . . . 51 D7
Midhopestones S Yorks . 186 C3
Midhurst W Sus 34 C5
Mid Lambrook Som . . . 28 D6
Midland Orkney 314 F3
Mid Lavant W Sus 22 B5
Midlem Borders 262 D2
Midlock S Lnrk 259 E11
Mid Main Highld 300 F4
Mid Mains Highld 300 F4
Midmar Aberds 293 C8
Mid Murthat Dumfries. . 248 D3
Midpark Argyll 255 F11
Midplaugh Aberds 302 F5
Midsomer Norton
 Bath 45 C7
Midtown Highld 307 L3
 Highld 308 C5
Midtown of Buchromb
 Moray 302 E3
Midtown of Glass
 Aberds 302 E4
Mid Urchany Highld. . . 301 E8
Mid Walls Shetland. . . . 313 H4
Midway Ches E 184 E6
 S Yorks 153 C7
Mid Yell Shetland. 312 D7
Miekle Toux Aberds . . . 302 D5
Migdale Highld. 309 K6
Migvie Aberds 292 C6
Milarrochy Stirl 277 C8
Milber Devon 14 G3
Milborne Port Som 29 D11
Milborne St Andrew
 Dorset. 18 B2
Milborne Wick Som. . . . 29 C11
Milbourne Northumb . . 242 B4
 Wilts. 62 B2
Milburn Aberds 302 E5
 Aberds 302 F6
 Cumb 231 F9
Milbury Heath S Glos. . 79 G11
Milcombe Oxon 101 E8
Milden Suff. 107 B9
Mildenhall Suff. 124 C4
 Wilts. 63 F7
Mile Brook Powys 114 C6
Mileham Norf 159 F7
Mile End Cambs. 140 G2
 Essex. 107 F9
 Glos. 79 C9
 London 67 C11
 Suff. 124 G6
 Devon 19 D8
Mile Oak Brighton. 36 F2
 Kent. 53 E7
 Shrops. 148 D6
 Staffs. 134 C3
Miles Green Staffs 168 F4
 Kent. 50 B4
Miles Hill W Yorks 205 F11
Milesmark Fife 279 D11
Miles Platting Gtr Man . 184 B5

 N Yorks. 205 D8
 N Yorks. 216 B5
 Perth 286 C5
 Perth 286 C5
 Shrops. 115 B10
 Shrops. 130 D5
 Shrops. 148 D6
 Suff. 127 D8
 Sur 50 E2
 Wilts. 31 B11
 W Isles 197 B10
Middleton Baggot
 Shrops 132 E2
Middleton Cheney
 Northants. 101 C9
Middleton Green Staffs. 151 B9
Middleton Hall
 Northumb 263 D11
Middleton-in-Teesdale
 Durham 232 F4
Middleton Junction
 Gtr Man 195 G11
Middleton Moor Norf . . 127 D8
Middleton of Rora
 Aberds 303 E10
Middleton One Row
 Darl. 225 C7
Middleton-on-Leven
 N Yorks 225 D9
Middleton-on-Sea
 W Sus 35 G7
Middleton on the Hill
 Hereford. 115 E10
Middleton-on-the-Wolds
 E Yorks 208 D4
Middleton Place Shrops 132 E2
Middleton Priors Shrops 132 E2
Middleton Quernhow
 N Yorks 214 D6
Middleton St George
 Darl. 224 C6
Middleton Scriven
 Shrops 132 F3
Middleton Stoney
 Oxon 101 G10
Middleton Tyas N Yorks 224 D4
Middletown Cumb 219 D9
 N Som 60 E3
 Powys 148 G6
 Warks 117 F11
Middle Town Scilly 1 F4
Middle Tysoe Warks . . . 100 C6
Middle Wallop Hants. . . 47 F9
Middle Weald M Keynes . 102 D5
Middlewich Ches E. . . . 167 B11
Middle Wick Glos. 80 F2
Middle Winterslow Wilts 47 G8
Middlewood Ches E . . . 184 E6
 Corn 11 F11
 S Yorks 186 C4
Middle Woodford Wilts . 46 F6
Middlewood Green
 Suff. 125 E11
Middleyard Glos. 80 E4
Middlezoy Som 43 G11
Middridge Durham 233 F11
Midelney Som 28 C6
Midfield Highld 308 C5
Midford Bath 61 G9
Midgard Borders 262 F3
Mid Garrary Dumfries . 237 B7
Midge Hall Lancs 194 C4
Midgeholme Cumb. . . . 240 F4
Midgham W Berks 64 F5
Midgley W Yorks 196 B4
 W Yorks 197 E9
Midhopestones S Yorks . 186 C3
Midhurst W Sus 34 C5
 E Sus 23 D10
 Glos. 80 B3
 Gtr Man 195 F8
 Kent. 55 C11
 Lincs 175 B8
 London 86 G2
 Suff. 125 C7
Mill Bank W Yorks 196 C4
 Highld 310 C5
 Kent. 71 F8
Millbank Aberds 303 E11
 Highld 310 C5
 Kent. 71 F8
Millbeck Cumb. 229 F11
Millbounds Orkney. . . . 314 C5
Millbreck Aberds 303 E10
Millbridge Sur 49 E10
Millbrook C Beds. 103 D10
 Corn. 7 E8
 Cambs 123 E9
 Cumb 211 C10
 Derbys 185 C7
 Devon 8 F6
 Soton. 32 E5
 Dumfries 236 D4
 Fife 287 G7
 Highld 299 E7
 N Som 59 G10
 Oxon 101 E8
 Pembs 73 E8
 Perth 286 F3
 Ptsmth 21 B9
 Stirl 285 G9
 S Yorks 197 G11
 W Dunb 277 G8
 Wilts. 45 G11
Mill Corner E Sus 38 C4
Milldale Staffs 169 E10
Mill Dam N Yorks 212 F3
Millden Lodge Angus . . 293 F7
Milldens Angus 287 B9
Millend Glos. 80 D3
 Glos. 80 F3
Mill End Bucks 65 C9
 Cambs 124 F3
 Glos. 81 C10
 Herts 85 G8
 Herts 104 E6
Mill End Green Essex . . 106 F2
Millendreath Corn 6 E5
Millerhill Midloth 270 B6
Miller's Dale Derbys . . 185 G10
Miller's Green Derbys. . 170 E3
 Essex. 87 D9
Millersneuk E Dunb . . . 278 G3
Millerston Glasgow . . . 268 B2
 S Yorks 197 G11
Mill Farm Aberds 303 C8
Millfield Pboro 138 C3
 T&W 243 F9
Millgate Lancs 195 D11
 Norf. 160 D3
Millgillhead Cumb 229 G2
Mill Green Cambs 106 B2
 Hants 64 G4
 Norf 142 G2
 Shrops 150 D3
 Suff. 107 C9
 Suff. 125 F9
 W Mid 133 C11
Millhalf Hereford. 96 B5
Millhall Kent. 53 B8
Mill Hall N Lnrk 237 E8
Mill Hayes Devon 27 E10
Mill Hill Blkburn. 195 B7
 Essex. 106 B2
 E Sus 23 D10
 Glos. 80 C2
 Kent. 55 C11
 London 86 G2
 Suff. 108 B5
Mill Hills Suff. 108 B5
Mill Hirst N Yorks 214 G3
Millholme Cumb. 221 G11
Millhill Devon 12 G5
Millhouse Argyll 275 F10
 Cumb 230 D3
Millhousebridge
 Dumfries. 248 F4
Millhouse Green
 S Yorks 197 G8
Millhouses S Yorks . . . 186 E4
 S Yorks 198 G2
Millikenpark Renfs . . . 267 C8
Millin Cross Pembs . . . 73 C7
Millington E Yorks. 208 C2
Millington Green Derbys 170 F3
Mill Lane Hants. 49 C9
Mill Meads London . . . 67 C11
Millmeece Staffs 150 C6
Millmoor Devon 27 E10
Millness Cumb 211 C10
Mill of Brydock Aberds . 302 D6
Mill of Chon Stirl. 285 G8
Mill of Haldane W Dunb . 277 E8
Mill of Kingoodie
 Aberds 303 G8
Mill of Lynebain Aberds . 302 F4
Mill of Muiresk Aberds . 302 E6
Mill of Rango Orkney . . 314 E2
Mill of Sterin Aberds . . 292 D5
Mill of Uras Aberds . . . 293 E10
Millom Cumb 210 C3
Millook Corn 11 B9
Millow C Beds. 104 C4
Mill Park Argyll 255 G8
Mill Place N Lincs 200 F3
Millpool Corn 11 G8
 Corn 2 C6
Millport N Ayrs 266 E3
Millquarter Dumfries. . 246 G4
Mill Shaw W Yorks 205 G11
Mill Side Cumb 211 C8
Mill Street Kent. 53 B7
 Norf 159 F11
 Suff. 107 D9
Milltack Aberds 303 D7
Millthorpe Derbys 186 F4
 Lincs 156 C2
Mill Throop Bmouth . . . 19 B8
Millthorpe Cumb. 222 G3
Milltimber Aberdeen . . 293 C10
Milltown Aberds 292 C4
 Corn. 6 C2
 Corn. 6 E2
 Derbys 170 C5
 Devon 40 F5
 Highld 301 D8
 Milltown of Aberdalgie
 Perth 286 E4
Milltown of Auchindoun
 Moray 302 E3
Milltown of Craigston
 Aberds 303 D7

Miles's Green W Berks . . 64 E3
Mile Town Kent 70 E2
Milfield Northumb 263 C10
Milford Derbys. 170 F5
 Devon 24 C2
 Powys 129 C11
 Shrops 149 E8
 Staffs 151 E9
 Sur 50 E2
 Wilts 31 B11
Milford Haven Pembs . . 72 D6
Milford on Sea Hants . . 19 C11
Milkhouse Water Wilts . 63 G7
Milkieston Borders . . . 270 F4
Milkwall Glos. 79 D9
Milkwell Wilts 30 C6
Milland W Sus 34 B4
Millarston Renfs 267 C9
Millbank Aberds 303 E11
 Highld 310 C5
 Kent. 71 F8
Mill Bank W Yorks 196 C4
Millbeck Cumb. 229 F11
Millbounds Orkney. . . . 314 C5
Millbreck Aberds 303 E10
Millbridge Sur 49 E10
Millbrook C Beds. 103 D10
 Corn. 7 E8
 Cumb 211 C10
 Derbys 185 C7
 Devon 8 F6
 Soton. 32 E5
Mill Brow Gtr Man 185 D7
Millburn S Ayrs. 257 D10
Millcombe Devon 8 F6
Mill Common Norf 142 C6
 Suff. 143 G8
Mill Corner E Sus 38 C4
Milldale Staffs 169 E10
Mill Dam N Yorks 212 F3
Millden Lodge Angus . . 293 F7
Milldens Angus 287 B9
Millend Glos. 80 D3
 Glos. 80 F3
Mill End Bucks 65 C9
 Cambs 124 F3
 Glos. 81 C10
 Herts 85 G8
 Herts 104 E6
Mill End Green Essex . . 106 F2
Millendreath Corn 6 E5
Millerhill Midloth 270 B6
Miller's Dale Derbys . . 185 G10
Miller's Green Derbys. . 170 E3
 Essex. 87 D9
Millersneuk E Dunb . . . 278 G3
Millerston Glasgow . . . 268 B2
 S Yorks 197 G11
Mill Farm Aberds 303 C8
Millfield Pboro 138 C3
 T&W 243 F9
Millgate Lancs 195 D11
 Norf. 160 D3
Millgillhead Cumb 229 G2
Mill Green Cambs 106 B2
 Hants 64 G4
 Norf 142 G2
 Shrops 150 D3
 Suff. 107 C9
 Suff. 125 F9
 W Mid 133 C11
Millhall Kent. 53 B8
Mill Hall N Lnrk 237 E8
Mill Hayes Devon 27 E10
Mill Hill Blkburn. 195 B7
 Essex. 106 B2
 E Sus 23 D10
 Glos. 80 C2
 Kent. 55 C11
 London 86 G2
 Suff. 108 B5
Mill Hills Suff. 108 B5
Mill Hirst N Yorks 214 G3
Millholme Cumb. 221 G11
Millhill Devon 12 G5
Millhouse Argyll 275 F10
 Cumb 230 D3
Millhousebridge
 Dumfries. 248 F4
Millhouse Green
 S Yorks 197 G8
Millhouses S Yorks . . . 186 E4
 S Yorks 198 G2
Millikenpark Renfs . . . 267 C8
Millin Cross Pembs . . . 73 C7
Millington E Yorks. 208 C2
Millington Green Derbys 170 F3
Mill Lane Hants. 49 C9
Mill Meads London . . . 67 C11
Millmeece Staffs 150 C6
Millmoor Devon 27 E10
Millness Cumb 211 C10
Mill of Brydock Aberds . 302 D6
Mill of Chon Stirl. 285 G8
Mill of Haldane W Dunb . 277 E8
Mill of Kingoodie
 Aberds 303 G8
Mill of Lynebain Aberds . 302 F4
Mill of Muiresk Aberds . 302 E6
Mill of Rango Orkney . . 314 E2
Mill of Sterin Aberds . . 292 D5
Mill of Uras Aberds . . . 293 E10
Millom Cumb 210 C3
Millook Corn 11 B9
Millow C Beds. 104 C4
Mill Park Argyll 255 G8
Mill Place N Lincs 200 F3
Millpool Corn 11 G8
 Corn 2 C6
Millport N Ayrs 266 E3
Millquarter Dumfries. . 246 G4
Mill Shaw W Yorks 205 G11
Mill Side Cumb 211 C8
Mill Street Kent. 53 B7
 Norf 159 F11
 Suff. 107 D9
Milltack Aberds 303 D7
Millthorpe Derbys 186 F4
 Lincs 156 C2
Mill Throop Bmouth . . . 19 B8
Millthorpe Cumb. 222 G3
Milltimber Aberdeen . . 293 C10
Milltown Aberds 292 C4
Milltown of Aberdalgie
 Perth 286 E4
Milltown of Auchindoun
 Moray 302 E3
Milltown of Craigston
 Aberds 303 D7

Milltown of Edinvillie
 Moray 302 E2
Milltown of Kildrummy
 Aberds 292 B6
Milltown of Rothiemay
 Moray 302 E5
Milltown of Towie
 Aberds 292 B6
Millwall London 67 D11
Milnacraig Angus. 286 B5
Milnathort Perth. 286 G5
Milner's Heath Ches W . 167 C7
Milngavie E Dunb. 277 G11
Milnquarter Falk 278 F6
Milnrow Gtr Man 196 E2
Milnsbridge W Yorks . . 196 D6
Milnshaw Lancs 195 B9
Milnthorpe Cumb 211 C9
 W Yorks 197 D10
Milo Carms 75 B9
Milson Shrops 116 C2
Milstead Kent 54 B2
Milston Wilts 47 D7
Milton Angus 287 C7
 Angus 292 G6
 Cambs 123 E9
 Cumb 211 C10
 Cumb 240 E3
 Derbys 152 D6
 Dumfries 236 D4
 Dumfries 237 B10
 Dumfries 247 G8
 Fife 287 F7
 Highld 299 E7
 Highld 300 C5
 Highld 300 D5
 Highld 300 E4
 Highld 301 B7
 Highld 301 E7
 Highld 310 D7
 Kent. 69 E7
 Moray 292 B2
 Moray 302 C5
 N Som 59 G10
 Oxon 83 G7
 Oxon 101 D8
 Pembs 73 D8
 Perth 286 F3
 Ptsmth 21 B9
 Som 29 F7
 Stirl 285 G9
 Stoke 168 F6
 S Yorks 197 G11
 W Dunb 277 G8
 Wilts. 45 G11
Milton Abbas Dorset . . 30 G4
Milton Bridge Midloth. . 270 C4
Milton Bryan C Beds. . . 103 E9
Milton Clevedon Som . . 45 F7
Milton Coldwells Aberds 303 F9
Milton Combe Devon . . . 7 B9
Milton Common Oxon . . 83 E11
Milton Coombe Devon . . 7 C10
Milton Damerel Devon . 24 E5
Miltonduff Moray 301 C11
Milton End Glos. 80 C2
 Glos. 81 E10
Milton Ernest Beds . . . 121 F10
Milton Green Ches W . . 167 D7
 Devon 12 F4
 Medway. 69 E8
Milton Heights Oxon . . 83 G7
Miltonhill Moray 301 C10
Milton Hill Devon 14 F4
 Oxon 83 G7
Miltonise Dumfries . . . 236 B3
Milton Keynes
 M Keynes 103 D7
Milton Keynes Village
 M Keynes 103 D7
Milton Lilbourne Wilts . 63 G7
Milton Malsor Northants 120 F4
Milton Morenish Perth. 285 D10
Milton of Auchinhove
 Aberds 293 C7
Milton of Balgonie Fife . 287 G7
Milton of Buchanan
 Stirl 277 C8
Milton of Campfield
 Aberds 293 C8
Milton of Campsie
 E Dunb 278 F3
Milton of Corsindae
 Aberds 293 C8
Milton of Cullerlie
 Aberds 293 C9
Milton of Cushnie
 Aberds 293 B7
Milton of Dalcapon
 Perth 286 B3
Milton of Drimmie
 Perth 286 B5
Milton of Edradour
 Perth 286 B3
Milton of Gollanfield
 Highld 301 D7
Milton of Lesmore
 Aberds 302 G4
Milton of Logie Aberds . 292 C6
Milton of Machany
 Perth 286 F2
Milton of Mathers
 Aberds 293 G9
Milton of Murtle
 Aberdeen 293 C10
Milton of Noth Aberds . 302 G5
Milton of Tullich Aberds . 292 D5
Milton on Stour Dorset. . 30 B3
Milton Regis Kent 70 F2
Milton Street E Sus 23 E8
Milton under Wychwood
 Oxon 82 B3
Milverstone Staffs 169 F9
Milverton Som 27 B10
 Warks 118 D6
Milwich Staffs 151 C9
Milwr Flint 181 G11
Mimbridge Sur 66 G3
Minard Argyll 275 D10
Minard Castle Argyll . . 275 D10
Minchington Dorset . . . 31 E7
Minchinhampton Glos. . 80 E5
Mincing Lane Bath 44 E2
Mindrum Northumb . . . 263 D8
Minehead Som 42 D3
Minera Wrex 166 E3
Minety Wilts 81 G8
Mingarrypark Highld. . . 289 C8
Mingearraidh W Isles . . 297 J3
Miningsby Lincs 174 C4
Minions Corn 11 G11
Minishant S Ayrs 257 F8
Minllyn Gwyn 147 G2
Minnes Aberds 303 G9

Minngearraidh W Isles . 297 J3
Minnigaff Dumfries . . . 236 C6
Minnonie Aberds 303 C7
Minnow End Essex 88 C2
Minnygap Dumfries . . . 248 D2
Minshull Vernon
 Ches E. 167 C11
Minskip N Yorks 215 G7
Minstead Hants 32 E3
Minsted W Sus 34 C5
Minster Kent 70 E3
 Kent 71 G10
Minsterley Shrops 131 C7
Minster Lovell Oxon . . 82 C4
Minsterworth Glos. . . . 80 B3
Minterne Magna Dorset. 29 G11
Minterne Parva Dorset . 29 G11
Minting Lincs 189 G11
Mintlaw Aberds 303 E10
Mintlaw Aberds 303 E10
Minto Borders 262 E3
Minto Kames Borders . . 262 E3
Mintsfeet Cumb 221 G10
Minwear Pembs. 73 C8
Minworth W Mid 134 E3
Mirbister Orkney. 314 E2
Mirehouse Cumb 219 B9
Mireland Highld 310 C7
Mirfield W Yorks 197 D8
Miserden Glos. 80 D6
Misery Corner Norf . . . 142 F5
Miskin Rhondda 58 C4
 Rhondda 77 F8
Misselfore Wilts 31 C8
Misson Notts 187 C11
Misterton Leics 135 G11
 Notts 188 C2
 Som 29 F7
Misterton Soss Notts . . 188 C2
Mistley Essex. 108 E3
Mistley Heath Essex . . . 108 E3
Mitcham London. 67 F9
Mitcheldean Glos. 79 B11
Mitchell Corn. 5 E7
Mitchellslacks
 Dumfries. 247 D11
Mitchelston Borders . . 271 F9
Mitchel Troy Mon. 79 C7
Mitcheltroy Common
 Mon. 79 D7
Mite Houses Cumb . . . 219 F11
Mitford Northumb 252 F5
Mithian Corn. 4 E4
Mithian Downs Corn . . . 4 F4
Mitton Staffs 151 F7
 Worcs 99 E8
Mixbury Oxon. 102 E2
Mixenden W Yorks 196 B5
Mixtow Corn 6 E2
Moat Cumb 239 C10
Moats Tye Suff. 125 F10
Mobberley Ches E. 184 F3
 Staffs 169 G8
Moblake Ches E 167 G11
Mobwell Bucks 84 E5
Moccas Hereford 97 C7
Mochdre Conwy 180 F4
 Powys 129 F11
Mochrum Dumfries . . . 236 E5
Mockbeggar Hants 31 F11
 Kent. 54 E6
 Medway. 69 E8
Mockerkin Cumb. 229 G7
Moclett Orkney 314 B4
Modbury Devon 8 E3
Moddershall Staffs 151 B8
Model Village Derbys . . 187 G8
 Warks 119 E8
Modest Corner Kent . . . 52 E5
Moelfre Anglesey 179 D8
 Conwy 181 G7
 Powys 148 D3
Moel Tryfan Gwyn 163 D8
Moel-y-crio Flint 165 B11
Moffat Dumfries 248 B3
Moffat Mills N Lnrk . . . 268 C5
Mogador Sur 51 C8
Moggerhanger C Beds . 104 B2
Mogworthy Devon 26 D5
Moira Leics 152 F6
Moity Powys 96 C3
Molash Kent 54 C5
Mol-chlach Highld 294 D6
Mold Flint 166 C2
Moldgreen W Yorks . . . 197 D7
Molehill Green Essex . . 105 G11
 Essex. 106 G4
Molescroft E Yorks 208 E6
Molesden Northumb. . . 252 G4
Molesworth Cambs . . . 121 B11
Molinnis Corn 5 D10
Moll Highld 295 B7
Molland Devon 26 B4
 Ches W 182 G5
 Oxon 101 B8
 S Yorks 198 G4
 W Yorks 207 F7
Monachty Ceredig 111 E10
Monachylemore Stirl . . 285 F8
Monar Lodge Highld . . 300 D2
Monaughty Powys 114 D4
Monboddo House
 Aberds 293 F9
Mondaytown Shrops . . 130 B6
Monemore Stirl 285 G9
Monevechadan Argyll. . 284 G5
Moneydie Perth 286 E4
Moneyacres E Ayrs . . . 267 E8
Moneyhill Herts 85 G8
Money Hill Leics 153 F7
Moneyrow Green
 Windsor 65 D11
Mongleath Corn 3 C7
Moniaive Dumfries . . . 247 E7
Monifieth Angus. 287 D8
Monikie Angus. 287 D8
Monimail Fife 286 F6
Monington Pembs 92 C2
Monk Bretton S Yorks . 197 F11
Monk End N Yorks 224 D5
Monken Hadley London . 86 F3
Monkerton Devon 14 C4
Monk Fryston N Yorks . 198 B4
Monk Hesleden Durham . 234 D5
Monkhide Hereford . . . 98 C2
Monkhill Cumb 239 F8
 Worcs 98 C3
Monkhopton Shrops . . 132 E2
Monkland Hereford . . . 115 F9
Monkleigh Devon 25 C7
Monknash V Glam 58 E2
Monkokehampton Devon 25 F9
Monkscross Corn 12 G3
Monkseaton T&W 243 C8
Monks Eleigh Suff. . . . 107 B9
Monk's Gate W Sus . . . 36 B2
Monks Heath Ches E . . 184 G4

Monk Sherborne Hants . 48 B6
Monkshill Aberds 303 E7
Monks Hill Kent. 53 E11
Monks Kirby Warks . . . 135 G9
Monk Soham Suff 126 D4
Monks Orchard London . 67 F11
Monk's Park Wilts 61 F11
Monkspath W Mid. 118 B2
Monks Risborough Bucks. 84 E4
Monksthorpe Lincs . . . 174 B6
Mon 78 A4
 W Yorks 206 F2
Monkston Park
 M Keynes. 103 D7
Monk Street Essex 106 F2
Monkswood Midloth . . 270 C6
 Mon 78 E5
Monkton Devon 27 G11
 Kent 71 G9
 Pembs 73 E7
 S Ayrs 257 D9
 T&W 243 E8
 V Glam 58 E2
Monkton Combe Bath . . 61 G9
Monkton Deverill Wilts . 45 F11
Monkton Farleigh Wilts . 61 F10
Monktonhall E Loth. . . 280 G6
Monkton Heathfield Som. 28 B3
Monkton Up Wimborne
 Dorset. 31 E8
Monkwearmouth T&W . 243 F9
Monkwood Hants 49 G7
Monkwood Green
 Worcs 116 E6
Monmarsh Hereford. . . 97 B10
Monmore Green W Mid . 133 D8
Monmouth Cap Mon . . 97 F7
Monmouth / Trefynwy
 Mon 79 C8
Monnington on Wye
 Hereford. 97 C7
Monreith Dumfries . . . 236 E5
Monreith Mains
 Dumfries. 236 E5
Montacute Som 29 D7
Montcliffe Gtr Man 195 E7
Montcoffer Ho Aberds . 302 C6
Montford Argyll 266 C2
 Shrops. 149 G8
Montford Bridge Shrops 149 F8
Montgarrie Aberds 293 B7
Montgomery Powys . . . 130 D4
Montgomery Lines
 Hants 49 C11
Monton Gtr Man. 184 B3
Montpelier Bristol 60 E5
Montrave Fife 287 G7
Montrose Angus 287 B11
Montsale Essex. 89 F7
Monwode Lea Warks . . 134 E5
Monxton Hants 47 E10
Monyash Derbys 169 C11
Monynusk Aberds 293 B8
Monzie Perth 286 E2
Monzie Castle Perth . . 286 E2
Moodiesburn N Lnrk . . 278 G3
Moolham Som 28 E5
Moon's Green Kent 38 B5
Moon's Moat Worcs. . . . 117 D11
Moonzie Fife 287 F7
Moor Som 28 D6
Mooradale Shetland. . . 312 F6
Moor Allerton W Yorks . 205 F11
Mooray Wilts 46 G3
Moorby Lincs 174 C3
Moorclose Cumb 228 F5
Moor Common Bucks. . 84 G4
Moorcot Hereford 115 F7
Moor Crichel Dorset . . . 31 F7
Moor Cross Devon 8 D2
Moordown Bmouth. . . . 19 C7
Moore Halton 183 E9
Moor Edge W Yorks . . . 205 F7
Moorend Glos. 239 G8
 Derbys. 170 F2
 Dumfries 239 C7
 Glos. 80 C5
 Glos. 80 E2
 Lancs 202 B3
 N Yorks 207 F7
 S Glos. 61 C7
Moor End Cambs. 105 B7
 C Beds 103 G9
 Durham 234 C2
 E Yorks 208 F2
 Glos. 99 G9
 Lancs 202 E3
 N Yorks 207 D7
 S Yorks 197 G11
 W Yorks 196 D4
 W Yorks 205 D8
Moored Cross Hereford . 98 H4
Moor End Field N Yorks . 215 F8
Moorends S Yorks 199 D7
Moorfield Derbys 185 C8
Moorgate Norf 160 C3
 S Yorks 186 C6
Moorgreen Hants. 33 D7
 Notts 171 F7
Moor Green Herts 104 F6
 Staffs 169 G7
 Wilts. 61 F11
 W Mid 133 G11
Moorhaigh Notts 171 C8
Moorhall Derbys 186 G4
Moor Hall W Mid 134 D2
Moorhampton Hereford . 97 B7
Moorhaven Village Devon. 8 D3
Moorhayne Devon 28 F3
Moorhead W Yorks 205 F9
Moor Head W Yorks . . . 197 B8
 W Yorks 197 B8
Moorhey Gtr Man. 196 G2
Moorhole S Yorks 186 E6
Moorhouse Cumb 239 F8
 Cumb 239 G9
 Notts 172 B3
 S Yorks 198 E3
Moorhouse Bank Sur . . 52 C2
Moorhouses Lincs. 174 D3
Moorland or Northmoor
 Green Som 43 G10
Moor Monkton N Yorks . 206 B6
Moor Monkton Moor
 N Yorks 206 B6
Moor of Balvack
 Aberds 293 B8
Moor of Granary
 Moray 301 D10
Moor of Ravenstone
 Dumfries. 236 E5
Moor Park Cumb 229 D7
 Hereford 97 C9

Moor Park continued
Herts 85 G9
Sur 49 D11
Moor Row Cumb 219 C10
Cumb 229 B10
Moorsholm Redcar 226 C3
Moorside Ches W 182 F3
Dorset 30 D3
Durham 233 B7
Gtr Man 195 G9
Gtr Man 196 F3
W Yorks 197 B8
W Yorks 205 F10
Moor Side Lancs 202 F5
Lancs 202 G4
Lincs 174 D2
W Yorks 197 B7
W Yorks 204 F6
Moorstock Kent 54 F6
Moor Street Kent 69 F10
Moorswater Corn 6 C4
Moorthorpe W Yorks 198 E3
Moor Top W Yorks 197 C7
Moortown Devon 12 B2
Devon 12 G6
Devon 25 C8
Hants 31 G11
IoW 20 E4
Lincs 189 B9
Telford 150 F2
W Yorks 206 F2
Morangie Highld 309 L7
Morar Highld 295 F8
Moravian Settlement
Derbys 153 B8
Morawelon Anglesey 178 E3
Morayhill Highld 301 E7
Morborne Cambs 138 E2
Morchard Bishop Devon 26 F3
Morchard Road Devon 26 G3
Morcombelake Dorset 16 C4
Morcott Rutland 137 C8
Morda Shrops 148 D5
Morden Dorset 18 B4
London 67 F9
Morden Green Cambs 104 C5
Morden Park London 67 F8
Mordiford Hereford 97 D11
Mordington Holdings
Borders 273 D8
Mordon Durham 234 F2
More Shrops 130 E6
Morebath Devon 27 C7
Morebattle Borders 263 E7
Morecambe Lancs 211 G8
More Crichel Dorset 31 F7
Moredon Swindon 62 B6
Moredun Edin 270 B5
Morefield Highld 307 K6
Morehall Kent 55 F8
Moreleggan Argyll 284 G6
Moreleigh Devon 8 E5
Morenish Perth 285 D9
Moresby Cumb 228 G5
Moresby Parks Cumb 219 B9
Morestead Hants 33 B8
Moreton Dorset 18 D2
Essex 87 D8
Hereford 115 E10
Mers 182 C3
Oxon 82 E6
Oxon 83 E11
Staffs 150 F5
Staffs 152 D2
Moreton Corbet
Shrops 149 E11
Moretonhampstead
Devon 13 D11
Moreton-in-Marsh Glos 100 E4
Moreton Jeffries
Hereford 98 B2
Moreton Morrell Warks 118 F6
Moreton on Lugg
Hereford 97 B10
Moreton Paddox Warks 118 G6
Moreton Pinkney
Northants 101 B11
Moreton Say Shrops 150 C2
Moreton Valence Glos 80 D3
Moretonwood Shrops 150 C2
Morfa Carms 56 B4
Carms 75 C9
Ceredig 110 G6
Gwyn 144 C3
Morfa Bach Carms 74 C5
Morfa Bychan Gwyn 145 B10
Morfa Dinlle Gwyn 162 D6
Morfa Glas Neath 76 D5
Morfa Nefyn Gwyn 162 G3
Morfydd Denb 165 F10
Morganstown Cardiff 58 C6
Morgan's Vale Wilts 31 C11
Moriah Ceredig 112 B2
Mork Glos 79 D9
Morland Cumb 231 G7
Morley Ches E 184 E4
Derbys 170 G5
Durham 233 F8
W Yorks 197 B9
Morley Green Ches E 184 E4
Morleymoor Derbys 170 G5
Morley Park Derbys 170 F5
Morley St Botolph
Norf 141 D11
Morley Smithy Derbys 170 G5
Mornick Corn 12 G2
Morningside Edin 280 G3
N Lnrk 268 D6
Morningthorpe Norf 142 E4
Morpeth Northumb 252 F6
Morphie Aberds 293 G9
Morrey Staffs 152 F2
Morridge Side Staffs 169 E8
Morrilow Heath Staffs 151 B9
Morris Green Essex 106 E4
Morriston / Treforys
Swansea 57 B7
Morristown V Glam 59 E7
Morston Norf 177 E8
Mortehoe Devon 40 D3
Morthen S Yorks 187 D7
Mortimer W Berks 65 G7
Mortimer's Cross
Hereford 115 E8
Mortimer West End
Hants 64 G6
Mortlake London 67 D8
Mortomley S Yorks 186 B4
Morton Cumb 230 D4
Cumb 239 G9
Derbys 170 C6
IoW 21 D8
Lincs 155 E11
Lincs 172 C5
Lincs 188 C4
Norf 160 F2
Notts 172 E2
S Glos 79 G10
Shrops 148 E5
Morton Bagot Warks 118 E2
Morton Common Shrops 148 E5
Morton Mains Dumfries 247 D9
Morton Mill Shrops 149 E11
Morton-on-Swale
N Yorks 224 G6
Morton Spirt Warks 117 G10
Morton Tinmouth
Durham 233 G9
Morton Underhill
Worcs 117 F10
Morvah Corn 1 B4
Morval Corn 6 D5
Morven Lodge Aberds 292 C5
Morvich Highld 295 C11
Highld 309 J7
Morville Shrops 132 E3
Morville Heath Shrops 132 E3
Morwellham Quay Devon 7 B8
Morwenstow Corn 24 E2
Mosborough S Yorks 186 E6
Moscow E Ayrs 267 G9
Mose Shrops 132 E5
Mosedale Cumb 230 E3
Moseley W Mid 133 D8
W Mid 133 G11
Worcs 116 F6
Moses Gate Gtr Man 195 F8
Mosley Common
Gtr Man 195 G8
Moss Argyll 288 E1
Highld 289 C8
S Yorks 198 E5
Wrex 166 E4
Mossat Aberds 292 B6
Mossbank Shetland 312 F6
Moss Bank Halton 183 C8
Mers 183 B8
Mossbay Cumb 228 F5
Mossblown S Ayrs 257 E10
Mossbrow Gtr Man 184 D2
Mossburnford Borders 262 F5
Mossdale Dumfries 237 B8
Mossedge Cumb 239 D11
Moss Edge Lancs 202 D4
Lancs 202 E4
Mossend N Lnrk 268 C4
Moss End Brack 65 E11
Ches E 183 F11
Mosser Mains Cumb 229 F8
Mossfield Highld 300 B6
Mossgate Staffs 151 B8
Mossgiel E Ayrs 257 D11
Mosshouses Borders 262 B2
Moss Houses Ches E 184 G5
Mosside Angus 287 B8
Moss Lane Ches E 184 G6
Mossley Ches E 168 C5
Gtr Man 196 G3
Mossley Brow Gtr Man 196 G3
Mossley Hill Mers 182 D5
Moss Nook Gtr Man 184 D4
Mers 183 C8
Moss of Barmuckity
Moray 302 C2
Moss of Meft Moray 302 C2
Mosspark Glasgow 267 C10
Moss Pit Staffs 151 E8
Moss Side Cumb 238 G5
Gtr Man 184 B4
Moss-side Highld 301 D8
Moss Side Lancs 193 G11
Lancs 194 C4
Lancs 202 G3
Mers 182 B6
Moss-side Moray 302 D5
Mosstodloch Moray 302 D3
Mosston Angus 287 C9
Mosstown Aberds 303 C10
Mossy Lea Lancs 194 E4
Mosterton Dorset 29 F7
Moston Ches E 168 C2
Ches W 182 G6
Gtr Man 195 G11
Shrops 149 D11
Moston Green Ches E 168 C2
Mostyn Flint 181 E11
Mostyn Quay Flint 181 E11
Motcombe Dorset 30 B5
Mothecombe Devon 8 F2
Motherby Cumb 230 F4
Motherwell N Lnrk 268 D5
Motspur Park London 67 F8
Mottingham London 68 E2
Mottisfont Hants 32 B4
Mottistone IoW 20 E4
Mottram in Longdendale
Gtr Man 185 B7
Mottram Rise Gtr Man 185 B7
Mottram St Andrew
Ches E 184 F5
Mott's Green Essex 87 B8
Mott's Mill E Sus 52 F4
Mouldsworth Ches W 183 G8
Moulin Perth 286 B3
Moulsecoomb Brighton 36 F4
Moulsford Oxon 64 C5
Moulsham Essex 88 D2
Moulsoe M Keynes 103 C8
Moultavie Highld 300 B6
Moulton Ches W 167 B11
Lincs 156 E6
Northants 120 D5
N Yorks 224 E4
Suff 124 E3
V Glam 58 E5
Moulton Chapel Lincs 156 F5
Moulton Eaugate Lincs 156 F6
Moulton Park Northants 120 E5
Moulton St Mary Norf 143 B7
Moulton Seas End Lincs 156 D6
Moulzie Angus 292 F4
Mounie Castle Aberds 303 G7
Mount Corn 4 D5
Corn 6 B2
Highld 301 E9
W Yorks 196 D5
Mountain Anglesey 178 E2
W Yorks 205 G7
Mountain Air Bl Gwent 77 D11
Mountain Ash / Aberpennar
Rhondda 77 F8
Mountain Bower Wilts 61 D10
Mountain Cross Borders 270 F2
Mountain Street Kent 54 C5
Mountain Water Pembs 91 G8
Mount Ambrose Corn 4 G4
Mount Ballan Mon 60 B3
Mount Batten Plym 7 E9
Mountbenger Borders 261 D8
Mountbengerburn
Borders 261 D8
Mountblow W Dunb 277 G9
Mount Bures Essex 107 E8
Mount Canisp Highld 301 B7
Mount Charles Corn 5 B10
Corn 5 E10
Mount Cowdown Wilts 47 C9
Mount End Essex 87 E7
Mount Ephraim E Sus 23 B7
Mounters Dorset 30 D3
Mountfield E Sus 38 C2
Mountgerald Highld 300 C5
Mount Gould Plym 7 D9
Mount Hawke Corn 4 F4
Mount Hermon Corn 2 F6
Sur 50 B4
Mount Hill S Glos 61 E7
Mountjoy Corn 5 C7
Mount Lane Devon 12 B3
Mountnessing Essex 87 F10
Mounton Mon 79 G8
Mount Pleasant Bucks 102 E3
Ches E 168 D4
Corn 5 C10
Derbys 152 D6
Derbys 152 F5
Derbys 170 F4
Devon 27 G11
Durham 233 E11
E Sus 23 E7
E Sus 36 D6
Flint 182 G2
Hants 19 B11
Kent 71 F10
London 85 G8
M Tydf 77 F9
Neath 57 B9
Norf 141 E9
Pembs 73 D8
Shrops 149 G9
Stockton 234 G4
Stoke 168 G5
Suff 106 B4
T&W 243 E7
Warks 135 F7
Worcs 99 D10
Worcs 117 E10
W Yorks 197 C8
Mount Sion Wrex 166 E3
Mount Skippett Oxon 82 B5
Mountsolie Aberds 303 D9
Mountsorrel Leics 153 F11
Mount Sorrel Wilts 31 C8
Mount Tabor W Yorks 196 B5
Mount Vernon Glasgow 268 C3
Mount Wise Corn 7 E9
Mousehill Sur 50 E2
Mousehole Corn 1 D5
Mousen Northumb 264 C4
Mousley End Warks 118 D4
Mouswald Dumfries 238 C3
Mouth Mill Devon 24 B3
Mowbreck Lancs 202 G4
Mow Cop Ches E 168 D5
Mowden Darl 224 B5
Essex 88 C3
Mowhaugh Borders 263 E8
Mowmacre Hill
Leicester 135 B11
Mowshurst Kent 52 D3
Mowsley Leics 136 F2
Moxby N Yorks 215 F11
Moxley W Mid 133 D9
Moy Argyll 255 E8
Highld 290 E6
Highld 301 F7
Moy Hall Highld 301 F7
Moy Ho Moray 301 C10
Moyles Court Hants 31 F11
Moylgrove / Trewyddel
Pembs 92 C2
Moy Lodge Highld 290 E6
Muasdale Argyll 255 C7
Muchalls Aberds 293 D11
Much Birch Hereford 97 E10
Much Cowardne Hereford 98 B2
Much Cowarne Hereford 98 B2
Much Dewchurch
Hereford 97 E9
Muchelney Som 28 C6
Muchelney Ham Som 28 C6
Much Hadham Herts 86 B5
Much Hoole Lancs 194 C3
Much Hoole Moss Houses
Lancs 194 C3
Much Hoole Town
Lancs 194 C3
Muchlarnick Corn 6 D4
Much Marcle Hereford 98 E3
Muchrachd Highld 300 F2
Much Wenlock Shrops 132 C2
Muckairn Argyll 289 F11
Muckernich Highld 300 D5
Mucking Thurrock 69 C7
Muckle Breck Shetland 312 G7
Mucklebridge Dorset 17 C8
Mucklestone Staffs 150 B4
Muckleton Norf 158 B6
Shrops 149 E11
Muckletown Aberds 302 G5
Muckley Shrops 132 D2
Muckley Corner Staffs 133 B11
Muckley Cross Shrops 132 D2
Muckton Lincs 190 E5
Muckton Bottom Lincs 190 E5
Mudale Highld 308 F5
Mudd Gtr Man 185 C7
Muddiford Devon 40 F5
Muddlebridge Devon 40 G4
Muddles Green E Sus 23 C8
Mudeford Dorset 19 C9
Mudford Som 29 D9
Mudford Sock Som 29 D9
Mudgley Som 44 D2
Mugdock Stirl 277 F11
Mugeary Highld 294 B6
Mugginton Derbys 170 G3
Muggintonlane End
Derbys 170 G3
Muggleswick Durham 232 B6
Mugswell Sur 51 C9
Muie Highld 309 J6
Muir Aberds 292 E2
Muircleugh Borders 271 F10
Muirden Aberds 303 D7
Muirdrum Angus 287 D9
Muiredge Fife 281 B7
Muirend Glasgow 267 C11
Muirhead Angus 287 D7
Fife 286 G6
Fife 287 F8
N Lnrk 268 B3
S Ayrs 257 C8
Muirhouse Edin 280 F4
N Lnrk 268 D5
Muirhouselaw Borders 262 D4
Muirhouses Falk 279 E10
Muirkirk E Ayrs 258 D5
Muirmill Stirl 278 E4
Muir of Alford Aberds 293 B7
Muir of Fairburn Highld 300 D4
Muir of Fowlis Aberds 293 B7
Muir of Kinellar
Aberds 293 B10
Muir of Miltonduff
Moray 301 D11
Muir of Ord Highld 300 D5
Muir of Pert Angus 287 D8
Muirshearlich Highld 290 E3
Muirskie Aberds 293 D10
Muirtack Aberds 303 F9
Muirton Aberds 303 D7
Highld 301 C7
Perth 286 E5
Perth 286 F3
Muirton Mains Highld 300 D4
Muirton of Ardblair
Perth 286 C5
Muirton of Ballochy
Angus 293 G8
Muiryfold Aberds 303 D7
Muker N Yorks 223 F8
Mulbarton Norf 142 C3
Mulben Moray 302 D3
Mulberry Corn 5 B10
Mulfra Corn 1 C5
Mulindry Argyll 254 B4
Mulla Shetland 313 G6
Mullardoch House
Highld 300 F2
Mullenspond Hants 47 D9
Mullion Corn 2 F5
Mullion Cove Corn 2 F5
Mumbles Hill Swansea 56 D6
Mumby Lincs 191 G8
Mumps Gtr Man 196 F2
Mundale Moray 301 D10
Munderfield Row
Hereford 116 G2
Munderfield Stocks
Hereford 116 G2
Mundesley Norf 160 B6
Mundford Norf 140 E6
Mundham Norf 142 D6
Mundon Essex 88 E5
Mundurno Aberdeen 293 B11
Munerigie Highld 290 C4
Muness Shetland 312 C8
Mungasdale Highld 307 K4
Mungrisdale Cumb 230 E3
Munlochy Highld 300 D6
Munsary Cottage Highld 310 E6
Munsley Hereford 98 C3
Munslow Shrops 131 F10
Munstone Hereford 97 C10
Murch V Glam 59 E7
Murchington Devon 13 D9
Murcot Worcs 99 C11
Murcott Oxon 83 B9
Wilts 81 G7
Murdieston Stirl 278 B3
Murdishaw Halton 183 E9
Murieston W Loth 269 C11
Murkle Highld 310 C5
Murlaggan Highld 290 D2
Highld 290 E5
Murra Orkney 314 F2
Murrayfield Edin 280 G4
Murrayshall Perth 286 E5
Murraythwaite Dumfries 238 C4
Murrell Green Hants 49 B8
Murrell's End Glos 98 E4
Glos 98 G5
Murrion Shetland 312 F4
Murrow Cambs 139 B7
Mursley Bucks 102 F6
Murston Kent 70 G2
Murthill Angus 287 B8
Murthly Perth 286 D4
Murton Cumb 231 G10
Durham 234 B3
Northumb 273 F9
Swansea 56 D5
T&W 243 C8
York 207 C8
Murton Grange
N Yorks 215 B10
Murtwell Devon 8 D5
Musbury Devon 15 C11
Muscliff Bmouth 19 B7
Muscoates N Yorks 216 C3
Muscott Northants 120 E2
Musdale Argyll 289 G11
Mushroom Green
W Mid 133 F8
Musselburgh E Loth 280 G6
Musselwick Pembs 72 D4
Mustard Hyrn Norf 161 F8
Muston Leics 154 B6
N Yorks 217 D11
Mustow Green Worcs 117 C7
Muswell Hill London 86 G3
Mutehill Dumfries 237 E8
Mutford Suff 143 F9
Muthill Perth 286 F2
Mutley Plym 7 D9
Mutterton Devon 27 G8
Mutton Hall E Sus 37 C9
Muxton Telford 150 G4
Mwdwl-eithin Flint 181 F11
Mwynbwll Flint 165 B11
Mybster Highld 310 D5
Myddfai Carms 94 F5
Myddle Shrops 149 E9
Myddlewood Shrops 149 E9
Myddyn-fych Carms 75 C10
Mydroilyn Ceredig 111 F9
Myerscough Lancs 202 F5
Myerscough Smithy
Lancs 203 G8
Mylor Bridge Corn 3 B8
Mylor Churchtown Corn 3 B8
Mynachdy Cardiff 59 D7
Rhondda 77 F8
Mynachlog-ddu Pembs 92 E2
Mynd Shrops 115 C7
Myndd Llandegai
Gwyn 163 B10
Myndtown Shrops 131 F7
Mynydd Bach Ceredig 112 B4
Mynydd-bach Mon 79 G7
Swansea 57 B7
Mynydd-bach-y-glo
Swansea 56 B6
Mynydd Bodafon
Anglesey 179 D7
Mynydd Fflint / Flint
Flint 182 G2
Mynydd Gilan Gwyn 144 E5
Mynydd-isa Flint 166 C3
Mynyddislwyn Caerph 77 G11
Mynydd-llan Flint 181 G11
Mynydd Marian Conwy 180 F5
Mynydd Mechell
Anglesey 178 D5
Mynyddygarreg Carms 74 D6
Mynytho Gwyn 144 C6
Myrebird Aberds 293 D9
Myrelandhorn Highld 310 D6
Myreside Perth 286 E6
Myrtle Hill Carms 94 E5
Mytchett Sur 49 B11
Mytchett Place Sur 49 C11
Mytholm W Yorks 196 B3
Mytholmes W Yorks 204 F6
Mytholmroyd W Yorks 196 B4
Mythop Lancs 202 G3
Mytice Aberds 302 F4
Myton Warks 118 E6
Myton Hall N Yorks 215 F8
Myton-on-Swale
N Yorks 215 F8
Mytton Shrops 149 F8

N

Naast Highld 307 L3
Nab Hill W Yorks 197 D7
Nab's Head Lancs 194 B6
Naburn York 207 D7
Nab Wood W Yorks 205 F8
Naccolt Kent 54 E4
Nackington Kent 55 C7
Nacton Suff 108 C4
Nadderwater Devon 14 C3
Nafferton E Yorks 209 B7
Na Gearrannan W Isles 304 D3
Nag's Head Glos 80 F5
Naid-y-march Flint 181 F11
Nailbridge Glos 79 B10
Nailsbourne Som 28 B2
Nailsea N Som 60 D3
Nailstone Leics 135 B8
Nailsworth Glos 80 F5
Nailwell Bath 61 G8
Nairn Highld 301 D8
Nalderswood Sur 51 D8
Nance Corn 4 G3
Nanceddan Corn 2 C2
Nancegollan Corn 2 C4
Nancemellin Corn 4 G2
Nancenoy Corn 2 D6
Nancledra Corn 1 B5
Nangreaves Lancs 195 D10
Nanhoron Gwyn 144 C5
Nanhyfer / Nevern
Pembs 91 D11
Nannau Gwyn 146 E4
Nannerch Flint 165 B11
Nanpantan Leics 153 F10
Nanpean Corn 5 D9
Nanquidno Corn 1 D3
Nanstallon Corn 5 B10
Nant Carms 74 B6
Denb 165 D11
Nant Alyn Flint 165 B11
Nant-ddu Powys 77 B8
Nanternis Ceredig 111 F7
Nantgaredig Carms 93 G9
Nantgarw Rhondda 58 B6
Nant-glas Powys 113 E9
Nantglyn Denb 165 C8
Nantgwyn Powys 113 B9
Nantithet Corn 2 E5
Nantlle Gwyn 163 E8
Nantmawr Shrops 148 E5
Nant Mawr Flint 166 C3
Nantmel Powys 113 D10
Nantmor Gwyn 163 F10
Nant Peris / Old Llanberis
Gwyn 163 D10
Nantserth Powys 113 C9
Nant Uchaf Denb 165 D8
Nantwich Ches E 167 E11
Nant-y-Bai Carms 94 C5
Nant-y-Bwch Bl Gwent 77 C10
Nant-y-cafn Neath 76 D4
Nantycaws Carms 75 B7
Nant y Caws Shrops 148 D5
Nant-y-ceisiad Caerph 59 B8
Nant-y-derry Mon 78 D4
Nant-y-felin Conwy 179 G11
Nant-y-ffin Carms 93 E11
Nantyffyllon Bridgend 57 C11
Nantyglo Bl Gwent 77 C11
Nant-y-gollen Shrops 148 D4
Nant-y-moel Bridgend 76 G6
Nant-y-pandy Conwy 179 G11
Nant-y-Rhiw Conwy 164 D4
Nantyronen Station
Ceredig 112 B3
Napchester Kent 55 D10
Naphill Bucks 84 F4
Napleton Worcs 99 B7
Napley Staffs 150 B4
Napley Heath Staffs 150 B4
Nappa N Yorks 204 C3
Nappa Scar N Yorks 223 G9
Napton on the Hill
Warks 119 E9
Narberth / Arberth
Pembs 73 C10
Narberth Bridge Pembs 73 C10
Narborough Leics 135 D10
Norf 158 G4
Narfords Som 28 F3
Narkurs Corn 6 D6
Narracott Devon 24 D5
Narrowgate Corner
Norf 161 F8
Nasareth Gwyn 163 E7
Naseby Northants 120 B3
Nash Bucks 102 E5
Hereford 114 E6
Kent 55 B9
London 68 G2
Newport 59 C10
Shrops 116 C2
Som 28 F6
Nashend Glos 80 D5
Nash End Worcs 132 G5
Nashes Green Hants 49 D7
Nash Lee Bucks 84 D4
Nash Mills Herts 85 E9
Nash Street E Sus 23 C8
Kent 68 F6
Nassington Northants 137 D11
Nastend Glos 80 D3
Nast Hyde Herts 86 D2
Nasty Herts 105 G7
Natcott Devon 24 C3
Nateby Cumb 222 D5
Lancs 202 E5
Nately Scures Hants 49 C8
Natland Cumb 211 B10
Natton Glos 99 E8
Naughton Suff 107 B10
Naunton Glos 100 G2
Worcs 99 D7
Naunton Beauchamp
Worcs 117 G9
Navant Hill W Sus 34 B6
Navenby Lincs 173 D7
Navestock Heath Essex 87 F8
Navestock Side Essex 87 F9
Navidale Highld 311 H4
Navity Highld 301 C7
Nawton N Yorks 216 C3
Nayland Suff 107 E9
Nazeing Essex 86 D6
Nazeing Gate Essex 86 D6
Nazeing Long Green
Essex 86 E6
Nazeing Mead Essex 86 D5
Neacroft Hants 19 B9
Nealhouse Cumb 239 G8
Neal's Green Warks 134 G6
Neames Forstal Kent 54 B5
Neap Shetland 313 H7
Near Hardcastle
N Yorks 214 F2
Near Sawrey Cumb 221 F7
Nearton End Bucks 102 F6
Neasden London 67 B8
Neasham Darl 224 C6
Neat Enstone Oxon 101 G7
Neath Abbey Neath 57 B8
Neatham Hants 49 E8
Neath / Castell-nedd
Neath 57 B8
Neath Hill M Keynes 103 C7
Neatishead Norf 160 E6
Neat Marsh E Yorks 209 G9
Neaton Norf 141 C8
Nebo Anglesey 179 C7
Ceredig 111 D10
Conwy 164 D4
Gwyn 163 E7
Nebsworth Warks 100 C3
Nechells W Mid 133 F11
Necton Norf 141 B7
Nedd Highld 306 F6
Nedderton Northumb 252 G6
Nedge Hill Som 44 C5
Telford 132 B4
Nedging Suff 107 B9
Nedging Tye Suff 107 B10
Needham Norf 142 G4
Needham Green Essex 87 B9
Needham Market Suff 125 G11
Needham Street Suff 124 D4
Needingworth Cambs 122 C6
Needwood Staffs 152 E3
Neen Savage Shrops 116 B3
Neen Sollars Shrops 116 C3
Neenton Shrops 132 F2
Nefod Shrops 148 B6
Nefyn Gwyn 162 G4
Neighbourne Som 44 D6
Neight Hill Worcs 117 F8
Neilston E Renf 267 D9
Neinthirion Powys 129 B9
Neithrop Oxon 101 C8
Nelly Andrews Green
Powys 130 B5
Nelson Caerph 77 F10
Lancs 204 F3
Nelson Village Northumb 243 B7
Nemphlar S Lnrk 269 G7
Nempnett Thrubwell
N Som 60 G4
Nene Terrace Lincs 138 B5
Nenthall Cumb 231 B11
Nenthead Cumb 231 C11
Nenthorn Borders 262 B5
Neopardy Devon 13 B11
Nepcote W Sus 35 F10
Nepgill Cumb 229 F7
Nep Town W Sus 36 D2
Nerabus Argyll 254 B3
Nercwys Flint 166 C2
Nerston S Lnrk 268 D2
Nesbit Northumb 263 C11
Ness Ches W 182 F4
Orkney 314 C4
Nesscliffe Shrops 149 F7
Nessholt Ches W 182 F4
Nesstoun Orkney 314 A7
Neston Ches W 182 F3
Wilts 61 F11
Netchells Green
W Mid 133 F11
Netham Bristol 60 E6
Nethanfoot S Lnrk 268 F6
Nether Alderley Ches E 184 F4
Netheravon Wilts 46 D6
Nether Blainslie
Borders 271 G10
Nether Booth Derbys 185 D10
Netherbrae Aberds 303 D7
Netherbrough Orkney 314 E3
Nether Broughton Leics 154 D3
Netherburn S Lnrk 268 F6
Nether Burrow Lancs 212 D2
Nether Burrows Derbys 152 B5
Netherbury Dorset 16 B5
Netherby Cumb 239 C9
N Yorks 206 D2
Nether Cassock
Dumfries 248 C6
Nether Cerne Dorset 17 B9
Nether Chanderhill
Derbys 186 G4
Netherclay Som 28 C3
Nether Compton Dorset 29 D9
Nethercote Oxon 101 C9
Warks 119 E10
Nethercott Devon 12 B3
Devon 40 F3
Oxon 101 G9
Som 42 G6
Nether Crimond Aberds 303 G8
Netherdale Shetland 313 H3
Nether Dalgliesh
Borders 249 B7
Nether Dallachy Moray 302 C3
Nether Edge S Yorks 186 E4
Netherend Glos 79 E9
Nether End Derbys 186 G3
Leics 154 G4
W Yorks 197 F8
Nether Exe Devon 26 G6
Netherfield E Sus 38 D2
M Keynes 103 D7
Notts 171 G10
Nethergate Norf 159 D11
Nether Glasslaw Aberds 303 D8
Nether Hall Leicester 136 B2
Netherhampton Wilts 31 B10
Nether Handley Derbys 186 F6
Nether Handwick Angus 287 C7
Nether Haugh S Yorks 186 B6
Nether Headon Notts 188 F2
Nether Heage Derbys 170 E5
Nether Heyford
Northants 120 F3
Nether Hindhope
Borders 263 G7
Nether Horsburgh
Borders 261 B8
Nether Howecleuch S
Lnrk 260 G2
Nether Kellet Lancs 211 F10
Nether Kidston Borders 270 G4
Nether Kinmundy
Aberds 303 E10
Nether Kirton E Renf 267 D9
Netherland Green Staffs 152 C2
Nether Langwith Notts 187 G8
Netherlaw Dumfries 237 E9
Netherlay Dorset 28 F6
Nether Leask Aberds 303 F10
Netherlee E Renf 267 D11
Nether Lenshie Aberds 302 E6
Netherley Aberds 293 D10
Mers 182 D6
Nether Loads Derbys 170 B4
Nethermill Dumfries 248 F2
Nethermills Moray 302 D5
Nether Monynut
Borders 272 C4
Nether Moor Derbys 170 B5
Nethermuir Aberds 303 E9
Netherne on-the-Hill
Sur 51 B9
Netheroyd Hill W Yorks 196 D6
Nether Padley Derbys 186 F3
Nether Park Aberds 303 D10
Netherplace E Renf 267 D10
Nether Poppleton York 207 B7
Netherraw Borders 262 E3
Nether Row Cumb 230 D2
Nether Savock Aberds 303 E10
Netherseal Derbys 152 G5
Nether Shiels Borders 271 F8
Nether Silton N Yorks 225 G9
Nether Skyborry Shrops 114 C5
Nether St Suff 125 E8
Netherstoke Dorset 29 F8
Nether Stowe Staffs 152 G2
Nether Stowey Som 43 F7
Nether Street Essex 87 C9
Herts 86 B6
Netherthird E Ayrs 258 F3
Netherthong W Yorks 196 F6
Netherthorpe Derbys 186 G6
S Yorks 187 E8
Netherton Aberds 303 E8
Angus 287 B9
Ches W 183 F8
Corn 11 G11
Cumb 228 D6
Devon 14 G3
Glos 81 E11
Hants 47 B11
Hereford 97 F10
Mers 193 G11
N Lnrk 268 E5
Northumb 251 B11
Oxon 82 F6
Perth 286 B5
Shrops 132 G4
Stirl 277 F11
W Mid 133 F8
Worcs 99 C9
W Yorks 196 E6
W Yorks 197 D9
Netherton of Lonmay
Aberds 303 C10
Nethertown Cumb 219 D9
Highld 310 B7
Lancs 203 F10
Staffs 152 F2
Nether Urquhart Fife 286 G5
Nether Wallop Hants 47 F10
Nether Warden
Northumb 241 D10
Nether Wasdale Cumb 220 E2
Nether Welton Cumb 230 B3
Nether Westcote Glos 100 G4
Nether Whitacre Warks 134 E4
Nether Winchendon or
Lower Winchendon
Bucks 84 C2
Netherwitton Northumb 252 E4
Netherwood E Ayrs 258 D5
Nether Worton Oxon 101 E8
Nether Yeadon
W Yorks 205 E10
Nethy Bridge Highld 301 G10
Netley Hants 33 F7
Netley Hill Soton 33 E7
Netley Marsh Hants 32 E4
Nettacott Devon 14 B4
Netteswell Essex 87 C7
Nettlebed Oxon 65 B8
Nettlebridge Som 44 D6
Nettlecombe Dorset 16 B6
IoW 20 F6
Nettleden Herts 85 C8
Nettleham Lincs 189 F8
Nettlestead Kent 53 C7
Suff 107 B11
Nettlestead Green Kent 53 C7
Nettlestone IoW 21 C8
Nettlesworth Durham 233 B11
Nettleton Glos 80 C6
Lincs 200 G6
Wilts 61 D10
Nettleton Green Wilts 61 D10
Nettleton Hill W Yorks 196 D5
Nettleton Shrub Wilts 61 D10
Nettleton Top Lincs 189 B10
Netton Wilts 46 F6
Neuadd Carms 94 G3
Nevendon Essex 88 G2
Nevern / Nanhyfer
Pembs 91 D11
Nevilles Cross Durham 233 C11
New Abbey Dumfries 237 C11
New Aberdour Aberds 303 C8
New Addington London 67 G11
Newall W Yorks 205 D10
Newall Green Gtr Man 184 D4
New Alresford Hants 48 G5
New Alyth Perth 286 C6
Newark Orkney 314 B7
Pboro 138 C4
Newark-on-Trent Notts 172 E3
New Arley Warks 134 F5
New Arram E Yorks 208 E6
Newarthill N Lnrk 268 D5
New Ash Green Kent 68 F6
New Balderton Notts 172 E4
Newball Lincs 189 F9
Newbarn Kent 55 F7
New Barn Kent 68 F6
New Barnet London 86 F3
New Barnetby N Lincs 200 E5
Newbarns Cumb 210 E4
New Barton Northants 121 E7
New Basford Nottingham 171 G9
Newbattle Midloth 270 B6
New Beaupre V Glam 58 E4
New Beckenham
London 67 E11
New Bewick Northumb 264 E3
Newbie Dumfries 238 D5
Newbiggin Cumb 210 F5
Cumb 211 D11
Cumb 219 G11
Cumb 230 F5
Cumb 231 B7
Cumb 231 F8
Durham 232 B5
Durham 232 F4
Durham 233 B8
N Yorks 213 B9
N Yorks 223 G9
Newbiggin-by-the-Sea
Northumb 253 F8
Newbigging Aberds 303 G7
Angus 287 D8
Borders 262 F6
Edin 280 F2
S Lnrk 269 F10
New-bigging Angus 286 C6
Newbiggings Orkney 314 B6
Newbiggin Hall Estate
T&W 242 D6
Newbiggin-on-Lune
Cumb 222 D4
New Bilton Warks 119 B9
Newbold Derbys 186 G5
Gtr Man 196 E2
Leics 136 B5
Leics 153 F8
Newbold Heath Leics 135 B8
Newbold on Avon
Warks 119 B9
Newbold on Stour
Warks 100 B4
Newbold Pacey Warks 118 F5
Newbolds W Mid 133 C8
Newbold Verdon Leics 135 C8
New Bolingbroke Lincs 174 D4
New Bolsover Derbys 187 G7
Newborough Pboro 138 B4
Staffs 152 D2
New Boston Mers 183 B9
New Botley Oxon 83 D7
Newbottle Northants 101 D10
T&W 243 G8
New Boultham Lincs 189 G7
Newbourne Suff 108 C5
New Bradwell M Keynes 102 C6
New Brancepeth
Durham 233 C10
Newbridge Bath 61 F8
Caerph 78 F2
Ceredig 111 F10
Corn 1 C4
Corn 4 G5
Corn 7 B7
Dumfries 237 B11
Edin 280 G2
E Sus 52 G3
Hants 32 D3
IoW 20 D4
Lancs 204 F3
N Yorks 216 B6
Oxon 82 E6
Pembs 91 E8
Shrops 148 D6
W Mid 133 D7
Wrex 166 G3
New Bridge Wrex 166 G3
Newbridge Green Worcs 98 D6
Newbridge-on-Usk Mon 78 G5
Newbridge-on-Wye
Powys 113 F10
New Brighton Flint 166 B3
Mers 182 C4
Wrex 166 E3
W Sus 22 B3
W Yorks 197 B9
W Yorks 205 F8
New Brimington Derbys 186 G6
New Brinsley Notts 171 E7
New Brotton Redcar 235 G9
Newbrough Northumb 241 D9
New Broughton Wrex 166 E4
New Buckenham Norf 141 E11
Newbuildings Devon 26 G3
New Buildings Bath 45 B7
Dorset 18 E5
Newburgh Aberds 303 D9
Aberds 303 G9
Borders 261 F8
Fife 286 F6
Lancs 194 E3
Newburn T&W 242 D5
Newbury Kent 54 B2
W Berks 64 F3
Wilts 45 E10
New Bury Gtr Man 195 F8
Newbury Park London 68 B2
Newby Cumb 231 G7
Lancs 204 D2
N Yorks 205 D11
N Yorks 212 E4
N Yorks 215 F7
N Yorks 225 C10
N Yorks 227 G10
Newby Bridge Cumb 211 B7
Newby Cote N Yorks 212 E4
Newby East Cumb 239 F11
Newby Head Cumb 231 G7
New Byth Aberds 303 D8
Newby West Cumb 239 G9
Newby Wiske N Yorks 215 B7
Newcastle Bridgend 58 D2
Mon 78 B6
Shrops 130 G4
Newcastle Emlyn / Castell
Newydd Emlyn Carms 92 C6
Newcastleton or Copshaw
Holm Borders 249 F11
Newcastle-under-Lyme
Staffs 168 F4
Newcastle upon Tyne
T&W 242 E6
New Catton Norf 160 G4
Newchapel Powys 129 G9
Staffs 168 E5
Sur 51 E11
Newchapel / Capel Newydd
Pembs 92 D4
New Charlton London 68 D2
New Cheltenham S Glos 61 E7
New Cheriton Hants 33 B9
Newchurch Bl Gwent 77 C11
Carms 93 G7
Hereford 115 G7
IoW 21 D7
Kent 54 G5
Lancs 195 C10
Mon 79 F7
Powys 114 G4
Staffs 152 E2
Newchurch in Pendle
Lancs 204 F2
New Clipstone Notts 171 C9
New Costessey Norf 160 G3
Newcott Devon 28 F2
New Coundon Durham 233 E10
New Cowper Cumb 229 B8
Newcraighall Edin 280 G6
New Crofton W Yorks 197 D11
New Cross Ceredig 112 B2
London 67 D11
Oxon 65 D9
Som 28 D6
New Cross Gate London 67 D11
New Cumnock E Ayrs 258 G4
New Deer Aberds 303 E8
New Delaval Northumb 243 B7
New Delph Gtr Man 196 F3
New Denham Bucks 66 C4
Newdigate Sur 51 E7
New Downs Corn 1 C3
Corn 4 E4
New Duston Northants 120 E4
New Earswick York 207 B8
New Eastwood Notts 171 F7
New Edlington S Yorks 187 B8
New Elgin Moray 302 C2
New Ellerby E Yorks 209 F9
Newell Green Brack 65 E11
New Eltham London 68 E2
New End Lincs 190 G2

Warks 118 E2
Worcs 117 F11
Newenden Kent 38 B4
New England Essex 106 C4
Lincs 175 D8
Pboro 138 C3
Som 28 E4
Newent Glos 98 F4
Newerne Glos 79 E10
New Farnley W Yorks 205 G10
New Ferry Mers 182 D4
Newfield Durham 233 E10
Durham 242 G6
Highld 301 B7
Stoke 168 E6
New Fletton Pboro 138 D3
Newford Scilly 1 G4
Newfound Hants 48 C5
New Fryston W Yorks 198 B3
Newgale Pembs 90 G6
New Galloway Dumfries 237 B8
Newgarth Orkney 314 E2
Newgate Lancs 194 F4
Norf 177 E9
Newgate Corner Norf 161 G8
Newgate Street Herts 86 D4
New Gilston Fife 287 G8
New Greens Herts 85 D10
New Grimsby Scilly 1 F3
New Ground Herts 85 C7
Newgrounds Hants 31 E11
Newhailes Edin 280 G6
New Hainford Norf 160 F4
Newhall Ches E 167 F10
Derbys 152 E5
Newhall Green Warks 134 F5
New Hall Hey Lancs 195 C10
Newhall House Highld 300 C6
Newhall Point Highld 301 C7
Newham Lincs 174 E3
Northumb 264 D5
New Hartley Northumb 243 B8
Newhaven Derbys 169 C11
Devon 24 C5
Edin 280 F5
E Sus 36 G6
New Haw Sur 66 G5
Newhay N Yorks 207 G9
New Headington Oxon 83 D9
New Heaton Northumb 273 G7
New Hedges Pembs 73 E10
New Herrington T&W 243 G8
Newhey Gtr Man 196 E2
Newhill Fife 286 F6
Perth 286 G5
S Yorks 186 B6
Newhills Aberdeen 293 C10
New Hinksey Oxon 83 E8
New Ho Durham 232 D3
New Holkham Norf 159 B7
New Holland N Lincs 200 C5
W Yorks 205 F7
Newholm N Yorks 227 C7
New Horwich Derbys 185 E8
New Houghton Derbys 171 B7
Norf 158 D5
Newhouse Borders 262 E2
N Lnrk 268 C5
Shetland 313 G6
New House Kent 68 E6
Newhouses Borders 271 G10
New Houses Gtr Man 194 G5
N Yorks 212 E6
New Humberstone
Leicester 136 B2
New Hunwick Durham 233 E9
New Hutton Cumb 221 G11
New Hythe Kent 53 B8
Newick E Sus 36 C6
Newingreen Kent 54 F6
Newington Edin 280 G5
Kent 55 F7
Kent 69 G11
Kent 71 F11
London 67 D10
Notts 187 C11
Oxon 83 F10
Shrops 131 G8
Newington Bagpath Glos 80 G4
New Inn Carms 93 D9
Devon 24 F6
Mon 79 E7
Pembs 91 E11
Torf 78 F4
New Invention Shrops 114 B5
W Mid 133 C9
New Kelso Highld 299 E9
New Kingston Notts 153 D10
New Kyo Durham 242 G5
New Ladykirk Borders 273 F7
New Lanark S Lnrk 269 G7
Newland Cumb 210 D6
E Yorks 199 B10
Glos 79 D9
Hull 209 G7
N Yorks 199 C7
Oxon 82 C5
Worcs 98 B5
Newland Bottom Cumb 210 C5
Newland Common
Worcs 117 E8
Newland Green Kent 54 D2
Newlandrig Midloth 271 C7
Newlands Borders 250 E2
Borders 262 E2
Cumb 229 G10
Cumb 230 D2
Derbys 170 F6
Dumfries 247 F11
Glasgow 267 C11
Highld 301 E7
Moray 302 D3
Northumb 242 F3
Notts 171 C9
Staffs 151 E11
Newlands Corner Sur 50 D4
Newlandsmuir S Lnrk 268 E2
Newlands of Geise
Highld 310 C4
Newlands of Tynet
Moray 302 C3
Newlands Park Anglesey 178 E3
New Lane Lancs 194 E2
New Lane End Warr 183 B10
New Langholm Dumfries 249 G9
New Leake Lincs 174 D6
New Leeds Aberds 303 D9
Newliston Edin 280 G2
Fife 280 C5
New Lodge S Yorks 197 F10
New Longton Lancs 194 B4
Newlot Orkney 314 E5
New Luce Dumfries 236 C3
Newlyn Corn 1 D5
Newmachar Aberds 293 B10
Newmains N Lnrk 268 D6
New Malden London 67 F8
Newman's End Essex 87 C8
Newman's Green Suff 107 C7
Newman's Place Hereford 96 B5
Newmarket Glos 80 F4
Suff 124 E2
W Isles 304 E6
New Marske Redcar 235 G8
New Marston Oxon 83 D8
New Marton Shrops 148 C6
New Micklefield
W Yorks 206 G4
Newmill Borders 261 G11
Corn 1 C5
Moray 302 D4
New Mill Aberds 293 E9
Borders 262 G2
Corn 1 C5
Corn 4 F6
Cumb 219 E11
Herts 84 C6
Wilts 63 G7
W Yorks 197 F7
Newmillerdam
W Yorks 197 D10
Newmill of Inshewan
Angus 292 G6
Newmills Corn 11 D11
Fife 279 D10
Highld 300 C6
New Mills Borders 271 F10
Ches E 184 E3
Corn 5 E7
Derbys 185 D7
Glos 79 E10
Hereford 98 D4
New Mills / Felin Newydd
Powys 129 C11
Newmills of Boyne
Aberds 302 D5
Newmiln Perth 286 D5
Newmilns E Ayrs 258 B2
New Milton Hants 19 B10
New Mistley Essex 108 E2
New Moat Pembs 91 F11
Newmore Highld 300 B6
Highld 300 D5
New Moston Gtr Man 195 G11
Newnes Shrops 149 C7
Newney Green Essex 87 D11
Newnham Cambs 123 F8
Glos 79 C11
Hants 49 C8
Herts 104 D4
Kent 54 B3
Northants 119 F11
Warks 118 E3
Newnham Bridge Worcs 116 D2
New Ollerton Notts 171 B11
New Oscott W Mid 133 E11
New Pale Ches W 183 G8
Newpark Fife 287 F8
New Park N Yorks 205 B11
New Parks Leicester 135 B11
New Passage S Glos 60 B4
New Pitsligo Aberds 303 D8
New Polzeath Corn 10 F4
Newpool Staffs 168 D5
Newport Corn 12 D2
Devon 40 G5
Dorset 18 C3
Essex 105 E10
E Yorks 208 G3
Glos 79 F11
Highld 311 G5
IoW 20 D6
Newport 59 B10
Norf 161 F10
Som 28 C4
Telford 150 F4
Newport-on-Tay Fife 287 E8
Newport Pagnell
M Keynes 103 C7
Newport / Trefdraeth
Pembs 91 D11
Newpound Common
W Sus 35 B9
Newquay Corn 4 C6
New Quay / Ceinewydd
Ceredig 111 F7
New Rackheath Norf 160 G5
New Radnor Powys 114 E4
New Rent Cumb 230 D5
New Ridley Northumb 242 F3
New Road Side N Yorks 204 E5
W Yorks 197 B7
New Romney Kent 39 C9
New Rossington
S Yorks 187 B10
New Row Ceredig 112 C4
Lancs 203 F8
N Yorks 226 C2
Newsam Green
W Yorks 206 G3
New Sarum Wilts 46 G6
New Sawley Derbys 153 C9
Newsbank Ches E 168 B4
New Scarbro W Yorks 205 G10
Newseat Aberds 303 E10
Aberds 303 F7
Newsells Herts 105 D7
Newsham Lancs 202 F6
Northumb 243 B8
N Yorks 215 C7
N Yorks 224 C2
New Sharlston
W Yorks 197 C11
Newsholme E Yorks 199 B8
Lancs 204 C2
W Yorks 204 F6
New Silksworth T&W 243 G9
New Skelton Redcar 226 B3
New Smithy Derbys 185 E9
Newsome W Yorks 196 E6
New Southgate London 86 G3
New Springs Gtr Man 194 F6
New Sprowston Norf 160 G4
New Stanton Derbys 153 B9
Newstead Borders 262 C3
Northumb 264 D5
Notts 171 E8
Staffs 168 G5
W Yorks 197 E11
New Stevenston N Lnrk 268 D5
New Street Kent 68 G6
Staffs 169 E9
Newstreet Lane Shrops 150 B2
New Swanage Dorset 18 E6
New Swannington Leics 153 F8
Newtake Devon 14 G3
New Thirsk N Yorks 215 C8
Newthorpe Notts 171 F7
N Yorks 206 G5
Newthorpe Common
Notts 171 F7
New Thundersley Essex 69 B9
Newtoft Lincs 189 D8
Newton Argyll 275 D11
Borders 262 E3
Borders 262 F2
Bridgend 57 F10
Cambs 105 B8
Cambs 157 G8
Cardiff 59 D8
C Beds 104 C4
Ches W 166 B6
Ches W 167 D8
Ches W 183 F8
Corn 5 C11
Cumb 210 E4
Derbys 170 D6
Dorset 30 E3
Dumfries 239 C7
Dumfries 248 E4
Gtr Man 185 B7
Hereford 96 C5
Hereford 96 E6
Hereford 115 D7
Hereford 115 G10
Highld 301 C7
Highld 301 E7
Highld 306 F7
Highld 310 E7
Lancs 202 F2
Lancs 202 G4
Lancs 203 C9
Lancs 211 E11
Lincs 155 B10
Mers 182 D2
Moray 301 C11
Norf 158 F6
Northants 137 G7
Northumb 242 E2
Notts 171 G11
Perth 286 D2
S Glos 79 G10
Shetland 312 E5
Shetland 313 K5
Shrops 132 D4
Shrops 149 C8
S Lnrk 259 C10
S Lnrk 268 C3
Som 42 F6
Staffs 151 D10
Suff 107 C8
Swansea 56 D6
S Yorks 198 G5
Warks 119 B10
Wilts 32 C2
W Loth 279 F11
W Mid 133 E10
Newton Abbot Devon 14 G3
Newtonairds Dumfries 247 G9
Newton Arlosh Cumb 238 F5
Newton Aycliffe
Durham 233 G11
Newton Bewley Hrtlpl 234 F5
Newton Blossomville
M Keynes 121 G8
Newton Bromswold
Northants 121 D9
Newton Burgoland
Leics 135 B7
Newton by Toft Lincs 189 D9
Newton Cross Pembs 91 F7
Newton Ferrers Devon 7 F10
Newton Flotman Norf 142 D4
Newtongrange Midloth 270 C6
Newton Green Mon 79 G8
Newton Hall Durham 233 B11
Northumb 242 D2
Newton Harcourt Leics 136 D2
Newton Heath
Gtr Man 195 G11
Newtonhill Aberds 293 D11
Highld 300 E5
Newton Hill W Yorks 197 C10
Newton Ho Aberds 302 G6
Newton Hurst Staffs 151 D11
Newtonia Ches E 167 B11
Newton Ketton Darl 234 G2
Newton Kyme N Yorks 206 E5
Newton-le-Willows
Mers 183 B9
N Yorks 214 B4
Newton Longville Bucks 102 E6
Newton Mearns
E Renf 267 D10
Newtonmill Angus 293 G8
Newtonmore Highld 291 D9
Newton Morrell
N Yorks 224 D4
Oxon 102 F2
Newton Mulgrave
N Yorks 226 B5
Newton of Ardtoe
Highld 289 B8
Newton of Balcanquhal
Perth 286 F5
Newton of Balcormo
Fife 287 G9
Newton of Falkland
Fife 286 G6
Newton of Mountblairy
Aberds 302 D6
Newton of Pitcairns
Perth 286 F4
Newton on Ayr S Ayrs 257 E8
Newton on Ouse
N Yorks 206 B6
Newton-on-Rawcliffe
N Yorks 226 G6
Newton on the Hill
Shrops 149 E9
Newton on the Moor
Northumb 252 B5
Newton on Trent Lincs 188 G4
Newton Park Argyll 266 B2
Mers 183 C9
Newton Peveril Dorset 18 B4
Newton Poppleford
Devon 15 D7
Newton Purcell Oxon 102 E2
Newton Regis Warks 134 B5
Newton Reigny Cumb 230 E5
Newton Rigg Cumb 230 E5
Newton St Boswells
Borders 262 C3
Newton St Cyres Devon 14 B3
Newton St Faith Norf 160 F4
Newton St Loe Bath 61 G8
Newton St Petrock Devon 24 E6
Newton Solney Derbys 152 D5
Newton Stacey Hants 48 E2
Newton Stewart
Dumfries 236 C6
Newton Tony Wilts 47 E8
Newton Tracey Devon 25 B8
Newton under Roseberry
Redcar 225 C11
Newton Underwood
Northumb 252 F4
Newton upon Derwent
E Yorks 207 D10
Newton Valence Hants 49 G8
Newton with Scales
Lancs 202 G4
Newton Wood Gtr Man 184 B6
New Totley S Yorks 186 F4
Newtown Argyll 284 G4
Bl Gwent 77 C11
Bucks 85 E7
Caerph 78 G2
Cambs 121 D11
Ches E 184 E6
Ches W 183 F8
Corn 2 D3
Corn 11 F11
Cumb 229 B7
Cumb 239 F9
Cumb 240 E2
Derbys 185 E7
Devon 26 B3
Dorset 29 G7
Falk 279 E9
Glos 79 E11
Glos 80 D3
Glos 99 E8
Gtr Man 194 F5
Gtr Man 195 G9
Hants 21 B8
Hants 32 C4
Hants 32 E3
Hants 33 D8
Hants 33 E10
Hants 33 F7
Hants 49 F8
Hants 49 G10
Hants 64 G3
Hereford 97 E10
Hereford 98 C2
Highld 290 C5
IoM 192 E4
IoW 20 C4
Mers 183 B7
Norf 143 B10
Northumb 252 C2
Northumb 263 C11
Northumb 264 D2
Oxon 65 C9
Poole 18 C6
Powys 130 E2
Rhondda 77 F9
Shrops 132 C2
Shrops 149 C9
Shrops 149 E8
Som 28 E3
Som 43 F9
Staffs 133 C9
Staffs 168 C6
Staffs 169 C9
Wilts 30 B6
Wilts 63 G10
W Mid 133 F11
Worcs 116 F5
Worcs 117 E7
New Town Bath 45 B9
Bath 60 G5
Dartford 68 E4
Dorset 30 C3
Dorset 30 D6
Dorset 31 D7
Dorset 31 F7
Edin 280 G4
Edin 280 G5
E Loth 281 G8
E Sus 37 C7
Glos 99 E10
Lancs 203 F8
Luton 103 G11
Maidstone 53 B7
Medway 69 G8
Oxon 100 F5
Reading 65 E8
Shetland 312 E6
Som 29 D9
Som 29 D11
Som 44 D3
Soton 33 E7
Swindon 63 C7
T&W 234 B2
T&W 243 E8
W Berks 64 D6
Wilts 46 C6
Wilts 63 E9
W Mid 133 B11
W Mid 133 D10
W Sus 35 B11
W Yorks 198 C3
Newtown-in-St Martin
Corn 2 E6
Newtown Linford Leics 135 B10
Newtown St Boswells
Borders 262 C3
Newtown Unthank Leics 135 C9
New Tredegar Caerph 77 E10
New Trows S Lnrk 259 B8
Newtyle Angus 286 C6
New Ulva Argyll 275 E8
New Village E Yorks 209 G7
S Yorks 198 F5
New Walsoken Cambs 139 B9
New Waltham NE Lincs 201 G9
New Well Powys 113 B11
New Wells Powys 130 D3
New Whittington Derbys 186 F5
New Wimpole Cambs 104 B6
New Winton E Loth 281 G8
New Woodhouses
Shrops 167 G9
New Works Telford 132 B3
New Wortley W Yorks 205 G11
New Yatt Oxon 82 C5
Newyears Green London 66 B5
New York Lincs 174 D2
N Yorks 214 G3
T&W 243 C8
New Zealand Wilts 62 D4
Nextend Hereford 114 F6
Neyland Pembs 73 D7
Niarbyl IoM 192 E3
Nib Heath Shrops 149 F8
Nibley Glos 79 D11
S Glos 61 C7
Nibley Green Glos 80 F2
Nibon Shetland 312 F5
Nicholashayne Devon 27 D10
Nicholaston Swansea 56 D4
Nidd N Yorks 214 G6
Niddrie Edin 280 G5
Nigg Aberdeen 293 C11
Highld 301 B8
Nigg Ferry Highld 301 C7
Nightcott Som 26 B5
Nilig Denb 165 D8
Nimble Nook Gtr Man 196 G2
Nimlet S Glos 61 E8
Nimmer Som 28 E4
Nine Ashes Essex 87 E9
Ninebanks Northumb 241 G7
Nine Elms London 67 D9
Swindon 62 B6
Nine Maidens Downs Corn 2 B5
Nine Mile Burn Midloth 270 D3
Nineveh Worcs 116 C3
Worcs 116 E2
Ninewells Glos 79 C9
Nine Wells Pembs 90 G5
Ninfield E Sus 38 E2
Ningwood IoW 20 D3
Ningwood Common IoW 20 D3
Ninnes Bridge Corn 2 B2
Nisbet Borders 262 D5
Nisthouse Orkney 314 E3
Shetland 313 G7
Nithbank Dumfries 247 D9
Niton IoW 20 F6
Nitshill Glasgow 267 C10
Noah's Arks Kent 52 B5
Noah's Green Worcs 117 E10
Noak Bridge Essex 87 G11
Noak Hill Essex 87 G11
London 87 G8
Nob End Gtr Man 195 F9
Nobland Green Herts 86 B5
Noblethorpe S Yorks 197 F9
Nobold Shrops 149 G9
Nobottle Northants 120 E3
Nob's Crook Hants 33 C7
Nocton Lincs 173 C9
Noctorum Mers 182 D3
Nodmore W Berks 64 D2
Noel Park London 86 G4
Nogdam End Norf 143 C7
Nog Tow Lancs 202 G6
Noke Oxon 83 C8
Noke Street Medway 69 E8
Nolton Pembs 72 B5
Nolton Haven Pembs 72 B5
No Man's Heath Ches W 167 F8
Warks 134 B5
Nomansland Devon 26 E4
Herts 85 C11
Wilts 32 D3
No Man's Land Corn 6 D5
Hants 33 B8
Noneley Shrops 149 D9
Noness Shetland 313 L6
Nonikiln Highld 300 B6
Nonington Kent 55 C9
Nook Cumb 211 C10
Noon Nick W Yorks 205 F8
Noonsbrough Shetland 313 H4
Noonsun Ches E 184 F4
Noonvares Corn 2 C3
Noranside Angus 292 G6
Norbiton London 67 F7
Norbreck Blkpool 202 E2
Norbridge Hereford 98 C4
Norbury Ches E 167 F9
Derbys 169 G10
London 67 F10
Shrops 131 E7
Staffs 150 E5
Norbury Common
Ches E 167 F9
Norbury Junction Staffs 150 E5
Norbury Moor Gtr Man 184 D6
Norby N Yorks 215 C8
Shetland 313 H3
Norchard Worcs 116 D6
Norcote Glos 81 E8
Norcott Brook Ches W 183 E10
Norcross Blkpool 202 E2
Nordelph Norf 139 C11
Nordelph Corner Norf 141 C10
Norden Dorset 18 E4
Gtr Man 195 E11
Norden Heath Dorset 18 E4
Nordley Shrops 132 D3
Norham Northumb 273 F8
Norham West Mains
Northumb 273 F8
Nork Sur 51 B8
Norland Town W Yorks 196 C5
Norleaze Wilts 45 C11
Norley Ches W 183 G9
Devon 25 G8
Norley Common Sur 50 E4
Norleywood Hants 20 B3
Norlington E Sus 36 E6
Normacot Stoke 168 G6
Normanby N Lincs 199 D11
N Yorks 216 C4
Redcar 225 B10
Normanby-by-Spital
Lincs 189 D7
Normanby by Stow
Lincs 188 E5
Normanby le Wold
Lincs 189 B10
Norman Cross Cambs 138 E3
Normandy Sur 50 C2
Norman Hill Glos 80 F3
Norman's Bay E Sus 23 D11
Norman's Green Devon 27 G9
Normanston Suff 143 E10
Normanton Derby 152 C6
Leics 172 G4
Lincs 172 F6
Notts 172 E2
Rutland 137 B8
Wilts 46 E6
W Yorks 197 C11
Normanton le Heath
Leics 153 G7
Normanton on Soar
Notts 153 E10
Normanton-on-the-Wolds
Notts 154 C2
Normanton on Trent
Notts 172 B3
Normanton Spring
S Yorks 186 E6
Normanton Turville
Leics 135 D9
Normoss Lancs 202 F2
Norney Sur 50 E2
Norr W Yorks 205 F7
Norrington Common
Wilts 61 G11
Norris Green Corn 7 B8
Mers 182 C5
Norris Hill Leics 152 F6
Norristhorpe W Yorks 197 C8
Norseman Orkney 314 E3
Northacre Norf 141 D9
Northall Bucks 103 G9
Northallerton N Yorks 225 G7
Northall Green Norf 159 G9
Northam Devon 24 B6
Soton 32 E6
Northampton Northants 120 E5
North Anston S Yorks 187 E8
North Ascot Brack 66 F2
North Aston Oxon 101 F9
Northaw Herts 86 E3
Northay Devon 28 G5
Som 28 E3
North Ayre Shetland 312 F6
North Baddesley Hants 32 D5
North Ballachulish
Highld 290 G2
North Barrow Som 29 B10
North Barsham Norf 159 C8
North Batsom Som 41 G10
Northbeck Lincs 173 G9
North Beer Corn 12 C2
North Benfleet Essex 69 B9
North Bersted W Sus 22 C6
North Berwick E Loth 281 D11
North Bitchburn Durham 233 E9
North Blyth Northumb 253 G8
North Boarhunt Hants 33 E10
North Bockhampton
Dorset 19 B9
Northborough Pboro 138 B3
Northbourne Bmouth 19 B7
Kent 55 C10
North Bovey Devon 13 E10
North Bradley Wilts 45 C11
North Brentor Devon 12 E5
North Brewham Som 45 F8
Northbridge Street
E Sus 38 C2
Northbrook Dorset 17 C11
Hants 33 D9
Hants 48 F4
Oxon 101 G9
Wilts 46 C4
North Brook End Cambs 104 C5
North Broomage Falk 279 E7
North Buckland Devon 40 E3
North Burlingham Norf 161 G7
North Cadbury Som 29 B10
North Cairn Dumfries 236 B1
North Camp Hants 49 C11
North Carlton Lincs 188 F6
Notts 187 E9
North Carrine Argyll 255 G7
North Cave E Yorks 208 G3
North Cerney Glos 81 D8
North Chailey E Sus 36 C5
Northchapel W Sus 35 B7
North Charford Wilts 31 D11
North Charlton
Northumb 264 E5
North Cheam London 67 F8
North Cheriton Som 29 B11
Northchurch Herts 85 D7
North Cliff E Yorks 209 D10
North Cliffe E Yorks 208 F3
North Clifton Notts 188 G4
North Close Durham 233 E11
North Cockerington
Lincs 190 C5
North Coker Som 29 E8
North Collafirth
Shetland 312 E5
North Common S Glos 61 E7
Suff 125 B9
North Connel Argyll 289 F11
North Cornelly Bridgend 57 E10
North Corner Corn 3 F7
S Glos 61 C7
North Corriegills
N Ayrs 256 C2
North Corry Highld 289 D10
Northcote Devon 27 G11
North Cotes Lincs 201 G11
Northcott Corn 24 F2
Devon 12 C2
Devon 27 E9
Devon 27 F10
North Country Corn 4 G3
Northcourt Oxon 83 F8
North Court Som 41 F11
North Cove Suff 143 F9
North Cowton N Yorks 224 E5
North Craigo Angus 293 G8
North Crawley
M Keynes 103 C8
North Cray London 68 E3
North Creake Norf 159 B7
North Curry Som 28 B4
North Dalton E Yorks 208 C4
North Darley Corn 11 G11
North Dawn Orkney 314 F4
North Deighton N Yorks 206 C3
North Denes Norf 161 G10
Northdown Kent 71 E11
North Dronley Angus 287 D7
North Drumachter Lodge
Highld 291 F8
North Duffield N Yorks 207 F9
Northdyke Orkney 314 D2
North Dykes Cumb 230 D6
North Eastling Kent 54 B3
Northedge Derbys 170 B5
North Elham Kent 55 E7
North Elkington Lincs 190 C3
North Elmham Norf 159 E9
North Elmsall W Yorks 198 E3
North Elmshall W Yorks 198 E3
North Elphinestone
E Loth 281 G7
Northend Bath 61 F9
Bucks 84 G2
Essex 89 E7
Essex 105 D10
Warks 119 G7
North End Bath 60 G6
Beds 103 B9
Beds 121 F10
Bexley 68 D4
Bucks 102 F4
Bucks 102 F6
Camden 67 B9
Cumb 239 F8
Devon 27 D10
Dorset 30 B4
Durham 233 C11
Essex 87 B11
Essex 106 D5
E Yorks 209 C9
E Yorks 209 E9
E Yorks 209 G11
Hants 31 D10
Hants 33 B9
Hants 64 G2
Leics 153 F11
Lincs 174 G2
Lincs 189 B8
Lincs 190 C5
Lincs 190 D6
Lincs 191 D7
Lincs 201 G10
N Lincs 200 C6
Norf 141 E10
Northumb 252 C4
N Som 60 F2
Ptsmth 33 G11
Som 28 B3
Wilts 81 G8
W Sus 35 F10
W Sus 35 G7
W Sus 51 F11
Northenden Gtr Man 184 C4
Northern Moor Gtr Man 184 C4
North Erradale Highld 307 L2
North Evington
Leicester 136 C2
North Ewster N Lincs 199 G10
North Fambridge Essex 88 F5
North Fearns Highld 295 B7
North Featherstone
W Yorks 198 C2
North Feltham London 66 E6
North Feorline N Ayrs 255 E10
North Ferriby E Yorks 200 B3
Northfield Aberdeen 293 C11
Borders 262 D3
Borders 273 B8
Edin 280 G5
E Yorks 200 B4
Highld 301 B7
M Keynes 103 C7
Northants 137 E7
Som 43 F9
W Mid 117 B10
Northfields Hants 33 B7
Lincs 137 B10
North Finchley London 86 G3
Northfleet Kent 68 E6
Northfleet Green Kent 68 E6
North Flobbets Aberds 303 F7
North Frodingham
E Yorks 209 C8
Northgate Lincs 156 D3
Som 27 B9
W Sus 51 F9
North Gluss Shetland 312 F5
North Gorley Hants 31 E11
North Green Norf 141 B10
Norf 142 F4
Suff 126 B6
Suff 126 E6
Suff 127 D7
North Greetwell Lincs 189 G8
North Grimston N Yorks 216 F6
North Halley Orkney 314 F5
North Halling Medway 69 F8
North Harrow London 66 B6
North Hayling Hants 22 C2
North Hazelrigg
Northumb 264 C3
North Heasley Devon 41 G8
North Heath W Berks 64 E3
W Sus 35 C9
North Hill Corn 11 F11
North Hillingdon London 66 C5
North Hinksey Oxon 83 D7
North Hinksey Village
Oxon 83 D7
North Ho Shetland 313 J5
North Holmwood Sur 51 D7
North Houghton Hants 47 G10
Northhouse Borders 249 B10
North Howden E Yorks 207 G11
North Huish Devon 8 D4
North Hyde London 66 D6
North Hykeham Lincs 172 B6
North Hylton T&W 243 F8
Northiam E Sus 38 B4
Northill C Beds 104 B2
Northington Glos 80 D2
Hants 48 F5
North Kelsey Lincs 200 G4
North Kelsey Moor
Lincs 200 G5
North Kensington London 67 C8
North Kessock Highld 300 E6
North Killingholme
N Lincs 200 D6
North Kilvington
N Yorks 215 B8
North Kilworth Leics 136 G2
North Kingston Hants 31 G11
North Kirkton Aberds 303 D11
North Kiscadale N Ayrs 256 D2
North Kyme Lincs 173 E11
North Laggan Highld 290 D4
North Lancing W Sus 35 F11
North Landing E Yorks 218 E4
Northlands Lincs 174 E4
Northlea Durham 243 G10
Northleach Glos 81 C10
North Lee Bucks 84 D4
North Lees N Yorks 214 E6
Northleigh Devon 15 B9
Devon 40 G6
North Leigh Kent 54 D6
Oxon 82 C5
North Leverton with
Habblesthorpe Notts 188 E3
Northlew Devon 12 B6
North Littleton Worcs 99 B11
North Looe Sur 67 G8
North Lopham Norf 141 G10
North Luffenham
Rutland 137 C8
North Marden W Sus 34 D4
North Marston Bucks 102 G5
North Middleton
Midloth 271 D7
Northumb 264 E2
North Millbrex Aberds 303 E8
North Molton Devon 26 B2
Northmoor Devon 24 D4
Oxon 82 E6
Northmoor Corner Som 43 G10
Northmoor Green or
Moorland Som 43 G10
North Moreton Oxon 64 B5
North Mosstown
Aberds 303 D10
North Motherwell N
Lnrk 268 D4
North Moulsecoomb
Brighton 36 F4
Northmuir Angus 287 B7
North Mundham W Sus 22 C5
North Muskham Notts 172 D3
North Newbald E Yorks 208 F4
North Newington Oxon 101 D8
North Newnton Wilts 46 B6
North Newton Som 43 G9
Northney Hants 22 C2
North Nibley Glos 80 F2
North Oakley Hants 48 C4
North Ockendon London 68 C5
Northolt London 66 C6
Northop Hall Flint 166 B3
Northop / Llan-eurgain
Flint 166 B2
North Ormesby Mbro 234 G6
North Ormsby Lincs 190 C3
Northorpe Lincs 155 F11
Lincs 156 B4
Lincs 188 B5
W Yorks 197 C8
North Otterington
N Yorks 215 B7
Northover Som 29 C8
Som 44 F3
North Owersby Lincs 189 C9
Northowram W Yorks 196 B6
Northpark Argyll 275 G11
North Perrott Som 29 F7
North Petherton Som 43 G9
North Petherwin Corn 11 D11
North Pickenham Norf 141 B7
North Piddle Worcs 117 G9
North Poorton Dorset 16 B6
Northport Dorset 18 D4
North Port Argyll 284 E4
North Poulner Hants 31 F11
Northpunds Shetland 313 L6
North Queensferry Fife 280 E2
North Radworthy Devon 41 G9
North Rauceby Lincs 173 F8
North Reddish Gtr Man 184 C5
Northrepps Norf 160 B4
North Reston Lincs 190 E5
North Rigton N Yorks 205 D11
North Ripley Hants 19 B9
North Rode Ches E 168 B5
North Roe Shetland 312 E5
North Row Cumb 229 E10
North Runcton Norf 158 F2
North Sandwick
Shetland 312 D7
North Scale Cumb 210 F3
North Scarle Lincs 172 B5
North Seaton Northumb 253 F7
North Seaton Colliery
Northumb 253 F7
North Sheen London 67 D7
North Shian Argyll 289 E11
North Shields T&W 243 D9
North Shoebury Sthend 70 B2
North Shore Blkpool 202 F2
Northside Aberds 303 D8
Orkney 314 D2
North Side Cumb 228 F6
Pboro 138 D5
North Skelmanae
Aberds 303 D9
North Skelton Redcar 226 B3
North Somercotes Lincs 190 B6
North Stainley N Yorks 214 D5
North Stainmore Cumb 222 B6
North Stifford Thurrock 68 C6
North Stoke Bath 61 F8
Oxon 64 B6
W Sus 35 E8
North Stoneham Hants 32 D6
North Street Hants 31 D11
Hants 48 G6
Kent 54 B4
Medway 69 E10
W Berks 64 E6
North Sunderland
Northumb 264 C6
North Synton Borders 261 E11
North Tamerton Corn 12 B2
North Tawton Devon 25 G11
North Thoresby Lincs 190 B3
North Tidworth Wilts 47 D8
North Togston Northumb 252 C6
Northton Aberds 293 C9
Northtown Orkney 314 G4
Shetland 313 M5
North Town Devon 25 F8
Hants 49 C11
Som 29 B10
Som 44 E5
Windsor 65 C11
North Tuddenham
Norf 159 G10
Northumberland Heath
London 68 D4
Northville Torf 78 F3
North Walbottle T&W 242 D5
North Walney Cumb 210 F3
North Walsham Norf 160 C5
North Waltham Hants 48 D5
North Warnborough
Hants 49 C8
North Water Bridge
Angus 293 G8
North Waterhayne Devon 28 F3
North Watford Herts 85 F10
North Watten Highld 310 D6
Northway Devon 24 C5
Glos 99 E8
Som 27 B10
Swansea 56 D5
North Weald Bassett
Essex 87 E7
North Weirs Hants 32 G3
North Wembley London 67 B7
North Weston N Som 60 D3
Oxon 83 D11
North Wheatley Notts 188 D3
North Whilborough Devon 9 B7
North Whiteley Moray 302 E4
Northwich Ches W 183 G11
Northwick S Glos 60 B5
Som 43 D11
Worcs 116 F6
North Wick Bath 60 F5
North Widcombe Bath 44 B5
North Willingham
Lincs 189 D11
North Wingfield Derbys 170 B6
North Witham Lincs 155 E8
Northwold Norf 140 D5
Northwood Derbys 170 C3
IoW 20 C5
Kent 71 F11
London 85 G9
Mers 182 B6
Shrops 149 C9
Staffs 168 G5
Stoke 168 F5
Northwood Green Glos 80 B2
Northwood Hills London 85 G9
North Woolwich London 68 D2
North Wootton Dorset 29 E11
Norf 158 E2
Som 44 E5
North Wraxall Wilts 61 D10
North Wroughton
Swindon 63 C7
Norton Devon 9 E7
Devon 24 B3
E Sus 23 E7
Glos 99 G7
Halton 183 E9
Herts 104 E4
IoW 20 D2
Mon 78 B6
Northants 120 E2
Notts 187 G9
N Som 59 G10
Powys 114 D6
Shrops 131 B11
Shrops 131 G9
Shrops 132 C4
Stockton 234 G4
Suff 125 D9
Swansea 56 D3
Swansea 56 D6
S Yorks 186 E5
S Yorks 198 D4
Wilts 61 C11
W Mid 133 G7
Worcs 99 B10
Worcs 117 G7
W Sus 22 B6
W Sus 22 D5
Norton Ash Kent 70 G3
Norton Bavant Wilts 46 E2
Norton Bridge Staffs 151 C7
Norton Canes Staffs 133 B10
Norton Canon Hereford 97 B7
Norton Corner Norf 159 D11
Norton Disney Lincs 172 D5
Norton East Staffs 133 B10
Norton Ferris Wilts 45 F9
Norton Fitzwarren
Som 27 B11
Norton Green Herts 104 G4
IoW 20 D2
Staffs 168 E6
W Mid 118 C3
Norton Hawkfield Bath 60 G5
Norton Heath Essex 87 E10

Rayleigh Essex 88 G4
Rayne Essex 106 G4
Rayners Lane London 66 B6
Raynes Park London 67 F8
Reabrook Shrops 131 C7
Reach Cambs 123 D11
Read Lancs 203 G11
Reader's Corner Essex 88 E2
Reading Reading 65 E8
Readings Glos 79 B10
Reading Street Kent 54 G2
Kent 71 F11
Readymoney Corn 6 E2
Ready Token Glos 81 E10
Reagill Cumb 222 B2
Rearquhar Highld 309 K7
Rearsby Leics 154 G3
Reasby Lincs 189 F9
Rease Heath Ches E 167 E10
Reaster Highld 310 C6
Reaulay Highld 299 D7
Reawick Shetland 313 J5
Reawla Corn 2 B4
Reay Highld 310 C3
Rechullin Highld 299 D8
Reculver Kent 71 F8
Red Ball Devon 27 D9
Redberth Pembs 73 E9
Redbourn Herts 85 C10
Redbournbury Herts 85 C10
Redbourne N Lincs 189 B7
N Lincs 200 G3
Redbridge Dorset 17 D11
London 68 B2
Soton 32 E5
Red Bridge Lancs 211 D9
Redbrook Mon 79 C8
Wrex 167 G8
Red Bull Ches E 168 D4
Staffs 150 B4
Redburn Highld 300 C5
Highld 301 E9
Northumb 241 E7
Redcar Redcar 235 G8
Redcastle Angus 287 B10
Highld 300 E5
Redcliff Bay N Som 60 D2
Redcroft Dumfries 237 B9
Redcross Worcs 117 C7
Red Dial Cumb 229 B11
Reddicap Heath W Mid 134 D2
Redding Falk 279 F8
Reddingmuirhead Falk 279 F8
Reddish Gtr Man 184 C5
Warr 183 D11
Redditch Worcs 117 D10
Rede Suff 124 F6
Redenhall Norf 142 G5
Redenham Hants 47 D10
Redesdale Camp
Northumb 251 D8
Redesmouth Northumb 251 G9
Redford Aberds 293 F9
Angus 287 C9
Dorset 29 F10
Durham 233 E7
W Sus 34 B5
Redfordgreen Borders 261 F9
Redgorton Perth 286 E4
Redgrave Suff 125 B10
Redheugh Angus 292 G6
Redhill Aberds 293 C9
Aberds 302 F6
Herts 104 E6
Notts 171 F9
N Som 60 G4
Shrops 131 B9
Shrops 150 G4
Staffs 150 D6
Sur 51 C9
Telford 150 G4
Red Hill Bmouth 19 B7
Hants 34 E2
Hereford 97 D10
Kent 53 C7
Leics 135 D10
Pembs 72 B6
Warks 118 F2
Worcs 117 G7
W Yorks 198 B2
Redhills Cumb 230 F6
Devon 14 C4
Redhouse Argyll 275 G9
Red House Common
E Sus 36 C5
Redhouses Argyll 274 G4
Redisham Suff 143 G8
Red Lake Telford 150 G3
Redland Bristol 60 D5
Orkney 314 D3
Redland End Bucks 84 E4
Redlands Dorset 17 E9
Som 44 G3
Swindon 81 G11
Redlane Som 28 E2
Redlingfield Suff 126 C3
Red Lodge Suff 124 C3
Red Lumb Gtr Man 195 D10
Redlynch Som 45 G8
Wilts 32 C2
Redmain Cumb 229 E8
Redmarley D'Abitot Glos 98 E5
Redmarshall Stockton 234 G3
Redmile Leics 154 B5
Redmire N Yorks 223 G10
Redmonsford Devon 24 D4
Redmoor Corn 5 C11
Redmoss Aberds 303 F8
Rednal Shrops 149 D7
W Mid 117 B10
Redpath Borders 262 B3
Red Pits Norf 159 D11
Redpoint Highld 299 C7
Red Post Corn 24 F3
Red Rail Hereford 97 F10
Red Rice Hants 47 E10
Red Rock Gtr Man 194 F5
Red Roses Carms 74 C2
Red Row Northumb 253 D7
Redruth Corn 4 G3
Red Scar Lancs 203 G7
Redscarhead Borders 270 G4
Redstocks Wilts 62 G2
Red Street Staffs 168 E4
Redtye Corn 5 C10
Redvales Gtr Man 195 F10
Red Wharf Bay Anglesey 179 E8
Redwick Newport 60 C2
S Glos 60 B4
Redwith Shrops 148 E6
Redworth Darl 233 G10
Reed Herts 105 D7
Reed End Herts 104 D6
Reedham Lincs 174 D2
Norf 143 C8
Reedley Lancs 204 F2
Reedness E Yorks 199 C9
Reed Point Lincs 174 E2
Reeds Beck Lincs 174 B2
Reedsford Northumb 263 C9
Reeds Holme Lancs 195 C10
Reedy Devon 14 D2
Reen Manor Corn 4 E5
Reepham Lincs 189 G8
Norf 159 E11
Reeth N Yorks 223 F10
Reeves Green W Mid 118 B5
Refail Powys 130 C3
Regaby IoM 192 C5
Regil Bath 60 G4
Regoul Highld 301 D8
Reiff Highld 307 H4
Reigate Sur 51 C9
Reigate Heath Sur 51 C8
Reighton N Yorks 218 D2
Reighton Gap N Yorks 218 D2
Reinigeadal W Isles 305 H4
Reisque Aberds 293 B10
Reiss Highld 310 D7
Rejerrah Corn 4 D5
Releath Corn 2 C5
Relubbus Corn 2 C3
Relugas Moray 301 E9
Remenham Wokingham 65 C9
Remenham Hill
Wokingham 65 C9
Remony Perth 285 C11
Rempstone Notts 153 E11
Remusaig Highld 309 J7
Rendcomb Glos 81 D8
Rendham Suff 126 E6
Rendlesham Suff 126 G6
Renfrew Renfs 267 B10
Renhold Beds 121 G11
Renishaw Derbys 186 F6
Renmure Angus 287 B10
Rennington Northumb 264 F6
Renshaw Wood Shrops 132 B6
Renton W Dunb 277 F7
Renwick Cumb 231 C7
Repps Norf 161 F8
Repton Derbys 152 D6
Reraig Highld 295 C10
Reraig Cot Highld 295 B10
Rerwick Shetland 313 M5
Rescassa Corn 5 G9
Rescobie Angus 287 B9
Rescorla Corn 5 D10
Resipole Highld 289 C9
Reskadinnick Corn 4 G2
Resolfen / Resolven
Neath 76 E4
Resolis Highld 300 C6
Resolven / Resolfen
Neath 76 E4
Restalrig Edin 280 G5
Reston Borders 273 C7
Cumb 221 F9
Restronguet Passage Corn 3 B8
Restrop Wilts 62 B5
Resugga Green Corn 5 D10
Reswallie Angus 287 B9
Retallack Corn 5 B8
Retew Corn 5 D8
Retford Notts 188 E2
Retire Corn 5 C10
Rettendon Essex 88 F3
Rettendon Place Essex 88 F3
Revesby Lincs 174 C3
Revesby Bridge Lincs 174 C4
Revidge Blkburn 195 B7
Rew Devon 9 G9
Devon 13 G11
Dorset 29 F11
Rewe Devon 14 B4
Rew Street IoW 20 C5
Rexon Devon 12 D4
Rexon Cross Devon 12 D4
Reybridge Wilts 62 F2
Reydon Suff 127 B9
Reydon Smear Suff 127 B9
Reymerston Norf 141 B10
Reynalton Pembs 73 D9
Reynoldston Swansea 56 C3
Rezare Corn 12 F3
Rhadyr Mon 78 E5
Rhaeadr Gwy / Rhayader
Powys 113 D9
Rhandir Conwy 180 G4
Rhandirmwyn Carms 94 C5
Rhayader / Rhaeadr Gwy
Powys 113 D9
Rhedyn Gwyn 144 C5
Rhegreanoch Highld 307 H5
Rhemore Highld 289 D7
Rhencullen IoM 192 C4
Rhenetra Highld 298 D4
Rhes-y-cae Flint 181 G11
Rhewl Denb 165 C10
Denb 165 F11
Shrops 148 C6
Wrex 149 B7
Rhewl-fawr Flint 181 E10
Rhewl-Mostyn Flint 181 E11
Rhian Highld 309 H5
Rhicarn Highld 307 G5
Rhiconich Highld 306 D7
Rhicullen Highld 300 B6
Rhidorroch Ho Highld 307 K6
Rhiews Shrops 150 B2
Rhifail Highld 308 E7
Rhigolter Highld 308 D3
Rhigos Rhondda 76 D6
Rhilochan Highld 309 J7
Rhippinllwyd Ceredig 92 C5
Ceredig 110 G6
Rhiroy Highld 307 L6
Rhitongue Highld 308 D6
Rhivichie Highld 306 D7
Rhiw Gwyn 144 D4
Rhiwabon / Ruabon
Wrex 166 G4
Rhiwbebyll Denb 165 B10
Rhiwbina Cardiff 59 C7
Rhiwbryfdir Gwyn 163 F11
Rhiwceiliog Bridgend 58 C3
Rhiwderin Newport 59 B9
Rhiwen Gwyn 163 C9
Rhiwfawr Neath 76 C2
Rhiwinder Rhondda 58 B4
Rhiwlas Gwyn 147 B8
Gwyn 163 B9
Powys 148 C3
Rhode Som 43 G9
Rhode Common Kent 54 B5
Rhodes Gtr Man 195 F11
Rhodesia Notts 187 F9
Rhodes Minnis Kent 55 E7
Rhodiad Pembs 90 F5
Rhonadale Argyll 255 D8
Rhondda Rhondda 77 F7
Rhonehouse or Kelton Hill
Dumfries 237 D9
Rhoose V Glam 58 F5
Rhos Carms 93 D7
Rhôs Denb 165 C10
Neath 76 E2
Rhos Powys 148 F5
Rhosaman Carms 76 C2
Rhosbeirio Anglesey 178 C5
Rhoscefnhir Anglesey 179 F8
Rhoscolyn Anglesey 178 F3
Rhôs Common Powys 148 F5
Rhoscrowther Pembs 72 E6
Rhosddu Wrex 166 E4
Rhos-ddû Gwyn 144 B5
Rhosdylluan Gwyn 147 D7
Rhosesmor Flint 166 B2
Rhosfach Pembs 92 F2
Rhos-fawr Gwyn 145 B7
Rhosgadfan Gwyn 163 D8
Rhosgoch Anglesey 178 D6
Powys 96 B3
Rhos-goch Powys 96 B3
Rhosgyll Gwyn 163 G7
Rhos Haminiog Ceredig 111 E10
Rhos-hill Pembs 92 C3
Rhoshirwaun Gwyn 144 D3
Rhos Isaf Gwyn 163 D7
Rhoslan Gwyn 163 G7
Rhoslefain Gwyn 110 B2
Rhosllanerchrugog
Wrex 166 F3
Rhôs Lligwy Anglesey 179 D7
Rhosmaen Carms 94 G2
Rhosmeirch Anglesey 179 F7
Rhosneigr Anglesey 178 G4
Rhosnesni Wrex 166 E5
Rhôs-on-Sea Conwy 180 E4
Rhosrobin Wrex 166 E4
Rhossili Swansea 56 D2
Rhosson Pembs 90 F4
Rhostrehwfa Anglesey 178 G6
Rhostryfan Gwyn 163 D7
Rhostyllen Wrex 166 F4
Rhoswiel Shrops 148 B5
Rhosybol Anglesey 178 D6
Rhos-y-brithdir Powys 148 E2
Rhosycaerau Pembs 91 D8
Rhosygadair Newydd
Ceredig 92 B4
Rhosygadfa Shrops 148 C6
Rhos-y-garth Ceredig 112 C2
Rhosygilwen Pembs 92 C4
Rhos-y-gwaliau Gwyn 147 C8
Rhos-y-llan Gwyn 144 B4
Rhos-y-Madoc Wrex 166 G4
Rhosymedre Wrex 166 G3
Rhos-y-meirch Powys 114 D5
Rhosyn-coch Carms 92 G5
Rhu Argyll 275 G9
Argyll 276 E5
Rhuallt Denb 181 F9
Rhubodach Argyll 275 F11
Rhuddall Heath Ches W 167 C9
Rhuddlan Ceredig 93 C9
Denb 181 F8
Rhue Highld 307 K5
Rhulen Powys 96 B2
Rhunahaorine Argyll 255 C8
Rhyd Ceredig 92 C5
Gwyn 163 G10
Powys 129 C9
Rhydaman / Ammanford
Carms 75 C10
Rhydargaeau Carms 93 F8
Rhydcymerau Carms 93 D11
Rhydd Worcs 98 B6
Rhyd-Ddu Gwyn 163 E9
Rhydd Green Worcs 98 B6
Rhydding Neath 57 B8
Rhydfudr Ceredig 111 D11
Rhydgaled Conwy 165 C7
Rhydgaled / Chancery
Ceredig 111 B11
Rhydlewis Ceredig 92 B6
Rhydlios Gwyn 144 C3
Rhydlydan Conwy 164 E5
Powys 129 E11
Rhydmoelddu Powys 113 B11
Rhydness Powys 96 C2
Rhydowen Carms 92 F3
Ceredig 93 B8
Rhyd-Rosser Ceredig 111 D11
Rhydspence Hereford 96 B4
Rhydtalog Flint 166 D2
Rhyd-uchaf Gwyn 147 B8
Rhydwen Gwyn 146 F4
Rhydwyn Anglesey 178 D4
Rhyd-y-Brown Pembs 91 G11
Rhyd-y-clafdy Gwyn 144 B6
Rhydycroesau Powys 148 C4
Rhyd-y-cwm Shrops 130 G3
Rhydyfelin Carms 92 D5
Ceredig 111 B11
Powys 129 E11
Rhondda 58 B5
Rhyd-y-foel Conwy 180 F6
Rhyd-y-fro Neath 76 D2
Rhydygele Pembs 91 G7
Rhyd-y-gwin Swansea 75 E11
Rhyd-y-gwystl Gwyn 145 B8
Rhydymain Gwyn 146 E6
Rhyd-y-meirch Mon 78 D4
Rhyd-y-meudwy Denb 165 E10
Rhydymwyn Flint 166 B2
Rhyd-y-pandy Swansea 75 E11
Rhyd-yr-onen Gwyn 128 C2
Rhyd-y-sarn Gwyn 163 G11
Rhydywrach Carms 73 B11
Rhyl Denb 181 E8
Rhymney Caerph 77 D10
Rhyn Wrex 148 B6
Rhynd Fife 287 E8
Perth 286 E5
Rhynie Aberds 302 G4
Highld 301 B8
Ribbesford Worcs 116 C5
Ribblehead N Yorks 212 D5
Ribble Head N Yorks 212 D5
Ribbleton Lancs 203 G7
Ribby Lancs 202 G4
Ribchester Lancs 203 F8
Riber Derbys 170 D4
Ribigill Highld 308 D5
Riby Lincs 201 F7
Riby Cross Roads Lincs 201 F7
Riccall N Yorks 207 F8
Riccarton E Ayrs 257 B10
Richards Castle
Hereford 115 D9
Richborough Port Kent 71 G10
Richings Park Bucks 66 D4
Richmond London 67 E7
N Yorks 224 E3
S Yorks 186 D6
Richmond Hill W Yorks 206 G2
Richmond's Green
Essex 106 F2
Rich's Holford Som 42 G6
Rickard's Down Devon 24 B6
Rickarton Aberds 293 E10
Rickerby Cumb 239 F10
Rickerscote Staffs 151 E8
Rickford N Som 44 B3
Rickinghall Suff 125 B10
Rickleton T&W 243 G7
Rickling Essex 105 E9
Rickling Green Essex 105 F10
Rickmansworth Herts 85 G9
Rickney E Sus 23 D10
Riddell Borders 262 E2
Riddings Derbys 170 E6
Riddlecombe Devon 25 E10
Riddlesden W Yorks 205 E7
Riddrie Glasgow 268 B2
Ridgacre W Mid 133 G10
Ridge Bath 44 B5
Dorset 18 D4
Hants 32 D4
Herts 86 E2
Lancs 211 G9
Som 28 F3
Wilts 46 G3
Ridgebourne Powys 113 E11
Ridge Common Hants 34 C2
Ridge Green Sur 51 D10
Ridgehill N Som 60 G4
Ridge Hill Gtr Man 185 B7
Ridge Lane Warks 134 E5
Ridgemarsh Herts 85 G8
Ridge Row Kent 55 E8
Ridgeway Bristol 60 D6
Derbys 170 E5
Derbys 186 E6
Kent 54 E5
Newport 59 B9
Pembs 73 D10
Som 45 D8
Staffs 168 E5
Ridgeway Cross Hereford 98 B4
Ridgeway Moor Derbys 186 E6
Ridgewell Essex 106 C4
Ridgewood E Sus 23 B7
Ridgmont C Beds 103 D9
Ridgway Shrops 131 F7
Sur 50 B4
Riding Gate Som 30 B2
Riding Mill Northumb 242 E2
Ridley Kent 68 G6
Northumb 241 E7
Ridley Stokoe Northumb 250 F6
Ridleywood Wrex 166 E6
Ridlington Norf 160 C6
Rutland 136 C6
Ridlington Street Norf 160 C6
Ridsdale Northumb 251 G10
Riechip Perth 286 C4
Riemore Perth 286 C4
Rienachait Highld 306 F5
Rievaulx N Yorks 215 B11
Riff Orkney 314 E4
Riffin Aberds 303 E7
Rifle Green Torf 78 D3
Rift House Hrtlpl 234 E5
Rigg Dumfries 239 D7
Riggend N Lnrk 278 G5
Rigsby Lincs 190 F6
Rigside S Lnrk 259 B9
Riley Green Lancs 194 B6
Rileyhill Staffs 152 F2
Rilla Mill Corn 11 G11
Rillaton Corn 11 G11
Rillington N Yorks 217 E7
Rimac Lincs 191 C7
Rimington Lancs 204 D2
Rimpton Som 29 C10
Rimswell E Yorks 201 B10
Rimswell Valley
E Yorks 201 B10
Rinaston Pembs 91 F9
Rindleford Shrops 132 D4
Ringasta Shetland 313 M5
Ringford Dumfries 237 D8
Ringing Hill Leics 153 F9
Ringinglow S Yorks 186 E3
Ringland Newport 59 B11
Norf 160 G2
Ringles Cross E Sus 37 C7
Ringlestone Kent 53 B9
Kent 53 B11
Ringley Gtr Man 195 F9
Ringmer E Sus 36 E6
Ringmore Devon 8 F3
Ring o' Bells Lancs 194 E3
Ringorm Moray 302 E2
Ring's End Cambs 139 C7
Ringsfield Suff 143 F8
Ringsfield Corner Suff 143 F8
Ringshall Herts 85 C7
Suff 125 G10
Ringshall Stocks Suff 125 G10
Ringstead Norf 176 E2
Northants 121 B9
Ringtail Green Essex 87 B11
Ringwood Hants 31 F11
Ringwould Kent 55 D11
Rinmore Aberds 292 B6
Rinnigill Orkney 314 G3
Rinsey Corn 2 D3
Rinsey Croft Corn 2 D4
Riof W Isles 304 E3
Ripe E Sus 23 C8
Ripley Derbys 170 E5
Hants 19 B9
N Yorks 214 G5
Sur 50 B5
Riplingham E Yorks 208 G5
Ripon N Yorks 214 E6
Ripper's Cross Kent 54 E3
Rippingale Lincs 155 D11
Ripple Kent 55 D10
Worcs 99 D7
Ripponden W Yorks 196 D4
Rireavach Highld 307 K5
Risabus Argyll 254 C4
Risbury Hereford 115 G10
Risby E Yorks 208 G6
Lincs 189 C10
Suff 124 D5
Risca Caerph 78 G2
Rise E Yorks 209 E9
Rise Carr Darl 224 B5
Riseden E Sus 52 G6
Kent 53 F8
Rise End Derbys 170 D3
Risegate Lincs 156 D4
Riseholme Lincs 189 F7
Risehow Cumb 228 E6
Riseley Beds 121 E10
Wokingham 65 G8
Rise Park London 87 G8
Nottingham 171 F9
Rishangles Suff 126 D3
Rishton Lancs 203 G10
Rishworth W Yorks 196 D4
Rising Bridge Lancs 195 B9
Risingbrook Staffs 151 E8
Risinghurst Oxon 83 D9
Rising Sun Corn 12 G3
Risley Derbys 153 B9
Warr 183 C10
Risplith N Yorks 214 F4
Rispond Highld 308 C4
Rivar Wilts 63 G10
Rivenhall Essex 88 B4
Rivenhall End Essex 88 B4
River Kent 55 E9
W Sus 34 C6
River Bank Cambs 123 D10
Riverhead Kent 52 B4
Rivers' Corner Dorset 30 E3
Riverside Cardiff 59 D7
Plym 7 D8
Stirl 278 C6
Worcs 117 D10
Riverside Docklands
Lancs 194 B4
Riverton Devon 40 G6
Riverview Park Kent 69 E7
Rivington Lancs 194 E6
Rixon Dorset 30 E3
Rixton Warr 183 C11
Roach Bridge Lancs 194 B5
Roaches Gtr Man 196 G3
Roachill Devon 26 C4
Roade Northants 120 G5
Road Green Norf 142 E5
Roadhead Cumb 240 C2
Roadmeetings S Lnrk 269 F7
Roadside Highld 310 C5
Roadside of Catterline
Aberds 293 F10
Roadside of Kinneff
Aberds 293 F10
Roadwater Som 42 F4
Road Weedon Northants 120 F2
Roag Highld 298 E2
Roa Island Cumb 210 G4
Roast Green Essex 105 E9
Roath Cardiff 59 D7
Roath Park Cardiff 59 D7
Roberton Borders 261 G10
S Lnrk 259 D10
Robertsbridge E Sus 38 C2
Robertstown Moray 302 E2
Rhondda 77 E8
Roberttown W Yorks 197 C7
Robeston Back Pembs 73 B9
Robeston Cross Pembs 72 D5
Robeston Wathen Pembs 73 B9
Robeston West Pembs 72 D5
Robhurst Kent 54 G2
Robin Hill Staffs 168 D6
Robin Hood Derbys 186 G3
Lancs 194 E4
W Yorks 197 B10
Robinhood End Essex 106 D4
Robin Hood's Bay
N Yorks 227 D9
Robins W Sus 34 B4
Robinson's End Warks 134 E6
Roborough Devon 7 C10
Devon 25 D9
Rob Roy's House Argyll 284 F5
Robroyston Glasgow 268 B2
Roby Mers 182 C6
Roby Mill Lancs 194 F4
Rocester Staffs 152 B2
Roch Pembs 91 G7
Rochdale Gtr Man 195 E11
Roche Corn 5 C9
Roche Grange Staffs 169 C7
Rochester Medway 69 F8
Northumb 251 D8
Rochford Essex 88 G5
Worcs 116 D2
Roch Gate Pembs 91 G7
Rock Caerph 77 F11
Corn 10 F4
Devon 28 G3
Neath 57 C9
Northumb 264 E6
Som 28 C4
Worcs 116 C4
W Sus 35 E10
Rockbeare Devon 14 C6
Rockbourne Hants 31 D10
Rockcliffe Cumb 239 E9
Dumfries 237 D10
Flint 182 G3
Lancs 195 C11
Rockcliffe Cross Cumb 239 E8
Rock End Staffs 168 D5
Rock Ferry Mers 182 D4
Rockfield Highld 311 L3
Mon 79 C7
Rockford Devon 41 D9
Hants 31 F11
Rockgreen Shrops 115 B10
Rockhampton S Glos 79 G11
Rockhead Corn 11 E7
Rockhill Shrops 114 B5
Rockingham Northants 137 E7
Rockland All Saints
Norf 141 D9
Rockland St Mary Norf 142 C6
Rockland St Peter Norf 141 D9
Rockley Notts 188 G2
Wilts 63 E7
Rockley Ford Som 45 C8
Rockness Glos 80 F4
Rockrobin E Sus 52 G6
Rocksavage Halton 183 E8
Rocks Park E Sus 37 C7
Rockstowes Glos 80 F3
Rockville Argyll 276 C4
Rockwell End Bucks 65 B9
Rockwell Green Som 27 C10
Rocky Hill Scilly 1 G4
Rodbaston Staffs 151 G8
Rodborough Glos 80 E4
Rodbourne Swindon 62 C6
Wilts 62 C2
Rodbourne Bottom Wilts 62 C2
Rodbourne Cheney
Swindon 62 B6
Rodbridge Corner
Essex 107 C7
Rodd Hereford 114 E6
Roddam Northumb 264 E2
Rodden Dorset 17 E8
Rodd Hurst Hereford 114 E6
Roddymoor Durham 233 D9
Rode Som 45 C10
Rodeheath Ches E 168 B5
Rode Heath Ches E 168 D3
Rode Hill Som 45 C10
Roden Telford 149 F11
Rodford S Glos 61 C7
Rodgrove Som 30 C2
Rodhuish Som 42 F4
Rodington Telford 149 G11
Rodington Heath
Telford 149 G11
Rodley Glos 80 C2
W Yorks 205 F10
Rodmarton Glos 80 F6
Rodmell E Sus 36 F6
Rodmer Clough
W Yorks 196 B3
Rodmersham Kent 70 G2
Rodmersham Green Kent 70 G2
Rodney Stoke Som 44 C3
Rodsley Derbys 170 G2
Rodway Som 43 F9
Telford 150 F3
Rodwell Dorset 17 F9
Roebuck Low Gtr Man 196 F3
Roecliffe N Yorks 215 F7
Roe Cross Gtr Man 185 B7
Roedean Brighton 36 G4
Roe End Herts 85 B8
Roe Green Gtr Man 195 G9
Herts 86 D2
Herts 104 E6
Roehampton London 67 E8
Roe Lee Blkburn 203 G9
Roesound Shetland 312 G5
Roestock Herts 86 D2
Roffey W Sus 51 G7
Rogart Highld 309 J7
Rogart Station Highld 309 J7
Rogate W Sus 34 C4
Roger Ground Cumb 221 F7
Rogerstone Newport 59 B9
Rogerton S Lnrk 268 D2
Roghadal W Isles 296 C6
Rogiet Mon 60 B3
Rogue's Alley Cambs 139 B7
Roke Oxon 83 G10
Rokemarsh Oxon 83 G10
Roker T&W 243 F10
Rollesby Norf 161 F8
Rolleston Leics 136 C4
Notts 172 E2
Rollestone S Yorks 186 E5
Wilts 46 E5
Rollestone Camp Wilts 46 E5
Rolleston-on-Dove
Staffs 152 D4
Rolls Mill Dorset 30 E3
Rolston E Yorks 209 D10
Rolstone N Som 59 G11
Rolvenden Kent 53 G10
Rolvenden Layne Kent 53 G11
Romaldkirk Durham 232 G5
Romanby N Yorks 225 G7
Roman Hill Suff 143 E10
Romannobridge Borders 270 F3
Romansleigh Devon 26 C2
Rome Angus 293 G7
Romesdal Highld 298 D4
Romford Dorset 31 F9
Kent 52 E6
London 68 B4
Romiley Gtr Man 184 C6
Romney Street Kent 68 G4
Rompa Shetland 313 L6
Romsey Hants 32 C5
Romsey Town Cambs 123 F9
Romsley Shrops 132 G5
Worcs 117 B9
Romsley Hill Worcs 117 B9
Ronachan Ho Argyll 255 B8
Ronague IoM 192 E3
Rondlay Telford 132 B4
Ronkswood Worcs 117 G7
Rood End W Mid 133 F10
Rookby Cumb 222 C6
Rook End Essex 105 E11
Rookhope Durham 232 C4
Rooking Cumb 221 B8
Rookley IoW 20 E6
Rookley Green IoW 20 E6
Rooks Bridge Som 43 C11
Rooksey Green Suff 125 G8
Rooks Hill Kent 52 C5
Rooksmoor Glos 80 E4
Rook's Nest Som 42 G5
Rook Street Wilts 45 G10
Rookwith N Yorks 214 B4
Rookwood W Sus 21 B11
Roos E Yorks 209 G11
Roose Cumb 210 F4
Roosebeck Cumb 210 F5
Roosecote Cumb 210 F4
Roost End Essex 106 C4
Rootham's Green Beds 122 F2
Rooting Street Kent 54 D3
Rootpark S Lnrk 269 E9
Ropley Hants 48 G6
Ropley Dean Hants 48 G6
Ropley Soke Hants 49 G7
Ropsley Lincs 155 C9
Rora Aberds 303 D10
Rorandle Aberds 293 B8
Rorrington Shrops 130 C5
Rosarie Moray 302 E3
Roscroggan Corn 4 G3
Rose Corn 4 E5
Roseacre Kent 53 B9
Lancs 202 F4
Rose-an-Grouse Corn 2 B2
Rose Ash Devon 26 C3
Rosebank E Dunb 278 G3
S Lnrk 268 F6
Rosebery Midloth 270 D6
Rosebrae Moray 301 C11
Rosebrough Northumb 264 D4
Rosebush Pembs 91 F11
Rosecare Corn 11 B9
Rosedale Herts 86 E4
Rosedale Abbey
N Yorks 226 F4
Roseden Northumb 264 E2
Rosedinnick Corn 5 B8
Rosedown Devon 24 C3
Rosefield Highld 301 D8
Rose Green Essex 107 F8
Suff 107 C9
Suff 107 D8
W Sus 22 D6
Rose Grove Lancs 204 G2
Rosehall Highld 309 J4
N Lnrk 268 C4
Rosehaugh Mains
Highld 300 D6
Rosehearty Aberds 303 C9
Rosehill Blkburn 195 C8
Corn 4 E5
Corn 5 C10
Gtr Man 184 D3
London 67 F9
Pembs 72 B5
Shrops 150 C3
T&W 243 D8
Rose Hill Bucks 66 C2
Derbys 153 B7
E Sus 23 B7
Gtr Man 195 F8
Lancs 204 G2
Oxon 83 E8
Suff 108 C3
Sur 51 D7
Roseisle Moray 301 C11
Roseland Corn 6 C5
Roselands E Sus 23 E10
Rosemarket Pembs 73 D7
Rosemarkie Highld 301 D7
Rosemary Lane Devon 27 E11
Rosemelling Corn 5 D10
Rosemergy Corn 1 B4
Rosemount Perth 286 C5
Rosenannon Corn 5 B9
Rosenithon Corn 3 E8
Roser's Cross E Sus 37 C9
Rose Valley Pembs 73 E8
Rosevean Corn 5 D10
Rosevear Corn 2 E5
Roseville W Mid 133 E8
Rosevine Corn 3 B9
Rosewarne Corn 2 B4
Corn 4 G2
Rosewell Midloth 270 C5
Roseworth Stockton 234 G4
Roseworthy Corn 2 B4
Corn 4 F5
Roseworthy Barton Corn 2 B4
Rosgill Cumb 221 B10
Rosherville Kent 68 E6
Roshven Highld 289 B9
Roskear Croft Corn 4 G3
Roskhill Highld 298 E2
Roskill House Highld 300 D6
Roskorwell Corn 3 E7
Rosley Cumb 230 B2
Roslin Midloth 270 C5
Rosliston Derbys 152 F4
Rosneath Argyll 276 E5
Ross Borders 273 C9
Dumfries 237 E8
Northumb 264 B4
Perth 285 E11
Rossett Wrex 166 D5
Rossett Green N Yorks 206 C2
Ross Green Worcs 116 E5
Rossie Ochill Perth 286 F4
Rossie Priory Perth 286 D6
Rossington S Yorks 187 B10
Rosskeen Highld 300 C6
Rossland Renfs 277 G8
Rossmore Poole 19 C7
Ross-on-Wye Hereford 98 G2
Roster Highld 310 F6
Rostherne Ches E 184 E2
Rostholme S Yorks 198 F5
Rosthwaite Cumb 220 C5
Cumb 220 G4
Roston Derbys 169 G10
Rosudgeon Corn 2 D3
Rosyth Fife 280 E2
Rotchfords Essex 107 E8
Rotcombe Bath 44 B6
Rothbury Northumb 252 C3
Rotherbridge W Sus 35 C7
Rotherby Leics 154 F3
Rotherfield E Sus 37 B9
Rotherfield Greys Oxon 65 C8
Rotherfield Peppard
Oxon 65 C8
Rotherham S Yorks 186 C6
Rotherhithe London 67 D11
Rothersthorpe Northants 120 F4
Rotherwas Hereford 97 D10
Rotherwick Hants 49 B8
Rothes Moray 302 E2
Rothesay Argyll 275 G11
Rothiebrisbane Aberds 303 F7
Rothiemay Crossroads
Moray 302 E5
Rothiemurchus Lodge
Highld 291 C11
Rothienorman Aberds 303 F7
Rothiesholm Orkney 314 D6
Rothley Leics 153 G11
Northumb 252 F2
Rothley Plain Leics 153 G11
Rothley Shield East
Northumb 252 E2
Rothmaise Aberds 302 F6
Rothwell Lincs 189 B11
Northants 136 G6
W Yorks 197 B10
Rothwell Haigh
W Yorks 197 B10
Rotsea E Yorks 209 C7
Rottal Angus 292 G5
Rotten End Essex 106 F4
Suff 127 D7
Rotten Green Hants 49 B9
Rotten Row W Berks 64 E5
W Mid 118 B3
Rottingdean Brighton 36 G5
Rottington Cumb 219 C9
Rotton Park W Mid 133 F10
Roud IoW 20 E6
Rougham Norf 158 E6
Suff 125 E8
Rougham Green Suff 125 E8
Rough Bank Gtr Man 196 E2
Roughbirchworth
S Yorks 197 G9
Roughburn Highld 290 E5
Rough Close Staffs 151 B8
Rough Common Kent 54 B6
Roughcote Staffs 168 G6
Rough Haugh Highld 308 E7
Rough Hay Staffs 152 E4
Roughlee Lancs 204 E2
Roughley W Mid 134 D2
Roughmoor Som 28 B2
Swindon 62 B6
Roughrigg N Lnrk 278 G6
Roughsike Cumb 240 B2
Roughton Lincs 174 C2
Norf 160 B4
Shrops 132 E5
Roughton Moor Lincs 174 C2
Roughway Kent 52 C6
Roundbush Essex 88 E5
Round Bush Herts 85 F10
Roundbush Green Essex 87 C9
Round Green Luton 103 G11
Roundham Som 28 F6
Roundhay W Yorks 206 F2
Round Maple Suff 107 C9
Round Oak Shrops 131 G7
W Mid 133 F8
Round's Green W Mid 133 F9
Roundshaw London 67 G10
Round Spinney
Northants 120 D5
Roundstonefoot
Dumfries 248 B4
Round Street Kent 69 F7
Roundstreet Common
W Sus 35 B9
Roundswell Devon 40 G4
Roundthorn Gtr Man 184 D4
Roundthwaite Cumb 222 E2
Roundway Wilts 62 G4
Roundyhill Angus 287 B7
Rousdon Devon 15 C11
Rousham Oxon 101 G9
Rous Lench Worcs 117 G10
Routenburn N Ayrs 266 C3
Routh E Yorks 209 E7
Rout's Green Bucks 84 F3
Row Corn 11 F7
Cumb 211 B8
Cumb 231 E8
Rowanburn Dumfries 239 B10
Rowanfield Glos 99 G8
Rowardennan Stirl 277 B7
Rowarth Derbys 185 D8
Row Ash Hants 33 E8
Rowbarton Som 28 B2
Rowberrow Som 44 B3
Row Brow Cumb 229 D7
Rowde Wilts 62 G3
Rowden Devon 13 B8
N Yorks 205 B11
Rowe Head Cumb 210 D5
Rowen Conwy 180 G3
Rowfoot Northumb 240 E5
Rowford Som 28 B2
Row Green Essex 106 G4
Row Heath Essex 89 B10
Rowhedge Essex 107 G10
Rowhill Sur 66 G4
Rowhook W Sus 50 G6
Rowington Warks 118 D4
Rowington Green
Warks 118 D4
Rowland Derbys 186 G2
Rowlands Castle Hants 34 E2
Rowlands Gill T&W 242 F5
Rowland's Green
Hereford 98 D3
Rowledge Sur 49 E10
Rowlestone Hereford 97 F7
Rowley E Yorks 208 G5
Shrops 130 B6
Rowley Green London 86 F2
Rowley Hill W Yorks 197 E7
Rowley Park Staffs 151 E8
Rowley Regis W Mid 133 F9
Rowley's Green W Mid 134 G6
Rowling Kent 55 C9
Rowly Sur 50 E4
Rownall Staffs 169 F7
Rowner Hants 33 G9
Rowney Green Worcs 117 C10
Rownhams Hants 32 D5
Row-of-trees Ches E 184 F4
Rowrah Cumb 219 B11
Rowsham Bucks 84 B4
Rowsley Derbys 170 B3
Rowstock Oxon 64 B3
Rowston Lincs 173 D9
Rowthorne Derbys 171 C7
Rowton Ches W 166 C6
Shrops 149 G7
Telford 150 F2
Rowton Moor Ches W 166 C6
Row Town Sur 66 G4
Roxburgh Borders 262 C5
Roxburgh Mains
Borders 262 D5
Roxby N Lincs 200 D2
N Yorks 226 B5
Roxeth London 66 B6
Roxton Beds 122 G3
Roxwell Essex 87 D10
Royal British Legion Village
Kent 53 B8
Royal Leamington Spa
Warks 118 D6
Royal Oak Darl 233 G10
Lancs 194 G2
N Yorks 218 D2
Royal's Green Ches E 167 G10
Royal Tunbridge Wells /
Tunbridge Wells Kent 52 F5
Royal Wootton Bassett
Wilts 62 C5
Roybridge Highld 290 E4
Royd S Yorks 197 G8
Roydhouse W Yorks 197 E8
Royd Moor S Yorks 197 G8
W Yorks 198 E2
Roydon Essex 86 D6
Norf 141 G11
Norf 158 E4
Roydon Hamlet Essex 86 D6
Royds Green W Yorks 197 B11
Royston Glasgow 268 B2
Herts 105 C7
S Yorks 197 E11
Royston Water Som 28 E2
Royton Gtr Man 196 F2
Ruabon / Rhiwabon
Wrex 166 G4
Ruaig Argyll 288 E2
Ruan High Lanes Corn 3 B10
Ruan Lanihorne Corn 5 G7
Ruan Major Corn 2 F6
Ruan Minor Corn 2 F6
Ruarach Highld 295 C11
Ruardean Glos 79 B10
Ruardean Hill Glos 79 B10
Ruardean Woodside
Glos 79 B10
Rubery Worcs 117 B9
Rubha Ghaisinis
W Isles 297 G4
Rubha Stoer Highld 306 F5
Ruchazie Glasgow 268 B3
Ruchill Glasgow 267 B11
Ruckcroft Cumb 230 C6
Ruckhall Hereford 97 D9
Ruckinge Kent 54 G4
Ruckland Lincs 190 F4
Rucklers Lane Herts 85 E9
Ruckley Shrops 131 C10
Rudbaxton Pembs 91 G9
Rudby N Yorks 225 D9
Ruddington Notts 153 C11
Ruddle Glos 79 C11
Rudford Glos 98 G5
Rudge Shrops 132 D6
Som 45 C10
Rudge Heath Shrops 132 D5
Rudgeway S Glos 60 B6
Rudgwick W Sus 50 G5
Rudhall Hereford 98 F2
Rudheath Ches W 183 G11
Rudheath Woods
Ches W 184 G2
Rudhja Garbh Argyll 289 E11
Rudley Green Essex 88 E4
Rudloe Wilts 61 E10
Rudry Caerph 59 B7
Rudston E Yorks 217 F11
Rudyard Staffs 169 D7
Ruewood Shrops 149 D9
Rufford Lancs 194 D3
Rufforth York 206 C6
Ruffs Notts 171 F8
Rugby Warks 119 B10
Rugeley Staffs 151 F10
Ruggin Som 27 D11
Ruglen S Ayrs 245 C7
Rugley Northumb 264 G5
Ruilick Highld 300 E5
Ruishton Som 28 C3
Ruisigearraidh W Isles 296 C5
Ruislip London 66 B5
Ruislip Common London 66 B5
Ruislip Gardens London 66 B5
Ruislip Manor London 66 B6
Ruiton W Mid 133 E8
Ruloe Ches W 183 G9
Rumach Highld 295 G8
Rumbling Bridge
Perth 279 B10
Rumbow Cottages
Worcs 117 B8
Rumburgh Suff 142 G6
Rumbush W Mid 118 B2
Rumer Hill Staffs 133 B9
Rumford Corn 10 G3
Falk 279 F8
Rumney Cardiff 59 D8
Rumsam Devon 40 G5

Sevenhampton Glos 99 G10
Swindon 82 G2
Seven Kings London 68 B3
Sevenoaks Kent 52 C4
Sevenoaks Common
Kent 52 C4
Sevenoaks Weald Kent . . 52 C4
Seven Sisters / Blaendulais
Neath 76 D4
Seven Springs Glos 81 B7
Seven Star Green Essex . 107 F8
Severn Beach S Glos 60 B4
Severnhampton Swindon . 82 G2
Severn Stoke Worcs 99 C7
Sevick End Beds 121 G11
Sevington Kent 54 E4
Sewards End Essex 105 D11
Sewardstone Essex 86 F5
Sewardstonebury Essex . . 86 F5
Sewell C Beds 103 G9
Sewerby E Yorks 218 F3
Seworgan Corn 2 C6
Sewstern Leics 155 E7
Sexhow N Yorks 225 D9
Sezincote Glos 100 E3
Sgarasta Mhor W Isles . . 305 J2
Sgiogarstaigh W Isles . . 304 B7
Sgiwen / Skewen Neath . . 57 B8
Shabbington Bucks 83 D11
Shab Hill Glos 80 B6
Shackerley Shrops 132 B6
Shackerstone Leics 135 B7
Shacklecross Derbys 153 C8
Shackleford Sur 50 D2
Shackleton W Yorks 196 B3
Shacklewell London 67 B10
Shacklford Sur 50 D2
Shade W Yorks 196 C2
Shadforth Durham 234 C2
Shadingfield Suff 143 G8
Shadoxhurst Kent 54 F3
Shadsworth Blkburn 195 B8
Shadwell Glos 80 G3
London 67 C11
Norf 141 G8
W Yorks 206 F2
Shaffalong Staffs 169 E7
Shaftenhoe End Herts . . 105 D8
Shaftesbury Dorset 30 C5
Shafton S Yorks 197 E11
Shafton Two Gates
S Yorks 197 E11
Shaggs Dorset 18 E3
Shakeford Shrops 150 D3
Shakerley Gtr Man 195 G7
Shakesfield Glos 98 E3
Shalbourne Wilts 63 G10
Shalcombe IoW 20 D3
Shalden Hants 49 E7
Shalden Green Hants 49 E7
Shaldon Devon 14 G4
Shalfleet IoW 20 D4
Shalford Essex 106 F4
Som 45 G8
Sur 50 D4
Shalford Green Essex . . 106 F4
Shalloch Moray 302 D3
Shallowford Devon 25 B11
Devon 41 E8
Staffs 151 D7
Shalmsford Street Kent . 54 C5
Shalstone Bucks 102 D2
Shamley Green Sur 50 E4
Shandon Argyll 276 D5
Shandwick Highld 301 B8
Shangton Leics 136 D4
Shankhouse Northumb . . 243 B7
Shanklin IoW 21 E7
Shannochie N Ayrs 255 E10
Shannochill Stirl 277 B10
Shanquhar Aberds 302 F5
Shanwell Fife 287 E8
Shanzie Perth 286 B6
Shap Cumb 221 B11
Shapridge Glos 79 B11
Shapwick Dorset 30 G6
Som 44 F2
Sharcott Wilts 46 B6
Shard End W Mid 134 F3
Shardlow Derbys 153 C8
Shareshill Staffs 133 B8
Sharlston W Yorks 197 D11
Sharlston Common
W Yorks 197 D11
Sharmans Cross W Mid . . 118 B2
Sharnal Street Medway . . 69 E9
Sharnbrook Beds 121 F9
Sharneyford Lancs 195 C11
Sharnford Leics 135 E9
Sharnhill Green Dorset . . 30 F2
Sharoe Green Lancs 202 G6
Sharow N Yorks 214 E6
Sharpenhoe C Beds 103 E11
Sharperton Northumb . . 251 C11
Sharples Gtr Man 195 E8
Sharpley Heath Staffs . . 151 B9
Sharpness Glos 79 E11
Sharpsbridge E Sus 36 C6
Sharp's Corner E Sus 23 B9
Sharpstone Bath 45 B9
Sharp Street Norf 161 E7
Sharpthorne W Sus 51 G11
Sharptor Corn 11 G11
Sharpway Gate Worcs . . 117 D9
Sharrington Norf 159 B10
Sharrow S Yorks 186 D4
Sharston Gtr Man 184 D4
Shatterford Worcs 132 G5
Shatterling Kent 55 B9
Shatton Derbys 185 E11
Shaugh Prior Devon 7 C10
Shavington Ches E 168 E2
Shaw Gtr Man 196 F2
Swindon 62 B6
W Berks 64 F3
Wilts 61 F11
W Yorks 204 F6
Shawbank Shrops 131 G9
Shawbirch Telford 150 G2
Shawbury Shrops 149 E11
Shawclough Gtr Man . . . 195 E11
Shaw Common Glos 98 F3
Shawdon Hall Northumb . 264 G3
Shawell Leics 135 G10
Shawfield Gtr Man 195 E11
Staffs 169 C9
Shawfield Head
N Yorks 205 C11
Shawford Hants 33 C7
Som 45 C9
Shawforth Lancs 195 C11
Shaw Green Herts 104 E5
Lancs 194 D4
N Yorks 205 C11
Shawhead Dumfries 237 B10
N Lnrk 268 C4
Shaw Heath Ches E 184 F3
Gtr Man 184 D5
Shawhill Dumfries 238 D6
Shawlands Glasgow 267 C11
Shaw Lands S Yorks . . . 197 F10
Shaw Mills N Yorks 214 G5
Shawsburn S Lnrk 268 E5
Shaw Side Gtr Man 196 F2
Shawton S Lnrk 268 F3
Shawtonhill S Lnrk 268 F3
Shay Gate W Yorks 205 F8
Sheandow Moray 302 F2
Shear Cross Wilts 45 E11
Shearington Dumfries . . . 238 D2
Shearsby Leics 136 E2
Shearston Som 43 G9
Shebbear Devon 24 F6
Shebdon Staffs 150 D5
Shebster Highld 310 C4
Sheddens E Renf 267 D11
Shedfield Hants 33 E9
Sheen Staffs 169 C10
Sheepbridge Derbys 186 G5
Sheepdrove W Berks 63 D10
Sheep Hill Durham 242 F5
Sheeplane C Beds 103 E8
Sheepridge Bucks 65 B11
W Yorks 197 D7
Sheepscar W Yorks 206 G2
Sheepscombe Glos 80 C5
Sheepstor Devon 7 B11
Sheepwash Devon 25 F7
Northumb 253 F7
Sheepway N Som 60 D3
Sheepy Magna Leics 134 C6
Sheepy Parva Leics 134 C6
Sheering Essex 87 C8
Sheerness Kent 70 E2
Sheerwater Sur 66 G4
Sheet Hants 34 C3
Shrops 115 C10
Sheets Heath Sur 50 B2
Sheffield Corn 1 D5
S Yorks 186 D5
Sheffield Bottom
W Berks 65 F7
Sheffield Green E Sus 36 C6
Sheffield Park S Yorks . . 186 D5
Shefford C Beds 104 D2
Shefford Woodlands
W Berks 63 E11
Sheigra Highld 306 C6
Sheildmuir N Lnrk 268 D5
Sheinton Shrops 132 C2
Shelderton Shrops 115 B8
Sheldon Derbys 169 B11
Devon 27 F10
W Mid 134 G3
Sheldwich Kent 54 B4
Sheldwich Lees Kent 54 B4
Shelf Bridgend 58 C2
W Yorks 196 B6
Shelfanger Norf 142 G2
Shelfield Warks 118 E2
W Mid 133 C10
Shelfield Green Warks . . 118 E2
Shelfleys Northants 120 F4
Shelford Notts 171 G11
Warks 135 F8
Shell Worcs 117 F9
Shelland Suff 125 E10
Shellbrook Leics 152 F6
Shelley Essex 87 E9
Suff 107 D10
W Yorks 197 E8
Shelley Woodhouse
W Yorks 197 E8
Shell Green Halton 183 D8
Shellingford Oxon 82 G4
Shellow Bowells Essex . . 87 D10
Shellwood Cross Sur 51 D8
Shelsley Beauchamp
Worcs 116 E4
Shelsley Walsh Worcs . . 116 E4
Shelthorpe Leics 153 F10
Shelton Beds 121 D10
Norf 142 E4
Notts 172 G3
Shrops 149 G9
Stoke 168 F5
Shelton Green Norf 142 E4
Shelton Lock Derby 153 C7
Shelton under Harley
Staffs 150 B6
Shelve Shrops 130 D6
Shelvin Devon 27 G11
Shelvingford Kent 71 F8
Shelwick Hereford 97 C10
Shelwick Green
Hereford 97 C10
Shenfield Essex 87 G10
Shenington Oxon 101 C7
Shenley Herts 85 E11
Shenley Brook End
M Keynes 102 D6
Shenleybury Herts 85 E11
Shenley Church End
M Keynes 102 D6
Shenley Fields W Mid . . 133 G10
Shenley Lodge
M Keynes 102 D6
Shenley Wood
M Keynes 102 D6
Shenmore Hereford 97 D7
Shennanton Dumfries . . . 236 C5
Shennanton Ho
Dumfries 236 C5
Shenstone Staffs 134 C2
Worcs 117 C7
Shenstone Woodend
Staffs 134 C2
Shenton Leics 135 C7
Shenval Highld 300 G4
Moray 302 G2
Shenvault Moray 301 E10
Shepeau Stow Lincs 156 G6
Shephall Herts 104 G5
Shepherd Hill W Yorks . . 197 C9
Shepherd's Bush London . 67 C8
Shepherd's Gate Norf . . 157 F11
Shepherd's Green Oxon . . 65 C8
Shepherd's Hill Sur 50 G2
Shepherd's Patch Glos . . 80 E2
Shepherd's Port Norf . . . 158 C3
Shepherdswell or
Sibertswold Kent 55 D9
Shepley W Yorks 197 F7
Sheppardine S Glos 79 F10
Shepperton Sur 66 F5
Shepperton Green Sur . . 66 F5
Shepreth Cambs 105 B7
Shepshed Leics 153 F9
Shepton Beauchamp
Som 28 D6
Shepton Mallet Som 44 E6
Shepton Montague Som . 45 G7
Shepway Kent 53 C9
Sheraton Durham 234 D4
Sherberton Devon 13 G8
Sherborne Bath 44 B5
Dorset 29 D10
Glos 81 C11
Sherborne St John Hants 48 B6
Sherbourne Warks 118 E5
Sherbourne Street Suff . 107 C9
Sherburn Durham 234 C2
N Yorks 217 D9
Sherburn Grange
Durham 234 C2
Sherburn Hill Durham . . 234 C2
Sherburn in Elmet
N Yorks 206 G5
Shere Sur 50 D5
Shereford Norf 159 D7
Sherfield English Hants . 32 C3
Sherfield on Loddon
Hants 49 B7
Sherfin Lancs 195 B9
Sherford Devon 8 G5
Dorset 18 C4
Som 28 C2
Sheriffhales Shrops 150 G5
Sheriff Hill T&W 243 E7
Sheriff Hutton N Yorks . . 216 F3
Sheriff's Lench Worcs . . 99 B10
Sheringham Norf 177 E11
Sherington M Keynes . . . 103 B7
Sheringwood Norf 177 E11
Shermanbury W Sus 36 D2
Shernal Green Worcs . . . 117 E8
Shernborne Norf 158 C4
Sherrard's Green Worcs . . 98 B5
Sherrardspark Herts 86 C2
Sherriffhales Shrops . . . 150 G5
Sherrington Wilts 46 F3
Sherston Wilts 61 B11
Sherwood Nottingham . . . 171 G9
Sherwood Green Devon . . 25 C9
Sherwood Park Kent 52 E6
Shettleston Glasgow 268 C2
Shevington Gtr Man 194 F4
Shevington Moor
Gtr Man 194 E4
Shevington Vale
Gtr Man 194 F4
Sheviock Corn 7 D7
Shewalton N Ayrs 257 B8
Shibden Head W Yorks . . 196 B5
Shide IoW 20 D5
Shiel Aberds 292 B4
Shiel Bridge Highld 295 D11
Shieldaig Highld 299 B8
Highld 299 D8
Shieldhall Glasgow 267 B10
Shieldhill Dumfries 248 F2
Falk 279 F7
S Lnrk 269 G10
Shield Row Durham 242 G6
Shielfoot Highld 289 C8
Shielhill Angus 287 B8
Invclyd 276 G4
Shifford Oxon 82 E5
Shifnal Shrops 132 B4
Shilbottle Northumb 252 B5
Shilbottle Grange
Northumb 252 B6
Shildon Durham 233 F10
Shillford E Renf 267 D8
Shillingford Devon 27 C7
Oxon 83 G9
Shillingford Abbot Devon 14 D4
Shillingford St George
Devon 14 D4
Shillingstone Dorset 30 E4
Shillington C Beds 104 E2
Shillmoor Northumb 251 B9
Shilton Oxon 82 D3
Warks 135 G8
Shilvington Northumb . . . 252 G5
Shimpling Norf 142 G3
Suff 125 G7
Shimpling Street Suff . . 125 G7
Shincliffe Durham 233 C11
Shiney Row T&W 243 G8
Shinfield Wokingham 65 F8
Shingay Cambs 104 B6
Shingham Norf 140 C5
Shingle Street Suff 109 C7
Shinner's Bridge Devon . . . 8 C5
Shinness Highld 309 H5
Shipbourne Kent 52 C5
Shipdham Norf 141 B9
Shipdham Airfield Norf . 141 B9
Shipham Som 44 B2
Shiphay Torbay 9 B7
Shiplake Oxon 65 D9
Shiplake Bottom Oxon . . . 65 C8
Shiplake Row Oxon 65 D9
Shiplate N Som 43 B11
Shiplaw Borders 270 F4
Shipley Derbys 170 G6
Northumb 264 F4
Shrops 132 D6
W Sus 35 C10
W Yorks 205 F8
Shipley Bridge Sur 51 E10
Shipley Common
Derbys 171 G7
Shipley Shiels Northumb 251 E7
Shipmeadow Suff 143 F7
Shippea Hill Sta Cambs . 140 F3
Shippon Oxon 83 F7
Shipston-on-Stour
Warks 100 C5
Shipton Bucks 102 F5
Glos 81 B8
N Yorks 207 B7
Shrops 131 E11
Shipton Bellinger Hants . 47 D8
Shipton Gorge Dorset . . . 16 C5
Shipton Green W Sus 22 C4
Shipton Lee Bucks 102 G4
Shipton Moyne Glos 61 B11
Shipton Oliffe Glos 81 B8
Shipton on Cherwell
Oxon 83 B7
Shipton Solers Glos 81 B8
Shiptonthorpe E Yorks . . 208 E3
Shipton-under-Wychwood
Oxon 82 B3
Shirburn Oxon 83 F11
Shirdley Hill Lancs 193 E11
Shirebrook Derbys 171 B8
Shirecliffe S Yorks 186 C4
Shiregreen S Yorks 186 C5
Shirehampton Bristol 60 D4
Shiremoor T&W 243 C8
Shirenewton Mon 79 G7
Shire Oak W Mid 133 C11
Shireoaks Derbys 185 E9
Notts 187 E9
Shires Mill Fife 279 D10
Shirkoak Kent 54 F2
Shirland Derbys 170 D6
Shirlett Shrops 132 D3
Shirley Derbys 170 G2
Hants 19 B9
London 67 F11
Soton 32 E6
W Mid 118 B2
Shirley Heath W Mid . . . 118 B2
Shirley holms Hants 19 B11
Shirley Warren Soton 32 E5
Shirl Heath Hereford . . . 115 F8
Shirrell Heath Hants 33 E9
Shirwell Devon 40 F5
Shirwell Cross Devon 40 F5
Shiskine N Ayrs 255 E10
Shitterton Dorset 18 C2
Shobdon Hereford 115 E8
Shobley Hants 31 F11
Shobnall Staffs 152 E4
Shobrooke Devon 26 G5
Shoby Leics 154 F3
Shocklach Ches W 166 F6
Shocklach Green
Ches W 166 F6
Shoeburyness S'thend 70 C2
Sholden Kent 55 C11
Sholing Soton 32 E6
Sholing Common Soton . . 33 E7
Sholver Gtr Man 196 F3
Shootash Hants 32 C4
Shooters Hill London 68 D2
Shootersway Herts 85 D7
Shoot Hill Shrops 149 G8
Shop Corn 10 G3
Corn 24 E2
Devon 24 E5
Shop Corner Suff 108 E4
Shopford Cumb 240 C3
Shopnoller Som 43 G7
Shopp Hill W Sus 34 B6
Shopwyke W Sus 22 B5
Shore Gtr Man 196 D2
W Yorks 196 B2
Shore Bottom Devon 28 G2
Shoreditch London 67 C10
Som 28 C2
Shoregill Cumb 222 E5
Shoreham Kent 68 G4
Shoreham Beach W Sus . . 36 G2
Shoreham-by-Sea
W Sus 36 F2
Shore Mill Highld 301 C7
Shoresdean Northumb . . 273 F9
Shores Green Oxon 82 D5
Shoreside Shetland 313 J4
Shoreswood Northumb . . 273 F8
Shoreton Highld 300 C6
Shorley Hants 33 B9
Shorncliffe Camp Kent . . . 55 F7
Shorncote Glos 81 F8
Shorne Kent 69 E7
Shorne Ridgeway Kent . . . 69 E7
Shorne West Kent 69 E7
Shortacombe Devon 12 D6
Shortacross Corn 6 D5
Shortbridge E Sus 37 C7
Short Cross W Mid 133 G9
Shortfield Common Sur . 49 E10
Shortgate E Sus 23 B7
Short Green Norf 141 F11
Shorthampton Oxon 100 G6
Shortheath Hants 49 F9
Sur 49 E10
Short Heath Derbys 152 G6
W Mid 133 C9
W Mid 133 E11
Shorthill Shrops 131 B8
Shortlands London 67 F11
Shortlanesend Corn 4 F6
Shortlees E Ayrs 257 B10
Shortmoor Devon 28 G2
Dorset 29 G7
Shorton Torbay 9 C7
Shortroods Renfs 267 B9
Shortstanding Glos 79 C9
Shortstown Beds 103 B11
Short Street Wilts 45 D10
Shortwood Glos 80 F4
S Glos 61 D7
Shorwell IoW 20 E5
Shoscombe Bath 45 B8
Shoscombe Vale Bath . . . 45 B8
Shotatton Shrops 149 E7
Shotesham Norf 142 D5
Shotgate Essex 88 G3
Shotley Northants 137 D8
Suff 108 D4
Shotley Bridge Durham . 242 G3
Shotleyfield Northumb . . 242 G3
Shotley Gate Suff 108 E4
Shottenden Kent 54 C4
Shottermill Sur 49 G11
Shottery Warks 118 G3
Shotteswell Warks 101 B8
Shottisham Suff 108 C6
Shottle Derbys 170 F4
Shottlegate Derbys 170 F4
Shotton Durham 234 D4
Durham 234 F3
Flint 166 B4
Northumb 242 B6
Northumb 263 C8
Shotton Colliery
Durham 234 C3
Shotts N Lnrk 269 C7
Shotwick Ches W 182 G4
Shouldham Norf 140 B3
Shouldham Thorpe Norf 140 B3
Shoulton Worcs 116 F6
Shover's Green E Sus 53 G7
Shraleybrook Staffs 168 F3
Shrawardine Shrops 149 F8
Shrawley Worcs 116 E6
Shreding Green Bucks . . . 66 C4
Shrewley Warks 118 D4
Shrewley Common
Warks 118 D4
Shrewsbury Shrops 149 G9
Shrewton Wilts 46 E5
Shripney W Sus 22 C6
Shrivenham Oxon 63 B8
Shropham Norf 141 E9
Shroton or Iwerne Courtney
Dorset 30 E5
Shrub End Essex 107 G9
Shrubs Hill Sur 66 F3
Shrutherhill S Lnrk 268 F5
Shucknall Hereford 97 C11
Shudy Camps Cambs . . . 106 C2
Shulishadermor Highld . 298 E4
Shulista Highld 298 B4
Shuna Ho Argyll 275 C8
Shurdington Glos 80 B6
Shurlock Row Windsor . . 65 E10
Shurnock Worcs 117 E10
Shurrery Highld 310 D4
Shurrery Lodge Highld . 310 D4
Shurton Som 43 E8
Shustoke Warks 134 E4
Shute Devon 15 B11
Devon 26 G5
Shute End Wilts 31 B11
Shutford Oxon 101 C7
Shut Heath Staffs 151 E7
Shuthonger Glos 99 D7
Shutlanger Northants . . 120 G4
Shutta Corn 6 E5
Shutt Green Staffs 133 B7
Shuttington Warks 134 B5
Shuttlesfield Kent 55 E7
Shuttlewood Derbys 187 G7
Shuttleworth Gtr Man . 195 D10
Shutton Hereford 98 F3
Shwt Bridgend 57 D11
Siabost bho Dheas
W Isles 304 D4
Siabost bho Thuath
W Isles 304 D4
Siadar W Isles 304 C5
Siadar Iarach W Isles . . . 304 C5
Siadar Uarach W Isles . . 304 C5
Sibbaldbie Dumfries 248 F4
Sibbertoft Northants . . . 136 G3
Sibdon Carwood Shrops 131 G8
Sibford Ferris Oxon 101 D7
Sibford Gower Oxon . . . 101 D7
Sible Hedingham Essex . 106 E5
Sibley's Green Essex . . . 106 F2
Sibsey Lincs 174 E5
Sibsey Fen Side Lincs . . . 174 E4
Sibson Cambs 137 D11
Leics 135 C7
Sibster Highld 310 D7
Sibthorpe Notts 172 F3
Notts 188 G2
Sibton Suff 127 D7
Sibton Green Suff 127 C7
Sicklesmere Suff 125 E7
Sicklinghall N Yorks 206 D3
Sid Devon 15 D8
Sidbrook Som 28 B3
Sidbury Devon 15 C8
Shrops 132 F3
Sidcot N Som 44 B2
Sidcup London 68 E3
Siddal W Yorks 196 C6
Siddick Cumb 228 E6
Siddington Ches E 184 G4
Glos 81 F8
Siddington Heath
Ches E 184 G4
Sidemoor Worcs 117 C9
Side of the Moor
Gtr Man 195 E8
Sidestrand Norf 160 B5
Sideway Stoke 168 G5
Sidford Devon 15 C8
Sidlesham W Sus 22 D5
Sidlesham Common
W Sus 22 C5
Sidley E Sus 38 F2
Sidlow Sur 51 D9
Sidmouth Devon 15 D8
Sidway Staffs 150 B5
Sigford Devon 13 G11
Sigglesthorne E Yorks . . 209 D9
Sighthill Edin 280 G3
Glasgow 268 B2
Sigingstone / Tresigin
V Glam 58 E3
Signet Oxon 82 C2
Sigwells Som 29 C10
Silchester Hants 64 G6
Sildinis W Isles 305 G4
Sileby Leics 153 F11
Silecroft Cumb 210 C2
Silfield Norf 142 D2
Silford Devon 24 B6
Silian Ceredig 111 G11
Silkstead Hants 32 C6
Silkstone S Yorks 197 F9
Silkstone Common
S Yorks 197 G9
Silk Willoughby Lincs . . . 173 G9
Silloth Cumb 238 G4
Sills Northumb 251 C8
Sillyearn Moray 302 D5
Siloh Carms 94 D4
Silpho N Yorks 227 G9
Silsden W Yorks 204 D6
Silsoe C Beds 103 D11
Silton Dorset 30 B3
Silverburn Midloth 270 C4
Silverdale Lancs 211 E9
Staffs 168 F4
Silverdale Green Lancs . 211 E9
Silver End Essex 88 B4
W Mid 133 F8
Silvergate Norf 160 D3
Silver Green Norf 142 E5
Silverhill E Sus 38 E3
Silver Hill E Sus 38 B2
Silverhill Park E Sus 38 E4
Silver Knap Som 29 C11
Silverknowes Edin 280 F4
Silverley's Green Suff . . . 126 B5
Silvermuir S Lnrk 269 F8
Silverstone Northants . . . 102 C3
Silver Street Glos 80 E3
Kent 69 G11
Som 27 C11
Som 44 G4
Worcs 117 B11
Silverton Devon 27 G7
W Dunb 277 F8
Silvertonhill S Lnrk 268 E4
Silvertown London 68 D2
Silverwell Corn 4 F4
Silvington Shrops 116 B2
Silwick Shetland 313 J4
Sim Hill S Yorks 197 G9
Simister Gtr Man 195 F10
Simmondley Derbys 185 C8
Simm's Cross Halton . . . 183 D8
Simm's Lane End Mers . . 194 G4
Simonburn Northumb . . . 241 C9
Simonsbath Som 41 F9
Simonsburrow Devon . . . 27 D10
Simonside T&W 243 E8
Simonstone Lancs 203 G11
N Yorks 223 G7
Simprim Borders 272 F6
Simpson M Keynes 103 D7
Pembs 72 B5
Simpson Cross Pembs . . . 72 B5
Simpson Green W Yorks . 205 F9
Sinclair's Hill Borders . . 272 E6
Sinclairston E Ayrs 257 F11
Sinclairtown Fife 280 C5
Sinderby N Yorks 214 C6
Sinderhope Northumb . . . 241 G8
Sinderland Green
Gtr Man 184 C2
Sindlesham Wokingham . . . 65 F9
Sinfin Derby 152 C6
Sinfin Moor Derby 153 C7
Singdean Borders 250 C3
Singleborough Bucks . . . 102 E5
Single Hill Bath 45 B8
Singleton Lancs 202 F3
W Sus 34 E5
Singlewell Kent 69 E7
Singret Wrex 166 D4
Sinkhurst Green Kent 53 E10
Sinnahard Aberds 292 B6
Sinnington N Yorks 216 B4
Sinton Worcs 116 E6
Sinton Green Worcs 116 E6
Sion Hill Bath 61 F8
Sipson London 66 D5
Sirhowy Bl Gwent 77 C11
Sisland Norf 142 D6
Sissinghurst Kent 53 F9
Sisterpath Borders 272 F5
Siston S Glos 61 D7
Sithney Corn 2 D4
Sithney Common Corn 2 D4
Sithney Green Corn 2 D4
Sittingbourne Kent 70 G2
Six Ashes Staffs 132 F5
Six Bells Bl Gwent 78 E2
Sixhills Lincs 189 D11
Six Hills Leics 154 E2
Sixmile Kent 54 E6
Six Mile Bottom Cambs 123 F11
Sixpenny Handley Dorset 31 D7
Sizewell Suff 127 E9
Skaigh Devon 13 C8
Skail Highld 308 E7
Skaill Orkney 314 C4
Orkney 314 E2
Orkney 314 F5
Skares E Ayrs 258 F2
Skateraw E Loth 282 F4
Skaw Shetland 312 B8
Shetland 312 G7
Skeabost Highld 298 E4
Skeabrae Orkney 314 D2
Skeeby N Yorks 224 E4
Skeete Kent 54 E6
Skeffington Leics 136 C4
Skeffling E Yorks 201 D11
Skegby Notts 171 C7
Notts 188 G3
Skegness Lincs 175 C9
Skelberry Shetland 313 G6
Shetland 313 M5
Skelbo Highld 309 K7
Skelbo Street Highld . . . 309 K7
Skelbrooke S Yorks 198 E4
Skeldyke Lincs 156 B6
Skelfhill Borders 249 C11
Skellingthorpe Lincs 188 G6
Skellister Shetland 313 H6
Skellorn Green Ches E . . 184 E6
Skellow S Yorks 198 E4
Skelmanthorpe W Yorks 197 E8
Skelmersdale Lancs 194 F3
Skelmonae Aberds 303 F8
Skelmorlie N Ayrs 266 B3
Skelmuir Aberds 303 E9
Skelpick Highld 308 D7
Skelton Cumb 230 D4
E Yorks 199 B9
N Yorks 223 E11
Redcar 226 B3
York 207 B7
Skelton-on-Ure
N Yorks 215 F7
Skelwick Orkney 314 B4
Skelwith Bridge Cumb . . 220 E6
Skendleby Lincs 174 B6
Skendleby Psalter Lincs 190 G6
Skene Ho Aberds 293 C9
Skenfrith Mon 97 G9
Skerne E Yorks 208 B6
Skerne Park Darl 224 C5
Skeroblingarry Argyll . . . 255 E8
Skerray Highld 308 C6
Skerricha Highld 306 D7
Skerryford Pembs 72 C6
Skerton Lancs 211 G9
Sketchley Leics 135 E8
Sketty Swansea 56 C6
Skewen / Sgiwen Neath . . 57 B8
Skewes Corn 5 B9
Skewsby N Yorks 216 E2
Skeyton Norf 160 D4
Skeyton Corner Norf 160 D5
Skiag Bridge Highld 307 G7
Skibo Castle Highld 309 L7
Skidbrooke Lincs 190 C6
Skidbrooke North End
Lincs 190 B6
Skidby E Yorks 208 G6
Skilgate Som 27 B7
Skillington Lincs 155 D7
Skinburness Cumb 238 F4
Skinflats Falk 279 E8
Skinidin Highld 298 E2
Skinner's Bottom Corn . . . 4 F4
Skinners Green W Berks . 64 F2
Skinnet Highld 308 C5
Skinningrove Redcar 226 B4
Skipness Argyll 255 B9
Skippool Lancs 202 E3
Skiprigg Cumb 230 B3
Skipsea E Yorks 209 B9
Skipsea Brough E Yorks . 209 C9
Skipton N Yorks 204 C5
Skipton-on-Swale
N Yorks 215 D7
Skipwith N Yorks 207 F9
Skirbeck Lincs 174 G4
Skirbeck Quarter Lincs . 174 G4
Skirethorns N Yorks 213 G9
Skirlaugh E Yorks 209 F8
Skirling Borders 260 B3
Skirmett Bucks 65 B9
Skirpenbeck E Yorks . . . 207 B10
Skirwith Cumb 231 E8
N Yorks 212 E4
Skirza Highld 310 C7
Skitby Cumb 239 D10
Skitham Lancs 202 E4
Skittle Green Bucks 84 E3
Skulamus Highld 295 C8
Skullomie Highld 308 C6
Skyborry Green Shrops . 114 C5
Skye Green Essex 107 G7
Skye of Curr Highld 301 G9
Skyfog Pembs 90 F6
Skyreholme N Yorks 213 G11
Slack Derbys 170 C4
W Yorks 196 B3
W Yorks 196 D5
Slackcote Gtr Man 196 F3
Slackhall Derbys 185 E9
Slackhead Moray 302 C4
Slack Head Cumb 211 D9
Slackholme End Lincs . . 191 G8
Slacks of Cairnbanno
Aberds 303 E8
Slad Glos 80 D5
Sladbrook Glos 98 F5
Slade Devon 27 F10
Devon 40 D4
Kent 54 C2
Pembs 72 B6
Slade End Oxon 83 G9
Slade Green London 68 D4
Slade Heath Staffs 133 B8
Slade Hooton S Yorks . . . 187 D8
Sladen Green Hants 48 C2
Sladesbridge Corn 10 G6
Slades Green Worcs 99 E7
Slaggyford Northumb . . . 240 G5
Slaidburn Lancs 203 C10
Slaithwaite W Yorks 196 E5
Slaley Derbys 170 D3
Northumb 241 F11
Slamannan Falk 279 G7
Slape Cross Som 43 F10
Slapewath Redcar 226 B2
Slapton Bucks 103 G8
Devon 8 G6
Northants 102 B2
Slateford Edin 280 G4
Slate Haugh Moray 302 C4
Slatepit Dale Derbys 170 B4
Slattocks Gtr Man 195 F11
Slaugham W Sus 36 B3
Slaughterbridge Corn 11 D8
Slaughterford Wilts 61 E10
Slaughter Hill Ches E . . . 168 D2
Slawston Leics 136 E5
Slay Pits S Yorks 199 F7
Sleaford Hants 49 F10
Lincs 173 F9
Sleagill Cumb 221 B11
Sleap Shrops 149 D9
Sleapford Telford 150 F2
Sleapshyde Herts 86 D2
Sleastary Highld 309 K6
Slebech Pembs 73 B8
Sledge Green Worcs 98 E6
Sledmere E Yorks 217 G8
Sleeches Cross E Sus 52 G5
Sleepers Hill Hants 33 B7
Sleetbeck Cumb 240 B2
Sleet Moor Derbys 170 E6
Sleight Dorset 18 B5
Sleights N Yorks 227 D7
Slepe Dorset 18 C4
Sliabhna h-Airde
W Isles 296 F3
Slickly Highld 310 C6
Sliddery N Ayrs 255 E10
Slideslow Worcs 117 C9
Sligachan Hotel Highld . 294 C6
Sligneach Argyll 288 G4
Sligrachan Argyll 276 C3
Slimbridge Glos 80 E2
Slindon Staffs 150 C6
W Sus 35 F7
Slinfold W Sus 50 G6
Sling Glos 79 D9
Gwyn 163 B10
Slingsby N Yorks 216 E3
Slioch Aberds 302 F5
Slip End C Beds 85 B9
Herts 104 D5
Slippery Ford W Yorks . . 204 E6
Slipton Northants 121 B9
Slitting Mill Staffs 151 F10
Slochd Highld 301 G8
Slockavullin Argyll 275 D9
Slogan Moray 302 E3
Sloley Norf 160 E5
Sloncombe Devon 13 D10
Sloothby Lincs 191 G7
Slough Slough 66 D3
Slough Green Som 28 C3
W Sus 36 B3
Slough Hill Suff 125 G7
Sluggan Highld 301 G8
Sluggans Highld 298 E4
Slumbay Highld 295 B10
Sly Corner Kent 54 G3
Slyfield Sur 50 C3
Slyne Lancs 211 F9
Smailholm Borders 262 B4
Smallbridge Gtr Man 196 D2
Smallbrook Devon 14 B3
Glos 79 E9
Smallburgh Norf 160 E6
Smallburn Aberds 303 E10
E Ayrs 258 D5
Smalldale Derbys 185 E11
Derbys 185 F9
Small Dole W Sus 36 E2
Small End Lincs 174 D6
Smalley Derbys 170 G6
Smalley Common
Derbys 170 G6
Smalley Green Derbys . . 170 G6
Smallfield Sur 51 E10
Smallford Herts 85 D11
Small Heath W Mid 134 F2
Smallholm Dumfries 238 B4
Small Hythe Kent 53 G11
Smallmarsh Devon 25 C10
Smallrice Staffs 151 C9
Smallridge Devon 28 G4
Smallshaw Gtr Man 196 G2
Smallthorne Stoke 168 E5
Small Way Som 44 G6
Smallwood Ches E 168 C4
Worcs 117 D10
Smallwood Green Suff . . 125 F8
Smallwood Hey Lancs . . . 202 D3
Smallworth Norf 141 G10
Smannell Hants 47 D11
Smardale Cumb 222 D4
Smarden Kent 53 E11
Smarden Bell Kent 53 E11
Smart's Hill Kent 52 E4
Smaull Argyll 274 G3
Smeatharpe Devon 27 E11
Smeaton Fife 280 C5
Smeeth Kent 54 F5
Smeeton Westerby
Leics 136 E3
Smelthouses N Yorks 214 G3
Smercleit W Isles 297 K3
Smerral Highld 310 F5
Smestow Staffs 133 E7
Smethcott Shrops 131 D9
Smethwick W Mid 133 F10
Smethwick Green
Ches E 168 C4
Smirisary Highld 289 B8
Smisby Derbys 152 F6
Smite Hill Worcs 117 F7
Smithaleigh Devon 7 D11
Smithbrook W Sus 34 C6
Smith End Green Worcs . 116 G5
Smithfield Cumb 239 D10
Smith Green Lancs 202 C5
Smithies S Yorks 197 F11
Smithincott Devon 27 E9
Smithley S Yorks 197 G11
Smith's End Herts 105 D8
Smiths Green Ches E 184 G4
Smith's Green Ches E . . . 168 E3
Essex 105 G11
Essex 106 C3
Smithston Aberds 302 G5
Smithstown Highld 299 B7
Smithton Highld 301 E7
Smithwood Green Suff . . 125 G8
Smithy Bridge Gtr Man . . 196 D2
Smithy Gate Flint 181 F11
Smithy Green Ches E 184 G2
Gtr Man 184 D5
Smithy Houses Derbys . . 170 F5
Smithy Lane Ends Lancs 194 E2
Smock Alley W Sus 35 D9
Smockington Leics 135 F9
Smoky Row Bucks 84 D4
Smoogro Orkney 314 F3
Smug Oak Herts 85 E10
Smyrton S Ayrs 244 G4
Smythe's Green Essex 88 B6
Snagshall E Sus 38 C3
Snaigow House Perth . . . 286 C4
Snailbeach Shrops 131 C7
Snails Hill Som 29 E7
Snailswell Herts 104 E3
Snailwell Cambs 124 D2
Snainton N Yorks 217 C8
Snaisgill Durham 232 F5
Snaith E Yorks 198 C6
Snape N Yorks 214 C5
Suff 127 F7
Snape Green Lancs 193 E11
Snape Hill Derbys 186 F5
S Yorks 198 G2
Snapper Devon 40 G5
Snaresbrook London 67 B11
Snarestone Leics 134 B6
Snarford Lincs 189 E9
Snargate Kent 39 B7
Snarraness Shetland 313 H4
Snatchwood Torf 78 E3
Snave Kent 39 B8
Sneachill Worcs 117 G8
Snead Powys 130 E6
Snead Common Worcs . . 116 D4
Sneads Green Worcs 117 D7
Sneath Common Norf 142 F3
Sneaton N Yorks 227 D7
Sneatonthorpe N Yorks . 227 D8
Snedshill Telford 132 B4
Sneinton Nottingham 153 B11
Snelland Lincs 189 E9
Snelston Derbys 169 G11
Snetterton Norf 141 E9
Snettisham Norf 158 C3
Sneyd Green Stoke 168 F5
Sneyd Park Bristol 60 D5
Snibston Leics 153 G8
Snig's End Glos 98 F5
Snipeshill Kent 70 G2
Sniseabhal W Isles 297 H3
Snitter Northumb 252 C2
Snitterby Lincs 189 C7
Snitterfield Warks 118 F4
Snitterton Derbys 170 C3
Snitton Shrops 115 B11
Snittongate Shrops 115 B11
Snodhill Hereford 96 C6
Snodland Kent 69 G7
Snods Edge Northumb . . . 242 G3
Snowden Hill S Yorks 197 G9
Snowdown Kent 55 C8
Snow End Herts 105 E8
Snow Hill Ches E 167 E10
W Yorks 197 C10
Snow Lea W Yorks 196 D5
Snowshill Glos 99 E11
Snow Street Norf 141 G11
Snydale W Yorks 198 D2
Soake Hants 33 E11
Soar Anglesey 178 G5
Carms 94 F2
Devon 9 G9
Gwyn 146 B2
Powys 95 E9
Soar-y-Mynydd
Ceredig 112 G5
Soberton Hants 33 D10
Soberton Heath Hants . . . 33 E10
Sockbridge Cumb 230 F6
Sockburn Darl 224 D6
Sockety Dorset 29 F7
Sodom Denb 181 G9
Shetland 313 G7
Wilts 62 C4
Sodylt Bank Shrops 148 B6
Soham Cambs 123 C11
Soham Cotes Cambs 123 B11
Soho London 67 C9
Som 45 D7
W Mid 133 F10
Solas W Isles 296 D4
Soldon Cross Devon 24 E4
Soldridge Hants 49 G7
Sole Street Kent 54 D5
Kent 69 F7
Solfach / Solva Pembs 90 G5
Solihull W Mid 118 B2
Solihull Lodge W Mid . . . 117 B11
Sollers Dilwyn Hereford . 115 F8
Sollers Hope Hereford 98 E2
Sollom Lancs 194 D3
Solva / Solfach Pembs 90 G5
Somerby Leics 154 G5
Lincs 200 F5
Somercotes Derbys 170 E6
Somerdale Bath 61 F7
Somerford Ches E 168 B4
Dorset 19 C9
Staffs 133 B7
Somerford Keynes Glos . . 81 G8
Somerley W Sus 22 D4
Somerleyton Suff 143 D9
Somersal Herbert
Derbys 152 B2
Somersby Lincs 190 G4
Somersham Cambs 123 B7
Suff 107 B11
Somers Town London 67 C9
Ptsmth 21 B8
Somerton Newport 59 B10
Oxon 101 F9
Som 29 B7
Suff 124 G6
Somerton Hill Som 29 B7
Somerwood Shrops 149 G11
Sompting W Sus 35 G11
Sompting Abbotts
W Sus 35 F11
Sonning Wokingham 65 D9
Sonning Common Oxon . . 65 C8
Sonning Eye Oxon 65 D9
Sontley Wrex 166 F4
Sookholme Notts 171 B8
Sopley Hants 19 B9
Sopwell Herts 85 D11
Sopworth Wilts 61 B10
Sorbie Dumfries 236 E6
Sordale Highld 310 C5
Sorisdale Argyll 288 C4
Sorley Devon 8 F4
Sorn E Ayrs 258 D3
Sornhill E Ayrs 258 C2
Sortat Highld 310 C6
Sotby Lincs 190 F2
Sothall S Yorks 186 E6
Sots Hole Lincs 173 C10
Sotterley Suff 143 G9
Soudley Shrops 131 E9
Shrops 150 D4
Soughley S Yorks 197 G7
Soughton / Sychdyn
Flint 166 B2
Soulbury Bucks 103 F7
Soulby Cumb 222 C4
Cumb 230 F5
Souldern Oxon 101 E10
Souldrop Beds 121 E9
Sound Ches E 167 F10
Shetland 313 H5
Shetland 313 J6
Sound Heath Ches E 167 F10
Soundwell S Glos 60 D6

394 Sou–Sto

Sourhope Borders 263 E8
Sourin Orkney 314 C4
Sourlie N Ayrs 266 G6
Sour Nook Cumb 230 C3
Sourton Devon 12 C6
Soutergate Cumb 210 C4
South Acre Norf 158 G6
South Acton London 67 D7
South Alkham Kent 55 E8
Southall London 66 C6
South Allington Devon 9 G10
South Alloa Falk 279 C7
Southam Cumb 219 C9
Glos 99 F9
Warks 119 E8
South Ambersham
W Sus 34 C6
Southampton Soton 32 E6
South Anston S Yorks 187 E8
South Ascot Windsor 66 F2
South Ashford Kent 54 E4
South Auchmachar
Aberds 303 E9
Southay Som 28 D6
South Baddesley Hants 20 B3
South Ballachulish
Highld 284 B4
South Balloch S Ayrs 245 D8
South Bank Redcar 234 G6
York 207 C7
South Barrow Som 29 B10
South Beach Northumb 243 B8
South Beach / Marian-y-de
Gwyn 145 C7
South Beddington
London 67 G9
South Benfleet Essex 69 B9
South Bents T&W 243 E10
South Bersted W Sus 22 C6
South Blainslie
Borders 271 G10
South Bockhampton
Dorset 19 B9
Southborough Bromley 68 F2
Kent 52 E5
Kingston-upon-Thames 67 F7
Southbourne Bmouth 19 C8
W Sus 22 B3
South Bramwith
S Yorks 198 E6
South Brent Devon 8 D3
South Brewham Som 45 F8
South Bromley London 67 C11
Southbrook Wilts 45 G10
South Broomage Falk 279 E7
South Broomhill
Northumb 252 D6
Southburgh Norf 141 C9
South Burlingham Norf 143 B7
Southburn E Yorks 208 C5
South Cadbury Som 29 B10
South Cairn Dumfries 236 C1
South Carlton Lincs 189 F7
Notts 187 E9
South Carne Corn 11 E10
South Cave E Yorks 208 G4
South Cerney Glos 81 F8
South Chailey E Sus 36 D5
South Chard Som 28 F4
South Charlton
Northumb 264 E5
South Cheriton Som 29 C11
Southchurch Sthend 70 B2
South Church Durham 233 F10
South Cliffe E Yorks 208 F3
South Clifton Notts 188 G4
South Clunes Highld 300 E5
South Cockerington
Lincs 190 D5
South Common Devon 28 G4
Southcoombe Oxon 100 F6
South Cornelly Bridgend 57 E10
South Corriegills
N Ayrs 256 C2
South Corrielaw
Dumfries 248 G5
Southcote Reading 65 E7
Southcott Corn 11 B9
Devon 24 D6
Wilts 47 B7
Southcourt Bucks 84 C4
South Cove Suff 143 G9
South Creagan Argyll 289 E11
South Creake Norf 159 B7
Southcrest Worcs 117 D10
South Crosland
W Yorks 196 E6
South Croxton Leics 154 G3
South Croydon London 67 G10
South Cuil Highld 298 C3
South Dalton E Yorks 208 D5
South Darenth Kent 68 F5
Southdean Borders 250 B4
Southdene Mers 182 B6
South Denes Norf 143 C10
Southdown Bath 61 G8
Corn 7 E8
South Down Hants 33 C7
Som 28 E2
South Duffield N Yorks 207 G9
South Dunn Highld 310 D5
South Earlswood Sur 51 D9
Southease E Sus 36 F6
South Elkington Lincs 190 D3
South Elmsall W Yorks 198 E3
South Elphinstone
E Loth 281 G7
Southend Argyll 255 G7
Bucks 65 B9
Glos 80 F2
London 67 E11
Oxon 83 E9
W Berks 64 D2
W Berks 64 E5
Wilts 63 E7
South End Beds 103 B10
Bucks 103 F7
Cumb 210 G4
E Yorks 209 E9
Hants 31 D10
South-end Herts 86 B6
South End N Lincs 200 C6
Norf 141 E9
Southend-on-Sea
Sthend 69 B11
Southerhouse Shetland 313 K5
Southerly Devon 12 D6
Southernby Cumb 230 D3
Southern Cross
Brighton 36 F3
Southernden Kent 53 D11
Southerndown
V Glam 57 G11
Southerness Dumfries 237 D11
Southern Green Herts 104 E6
South Erradale Highld 299 B7
Southery Norf 140 E2
Southey Green Essex 106 E5
South Fambridge Essex 88 F5
South Farnborough
Hants 49 C11
South Fawley W Berks 63 C11
South Ferriby N Lincs 200 C3
Southfield Northumb 243 B7
South Field E Yorks 200 B4
Windsor 66 D3
Southfields London 67 E9
Thurrock 69 C7
Southfleet Kent 68 E6
South Flobbets Aberds 303 F7
Southford IoW 20 F6
South Garth Shetland 312 D7
South Garvan Highld 289 B11
Southgate Ceredig 111 A11
London 86 G3
Norf 159 C7
Norf 160 E2
Swansea 56 D5
W Sus 51 F9
South Glendale W Isles 297 K3
South Gluss Shetland 312 F5
South Godstone Sur 51 D11
South Gorley Hants 31 E11
South Gosforth T&W 242 D6
South Green Essex 87 G11
Essex 89 B8
Kent 69 G11
Norf 157 F10
Norf 159 G11
Suff 126 B3
South Gyle Edin 280 G3
South-haa Shetland 312 E5
South Hackney London 67 C11
South Ham Hants 48 C6
South Hampstead London 67 C9
South Hanningfield Essex 88 F2
South Harefield London 66 B5
South Harrow London 66 B6
South Harting W Sus 34 D3
South Hatfield Herts 86 D2
South Hayling Hants 21 B10
South Hazelrigg
Northumb 264 C3
South Heath Bucks 84 E6
Essex 89 B10
South Heighton E Sus 23 E7
South-heog Shetland 312 E5
South Hetton Durham 234 B3
South Hiendley
W Yorks 197 E11
South Hill Corn 12 G2
N Som 43 B10
Pembs 72 C4
South Hinksey Oxon 83 E8
South Hole Devon 24 C2
South Holme N Yorks 216 D3
South Holmwood Sur 51 D7
South Hornchurch
London 68 C4
South Huish Devon 8 G3
South Hykeham Lincs 172 C6
South Hylton T&W 243 F9
Southill C Beds 104 C3
Dorset 17 E9
Southington Hants 48 D4
South Kelsey Lincs 189 B8
South Kensington London 67 D9
South Kessock Highld 300 E6
South Killingholme
N Lincs 201 D7
South Kilvington
N Yorks 215 C8
South Kilworth Leics 136 G2
South Kirkby W Yorks 198 E2
South Kirkton Aberds 293 C9
South Kiscadale N Ayrs 256 D2
South Knighton Devon 14 G2
Leicester 136 C2
South Kyme Lincs 173 F11
South Lambeth London 67 D10
South Lancing W Sus 35 G11
Southlands Dorset 17 F9
South Lane S Yorks 197 F9
Southleigh Devon 15 C10
South Leigh Oxon 82 D5
South Leverton Notts 188 E3
South Littleton Worcs 99 B11
South Lopham Norf 141 G10
South Luffenham
Rutland 137 C8
South Malling E Sus 36 E6
Southmarsh Som 45 G8
South Marston Swindon 63 B7
Southmead Bristol 60 D5
South Merstham Sur 51 C9
South Middleton
Northumb 263 E11
South Milford N Yorks 206 G5
South Millbrex Aberds 303 E8
South Milton Devon 8 G4
South Mimms Herts 86 E2
Southminster Essex 89 F7
South Molton Devon 26 B2
Southmoor Oxon 82 F5
South Moor Durham 242 G5
South Moreton Oxon 64 B5
South Mundham W Sus 22 C5
South Muskham Notts 172 D3
South Newbald E Yorks 208 F4
South Newbarns Cumb 210 F4
South Newington Oxon 101 E8
South Newsham
Northumb 243 B8
South Newton Wilts 46 G5
South Normanton
Derbys 170 D6
South Norwood London 67 F10
South Nutfield Sur 51 D10
South Ockendon Thurrock 68 C5
Southoe Cambs 122 E3
Southolt Suff 126 D3
South Ormsby Lincs 190 F5
Southorpe Pboro 137 C11
South Ossett W Yorks 197 D9
South Otterington
N Yorks 215 B7
Southover Dorset 17 C8
E Sus 36 F6
E Sus 37 B11
South Owersby Lincs 189 C9
Southowram W Yorks 196 C6
South Oxhey Herts 85 G10
South Park Sur 51 D8
South Pelaw Durham 243 G7
South Perrott Dorset 29 F7
South Petherton Som 28 D6
South Petherwin Corn 12 E2
South Pickenham Norf 141 C7
South Pill Corn 7 D8
South Pool Devon 8 G5
South Poorton Dorset 16 B6
Southport Mers 193 D10
South Port Argyll 284 E4
Southpunds Shetland 313 L6
South Quilquox Aberds 303 F8
South Radworthy Devon 41 G9
South Rauceby Lincs 173 F8
South Raynham Norf 159 E7
South Reddish Gtr Man 184 C5
Southrepps Norf 160 B5
South Reston Lincs 190 E6
Southrey Lincs 173 B10
Southrop Glos 81 E11
Oxon 101 E7
Southrope Hants 49 E7
South Ruislip London 66 B6
South Runcton Norf 140 B2
South Scarle Notts 172 C4
Southsea Ptsmth 21 B8
Wrex 166 E4
South Shian Argyll 289 E11
South Shields T&W 243 D9
South Shore Blkpool 202 G2
South Side Durham 233 F8
Orkney 314 D5
South Somercotes Lincs 190 C6
South Stainley N Yorks 214 G6
South Stainmore Cumb 222 C6
South Stanley Durham 242 G5
South Stifford Thurrock 68 D6
Southstoke Bath 61 G8
South Stoke Oxon 64 C6
W Sus 35 F8
South Stour Kent 54 F4
South Street E Sus 36 D5
Kent 54 B5
Kent 68 G6
Kent 69 G10
Kent 70 F6
London 52 B2
South Tawton Devon 13 C9
South Tehidy Corn 4 G3
South Thoresby Lincs 190 F6
South Tidworth Wilts 47 D8
South Tottenham
London 67 B10
Southtown Norf 143 B10
Orkney 314 G4
Som 28 D4
Som 44 F5
South Town Devon 14 E5
Hants 49 F7
South Twerton Bath 61 G8
South Ulverston Cumb 210 D6
South View Hants 48 C6
Southville Devon 8 G4
Torf 78 F3
South Voxter Shetland 313 G5
Southwaite Cumb 230 C4
South Walsham Norf 161 G7
Southwark London 67 D10
South Warnborough
Hants 49 D8
Southwater W Sus 35 B11
Southwater Street
W Sus 35 B11
Southway Plym 7 C9
Som 44 E4
South Weald Essex 87 G9
South Weirs Hants 32 G3
Southwell Dorset 17 G9
Notts 172 E2
South Weston Oxon 84 F2
South Wheatley Corn 11 C10
Notts 188 D3
South Whiteness
Shetland 313 J5
Southwick Hants 33 F10
Northants 137 E10
Som 43 D11
T&W 243 F9
Wilts 45 B10
W Sus 36 F2
South Widcombe Bath 44 B5
South Wigston Leics 135 D11
South Willesborough
Kent 54 E4
South Willingham
Lincs 189 E11
South Wimbledon London 67 E9
South Wingate Durham 234 E4
South Wingfield Derbys 170 D5
South Witham Lincs 155 F8
Southwold Suff 127 B10
South Wonford Devon 24 F5
South Wonston Hants 48 F3
Southwood Derbys 153 E7
Hants 49 B10
Norf 143 B7
Som 44 G5
Worcs 116 E4
South Woodford London 86 G6
South Woodham Ferrers
Essex 88 F4
South Wootton Norf 158 E2
South Wraxall Wilts 61 G10
South Yardley W Mid 134 G2
South Yarrows Highld 310 E7
South Yeo Devon 25 G8
South Zeal Devon 13 C9
Soval Lodge W Isles 304 F5
Sowber Gate N Yorks 215 B7
Sowerby N Yorks 215 C8
W Yorks 196 C4
Sowerby Bridge
W Yorks 196 C5
Sowerby Row Cumb 230 D3
Sower Carr Lancs 202 E3
Sowley Green Suff 124 G4
Sowood W Yorks 196 D5
Sowood Green W Yorks 196 D5
Sowton Devon 14 C5
Sowton Barton Devon 14 D2
Soyal Highld 309 K5
Soyland Town W Yorks 196 C4
Spacey Houses N Yorks 206 C2
Spa Common Norf 160 C5
Spalding Lincs 156 E4
Spaldington E Yorks 207 G11
Spaldwick Cambs 122 C2
Spalford Notts 172 B4
Spanby Lincs 155 B11
Spango Invclyd 276 G4
Spanish Green Hants 49 B7
Sparham Norf 159 F11
Sparhamhill Norf 159 F11
Spark Bridge Cumb 210 C6
Sparkbrook W Mid 133 G11
Sparkford Som 29 B10
Sparkhill W Mid 133 G11
Sparkwell Devon 7 D11
Sparl Shetland 312 G5
Sparnon Corn 1 E3
Sparnon Gate Corn 4 G3
Sparrow Green Norf 159 G9
Sparrow Hill Som 44 C2
Sparrowpit Derbys 185 E9
Sparrow's Green E Sus 52 G6
Sparsholt Hants 48 G2
Oxon 63 B10
Spartylea Northumb 232 B3
Spath Staffs 151 B11
Spaunton N Yorks 226 G4
Spaxton Som 43 F8
Spean Bridge Highld 290 E4
Spear Hill W Sus 35 D10
Spearywell Hants 32 B4
Speckington Som 29 C9
Speed Gate Kent 68 F5
Speedwell Bristol 60 E6
Speen Bucks 84 F4
W Berks 64 F3
Speeton N Yorks 218 E2
Speke Mers 182 E6
Speldhurst Kent 52 E5
Spellbrook Herts 87 B7
Spelsbury Oxon 101 G7
Spelter Bridgend 57 C11
Spen W Yorks 197 B7
Spencers Wood
Wokingham 65 F8
Spen Green Ches E 168 C4
Spennells Worcs 116 C6
Spennithorne N Yorks 214 B2
Spennymoor Durham 233 E11
Spernall Warks 117 E11
Spetchley Worcs 117 G7
Spetisbury Dorset 30 G6
Spexhall Suff 143 G7
Speybank Highld 291 C10
Spey Bay Moray 302 C3
Speybridge Highld 301 G10
Speyview Moray 302 E2
Spillardsford Aberds 303 D10
Spilsby Lincs 174 B6
Spindlestone Northumb 264 C5
Spinkhill Derbys 187 F7
Spinney Hill Northants 120 E5
Spinney Hills Leicester 136 C2
Spinningdale Highld 309 L6
Spion Kop Notts 171 B9
Spirthill Wilts 62 D3
Spital Mers 182 E4
Windsor 66 D3
Spitalbrook Herts 86 D5
Spitalfields London 67 C10
Spitalhill Derbys 169 F11
Spital Hill S Yorks 187 C10
Spital in the Street
Lincs 189 D7
Spital Tongues T&W 242 D6
Spithurst E Sus 36 D6
Spittal Dumfries 236 D5
E Loth 281 F9
E Yorks 207 C11
Highld 310 D5
Northumb 273 E10
Pembs 91 G9
Stirl 277 D10
Spittalfield Perth 286 C5
Spittal Houses S Yorks 186 B5
Spittal of Glenmuick
Aberds 292 E5
Spittal of Glenshee
Perth 292 F3
Spittlegate Lincs 155 C8
Spixworth Norf 160 F4
Splatt Corn 10 F4
Corn 11 D10
Devon 25 F10
Som 43 F8
Splayne's Green E Sus 36 C6
Splott Cardiff 59 D7
Spofforth N Yorks 206 C3
Spondon Derby 153 B8
Spon End W Mid 118 B6
Spon Green Flint 166 C3
Spooner Row Norf 141 D11
Spoonleygate Shrops 132 D6
Sporle Norf 158 G6
Spotland Bridge
Gtr Man 195 E11
Spott E Loth 282 F3
Spratton Northants 120 C4
Spreakley Sur 49 E10
Spreyton Devon 13 B9
Spriddlestone Devon 7 E10
Spridlington Lincs 189 E8
Sprig's Alley Oxon 84 F3
Springbank Glos 99 G8
Spring Bank Cumb 229 G10
Springboig Glasgow 268 C3
Springbourne Bmouth 19 C8
Springburn Glasgow 268 B2
Spring Cottage Leics 152 F6
Spring End N Yorks 223 F9
Springfield Argyll 275 F11
Caerph 77 F11
Dumfries 239 D8
Essex 88 D2
Fife 287 F7
Gtr Man 194 F5
Highld 300 C6
M Keynes 103 D7
Moray 301 D10
W Mid 133 D8
W Mid 133 F9
W Mid 133 G11
Springfields Stoke 168 G5
Spring Gardens Som 45 D9
Spring Green Lancs 204 E4
Spring Grove London 67 D7
Springhead Gtr Man 196 G3
Springhill E Renf 267 D10
IoW 20 B6
N Lnrk 269 D7
Staffs 133 B11
Staffs 133 C9
Spring Hill Gtr Man 196 F2
Lancs 195 B8
W Mid 133 D7
Springholm Dumfries 237 C10
Springkell Dumfries 239 B7
Spring Park London 67 F11
Springside N Ayrs 257 B9
Springthorpe Lincs 188 D5
Spring Vale S Yorks 197 G9
Spring Valley IoM 192 E4
Springwell Essex 105 C10
T&W 243 F7
T&W 243 F9
Springwells Dumfries 248 E3
Sproatley E Yorks 209 G9
Sproston Green Ches W 168 B2
Sprotbrough S Yorks 198 G4
Sproughton Suff 108 C2
Sprouston Borders 263 B7
Sprowston Norf 160 G4
Sproxton Leics 155 E7
N Yorks 216 C2
Sprunston Cumb 230 B3
Spunhill Shrops 149 C8
Spurlands End Bucks 84 F5
Spurstow Ches E 167 D9
Spurtree Shrops 116 D2
Spynie Moray 302 C2
Spyway Dorset 16 C6
Square and Compass
Pembs 91 E7
Squires Gate Blkpool 202 G2
Sraid Ruadh Argyll 288 E1
Srannda W Isles 296 C6
Sronphadruig Lodge
Perth 291 F9
Stableford Shrops 132 D5
Staffs 150 B6
Stacey Bank S Yorks 186 C3
Stackhouse N Yorks 212 F6
Stackpole Pembs 73 F7
Stackpole Quay Pembs 73 F7
Stacksford Norf 141 E11
Stacksteads Lancs 195 C10
Stackyard Green Suff 107 B9
Staddiscombe Plym 7 E10
Staddlethorpe E Yorks 199 B10
Staddon Devon 24 C3
Devon 24 G5
Staden Derbys 185 G9
Stadhampton Oxon 83 F10
Stadhlaigearraidh
W Isles 297 H3
Stadmorslow Staffs 168 D5
Staffield Cumb 230 C6
Staffin Highld 298 C4
Stafford Staffs 151 E8
Stafford Park Telford 132 B4
Stafford's Corner Essex 89 B7
Stafford's Green Dorset 29 C10
Stagbatch Hereford 115 F9
Stagden Cross Essex 87 C10
Stagehall Borders 271 G9
Stagsden Beds 103 B9
Stagsden West End
Beds 103 B9
Stag's Head Devon 25 B11
Stainburn Cumb 228 F6
N Yorks 205 D10
Stainby Lincs 155 E8
Staincliffe W Yorks 197 C8
Staincross S Yorks 197 E10
Staindrop Durham 233 G8
Staines Green Herts 86 C3
Staines-upon-Thames
Sur 66 E4
Stainfield Lincs 155 D11
Lincs 189 G10
Stainforth N Yorks 212 F6
S Yorks 198 E6
Staining Lancs 202 F3
Stainland W Yorks 196 D5
Stainsacre N Yorks 227 D8
Stainsby Derbys 170 B6
Lincs 190 G4
Stainton Cumb 211 B10
Cumb 230 F5
Cumb 239 F9
Durham 223 B11
Mbro 225 C9
N Yorks 224 F2
S Yorks 187 C9
Stainton by Langworth
Lincs 189 F9
Staintondale N Yorks 227 F9
Stainton le Vale Lincs 189 C11
Stainton with Adgarley
Cumb 210 E5
Stair Cumb 229 G10
E Ayrs 257 E10
Stairfoot S Yorks 197 F11
Stairhaven Dumfries 236 D4
Staithes N Yorks 226 B5
Stakeford Northumb 253 F7
Stake Hill Gtr Man 195 F11
Stakenbridge Worcs 117 B7
Stake Pool Lancs 202 D4
Stalbridge Dorset 30 D2
Stalbridge Weston
Dorset 30 D2
Stalham Norf 161 D7
Stalham Green Norf 161 E7
Stalisfield Green Kent 54 C3
Stallen Dorset 29 D10
Stallingborough
NE Lincs 201 E7
Stalling Busk N Yorks 213 B8
Stallington Staffs 151 B8
Stalmine Lancs 202 D3
Stalmine Moss Side
Lancs 202 D3
Stalybridge Gtr Man 185 B7
Stambermill W Mid 133 G8
Stamborough Som 42 F4
Stambourne Essex 106 D4
Stambourne Green
Essex 106 D4
Stamford Lincs 137 B10
Stamford Bridge
Ches W 167 B7
E Yorks 207 B10
Stamfordham Northumb 242 C3
Stamford Hill London 67 B10
Stamperland E Renf 267 D11
Stamshaw Ptsmth 33 G10
Stanah Cumb 220 B6
Lancs 202 E3
Stanborough Herts 86 C2
Stanbridge C Beds 103 G9
Dorset 31 G8
Stanbridgeford C Beds 103 G9
Stanbrook Essex 106 F2
Worcs 98 B6
Stanbury W Yorks 204 F6
Stand Gtr Man 195 F9
N Lnrk 268 B5
Standburn Falk 279 G8
Standeford Staffs 133 B8
Standen Kent 53 E11
Standen Hall Lancs 203 E10
Standen Street Kent 53 G10
Standerwick Som 45 C10
Standford Hants 49 G10
Standford Bridge
Telford 150 E4
Standingstone Cumb 229 B11
Cumb 229 E7
Standish Glos 80 D4
Gtr Man 194 E5
Standish Lower Ground
Gtr Man 194 F5
Standlake Oxon 82 E5
Standon Hants 32 B6
Herts 105 G7
Staffs 150 B6
Standon Green End Herts 86 B5
Stane N Lnrk 269 D7
Stanecastle N Ayrs 257 B8
Stanfield Norf 159 E8
Stoke 168 E5
Stanford C Beds 104 C3
Kent 54 F6
Norf 141 E7
Shrops 148 G6
Stanford Bishop
Hereford 116 G3
Stanford Bridge Worcs 116 D4
Stanford Dingley
W Berks 64 E5
Stanford End Wokingham 65 G8
Stanford Hills Notts 153 E10
Stanford in the Vale
Oxon 82 G4
Stanford-le-Hope
Thurrock 69 C7
Stanford on Avon
Northants 119 B11
Stanford on Soar Notts 153 E10
Stanford on Teme
Worcs 116 D4
Stanford Rivers Essex 87 E8
Stanfree Derbys 187 G7
Stanground Pboro 138 D4
Stanhill Lancs 195 B8
Stanhoe Norf 158 B6
Stanhope Borders 260 D4
Durham 232 D5
Kent 54 E3
Stanion Northants 137 F8
Stank Cumb 210 E4
Stanklyn Worcs 117 C7
Stanks W Yorks 206 F3
Stanley Derbys 170 G6
Durham 242 G5
Lancs 194 F3
Notts 171 C7
Perth 286 D5
Shrops 132 G3
Shrops 132 G5
Staffs 168 E6
Wilts 62 E3
W Yorks 197 C10
Stanley Common
Derbys 170 G6
Stanley Crook Durham 233 D9
Stanley Downton Glos 80 E4
Stanley Ferry W Yorks 197 C11
Stanley Gate Lancs 194 G2
Stanley Green Ches E 184 E5
Poole 18 C6
Shrops 149 B10
Stanley Hill Hereford 98 C3
Stanley Moor Staffs 168 E6
Stanley Pontlarge Glos 99 E9
Stanleytown Rhondda 77 G8
Stanlow Ches W 182 F6
Staffs 132 D5
Stanmer Brighton 36 F4
Stanmore Hants 33 B7
London 85 G11
Shrops 132 E4
W Berks 64 D3
Stanner Powys 114 F5
Stannergate Dundee 287 D8
Stannersburn Northumb 250 F6
Stanners Hill Sur 66 G3
Stanningfield Suff 125 F7
Stanningley W Yorks 205 G10
Stannington Northumb 242 B6
S Yorks 186 D4
Stanpit Dorset 19 C9
Stansbatch Hereford 114 E6
Stansfield Suff 124 G5
Stanshope Staffs 169 E10
Stanstead Suff 106 B6
Stanstead Abbotts Herts 86 C5
Stansted Kent 68 G6
Stansted Airport Essex 105 G11
Stansted Mountfitchet
Essex 105 G10
Stanthorne Ches W 167 B11
Stanton Glos 99 E11
Mon 96 G6
Northumb 252 F4
Staffs 169 F10
Suff 125 C9
Stantonbury M Keynes 102 C6
Stanton by Bridge
Derbys 153 D7
Stanton-by-Dale Derbys 153 B9
Stanton Chare Suff 125 C9
Stanton Drew Bath 60 G5
Stanton Fitzwarren
Swindon 81 G11
Stanton Gate Notts 153 B9
Stanton Harcourt Oxon 82 D6
Stanton Hill Notts 171 C7
Stanton in Peak Derbys 170 C2
Stanton Lacy Shrops 115 B9
Stanton Lees Derbys 170 C3
Stanton Long Shrops 131 E11
Stanton-on-the-Wolds
Notts 154 C2
Stanton Prior Bath 61 G7
Stanton St Bernard Wilts 62 G5
Stanton St John Oxon 83 D9
Stanton St Quintin Wilts 62 D2
Stanton Street Suff 125 D9
Stanton under Bardon
Leics 153 G9
Stanton upon Hine Heath
Shrops 149 E11
Stanton Wick Bath 60 G6
Stantway Glos 80 C2
Stanwardine in the Fields
Shrops 149 E8
Stanwardine in the Wood
Shrops 149 D8
Stanway Essex 107 G8
Glos 99 E11
Stanway Green Essex 107 G9
Suff 126 C4
Stanwell Sur 66 E5
Stanwell Moor Sur 66 E4
Stanwick Northants 121 C9
Stanwick-St-John
N Yorks 224 C3
Stanwix Cumb 239 F10
Stanycliffe Gtr Man 195 F11
Stanydale Shetland 313 H4
Staoinebrig W Isles 297 H3
Stape N Yorks 226 G5
Stapehill Dorset 31 G9
Stapeley Ches E 167 F11
Stapenhill Staffs 152 E5
Staple Kent 55 B9
Som 42 E6
Staplecross E Sus 38 C3
Staple Cross Devon 27 C8
Staplefield W Sus 36 B3
Staple Fitzpaine Som 28 D3
Stapleford Cambs 123 G9
Herts 86 B4
Leics 154 F6
Lincs 172 D5
Notts 153 B9
Wilts 46 F5
Stapleford Abbotts Essex 87 G8
Stapleford Tawney Essex 87 F8
Staplegrove Som 28 B2
Staplehay Som 28 C2
Staple Hill S Glos 61 D7
Worcs 117 C9
Staplehurst Kent 53 E9
Staple Lawns Som 28 D3
Staplers IoW 20 D6
Staples Hill W Sus 35 B8
Staplestreet Kent 70 G5
Stapleton Bristol 60 D6
Cumb 240 C2
Hereford 114 D6
Leics 135 D8
N Yorks 198 D4
N Yorks 224 C5
Shrops 131 C9
Som 29 C7
Stapley Som 27 E11
Staploe Beds 122 E2
Staplow Hereford 98 C3
Stapness Shetland 313 J4
Star Fife 287 G7
Pembs 92 E4
Som 44 B2
Stara Orkney 314 D2
Starbeck N Yorks 206 B2
Starbotton N Yorks 213 E9
Starcross Devon 14 E5
Stareton Warks 118 C6
Stargate T&W 242 E5
Star Hill Mon 79 E7
Starkholmes Derbys 170 D4
Starling Gtr Man 195 E9
Starlings Green Essex 105 E9
Starr's Green E Sus 38 D3
Starston Norf 142 G4
Start Devon 8 G6
Startforth Durham 223 B10
Start Hill Essex 105 G10
Startley Wilts 62 C2
Startop's End Bucks 84 C6
Starveall S Glos 61 B9
Starvecrow Kent 52 D5
Statenborough Kent 55 B10
Statford St Andrew Suff 127 E7
Statham Warr 183 D11
Stathe Som 28 B5
Stathern Leics 154 C5
Station Hill Cumb 229 B11
Station Town Durham 234 D4
Statland Common
Norf 141 D10
Staughton Green Cambs 122 D2
Staughton Highway
Cambs 122 E2
Staughton Moor Beds 122 E2
Staunton Glos 79 C8
Glos 98 F5
Staunton in the Vale
Notts 172 G4
Staunton on Arrow
Hereford 115 E7
Staunton on Wye
Hereford 97 B7
Staupes N Yorks 205 B10
Staveley Cumb 211 B7
Cumb 221 F9
Derbys 186 G6
N Yorks 215 G7
Staveley-in-Cartmel
Cumb 211 B7
Staverton Devon 8 C5
Glos 99 G7
Northants 119 E10
Wilts 61 G11
Staverton Bridge Glos 99 G7
Stawell Som 43 F11
Stawley Som 27 C9
Staxigoe Highld 310 D7
Staxton N Yorks 217 D10
Staylittle Ceredig 128 F2
Staylittle / Penffordd-Lâs
Powys 129 E7
Staynall Lancs 202 E3
Staythorpe Notts 172 E3
Stead W Yorks 205 D8
Steam Mills Glos 79 B10
Stean N Yorks 213 E11
Steanbow Som 44 F5
Stearsby N Yorks 216 E2
Steart Som 29 B9
Som 43 D9
Stebbing Essex 106 G3
Stebbing Green Essex 106 G3
Stechford W Mid 134 F2
Stede Quarter Kent 53 F11
Stedham W Sus 34 C5
Steel Northumb 241 F10
Northumb 251 G9
Steel Bank S Yorks 186 D4
Steel Cross E Sus 52 G4
Steelend Fife 279 C10
Steele Road Borders 250 E2
Steeleroad-end Borders 250 E2
Steel Green Cumb 210 D3
Steel Heath Shrops 149 B10
Steen's Bridge
Hereford 115 F10
Steep Hants 34 B2
Steephill IoW 21 F7
Steep Lane W Yorks 196 C4
Steeple Dorset 18 E4
Essex 88 E6
Steeple Ashton Wilts 46 B2
Steeple Aston Oxon 101 F9
Steeple Barton Oxon 101 G8
Steeple Bumpstead
Essex 106 C3
Steeple Claydon Bucks 102 F3
Steeple Gidding Cambs 138 G2
Steeple Langford Wilts 46 F4
Steeple Morden Cambs 104 C5
Steep Marsh Hants 34 B3
Steeraway Telford 132 B3
Steeton W Yorks 204 E6
Stein Highld 298 D2
Steinmanhill Aberds 303 E7
Stella T&W 242 E5
Stelling Minnis Kent 54 D6
Stelvio Newport 59 B9
Stembridge Som 28 C6
Swansea 56 C3
Stemster Highld 310 C5
Stemster Ho Highld 310 C5
Stenalees Corn 5 D10
Stenaquoy Orkney 314 C5
Stencoose Corn 4 F4
Stenhill Devon 27 E9
Stenhouse Dumfries 247 E8
Edin 280 G4
Stenhousemuir Falk 279 E7
Stenigot Lincs 190 E3
Stennack Corn 2 B5
Stenness Shetland 312 F4
Stenscholl Highld 298 C4
Stenso Orkney 314 D3
Stenson Derbys 152 D6
Stenton E Loth 282 G2
Fife 280 B5
Stentwood Devon 27 F10
Stenwith Lincs 154 B6
Stepaside Corn 5 G9
Pembs 73 D10
Powys 129 F11
Stepping Hill Gtr Man 184 D6
Steppingley C Beds 103 D10
Stepps N Lnrk 268 B3
Sterndale Moor Derbys 169 B10
Sternfield Suff 127 E7
Sterridge Devon 40 D5
Stert Wilts 46 B4
Sterte Poole 18 C6
Stetchworth Cambs 124 F2
Stevenage Herts 104 G4
Steven's Crouch E Sus 38 D2
Stevenston N Ayrs 266 G5
Stevenstone Devon 25 D8
Steventon Hants 48 D4
Oxon 83 G7
Shrops 115 C10
Steventon End Essex 105 C11
Stevington Beds 121 G9
Stewards Essex 87 D7
Steward's Green Essex 87 E7
Stewartby Beds 103 C10
Stewarton Argyll 255 F7
E Ayrs 267 F8
Stewkley Bucks 103 F
Stewkley Dean Bucks 102 F
Stewley Som 28 D
Stewton Lincs 190 D
Steyne Cross IoW 21 D
Steyning W Sus 35 E1
Steynton Pembs 72 D
Stibb Corn 24 E
Stibbard Norf 159 D
Stibb Cross Devon 24 E
Stibb Green Wilts 63 G
Stibbington Cambs 137 D1
Stichill Borders 262 B
Sticker Corn 5 E
Stickford Lincs 174 D
Stick Hill Kent 52 E
Sticklepath Devon 13 C
Devon 40 G
Som 28 E
Som 42 F
Sticklinch Som 44 F
Stickling Green Essex 105 E
Stickney Lincs 174 D
Stiffkey Norf 177 E
Stifford's Bridge Hereford 98 B
Stiff Street Kent 69 G1
Stileway Som 44 E
Stillingfleet N Yorks 207 E
Stillington N Yorks 215 F1
Stockton 234 G
Stilton Cambs 138 F
Stinchcombe Glos 80 F
Stinsford Dorset 17 C
Stiperstones Shrops 131 C
Stirchley Telford 132 B
W Mid 133 G1
Stirkoke Ho Highld 310 D
Stirling Aberds 303 E
Stirl 278 C
Stirtloe Cambs 122 D
Stirton N Yorks 204 C
Stisted Essex 106 G
Stitchcombe Wilts 63 F
Stitchin's Hill Worcs 116 G
Stithians Corn 2 B
Stittenham Highld 300 B
Stivichall W Mid 118 B
Stixwould Lincs 173 B
Stoak Ches W 182 G
Stobhill Northumb 252 G
Stobhillgate Northumb 252 F
Stobieside S Lnrk 258 B
Stobo Borders 260 B
Stoborough Dorset 18 D
Stoborough Green
Dorset 18 D
Stobs Castle Borders 250 B
Stobshiel E Loth 271 C
Stobswood Northumb 252 E
Stock Essex 87 F1
Lancs 204 D
N Som 60 G
Stockbridge Hants 47 G1
S Yorks 198 F
W Sus 22 C
W Yorks 205 E
Stockbridge Village
Mers 182 C
Stockbury Kent 69 G1
Stockcross W Berks 64 F
Stockend Glos 80 D
Stocker's Head Kent 54 C
Stockerston Leics 136 C
Stockfield W Mid 134 G
Stock Green Worcs 117 F
Stockheath Hants 22 B
Stock Hill Suff 125 D
Stockholes Turbary
N Lincs 199 F
Stockiemuir Stirl 277 E
Stocking Hereford 98 E
Stockingford Warks 134 E
Stocking Green Essex 105 D
Stocking Pelham Herts 105 F
Stockland Devon 28 G
Stockland Bristol Som 43 E
Stockland Green Kent 52 E
W Mid 133 E1
Stockleigh English Devon 26 F
Stockleigh Pomeroy
Devon 26 G
Stockley Wilts 62 F
Stocklinch Som 28 D
Stockport Gtr Man 184 C
Stocksbridge S Yorks 186 B
Stocksfield Northumb 242 E
Stocks Green Kent 52 D
Stockstreet Essex 106 G
Stockton Hereford 115 E1
Norf 143 E
Shrops 130 C
Shrops 132 D
Telford 150 F
Warks 119 E
Wilts 46 F
Stockton Brook Staffs 168 E
Stockton Heath Warr 183 D1
Stockton-on-Tees
Stockton 225 B
Stockton on Teme
Worcs 116 D
Stockton on the Forest
York 207 B
Stocktonwood Shrops 130 C
Stockwell Devon 27 G
Glos 80 C
London 67 D1
Stockwell End W Mid 133 C
Stockwell Heath Staffs 151 E1
Stockwitch Cross Som 29 C
Stockwood Bristol 60 F
Dorset 29 F
Stock Wood Worcs 117 F
Stockwood Vale Bath 60 F
Stodday Lancs 202 B
Stodmarsh Kent 71 G
Stody Norf 159 C1
Stoer Highld 307 G
Stoford Som 29 E
Wilts 46 F
Stoford Water Devon 27 F
Stogumber Som 42 F
Stogursey Som 43 E
Stoke Devon 24 C
Hants 22 C
Hants 48 C
Medway 69 D1
Plym 7 D
Suff 108 C
W Mid 119 B
Stoke Abbott Dorset 29 G
Stoke Albany Northants 136 F
Stoke Aldermoor
W Mid 119 B
Stoke Ash Suff 126 C
Stoke Bardolph Notts 171 G1
Stoke Bishop Bristol 60 D
Stoke Bliss Worcs 116 E
Stoke Bruerne Northants 102 B
Stoke by Clare Suff 106 C
Stoke-by-Nayland Suff 107 D

Durham 233 E10
odlachie Aberds 293 B8
odmorden W Yorks 196 C2
odpool Corn 4 G4
odrig Borders 261 F10
odwick S Yorks 187 E7
oft Cambs 123 F7
Lincs 155 F11
Shetland 312 F6
Warks 119 C9
oft Hill Durham 233 F9
Lincs 174 C2
oft Monks Norf 143 E8
oft next Newton Lincs 189 D8
oftrees Norf 159 D7
ofts Highld 310 C7
oftshaw W Yorks 197 B7
oftwood Norf 159 G9
ogston Northumb 252 C6
okavaig Highld 295 D8
okers Green Oxon 65 D8
okyngton London 67 C7
olastadh a Chaolais
W Isles 304 E3
olastadh bho Thuath
W Isles 304 D7
olborough Corn 11 F9
olcarne Corn 2 B5
Corn 2 C5
olcarne Wartha Corn 2 B5
oldish Corn 5 D8
olgus Mount Corn 4 G3
olhurst E Sus 53 G7
olladine Worcs 117 F7
olland Som 42 G6
ollard Farnham Dorset 30 D6
ollard Royal Wilts 30 D6
oll Bar Mers 183 C7
Rutland 137 B10
S Yorks 198 F5
ollbar End W Mid 119 B7
oll End W Mid 133 E9
ollerford Dorset 17 B7
oller Fratrum Dorset 17 B7
oller Porcorum Dorset 17 B7
ollerton Notts 154 C2
N Yorks 215 G10
oller Whelme Dorset 29 G8
ollesbury Essex 89 C7
ollesby Mbro 225 B10
olleshunt D'Arcy Essex 88 C6
olleshunt Knights Essex 88 C6
olleshunt Major Essex 88 C5
ollie Highld 300 D5
oll of Birness Aberds 303 F10
olm W Isles 304 E6
olmers Herts 86 E4
olpuddle Dorset 17 C11
olskithy Corn 4 G3
olvaddon Downs Corn 4 G3
olvah Highld 291 D10
olworth London 67 F7
omaknock Perth 286 E2
om an Fhuadain
W Isles 305 G5
omatin Highld 301 G8
ombreck Highld 300 F6
ombui Perth 286 B2
omchrasky Highld 290 B4
omdoun Highld 290 C3
omich Highld 300 B6
Highld 300 G3
omich House Highld 300 E5
omintoul Aberds 292 D3
Moray 292 B3
omlow Warks 119 E9
omnaven Moray 302 F4
omnavoulin Moray 302 G2
omperrow Corn 4 G5
ompkin Staffs 168 E6
ompset's Bank E Sus 52 G2
omsleibhe Argyll 289 F8
omthorn Derbys 185 F9
on Mon 78 F5
on Breigam V Glam 58 D3
onbridge Kent 52 D5
onderghie Dumfries 236 F6
ondu Bridgend 57 E11
one Som 27 C10
onedale Som 27 C10
one Green Som 27 C11
ong Kent 53 D10
Shrops 132 B5
W Yorks 205 G10
onge Leics 153 E8
onge Corner Kent 70 F2
onge Fold Gtr Man 195 F8
onge Moor Gtr Man 195 E8
ong Forge Shrops 132 B5
ong Green Kent 54 C3
ongham Sur 49 D11
ongland Dumfries 237 D8
ong Norton Shrops 132 B5
ong Park W Yorks 205 F9
ong Street W Yorks 205 G9
ongue Highld 308 D5
ongue End Lincs 156 F3
ongwell M Keynes 103 C7
ongwynlais Cardiff 58 C6
onmawr Neath 57 B10
onna / Tonnau Neath 57 B9
onnau / Tonna Neath 57 B9
on-Pentre Rhondda 77 F7
on-teg Rhondda 58 B5
ontine Lancs 194 G4
onwell Herts 86 B4
onypandy Rhondda 77 G7
on-y-pistyll Caerph 77 F11
onyrefail Rhondda 58 B4
oot Baldon Oxon 83 E9
oothill Hants 32 D5
Swindon 62 C6
W Yorks 196 C6
oot Hill Essex 87 E8
Staffs 169 G9
ooting Graveney London 67 E9
opcliffe N Yorks 215 D8
W Yorks 197 B9
opcroft Norf 142 E5
opcroft Street Norf 142 E5
op End Beds 121 E10
op Green Notts 172 F3
opham S Yorks 198 D6
opleigh W Sus 34 D6
op Lock Gtr Man 194 F6
op of Hebers Gtr Man 195 F11
op o' th' Lane Lancs 194 C5
op o' th' Meadows
Gtr Man 196 F3
oppesfield Essex 106 D4
oppings Gtr Man 195 E8
oprow Norf 142 D3
opsham Devon 14 D5
op Valley Nottingham 171 F9
orbeg N Ayrs 255 E10
orboll Farm Highld 309 K7
orbothie N Lnrk 269 D7
orbreck Highld 309 J7
orbrex Stirl 278 C5
orbryan Devon 8 B6
orbush N Lnrk 268 D6
Torcross Devon 8 G6
Torcroy Highld 291 D9
Tore Highld 300 D6
Torfrey Corn 6 E2
Torgyle Highld 290 B5
Torinturk Argyll 275 G9
Torkington Gtr Man 184 D6
Torksey Lincs 188 F4
Torlum W Isles 296 F3
Torlundy Highld 290 F3
Tormarton S Glos 61 D9
Tormisdale Argyll 254 B2
Tormitchell S Ayrs 244 E6
Tormore Highld 295 E8
N Ayrs 255 D9
Tornagrain Highld 301 E7
Tornahaish Aberds 292 C4
Tornapress Highld 299 E8
Tornaveen Aberds 293 C8
Torness Highld 300 G5
Toronto Durham 233 E9
Torpenhow Cumb 229 D10
Torphichen W Loth 279 G9
Torphin Edin 270 B4
Torphins Aberds 293 C8
Torpoint Corn 7 E8
Torquay Torbay 9 C8
Torquhan Borders 271 F8
Torr Devon 7 E11
Devon 8 C2
Torra Argyll 254 B4
Torran Argyll 275 C9
Highld 298 E5
Highld 301 B7
Torrance E Dunb 278 G2
Torrans Argyll 288 G6
Torranyard N Ayrs 267 G7
Torre Som 42 E4
Torbay 9 C8
Torridon Highld 299 D9
Torridon Ho Highld 299 D8
Torries Aberds 293 B8
Torrin Highld 295 C7
Torrisdale Highld 308 C6
Torrisdale Castle Argyll 255 D8
Torrisdale-Square
Argyll 255 D8
Torrish Highld 311 H3
Torrisholme Lancs 211 G9
Torroble Highld 309 J5
Torroy Highld 309 K5
Torrpark Corn 11 D10
Torry Aberdeen 293 C11
Aberds 302 F4
Torryburn Fife 279 D10
Torsonce Borders 271 G9
Torsonce Mains Borders 271 G9
Torterston Aberds 303 E10
Torthorwald Dumfries 238 B2
Tortington W Sus 35 F8
Torton Worcs 116 C6
Tortworth S Glos 80 G2
Torvaig Highld 298 E4
Torver Cumb 220 G5
Torwood Falk 278 E6
Torwoodlee Mains
Borders 261 B11
Torworth Notts 187 D11
Tosberry Devon 24 C3
Toscaig Highld 295 B9
Toseland Cambs 122 E4
Tosside N Yorks 203 B11
Tostock Suff 125 E9
Totaig Highld 295 C10
Highld 298 D2
Totardor Highld 294 B5
Tote Highld 298 E4
Totegan Highld 310 C2
Tote Hill Hants 32 C4
W Sus 34 C5
Totford Hants 48 F5
Totham Hill Essex 88 C5
Totham Plains Essex 88 C5
Tothill Lincs 190 E6
Tot Hill Hants 64 G3
Totland IoW 20 D2
Totley S Yorks 186 F4
Totley Brook S Yorks 186 E4
Totley Rise S Yorks 186 E4
Totmonslow Staffs 151 B9
Totnell Dorset 29 F10
Totnes Devon 8 C6
Totnor Hereford 97 E11
Toton Notts 153 C10
Totronald Argyll 288 D3
Totscore Highld 298 C3
Tottenham London 86 G4
Tottenham Hale London 67 B10
Tottenhill Norf 158 G2
Tottenhill Row Norf 158 G2
Totteridge Bucks 84 G5
London 86 G2
Totternhoe C Beds 103 G9
Totteroak S Glos 61 C8
Totterton Shrops 131 F7
Totties W Yorks 197 F7
Tottington Gtr Man 195 E9
Norf 141 D7
Tottlebank Cumb 210 C6
Tottleworth Lancs 203 G10
Totton Hants 32 E5
Touchen End Windsor 65 D11
Toulston N Yorks 206 E5
Toulton Som 43 G7
Toulvaddie Highld 311 L2
Tournaig Highld 307 L3
Toux Aberds 303 D9
Tovil Kent 53 C9
Towan Corn 10 G3
Towan Cross Corn 4 F4
Toward Argyll 266 B2
Towcester Northants 102 B3
Towednack Corn 1 B5
Towerage Bucks 84 G4
Tower End Norf 158 F3
Tower Hamlets Kent 55 E10
Towerhead N Som 44 B2
Tower Hill Ches E 184 F6
Devon 12 C3
Essex 108 E5
Herts 85 E8
Mers 194 G2
Sur 51 D7
W Mid 133 E11
W Sus 35 B11
Towersey Oxon 84 D2
Tow House Northumb 241 E7
Towie Aberds 292 B6
Aberds 302 G5
Aberds 303 C8
Towiemore Moray 302 E3
Tow Law Durham 233 D8
Town Barton Devon 14 C2
Townend Derbys 185 E9
Staffs 151 B9
W Dunb 277 F8
Town End Bucks 84 F3
Cambs 139 D8
Cumb 211 B7
Cumb 211 C8
Cumb 212 C2
Cumb 220 D6
Cumb 221 E8
Cumb 221 F7
Cumb 231 F8
Derbys 185 F11
E Yorks 207 C10
Mers 183 D7
W Yorks 196 D5
Townfield Durham 232 B5
Town Fields Ches W 167 B10
Towngate Cumb 230 B6
Lincs 156 G2
Town Green Gtr Man 183 B9
Lancs 194 F2
Norf 161 G7
Townhead Argyll 275 G11
Cumb 229 D7
Cumb 230 D6
Cumb 231 E8
Dumfries 237 E8
N Lnrk 268 B4
Northumb 251 E9
S Ayrs 244 C6
S Yorks 186 E4
S Yorks 197 G7
Town Head Cumb 220 D6
Cumb 221 E8
Cumb 222 C2
Cumb 222 C3
Cumb 231 F7
Cumb 231 F8
Cumb 231 G8
Cumb 231 G9
Derbys 185 F11
N Yorks 204 B2
N Yorks 212 F5
Staffs 169 F8
W Yorks 204 D6
Townhead of Greenlaw
Dumfries 237 C9
Townhill Fife 280 D2
Swansea 56 C6
Townhill Park Hants 33 E7
Town Kelloe Durham 234 D3
Townlake Devon 12 G4
Townland Green Kent 54 G2
Town Lane Gtr Man 183 B11
Town Littleworth E Sus 36 D6
Town of Lowton Mers 183 B10
Town Park Telford 132 B3
Town Row E Sus 52 G5
Townsend Bath 44 B5
Bucks 84 D2
Devon 25 B10
Herts 85 D10
Oxon 63 B11
Pembs 72 D4
Som 44 C4
Stoke 168 F6
Wilts 46 B3
Wilts 46 B4
Towns End Hants 48 B5
Som 30 D2
Town's End Bucks 102 G2
Dorset 18 B3
Dorset 18 E5
Dorset 29 F9
Som 45 D7
Townsend Fold Lancs 195 C10
Townshend Corn 2 C3
Town Street Glos 98 F6
Townwell S Glos 79 G11
Town Yetholm Borders 263 D8
Towthorpe E Yorks 217 G8
York 207 B8
Towton N Yorks 206 F5
Towyn Conwy 181 F7
Toxteth Mers 182 D5
Toynton All Saints Lincs 174 C5
Toynton Fen Side Lincs 174 C5
Toynton St Peter Lincs 174 C6
Toy's Hill Kent 52 C3
Trabboch E Ayrs 257 E10
Traboe Corn 2 E6
Trabrown Borders 271 F10
Tracebridge Som 27 C9
Tradespark Highld 301 D8
Orkney 314 F4
Trafford Park Gtr Man 184 B3
Traigh Ho Highld 295 F8
Trallong Powys 95 F9
Trallwn Rhondda 77 G9
Swansea 57 B7
Tramagenna Corn 11 E7
Tram Inn Hereford 97 E9
Tranch Torf 78 E3
Tranent E Loth 281 G8
Tranmere Mers 182 D4
Trantlebeg Highld 310 D2
Trantlemore Highld 310 D2
Tranwell Northumb 252 G5
Trapp Carms 75 B11
Traprain E Loth 281 F11
Trap's Green Warks 118 D2
Trapshill W Berks 63 G11
Traquair Borders 261 C8
Trash Green W Berks 65 F7
Travellers' Rest Carms 74 B5
Trawden Lancs 204 F4
Trawscoed Powys 95 E11
Trawsfynydd Gwyn 146 B4
Trawsnant Ceredig 111 D11
Treadam Mon 78 B5
Treaddow Hereford 97 G10
Treal Corn 2 F6
Trealaw Rhondda 77 G8
Treales Lancs 202 G4
Trearddur Anglesey 178 F3
Treaslane Highld 298 D3
Treath Corn 3 D7
Treator Corn 10 F4
Tre-Aubrey V Glam 58 E4
Trebanog Rhondda 77 G8
Trebanos Neath 76 E2
Trebarber Corn 5 C7
Trebartha Corn 11 F11
Trebarwith Corn 11 D7
Trebarwith Strand Corn 10 D6
Trebeath Corn 11 D11
Tre-Beferad V Glam 58 F3
Trebell Green Corn 5 C11
Treberfydd Powys 96 F2
Trebetherick Corn 10 F4
Trebilcock Corn 5 C9
Treble's Holford Som 43 G7
Tre-boeth Swansea 57 B7
Treborough Som 42 F4
Trebudannon Corn 5 C7
Trebullett Corn 12 F2
Treburgett Corn 11 F7
Treburgie Corn 6 C4
Treburley Corn 12 F3
Treburrick Corn 10 G3
Trebyan Corn 5 C11
Trecastle Powys 95 F7
Trecenydd Caerph 58 B6
Trecott Devon 25 G10
Trecwn Pembs 91 E9
Trecynon Rhondda 77 E7
Tredannick Corn 10 G6
Tredaule Corn 11 E10
Tredavoe Corn 1 D5
Treddiog Pembs 91 F7
Tredegar Bl Gwent 77 D10
Trederwen Powys 148 F5
Tre-derwen Powys 148 F4
Tredethy Corn 11 G7
Tredington Glos 99 F8
Warks 100 C5
Tredinnick Corn 1 C4
Corn 5 D10
Corn 6 B3
Corn 6 D4
Corn 10 G4
Tredogan V Glam 58 F5
Tredomen Caerph 77 G10
Powys 96 E2
Tredown Devon 24 D2
Tredrizzick Corn 10 F5
Tredunnock Mon 78 G5
Tredustan Powys 96 E2
Tredworth Glos 80 B4
Treen Corn 1 B4
Corn 1 E3
Treesmill Corn 5 D11
Treeton S Yorks 186 D6
Trefaes Gwyn 144 C5
Trefanny Hill Corn 6 D4
Trefasser Pembs 91 D7
Trefdraeth Anglesey 178 G6
Trefdraeth / Newport
Pembs 91 D11
Trefecca Powys 96 E2
Trefechan Ceredig 111 A11
M Tydf 77 D8
Wrex 166 F3
Trefeglwys Powys 129 E9
Trefeitha Powys 96 E2
Trefenter Ceredig 112 D2
Treffgarne Pembs 91 G9
Treffynnon Pembs 90 F6
Treffynnon / Holywell
Flint 181 F11
Trefgarn Owen Pembs 91 F7
Trefil Bl Gwent 77 C10
Trefilan Ceredig 111 F11
Trefin / Trevine Pembs 90 E6
Treflach Shrops 148 D5
Trefnanney Powys 148 F4
Trefnant Denb 181 G9
Trefonen Shrops 148 D5
Trefor Anglesey 178 E5
Gwyn 162 F5
Treforda Corn 11 E7
Treforest Rhondda 58 B5
Treforgan Ceredig 92 B4
Tre-Forgan Neath 76 D3
Treforys / Morriston
Swansea 57 B7
Trefriw Conwy 164 C3
Trefrize Corn 12 F2
Tref y Clawdd / Knighton
Powys 114 C5
Trefynwy / Monmouth
Mon 79 C8
Tregada Corn 12 E2
Tregadgwith Corn 1 D4
Tregadillett Corn 12 E2
Tre-gagle Mon 79 D8
Tregaian Anglesey 178 F6
Tregajorran Corn 4 G3
Tregamere Corn 5 C8
Tregardock Corn 10 E6
Tregare Mon 78 C6
Tregarland Corn 6 D5
Tregarlandbridge Corn 6 D4
Tregarne Corn 3 E7
Tregaron Ceredig 112 F3
Tregarrick Mill Corn 6 D4
Tregarth Gwyn 163 B10
Tregath Gwyn 163 B10
Tregatillian Corn 5 C8
Tregatta Corn 11 D7
Tregavarah Corn 1 D4
Tregear Corn 2 E5
Tregeare Corn 11 D10
Tregeiriog Wrex 148 C3
Tregele Anglesey 178 C5
Tregellist Corn 10 F6
Tregeseal Corn 1 C3
Tregew Corn 3 C8
Tre-Gibbon Rhondda 77 E7
Tregidden Corn 3 E7
Treginnis Pembs 90 G4
Treglemais Pembs 90 F6
Tregole Corn 11 B9
Tregolls Corn 2 B6
Tregolwyn / Colwinston
V Glam 58 D2
Tregona Corn 5 B7
Tregonce Corn 10 G4
Tregonetha Corn 5 C9
Tregonna Corn 10 G4
Tregonning Corn 5 D7
Tregony Corn 5 G8
Tregoodwell Corn 11 E8
Tregorden Corn 10 G6
Tregorrick Corn 5 E10
Tregoss Corn 5 C9
Tregoyd Powys 96 D4
Tregoyd Mill Powys 96 D3
Tregreenwell Corn 11 E7
Tregrehan Mills Corn 5 E10
Tregroes Ceredig 93 C8
Tregullon Corn 5 C11
Tregunna Corn 10 G5
Tregurrian Corn 5 B7
Tregurtha Downs Corn 2 C2
Tre Gwyr / Gowerton
Swansea 56 B5
Tregyddulan Pembs 91 D7
Tregynon Powys 129 D11
Tre-gynwr Carms 74 B6
Trehafod Rhondda 77 G8
Trehafren Powys 129 E11
Trehan Corn 7 D8
Treharris M Tydf 77 F9
Trehemborne Corn 10 G3
Treherbert Rhondda 76 F6
Tre-hill V Glam 58 E5
Trehunist Corn 6 C6
Tre-Ifor Rhondda 77 D7
Trekeivesteps Corn 11 G10
Trekenner Corn 12 F2
Trekenning Corn 5 C8
Treknow Corn 11 D7
Trelales / Laleston
Bridgend 57 F11
Trelan Corn 2 F6
Tre-lan Flint 165 B11
Trelash Corn 11 C9
Trelassick Corn 5 E7
Trelawnyd Flint 181 F9
Trelech Carms 92 E5
Treleddyd-fawr Pembs 90 F5
Treleigh Corn 4 G4
Treletert / Letterston
Pembs 91 F8
Trelew Corn 3 B8
Trelewis M Tydf 77 F10
Treligga Corn 11 E7
Trelights Corn 10 F5
Trelill Corn 10 F6
Trelion Corn 5 E8
Treliske Corn 4 F6
Trelissick Corn 3 B8
Treliver Corn 5 B9
Trellech Mon 79 D8
Trelleck Grange Mon 79 E7
Trelogan Flint 181 E10
Treloquithack Corn 2 D5
Trelowia Corn 6 D5
Trelowth Corn 5 E9
Trelystan Powys 130 C5
Tremadog Gwyn 163 G9
Tremail Corn 11 D9
Tremain Ceredig 92 B4
Tremaine Corn 11 D10
Tremains Bridgend 58 D2
Tremar Corn 6 B5
Trematon Corn 7 D7
Trematon Castle Corn 7 D8
Tremayne Corn 2 B4
Trembraze Corn 6 B5
Tremedda Corn 1 B5
Tremeirchion Denb 181 G9
Tremethick Cross Corn 1 C4
Tremore Corn 5 C10
Tremorebridge Corn 5 C10
Tremorfa Cardiff 59 D8
Tre-Mostyn Flint 181 F10
Trenance Corn 4 C6
Corn 5 B7
Corn 5 C9
Corn 10 G4
Trenant Corn 6 B4
Corn 10 G5
Trenarren Corn 5 F10
Trenay Corn 6 B3
Trench Telford 150 G3
Trench Green Oxon 65 D7
Trench Wood Kent 52 D5
Trencreek Corn 4 C6
Trencrom Corn 2 B2
Trendeal Corn 5 E7
Trenear Corn 2 C5
Treneglos Corn 11 D10
Trenerth Corn 2 B4
Trenewan Corn 6 E3
Trengune Corn 11 C9
Trenhorne Corn 11 F11
Treningle Corn 5 B10
Treninnick Corn 4 C6
Trenoon Corn 2 F6
Trenoweth Corn 3 C7
Trent Dorset 29 D9
Trentham Stoke 168 G5
Trentishoe Devon 40 D6
Trentlock Derbys 153 C9
Trent Vale Stoke 168 G5
Trenwheal Corn 2 C4
Treoes V Glam 58 D2
Treopert / Granston
Pembs 91 E7
Treorchy / Treorci
Rhondda 77 F7
Treorci / Treorchy
Rhondda 77 F7
Treowen Caerph 78 F2
Powys 130 E2
Tre-pit V Glam 58 E2
Trequite Corn 10 F6
Tre'r-ddôl Ceredig 128 E3
Trerhyngyll V Glam 58 D4
Trerise Corn 2 F6
Trer Ilai / Leighton
Powys 130 B4
Trerose Corn 3 D7
Trerulefoot Corn 6 D6
Tresaith Ceredig 110 G5
Tresamble Corn 3 B7
Tresarrett Corn 11 G7
Tresavean Corn 2 B6
Tresawle Corn 5 F7
Tresawsen Corn 4 F5
Trescoll Corn 5 C10
Trescott Staffs 132 D6
Trescowe Corn 2 C3
Tresean Corn 4 D5
Tresevern Croft Corn 2 B6
Tresham Glos 80 G3
Tresigin / Sigingstone
V Glam 58 E3
Tresillian Corn 5 F7
Tresimwn / Bonvilston
V Glam 58 E5
Tresinney Corn 11 E8
Tresinwen Pembs 91 C7
Treskerby Corn 4 G4
Treskillard Corn 2 B5
Treskilling Corn 5 D10
Treskinnick Cross Corn 11 B10
Treslothan Corn 2 B5
Tresmeer Corn 11 D10
Tresowes Green Corn 2 D3
Tresoweshill Corn 2 D4
Tresparrett Corn 11 C8
Tresparrett Posts Corn 11 C8
Tressady Highld 309 J7
Tressait Perth 291 G10
Tresta Shetland 312 D8
Shetland 313 H5
Treswell Notts 188 F3
Treswithian Corn 4 G2
Treswithian Downs Corn 4 G2
Tre-Taliesin Ceredig 128 E3
Trethellan Water Corn 2 B6
Trethevy Corn 11 D7
Trethewell Corn 3 B9
Trethewey Corn 1 E3
Trethillick Corn 10 F4
Trethomas Caerph 59 B7
Trethosa Corn 5 E8
Trethowel Corn 5 E10
Trethurgy Corn 5 D10
Tretio Pembs 90 F5
Tretire Hereford 97 G10
Tretower Powys 96 G3
Treuddyn Flint 166 D3
Trevadlock Corn 11 F11
Trevail Corn 4 D5
Trevalga Corn 11 D7
Trevalgan Corn 1 A5
Trevalyn Wrex 166 D5
Trevance Corn 10 G4
Trevanger Corn 10 F5
Trevanson Corn 10 G5
Trevarrack Corn 1 C5
Trevarren Corn 5 C8
Trevarrian Corn 4 B6
Trevarrick Corn 5 G9
Trevarth Corn 4 G4
Trevaughan Carms 73 B11
Carms 93 G7
Tre-vaughan Carms 93 G8
Treveal Corn 1 A5
Trevegean Corn 1 D3
Treveighan Corn 11 F7
Trevellas Corn 4 E4
Trevelmond Corn 6 C4
Trevelver Corn 10 G5
Trevemper Corn 4 D6
Treven Corn 11 D7
Trevena Corn 2 D4
Trevenen Corn 2 D5
Trevenen Bal Corn 2 D5
Trevenning Corn 11 F7
Treveor Corn 5 G9
Treverbyn Corn 5 D10
Corn 6 B4
Treverva Corn 3 C7
Trevescan Corn 1 E3
Trevethin Torf 78 E3
Trevia Corn 11 E7
Trevigro Corn 6 B6
Trevilder Corn 10 G6
Trevilla Corn 3 B8
Trevilson Corn 4 D6
Trevine Corn 10 F5
Trevine / Trefin Pembs 90 E6
Treviscoe Corn 5 D8
Treviskey Corn 2 B6
Trevithal Corn 1 D5
Trevoll Corn 4 D6
Trevone Corn 10 F3
Trevor Wrex 166 G3
Trevorrick Corn 10 G4
Trevor Uchaf Denb 166 G2
Trevowah Corn 4 D5
Trevowhan Corn 1 B4
Trew Corn 2 D4
Trewalder Corn 11 E7
Trewarmett Corn 11 D7
Trewartha Corn 2 B2
Corn 3 B10
Trewassa Corn 11 D8
Treween Corn 11 E10
Trewellard Corn 1 C3
Trewen Corn 11 E7
Corn 11 E11
Mon 79 G7
Trewennack Corn 2 D5
Trewennan Corn 11 E7
Trewern Powys 148 G5
Trewetha Corn 10 E6
Trewethen Corn 10 F6
Trewethern Corn 10 F6
Trewey Corn 1 B5
Trewidland Corn 6 D5
Trewindle Corn 6 C2
Trewint Corn 6 C5
Corn 11 B9
Corn 11 E10
Trewithian Corn 3 B9
Trewithick Corn 11 D11
Trewollock Corn 5 G10
Trewoodloe Corn 12 G2
Trewoofe Corn 1 D4
Trewoon Corn 2 F5
Corn 5 E9
Treworga Corn 5 G7
Treworgan Common
Mon 78 D6
Treworlas Corn 3 B9
Treworld Corn 11 C8
Trewornan Corn 10 G5
Treworrick Corn 6 B4
Treworthal Corn 3 B9
Trewyddel / Moylgrove
Pembs 92 C2
Trewyn Devon 24 G4
Tre-wyn Mon 96 G6
Treyarnon Corn 10 G3
Treyford W Sus 34 D4
Trezaise Corn 5 D9
Trezelah Corn 1 C5
Triangle Glos 79 E8
Staffs 133 B11
W Yorks 196 C4
Trickett's Cross Dorset 31 G9
Triffleton Pembs 91 G9
Trillacott Corn 11 D11
Trimdon Durham 234 E3
Trimdon Colliery
Durham 234 D3
Trimdon Grange
Durham 234 D3
Trimingham Norf 160 B5
Trimley Lower Street
Suff 108 D5
Trimley St Martin Suff 108 D5
Trimley St Mary Suff 108 D5
Trimpley Worcs 116 B5
Trimsaran Carms 75 E7
Trims Green Herts 87 B7
Trimstone Devon 40 E3
Trinafour Perth 291 G9
Trinant Caerph 78 E2
Tring Herts 84 C6
Tringford Herts 84 C6
Tring Wharf Herts 84 C6
Trinity Angus 293 G8
Devon 27 F7
Edin 280 F4
Trinity Fields Staffs 151 D8
Trisant Ceredig 112 B4
Triscombe Som 43 F7
Trislaig Highld 290 F2
Trispen Corn 4 E6
Tritlington Northumb 252 E6
Troan Corn 5 D7
Trochry Perth 286 C3
Trodigal Argyll 255 E7
Troearhiwgwair
Bl Gwent 77 D11
Troedrhiwdalar Powys 113 G9
Troedrhiwffenyd Ceredig 93 C8
Troedrhiwfuwch Caerph 77 E10
Troedyraur Ceredig 92 B6
Troedyrhiw M Tydf 77 E9
Trofarth Conwy 180 G5
Trolliloes E Sus 23 C10
Tromode IoM 192 E4
Trondavoe Shetland 312 F5
Troon Corn 2 B5
S Ayrs 257 C8
Trooper's Inn Pembs 73 C7
Trosaraidh W Isles 297 K3
Trossachs Hotel Stirl 285 G9
Troston Suff 125 C7
Trostre Carms 56 B4
Trostrey Common Mon 78 E5
Troswell Corn 11 C11
Trotshill Worcs 117 F7
Trotten Marsh W Sus 34 B4
Trottiscliffe Kent 68 G6
Trotton W Sus 34 C4
Trough Gate Lancs 195 C11
Troutbeck Cumb 221 E8
Cumb 230 F3
Troutbeck Bridge Cumb 221 F8
Troway Derbys 186 F5
Trowbridge Cardiff 59 C8
Wilts 45 B11
Trowell Notts 153 B9
Trow Green Glos 79 D9
Trowle Common Wilts 45 B10
Trowley Bottom Herts 85 C9
Trows Borders 262 C5
Trowse Newton Norf 142 B4
Troydale W Yorks 205 G10
Troy Town Kent 52 D2
Kent 54 E5
Medway 69 F8
Truas Corn 11 D7
Trub Gtr Man 195 F11
Trudoxhill Som 45 E8
Trueman's Heath
Worcs 117 B11
True Street Devon 8 C6
Trull Som 28 C2
Trumaisgearraidh
W Isles 296 D4
Trumfleet S Yorks 198 E6
Trumpan Highld 298 C2
Trumpet Hereford 98 D3
Trumpington Cambs 123 F8
Trumpsgreen Sur 66 F3
Trunch Norf 160 C5
Trunnah Lancs 202 E2
Truro Corn 4 G6
Truscott Corn 12 D2
Trusham Devon 14 E3
Trusley Derbys 152 B5
Trussall Corn 2 D5
Trussell Corn 11 D10
Trusthorpe Lincs 191 E8
Truthan Corn 4 E6
Truthwall Corn 2 C2
Trwstllewelyn Powys 130 D3
Tryfil Anglesey 178 E6
Trysull Staffs 133 E7
Trythogga Corn 1 C5
Tubbs Mill Corn 5 G9
Tubney Oxon 82 F6
Tubslake Kent 53 G9
Tuckenhay Devon 8 D6
Tuckermarsh Devon 7 B8
Tuckerton Som 28 B3
Tuckhill Shrops 132 F5
Tuckingmill Corn 4 G3
Corn 11 F7
Wilts 30 B6
Tucking Mill Bath 61 G9
Tuckton Bmouth 19 C8
Tuddenham Suff 108 B3
Suff 124 C4
Tuddenham St Martin
Suff 108 B3
Tudeley Kent 52 D6
Tudeley Hale Kent 52 D6
Tudhay Devon 28 G4
Tudhoe Durham 233 D11
Tudhoe Grange
Durham 233 E11
Tudor Hill W Mid 134 D2
Tudorville Hereford 97 G11
Tudweiliog Gwyn 144 B4
Tuebrook Mers 182 C5
Tuesley Sur 50 E3
Tuesnoad Kent 54 E2
Tuffley Glos 80 C4
Tufnell Park London 67 B9
Tufton Hants 48 D3
Pembs 91 F10
Tugby Leics 136 C5
Tugford Shrops 131 F11
Tughall Northumb 264 D6
Tulchan Lodge Angus 292 F3
Tullecombe W Sus 34 B4
Tullibardine Perth 286 F3
Tullibody Clack 279 B7
Tullich Argyll 284 F4
Highld 299 E9
Highld 300 G6
Tullich Muir Highld 301 B7
Tulliemet Perth 286 B3
Tulloch Aberds 293 F9
Aberds 303 F8
Highld 290 E5
Perth 286 E4
Tulloch Castle Highld 300 C5
Tullochgorm Argyll 275 D10
Tulloch-gribban Highld 301 G9
Tullochroisk Perth 285 B11
Tullochvenus Aberds 293 C7
Tulloes Angus 287 C9
Tullybannocher Perth 285 E11
Tullybelton Perth 286 D4
Tullycross Stirl 277 D9
Tullyfergus Perth 286 C6
Tullymurdoch Perth 286 B5
Tullynessle Aberds 293 B7
Tulse Hill London 67 E10
Tumbler's Green Essex 106 F6
Tumble / Y Tymbl Carms 75 C8
Tumby Lincs 174 D2
Tumby Woodside Lincs 174 D3
Tummel Bridge Perth 285 B11
Tumpy Green Glos 80 E2
Tumpy Lakes Hereford 97 B10
Tunbridge Hill Medway 69 E10
Tunbridge Wells / Royal
Tunbridge Wells Kent 52 F5
Tunga W Isles 304 E6
Tungate Norf 160 D5
Tunley Bath 45 B7
Glos 80 E6
Tunnel Hill Worcs 98 C6
Tunnel Pits N Lincs 199 G8
Tunshill Gtr Man 196 E2
Tunstall E Yorks 209 G12
Kent 69 G11
Lancs 212 E2
Norf 143 B8
N Yorks 224 F4
Staffs 150 D5
Stoke 168 E5
Suff 127 G7
T&W 243 G9
Tunstead Derbys 185 G10
Gtr Man 196 G4
Norf 160 E5
Tunworth Hants 49 D7
Tupsley Hereford 97 C10
Tupton Derbys 170 B5
Turbary Common Poole 19 C7
Turfdown Corn 5 B11
Turf Hill Gtr Man 196 E2
Turfholm S Lnrk 259 B8
Turfmoor Devon 28 G3
Shrops 149 F7
Turgis Green Hants 49 B7
Turin Angus 287 B9
Turkdean Glos 81 B10
Turkey Island Hants 33 E9
W Sus 34 D3
Turkey Tump Hereford 97 F10
Tur Langton Leics 136 E4
Turleigh Wilts 61 G10
Turleygreen Shrops 132 F5
Turlin Moor Poole 18 C5
Turmer Hants 31 F10
Turn Lancs 195 D10
Turnalt Argyll 275 C9
Turnastone Hereford 97 D7
Turnberry S Ayrs 244 B6
Turnchapel Plym 7 E9
Turnditch Derbys 170 F3
Turner Green Lancs 203 G8
Turner's Green E Sus 23 B10
E Sus 52 G6
Warks 118 D3
W Berks 64 F4
Turners Hill W Sus 51 F10
Turners Puddle Dorset 18 C2
Turnerwood S Yorks 187 E8
Turnford Herts 86 E5
Turnhouse Edin 280 G3
Turnhurst Stoke 168 E5
Turnstead Milton
Derbys 185 E8
Turnworth Dorset 30 F4
Turrerich Perth 286 D2
Turriff Aberds 303 D7
Tursdale Durham 234 D2
Turton Bottoms Blkburn 195 D8
Turves Cambs 138 D6
Turves Green W Mid 117 B10
Turvey Beds 121 G8
Turville Bucks 84 G3
Turville Heath Bucks 84 G2
Turweston Bucks 102 D2
Tushielaw Borders 261 F8
Tutbury Staffs 152 D4
Tutnall Worcs 117 C9
Tutnalls Glos 79 E10
Tutshill Glos 79 G8
Tutt Hill Kent 54 D3
Tuttington Norf 160 D4
Tutts Clump W Berks 64 E5
Tutwell Corn 12 F3
Tuxford Notts 188 G2
Twatt Orkney 314 D2
Shetland 313 H5
Twechar E Dunb 278 F4
Tweedale Telford 132 C4
Tweeddaleburn Borders 270 E5
Tweedmouth Northumb 273 E9
Tweedsmuir Borders 260 E3
Twelve Heads Corn 4 G5
Twelve Oaks E Sus 37 C11
Twelvewoods Corn 6 B4
Twemlow Green Ches E 168 B3
Twenties Kent 71 F10
Twenty Lincs 156 E3
Twerton Bath 61 G8
Twickenham London 67 E7
Twigworth Glos 98 G6
Twineham W Sus 36 D3
Twineham Green W Sus 36 C3
Twinhoe Bath 45 B8
Twinstead Essex 107 D7
Twinstead Green Essex 106 D6
Twiss Green Warr 183 B11
Twist Devon 28 G3
Twiston Lancs 204 E2
Twitchen Devon 41 G9
Shrops 115 B7
Twitchen Mill Devon 41 G9
Twitham Kent 55 B9
Twitton Kent 52 B4
Two Bridges Devon 13 G8
Glos 79 D11
Two Burrows Corn 4 F4
Two Dales Derbys 170 C3
Two Gates Staffs 134 C4
Two Mile Ash M Keynes 102 D6
W Sus 35 B10
Two Mile Hill Bristol 60 E6
Two Mile Oak Cross Devon 8 B6
Two Mills Ches W 182 G5
Two Pots Devon 40 E4
Two Waters Herts 85 D9
Twr Anglesey 178 E2
Twycross Leics 134 C6
Twydall Medway 69 F9
Twyford Bucks 102 F3
Derbys 152 D6
Dorset 30 D5
Hants 33 C7
Leics 154 G4
Lincs 155 E8
Norf 159 E10
Oxon 101 D9
Shrops 148 D6
Wokingham 65 D9
Worcs 99 B10
Twyford Common
Hereford 97 D10
Twyn-Allws Mon 78 C3
Twynholm Dumfries 237 D8
Twyning Glos 99 D7
Twyning Green Glos 99 D8
Twynllanan Carms 94 G5
Twynmynydd Carms 75 C11
Twyn Shôn-Ifan Caerph 77 G11
Twynyrodyn M Tydf 77 D9
Twyn-yr-odyn V Glam 58 E6
Twyn-y-Sheriff Mon 78 D6
Twywell Northants 121 B9
Tyberton Hereford 97 D7
Tyburn W Mid 134 E2
Tyby Norf 159 D11
Ty-coch Swansea 56 C6
Tycroes Carms 75 C10
Tycrwyn Powys 148 F2
Tyddewi / St Davids
Pembs 90 F5
Tydd Gote Lincs 157 F9
Tydd St Giles Cambs 157 F8
Tydd St Mary Lincs 157 F8
Tyddyn Powys 129 F9
Tyddyn Angharad Denb 165 F9
Tyddyn Dai Anglesey 178 C6
Tyddyn-mawr Gwyn 163 G9
Ty-draw Conwy 164 D5
Swansea 57 C7
Tye Hants 22 C2
Tye Common Essex 87 G11
Tyegate Green Norf 161 G7
Tye Green Essex 87 C10
Essex 87 D7
Essex 87 F11
Essex 105 D11
Essex 105 G10
Essex 106 G5
Tyersal W Yorks 205 G9
Ty-fry Mon 78 F6
Tyganol V Glam 58 E4
Ty-hen Carms 92 G6
Gwyn 144 C3
Ty-isaf Carms 56 B4
Tyla Mon 78 C2
Tylagwyn Bridgend 58 B2
Tyldesley Gtr Man 195 G7
Tyle Carms 94 F3
Tyle-garw Rhondda 58 C4
Tyler Hill Kent 70 G6
Tylers Causeway Herts 86 D3
Tylers Green Bucks 84 G6
Tyler's Green Essex 87 D8
Sur 51 C11
Tyler's Hill Bucks 85 E7
Ty Llwyn Bl Gwent 77 D11
Tylorstown Rhondda 77 F8
Tylwch Powys 129 G9
Ty-mawr Anglesey 179 D7
Ty Mawr Carms 93 C10
Ty-mawr Conwy 181 F7
Ty Mawr Cwm Conwy 164 F6
Tynant Rhondda 58 B5
Ty-nant Conwy 165 G7
Gwyn 147 D8

County and unitary authority boundaries

Ordnance Survey National Grid

The blue lines which divide the Navigator map pages into squares for indexing match the Ordnance Survey National Grid and correspond to the small squares on the boundary map below. Each side of a grid square measures 10km on the ground.

The National Grid 100-km square letters and kilometre values are indicated for the grid intersection at the outer corners of each page. For example, the intersection SE6090 at the upper right corner of page 215 is 60km East and 90km North of the south-west corner of National Grid square SE.

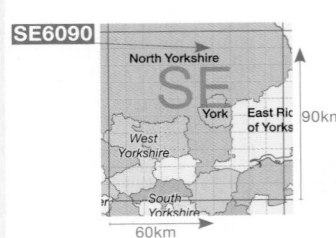
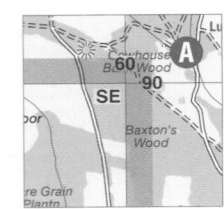

Using GPS with Navigator mapping

Since Navigator Britain is based on Ordnance Survey mapping, and rectified to the National Grid, it can be used with in-car or handheld GPS for locating identifiable waypoints such as road junctions, bridges, railways and farms, or assessing your position in relation to any of the features shown on the map.

On your receiver, choose British Grid as the location format and for map datum select Ordnance Survey (this may be described as Ord Srvy GB or similar, or more specifically as OSGB36). Your receiver will automatically convert the latitude/longitude co-ordinates transmitted by GPS into compatible National Grid data.

Positional accuracy of any particular feature is limited to 50–100m, due to the limitations of the original survey and the scale of Navigator mapping.

For further information see www.gps.gov.uk

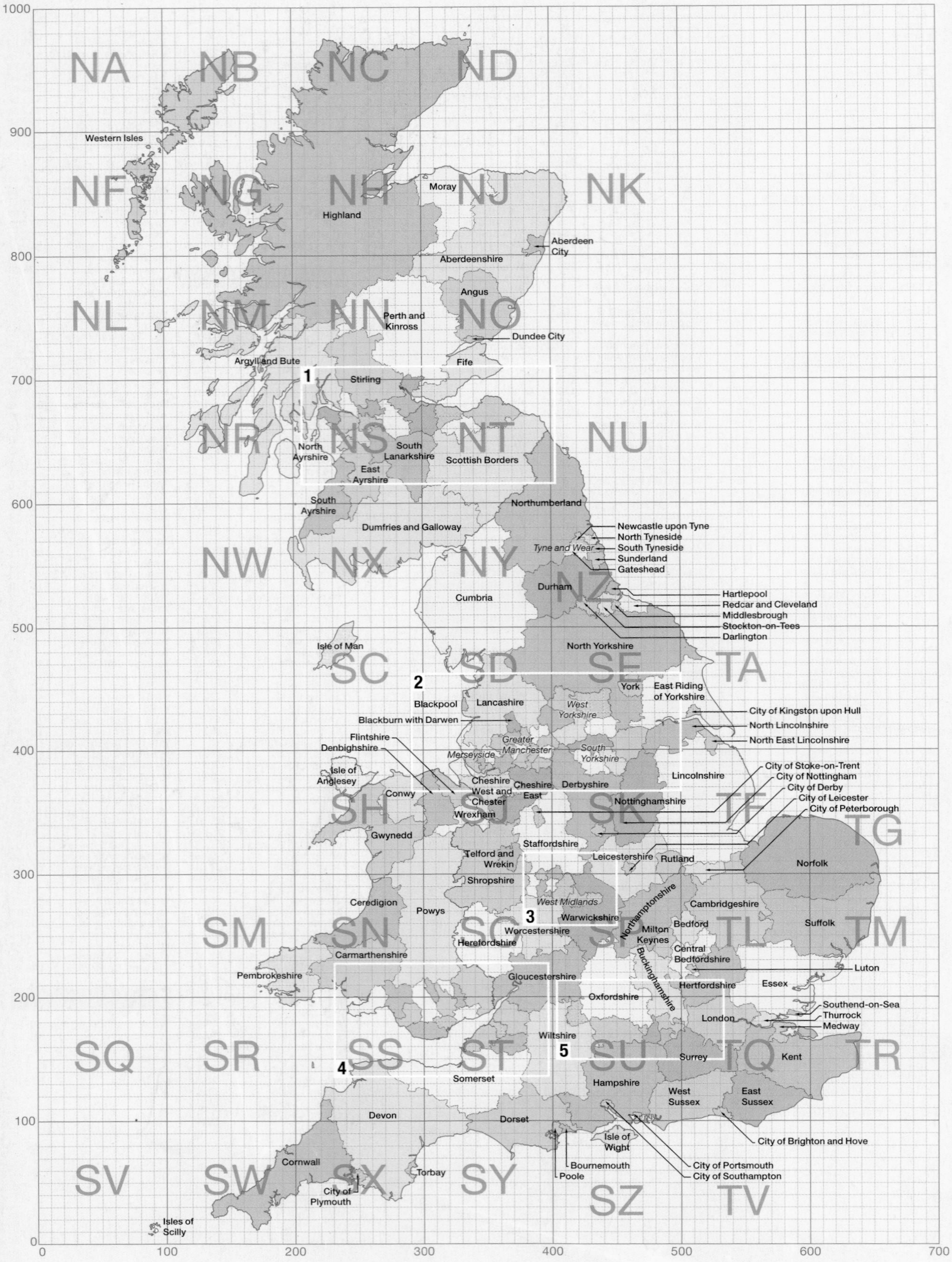

Greater London

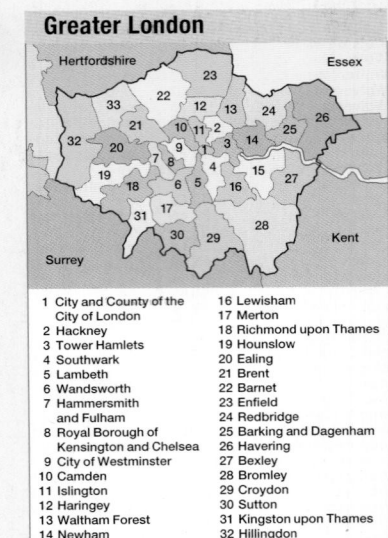

1 City and County of the City of London
2 Hackney
3 Tower Hamlets
4 Southwark
5 Lambeth
6 Wandsworth
7 Hammersmith and Fulham
8 Royal Borough of Kensington and Chelsea
9 City of Westminster
10 Camden
11 Islington
12 Haringey
13 Waltham Forest
14 Newham
15 Greenwich
16 Lewisham
17 Merton
18 Richmond upon Thames
19 Hounslow
20 Ealing
21 Brent
22 Barnet
23 Enfield
24 Redbridge
25 Barking and Dagenham
26 Havering
27 Bexley
28 Bromley
29 Croydon
30 Sutton
31 Kingston upon Thames
32 Hillingdon
33 Harrow

1 Central Scotland

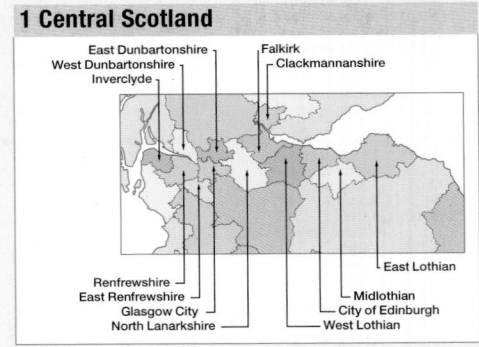

2 Northern England

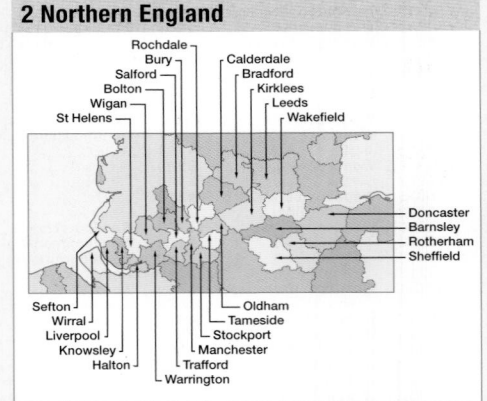

3 West Midlands

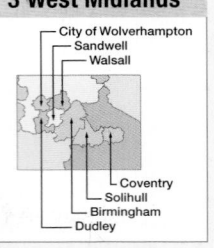

4 South Wales and Bristol area

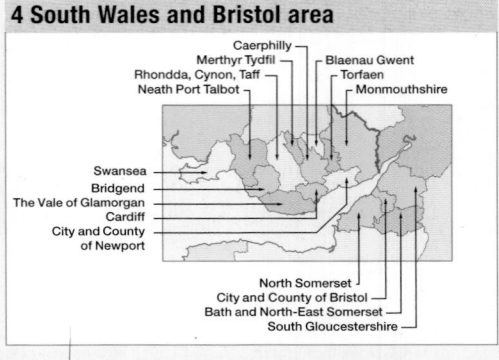

5 Thames Valley

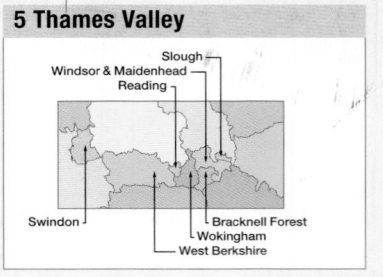